SMALL WORLD

Readings in Sociology

Second Edition

SMALL WORLD
Readings in Sociology

Second Edition

Edited by

Lorne Tepperman
James Curtis
Susannah J. Wilson
Alan Wain

Prentice Hall Canada Inc.
Scarborough, Ontario

Canadian Cataloguing in Publication Data

Main entry under title:

Small world : readings in sociology

2nd ed.
ISBN 0-13-613704-0

1. Sociology.   I. Tepperman, Lorne, 1943–   .

HM51.S634   1997   301   C96-931835-9

 © 1997 Prentice-Hall Canada Inc., Scarborough, Ontario
A Division of Simon & Schuster/A Viacom Company

Prentice-Hall, Inc., Upper Saddle River, New Jersey
Prentice-Hall International (UK) Limited, London
Prentice-Hall of Australia, Pty. Limited, Sydney
Prentice-Hall Hispanoamericana, S.A., Mexico City
Prentice-Hall of India Private Limited, New Delhi
Prentice-Hall of Japan, Inc., Tokyo
Simon & Schuster Southeast Asia Private Limited, Singapore
Editora Prentice-Hall do Brasil, Ltda., Rio de Janeiro

ISBN 0-13-613704-0

Vice President, Editorial Director: Laura Pearson
Acquisitions Editor: Rebecca Bersagel
Editorial Assistant: Shoshana Goldberg
Production Editor: Amber Wallace
Copy Editor: Karen Alliston
Production Coordinator: Deborah Starks
Permissions: Marijke Leupen
Art Director: Mary Opper
Cover Design: Ignition Design and Communications / Kyle Gell
Cover Image: PhotoDisc
Page Layout: Ignition Design and Communications

1 2 3 4 5   RRD   01 00 99 98 97

Printed and bound in the United States.

Visit the Prentice Hall Canada Web site! Send us your comments, browse our catalogues, and more.
www.phcanada.com Or reach us through e-mail at **phabinfo_pubcanada@prenhall.com**

TABLE OF CONTENTS

SECTION 4: CLASS AND SOCIAL STRATIFICATION 76

SECTION 5: RACE AND ETHNIC RELATIONS 99

SECTION 6: GENDER RELATIONS 127

SECTION 10: COMMUNICATIONS MEDIA 228

SECTION 11: RELIGION 252

Preface

Today's students realize that events in other parts of the world influence their own lives. Political unification in Europe, economic prosperity in the Pacific Basin, environmental destruction in South America, military conflict in the Middle East, and famine and epidemic in Central Africa will all affect them in one way or another. What's more, the worldwide forces of industrialization and democratization have affected different parts of the world in different ways.

Amid this general awareness of unpredicted change in a shrinking world, more and more people recognize that social life is changing too. Theoretical and practical concerns have led researchers to focus their attention on the possible futures of our social institutions. They have begun to look for clues about the future of social change in other societies, where social life is different from our own. They have also looked into history for clues to the trends and forces that will shape social life in North America.

A rapidly changing world calls for new kinds of textbooks. Instructors in sociology need textbooks that talk about social life in ways their undergraduate students can relate to in this fluid, changeable world. Students need books that will teach them about the world and its variety while introducing the topics and traditions of sociology. In particular, Canadian students want materials that will show their own society in a global context, against the backdrop of changes taking place in other parts of the world.

We believe that the only way for students to learn about the various influences on social life in a modern world, and the kinds of institutional arrangements that support them, is to study sociology from an international perspective. That is what this book aims to provide. Some of the excerpts are cross-nationally comparative, while others are case studies based on the country's own frame of reference. All sections of this book contain excerpts from a variety of countries and perspectives.

Professional social scientists have written all of the excerpts in this book. Since professional writing is often telegraphic and sometimes obscure, each excerpt in *Small World* is introduced by a few paragraphs describing the purpose and setting the context of the piece. As well, each section of the book is introduced by a brief essay that foreshadows and integrates the excerpts that follow.

Because of the great diversity of materials and approaches, learning aids play a critical role in making this book a success. Each section ends with discussion questions and exercises that help the student understand and review the pieces. These questions will stimulate classroom discussion by suggesting unresolved issues and calling attention back to earlier readings.

Again, the purpose of this review material is to help students unpack the case studies they are reading and find links among them. In this way we guide the student to seeing meaningful patterns in what is, admittedly, a world's worth of material.

What's New: A Comparative Outlook. This edition of *Small World* builds on the strengths of the earlier edition, but provides more Canadian content and an explicitly comparative focus.

In this edition we repeatedly ask the question, "How is this similar to Canadian society and how is it different?" Canadian and international readings have been chosen to highlight important similarities and differences. There are two useful results of this strategy: one is to throw Canada's uniqueness into clearer perspective. The other is to show that social life in the modern world—the "global village" as Marshall McLuhan called it—is similar in many ways, whether we are considering Canada, Chile, or China, the United States or the Ukraine.

What's New: More Canadian Content. This edition of *Small World* keeps the best international articles that were included in the first edition and replaces the rest with interesting and important articles on Canadian society. In the book as a whole, about half of the articles are now Canadian. The themes and issues raised in an article about Canada connect with themes and issues in articles discussing other societies. Discussion and review questions make the comparisons explicit, helping students to view Canadian society in a new light.

What's New: Four Additional Topics. In direct response to requests by instructors of sociology, we have added four new topic areas to this book: education, mass media, religion, and health. To keep the book the same size (and cost) as the first edition, we have reduced the number of articles per section from four to three. In this way, we have met the demand for more variety and Canadian content while keeping the same size as before.

In Closing: To prepare this revision, we have looked at abstracts and articles from scores of different journals. If there could have been a better selection of timely, well-written excerpts, we would have provided it. We have had a lot of fun and excitement putting this book together. We hope you enjoy it too.

ACKNOWLEDGEMENTS

This has been a team effort from the beginning, and we think it has worked out pretty well; judge for yourself. What made it possible is the fact that we have all worked together in pairs and trios several times before; and we have, most of us, worked with Prentice Hall Canada before.

So our thanks go to Prentice Hall Canada, and especially to Acquisitions Editor Rebecca Bersagel for seeing merit in what we are trying to do in this book. Shoshana Goldberg, the Editorial Assistant, and Production Editor Amber Wallace shepherded the book through the usual hoops, seeing that everything went smoothly. Along with Shoshana, Charles Tepperman got us many of the permissions to reprint these articles. Karen Alliston edited the copy, making sure that all the pieces fit together in a sensible and understandable way. We would also like to thank our reviewers for their contributions: Francis Adu-Febiri, Camosun College; Deborah Beaulieu, Brock University; Sheldon Goldenberg, University of Calgary; and Maureen Murphy-Fricker, Laurentian University. Finally, our main thanks go to the authors whose articles we have excerpted here, and who have allowed us to reprint them in a shortened form. This book could not have existed without their insights and efforts. (You may want to read some of these articles in their original, unabridged form. We have provided the source references for this purpose.)

We continue to dedicate this book to Canadian undergraduate students who, if our experience serves as any guide, are struggling to understand what is going on in this rapidly changing, exciting, and sometimes terrifying world.

SECTION 1   CULTURE

Introduction

Sociologists and biologists both use the word "culture" in their work. To the biologist a culture is what results from the cultivation of living material in prepared nutrient material. Biologists grow cultures in plastic Petri dishes as a routine part of their research. By preparing the nutrients in one way, they can grow one kind of culture; by altering their preparation, they cause another kind of culture to grow. Biologists sometimes use the word culture as a verb, meaning "to grow in a prepared nutrient media."

Sociologists use the word culture in a more expansive but related way. They cast society, rather than the scientist, in the role of culture grower. And the kinds of culture sociologists study would never fit into the small, neatly controllable space of a Petri dish. In fact sociologists, unlike biologists, see themselves as immersed in the cultures they are studying. Like biologists, sociologists may hope that cultures can be engineered, altered, and manipulated for the benefit of humanity. But unlike biologists, sociologists must also accept that to some extent they themselves have been engineered, altered, and manipulated by their own cultures too. The excerpt by Neil Smelser in this section, for example, describes American sociology as an academic discipline influenced by the culture that spawned it.

THE SOCIOLOGICAL DEFINITION OF CULTURE

To sociologists, culture is the integrated pattern of human behaviour that grows out of the human capacity for transferring knowledge from one generation to the next. This pattern of behaviour includes thoughts, actions, words, and artifacts. As such, culture has five main characteristics worth noting: it is learned, comprehensive, integrated, definitive, and enduring.

Culture Is Learned

Culturally influenced behaviour is what's left after the influence of human nature has been accounted for. For example, a sex drive is part of human nature. But cultural norms (or standards), cultural taboos (or prohibitions), and cultural traditions and rituals influence how that drive is channelled. Culture influences how and whom we court, what we find attractive, how we feel about promiscuity or fidelity, the kinds of marriages and families we form, and even the kinds and frequency of sexual intercourse we choose.

In this sense, human culture is every bit as artificial and "unnatural" as the Petri dish cultures that biologists grow. Human nature provides only the raw materials for culture-making. And different societies—different social laboratories if you will—can and have channelled human nature into a startling variety of different forms.

Culture Is Comprehensive

The fact that culture influences virtually every aspect of social life—from the way we talk, walk, dress, eat, work, play, even to the way we die—can, paradoxically, sometimes make the effect of culture hard to detect. We are immersed in culture just as we are immersed in air, or as a fish is immersed in water. Because culture is ubiquitous, it is easy to take it for granted.

Two tools sociologists use to discover the influence of culture on a society are historical and cross-cultural analyses. Such studies help reveal which customs, beliefs, values, and social practices are universal and which vary from one time period to another or from one society to another. It's reasonable to assume that practices that vary widely from one social setting to the next have been influenced by cultural factors.

But we must be careful in assuming that widespread social practices necessarily reflect the predilections of human nature. Sometimes social practices are attributable to "diffusion," which is the term used when one society learns of and adopts the practices of another culture. Diffusion can be a voluntary and two-way process. But it can also occur as a result of "cultural imperialism," which occurs when a stronger society's culture overwhelms and displaces the culture of a weaker one. Robert Washington's excerpt in this section shows the influence of cultural imperialism on international race relations. Many societies once colonized by the West have now acquired its prevailing racial prejudices. One benefit of a cross-cultural perspective is that it can lead us to re-examine our complacent assumption that we do what we do only because "it's natural for us to behave like this." Recognizing that culture also affects social behaviour raises the possibility that changing a cultural environment may also lead to improvements in social behaviour.

Culture Is Integrated

On the other hand, cultural behaviour can be quite difficult to understand, let alone change. Sociologists who want to understand culture have to do much more than record objective data about whether a particular cultural practice has been observed or not. The sociologist's job is to interpret the meaning or significance of a cultural phenomenon within a specific cultural context. The interpretation of what cultural phenomena signify is called "semiotics."

The interpretation of cultural phenomena can be tricky because the exact same act can mean vastly different things in different cultural contexts. This fact is recognized in the concept of "cultural relativism." A failure to take cultural relativism into account occurs, for example, when a person's behaviour inadvertently slights someone who comes from a different cultural background. Such slights happen because an act that is neutral or even complimentary from one cultural perspective may be interpreted as rude from another perspective.

The belief that the components of culture are all integrated or tied together to form a coherent picture leads sociologists to search for and find a context for interpreting phenomena within that culture. In other words, the theory is that once you have a general idea of what the Canadian or Japanese or Italian "way" is, you are better able to see specific cultural practices as expressions of that way of being.

Culture Is Definitive

Because cultural practices are thought to signify or mean something, culture is seen as a key to understanding its creators and practitioners. Just as individuals make fashion statements or political statements or personal statements with their behaviour, so do whole societies make cultural statements. What a people does goes a long way towards defining who they are. The excerpt in this section by Neil Earle, for example, looks at what Canadians' collective love of hockey says about us as a people.

Culture Endures

Finally, culture endures. Despite an endless string of changing superficial fads and fashions there is also an underlying continuity to social life. One function of culture is to remind us, through myths (or stories), ritual celebrations, and public holidays, about the historical origins of why we behave as we do. In tracing the origins of things, cultural scholars have found that we aren't just heirs to a Canadian past but to the historical influences of other cultures too. For example, much of what we do and who we are is deeply rooted in the traditions of Judeo-Christian civilization and of the whole Western world.

ARTICLE 1.1

Neil J. Smelser

CULTURAL INFLUENCES ON SOCIOLOGY

INTRODUCTION

Sociologists who study culture are in a paradoxical situation. They are both participants integrated into their own culture and detached observers of it. As social scientists they strive to be unbiased, objective, and value-neutral observers. But as normal citizens they have many of the same cultural biases, interests, and preferences as do their neighbours.

The following excerpt by Neil Smelser examines how these dual roles are reconciled in American sociology. He shows that although culture influences sociologists, it does not dictate to them in any narrow and limiting way. Culture seems mainly to influence the attitudes most sociologists will tend to take towards certain sociological topics. Like their fellow citizens,

Smelser, Neil J. (1989). "External Influences on Sociology," *International Sociology*, 4(4), December, 419–429. Reprinted by permission.

American sociologists will tend to find some theories and phenomena inherently more inter-esting than others.

But Smelser also points out that a number of countervailing influences guarantee that sociological opinion will become neither monolithic nor a mere weather vane for mainstream American culture. Among these influences are the legacy of work by previous generations of sociologists, the voice of dissenting minorities within the discipline, and the influence of exter-nal, non-American cultures.

In short, it's true that sociology can and should be viewed as a product of the culture that spawns it. But it's also true that different mixes of cultural influences produce a variety of products and subcultures. So the question of what's American about American sociology, or Canadian about Canadian sociology, is a complicated one.

There is a multiplicity of cultural, economic, political and organisational influences in the evolution of a field of knowledge as large and complex as sociology. To speak of cultural influences is to suggest that major motifs and emphases in any national sociological tradition will reflect the implications of the major value and ideological components of the larger culture that harbours it. Several examples come readily to mind:

- In Latin American sociology, there is a special emphasis on the political and class dimensions. It has been declared that even though the starting point of inquiry may be work, health, or social protest, all sociological analysis in Latin America ends up as political analysis. This is clearly an exaggeration, but any review of theoretical writings and empirical research in these countries reveals the salience of that theme.

- In Great Britain is found a special scholarly fascination with social stratification and social classes, and the manifestation of these in all other areas of social life, such as education, culture and family.

- Sociological theory in the Soviet Union and the socialist countries of Eastern Europe was for a long time under the ideological shadow of often orthodox Marxist-Leninist doctrines that proscribed official interpretations of capitalist and socialist societies that left little room for the development of alternative lines of thought; as that shadow has lifted sociological theory is becoming increasingly variegated.

- American research on social stratification has stressed individual mobility more than collective mobility, and upward mobility more than downward mobility. These emphases can be seen as manifesting a special preoccupation with the American cultural value of individual achievement. That research also has focussed on rates of individual mobility over time and above all with blockages to mobility (e.g., racial discrimination) which no doubt reveals a sensitivity to the degree to which the American cultural value of equality of opportunity is or is not being realised (Blau and Duncan, 1967).

Turning to the American value system more generally, it is possible to cull from the insights of various observers and analysts (Tocqueville, 1841; Parsons, 1951; Williams, 1963) a number of recurrent themes:

- individualism, with an assumption of responsibility for one's conduct;
- mastery of nature and of one's fate;
- voluntary cooperation as the basis of interaction;
- social order based on moral consensus, as contrasted with hierarchical ordering, class or authority (consistent with the early Republican rejection of European patterns of monarchy and aristocracy);
- pragmatism, incrementalism, and reform as principles of social changes;
- a resultant optimism.

It would be a serious oversimplification to argue that these themes have dominated American sociology, and, more broadly, the behavioural and social sciences in general, but it would also be a mistake to ignore them.

Similar continuities might be observed in many schools of thought that have had indigenous American origins. It can be argued, for example, that role theory is based on the assumption of socialisation into, and more or less voluntary compliance with, the "expectations" of others, and the mechanisms of social control associated with role theory stress conformity rather than obedience to authority or submission to coercion. The school of symbolic interaction, rooted in the pragmatic philosophies of Dewey, Mead and Blumer conceive of the actor as an agent, an active user and manipulator of his or her symbolic environment, and not in any way enslaved by the structural forces of society, by instinct, or by mechanical principles such as behavioural conditioning; in this sense the tenets of symbolic interactionism can be regarded as a kind of celebration of individual mastery and freedom, in contrast to the more deterministic theories against which it is counterpoised. Much of exchange theory, too, while it has origins in economic theories of competition, shares with these the underlying assumption that exchange is a matter of freely supplying and demanding resources and rewards to and from others. And, finally, the central features of Parsonian sociology, and functionalism in general, are voluntarism and consensus around a moral order.

To point out these continuities, of course, is to simplify matters greatly. American sociology has been characterised also by theoretical formulations that stand in critical dialogue with these strands and stress themes of inequality, domination and coercion. Many of these theories are of European origin, and have found their way into American sociology through the works of those who came from Europe (for example, Sorokin, 1927) or studied in Europe (e.g., Parsons, 1937), or who were otherwise inspired by the European masters (e.g., Mills, 1956).

These system/collectivist/critical/radical perspectives have themselves come to constitute a major part of sociology in the United States, and continue to be nourished by the more contemporary contributions of European scholars, such as Habermas, Touraine, Bourdieu, Giddens, and others. The field can be regarded as a kind of continuous dialogue and ferment among these strands of thought, some consonant with and some in critical opposition to the dominant themes of the American cultural tradition.

This notion of a continuous cultural dialogue within the discipline is closely connected with an observable but not very well understood phenomenon of the periodic rise and fall of the great historic figures of the field in sociological research and explanation. Durkheim and Freud held great sway in the two post-war decades in American sociology and social science generally, but the fortunes of both, especially the latter, have now faded somewhat and the neo-Marxian and neo-Weberian themes have risen in salience. European sociology has witnessed an ebbing of Marxian sociology as such, but continues to generate and nurture theories which cannot be described as Marxian but which retain some distinctive thread of Marxian thought, such as the ideas of domination and protest (new critical theory and the new social movements school, for example). As indicated, we do not understand the vicissitudes of the masters very well. Some of these might be a generational matter; one cohort of sociologists may embrace and make productive use of the insights of a Tocqueville or a Freud, while the next, facing new intellectual problems, and perhaps eager to distance itself from the work of its teachers, will forsake those figures and resurrect others; still another cohort will call up the heroes of their teachers' teachers. In any event, this invocation of the notion of a kind of myriad of cultural dialogues within sociology that mirror large cultural themes brings into question the strict distinction between internal and external influences on the evolution of a field of inquiry.

KEEPING UP WITH SOCIETY

One of the key influences in the development of sociology is the fact that much of its subject-matter is dictated by real and perceived social trends in the larger society. If one examines the rise of new areas of interest in the past several decades, one will find the family and unemployment emerging in the years of the Great Depression, propaganda and public opinion and rumour in World War II, a burst of new interests in the sociology of poverty, sociology of education, sociology of youth and feminist sociology in the 1960s and immediately thereafter, and environmental sociology, the sociology of energy, and the sociology of risk more recently. All these are evident reactions to social problematics.

The rise and fall of major figures, mentioned before, might also be explained in part by the changing historical circumstances of any given society. The evident rise of interest in Marx and Weber in the United States in the 1960s and 1970s can be regarded as a kind of intellectual mirror of the group conflict and political turmoil of those decades. It also makes sense in that, as colonial countries are struggling under the yoke of the colonial powers and subsequently are fighting to consolidate their own independence, they may turn to the Marxian notions of exploitation and dominance to enlighten their understanding; when they move actively into the phase of building institutions and promoting economic growth, the theories of a Joseph Schumpeter might appear more attractive.

A closely related tendency to these is for our subject-matter to run ahead of the conceptual frameworks under which we study it. The most important illustration of this concerns the study of international relations and international interdependencies. If we examine our major sociological heritage, it is apparent that most of our theories are based on the postulate that most of what transpires in social life does so within single societies and, indeed, intra-societal forces are the main operative determinants. Put another way, sociologists have tended to regard the single society, nation or culture as the principal unit of analysis for their studies. When we look around the contemporary world, however, it is apparent that the relevance of this kind of approach grows less and less. Nations grow more dependent on one another; the major forces affecting the decisions of national governments are not within the hands of national decision-makers but outside their control; in short, it is systems of societies, not single societies, that constitute the most important level of analysis. Accordingly, analyses built on the idea of single societies, states, nation-based ideologies, and the like, are less powerful. But, with few exceptions, the corpus of our inherited traditions does not provide very many theories and frameworks for moving to the higher systemic levels.

INFLUENCES FROM SCIENCE

One of the remarkable features of human history during the past several hundred years is the extent to which science as a culture has come to be such a dominant feature of Western culture in general.

It is important to recognise, moreover, that as the scientific impulse emerged in one intellectual area after another, it arose in a unique historical context, and its character was influenced by that context. Here the contrast between the histories of European and American sociology are instructive. The emergence of the field in continental Europe—associated above all with the efforts of Emile Durkheim and Max Weber—occurred in two principal contexts: first, the distinctive emphases in European social thought, and second, the simultaneous emergence of the scientific impulse in economics and psychology. With respect to the first, European sociology oriented itself above all to the intellectual traditions of European thought as represented in the study of history, philosophy, law, and the classics in the academy and in the critical intellectual traditions focussing on the state, social classes and the economy, to be found both in the academy and in the more general intellectual life of those countries. It also oriented itself to the emerging social-scientific emphases of the day, as Durkheim's negative polemic toward psychology and Weber's suspicion of the assumptions of formal economics reveal this second stress. The current preoccupations of European sociology with macroscopic and critical issues—phenomenology excepted—of the state, classes and the economy, and the critical treatment of each bears witness to the power of these traditions.

America is something of an exception. Just as its nation arose without the necessity to fight off the burdens of European feudalism, so its sociology arose in a context that did not include (with exceptions to be noted presently) the peculiar intellectual history of European nations. Our sociology grew up in two major intellectual and social contexts. First, it made its appearance in the public institutions of higher education in this country several decades after the passage of the Morell Act of 1862, which solidly established the scientific and applied impulses (mechanical and agricultural) in American higher education; a related part of this development was that economics and psychology preceded sociology, and had fully adopted the scientific "definition" of their own fields. Second, in the 1890s, the reform theme was in the air and sociology picked up that theme from both the social gospel and the progressivist movements. It is not surprising that sociology, struggling to establish its legitimacy in those days, picked up the twin themes of scientific respectability and social reform as its motifs to broadcast to the academy and to the larger society. Those themes persist to the present day. These themes also fit comfortably into American cultural emphases on pragmatism, reform and optimism identified in the previous section.

POLITICAL INFLUENCES

We know enough about the systemic character of societies to be able to assert with confidence that sociology—or any other field of inquiry, for that matter—never exists in isolation from the polity, but is embedded in its complex ways. In particular, sociology's general relations with national governments and its many publics are always fraught with uncertainty and ambivalence. These relations may be likened to a troubled marriage. The two partners may constantly irritate one another as governments and publics raise ideological concerns and pressures that threaten to compromise the freedom of thinkers and researchers in the discipline, and sociologists forever generate information and ways to describe social events and situations that have an unsettling, needling, and even debunking effect. At the same time the two may find that they cannot live without one another, governments and publics being dependent on data, information and perspectives for their policies and their interpretations of the social world, and sociology requiring autonomy as well as financial and institutional support. This inevitable ambivalence can be resolved in a variety of ways. Sociology may be afforded a free and happy welcome as part of the academy; it may be given only low status and a bad press in the public eye; or it may be constantly hounded to be something that it is not or driven underground altogether by oppressive measures.

One of the remarkable features of American sociology is that it has been housed in academic departments in universities, which have as a matter of historical fact been institutionally removed from the political winds, despite periodic forays of interested legislators and usually right-wing political groups that have imperiled academic freedom in universities. This is a relative statement, of course, but if one compares the American case with others—including those of Eastern European societies—the field has emerged as one which is, by and large, non-politicised from the standpoint of its environment.

As the functions of the state have grown, and the welfare state in particular, sociology and the other social sciences have taken on a different kind of political significance. Government agencies, pursuing their various missions, are inevitably called upon to justify both their concerns with societal problems and their policies relating to these problems in terms of some kind of factual base. In establishing this kind of empirical scope, various political agencies have borrowed both methods (mainly survey) and findings from sociology and the other social sciences, giving them applied or political significance, if you will. In many respects the research carried out by agencies is very similar to social science research in general.

Where sociology has come under greater political influence is not in its significance as an academic discipline in the university setting, but in its significance as a science based on research, with the support for that research coming from the science establishment (and ultimately from the Congress and the Executive branch); it is the case, furthermore, that the phenomenon of research has a political dimension.

REFERENCES

Blau, P. and O. D. Duncan (1967). *The American Occupational Structure*. New York: Wiley.

Mills, C. W. (1956). *The Power Elite*. New York: Oxford University Press.

Parsons, T. (1937). *The Structure of Social Action*. New York: Macmillan.

Parsons, T. (1951). *The Social System*. Glencoe, Ill.: The Free Press.

Sorokin, P. (1928). *Contemporary Sociological Theories*. New York: Harper.

Tocqueville, A. de (1841). *Democracy in America*. New York: J. & H.G. Langley.

Williams, R. (1963). *American Society: A Sociological Interpretation*. New York: Knopf.

A R T I C L E   1 . 2

Robert E. Washington

IMPERIALISM AND THE WORLD SYSTEM OF RACIAL STRATIFICATION

INTRODUCTION

Adopting some other society's culture is often criticized on the grounds that it will be a bad fit. The theory is that each people deserve and need to make their own culture so that it will reflect their own uniqueness. But the following excerpt highlights an additional, related argument against adopting someone else's culture. It suggests that if you adopt a different culture you may end up picking up ideas, values, and attitudes that will be positively harmful to you and others.

In this case Washington has in mind the West's assumptions about the racial superiority of white people. He argues that the West's racial hierarchy, which puts whites at the top, blacks at the bottom, and browns (i.e. everybody else) in between, now has worldwide currency. According to Washington, these racist attitudes are an implicit part of Western culture and so get exported around the world along with such Western cultural products as movies, magazines, music, radio programs, and television shows. People may tune in because they are fasci-

Washington, Robert E. "Brown Racism and the Formation of a World System of Racial Stratification," *International Journal of Politics, Culture and Society*, 4(2), 209–227. Reprinted by permission of Human Sciences Press, Inc.

*nated by and attracted to images and tales of Western (and predominantly American) afflu-
ence and lifestyles. But along with those images and stories Third World consumers are being
exposed to implicitly racist assumptions.*

*Washington points out that overt racism against blacks now exists in many "brown"
societies that have had little actual contact with large numbers of black people. One of the
consequences of "brown racism" is that it hampers efforts to create a unified opposition to
racism among the non-white peoples of the world.*

Probably no problem of race relations in the contemporary world has been more
free from critical scrutiny than brown racism. I use "brown" here in the figurative
sense, as a reference to the neither white nor black but colored peoples of the third
world (the Chinese, East Indians, Filipinos, Mestizos, etc.). These peoples occupy
an intermediate position along the black-white spectrum of color classification. By
brown racism, I refer to the prevalence of prejudice among these fair complexioned
colored groups and societies toward blacks, especially those of African ancestry.

Brown racism is commonplace throughout the third world. In what follows I
shall contend that the current form of brown racism, and the global system of racial
stratification through which it is manifested, are post-colonial adaptions of white
Western imperialism and are effected through the latter's cultural hegemony in
third world societies.

THE EMERGENCE OF BROWN RACISM

European colonial expansion into Asia, Africa, and the Americas was legitimated
by beliefs in white racial superiority. As one author has noted:

> The dilemma of the imperialist democracy was much more happily solved if "the
> native" was permanently and genetically inferior. . . . It seemed manifest that evo-
> lution had culminated in the people of North-Western Europe and North America,
> who dominated the world and, in their own eyes, surpassed all others in skill, intel-
> ligence, beauty and moral standards. (Mason, 1970a:31–33)

Often European colonial conquests were viewed as religiously mandated obligations to spread Western civilization and assume control over the backward people
of color throughout the world.

The effect of early European colonial conquests was the emergence of localized dual layered systems of racial stratification comprised of white Europeans at
the top and "natives" at the bottom. "In European colonies all natives were treated alike, regardless of the numerous distinctions they made among themselves"
(Shibutani, 1969, 1969:201). These localized dual layered systems of racial stratification, however, were seldom of long duration. Either because of a shortage of
European women or the importation of nonwhite laborers from other regions or
both, they evolved into multi-layered stratification systems which were maintained by direct European colonial domination (Ballhatchet, 1980; Mason, 1970a;
Schermerhorn, 1970).

In one type of situation, where sexual relations between European men and native females resulted in offspring, a status distinction was established between those of mixed race and those born of the native population. The dominant European groups drew boundaries of the color line, placing the mixed race group into a separate and intermediate racial category.

The appearance of these mixed race European-native groups in colonies and their identification with the Europeans resulted in the first pattern of brown racism: the antipathy of mixed race groups toward the native groups.[1] The antipathy of these mixed race groups resulted from their having internalized the color valuations of the European colonials and from the superior status privileges granted them—such as separate schools, better employment opportunities, and in some cases, the right to emigrate to the mother country. These privileges were denied to the darker skinned native groups.

Early manifestations of brown racism were also evidenced in situations where there was importation of groups from one colonial region to another for the purpose of providing labor. Such policies often resulted in the co-presence of brown skinned and black African groups.

What is significant about the above patterns is the formation of localized multi-layered stratification systems comprised of white Europeans at the top, mixed race and/or brown groups in the middle, and Africans at the bottom (Morner, 1970). Interestingly, the status distinction between browns and blacks originated by European colonials became so ingrained that the moral objections to the abuse of browns were seldom extended to blacks (Mason, 1970a; Rout, 1976). As one British student of racial relations notes in reference to Brazil,

> It is pertinent to recall that many of the liberal Portuguese who . . . championed the cause of the South American Indians at this time, did not regard the enslavement of Negroes as wrongful or protest so strongly about their ill treatment. (Banton, 1967:259)

It is also noteworthy that Mahatma Ghandi, who began his resistance movement against the racial policies of British colonialism in South Africa, restricted his protest to the treatments of Indians. He ignored the plight of the much larger and more severely oppressed African group. The pariah status imposed on Africans was deliberately contrived to prevent integration of brown and black communities and thereby fragment opposition to white European colonial domination.

During the colonial era, to briefly recapitulate, brown racism arose out of European administrative and military domination and the status gradations the latter created through elaborating a racially based ideology.

THE TRANSITIONAL ANTI-COLONIAL PHASE
AND THE ILLUSION OF UNITY

Throughout much of the third world, the post World War Two era was characterized by national independence movements oriented to both anti-colonial and anti-racist ideology. Among third world intellectuals and political elites of color a feeling of unity evolved based on the view that racism was the prejudice of white Westerners toward nonwhites.

The high point in this movement of solidarity among third world leaders of color was the conference in Bandung, Indonesia in 1955. In the words of a *Newsweek Magazine* article:

> The Columbo Powers (India, Pakistan, Ceylon, Burma, and Indonesia) convoked an unprecedented conference of officials from 30 Asian and African nations, representing more than half of the world's people. . . . The sponsoring powers seemed to be aiming vaguely at a sort of Monroe Doctrine against colonialism. Their basic philosophy was that Asian and African nations have some common destiny, freeing them from the power politics of the white race and setting them aside from the Atlantic and Soviet blocs. (*Newsweek*, 1955:32)

The effects of a number of world shaking events led up to this movement of third world unity. First, there were Marxist influences. As one author has noted, "Lenin's dicta . . . that 'colonialism is the worst and the most extreme form of capitalism, but also its last' could not fail to impress anti-imperialists from Asia and Africa" (Kimble, 1973:3).

Second, there was the feeling of a bond among non-white peoples influenced by the shared experiences of racial oppression. In fact, as early as the beginning of the century, we can see an assertion of this view of a simple white/nonwhite division of the world in the declaration of W. E. B. DuBois, the black American pan-Africanist leader, that, "the problem of the twentieth century is the problem of the color line" (Tuttle, 1973:65). This sentiment was echoed by Richard Wright, the exiled black American writer, who attended the Bandung Conference and characterized that gathering as a meeting of "the despised, the insulted, the hurt, the dispossessed—in short—the underdogs of the human race" (Wright, 1956:12).

The spirit of Bandung fueled the anti-colonial movement and gave it a new impetus.

Significantly, however, no one mentioned the color prejudice of brown groups toward Africans. Apparently that prejudice was deemed insignificant in the face of the overwhelming force of European colonial domination and the deep-rootedness of white racism. No doubt some were motivated not to mention the brown racism issue because of its potentially disruptive effect on the solidarity of the anti-colonial struggle.

A WORLD SYSTEM OF RACIAL STRATIFICATION EMERGES

Western imperialism during the post World War Two era shifted from a colonial to a neo-colonial form of domination. White Western capitalism forged ties of economic dependency between itself and the former colonies as well as those third world regions that had escaped colonialism.

While much has been written about the economics of neo-colonialism, too little attention had been paid to its cultural process. What had been previously achieved through direct administrative and military control was achieved during the post war era through cultural hegemony—the propagation of Western values through which third world peoples are conditioned to acceptance of a world view that facilitates Western economic domination. Two crucial preconditions lay behind this development: the political displacement of direct European colonial control and the transformation of the technology of cultural communication. Under the control of white Western nations, this new technology of cultural communication facilitated the diffusion of Western popular culture—via films, radio, television, etc.—throughout the third world.

Among the values diffused by Western culture are color valuations based on ideological assumptions of white superiority. This is evidenced in the consistency of race/color rankings throughout the contemporary world.

The valuations underlying this global stratification system are perceived not as racial but modern because white Western films, magazines, television and news publications project such values in a subliminal form. Thus, the images of white superiority propagated by these cultural products largely escape the notice of the recipient societies. Indeed, the same cultural influences that create attractions to hamburgers, Western music, Western clothing fashions and Western style home furnishings also create attractions to Western categories of color valuation. Third world societies, subjected to this cultural hegemony, soon began to evidence clear tendencies toward brown racism—manifested in positive valuations of whiteness and negative valuations of blackness.

Whereas the colonial form of brown racism was the result of contacts between browns and blacks, the neo-colonial form often exists independent of such contact. Thus, when we find these negative valuations of blackness in an ideological form (that is, expressed in terms of beliefs about the biological inferiority of blacks) in societies that have had no contact with blacks except that derived from white Western cultural media, we must conclude these are products of white Western culture.

THE MANIFESTATIONS OF BROWN RACISM

What is most striking is the extent of antipathy toward blacks among brown groups throughout the world. This antipathy, based on beliefs about the innate inferiority of Africans—beliefs which typically precede contacts with the latter, is the result of the assimilation of white Western culture in the post colonial era. An illustration of how these negative race/color categories are formed is provided by the experience of black American soldiers when first stationed in Oahu, Hawaii, during World War Two.

> The presence of a large number of white soldiers from the mainland had much to do with the importation of stereotyped conceptions. At first, many Hawaiian girls treated the Negroes like all other soldiers, but they soon found themselves under pressure to make distinctions. Girls who danced with Negroes at the U.S.O. were ostracized; in time most hostesses refused to dance with Negroes, even though they had initially assumed that they were to entertain all servicemen. (Shibutani, 1969:205)

Parallel problems are encountered by blacks in China. In May 1986 at Tianjin University, a skirmish between African and Chinese students occurred. It was a five hour long rock and bottle throwing brawl between 300–500 Chinese students and approximately 18 foreign (mostly African) students (Scott, 23 June, 1986:51). Shortly afterwards, in June 1986, as a result of the incident, there was a mass demonstration of 200 African students in Beijing to highlight racism in China. Complained one African student from Togo, "The Chinese do not consider us human" (Scott, 19 June, 1986:20).

According to the African Student Union (which monitors cases of racism against African students), "most cases of trouble with university or government authorities involve Africans who dated Chinese women" (Scott, 23 June, 1986:51).

Brazil—another society that evidences a pervasive brown racism—is often mistakenly thought to be free of racial prejudice, because the few blacks who attain upper class status are socially defined as whites. However, this token exemption in no way obviates the negative categorization of blackness. As one scholar has pointed out:

> The Brazilian outlook assumes that everyone would like to be white and that the whiter a person is the higher he is likely to be in the social status scale . . . The psychological effects upon dark skinned people of a wholesale desire for whitening are also unfavorable. They entail acceptance by dark people of the belief that whites are justified in discriminating against them. (Banton, 1967:280)

This pattern is hardly restricted to societies where blacks constitute a minority. We see a similar hierarchy of race/color in the West Indies where the majority populations are black. Referring to Jamaica, Henriques notes: "The important point is that all the different groups, from the black to the white, accept that the European is the ideal and the Negro inferior" (Henriques, 1964:128).

Hundreds of illustrations of brown racism could be cited.[2] Its prevalence in such countries as Mexico, Saudi Arabia, Sudan, Dominican Republic, Thailand, Morocco, and Venezuela is documentable.

THE SOCIAL PSYCHOLOGICAL DYNAMICS BEHIND BROWN RACISM

Like any other racism, brown racism is based on a culturally embedded categorical system of classification. In this instance, the system is absorbed concomitant with Westernization. This process facilitates the largely unconscious assignment of negative valuations to blacks based solely on their physical appearance. However, it does not explain the social psychological functions of those valuations. To explain this, it is necessary to understand the psychological implications of the Western white oriented racial stratification system from which brown racism derives. That stratification system is distinguished by the following characteristics:

1. It is based on the ideal of white racial features.
2. It consists of a continuum of color valuation—that is, the further away one's group is from the ideal, the lower its status.

3. Because the system has a positive and a negative node, it possesses only two unambiguously defined statuses: whiteness at the top and blackness at the bottom.

For individuals and groups who fit neither the positive or negative ideal, the consequences for their color/racial identity of acculturating the white Western world view (i.e., Westernization) are marginalization and psychological anxiety. Because they occupy an ambiguously defined position, browns fear being categorically identified with blacks. Their preoccupation with segregating themselves from blacks reflects their desire to avoid the stigma associated with blackness. This helps to explain why there is considerably more fraternization between whites and blacks and whites and browns than between browns and blacks. Whites, who possess the clearly defined superior status in the racial hierarchy, need not fear being subsumed under the same category as blacks. Whereas browns, lacking such a clearly defined superior status, are plagued by this fear. And for this reason, they exert strenuous energy to segregate themselves from blacks.

It is not only brown groups' repulsion from blacks but also their attraction to whites—indeed in many cases their aspirations for whiteness—that are produced by marginalization and the attendant psychological anxiety. This helps us to understand another curious fact. Among brown/white, black/white and brown/black rates of intermarriage, the latter are always—and by a considerable degree—the lowest. And in those few instances where members of a brown group marry a black person, they will tend to be ostracized by their community.

It might be argued that these low intermarriage rates between browns and blacks are merely the effect of ethnic differences, i.e., of the desires of brown groups to retain their distinctive ethnic cultures. However, this thesis fails to account for the consistently higher rates of intermarriage of browns to whites and to members of other brown groups who have different ethnic backgrounds.

Insofar as brown groups internalize the Western world view, they will experience a psychological need to distance themselves from blacks in order to validate their claims to superior racial status within the hierarchy of Western white color valuations. Thus, their anxiety about their racial status has the paradoxical effect of causing them to inadvertently support the principle of white superiority and the hierarchy of color stratification. That is, it causes them to support the system which also defines them as inferior.

ENDNOTES

[1] This incipient pattern of brown racism differs from the modal pattern in that it was not characterized by Afrophobia. Nevertheless, it shared the basic characteristics of the modal pattern—identification with whites and antipathy toward the darker skinned native population.

[2] Actually, symptoms of brown racism can be found among groups with African ancestry. For instance, until relatively recently, fair complexioned African Americans (e.g., often those of mixed racial backgrounds) tended to express prejudice against darker skinned African Americans (see Urdy *et al.*, 1971:722–733).

REFERENCES

Ballhatchet, K. (1980). *Race, Sex and Class Under the Raj.* New York: St. Martin Press.

Banton, M. (1967). *Race Relations.* New York: Basic Books.

Henriques, F. (1964). *Jamaica.* New York: London and Maxwell.

——— (1975). *Children of Conflict.* New York: E. P. Dutton.

Kimble, D. (1973). *The Afro-Asian Movement.* Jerusalem: Israel Universities Press.

Mason, P. (1970). *Patterns of Dominance.* Oxford, England: Oxford University Press. *Race Relations,* Oxford, England: Oxford University Press.

Morner, M. (1967). *Race Mixture in the History of Latin America.* New York: Little Brown.

——— (1970). *Race and Class in Latin America.* New York: Columbia University Press.

Newsweek (1955). "Asia—A Place in the Sun," 17 January.

Schermerhorn, R. A. (1976). *Comparative Ethnic Relations.* New York: Random House,

Schiller, H. I. (1976). *Communication and Cultural Domination.* White Plains, N.Y.: International Arts and Sciences Press.

Scott, M. (1986). "Blacks and Red Faces," *Far Eastern Economic Review,* 132, 19 June.

——— (1986). "Black Students and the Tide of Prejudice," *Far Eastern Economic Review,* 132, 23 June.

Shibutani, T. and K. Kwan (1969). *Ethnic Stratification.* New York: McMillan.

Tuttle, W. M. (ed.) (1973). *W. E. B. DuBois.* Englewood Cliffs, N.J.: Prentice Hall.

Urdy, J. R., K. E. Bauman, and C. Chase (1971). "Skin Color, Status, and Mate Selection," *American Journal of Sociology,* 76 (Jan.).

Wright, R. (1956). *The Color Curtain.* Cleveland and New York: The World Publishing Co.

Neil Earle

HOCKEY AS CANADIAN POPULAR CULTURE: TEAM CANADA 1972, TELEVISION AND THE CANADIAN IDENTITY

INTRODUCTION

If it's true that people reveal themselves in unguarded moments, then Canadians, as a people, should be fairly inscrutable. By international standards, we are a pretty reserved bunch. We are masters of understatement and known as a generally quiet, low-key, self-effacing people. When the world thinks of "machismo," "chutzpah," "chauvinism," or swaggering, bragging super-patriots, Canadians are never the first people who come to mind. Nor, unfortunately, do we have much of a reputation for having passion, soul, or "joie de vivre."

But there is one exception to all of the above. If you want to see Canadians shed their reserve, get happily excited, grow loud and become aggressively boastful, then go to a hockey game. Better yet, go to an international hockey game between Canada and an arch-rival like Russia.

In the following excerpt, Neil Earle examines what the eight-game 1972 Team Canada versus the Soviet Union series meant to ordinary Canadians. As Earle points out, the way Canadians reacted to that series suggests that hockey is definitely not "just a game" to Canadians. Who won that series was something that mattered greatly to millions of Canadians.

A sub-theme of Earle's excerpt is the role of television in creating and reinforcing cultural myths. He points out that there is not only a strong affinity between Canadians and hockey but also between hockey and television. Television was the perfect theatre for elevating the series from a sporting event to a great drama.

It is commonplace to assert that ice hockey signifies something about Canadian culture. Yet what it might signify has not been explored at any length by scholars. The 1972 Canada-Soviet series can serve as a useful model to probe certain questions. How does electronic technology impact upon a mass audience? Is there a bardic function for television?

Earle, Neil (1995). "Hockey as Canadian Popular Culture: Team Canada 1972, Television and the Canadian Identity," *Journal of Canadian Studies*, 30(2), Summer, 107–123.

The Canada-Soviet Series of September 1972 offers an especially useful paradigm for a study of "our game" on two levels: first, the series occasions reflection on the cultural nexus of the great national pastime; and second, electronic technology was sufficiently developed by 1972 to allow a sustained probe into its codes and structures. Especially interesting is mass technology's capacity to transform play into a form of collective drama.

For 27 days in September 1972 Canadian television was the matrix for a sports event that has become an enduring folk memory, a cultural text. For once, disparate notions of class, ethnicity and gender were welded into a rare Canadian moment. Millions of adult Canadians reserve hallowed psychic space for the memory of Paul Henderson's winning goal in Game Eight of the 1972 Canada-Soviet series.

Doug Beardsley's personalized account of the game, *Country on Ice*, argues that in Canada hockey is played for its own sake, for the fact that almost every Canadian has been touched by its mystery and mystique. Hockey is played with equal relish on both sides of the Ottawa River. Ice hockey has been called the "common coin" of Canada.

Televised hockey elevated the game into a national preoccupation. Canadian content is alive and well on prime time each April to June, as the Stanley Cup playoff series skate their seemingly interminable way across the nation's television screens.

Television is suited to the game's strengths. Hockey is a transition game—everyone gets a chance to play, and it is one of the few games where players can change "on the fly." Crucially, the spectators are very much part of the action in the confined, enclosed arena; they are close to the ice surface. This serves to heighten the intensity of crowd reactions, reactions which the cameras and microphones can easily amplify. It is not extravagant to assert a parallel between televised hockey's participatory dynamic and the presentational and affective aspects of Greek and Shakespearean drama, the Odeon and the "wooden O."

Hockey's speed and intensity played well to the myth of a rough, tough game demanding skill, effort, commitment, endurance. "It was the Canadian game because we had created it. . . . It suited a land in which the winter always loomed so large," explains Rutherford. "Even more the game fitted an image of Canadian manhood."[1] If there is no Canadian Stalingrad or Marathon, might not the Stanley Cup playoffs and the international Canada Cup competitions form an imaginative substitute? Ward Cornell, a broadcaster from the 1960s, expressed one aspect of hockey's overweening maleness: "We're tough, rugged guys from the North," he expostulated half-jokingly to Rutherford. The element of catharsis encouraged the "juvenile" facets of the game ("Stand your ground, don't back down from a fight!"), the ugly primitivism that led inevitably to the outcries and protests against hockey violence.

Yet hockey reflects another part of the male sensibility that televised hockey magnifies and transmits. This was and *is* the game's evocation of a peculiarly Canadian paradisiacal myth, the appeal to "the boy inside the man," a myth that intelligent students and players of the game have captured. Ken Dryden is a former goal-tender in the National Hockey League. One of the photographs in Dryden's *Home Game: Hockey and Life in Canada* is simply and tellingly entitled "Icons." It features a photograph of the Montreal Forum scoreboard imposed upon a two-page spread of boys in toques and sweaters playing shinny on a slough in St. Denis,

Saskatchewan.[2] The picture brilliantly captures hockey's imaginative hold over millions of Canadian males. The image of the boy with his hockey stick on the outdoor pond evokes something distinctive—"the true North strong and free."

This is the romance of hockey; play as idyll. The mysterious bonding of millions of Canadian males to "the game" traces back to the pond, the slough, the indoor rink; to the iced driveway, to the time when they, in their youthful fantasies, were Gordie Howe or Bobby Orr or Wayne Gretzky. Here is hockey's cultural core, the central explanation for its mystical attraction for prime ministers and pipe-fitters, for Nobel Prize winners and new immigrants.

One could argue that Canadians are involved in collective myth-making when watching hockey telecasts. The mass audience "decodes" the game. On one level, there is a straightforward hero-worship dynamic at work. Yet there are hidden duplicities as well. Some enjoy the "we're rough, tough guys from the North" message; hence, hockey's violence has never hurt its ratings. Others more likely enjoy the social segmentation noted by Rutherford. ("Where are all the women?" said one wife to her husband during her first game at Maple Leaf Gardens.) Then, as the wrestling phenomenon illustrates, excess possesses its own appeal. The striking uniforms, the crowd noises, the body checks—these aspects of excess throw into bold relief conventional notions of decorum, propriety and law and order. Hockey's very physicality is part of its appeal.

The series with the USSR stirred potent cultural signifiers. Ken Dryden wrote at the time: "[A]s far as the vast majority of Canadians are concerned, this series was not conceived in a spirit of brotherhood and understanding but as a means of putting down the Russians and asserting our claim to hockey supremacy."[3]

Some 15 million Canadians shared in the vicarious climax when Henderson scored for Canada. Scott Young remembered the excitement the series generated in the country: "Nothing to match the excitement of this series had ever happened in Canada; rarely anywhere in any sport."[4]

Ken Dryden also caught the embedded nationalist agenda:

> The talk all through the summer of 1972 was about the series. And because Canada was the best and sure to win, Canadians couldn't wait for the series to begin. It would be a glorious "coming out" party, a celebration of us. This gave to it a more fundamental dimension. For though much may be special about Canada, surrounded as it is historically and geographically by countries that are bigger, richer, more powerful, whose specialness seems more obvious, we cling to every symbol. A game is a game. But a symbol is not. We had to win this series.[5]

Dryden is right: symbols are important. The team's name—"Team Canada"—was rife with meaning, cast in a form that would be easily translatable into both French and English, thus fitting the bilingual ethos of the times. Little wonder that the 2 September 1972 opening night at the prestigious Montreal Forum resembled, in retrospect, the first act of a national drama.

The opening moments exploded with emotional energy and harbingers. Esposito scored for Canada after the first 30 seconds, Paul Henderson six minutes later. But in the next 53 minutes, recalled Dryden, "Team Canada's players, its fans, Canadians, could feel everything slipping away."[6] After such an explosive start the Soviets doggedly fought back to win 7–3. It was the worst of all possible scenarios: Team Canada humbled in one of the holy of holies of Canadian hockey, the Montreal Forum. The nightmarish spectacle that was to engage the entire nation for the next few days was launched.

As the continued fascination with "horror" movies reveals, popular culture is pleasurable when it takes on nail-biting intensity.

The nation-wide audience knew that according to the tried and true rhythm of playoff hockey, this second game would be crucial. The feeling in Maple Leaf Gardens was palpable. The cameras framed a bright red maple leaf on the television screens of the millions who watched: "There existed in historic Maple Leaf Gardens that night more stifling pressure than excitement . . . though the support of the fans was staggering. In conservative Toronto, where the fans are generally quite reserved . . . on this night they stood as one and chilled the air singing the national anthem. But there also remained a sharp sense of trepidation, of apprehension. This sense no longer pertained to what the opposition would bring, but the home team."[7]

The cameras and commentary were relaying "bardic television," functioning as an electronic stage bringing together viewers from the Atlantic and Pacific coasts. It superbly transmitted tragic pity and fear. Once again the Chorus-like presence of Foster Hewitt accentuated the strained emotion. A hapless Team Canada felt the sting of tragic reversal: after Game One a solid majority of their countrymen condemned them for refusing to shake hands with the Soviets, a convention of international hockey. That night, however, Maple Leaf Gardens was the venue for the spectacle of redemption: Team Canada won 4–1. It was to be their most decisive victory of the series.

Yet, the redemptive drama that unfolded in Game Two was only a prelude to the theatre of the absurd that would characterize Games Three and Four. Game Three was a heartbreaking encounter. The Canadians gave up two leads on brilliant short-handed goals by the Soviets. Team Canada was thankful to skate away with a 4–4 tie. A feeling of impending doom was intensifying as Game Four loomed in Vancouver.

The ambivalence about Team Canada that was building up across the country is best expressed in theatrical terms: the footlights were definitely down; the spectators were very much part of the action, and they were angry.

On 8 September 1972, the Vancouver fans chose revenge. The feverish fourth game in British Columbia saw Team Canada crushed 5–2. Worse, it was a loss Team Canada perhaps made inevitable by drawing two silly minor penalties in the first 10 minutes. The "home" part of the series had ended with the Soviets holding a commanding 2-1-1 lead. The final four games were to be played in Moscow. Ken Dryden later related: "It seemed as though it had all slipped beyond us." Then came an unusual chain of events. First, the players, seared by the reaction of the Vancouver fans, steeled their determination and decided to "win it for themselves."[8] Second, what Horace Newcomb has called "the aesthetics of television" began to emerge as a factor in its own right. Television, claims Newcomb, has a bias for intimacy: "Television is at its best when it offers us faces, reactions, explorations of emotions registered by human beings. The importance is not placed on the action, though that is certainly vital as stimulus. Rather, it is on the reaction to the action, to the human response."[9]

Not action but reaction—an interesting thesis. That wild night in Vancouver did not end with Team Canada's loss. Something else happened. Television beamed the spectacle of a totally believable Phil Esposito—his "sad-eyed, washed-out face, bathed with the sweat of the world," in Dryden's words—speaking "heart to heart" with the Canadian public. Esposito, who had emerged as the unofficial leader of Team Canada, had his moment of personal angst captured in close-up by the camera as waves of frustration convulsed his countrymen. Yet Esposito treated the audience to what television does so effectively, some would say too effectively: the personalizing and humanizing of a complex, mass spectacle: "To the people of Canada, we're trying our best. . . . The people boo us. We're all disappointed, disenchanted. I can't believe people are booing us. If the Russians boo their players like some of our Canadian fans—not all, just some—then I'll come back and apologize. We're completely disappointed. I can't believe it. We're trying hard. Let's face facts. They've got a good team. We're all here because we love Canada. It's our home and that's the only reason we came."[10]

The "intimate" medium was about to transform the 30-odd players of Team Canada into "our guys," an embattled little family up against life's bewildering complexities and letdowns. This was what television had been transmitting and celebrating for decades.

If there was intimacy there was also *continuity*, the second of Newcomb's televisual aesthetics. Prime time's dynamics helped make Team Canada as familiar as extended family: Clarke and Cournoyer, Henderson and Ratelle, Esposito and the Mahovlich brothers. Heroes are often found in defeat, as the reputations of Winston Churchill, Charles de Gaulle and John Diefenbaker can attest. The shrill voice of Foster Hewitt crackling across the ether from the grim and dour Soviet capital for the last four games thus deepened the element of participatory drama. In Ken Dryden's words, those scratchy transmissions over the pole came embedded with their own dramatic intensity, "momentous with distance . . . never certain of getting through."[11]

Canadians watching the telecast of 22 September 1972 from Moscow by now were involved in something deeper than sport. There was an element of heroic daring in the fact of a middle power contending with the largest national land mass in the world, a nuclear-armed super-power at the time, for hockey supremacy. The very audacity of the attempt seemed heroic. The fight had to be played out to the final seconds, according to the prescribed codes of sport. If this was not Newcomb's "mythic model," then what was?

Team Canada lost their first game in Moscow 5-4. Yet the Canadians "were adjusting, adapting, experimenting . . . now able to break up the Soviets' intricate passing plays." Thus Game Six was do-or-die for Team Canada, a spiritual *ne plus ultra*. They chose to "do." Game Six produced the first Canadian victory since that seemingly long-ago night in Toronto. It was noted for something else as well: a particular piece of infamy that starkly reflects hockey's darker side. Canada's Bobby Clarke purposely set out to "tap" and thus sabotage the speedy Russian Kharlamov's ankle. Years later Clarke was only mildly repentant: "It's not something I would've done in an NHL game, at least I hope I wouldn't. But that situation . . . at that stage in the series, with everything that was happening, it was necessary."[12]

"With everything that was happening"—if there was little grace in Clarke's confession there was admittedly some in his candour. For by now these were obviously more than just hockey games; the whole experience had been lifted beyond sport. The series was pointing to something beyond itself, something primal, something of hockey's own elemental origins.

The telecasts revealed more and more of the pride as well as the insecurity welling up from deep inside the psyche of a young nation at a "coming out party" with the whole world watching. The emotional intensity of this electronic drama stunned all the participants. "Some of them [the players] after that series were never the same," Tony Esposito related years later.

After Team Canada pulled together for a 4–3 victory in a wild stick-swinging Game Seven to tie the series, the stage was set for the final resolution, the eighth and final game of the series. "The game was broadcast on both CBC and CTV. All other programming came to a stop. Canada's population in 1972 was 21.8 million. On this Thursday afternoon, a work day, 7.5 million watched."[13] Foster Hewitt had been saying "Hello Canada!" for decades, but it never seemed to resonate with such meaning before. For, in an amazing moment of postmodern reflexivity, it was Foster Hewitt "playing" Foster Hewitt that added to the sense of other-worldliness that last night in Moscow.

The last four games no doubt evoked another shared folk memory. There was the weighted sociological meaning of over four decades of small-town families huddled around the radio as Foster Hewitt's voice came crackling from one of the few big cities in Canada at the time.

On 28 September 1972, 12 million Canadians heard that voice say they were the best in the world at hockey. It was a unique Canadian epiphany. A Soviet coach commented years later: "We do not have the spirit to draw on that these Canadians do." To him, the Canadian players had "a light that cannot be put out. . . . You defeat them sometimes, but you discourage them never."[14] What was the source of that light? Was it money and commercialism? Was it the male physicality and exclusiveness? Or perhaps it was something much deeper—the intensification and celebration of a collective myth as enhanced by electronic technology.

The national fervour unleashed across the country was unprecedented in modern, peace-time Canada. Ontario Education Minister Tom Wells intervened to allow half a million elementary and secondary school students in the province to watch or listen to the final game in school auditoriums or cafeterias.

The *Calgary Herald*, whose front page on 28 September pictured a crowd of Calgarians watching the game in a downtown department store, a scene "undoubtedly repeated in stores, offices and living rooms across the country," recorded how actor William Hutt, declaiming King Lear at Stratford, Ontario, paused dramatically during the storm scene to announce the score to the 2,000 students in his audience.[15]

Hockey, for all its regrettable "male-only" encodements, its violence and occasional juvenility, serves as a primal source of identity-reinforcement for Canadians. It is rooted in a paradisiacal locus of the imagination, drawing upon the game's rural, northern signifiers. Playing hockey on the ponds that dot the frozen landscape for many appears to be nothing less than a Canadian rite of passage, a vital part of the acculturation process.

If the 1972 series was a Canadianized form of the Persian-Greek Wars, and Foster Hewitt—to stretch the metaphor—was our electronically relayed Homer with a microphone, then television served as national theatre. The tiny screen became the locus for "the time of heroes." Television's bias for intimacy helped enshrine one of those rare shared moments of collective national myth, an electronically catalyzed national drama.

The 1972 series lives on in the popular imagination. It demonstrated as never before or since that televised hockey, perhaps the most characteristic artifact of Canada's popular culture, points to a desire for something essential about Canadians as a northern people. Winter, with its abstract black and white patterns, its long shadows and desolation, has nurtured—perhaps to their surprise—a nation of myth-makers after all.

ENDNOTES

[1] Rutherford, *When Television Was Young*, 248.

[2] Ken Dryden and Roy MacGregor, *Home Game: Hockey and Life in Canada* (Toronto: McClelland and Stewart, 1989), 4–5.

[3] Ken Dryden with Mark Mulvoy, *Face-Off At The Summit* (Toronto: Little, Brown, 1973), 65.

[4] Scott Young, *Hello Canada! The Life and Times of Foster Hewitt* (Toronto: Seal Books, 1985), 172.

[5] Dryden and MacGregor, *Home Game*, 202. Dryden's summation of the series in Chapter Five has a fine postmodern ring in its title, "No Final Victories."

[6] Ibid.

[7] Ibid., 64–65.

[8] Ibid., 94, 97, 102.

[9] Horace Newcomb, *TV: The Most Popular Art* (New York: Anchor Press, 1974), 245–246.

[10] Scott Morrison, *The Days Canada Stood Still: Canada vs USSR* (Toronto: McGraw Hill, 1989), 95.

[11] Dryden and MacGregor, *Home Game*, 194.

[12] Morrison, *The Days Canada Stood Still*, 151, 167.

[13] Dryden and MacGregor, *Home Game*, 194.

[14] Ibid., 36.

[15] "Canadians flip as Russians slip—WE'RE THE CHAMPS." *Calgary Herald*, 29 September 1972.

QUESTIONS

DISCUSSION QUESTIONS

1. In your experience, how do cultural differences make communication between people difficult?

2. What kinds of assumptions do people from your own cultural background tend to make about life and the way society works?

3. Immigrants to Canada leave their home culture behind. Thinking of the immigrants to Canada whom you know, what things do you think they miss the most about their original culture?

4. One kind of cultural message conveyed by the Western-dominated worldwide media concerns what fashions and what physical features are considered to be beautiful. Is this message appreciative of a wide variety of cultural definitions of beauty, or does a Western image predominate?

DATA COLLECTION EXERCISES

1. The fact that women live longer than men could be attributed either to biology or to culture. Find some historical data on whether the life expectancy gap between genders has always been about the same as it is today. Also, compare Canada's gender gap in life expectancy to that of other countries.

2. Research the gender, ethnicity, age, and income level of sociologists on the faculty at a major university. Does this help to explain the main concerns of modern sociology?

3. Try changing your lifestyle for a month by ceasing to use as much modern technology as is feasible. For example, stop using your TV, stereo, microwave, telephone, car, etc. Record whether your new lifestyle has led to any changes in the way you think and feel about life.

4. Analyze a grade school reader in terms of the cultural values that its stories portray.

WRITING EXERCISES

1. The Canadian sports scene has changed since the 1972 Canada-Soviet hockey series; pro hockey now has to share the spotlight with major league baseball and basketball. Write a brief (500-word) essay on whether or not hockey remains as important to Canadians as it was in 1972.

2. Write a brief (500-word) opinion piece accounting for why people around the world seem so receptive to American mass culture; or why the market for foreign cultural products (i.e. movies, music) is relatively small in North America.

3. Write a brief (500-word) essay on the limits of tolerance of subcultures. In your essay, describe when, if ever, you think a dominant culture would be justified in forbidding the cultural practice of a minority group. For example, should the dominant culture tolerate polygamy, tax evasion, child labour, refusal to serve in the military, unlicensed medical practice, or sex discrimination out of respect for a subculture's right to self determination?

4. Write a brief (500-word) essay on whether it is possible for a social scientist to achieve an objective view of his or her own culture.

SUGGESTED READINGS

1. Atwood, Margaret (1972). *Survival: A Thematic Guide to Canadian Literature.* Toronto: Anansi. This book is an attempt by one of Canada's most famous writers to see what can be learned about the Canadian national identity by examining its literature. Her thesis is that one of the recurring themes in our literature is our attempts to define ourselves as survivors in a vast and often hostile land.

2. Harris, Marvin (1989). *Our Kind: The Evolution of Human Life and Culture.* New York: Harper & Row. Harris is an anthropologist who takes all of human history as his subject. In this book he tries to offer plausible explanations of why various cultural institutions and practices came into being.

3. Morris, Desmond (1967). *The Naked Ape: A Zoologist's Study of the Human Animal.* London: Jonathan Cape. This book tries to unravel the "nature versus nurture" mystery by starting from the nature perspective. It's an attempt to see how much of modern cultural behaviour can be attributed to the nature of the human beast.

SECTION 2   SOCIALIZATION

Introduction

Socialization is the process of learning cultural values and norms. People learn to be different (or the same). People who grow up in a particular culture internalize a similar "package" of norms, beliefs, and values. The more generally people accept this "package," the more smoothly the group will function. Sociologists call this smooth functioning "social integration."

Socialization begins at birth and continues throughout our lives. The most intense learning occurs when we are young, so we call this "primary socialization." Children have less power than adults, so primary socialization is more or less imposed. Through socialization children learn to conform to adult expectations about the right ways of managing physical needs, manners, and morals. For example, young children learn to be hungry at mealtime, sleep when it is dark, and so on.

By contrast, "secondary socialization" is an ongoing process of learning throughout the life cycle. It occurs as we anticipate and adjust to new experiences and new situations.

How does the more basic process of primary socialization occur? Symbolic interactionism, an important theoretical approach in sociology, has provided us with insight into this process. It argues that people actively participate in their own socialization. George H. Mead (1863-1931) and Charles H. Cooley (1864-1929), two American sociologists, were key influences in developing this symbolic interactionist perspective. In fact, they influenced the way most sociologists think about socialization.

Both were interested in how people develop a sense of self. Cooley believed children are born with an instinctive capacity for self development that unfolds through social interaction. A key element in the development of the self is the perception of others' reactions to us. Cooley's concept of "the looking-glass self" captures this idea: "*I* feel about me the way I think *you* think about me."

Mead was interested in the ways we learn to present ourselves in different social situations. According to Mead, we learn symbolically through role-taking. As children, our behaviour comes to combine instinctive reaction and imitation. Mead called this the "pre-play" stage. Later, during the "play" stage, children learn to take on the roles of others. They objectify their experience by seeing themselves from other people's point of view. Then, in the subsequent "game" stage, children learn to handle several roles at once. In this way, they learn to anticipate the behaviour of others.

Finally, children learn to internalize general social expectations by imagining how others will act and react. At this "generalized other" stage the child has a sense of self and can react in a socially approved way.

Social meanings are based on assumptions about other people's understandings and intentions, so they are always more or less ambiguous. In this sense, they are subject to ongoing interpretation and negotiation. In most situations, previous experience helps us to imagine new experiences, so we become good at what sociologists call "anticipatory socialization." There are many social arrangements that make anticipatory socialization easier. Some examples include university initiation weeks, new employee orientation programs, parenting support groups, and pre-retirement courses.

Sometimes new situations are so strange that we cannot rely on previous experience to tell us how to act. Then we may enter a period of resocialization. An extreme example of resocialization is military "boot camp." Similarly, whenever we change important roles—as we do in divorce, relocation, or career change—we may need a period of disengagement before we can establish new relationships.

NATURE VERSUS NURTURE

Socialization is not something that "happens to us" so much as something in which we actively engage. Because of their individual differences, people experience socialization differently. And our socialization experience inevitably depends on a combination of personality and social experiences. For example, the same family may socialize sons differently than daughters, first-born children differently than later children, and so on.

One of the big questions in social science—a question that puzzles sociologists and psychologists alike—is how much of "what we are" is determined by socialization and how much is inborn. This question is sometimes called "the nature versus nurture debate." The assumption that nature dominates us is called "biological determinism." The opposite of biological determinism is "social determinism," which at its extreme gives us an "oversocialized" view of human nature.

In the past people believed that behavioural differences were (for the most part) genetically determined. That is, people are born with certain aptitudes and dispositions, including an aptitude for good or evil. People even applied this point of view to explaining differences between races and differences between men and women.

Today, we are more conscious of the weakness in this line of reasoning. It's one thing to say that nature helps explain individual differences, and quite another to say that it explains group differences. Some recent evidence indicates that many differences once thought to be innate are really the result of socialization. However, the question remains unresolved. The relative weights of nature and nurture continue to interest researchers.

Consider the focus of the current attention on male-female differences. Some argue that gender differences develop because parents react to innate differences in their children. In other words, girls become more verbal than boys because they are more receptive to verbal interactions with their parents. Boys become more physically aggressive because they respond more positively to aggressive play.

Others argue that parents reinforce behaviour in a way that is consistent with their (cultural) expectations and stereotypes. In fact, parents begin to think differently about male and female children even before birth! For example, they assume a large and active fetus will be turn out to be a baby boy.

It seems likely that gender differences in adults are the result of gender-based socialization interacting with some innate biological differences. To draw attention to this interplay, sociologists distinguish between sex (the biological fact of maleness or femaleness) and gender (the social distinction between maleness and femaleness). Then they re-phrase traditional assumptions about sex differences as research questions about gender learning.

THE CONTEXT OF SOCIALIZATION

For most young children throughout the world, the family is the most significant "agent of socialization." Other "agents" include friends, school, church, volunteer organizations, and the media. What distinguishes these agents from all other social institutions that influence us is intent. Agents of socialization consciously try to socialize us.

We generally assume that parents are the best people to socialize children. Many people regret that so many young children are required to spend so much time at day care or in school, away from parental influence. We sometimes long for a simpler time when mothers stayed home with young children, ignoring the structural inequalities this reflected. The first excerpt in this section describes an interesting exception to our usual assumptions. The children of Oneida were raised in an intentionally non-family communal setting. This community provided well-supervised day care for very young children at a period in American history before universal education.

The second excerpt is an interesting contrast to the first in that it too raises questions about child care. This time the setting is Scandinavia, where day care and women's employment are taken for granted. However, as Wolfe points out, there are some reasons to be cautious about the Scandinavian system.

Not everything children learn from parents in family settings is desirable. There is increased evidence that violence, and a tolerance for violence, is learned. A significant number of batterers in MacLeod's Canadian study (see excerpt 2.3) were abused as children, as were a significant number of abused wives. From other recent studies we also know that date violence is common, and that much marital abuse began as date abuse. These adults, it seems, were socialized to be violent.

S. Matarese and P. G. Salmon

THE CHILDREN OF ONEIDA

INTRODUCTION

Families are the most important influence on the early development of most Canadians. But this excerpt describes how a group of American children were socialized outside the context of family living, by the community as a whole.

In the mid-1800s the Oneida community was established in New York state by a religious leader named John Noyes. Reverend Noyes' followers agreed not to marry or form attachments to one particular partner, but rather to define themselves as part of a community-wide "complex" marriage.

Children born into the community remained with their mothers until they were weaned. After that, the whole community raised them. Noyes strongly discouraged close relationships between mothers and their children. Indeed he thought any close bonds, even friendship, would disrupt the group, so he devised ways of preventing their formation.

Noyes may have disregarded the emotional needs of his followers, but materially he provided for them very well. At a time when few American children received a formal education, children in the Oneida community received both day care and schooling. They learned to read and write, and later they integrated their schoolwork with useful labour in a kind of nineteenth century "work-study program." Noyes may have had strange views about marriage and sexuality, but he and his group created a "modern" and inventive way of socializing children.

One of history's most remarkable experiments in family organization is found in the Oneida Community, a religious utopia which flourished in northwestern New York State during the nineteenth century. Its social structure and child-rearing practices represented a radical alternative to patterns of community organization based upon the nuclear family. Some of the community's children were the result of one of the earliest experiments in human eugenics. All were raised communally according to religious ideals which stressed cooperation and non-exclusive attachments among community members. The purpose of this essay is to provide a broad overview of the community's unique social organization and resultant child-rearing practices.

Founded in 1848 by radical theologian John Humphrey Noyes, the Oneida Community was based upon the doctrine of "Perfectionism" which held that through union with God, persons could live lives free from sin.[1] Noyes and his

Matarese, S. and P.G. Salmon (1983). "Heirs to the Promised Land: The Children of Oneida," *International Journal of Sociology of the Family*, 13(2), Autumn, 35–43. Reprinted by permission.

three hundred followers sought to emulate the primitive apostolic church in which "believers possessed one heart and one soul and held all things in common."[2] These principles gave Oneida some of its most distinctive features: economic communism, communal sleeping and dining arrangements, government by mutual criticism and collective labour in agriculture, manufacturing and light industry.

The communal ideal extended even to sexual relations and resulted in the controversial practice: "complex marriage."[3] Under this systems, monogamous relationships were forbidden and adults were encouraged to have sexual relations with a wide variety of partners. Central to the institution was the practice of "male continence," a method of birth control which allowed the community to separate the propagative from the social functions of sex.[4]

During the first twenty years of the community's history, the number of births was intentionally limited, averaging fewer than two a year.[5] By 1868, however, Noyes had become mindful of the need to develop a new generation of Oneidans to carry out his ideals. He initiated an experiment in human breeding which he called "stirpiculture."[6] During the next ten years, fifty-eight children were born as a result of these selected pairings.

According to "Perfectionist" doctrine, children belonged to the entire community, and the women were exhorted to understand they produced children not for their own satisfaction, but for God and communism. Noyes maintained the love of the community was superior to the "special love" engendered by exclusive child-parent bonding. The community's newspaper, the Oneida *Circular*, emphasized the need to "communize the children as completely as we have all other possessions."[7]

In keeping with this doctrine, the community assumed primary responsibility for child-rearing. There were several reasons for this. First, Noyes wanted to ensure that socialization was standardized as far as possible. To this end, he appointed as caretakers a small group of his most loyal and trusted followers. Second, Noyes feared that an intense attachment between parents and children would threaten the system of complex marriage by encouraging exclusionary loyalties.[8]

Separating parents and children took place in stages. During the first year of life, children were cared for by their mothers, much as in any traditional family. At the age of weaning, however, the community began to take a more active and intrusive role. At this time, children were placed in the community's nursery during the day. This nursery was located in a special wing of the Mansion House, the main residence of the community's members. Here they encountered for the first time not only new caretakers, but other children of comparable age. The intent was to wean the child not only physically, but psychologically. This process was virtually completed when at age three they were moved into communal sleeping quarters which further curtailed the amount of maternal-child contact. Although parents and children were allowed time together during the day, this marks the point at which parental—especially maternal—influence ceased to have a decisive impact on the child's day-to-day behaviour.

Since Noyes opposed what he termed "philoprogenitiveness," that is, special loyalty or love for one's own progeny,[9] it is surprising that he permitted mothers and children virtually unrestricted access to each other during the infant's first fourteen months. Sustained contact of this duration allowed ample time for the formation of strong maternal-child attachment. This resulted in powerful emotional ties that ran counter to the spirit of communal love. The subsequent separation of mother and child was apparently quite traumatic, especially for the mother.

Although the advantages of communal care were publicly supported by women's testimonials in the Oneida *Circular,* memoirs of the community's children reveal considerably more ambivalence on the part of their mothers. For example, Pierrepont Noyes' autobiography poignantly describes weekly meetings in his mother's room in which she lavished affection upon him as though trying to make up for lost opportunity. He recalled she frequently interrupted his play to ask, "Darling, do you love me?"[10] Yet toward the end of their visits, she became aloof if it appeared he would resist returning to the Children's House. To a young child, this abrupt change in demeanor must have been confusing. For the mothers, it created strong feelings of conflict. They needed an outlet for the love that had developed during the child's first year. On the other hand, they were aware of the community's practice of temporarily suspending visiting privileges between parents and children for displays of "special love."[11] This is illustrated in Corinna Ackley Noyes' recollection of a chance encounter with her mother during a two-week enforced separation:

> I caught a glimpse of (my mother) passing through a hallway near the Children's House and rushed after her screaming. She knew—what I was too young to know—that if she stopped to talk to me another week might be added to our sentence. Hoping, I suppose, to escape, she stepped quickly into a nearby room. But I was as quick as she. I rushed after her, flung myself upon her, clutching her around the knees, crying and begging her not to leave me, until some Children's House mother, hearing the commotion, came and carried me away.[12]

Between the ages of three and six, the children spent their days in the East Room, appointed much like modern-day nurseries. Toys and playthings were provided, which the children were expected to share in a non-possessive fashion.[13]

Although play was encouraged, Oneida's philosophy of child-rearing emphasized constant instruction and training. As a result, even young children's schedules were planned to allow ample time for many activities which were explicitly instructional. The young children arose at 5:35 every morning. After washing and dressing, they had a brief exercise period, breakfast and a session of Bible reading. At this point children participated in work, recreation and religious training that filled most of the day. By seven o'clock, the youngest children were in bed; the older ones retired an hour later.[14]

EDUCATION

At age six, children were moved to the South Room and formal education began. Formal education was required of all children, and encompassed primary and secondary grades. Instruction was provided in a range of subjects, including reading, spelling, grammar, composition, arithmetic, algebra and Latin.[15] Although books and other instructional aids were available, students were encouraged to master these subjects through discussion and class reports rather than by memorization.[16]

A community University was planned but never materialized. Several young men received college educations subsidized by the community. They received training in applied areas, such as medicine, which they were then expected to practice within the community.[17]

In addition to their schoolwork, the older children were required to work in the community's agricultural and manufacturing activities. On an average day, children devoted approximately equal time to work and formal studies. In addition to farming, carpentry, and housekeeping, children's jobs included the production of traps, boxes, and traveling bags.[18] Despite the community's stated belief in sexual equality, young women were most often channeled into traditional women's work including laundry, sewing and housekeeping services.

An important aspect of socialization concerns the manner in which a community responds to transgressions. At Oneida, people other than biological parents played a significant role in socializing and disciplinary activities. Children were accountable not only to the community's adult members, but to God and their peers. Accountability to adults took the form of frequent "criticisms," a practice in which even young children were apprised of their flaws by a group of adults and provided with guidelines for rectifying their mistakes. These criticisms had religious overtones as well, for children were encouraged to "confess Christ" and thereby restore themselves to good standing in the spiritual realm. Children were also encouraged to monitor one another's behaviour, and to report transgressions to appropriate adults.[19]

DISCIPLINE

Noyes had a liberal attitude toward discipline and discouraged corporal punishment.[20] Instead, efforts were made to talk and reason with young offenders. Adults were encouraged to use positive rewards and incentives to encourage behavior consistent with community norms. For example, one Children's House worker initiated a club known as the "Order of the O and F" (Obedient and Faithful), giving badges for good behaviour.[21]

Descriptions of the children generally portray them as cheerful, energetic and well-behaved. Compared with children outside the community, they were perceived as highly cooperative and mutually supportive.[22] They were also physically robust: a medical report by Dr. Theodore Noyes revealed they were taller and heavier then a sample of children taken from a Boston school.[23]

Among the most controversial features of the community's child-rearing practices was sexual initiation. This occurred at a young age, in some cases predating puberty.[24] At the age of 10 to 12, children were considered to be adults and moved into individual rooms in the Mansion House. There their sexual initiation took place. Young boys were paired with women past child-bearing age; girls were initiated primarily by Noyes himself.

The practice of sexually pairing young and old members of the community was based upon the doctrine of "ascending fellowship," a reflection of Noyes' belief that community members ranged in ascending order from those who were the least to those who were the most nearly perfect. He argued persons who were at lower levels of spiritual development should associate with their superiors; hence the term, "ascending fellowship."[25] In general, it was felt older persons were spiritually more advanced than their younger counterparts. When applied to complex marriage, this principle dictated younger persons should be paired with older persons of the opposite sex. This arrangement was buttressed by systematic segregation of young men and women between the ages of 12 through 25 to curb what Noyes termed "horizontal fellowship." This referred to the natural attractions of young people for one another.[26] Noyes believed children experienced "amative desires" when quite young, and apparently thought it best to channel such sexual energies in ways which promoted community solidarity.[27] Specifically, he wished to avoid the intergenerational conflict responsible for the demise of earlier communal efforts.

THE DISSOLUTION OF THE COMMUNITY

Despite his best efforts, many of the offspring grew dissatisfied with community life and thereby contributed to its dissolution.

Several reasons explain this unanticipated outcome. First, though raised under conditions that promoted social homogeneity, children of the Oneida community were not preselected for specific spiritual or moral values as their forebears had been. This is true even of the stirpicults, who were presumed by Noyes to have inherited their parents' moral and spiritual commitment.[28] There is implied in this a perhaps unfounded faith both in the powers of environmental control and the mechanisms of heritability.

Educational factors contributed as well. Children sent to college developed a perspective on life that transcended the community's boundaries. Those who returned often did so with criticisms of the existing social order.[29] Even those whose education took place within the community grew dissatisfied. For one thing, Noyes encouraged a spirit of scientific inquiry in the educational process that undoubtedly undermined the faith and obedience which had been fundamental to the Perfectionist creed.[30] Second, the children's teachers lacked the charismatic qualities that had aided Noyes in converting people to Perfectionism. Moreover, aside from his role in sexually initiating young women, Noyes appears to have been remote from the day-to-day activities of the children.

Finally, despite Noyes' emphasis on "ascending fellowship," children developed strong peer attachments. They ate, slept, studied, worked and played together beginning at a very early age. This fostered solidarity vis-a-vis adults. They founded secret societies, resisted pressures to report on one another, and proved to be mutually supportive in the face of adult intrusions.[31] Despite frequent contact with older community members in sexual encounters, they retained a loyalty to their own cohort.

The Oneida experiment came remarkably close to achieving a system of child-rearing in which environmental factors and heritability were successfully controlled. Under such highly regulated conditions, it may come as a surprise that the community was racked by internal dissent and ultimately dissolved. This outcome attests to the difficulties in reshaping traditional family structure and insuring the continuity of the resultant changes from one generation to the next.

ENDNOTES

1   Noyes (1849).

2   Oneida (1867:11).

3   Carden (1969:49–61).

4   Noyes (1866).

5   Oneida (1875:19).

6   Noyes (1875).

7   Oneida *Circular*, June 5, 1868.

8   Barren and Miller, eds. (1875:282). An early community statement of "general principles" regarding the relationship of parents to children also declared that love between
adult men and women was a "superior passion" to love between adults and children.
Oneida *Circular*, January 29, 1863.

9   Oneida *Circular*, October 5, 1868.

10   Noyes (1937:65–67).

11   Carden (1969:63–66).

12   Corinna Ackley Noyes (1960:16).

13   Oneida *Circular*, June 15, 1868.

14   Oneida *Circular*, October 29, 1857.

15   Robertson (1970:182–185).

16   Oneida (1850:15).

17   Robertson (1970:178).

18   Noyes (1937:101).

19   Pierrepont Noyes (1937:51).

20   Oneida (1850:13–14).

21   Kanter (1972:14).

22   Noyes (1937:148).

23   Theodore Noyes (1878:2).

24   Van de Warker (1884:789).

25   Carden (1969:52–53).

26   Oneida *Circular*, April 4, 1864.

27   Van de Warker (1884:789).

28   Parker (1935:264). Parker quotes Noyes as follows:
I can tell just when all this repeating of troubles is going to end. It will be when wisdom
and righteousness are fixed in the blood, so that the lessons which the parents have
learned by experience, the children will have in them when they are born. . . .
Educating (children) is not going to do it, only as it helps the process of breeding. It is
breeding that is going to finish the work.

29   Noyes' eldest son. Theodore, for example, was an avowed agnostic. See Carden
(1969:96).

30   Oneida *Circular*, January 4, 1869.

31   Pierrepont Noyes (1937:49,112).

REFERENCES

Carden, Maren Lockwood (1969). *Oneida: Utopian Community to Modern Corporation.* Baltimore: Johns Hopkins Press.

Kanter, Rosabeth (1972). *Commitment and Community.* Massachusetts: Harvard University Press.

Noyes, Corinna Ackley (1960). *The Days of My Youth.* Utica, New York: Widtman Press.

Noyes, John Humphrey (1849). *Confessions of John Humphrey Noyes, Part 1: Confessions of Religious Experience: Including a History of Modern Perfectionism.* Oneida, New York.

———— (1866). *Male Continence.* Oneida, New York: Office of the Circular.

———— (1875). Essay on Scientific Propagation. Oneida, New York: Oneida Community.

———— (1875). *Home Talks.* Edited by Alfred Barron and George Noyes Miller. Oneida, New York: Oneida Community.

Noyes, Pierrepont (1937). *My Father's House: An Oneida Boyhood.* New York: Farrar and Rinehart.

Noyes, Theodore (1878). Report on the Health of Children in the Oneida Community. Oneida, New York: Oneida Community.

Oneida (1850). *Second Annual Report of the Oneida Association.* Oneida, New York: Leonard and Co., Printers.

———— (1864–1879). *The Circular.* Oneida, New York: Oneida Community: Thirteen Volumes.

———— (1867). Handbook of the Oneida Community. Wallingford, Connecticut: Office of the Circular

———— (1875). Handbook of the Oneida Community 1875. Oneida, New York: Office of the Circular.

Parker, Robert Allerton (1935). *A Yankee Saint.* New York: G. P. Putnam's Sons.

Robertson, Constance Noyes (1970). *Oneida Community: An Autobiography.* New York: Syracuse University Press.

Van de Warker, Ely (1884). "A Gynecological Study of the Oneida Community," *The American Journal of Obstetrics and Diseases of Women and Children*, XVIII:785–810.

Alan Wolfe

THE DAY-CARE DILEMMA: A SCANDINAVIAN PERSPECTIVE

INTRODUCTION

In many societies, including Canada's, it is assumed that parents provide the best care for young children. Of the alternatives, regulated day care is presumed to be better than unregulated care. However, as Wolfe points out in this excerpt, "one should never forget that day care is provided primarily to serve parents and only secondarily to serve children."

In Canada regulated child care is expensive and in short supply. Less than 20 percent of Canadian children attend licensed day care facilities. Most children of employed parents in Canada are cared for by sitters. Many of these sitters may be family members, since one-third of them are not paid. In Scandinavia, public day care is much more generally available. North Americans often look to Scandinavian countries with envy because of their supportive family policies, but as this excerpt makes clear, there are some disadvantages to the Scandinavian system. Children may not be as well served by a system that rests on the assumption that parents' primary responsibility is employment. Wolfe argues against turning the problem of child care over to government, and points out the advantage of parental work flexibility.

You may want to read this excerpt a second time, and think about the problem again, after reading the excerpts on employed parents and the division of housework (excerpt 6.3) and "brave new families" (excerpt 7.3).

Nowhere is the public commitment to child care more extensive than in Scandinavia. Sweden and Denmark have both committed themselves to providing full-time institutional care for children from the age of three months until they begin school (typically at age seven).

According to a recent study by the quasi-official Social Research Institute of Denmark, only 5 percent of Danish children under the age of six are being raised full-time by their mothers at home; fewer than 20 percent are being watched at home by working parents on shifts, mothers on pregnancy leave, unemployed parents, or parents who work at home. Twenty-one percent are in private day care and 55 percent are in public day care. In Sweden fewer children are in public day care, in part because of more generous maternity leaves. (The Swedish Social Democrats recently committed themselves to full maternity benefits for eighteen

Wolfe, A. (1989). "The Day-Care Dilemma: A Scandinavian Perspective," *The Public Interest*, 95, Spring, 14–23.

months, a policy that would greatly lower reliance on public day care for infants.) About a third of Swedish children remain at home with their mothers, but that minority will probably continue to shrink.

Enthusiasts for public day care rightly point out that there are few latchkey children in Scandinavia, and that children in day care are better nourished and more self-sufficient than children who stay at home. If the American and Scandinavian ways of raising children were the only ones from which to choose, the latter would be preferable by most criteria. Yet one should never forget, especially when turning to Scandinavia for lessons relevant to America, that public day care is provided primarily to serve parents and only secondarily to serve children.

DAY CARE'S EFFECT ON CHILDREN

There is no unambiguous answer to the question of whether extensive public day care is better for children than the "traditional" family. Bengt-Erik Andersson, a Swedish educational psychologist, carried out a longitudinal study of 119 Stockholm and Gothenberg children from their first to their eighth years. He found that age of entry into public day care was a consistent predictor of success later on: children who began attending day care earlier fared better when they reached school.

Andersson and Lars Dencik (who has studied the lives of small children in Scandinavia) both conclude that the day-care system works well. Yet the matter is far from settled. A governmental commission on the status of children in Denmark, contradicting more optimistic studies, wrote in 1981 of a "closed child's world" cut off from adult life. Echoing that report, the National Association of School Psychologists found:

> It is becoming more common that children who are beginning school are antisocial, loud, and confused. They are uncertain, unhappy, and badly in need of contact. They do not have the awareness that early beginners in school once had and they are missing moral conceptions. They have no respect for elders and are untrained in using their body and their hands. Many are passive or aggressive and they do not understand ordinary reprimands.

Ultimately, however, no amount of empirical research can resolve all the questions about day care. And even if the experts unanimously supported day care, nearly all Scandinavians—especially women—would still feel guilty about relying extensively on government to watch their children for them. Most people know that specific children have specific needs, and that parents are in the best position to know what those needs are.

Even in an ideal world, where parents could be sure that the strangers who cared for their children nonetheless loved them as their own and spared no expense in helping them, leaving one's children in the care of others would probably still cause guilt. And the Scandinavian system is far from ideal. Though Swedish taxpayers pay approximately $10,000 per year for every child in public day care, a series of problems plagues day-care institutions—nearly all of them having to do with money.

CONFLICTS OF EQUITY AND OBLIGATION

Waiting lists abound for public day care in Scandinavia. In Denmark, which has the most extensive system of institutionalized care, two-thirds of the counties have waiting lists. A child growing up in Aalborg may not obtain a place in public day care until it is too late to use it. Rural areas (in Norway, for example) tend to have longer waiting lists than urban areas.

The most serious distributional imbalances, however, are class-related. Middle-class people in all three Scandinavian countries rely on public day care more than working-class people. Day-care centers are open only during the day, making them unavailable for those who work nights and weekends. They are often not trusted by immigrant men, who are afraid their children will become assimilated and their wives more conversant with their rights. Middle-class users know how to gain and keep access to public day-care institutions and are far better organized to take advantage of available services than working-class users.

As a result the moral solidarity of the welfare state is cracking, if only slightly. Rather than symbolizing equal treatment for all and fostering collectivity, public day care reinforces the growing tendency of individuals in welfare states to calculate which programs provide enough benefits to compensate for the taxes imposed. Using day care is a way in which middle-class people use the state to hire others to perform tasks they once did themselves.

A second series of problems faces those who obtain places for their children. Bengt-Erik Andersson's study emphasized that good day care can work well. Not all public day care is good, however. The most serious problem is the rate of job turnover in day-care institutions. Many day-care workers are young women who have recently joined the labor force and are willing to put up with the low pay. They leave when marriage or a new job beckons. If a child enters a day-care at age three (all the Scandinavian countries have separate institutions for those under three and those over), it is likely that all the original workers will have left by the time the child starts school. The only way to correct this problem is to increase the pay and status of day-care work, but given fiscal constraints, that would decrease the availability of day care.

"Good" day care also falls victim to bureaucratization. Nothing horrifies Scandinavians more than the stories of child abuse coming from the United States, where day care is poorly regulated. (For that reason alone, the Scandinavian system is superior.) But overregulation can also cause problems. Government provision of a service comes complete with relatively inflexible rules, an overemphasis on procedures, and discussions framed by an emphasis on rights, often to the exclusion of obligations.

Many day-care workers are mothers of small children. These women are often idealistic and caring but tend toward the left politically and are highly aware of their trade-union benefits. Insistent on their rights—such as periodic vacations, routine coffee breaks, and regular working hours—they often feel torn between solidarity to their colleagues and concern for the children in their care. Women who raise children at home must balance their obligation to themselves with their obligation to their children. Women who raise the children of others as a career have far more obligations to balance: to themselves, to their colleagues, to their own children, and to the children they are watching. As obligations proliferate, the children's needs may get lost in the shuffle.

PROVIDING SERVICE AND RESTRICTING CHOICES

If there is a consensus among the experts on children in the Scandinavian countries, it runs as follows: public day care can help build a child's healthy feelings of autonomy—but only if care is limited to about twenty hours a week. Less than that, and children become withdrawn. More, and they tend to become aggressive. Common sense, then, would suggest that children spend part of their time in public day-care facilities, and that parents work only part-time when their children are small.

Common sense, however, has not won out. Part of the reason is economic. Rapidly changing economic conditions have made it enormously difficult for Scandinavians not to exercise their right to full-time day care. Inflation and tax rates of 50 percent or more have combined to decrease the typical family's ability to live on one or one and one-half incomes. Knowing that day care is available makes it possible for employers to keep wages down, for the state to keep taxes up, and for husbands to encourage their wives to work without taking on additional child-care responsibilities themselves. As a result, most couples have little choice but to work full-time and send their children to day care.

In addition, the bureaucratization of a public service like day care makes it difficult to accommodate part-time users. Part-time work tends to be opposed by many women's organizations, which are committed to the idea of full equality for women in the labor market. Day-care workers themselves support full-time work to protect the integrity of their jobs. Once day care is brought into the public sector, with its strong unions and firm rules, it loses much of its flexibility. Efforts by parents to play a greater role in the governance of day-care centers, for example, are often opposed by a variety of entrenched interests.

Studies of public opinion indicate continued support for public day care. But subtle shifts have taken place. Instead of arguing that day care is a positive good, recent research suggests it does no harm. Surveys indicate that women want to work part-time when their children are very small. Day care, in short, is an imperfect solution to the conflict between the needs of parents and those of their young children. Given one goal—equality between the sexes in the workplace—Scandinavians support public day care. Given another—doing what is best for their own children—they try to find ways to limit their reliance upon it.

SERVICE FOR "THE HARRIED LEISURE CLASS"

One of Sweden's most respected economists, Staffan B. Linder once wrote a book called *The Harried Leisure Class*. The book describes trends that affect most Scandinavians. In all the Scandinavian countries people are working longer hours than ever before. Scandinavians lead busy lives. Both parents have jobs. Store hours in Denmark and Norway are highly restricted, and so most Scandinavians must do all their shopping in the last half hour of the day or in three hours on Saturday morning. And even though Scandinavians now have fewer children, they still have some, whose needs must be met as well.

The pressures of work and family life make nearly everyone touchy and make feeling guilty a national pastime. Fathers have always spent too little time with their children. Now mothers have joined them. The state has filled in because somebody has to watch children when everyone else is busy.

Recognizing that public day care has been advanced in the interest of parents would help to improve it. So long as people assume that children will be better off because of public day care, they will be likely to rely upon it too much. But the dissatisfaction and guilt felt by many Scandinavian parents indicate that parents realize government ought to support families, not replace them.

How should Scandinavians reform their day-care policies? Berkeley professor Neil Gilbert has suggested the period when parents have small children ought to be viewed as a special phase in the life cycle. Parents who stay home serve not only their own children, but society as well, by reducing the cost to others. Such parents ought therefore to be given credit. Gilbert suggests mothers who raise their own children could be given preferential treatment when applying for civil-service employment after their children have grown older, or perhaps advanced standing at educational institutions. In Scandinavian societies, proposals have been advanced, usually by conservative and religious parties, to pay mothers who stay home with their own children, since almost any such program would cost less than public day care.

Nearly all of these proposals are opposed by unions, women's organizations, and the Social Democratic parties. The logic of the modern welfare state stresses universalization and equality; it is consequently reluctant to admit the need for exceptions. Given these political realities, reforms are more likely to come in the form of new targeted benefits, such as extended parental leave. An eighteen-month parental-leave policy, at full pay with job guarantees, would enable parents to stay at home with their infants without sacrificing their careers.

Governmental wage supplements would let couples decide for themselves how to allocate their responsibilities. Each parent could work three-quarter time while the children were young, or one could work full-time and the other half. It would even be possible for one to work time and a half while the other stayed home. Government would insure that families were paid the equivalent of two incomes—since families with small children tend to have high expenses—while leaving parents enough time to rely on public day care only twenty hours a week and to care for their children the rest of the time. At the same time, struggles over gender roles would be left to individual wives and husbands, since they would have to negotiate their own agreements about who is to spend more time with the children. Most important, the wage-supplement program would probably cost less than the universal provision of public child care.

LESSONS FOR THE U.S.

America has not yet made any serious public commitment to day care, relying instead upon a hodgepodge of solutions that is worse than Scandinavian programs for both parents and children. But patterns of American family life have changed; two-career families are here to stay. There is a positive role for government to play in offsetting the costs of the change.

It is clearly unwise, however, to turn the problem of raising the children of two-career families entirely over to government. In dealing with the intimate concerns of family life, strict rules and bureaucratic procedures work less well than intuition, common sense, and flexibility. Part-time work may conflict with the goal of equal pay for women, but it makes sense for children. Voucher schemes—which the Bush administration is likely to propose—should be designed to give parents flexibility. User fees for public day care are not inappropriate; those who have resources ought to pay more so that those who lack resources can benefit.

There is little chance, given American conservatism and the limits on our fiscal resources, that we will soon establish a system of universal day care subsidized by government. Instead of bemoaning that fact as evidence of backwardness, we Americans ought instead to appreciate the advantages that being backward provides. A society that loves children will use the state to provide for them, but will also allow parents the time to be with them.

A R T I C L E   2 . 3

Linda MacLeod

WIFE BATTERING IN CANADA

INTRODUCTION

Linda MacLeod estimates that each year a million Canadian women are beaten by their partners. In recent years, over half of all female victims of homicide in Canada were killed by someone with whom they shared a domestic relationship. Typically, marital homicide is related to wife battering: wives who kill their husbands do so in self-defence. Other wives are killed by abusive husbands in an escalating cycle of abuse.

The excerpt begins by outlining two explanations of wife battering: power-based theories and learning theories. Power-based theories suggest that wife battering is an extension of socially accepted expressions of male power; that men physically assert themselves in order to re-establish dominance over their wives. MacLeod, however, finds little support for this theory in her research.

By contrast, learning theories focus on the consistent finding that a high proportion of abusers and survivors of abuse were abused as children, and in turn abuse their own children.

MacLeod, Linda (1987). *Battered but not Beaten: Preventing Wife Battering in Canada.* Reprinted by permission of the Canadian Advisory Council of the Status of Women, Ottawa.

In other words, both men and women learn to abuse (or accept abuse) as a response to frustration. Neither abusers nor survivors have learned other, more appropriate ways of dealing with failure or frustration. If violent behaviour is learned, we must focus our energies on early prevention strategies. Family Studies courses that teach young people appropriate problem-solving and stress-reduction techniques may forestall violence in the short and in the long term.

Battered women and batterers come from all walks of life. They may be working outside the home or in the home. They may be unemployed or have a steady job. They may be rich or poor, well-educated or illiterate, of any nationality or race, young or old, with or without children.

Despite the difficulty of understanding wife battering, two major types of explanation have been widely used to respond to battered women, their children, and the men who batter them.

POWER-BASED THEORIES

These theories explain that violence against women is perpetuated by society's power structure which makes men dominant over women through the creation of separate and unequal roles for each gender. This dominance is reinforced through institutional rules and structures based on male supremacy.

As staff members of the Women's Research Centre in Vancouver have stated:

> Wife assault is a reality in our society because men have the socially ascribed authority to make the rules in marriage, and because violence against their wives is accepted in the eyes of society, as an appropriate instrument of control. The social and economic structure of marriage as an institution in which women are dependent on men, requires this assignment of authority to men.[1]

Power-based theories of wife battering emphasizing sex-based inequality and the patriarchal structure of society have gained acceptance by policy-makers and service-providers in this field. This explanation for wife battering appears in most writings on the subject and helps guide intervention services for battered women, their partners, and their children.

Research on the power dynamics in battering families also asserts that power is more highly valued in battering families than in non-battering families. On the surface, this power may not always overtly rest with the man. However, research findings suggest that, in families where the woman is dominant in terms of decision-making or earning power, or where the woman is perceived to be superior in some other way, violence is often used by the man to shift the balance of power. Many counsellors reported that many men resort to physical violence when they feel their wives are more articulate than they are. These men frequently complain that they can't win an argument with their wives, so they "shut them up" by the use of force.

In power-based theories, the acceptance and social reinforcement of violence in the family is a means to establish and to maintain the male in a dominant relationship over his wife.

Because male roles are socially created as dominant over female roles,

> Wife assault arises out of the socio-cultural belief that women are less important and less valuable than men and so are not entitled to equal status and respect. Thus, central to the task of dealing with the problem of wife assault is the need to recognize that wife assault is a social problem experienced by many Canadian women each year rather than an isolated interpersonal problem between two particular spouses.[2]

LEARNING THEORIES

Learning theorists argue that witnessing or suffering violence teaches people to use violence to try to solve problems or deal with stress.[3] This argument is supported by research and by statements from service-providers which reveal that many batterers come from families where their mothers were battered and/or where they themselves were physically, sexually, or psychologically abused as children.[4] These findings are corroborated by the statistics collected for this study. Sixty-one percent of the partners of the women who stayed in transition houses in 1985 had been abused as children. Thirty-nine per cent of the battered women reported being physically abused as children, 24 percent reported being sexually abused, and 48 percent reported being emotionally abused as well. Of the women who said they physically abused their own children, 69 percent said they had themselves been physically abused during their childhood.

Learning theorists also argue that the use of violence as a discipline tool can teach violence. In this vein, researchers report a "strong relationship between parental punishment and aggression" and suggest that

> increasing evidence indicates that a high price is paid for maintaining order in the family through violence. The norms that legitimate violence assure a family institution and a society characterized by violence for years to come.[5]

Learning theorists also frequently explain the perpetuation of violence by stating that victims, friends, and society as a whole unintentionally reinforce the violence.

> The victim after the beating, may indeed do as he insists; others may treat him with more respect and often he feels more in control. Even if he feels remorseful or guilty about her injuries he (and sometimes the victim herself) tends to blame the victim for "causing" him to "lose control." He denies responsibility for the negative behaviour. Due to the tacit acceptance of family violence in society and to the lack of clear messages that his violent behaviour must stop, his violence is rarely punished.[6]

Finally, learning theorists suggest that witnessing violence vicariously can teach some men to use violence within or outside the family. This tenet has created concern about pornography as a teaching tool for violence.

These types of explanations, one based on the structure of power in our society, the other on learning theory, have clarified our understanding of wife battering, and have helped to guide intervention efforts. Yet many shelter workers and other service-providers lamented, "These theories that seem so clear to us just don't seem to ring true for too many of the women who come to us."

HOW DO BATTERED WOMEN UNDERSTAND THE BATTERING?

Battered women speak of a shifting, ambiguous power. They spoke sometimes of feeling powerless against their partners. They also spoke of their power in the relationship and of the powerlessness of their partners. Many believe women are more powerful than men, as the quote below elucidates:

> I can't quite make sense of what the women here [at the shelter] are saying about the patriarchal structure of society and about power and society making men more powerful and all that. When I was growing up, my mother was for sure stronger than my Dad in every way but physically. She was smarter, could do more, and more people respected her. I think it's the same with my husband and me. There's no way he's stronger than me, except physically, and that's why he hits me, because he feels so low.

Other women elaborated this theme in terms of a mother-son model of relationships between themselves and their partners.

> My husband and all the men I've ever known are like little boys. We're really like their mothers, underneath. Everyone keeps telling me to leave him; they say he'll destroy me. But they don't know how strong I am and how weak he is underneath.

Others spoke of the power they feel in the relationship.

> Sure I feel sorry for him. He says he would have nothing without me and the kids. I know he's pretty rotten sometimes. But he really needs me. I guess that's why I keep going back. He makes me feel important.

Still others spoke of their partners as victims or losers in society.

> You can talk about men being powerful in our society if you want, but you're not talking about my husband. My husband's never had any power in his whole life. He's never had a chance. He was born poor. He was born Indian. He's never felt better than anyone. He's never felt better than me. It's because he's so low that he hits me.

Many battered women do not feel like powerless victims, and will not respond positively to services which treat them like victims instead of survivors.

These experiences remind us of the complexity of the realization of power in individual relationships. They also remind us that power in our society is not just gender-based; it is also class-, race-, and age-based.

Many battered women also understand battering as something that "got out of hand," as an extension of a normal part of a normal relationship. Many battered women feel their relationship started out much like any other relationship and, in fact, some emphasize that they feel they had an unusually loving, intense, and close relationship.

Intimate relationships, by definition, generate a wide range of emotions. The image of romantic love idealized in our society is characterized by highs and lows. Being "in love" is living "on the edge," participating in a kind of emotional aerobics. The socially accepted use of drugs, the preoccupation with "having it all," with creative stress, the fitness craze, and even our social addiction to soap operas and violent television shows emphasize high energy and intense emotional highs and lows.

For these reasons, wife battering at the outset is often difficult to prevent, or even to identify, because some violence (rough sexual play and psychological games intended to elicit jealousy) is intertwined with our ideal of "being in love" (isolation and possessiveness). In different socio-economic groups, this violence may be more or less psychological, or more or less physical, but the romantic desire to be alone together in a private world and the desire to have constant physical contact with your loved one are simply the "positive" faces of the jealousy and isolation which become part of most wife-battering experiences.

Battered women often talk of the intensity of their love for the batterer. Throughout this study, many battered women made the following kinds of statements: "I've never had better sex with anyone," "I just can't believe he'd hit me. I know he really loves me as much as I love him," "No one's ever loved me the way he does." Battered women also speak of the highs and lows of the relationship:

> You know, life was a roller-coaster with Bill. In the end, of course, that became unbearable—all the tension. But in the beginning, it was just so thrilling. I never wanted to come down.

Many battered women are guilty of no greater "weakness" than being in love with being in love. It's their attempt to stay in love, to retain an idealized vision of their partner, that often prevents many battered women from realizing they are being battered until the battering has become a part of life.

Women who are battered do not generally define themselves as battered the first time they are battered. In fact, because wife battering includes emotional, verbal, and financial battering, as well as physical and sexual battering, it may be difficult to define when the first incident actually occurred. This ambivalence is evident in the words battered women use to describe their early experiences with the batterer. It is not uncommon for battered women to say:

> I was flattered by his jealousy at first–I thought it meant he loved me. He said he would rather stay home, just with me, than go out with friends. I loved the attention and closeness at first. I thought he was the most romantic man in the world.

Even the first case of physical abuse is not always clear-cut. In many cases, the woman is "just pushed." While pushing can result in severe injuries, depending on the location of the push—down the stairs, over a chair, into a pot of boiling water on the stove, etc.—the push itself can be easily re-interpreted by the batterer and by the woman who is battered as something minor. The results of the push can be viewed as an accident.

> I was just baffled the first time he hit me. It wasn't really a hit, you know, not like a punch or even a slap; he just pushed me really hard. I broke an arm, but it was from falling backward over a chair, not from his push.

Another woman's statement mirrors these sentiments:

> I couldn't believe my husband had hit me. I just kept asking, is this the same man who loves me so much that he can't stand it if another man talks to me? It was really easy for me to accept his explanation that he'd had a hard day at work and a

little too much to drink. I couldn't see anything else without having to ask if he really did love me, and that was just too painful. It wasn't until much later, years of violence later, that I could see that the way he loved me—his jealousy, his posses-siveness—were also part of the violence.

Is this "illogic" really so different from the logic which we call compromising, or "forgiving and forgetting," when it does not involve identifiable violence?

While violence almost always escalates, it may not do so for months or years. The result is that women accept the violence as unpleasant but bearable, given the good things about the relationships (and most battering relationships do still pro-vide sporadic periods of closeness during the honeymoon phases of the violence) until they are so enmeshed in the cycle of violence and so demoralized and trapped by it that they can't "just leave."

Many service-providers, and even women who have been battered, counsel that leaving or calling the police "the first time it happens" is the most effective way to ensure it won't happen again. However, given that it may be hard to define "that first incident," especially since definitions of intolerable violence are culturally relative and since most women have a lot of emotional and practical investment in their relationships, this advice frequently has an unreal, hollow ring to it.

American author Susan Schechter points to the "normalcy" of the early reactions of most battered women, at least in terms of the current "rules" of intimate relation-ships, in her comment: "Most people feel ambivalent when ending a long-term rela-tionship. Major change is always difficult, often slowly and haltingly undertaken."[7]

There is growing evidence that leaving provides no guarantee the battering will stop and may even escalate the violence. In the present study, 12 percent of the women were separated or divorced. Anecdotal information suggests the majority of these women were battered by their ex-husbands, some by new partners. Michael Smith, in his telephone survey of 315 Toronto women, found that, while the rate of abuse for all women interviewed was 18.1 percent, for women who were sepa-rated or divorced, the rate jumped to 42.6 percent.[8]

The reactions of most battered women are often strong and logical and must be treated this way if we are to reach out to battered women and provide services for them which "ring true," will be helpful, and will be used by a greater number of bat-tered women. It is easy to scoff at, or be discouraged by, the astonished response of many women to the suggestion that they leave their violent husbands: "But he's my husband, and the father of my children. I can't just abandon him." It's easy from an outside vantage point which assumes the batterer, the battered wife, their relation-ship, or all three are defective, to dismiss as misguided sentiment the woman's heroic attempts to keep her marriage together, to keep her children from knowing about the violence, to insist that she loves her husband. The woman's actions and statements are easy to dismiss as long as we assume the battered woman, along with her partner and their relationship, are somehow different from us in terms of the basic personali-ty of the man and woman and in terms of the initial quality of the relationship.

However, as this study has established repeatedly, research shows that battered women do not fit one psychological or socio-economic mould. Few common charac-teristics which are not the direct result of the battering have been cited. In fact, in the one study known to the author where the personality traits of battered women before the violence were discussed, Lenore Walker found women who are battered "perceive themselves as more liberal than most" in their relationships with men[9]—a far cry from the stereotype of the battered woman as a traditional woman totally oppressed by, and dependent on, her partner.

It is after prolonged battering, as a result of the battering, that battered women begin to display certain similar psychological traits. After prolonged battering, women suffer from low self-esteem and isolation. They are emotionally dependent on the batterer, are compliant, feel guilty, and blame themselves for the violence, and yet demonstrate great loyalty to the batterer. Not only do they want the relationship to continue, they state they are staying for the sake of the family. They believe the batterers' promises to change and frequently believe the violence would stop if only their partners would get the one lucky break they've always wanted.[10]

To understand the actions and perceptions of battered women, it is important to think of how we all act in relationships, what we want, and the extent to which many of us will go to preserve a relationship. As one shelter worker poignantly said:

> Relationships are hard to come by. Sure we should help women know that they have worth outside their marriages, but a marriage isn't just status and a piece of paper . . . it's warmth, belonging, and a future. Battered women don't always get these good things out of their relationships, but most of them did in the beginning, and they just keep hoping it will come back. People will go to any lengths to feel loved, and love is not just waiting around the next corner for every battered woman who leaves her batterer.

Even the majority of women who report the violence do so out of hope that she and her partner will be helped to return to their pre-violent state. Of course, she may also hope she will get attention and be listened to because she is frequently lonely and unnurtured as a result of the isolation most batterers impose on their victims. She may also hope he will be punished or "get his just deserts." But behind it all, she often just wants them to be happy again. The importance of these hopes should not be diminished.

Unfortunately many of the services which have been created for battered women and for their partners have been built on the assumption that the relationship is not worth saving and ignore or belittle the woman's hopes to save and rekindle it. The hope of the service-providers is most often to save or protect the woman as an individual or to help or change the batterer as an individual in some way. This well-intentioned, institutional hope often buries the woman's pleas for a different kind of help. This discrepancy between the battered woman's hopes and the hopes of the service-providers renders many of the initiatives taken inappropriate and frustrating for the women who are battered and contributes to the burnout and despair of the people who try to help the women, their children, and their partners.

ENDNOTES

[1] Helga Jacobson, Co-ordinator. *A Study of Protection for Battered Women* (Vancouver: Women's Research Centre, 1982). p. 5.

2 Marion Boyd, ed. *Handbook for Advocates and Counsellors of Battered Women* (London, Ontario: London Battered Women's Advocacy Clinic Inc., 1985), pp. 12–13.

3 Anne Ganley, "Causes and Characteristics of Battering Men," in *Wife Assault Information Kit* (Victoria: Ministry of the Attorney General. April 1986), pp. 68–69.

4 Research supporting this hypothesis is summarized in Straus and Hotaling, *The Social Causes*, pp. 14–15.

5 Ibid., p. 15.

6 Ganley, "Causes and Characteristics," p. 70.

7 Susan Schechter, *Women and Male Violence: The Visions and Struggles of the Battered Women's Movement* (Boston: South End Press, 1982), p. 20.

8 Michael D. Smith, *Woman Abuse: The Case for Surveys by Telephone*. The LaMarsh Research Programme Reports on Violence and Conflict Resolution. Report #12 (Toronto: York University, November 1985), p. 29.

9 Walker, "The Battered Woman Syndrome Study," p. 8.

10 Alberta, Social Services and Community Health, Breaking the Pattern: *How Alberta Communities Can Help Assaulted Women and Their Families* (Edmonton: November 1985), p. 17.

QUESTIONS

DISCUSSION QUESTIONS

1. In countries like Somalia or the former Yugoslavia, many children are socialized by the experience of war. In a sense, they come to think of war as "normal." Is there a realistic hope for peace among people who grow up expecting war?

2. Brainstorm a list of Canada-U.S. differences. (Follow the most important rule of brainstorming: don't evaluate people's ideas until you have finished collecting and listing as many as you possibly can.) Then, try to reach a consensus on the list—which ideas should go and which should stay. Finally, explore the question of how the differences between Canadians and Americans are learned.

3. Wolfe implies that there may be advantages to our more haphazard day care system over the more highly structured Scandinavian system. Do you agree? Why or why not?

4. Which of the two theories of wife-battering described by MacLeod do you find has the greatest "face validity" (i.e., makes the best common sense)?

DATA COLLECTION EXERCISES

1. Interview young parents about their socialization practices. Ask them about the ways their goals and expectations differ from the ways they were socialized.

2. Collect biographical data on several notorious deviants (e.g., Bundy, Hitler, Bernardo). To what extent does faulty socialization account for their behaviour? Is looking for explanations in socialization a thinly disguised version of mother-blaming?

3. Interview a student who has attended college or university outside Canada. Ask about the differences that he or she has experienced in classroom attitudes and behaviour, and about the roles of student and teacher.

4. Are children's cartoons too violent? Watch two hours of television cartoons with a partner and document the types and frequencies of violent action.

WRITING EXERCISES

1. Go to the library and find out what you can about the "rise and fall" of the Oneida community. In a brief (500-word) essay, indicate if the community's demise was in any way due to the unusual socialization of children born into the commune.

2. In a brief (500-word) essay, analyze how gender socialization might have influenced the educational and occupational choices you have made so far. What people and what factors influenced your choices? Did your parents or grandparents have the same range of choices?

3. Can a majority of people living in an advanced capitalist society embrace universalistic values? Give your answer in a brief (500-word) essay.

4. Are some people poor and other people rich because of the ways they were socialized? Answer in a brief (500-word) essay.

SUGGESTED READINGS

1. Elkin, Frederick and Gerald Handel (1989). *The Child and Society: The Process of Socialization*, Fifth Edition. New York: Random House. This is a classic reference work for anyone interested in knowing more about the topic of socialization.

2. Handel, Gerald (1988). *Childhood Socialization*. New York: Adeline de Gruyter. This is a collection of nineteen articles dealing with such topics as the family, schools, peer groups, and television as agents of gender and class socialization. Several of these articles look beyond the North American context.

3. Kostash, Myrna (1987). *No Kidding: Inside the World of Teenage Girls.* Toronto: McClelland and Stewart. This Canadian study is a rich analysis of the teen years, based on lengthy interviews with teenage girls who talk candidly about boys, friends, family, and sex.

SECTION 3   DEVIANCE AND CONTROL

Introduction

Philosopher Thomas Hobbes believed that the State is the source of social order and the basis for all that is good and stable in human life. But anthropological and sociological evidence gives us reason to think that Hobbes was wrong.

In different parts of the world anthropologists have studied small, pre-industrial societies that have little "government" and no written laws. Yet these societies seem to work well. This raises the question of whether we really need a state—with its laws, courts, police forces, and a standing army—to enforce social order. After all, in any society there exist many social ties that help to maintain order without state intervention. These ties include kinship, economic exchange, and a shared culture.

And, unlike Hobbes, modern sociologists deny that social disorder is abnormal. From a sociological standpoint, rule-breaking is a normal part of society. Rule-breakers are usually normal members of an alternate, or deviant, social order. By this standard, deviance is conformity to a set of values and norms that many (often middle-class) people don't want to accept as legitimate.

We are all creating and enforcing the social order all the time. As we do so, we decide whether, when, and how we should make exceptions to the rules that we and other people have created. Nothing is absolutely and permanently normal or abnormal, deviant or conforming. Standards of behaviour are always being negotiated. Our rules of conduct are all being socially invented all the time.

It follows that nothing is deviant in itself. An act becomes deviant only when members of the community react in ways that indicate it is so. And in a pluralistic society like ours, people differ widely in deciding which behaviours are deviant. Sociology's job is to study how competing social and moral orders come into existence. Sociologists want to know how people in everyday life create and defend social orders they find particularly appealing.

There is a great deal of consensus about some forms of deviance—murder, for example. We are often shocked and fascinated to learn the facts about murderers. (See excerpt 3.1 below, on "kids who kill," for more on this topic.) But murder aside, people disagree about the acceptability of other types of behaviour. (See excerpt 3.2, which discusses differences in the perception of deviant acts in the U.S., India, and Kuwait.) They also disagree about the punishment that a deviant act deserves.

Like beauty, deviance is in the eye of the beholder. The more deviant an act seems to a majority of community members, the stronger the reaction it provokes. Thus the perceived seriousness of a deviant act is known only by the efforts people make to control or punish that act.

THEORIES OF DEVIANCE AND CONTROL

Usually we think of crime as causing, or calling for, formal social control. The actions of police, courts, and prisons can be seen as a response to crime. However social control also "causes" crime. If there were no laws and police officers, there would be no crime and criminals. All schools of sociology recognize this fact, but they view the relationship between social control and crime differently.

Structural-Functional Theories

Structural functionalists show that both deviance and social control perform valuable social functions. Deviance is found in every social group. In that sense, deviance—even crime—is a "normal" aspect of social life; it may even benefit society.

One version of this approach is *anomie theory*, developed by Robert Merton (1957). According to this theory, deviant behaviour is a normal, functional response to unequal opportunities for success in our society. Merton calls one deviant response "innovation": the development of illegitimate, even criminal, means for achieving success.

"Innovation" is most likely to occur among poor people who have been socialized to desire success but have little hope of gaining it legitimately. According to sociologist Daniel Bell, that is why crime is a widely practised method of achieving upward mobility in North America, where everyone yearns for success.

By this interpretation, crime is "functional" because it allows poor people to keep believing in those traditional values and institutions that nonetheless work to their disadvantage. Yet, there are many senses in which crime is not functional to society. Consider the women and children victimized by violent men, as described in excerpt 3.3 below. No one really benefits from these crimes, so functional theory does not seem to work here. We need another theory to explain the persistence of crime and social control.

Conflict Theories

As we noted above, deviance occurs only when we apply rules to human behaviour. Yet, it matters who makes these rules. According to conflict theorists, knowing who makes the rules, and why, is the key to understanding deviance and control.

Conflict theorists show that social control extends social inequality into the realm of law. In every society, some people have more power than others. They use power to protect their own values, interests, and possessions. That means getting the government to make, and the police to enforce, laws that protect their own interests. Legal institutions offer less to the poor and powerless.

From a conflict perspective the study of deviance and control is the study of law-making: why governments make certain laws, and who these laws favour. Neither deviance nor control is functional to society as a whole. Rather, social control serves one particular group at the expense of another. For example, police officers' reluctance to intervene in violent domestic disputes (which usually victimize women) works to the advantage of abusive men.

But there are problems with this approach to crime and deviance. Despite class and gender differences, people generally agree about the enforcement of laws.

And, although conflict theory depicts poor people as victims of the police and courts, they are more often the victims of criminals. So it is worthwhile to examine what the third major school of sociology, symbolic interactionism, says about the ways people interpret deviance and control.

Symbolic Interactionist Theories

Symbolic interactionists focus on the ways that social control affects deviant actors. Out of this approach comes the study of labelling and "deviant subcultures."

Labelling theory assumes that deviance is largely a result of the reactions of others. Labelling theorists do not try to explain why someone engages in deviant behaviour: everyone does it sometimes. Instead they study what happens to people after they have been caught in the act and labelled deviant.

This means that labelling theorists begin by looking at the act of labelling itself. They show that the application of a label is stigmatizing. *Stigmas*—marks of shame or social disgrace—discredit people. What's more, people who are seen as deviant by others may come to see themselves in the same way. They will now be more likely to engage in repeated deviant behaviour, because it fits their new self-image. Recidivism (or repeated deviant behaviour) is what labelling theorists call *secondary deviation*.

The interactionist approach also focuses on the fact that some people are more likely than others to learn how to be deviant. Edwin Sutherland's "differential association theory" assumes that deviant people actually conform to the norms and values of deviant subcultures. A *deviant subculture* contains norms and beliefs that the larger society considers deviant, even immoral. Members of a deviant subculture dress, act, and talk in ways that emphasize differences between their group and competing groups (e.g., rival gangs) or "straight" society. Some people have more opportunity to learn the lifestyle of the deviant subculture, and less opportunity to learn the mainstream culture. No wonder they break society's rules.

According to this interpretation, deviance is normal, not pathological. Controlling deviant behaviour means controlling people's conformity to the rules of deviant groups. So, in reading the excerpts that follow, remember that deviance is relative. There are always disagreements about "right" and "wrong." Social order is always changing. And agencies of social control have their own goals to serve—which do not always consider the "good of society" as a whole.

William Meloff and Robert A. Silverman

CANADIAN KIDS WHO KILL[1]

INTRODUCTION

In Canada and elsewhere, according to some reports, the average age of criminals is dropping. More teenagers and even younger children are allegedly committing crimes. The law often prevents them from being charged, convicted, or punished. What are the characteristics of these criminals and their crimes?

This excerpt looks at one particular crime—homicide—and compares the behaviour of Canadian and American "kids who kill." It finds that, in both countries, homicides involving one victim are usually committed by a single acquaintance, friend, or family member. As emotional acts, they are like the murders of women that Gartner discusses in excerpt 3.3. Generally, younger children are more likely to kill family members, while older children are more likely to kill strangers and to kill during the commission of a crime. Shooting is the most common means of homicide, followed by stabbing and beating. Homicides by two or more offenders are more often carried out against strangers, or during the process of committing another crime such as theft or rape. As usual, boys are much more likely to kill than are girls.

The study also contributes to our understanding of the differences between Canadian and American society. American kids who kill are far more likely to act in groups, use guns, and victimize acquaintances—in short, to participate in gang-type warfare. This may be related to the greater prevalence of drug use in the United States. Probably it is also related to the greater availability of guns and the larger number of gangs in American cities.

Recently in Canada, a great deal of publicity has been given to cases of individuals charged with homicide under the *Young Offenders Act*. The sensationalist tone of the media in these instances has implied that the number of homicides committed by youth is high, and that these offenders are receiving inordinately light sentences for crimes that in the adult world would be treated much more severely. The inference is that the youth who kill are incorrigible criminals who murder during the commission of other crimes and that there is little or no deterrent value to the sentences under the Act. As an initial step in the objective analysis of factors involved in youth homicide, it is instructive to examine some of the characteristics of offenders, victims, and the circumstances under which the act was committed. It is useful as well to compare the Canadian data with corresponding data from the United States in order to determine the similarities and differences which may obtain between the two countries.

Meloff, William and Robert A. Silverman (1992). "Canadian Kids Who Kill," *Canadian Journal of Criminology*, January, 15–34.

The few sociological/criminological studies of youth homicide that have been done are from the United States and for the most part draw their data from single geographical areas. (For instance, Goetting (1989) uses 55 cases from a 7-year period in Detroit; Zimring (1984) uses 286 cases of children under 16 and 1,111 cases of youth between 16 and 19 from New York between 1973 and 1980.) The only recent national American study that encompasses all types of juvenile homicide was done by Rowley, Ewing, and Singer (1987).

Findings from these studies provide the research questions and points of comparison for this research. Specifically, we will pursue the following issues raised with regard to youth homicide in Canada:

1. Following Zimring, we will undertake an examination of age-specific homicide rates for youth under 18. We expect the homicide rate to rise with age. Further, as the homicide rate in Canada is between 1/3 and 1/4 that of the U.S., we expect rates of Canadian juvenile homicide to be substantially lower than rates found by Zimring.

2. Combining findings from Zimring (1981) and Rowley *et al.* (1987), we predict that multiple offenders are more likely to be involved in youth homicide in distant rather than close social relationships.

3. While the American studies show that most youth homicide involves guns (Goetting 1989; Zimring 1981), we predict that a lower proportion of youth homicides in Canada will involve guns due to stringent gun laws. Further, when guns are used, they will more likely be used by older youth who are more familiar with these weapons and have easier access to them.

4. In the United States, less than 20% of youth homicides involve close relatives (Goetting 1989; Rowley *et al.*, 1987). Given the overall pattern of homicide in Canada (Silverman and Kennedy 1987), we predict that a higher proportion of Canadian youth homicides will involve close relatives and, conversely, that there will be proportionately fewer stranger- and crime-based homicides.

5. A higher proportion of younger than older offenders will be involved in killing relatives (Rowley *et al.* 1987).

6. The closer the social relationship, the less likely theft will be involved (Rowley *et al.* 1987).

7. Race plays an important part in studies of homicide in the United States (see for instance, Block 1985; Messner 1983). While the situation is not directly comparable to Canada, we can predict that most youth homicide is intra-racial; the victims and offenders will come from the same racial group. With regard to race, the American literature has also been concerned with social relationships and race of offenders. This study will also examine the social relationship component of the offence.

Since the proportion of Canadian Indians involved in homicide in Canada is far higher than their proportion in population (about 2% of the population and 14% involvement in homicide), it is reasonable to predict that the proportion of Canadian Indian youth involved in homicide is higher than their proportion in the population.

8. Finally, we predict that males will be the predominant perpetrators of youth homicide. When females kill, they will most likely kill a male. Further, we predict that females kill family members proportionately more often than males (Goetting 1989).

METHOD AND MEASUREMENT

This analysis is based on data collected by the Canadian Centre for Justice Statistics, Statistics Canada. The data encompass the years from 1961–1983 and are reported to Statistics Canada via a "homicide return." Each reporting police department in the country regularly completes homicide returns which contain information about victims, offenders, offences, and court appearances. For this study we use only data collected about victims, offenders, and offences. Within the data set are cases of multiple offenders and victims which are extremely difficult to include in an analysis. The solution in this paper is to use only the first victim/offender combination (the most intimate grouping) for the analysis (Silverman and Kennedy 1987). First and second degree murder are the focus of this study, as manslaughter and infanticide data were only recorded after 1974. A total of 53 cases of manslaughter and 14 cases of infanticide are excluded.

Youth are defined as any individual under the age of 18 regardless of the legal prerequisites for qualification as a "young offender" under the *Young Offenders Act.* The bulk of the analysis is concerned with individuals under the age of 18 who commit the crimes of first or second degree murder.

In this paper, victim-offender relationship is of prime importance. Relationship has been coded as the most intimate relationship between an offender and a victim. The rather extensive Statistics Canada listing of relationships has been collapsed as follows. *Parents* includes natural, step, and common-law parents. Heide (1988) suggests that it may not be wise to combine these types of parents as the relationships between natural parents and children and step parents and step children may be very different. While this may be true, only about 2% of all relationships were step or common-law so combining them with the natural parent category seemed to be most appropriate. A second category is *siblings* who kill each other. These include natural, step, common-law, and foster brothers and sisters. Again, the small number in each group made combination the most logical procedure. *Other family* refers to any kinship relationship that is not covered by the first two categories (e.g., cousins, grandparents, aunts, and uncles). The fourth category is comprised of *friends and acquaintances.* (In the tables, this category is named "other relationship.") Category five refers to victims and offenders for whom *no relationship* was known (for example, strangers) while category 6 includes those events that were precipitated by a *crime* other than the homicide (for example, theft).

Gender and age are available for both offenders and victims. Those under 13 have been grouped. For purposes of the analysis of race, only caucasians and Canadian Indians are examined. There are 23 cases of "other" races (e.g., black, oriental, Inuit) which have been deleted from the analysis of race, as when they are broken down they generate too many categories with too few cases and when grouped they make no theoretical sense.

SUMMARY OF FINDINGS

To a limited extent, we were able to replicate Zimring's (1984, 1981) studies using Canadian data. Direct comparisons are probably not appropriate as Zimring used data from New York City for a 5-year period while we used nationwide data for a 22-year period. Nonetheless, the age pattern in which homicide rates rise with age of offender were duplicated. However, the New York data reveals rates ten times that of Canada. This is a rather dramatic finding and one that might lead to further research with more comparable data sets. Given the drug situation in the United States when compared to that in Canada, it might be reasonable to predict a nation-wide rate of juvenile homicide in the United States that far exceeds that in Canada.

Most youth homicide in Canada consists of single victims and single offend-ers, multiple victims or both. As relational distance between offender and victim increases, so too does the probability of victimization by more than one offender. In the United States, Rowley *et al.* (1987) made similar observations. Crime-based homicide was the most likely to have multiple offenders as perpetrators. The association between relational distance and the presence of multiple offenders is direct. In the case of family relationships, it is likely that the precipitating event leading to the homicide is an emotional outburst that usually involves interaction between one offender and one victim. The predation that is associated with crime-based homicide can often more easily be carried out by multiple offenders. In fact, the event will not usually have homicide as a primary goal. Homicide will occur as a result of implementation of action to achieve the crime goal (usually theft or sex).

While the Canadian data confirm the general findings of Rowley *et al.* that most homicide involves single offenders and victims, there are some interesting dif-ferences between the United States and Canadian data. For instance, when strangers are victims in Canada, a single offender is involved 67% of the time while the similar figure for the United States is only 31%. In fact, for every category of social relationship there is substantially more multiple offender perpetration in the United States than in Canada. Other than the possibility of drug-related events, there is no immediately forthcoming explanation for this phenomenon.

While the proportion of gun use in Goetting's (1989) Detroit study was far higher than the Canadian case, shooting was still the most common means of homicide commission among Canadian youth. As in the American studies, shoot-ing is followed by stabbing and beating as means of homicide commission. Contrary to our prediction, younger children (below 15) are more likely to use guns than are older children (15–17). This suggests that older children are more likely to be involved in internecine conflict in which guns are not available (for instance, in street fights) while younger children find guns a great equalizer when they are available (i.e., in the home). The Canadian data lend some sup-port to this notion as 74% of shooting homicides by children under 15 occur in the victim's home (compared to only 55% for older youth). No other type of homicide (beating, stabbing, other) occurs in the victim's home more than 49% of the time.

About one-third of the Canadian juvenile homicide involves a family member. This proportion is almost twice as high as the similar proportion reported in two American studies (Goetting 1989; Rowley *et al.* 1987). When all Canadian homicides are examined, it is found that family homicide plays a significant role (Silverman and Kennedy 1987). The lower proportion of family homicide in the United States results from higher proportions of more distant relationships. For instance, Rowley *et al.* (1987) found that 33% involved strangers and 49% involved "acquaintances." The comparable Canadian figures are 31% strangers (including crimes) and 35% friends and acquaintances. Canadian juveniles are more likely to kill people with whom they share a more intimate relationship than are American youth. The explanation for these differences most probably lies in homicides associated with the drug trade in the United States as well as with structural and cultural differences in the two countries.

The proportion of youth involved in crime-related homicide in the Detroit study was 22% (Goetting 1989) while in the Rowley *et al.* (1987) study about 20% of the events involved a stranger-theft relationship.[2] The proportion of crime involvement in our study is a very similar 23%. Crime involvement was inversely related to relational distance. Closer relationships were much less likely to involve a crime in addition to the homicide. While Canadian youth are involved in higher proportions of more intimate kinds of homicide than American juveniles, it is intriguing that they are involved in similar proportions of crime-based homicide (though Rowley *et al.* are only concerned with theft).

Consistent with our predictions and with earlier findings, younger children are more likely to kill family members than are older children. Similarly, older juveniles are more likely to be involved in crime-based and stranger homicide than are younger juveniles. It is likely that younger children are involved in emotional situations involving those with whom they spend the most time (family) while older juveniles are engaged in more wide-ranging activities that lead to homicide.

Most Canadian juvenile homicide is committed by caucasians against caucasians but Canadian Indian perpetrators are represented in the homicide-committing population in proportions far out-stripping their proportion in the population.[3] Canadian Indians are far more likely than caucasians to kill someone with whom they have a close social relationship. Canadian Indian youth are rarely involved in crime-related homicide or in homicides against strangers. The reason for the differences in the targets between the two groups is probably related to the living arrangements of natives. That is, Indians on a reserve are more likely to be in proximity of family than either urban natives or urban caucasians. Our data does not indicate reserve/non-reserve status so this will have to remain a hypothesis for the present.

As in virtually all studies of homicide, we find that males are the most likely perpetrators. About 11% of our sample and 13% of Rowley *et al.*'s were female. Like Rowley *et al.* (1987), we found that females were more likely to kill family members and less likely to be involved in crime-based homicide than were males. However, distinguishing this group from Rowley *et al.* was the finding that

Canadian female juveniles were somewhat more likely than males to kill strangers. If strangers are combined with crime-based homicide then Canadian females are still about twice as likely (proportionally) as their American counterparts to be involved in this type of crime. No explanation for these differences is apparent but as indicated earlier it may simply be an artifact of the small numbers of Canadian female juveniles who commit homicide.

In this paper, we have replicated some of the findings of American studies and have found some differences between American and Canadian juvenile homicide. While juvenile homicide only constitutes about 7% of all homicides in either country, it is an interesting and important area of study insofar as it sheds light on this highly emotional area of youth violence which seems to be such a favorite media topic. The clearly documented fact that most youth homicides involve relatives or acquaintances of the perpetrator tends to cast considerable doubt on the popular premise that the incidence of random youth violence as manifested in homicide is sharply increasing in Canadian society.[4] The old maxim that one is in significantly more danger from murder at the hands of a relative or friend than from a stranger appears to hold true for the youthful offender as well as the adult offender.

ENDNOTES

[1] This research was supported by the Contributions Grant of the Solicitor General of Canada and by the Canadian Centre for Justice Statistics, Statistics Canada.

[2] Calculated from data presented by Rowley *et al.* (1987).

[3] It is difficult to calculate the proportion of Indian youth in the Indian population but it is noteworthy that Canadian Indians comprise only about 2% of the Canadian population as a whole.

[4] In fact, using our definition of youth, the rate of youth homicide has been stable or decreasing recently (Silverman 1990).

REFERENCES

Block, Carolyn (1985). Lethal Violence in Chicago Over Seventeen Years: Homicides Known to the Police 1965–1981. Chicago: Illinois Criminal Justice Information Authority.

Cormier, B., C. Angliker, P. Gagne, and B. Markus (1978). "Adolescents who kill a member of the family," in J. Eekelaar and S. Katz (eds.), Family Violence: An International and Interdisciplinary Study. Toronto: Butterworths.

Cornell, D., E. Benedek, D. Benedek (1987). "Characteristics of Adolescents Charged with Homicide: Review of 72 Cases," Behavioral Sciences and the Law. 5(1):11–23.

Crimmins, S. (1988). "Parricide vs. suicide in adolescents: The dilemma of them or me." Paper presented to the Annual Meetings of the American Society of Criminology, Chicago, Nov.

Easson W.M. and R.M. Steinhilber (1961). "Murderous aggression by children and adolescents," Archives of General Psychiatry, 127(1):74–78.

Goetting, A. (1989). "Patterns of homicide among children," Criminal Justice and Behavior, 16(1):63–80.

Heide, K. (1988). "Parricide committed by adolescents." Paper presented to the Annual Meetings of the American Society of Criminology, Chicago, Nov.

Heide, K. (1987). "Parricide: Nationwide incidence and correlates." Paper presented at the Annual Meetings of the American Society of Criminology, Montreal, Nov.

Heide, K. (1986) "Taxonomy of murder: Motivational dynamics behind the homicidal acts of adolescents," Journal of Justice Issues, 1(1):3–19.

Markus, B. and B. Cormier (1978). "A preliminary study of adolescent murderers." Paper presented to the Annual Meeting of the American Academy of Psychiatry and the Law, Montreal, Oct.

Messner, S. (1983). "Regional and racial effects on the urban homicide rate: The subculture of violence revisited," American Journal of Sociology, 88(5):997–1007.

McNight, C., J.W. Mohr, R. Quinsey, and J. Orochko (1966). "Matricide and mental illness," Canadian Psychiatric Association Journal, 1(2):99–106.

Mones, P. (1985). "The relationship between child abuse and parricide," in E. Newberger and R. Bourne (eds.), Unhappy Families. Littleton, Mass:PSG.

Morris, G. (1985). The Kids Next Door: Sons and Daughters Who Kill Their Parents. New York: William Morrow.

Rowley, J., C.P. Ewing, and S. Singer (1987). "Juvenile homicide: The need for an interdisciplinary approach," Behavioral Sciences and the Law, 5(1):1–10.

Russell, D. (1965). "A study of juvenile murderers," Journal of Offender Therapy, 9(3):55–86.

Russell, D. (1984). "A study of juvenile murderers of family members," International Journal of Offender Therapy and Comparative Criminology, 28(3):177–92.

Sargent, D. (1962). "Children who kill—a family conspiracy," Social Work, 7:35–42.

Scherl, D and J. Mack (1966). "A study of adolescent matricide," Journal of the American Academy of Child Psychiatry, 5(2):569–93.

Silverman, Robert A. (1990). "Trends in youth homicide: Some unanticipated consequences of a change in the law," Canadian Journal of Criminology, 32(4):651–656.

Silverman, Robert A. and Kennedy L. (1987). "Relational distance and homicide: The role of the stranger," Journal of Criminal Law and Criminology, 78(2):272–308.

Sorrells, J. (1977). "Kids who kill," Crime and Delinquency, July:312–320.

Sorrells, J. (1980). "What can be done about juvenile homicide," Crime and Delinquency, April:152–161.

Steinmetz, Susan (1978). Sibling Violence, in J. Eekelaar and S. Katz (eds.), Family Violence: An International and Interdisciplinary Study. Toronto: Butterworths.

Toupin, J. (1988). "Adolescent murderers," paper presented to the Annual Meetings of the American Society of Criminology, Chicago, Nov.

Zimring, F. (1981). "Kids, groups and crime: Some implications of a well kept secret," Journal of Criminal Law and Criminology, 72(3):867–885.

Zimring, F. (1984). "Youth homicide in New York: A preliminary analysis," Journal of Legal Studies, XIII:81–99.

Sandra Evans Skovron, Joseph E. Scott,
and P. Kamalakara Rao

HOW OFFENSES ARE PERCEIVED IN THE UNITED STATES, INDIA AND KUWAIT

INTRODUCTION

We are used to thinking that the ways Canadians define deviant behaviour are sensible and natural, even inevitable. Yet this excerpt shows that there are variations in the ways people view different types of deviance, and even crimes. Canadian views come closest to those expressed by Americans in the study described below.

In surveys carried out in the United States, India, and Kuwait, students rated the severity of different penalties. They then evaluated the seriousness of deviant acts by assigning penalties to them. Respondents in the three countries rated the penalties, and the seriousness of deviant acts, similarly to a great extent. However, there was one important difference in the ratings. Kuwaiti respondents treated offences against morals much more severely than did the Indian and American respondents.

Kuwaitis considered these offences against morals—which included such acts as adultery, atheism, and homosexuality—to be just as serious as armed robbery and manslaughter, and they wanted to penalize them similarly. This desire to punish offences against morality reflects Islamic religious teaching in Kuwait (and indeed, in much of the Islamic world). It also shows the reluctance of pious Muslims to distinguish between sacred and secular, or church and state, concerns.

As a result, this excerpt shows the effect of secularization on views of morality and deviance. In secular societies like Canada and the United States, people of different cultural or religious origins make similar evaluations of good and evil. Since there is less agreement on what is "moral" behaviour, they punish immoral behaviour less severely.

There is little research that addresses the perceived seriousness of crime from a cross cultural perspective. This paper extends the research on cross cultural perceptions of crime seriousness by examining perceptions of a wide range of offenses and

Skovron, Sandra Evans, Joseph E. Scott and P. Kamalakara Rao (1987). "Cross Cultural Perceptions of Offense Severity: The United States, India and Kuwait," *International Journal of Comparative and Applied Criminal Justice*, 11(1), Spring, 47–60. Reprinted by permission.

sanctions for respondents from three very different cultures: namely, the United States, India, and Kuwait.[1]

The seriousness of thirty-seven offenses were rated by having respondents assign one of seventeen penalties to each offense. The severity of the seventeen penalty categories were in turn ranked by respondents. As a first step in calculating the perceived seriousness of offenses, the severity ratings of the penalty categories must be analyzed.

There are only slight differences in the penalty rank ordering among the United States, Indian, and Kuwaiti respondents. It may be concluded that the rank order of penalties is essentially similar for the United States, Indian, and Kuwaiti respondents. The perceived seriousness of penalties was essentially similar despite the inclusion of non-traditional and unfamiliar penalties in the penalty list.[2]

THE PERCEIVED SERIOUSNESS OF OFFENSES

Respondents were asked to rate the seriousness of thirty-seven offense vignettes by assigning one of the seventeen penalty categories to each offense. The mean seriousness scores for the penalty categories were used to calculate the mean seriousness score for each offense. The mean seriousness score for each offense was calculated by summing the seriousness scores of the assigned penalties and then dividing by the number of respondents. This process was repeated for all three samples and yielded seriousness scores for the three groups for the thirty-seven offense items. The offenses were then rank ordered for each group of respondents. The rank ordering of offenses for the United States sample could then be compared to the rank ordering for the Indian and Kuwaiti respondents. The rank ordered offenses for the United States sample, as well as the seriousness scores for all three samples, are presented in Table 1.

Table 1 reveals a number of similarities in the rank ordering of offenses for the United States and Indian samples. However, some differences may be noted. A number of property offenses were perceived much less seriously by the Indian respondents than by the United States respondents. For example, the Indian students ranked items 8 and 11, both property offenses, considerably less seriously than their United States counterparts. There were also differences with regard to white collar offenses. The Indian respondents rated a number of white collar offenses, for example items 14, 15, 16, 24, and 26, more seriously than did the United States respondents.

The rank order of the seriousness ratings of the Kuwaiti respondents differ from those of both the United States and Indian respondents.

To further examine these differences, the offense items were examined by groups or categories of offenses. For purposes of analysis, the offenses were grouped into four categories: violent offenses (items 1, 2, 3, 4, 6, 7, 8, and 10), property offenses (items 11, 12, 13, 20, and 23), white collar offenses (items 14, 15, 16, 17, 24, 25, and 26), and morals offenses (items 9, 18, 19, 21, 27, 28, 29, 30, 31, 32, 33, 34, 35, 36, and 37). Items 22 and 5 were accidental crimes and thus were not placed into any category for this analysis. Mean seriousness scores were then calculated for each category of offense. These scores are presented in Table 2.

TABLE 1 Rank Order Of Thirty-Seven Offenses from Most to Least Serious

Offense	United States N = 535		India N = 300		Kuwait* N = 599	
	Mean Sanction	Rank	Mean Sanction	Rank	Mean Sanction	Rank
A man killed his wife during an argument.	13.163	1	10.883	1	12.353	6
An individual kidnapped a woman to rape her.	12.120	2	10.778	2	12.804	4
A man stabbed his wife with a knife during an argument.	11.974	3	8.921	7	11.557	8
An individual committed a forcible rape.	11.504	4	10.003	5	13.202	2
A man killed a little girl with his car while driving under the influence of alcohol.	11.403	5	9.856	6	11.407	10
An individual intending only to injure someone by throwing a stone accidentally killed him.	10.827	6	8.590	9	8.743	25
An individual forced a woman into prostitution.	10.396	7	10.267	3	13.041	3
An individual robbed a store with a gun.	10.112	8	8.416	12	11.200	12
An individual sold illegal drugs.	9.664	9	7.649	15	11.250	11
An individual threw burning liquid in someone's face which caused scars.	9.576	10	10.042	4	10.141	15
An individual burglarized a neighbor's home.	9.149	11	3.062	36	10.515	14
An individual set fire to a warehouse.	9.041	12	8.295	14	9.738	21
An individual stole things worth about $100.	8.799	13	7.596	16	8.543	28

TABLE 1 Cont'd

Offense	Mean Sanction	Rank	Mean Sanction	Rank	Mean Sanction	Rank
An individual sold company secrets to another company.	7.931	14	8.558	10	7.880	31
An individual forged an official document.	7.679	15	8.357	13	8.509	29
A businessman bribes a government official for a contract.	7.607	16	8.612	8	8.810	23
An individual loaned money at a high interest rate.	7.226	17	6.856	20	8.235	30
An individual used drugs.	6.802	18	6.965	19	9.403	20
An individual committed perjury.	6.734	19	5.643	28	9.457	19
A person forged a check.	6.530	20	8.446	11	8.618	27
An individual operated a public gambling house.	5.805	21	7.170	17	9.977	16
An individual accidentally shot another while hunting.	5.624	22	6.820	21	5.764	35
A young boy stole an automobile.	5.355	23	6.002	26	4.942	37
An employee took a car as a bribe.	5.264	24	7.056	18	7.512	32
An executive falsely advertised the quality of a product.	4.824	25	6.642	25	5.622	36
An individual falsely advertised prices.	4.755	26	6.685	23	6.205	34
A pharmacist sold drugs for an abortion.	4.722	27	5.456	30	8.881	23
A physician performed an illegal abortion.	4.699	28	3.872	34	8.702	26
A woman engaged in prostitution.	3.818	29	5.561	29	11.956	7

TABLE 1 Cont'd

Offense	Mean Sanction	Rank	Mean Sanction	Rank	Mean Sanction	Rank
An individual accused a woman of adultery without adequate proof.	3.179	30	6.664	24	9.808	17
A married man committed adultery.	3.100	31	6.095	27	12.789	5
A married woman committed adultery.	3.062	32	6.773	22	13.539	1
An individual insulted someone's honor in front of others.	2.823	33	4.646	32	7.258	33
A male engaged in homosexuality.	2.810	34	5.360	31	11.518	9
A woman had an illegal abortion.	2.731	35	4.339	33	9.355	22
An individual abandons religion and espouses atheism.	1.476	36	3.340	35	10.587	13
A single man committed fornication.	1.295	37	1.000	37	9.532	18

*Permission was obtained from Al-Thakeb, F. and J. E. Scott (1981). *International Journal of Comparative and Applied Criminal Justice,* 5 (Winter): 129–143.

TABLE 2 Mean Seriousness of Offense Category: United States, India, and Kuwait

Offense	United States Mean Seriousness	India Mean Seriousness	Kuwait* Mean Seriousness
Violent	11.209	9.737	11.650
Property	7.775	6.680	8.399
White Collar	6.075	7.538	7.840
Morals	4.100	5.369	10.494

*Permission was obtained from Al-Thakeb, F. and J. E. Scott (1981). *International Journal of Comparative and Applied Criminal Justice,* 5 (Winter): 129–143.

As may be seen in Table 2, the United States respondents perceived violent offenses most seriously, with a mean seriousness score of 11.209, followed by property offenses (7.775), white collar offenses (6.075), and morals offenses (4.100). The rank order of offenses for Indian respondents was somewhat different. The Indian respondents also ranked violent offenses as the most serious offense category, although their mean seriousness score was somewhat less than for the United States respondents (9.737 as compared to 11.209). The second most serious offense category for the Indian respondents was white collar offenses (7.538), followed by property offenses (6.680), with the morals offenses ranked as the least serious (5.369). The Indian respondents perceived white collar offenses somewhat more seriously and property offenses somewhat less seriously than did the United States respondents.

The Kuwaiti respondents differ considerably from the other two samples in their ranking of offense categories. They do rank violent offenses as being most serious (11.650). However, the Kuwaiti respondents ranked morals offenses nearly equal in seriousness to violent offenses (mean seriousness = 10.494). In fact the single most serious offense as ranked by the Kuwaiti respondents was a morals offense. "A married woman committed adultery." The United States and Indian samples both rated morals offenses as the least serious offense category. The Kuwaiti respondents ranked property offenses and white collar offenses as the third and fourth most serious category of offense respectively.

Removal of the morals offenses increased the similarity between the Kuwaiti and Indian and United States samples.

DISCUSSION AND IMPLICATIONS

This research has demonstrated remarkable similarity with regard to perceptions of the severity of both sanctions and offenses for comparable samples of United States, Indian, and Kuwaiti respondents. The perceptions of the three sampled groups were essentially comparable with regard to perceptions of the severity of the seventeen sanctions. This finding is particularly remarkable inasmuch as a number of penalties which were unfamiliar to the respondents from some countries were included on the list of penalty categories. For example, such sanctions as "civil death and no job," "banishment," "severing a limb," "whipping," and "stoning to death" are certainly unfamiliar to United States respondents and are not used as sanctions in Western legal systems. Many of these penalties, in particular "severing a limb" and "banishment" are also unfamiliar to most Indian respondents. Despite this, the three groups of respondents were in essential agreement with regard to the perceived seriousness of these penalties.

There was also essential agreement among the United States and Indian respondents with regard to the perceived seriousness of the 37 offense items. Despite a few differences, such as the greater perceived severity of white collar offenses for the Indian students and the greater perceived severity of property offenses for the United States students, marked similarity in perceptions was demonstrated overall.

Consistent with previous research (Scott and Al-Thakeb, 1977; Evans and Scott, 1984) the Kuwaiti sample was the most divergent. However, the differences were largely attributable to the morals offenses. There was a marked degree of similarity to the other samples on the rankings of violent, property, and white collar offenses. Despite the widely divergent cultures, standards, and practices in the United States, India, and Kuwait, this research has, with the exception of morals offenses, demonstrated a high degree of consensus with regard to the perceived seriousness of both sanctions and offenses.

ENDNOTES

[1] University students were used in order to obtain a sample most comparable to the samples from other cultures to be included in this study. It is recognized that student samples are often criticized as being non-generalizable to the wider population. In this research, a student sample was selected because it provides the most control and comparability for the cross cultural comparison. Previous research (Rossi et al., 1974; Evans, 1981; Evans and Scott, 1982a) has indicated that demographic characteristics of respondents such as age, education, and social class have little or no impact on seriousness perceptions. The fact that students' perceptions of offense severity do not differ markedly from those of the general public is illustrated by the similarities between the United States students' seriousness ratings obtained in this study and those obtained for a community sample in an earlier study (Scott and Al-Thakeb, 1977).

[2] The nontraditional penalties are: Civil Death and No Job; Whipping; Banishment; Sever Limb; and Stone to Death.

REFERENCES

Al-Thakeb, Fahed and Joseph E. Scott (1981). "The Perceived Seriousness of Crime in the Middle East," *International Journal of Comparative and Applied Criminal Justice,* 5(2): 129–143.

Evans, Sandra S. (1981). *Measuring the Seriousness of Crime: Methodological Issues and a Cross Cultural Comparison.* Unpublished Dissertation, The Ohio State University.

Evans, Sandra S. and Joseph E. Scott (1982a). "Analyzing the Perceived Seriousness of Crime Cross Culturally: The Impact of Respondent Characteristics," presented at the X World Congress of Sociology, August, 15–20, 1982, Mexico City.

Rossi, Peter, Emily Waite, Christine Bose, and Richard Berk (1974). "The Seriousness of Crimes: Normative Structure and Individual Differences," *American Sociological Review,* 39:224–237.

Scott, Joseph E. and Fahed Al-Thakeb (1977). "The Public's Perception of Crime: Scandinavia, Western Europe, the Middle East and the United States," in C. Ronald Huff (Ed.) *Contemporary Corrections,* Beverly Hills, CA: Sage.

Rosemary Gartner

PATTERNS OF VICTIMIZATION AROUND THE WORLD

INTRODUCTION

Canadians increasingly feel that more needs to be done to protect and empower victims of violence. But what can be done? In hopes of answering that question, a growing number of researchers have turned to studying who gets hurt, why some kinds of people are more likely to get hurt than others, and how victimization is a characteristic of societies, not individuals.

This excerpt looks at violence against women and children—criminal acts that are usually committed by intimates. (On this, see also excerpt 2.3.) Gartner finds social patterns that predict higher and lower risks of violence across a wide range of societies. These "risk factors" include women's education and their participation in the paid work force. Violence against women increases as women make the transition to independence and more participation in public life. When gender equality is well established, violence diminishes.

Other research by Gartner shows that men are more likely to kill spouses or girlfriends who are leaving or have left them. By making it possible for women to leave abusive relationships, equality (paradoxically) makes murder "normal"—at least until men adjust to a new way of thinking about intimate relations.

This suggests a certain inevitability about the upsurge in violence against women and children. However, even if domestic violence is a societal problem, individuals must prevent it and punish it. And, these data say, inevitably the problem will diminish.

The mass slaying of 14 women at the University of Montreal in December 1989 shocked all Canadians deeply, but had especially profound effects on women. After the tragedy, many expressed concern about whether it signaled a trend in violence against females—a sort of "backlash" in response to the movement of women into arenas traditionally dominated by males. Those reacting against this fear have noted the Montreal killings were unprecedented and atypical. But, while the likelihood of more massacres of women is extremely remote, is it not possible that such backlash violence could be increasingly directed against individual women in less spectacular, but no less deadly incidents?

This question prompted me to look at the relationship between changing gender roles and women's vulnerability to violence (Gartner, 1990b). While females

Gartner, Rosemary (1992). "Patterns of Victimization," in L. Tepperman and J. Curtis (eds.), *Everyday Life*. Toronto: McGraw-Hill Ryerson. Reprinted by permission.

are the victims of homicide less often than males, the size of this female protective advantage varies considerably. For example, in Italy and the United States since 1950, males have faced risks of homicide three times greater than females' risks. In other societies, this female advantage has been negligible: in the 1980s in Denmark and England, for instance, women were killed almost as often as were men. There is much less variation across societies in who kills women. Males are the perpetrators in over 80 percent of the killings of females, and in about 90 percent of the killings of adult females.

FEMALE HOMICIDES AND GENDER INEQUALITY

Anthropological and historical evidence shows that the killing of women is relatively infrequent, and the gender gap in homicide is relatively large, in many societies that are sharply gender-stratified (Curtis, 1974). In these societies, family arrangements are especially patriarchal, women are not allowed to participate in economically productive activities (or their economic activities are devalued), and females are socialized to be extremely passive and subservient. Yet despite these disadvantages, women appear to be at much less risk of homicide than are men. On the other hand, in many societies where gender inequality is less pronounced, women's risks of being killed are closer to men's risks. This suggests women in contemporary western societies might come to face risks of being killed similar to men's as various forms of gender inequality and discrimination diminish.

To explore this issue, I collected homicide victimization rates of females and males in 18 developed nations for the years 1950 to 1980. I also gathered information on the roles and status of women, and on gender inequality in each nation. This included women's participation in the labour force and in higher education, gender segregation in occupations, and the rate at which women had children outside of marriage, got divorced, and delayed marriage past their early twenties.

Two perspectives on the relationship between greater gender equality and female homicide can be distinguished. One, the "criminal opportunity" approach, deals largely with homicides in the public domain. According to this approach, criminal victimization, such as murder, occurs when a motivated offender encounters a suitable target (victim) in the absence of capable guardians (Hindelang et al., 1978; Cohen and Felson, 1979). How people move through the routine daily activities of life—where they spend time, how many and what types of people they spend time with—all influence their opportunities for being homicide victims. It follows that where women's and men's activities are more alike, their chances of being killed ought to be more alike.

A second perspective on the gender gap in homicide is suggested by feminist discussions of changing gender relations. According to this view, with reductions in gender inequality, women should be freer to avoid or to challenge male domination in a number of spheres of social life. Thus, where women have more alternatives to violent relationships with men, or more resources to protect themselves from victimization, their risks of being killed should be lower than where their choices and opportunities are more limited, if this view is correct.

This approach is more general than the criminal opportunity perspective, in that it can be applied to homicides in both the public and private domains. Women with more resources can leave abusive relationships more easily. They can also protect themselves more adequately in their public lives, for example, by choosing to live in safer neighbourhoods or taking taxis rather than walking late at night. Moreover, women with more resources can direct them toward collective advantages. For instance, they can lobby for more public protection of women, through changes in the substance and enforcement of laws against violence toward women.

TABLE 1   Mean Sex- and Age-Specific Homicide Victimization Rates[a] for 18 Nations, 1965-1984

Country	Males over age 14	Females over age 14	Children aged 5-14	Children 1-4	Infants under 1 year
United States	14.92	4.18	.99	2.11	5.40
Finland	4.89	1.51	.55	.89	6.92
Canada	3.28	1.55	.58	1.04	3.17
Italy	2.45	.69	.24	.22	.80
Australia	2.30	1.41	.51	1.06	3.00
Austria	1.67	1.20	.48	.89	6.81
Belgium	1.53	1.13	.33	.73	.98
West Germany	1.48	1.03	.56	1.03	5.59
New Zealand	1.46	.83	.38	1.71	4.49
Sweden	1.41	.83	.44	.84	1.36
France	1.39	.79	.26	.48	1.92
Japan	1.34	.74	.80	2.26	7.64
Norway	1.20	.59	.23	.35	1.80
Ireland	1.09	.43	.10	.18	2.05
Switzerland	1.04	.81	.51	.75	4.57
Netherlands	1.00	.51	.21	.43	1.63
England & Wales	.88	.71	.28	.99	4.30
Denmark	.75	.78	.65	.83	2.21
Mean, all 18 nations	2.45	1.10	.45	.93	3.65

[a]All rates are calculated per 100,000 persons in the appropriate sex or age group, except rates for infants, which are calculated per 100,000 live births.

Source: *World Health Statistics Annual*, World Health Organization, Switzerland.

The criminal opportunity perspective and the feminist approach seem to predict different outcomes for changes in gender stratification. The former suggests that gender equality increases the likelihood of women being killed, whereas the latter predicts that gender equality *reduces* the likelihood of women being killed.

Both may be right, however. Gender stratification is a complex phenomenon. It is composed of both differences in the *roles* and *activities* women and men perform, as well as differences in the *status* and *power* women and men hold. With greater gender equality in *roles*, women's daily activities could expose them to more dangerous situations.

This could increase the opportunities for female victimization. However, with greater gender equality in *status*, women could individually and collectively claim more control over their lives and their environments. This could decrease the opportunities for female victimization.

In other words, changes in gender stratification could operate to increase or decrease homicides of females, depending on which process had the strongest effects.

These processes may operate within different time frames and unfold at different speeds. Over the last few decades, the greatest changes in women's lives have been in their day-to-day activities, as they have moved into the labour force in unprecedented numbers, taken on a wider array of non-domestic responsibilities, and moved away from lives circumscribed largely by family ties. So gender inequality in roles has declined at a fairly steady pace.

Gender inequality in status, however, has been more obdurate. More women are working outside the home and heading households. But gains in status have not kept pace with changes in women's roles. For example, women's economic status has improved little in the last few decades, either in an absolute sense or relative to males. There are many disturbing examples of this, from the continued gender gap in wages to the growing proportion of poor households headed by females.

These differences suggest that recent changes in women's roles and changes in women's status may have had countervailing effects on women's risks of being killed. Moreover, improvements in women's status, however gradual, may have slowed any increase in women's risks of victimization by counteracting the risk-enhancing effects of women's less traditional roles.

To explore these issues, I combined and analyzed the time-series data on women's roles, status, and homicide for all 18 nations. The patterns I found, then, are general, applicable across these nations. I discovered:

- where women are less embedded in *traditional family and reproductive roles*—that is, where they had children out of wedlock more often, divorced more often, and delayed marriage longer—their risks of being killed were higher, and the gender gap in homicide was less pronounced.

- where women competed with men for *economically productive roles*—that is, where women made up a larger proportion of the paid labour force, and where occupations were less gender-stratified—their risks of being killed were also higher, and the gender gap in homicide was less pronounced.

- however, where women had *greater access to higher education* (and, I would argue, to the status, resources, and power that higher education confers) their risks of being killed eventually declined, and the gender gap in homicide did not narrow.

So, changes in women's roles and changes in women's status appeared to have counterbalancing effects on their risks of being killed. However, as anticipated, gains in women's status seemed to take time to translate into protection against violence. In the short run, as women assumed a greater range of roles and responsibilities, they also became more vulnerable to violence.

I decided to explore a bit further. Did women's less traditional roles always lead to greater risks, or did this depend on how much status women had? Perhaps where gender differences in status were less pronounced, women did not face increased risks of homicide when they moved into non-traditional roles; whereas where gender differences in status remained large, women were vulnerable when they took on more non-traditional roles.

I divided the 18 nations into two groups, depending on the level of female status in the nations (measured by female college enrollments). Some nations in the "high status" group were Canada, Sweden, Finland, and the United States; "low status" nations included Ireland, Japan, Italy, and the Netherlands. I found it was only in the low status group that women's less traditional roles substantially raised their risks of being killed. In the high status group of nations, the rate at which women were killed did not rise as gender differences in roles diminished.

It appears, then, that in societies that allowed fuller participation of women in higher education—a major avenue to higher status—women were not as likely to lose their protective advantage as they competed with men in the labour force or as they moved out of traditional domestic arrangements. Thus, the context within which women participate seems to determine their vulnerability to violence.

What do these findings have to tell us about Marc Lepine's murder of 14 women at the University of Montreal? At first glance, the Montreal killings do not seem to fit the general pattern I found. They occurred in Canada, a nation with relatively high female status. The setting was a university, a source of advances in women's status. On the other hand, most of the women killed were engineering students; they had entered a traditionally male-dominated field. And the verbal and written comments Lepine left behind indicated he was resentful and infuriated by "feminists" and other women who sought opportunities in less traditionally female ways. For him, such women had prevented his success professionally and personally.

Thus, I think the Montreal massacre can be seen both as part of a more general phenomenon of male backlash violence against women, and as a particularly aberrant expression of that pattern. In other words, Lepine's hostility toward successful women cannot be dismissed as merely the attitude of one isolated and psychotic individual. At the same time, it would be a mistake to conclude that seeking gender equality through higher education or professional advancement is a risky strategy for Canadian women.

CHILD HOMICIDES, FAMILY STRUCTURE, AND WELFARE SPENDING

The analysis of homicides of females was based on the knowledge that their killers are usually men. That is why it was important to focus on gender relations in explaining changes in women's risks of victimization. Similarly, studying the homicides of children requires some knowledge of who presents the greatest risks to children's lives, and under what circumstances.

Children, like women, face the greatest risks from people they are related to or living with. For infants, the most likely killer is a parent; as children grow older, the risks from their parents decrease, while the risks from other family members or other persons who know them well grow.

Certain types of family structures are known to increase children's vulnerability to violent victimization, including homicide. For example, children with young parents, single parents, step or foster-parents, or many young siblings face elevated risks of being physically abused or killed (Daly and Wilson, 1988). Where such families are also exposed to economic stresses, children's risks are especially high.

These well-known patterns have been explained in different ways. The "systems" or ecological approach proposes that a group's balance of resources for coping with stressors determines the level of violence in the group. From this approach, the family is a microsystem that is sometimes structured to limit the extent to which resources can be marshaled to cope with stressors (Garbarino, 1981). Where parents have fewer personal and social resources to draw on, where they are isolated from support systems, and where family size exceeds resource capacity, child abuse and homicide should be greater.

According to a systems approach, this relationship between family risk factors and violence against children operates at two levels. Not only will individual families that are isolated and resource-poor be particularly prone to child abuse. In addition, large numbers of such families in a social system (for example, a neighbourhood, city, or nation) can raise the risks of violence for all families in the system. This occurs because networks of informal control and support become weakened in the system as a whole.

A second explanation of the higher risks of homicide for children in certain family settings is provided by evolutionary psychology (Daly and Wilson, 1988). According to this perspective, through natural selection, individual decision making is oriented toward promoting one's genetic posterity or reproductive fitness. Consequently, the likelihood of infanticide is greater where a child is

> of dubious quality, . . . where there is some doubt that the offspring in question is indeed the putative parent's own [and where there are] extrinsic circumstances that might bode ill for a particular childrearing effort: food scarcities, a lack of social support, overburdening from the demands of older offspring, and so forth. (Daly and Wilson, 1988:44)

According to an evolutionary perspective, certain family structures or parental characteristics may increase the likelihood of child homicide, even when they are not accompanied by resource constraints. For example, teenage mothers should be more likely than older mothers to kill their children, in part because the potential future reproduction of teenage mothers is greater. Children raised by step-parents and unrelated caregivers should be at greater risk of violence, in part because these children do not enhance the reproductive fitness of their caregivers. Furthermore, maternal characteristics that are associated with premature, underweight, and less healthy babies should also be associated with elevated risks of child homicide.

The systems approach and the evolutionary perspective identify similar types of risk factors for children. According to both, where there are more single and very young mothers, non-intact families, and families with many young children, child homicide rates should be higher. Furthermore, where systems of social and economic support for families are less developed and less generous, child homicide rates should also be higher. I examined these predictions using child homicide data from the same set of nations described earlier for the years 1965 to 1984 (Gartner, 1991). I also collected data on family structures and welfare spending in these nations, including information on births to teenage and single mothers, divorce rates, and the ratio of young children to adult women in the population. A number of these high-risk characteristics of families increased between the late 1960s and the late 1970s in these nations. For example, divorce rates more than doubled, and rates of births to teenage and single mothers also grew. I asked if these changes in family structure were associated with changes in the homicide rates of infants and young children and found:

- infants under the age of one were more likely to be killed where rates of births to teenage mothers were higher, and where government spending on welfare programs was more limited;
- children aged one to four were more likely to be killed where rates of births to teenage mothers and to single mothers were higher, where divorce rates were higher, and where government spending on welfare programs was more limited.

Both the systems and the evolutionary approaches suggest that the risks associated with certain family structures can be lessened by providing families with resources to deal with the stresses they face. One way to do this is through government programs designed to alleviate economic deprivation.

To look at this issue, I divided the nations into two groups: one had higher than average government spending on welfare programs, while the other had lower than average spending. I then analyzed family structures and child homicide in these two groups. This analysis revealed that

- in nations where welfare programs were less generous, the risks associated with certain family structures were much greater than in nations where welfare programs were more generous.

In other words, higher government spending on social welfare was associated with lower risks of violence against children that resulted from the prevalence of particular family structures.

CONCLUSION

There are two important implications of these studies of female and child homicides. First, they show that social processes and structures can raise the risks of being killed for all members in society, regardless of gender or age. Second, they show that some social processes and structures pose particular risks for females and children. Therefore, theories of homicide based solely on studies of males are likely to be inadequate or even misleading when applied to females and children.

REFERENCES

Cohen, Lawrence E. and Marcus Felson (1979). "Social change and crime rate trends: A routine activity approach," *American Sociological Review*, 44:588–607.

Curtis, Lynn (1974). *Criminal Violence: National Patterns and Behavior*. Lexington, MA: D.C. Heath.

Daly, Martin and Margo Wilson (1988). *Homicide*. New York: Aldine de Gruyter.

Garbarino, James (1981). "An ecological approach to child maltreatment," pp. 228–267 in L. H. Pelton (ed.), *The Social Context of Child Abuse and Neglect*. New York: Human Sciences Press.

Gartner, Rosemary (1990b). "Gender stratification and the gender gap in homicide victimization," *Social Problems*, 37:593–612.

——— (1991). "Family structure, welfare spending, and child homicide in developed democracies," *Journal of Marriage and the Family*, 53.

Hindelang, Michael J., Michael R. Gottfredson, and James Garofalo (1978). *Victims of Personal Crime: An Empirical Foundation for a Theory of Personal Victimization*. Cambridge, MA: Ballinger.

QUESTIONS

DISCUSSION QUESTIONS

1. Evidence suggests that as the rate of crimes committed by older Canadians drops, the rate of crimes committed by juveniles increases. If this is true, how do you explain these two findings? Are they related in any way?

2. Is there a likely relationship between crimes against women and crimes committed by children and adolescents? Propose a theory that links these two types of crime.

3. According to Gartner, why are women safer from domestic violence in societies like that of Kuwait, which take moral violations by wives more seriously than does our own society?

4. What differences do you expect to find in the ways Americans, Indians, and Kuwaitis assess the seriousness of murders committed by children? Explain your answer.

DATA COLLECTION EXERCISES

1. What kind(s) of data would you collect to test the hypothesis that abused children, or the children of abused women, are more likely than other children to commit violent crimes?

2. How might societies differ in the degree of seriousness they attach to the crimes that Gartner discusses in her excerpt? See if you can find a society where violence against women and children is considered unimportant, or undeserving of harsh penalties.

3. Historically, how have the Canadian courts punished men who have been convicted of beating their wives? Collect data from the nineteenth century to answer this question.

4. Using published materials, collect information about abused Canadian women and children. How likely are they to end up "on the street"—homeless, as beggars or engaged in prostitution?

WRITING EXERCISES

1. "Capital punishment is just as appropriate for kids who kill as it is for adults who kill." Write 500 words defending or opposing this view.

2. "In the old days, children were well-behaved and wives obeyed their husbands. Crime is a problem today because this authority system broke down." Write 500 words commenting on this statement.

3. Based on the data provided in excerpt 3.2, write a 500-word essay describing the Kuwaiti view of right and wrong.

4. "The ways people evaluate offences against women and children tell us a great deal about ideas of equality in that society." Do you agree? Answer in a brief (500-word) essay.

SUGGESTED READINGS

1. Levinson, David (1989). *Family Violence in Cross-Cultural Perspective*, pp. 9-38. Frontiers of Anthropology, Volume 1. Newbury Park: Sage Publications. This essay uses the Human Relations Area Files to find out typical characteristics of societies in which family violence is common, and why domestic violence is justified in different ways in different societies.

2. Bell, Daniel (1958). *The End of Ideology*. In this book Bell makes his famous claim that crime is as American as apple pie—a "queer ladder of success" in a society driven by the desire for success. What would he have to say about the evidence of high and rising rates of crime in Moscow, Calcutta, and Paris?

3. Williams, Holly Ann (1990). "Families in refugee camps," *Human Organization*, Vol. 49, No. 2, 100-109. As civil wars rage around the world, families are forced from their home communities into refugee camps and other temporary shelters. This article shows that when family members become refugees traditional social controls break down and deviance, even violence, increases.

SECTION 4   CLASS AND SOCIAL STRATIFICATION

Introduction

Ever since the origin of the discipline in nineteenth century European social thought, sociology has been concerned with the sources and consequences of social inequality. The problem of social inequality has been so central to sociology that some see it as one of the field's three "classic questions"—even as *the* problem in sociology." In his book *Class Tells: On Social Inequality in Canada* (Second Edition), Alfred Hunter claims that the strong interest in social inequality "lies in the fact that it seeps into and shapes so many aspects of our experience, even if we are not always (or even often) aware of its presence and effects. It is not something which affects only some people or touches only some isolated corner of our lives." In fact, it touches all parts of all of our lives.

Every society that sociologists have studied has manifested social inequality. By *social inequality* we mean differences in access to scarce and valued resources of ownership, income, occupational prestige, power, and so on. All societies have at least some inequality, particularly in access to the scarce resource of power and leadership positions. For example, some people get to fill leadership positions and others do not; and men typically have more power than women.

Such differences in power are not the only forms of social inequality. Many societies contain marked differences in ownership, wealth, income, and prestige. And, time and again, we find that these resources are more easily obtained by men than women, by majority racial and ethnic groups than by minority groups, and by people of higher (rather than lower) social class backgrounds. In short, people with power in societies have seen to it that things are arranged so that gender, race, and social class are "used" to distribute scarce resources.

VARIETIES OF STRUCTURED INEQUALITY

Another way of saying the same thing is that all societies have "policies" concerning the distribution of scarce resources. These policies are specified both in laws (e.g., laws concerning private property in Canada) and in various norms (e.g., rules on advancement in bureaucratic workplaces). Taken together, these laws and norms form the basis of a *stratification system*.

In any stratification system, the same types of inequalities occur with each new generation. Inequalities between people persist because the same "rules of the game" persist. Researchers working from two different sociological theories have identified two distinct types of social inequality. One theory comes out of the work of Karl Marx and emphasizes economic ownership. The other comes out of the work of Max Weber and emphasizes more varied forms of inequality—including income and wealth, occupational prestige, and power.

Social Class

According to the Marxian approach, *social classes* exist in all capitalist societies, and are defined by ownership of the means of production and labour power. The "means of production" may include the machines, buildings, land, and materials used in the production of goods and services. The owners of the means of production, or their agents, buy "labour power"—people's physical and mental capacity to work for wages (or salaries).

With this relationship in mind, Marxists identify three main classes. The *bourgeoisie*, or capitalist class, own the means of production, purchase labour power, and accumulate wealth from surplus value created by workers' labour. The *petite bourgeoisie* own their means of production, work for themselves, and do not employ others. The *proletariat*, or working class, do not own the means of production and sell their labour power for wages.

Marxists believe that a conflict of interests is inherent in the organization of capitalism. On the one side, capitalists try to keep wages low and productivity high to maximize their wealth; on the other, workers try to increase their share of the wealth by winning higher wages and improving their working conditions.

Socio-Economic Status

This is an important part of the story, but not the only story. For example, non-Marxists claim that social classes can also be defined through inequalities in income, occupational prestige, and power. Non-Marxists often study these forms of social inequality to the neglect of social class in the Marxian sense. In practice, people ranked on income, prestige, and power may fall into different ranks within these different dimensions. For example, people in the middle-income category may receive quite different degrees of prestige for their different jobs, depending on whether they earn their income in white-collar or blue-collar work. Likewise, people with the same amount of income may enjoy very different amounts of control, or authority, in the workplace.

POVERTY

So far the topic of inequality sounds very abstract and dry. It becomes much less so when we look at concrete cases of social inequality in Canada and other countries, as we do in the following excerpts. And it becomes positively dramatic when we confront some very sobering facts about poverty.

When sociologists distinguish between relative and absolute poverty, they are distinguishing between very different kinds of poor people. Under conditions of *absolute poverty*, people do not even have enough of the basic necessities—food, shelter, and medicine, for example—for physical survival.

By contrast, *relative poverty* must be judged in terms of the general living standards of a given society or social group. What people consider "poor" varies from one society to another and, within a given society, from one group to another. In North America, we would consider people with much less than the average income to be "poor," even though most of them have enough money to survive physically.

Governments usually measure poverty in relation to "low income cut-off points" that vary according to the size of the family and of the community in which it lives. Large families who live in large communities generally need more money to live at a given level than do smaller families in smaller communities. Welfare legislation suggests that the amount of government assistance provided to poor people depends as much on the perceived causes of their poverty as it does on the extent of their poverty.

For example, old people and the physically disabled typically receive the most help. Apparently we consider them the blameless or "deserving poor." Single mothers and chronically unemployed people receive less generous and secure assistance, since many consider them the "undeserving poor." Welfare payments to this latter group fail to meet actual living expenses—especially for people living in large cities where rents are high. Many believe that if welfare payments were higher than the minimum wage, unemployed people would be reluctant to get off welfare and take a job.

Yet many unemployed people cannot find a job. In some regions and for some groups the unemployment rate has been very high. Certain groups, such as female lone parents of small children, cannot afford to pay the day care costs that would allow them to take a job. Others, such as the physically disabled, cannot find a job suitable to their ability (or disability).

Of all age groups, children are the most numerous and blameless victims of poverty. Their poverty demonstrates the error in thinking that a poor person has only him- or herself to blame. It is clear that the poverty of children is due to forces beyond their control, particularly the inability of parents to find work and the inadequacy of social supports (like free day care) that would permit them to hold jobs.

The poverty problem in Canada is not going to get better without decisive actions that include (1) the creation of new jobs; (2) job retraining for people whose job skills are inappropriate; and (3) social supports, such as free, good-quality day care, for women who need to go out and earn an income. The following excerpts—on poverty in the villages in Bangladesh and among the urban black "underclass" of America—demonstrate that there is much in common across societies in both the causes of and necessary solutions to poverty.

Don Black and John Myles

INDUSTRIALIZATION AND THE CLASS STRUCTURE IN CANADA, THE UNITED STATES, AND SWEDEN

INTRODUCTION

This excerpt puts the class structure of Canada in comparative perspective by considering Canada's system in relation to that of the United States and Sweden. Black and Myles use a modified version of the Marxian class categories described above, making further distinctions between large and small employers and between workers, managers, and supervisors.

The authors expect that major differences among the three countries will be found in the ways that management and economic ownership are organized, and this turns out to be the case. Canada is shown to have relatively more managers and supervisors than Sweden and fewer than the United States. Also, the bourgeoisie is relatively smaller in Canada than in the United States or Sweden.

Black and Myles attribute these differences in part to the high level of foreign ownership in the Canadian economy. In effect, Canadians manage what Americans own. Even Sweden, a small, late-developing country like Canada, has a larger share of home-grown capitalists. To find out the reasons why Canada is comparatively low in this regard you may want to read a book by Gordon Laxer (see Suggested Readings below).

In large part, the evolution of capitalism in Canada explains these differences. But the Canadian state has also evolved differently, taking a major role in the country's social and economic development. For a different slant on a related topic, read excerpt 14.3 on the political (and moral) regulation of single mothers.

This paper will address a comparative analysis of the class structures of Canada, the United States, and Sweden. Our general conclusion will be that the Canadian class structure continues to bear the imprint of "uneven development" that is reflected in the size and composition of both the petite bourgeoisie and the working class. We also conclude that dependent industrialization has resulted in the "Americanization" of the Canadian class structure. Within those sectors of the

Black, Don and John Myles (1986). "Dependent Industrialization and the Canadian Class Structure: A Comparative Analysis of Canada, the United States, and Sweden," *Canadian Review of Sociology and Anthropology*, 23(2), May, 157–181. Reprinted by permission.

economy traditionally dominated by U.S. capital (and U.S. labour unions), Canada has developed a class structure that is distinctively American. The result is a much greater dispersion of capitalist functions within the labour force.

These conclusions are based on the analysis of identical national surveys conducted in the United States, Sweden, and Canada between 1980 and 1983. In the following sections we briefly outline the conceptualization of classes and the data that provide the bases for these conclusions.

CONCEPTUALIZING THE STRUCTURE OF CLASS RELATIONS

Class location is defined as a position in a structure of power within which producing occurs. Hence, the term class structure refers to the distribution of effective powers over the forces of production including money capital, the means of production, and labour. The schema guiding the analysis is derived from the work of Erik Wright (1978).

The Bourgeoisie, the Petit Bourgeoisie, and Small Employers

The traditional bourgeoisie is defined simultaneously by legal ownership of the means of production and the purchase of the labour power of others. The latter distinguishes such positions from petits bourgeois positions where no labour power other than that of the owner is employed in production. Operationally, these two types of positions are easily distinguished by differentiating between the self-employed who do and do not have employees. What critically distinguishes between these two classes is whether the surplus value produced originates from the owner's own labour power or the labour power of others. Between these two conditions, however, is the situation of many small employers who continue to produce much of the surplus product themselves but also exploit the labour of others. For present purposes, small employers are arbitrarily distinguished from the bourgeoisie by their employment of more or less than ten persons. Given the nature of national random samples, most members of the bourgeoisie captured by this method are at best small capitalists and for most purposes we shall simply collapse "small" and "large" employers into a single category.

Managers and Supervisors

Managers and supervisors are distinguished by the fact that while they lack legal ownership of the means of production, they participate directly in the functions of capital, that is in control over capital, labour, and the means of production. Managers are identified by responses to a complex set of questions concerning participation in policy-making decisions with respect to the allocation of capital, labour, and the means of production within the enterprise. A separate category of "advisor-managers" is also used to identify those who provide advice in the decision-making process but do not directly make decisions. In most of our analyses we do not distinguish between advisor-managers and other managers because of the small size of the advisor category.

Supervisors include those employees who do not participate in making policy decisions but who do exercise authority over others. In constructing this category two forms of authority were identified: 1) sanctioning authority—an employee who is able to impose positive or negative sanctions on others; and 2) task authority—responsibility for coordinating the labour of others. Those with task authority are included in the supervisory category only if they are also part of the formal hierarchy. Nominal supervisors—persons in the formal hierarchy but with neither sanctioning nor task authority—are not included.

Workers and Semiautonomous Employees

The working class in Wright's formulation is a residual category, defined by the absence of direct or indirect powers over the disposition of capital, labour, or the means of production. But were we to define the working class simply as all those who do not participate in the managerial-supervisory chain of command, numerous occupational groups with at least an ambiguous relation to the working class would be relegated to the working class. These include university professors, social workers, engineers, and various other professional and semi-professional groups neither participating in the decision-making process nor controlling the labour of others. Wright deals with this problem by constructing a category of "semiautonomous" employees defined as wage-earners for whom the process of proletarianization is relatively incomplete (i.e. those employees who retain control over how they do their work and have at least some control over what they produce). Operationally, they are identified by a coding procedure based on responses to an open-ended question in which respondents provide examples of how they are able to design and otherwise control important aspects of their work (see Wright, Costello, Hachen, and Sprague, 1982).

THE CLASS STRUCTURES OF CANADA, THE UNITED STATES, AND SWEDEN

Despite obvious (and expected) similarities in the class structure of the three countries, there are notable differences.

First, Canada has a much larger petit bourgeoisie and, correspondingly, a smaller bourgeoisie than either Sweden or the United States.

Second, Canada has a smaller managerial and supervisory apparatus than the United States but a larger one than Sweden. The key to this difference lies at the supervisory rather than the managerial level. This becomes more apparent from the distributions in panel B where the self-employed are excluded and "managers" are broken down into decision-making managers and managers who only advise in the decision-making process.

TABLE 1 The Class Structures of Canada, the United States, and Sweden (%)

A) Total Labour Force

	Canada	U.S.	Sweden
Large employers	0.9	1.8	0.7
Small employers	2.8	6.0	4.7
Petit bourgeoisie	12.3	6.8	5.3
Managers	14.6	17.1	14.7
Supervisors	10.0	12.7	7.0
Semiautonomous employees	16.0	9.4	16.8
Workers	43.4	46.0	50.9
Total	100 (1756)	100 (1415)	100 (1133)

B) Wage Earners

	Canada	U.S.	Sweden
Decision-making managers	14.1	14.8	12.7
Advisor-managers	3.3	5.2	3.8
Supervisors	11.9	14.9	7.8
Semiautonomous employees	19.1	11.0	18.8
Workers	51.6	54.0	57.0
Total	100 (1474)	100 (1207)	100 (1012)

NOTE: N is in parentheses

Third, in contrast to the preceding pattern, Canada and Sweden are remarkably similar with respect to the relative number of semiautonomous employees and, here, it is the United States that proves to be the exception where only 11 percent of all wage-earners fall into this category compared to 19 percent of all wage-earners in Canada and Sweden.

Fourth, the result of a much larger petit bourgeoisie than either the United States or Sweden, a high proportion of semiautonomous workers relative to the United States, and a large supervisory apparatus relative to Sweden, is that Canada has the smallest "working class" of the three countries though the difference between Canada and the United States is not large.

These differences underline the two distinct problems that must be addressed in comparing the class structure of Canada with those of the United States and Sweden. On the one hand, Canada has a larger proportion of petit bourgeois locations and, on the other hand, it has a different distribution of autonomy and authority within the wage-earning population of the class structure. While the relative size of the wage-earning population is certainly related to the size of the petit bourgeoisie, its composition is not.

SOME FURTHER CONSIDERATIONS

Relative to the class structures of Sweden and the United States, there is evidence of the "distortions" in Canada's class structure. There are two notable features. First, Canada does have a distinctive occupational and industrial composition, and the size of the working class in Canada reflects these differences. Although Canada's industrial structure per se is of only minor importance in accounting for differences in the size of the working class, the occupational composition of the employed work force is significant. Smaller blue-collar work force is the major component accounting for Canada's smaller working class. What is striking about this is, of course, that there are no comparable effects of occupational or industrial composition in explaining U.S–Swedish differences in class structure.

A second feature of the Canadian class structure is Canada's larger petite bourgeoisie and, correspondingly, fewer small and large employers. Although Canada's large petite bourgeoisie is mostly a product of the persistence of petit bourgeois production in agriculture, it is also the case that petty commodity production has been more persistent within the Canadian transformative sector than in the U.S. or Sweden. In addition, the typical Canadian employee works for a smaller firm than Swedish or American employees. Both patterns would appear to reflect the truncated character of capitalist development in Canada.

But by far the most striking feature is the extent of incorporation of American practices for organizing class relations in the Canadian workplace. This is reflected in the apparent "overmanagement" of the Canadian working class and the tendency to incorporate employees into the administrative apparatus while simultaneously limiting the autonomy of those excluded from it, particularly in those sectors where the American branch plant has been dominant. It is the degree to which the Canadian class structure is Americanized that constitutes its most distinctive feature, and, to the extent that the American class structure itself is a curiosity among the advanced capitalist countries, this is also its most distinctive "distortion."

REFERENCES

Wright, Erik Olin (1978). *Class, Crisis and the State.* London: NLB.

Wright, Erik Olin, Cynthia Costello, David Hachen, and Joey Sprague (1982). "The American class structure," *American Sociological Review* 47: 709–26.

Mohammed Sadeque

SURVIVAL CHARACTERISTICS OF THE POOR IN A BANGLADESH VILLAGE

INTRODUCTION

Oppressively poor living conditions are the lot of many people throughout the world. We see a graphic example of this condition in this excerpt on village life in Bangladesh, where many people are far worse off than the poorest Canadians.

There, the working lives of poor people are filled with uncertainty. Some spend every day looking for whatever work they can find, without great likelihood of finding work at all. And there is a constant threat of employers hiring outside workers for cheaper wages.

At the best of times, a family's income is scarcely enough to meet its basic needs. Food is the number one priority of families; many spend their entire income on it. The residents of Rajshahi live in dilapidated, unsafe huts, and in filthy surroundings. Many are in poor health.

Poverty has also had a disastrous effect on family life. In these families, tensions are high, and divorce and desertion are common. Education of children is unimportant to these villagers because they see no hope of their children's lives being any better than their own. As a result there is a high dropout rate among those who begin school, and few children complete even a minimal education. People here will never have stable employment and a stable income until they improve their education. Unfortunately, they cannot improve their education until they have stable employment and a stable income.

In Bangladesh, poverty has been one of the major concerns in social studies in recent years. The present study adopted a multidimensional stance to analyze the interrelationship between economic and non-economic features of deprivation and their impact on the survival of the poor. The study is expected to help develop appropriate social policies for Bangladesh where methods for mobilizing the poor do not exist.

VILLAGE MEHERCHANDI

The study village was located on the northern border of the University of Rajshahi. Two criteria—land ownership and income—were adopted to single out the poor

Sadeque, Mohammed (1986). "The Survival Characteristics of the Poor: A Case Study of a Village in Bangladesh," *Social Development Issues,* 10(1), Spring, 11–27. Reprinted by permission.

households which constituted about 86 percent of the 632 households in the study village. The *Second Five Year Plan of Bangladesh* estimates the number of poor and extremely poor at 83 percent and 53 percent, respectively (Bangladesh Planning Commission, 1980).

TABLE 1 Land Ownership in Meherchandi

Land Holding	Percentage of Total Households	Percentage of Total Land
Landless	39.24	—
Less than 1 acre	21.84	6.28
1.00-2.50 acres	23.58	26.93
2.50-5.00 acres	8.70	21.08
5.00-7.50 acres	3.80	16.68
7.50-12.50 acres	1.58	11.33
Over 12.50 acres	1.26	17.70
Total	100.00	100.00

Location, cost consideration, and familiarity with the community prompted the selection of the study village. Data were collected in three stages: preliminary survey of all households in the village, an intensive interview of selected households, and 12 case studies.

PRESENTATION OF THE FINDINGS

Income-Earning Activities

The daily wage earners had to undertake whatever work they could manage on a day-to-day basis for eking out a bare subsistence. The day laborers were faced with uncertain employment opportunities due to the seasonal nature of agricultural and non-agricultural income-earning activities, unfavorable natural conditions, and the pressure of outside laborers. Others who had relatively stable sources of income could not count on any single activity throughout the year, and had to engage in additional activities to supplement their income.

On the basis of the major income-earning activities, we broadly categorized the households into eight specific groups: day laborers, small farmers, petty service holders, rickshaw pullers, petty traders, artisans, and beggars. The day laborers were the largest group. They constituted 40 percent of the households at the preliminary survey stage.

The monthly average household income of the classified categories based on data collected at the interview phase indicates very low income levels. The average monthly income of all the categories was about Tk.377, or roughly U.S.$13 (1 taka = $0.035). An average household size of 5.48 persons put the per capita monthly income at slightly more than two dollars, which is about one-fourth of the pre-sumed national per capita income in Bangladesh.

The findings in regard to income were supported by case studies. The abysmal-ly low income of the day laborers, service holders, and beggars was confirmed by the case studies.

Meeting Basic Needs

The poor spent all or most of their income for consumption purposes only. Analysis of a month's expenditures shows that more than 90 percent of the total expenses were for daily food requirements (Table 2).

The various household categories show a similar expenditure pattern. Four households (Cases II, III, XI, and XII) spent their entire yearly income on food. Four others (Cases I, IV, VI, and VIII) allocated nearly 90 percent for food. The remaining four cases had to divert part of their incomes for meeting extraordinary expenses such as payment of marriage gift, purchase of medicine, etc. In other words, they decreased food intake to meet other unavoidable expenses.

The poor adopted varied means to survive a decrease in income: credit-buying from village grocers, informal loans, institutional credit, disinvestment of assets (if any) or, in extreme circumstances, starvation.

TABLE 2 Expenditure Pattern of Poor Households in a Particular Month

Expenditure Item	Percentage of Total Expenses
Rice	47.11
Wheat	15.73
Pulses	3.16
Vegetables	5.06
Other Foodstuffs	20.08
Cloth	6.15
Medicine and Medical Expenses	1.53
Recreation	0.82
Social Responsibility	0.36
Total	100.00

Since they purchased foodstuffs daily, they were subject to recurring price fluc-tuations. Certain essential items of daily living for the years 1981–1983 demon-strated wide variations in local prices.

Because their earnings were uncertain and irregular, so was their food-intake pattern. It was clearly linked to income and the manner in which it was earned. Thus, they had little control over what and when they ate. Food-intake information for a particular 24-hour day and for a particular month strongly suggests the poor recorded a much lower intake of carbohydrates (their dominant form of food) than the desirable minimum of 450 grams of rice/wheat per capita per day.

Food-intake information from the twelve case studies collected for two consecutive months on a weekly basis shows an equally depressing picture. None of these households could afford a minimum carbohydrate diet.

The vast majority of households cooked rice and/or wheat only once in the evening and ate the evening's leftover, if available, the next morning. The curry consisted of leafy vegetables or *marichbata*, a peculiar combination of onions, chilies, and mustard oil. None of the households purchased any fish or meat from the market.

This near-starvation diet had a deleterious impact on health. About one-fourth of all members in the households studied and one-half of the labor force reportedly were suffering from diseases. The incidence of chronic and severe gastrointestinal diseases on a wide scale was clearly indicated. Deficiency diseases related to malnourishment seemed to be highly concentrated among the poorest households.

Health problems were exacerbated by at least two conditions: first, their huts (78 percent had a one-room dwelling of about 127 sq. ft.) were made of rustic material, were substandard, dilapidated, and unsafe, and they lacked the minimum facilities of rest, sleeping, and healthful living; second, their living environment was filthy, as only 15 percent used service latrines, whereas the vast majority evacuated their bowels in the fields and banks of tanks, polluting soil and water. Moreover, 50–80 percent of the households utilized home remedies, faith healing, and herbal medicines, and went to locally available quack alopaths and homeopaths when disease conditions deteriorated. Most people had no awareness of prevention.

Education of children was not conceived of as relevant to the realities of living. They could not imagine that the lifestyle of their children could differ from theirs. Only about 25 percent of the children were attending primary schools. The dropout phenomenon was also colossal. Most school-aged boys and girls had to help their parents with household tasks, collect firewood, or earn an income.

In summary, food was the overriding need. Families were so engrossed in meeting this requirement that the rest of their basic needs were grossly neglected— consciously or unconsciously.

Impact on Family and Kinship Relationships

Economic insecurity and hardship and the consequent interpersonal complications appeared to pave the way for the division of joint families into nuclear ones. About 85 percent of the poor households could be classified as nuclear. This division took place upon any pretext. At times, far-sighted parents took the initiative in setting up separate households for married sons in the interest of amity or to make them independent. All the cases except one were nuclear in the present study.

Many of the nuclear families were wracked by internal conflicts and mutual distrust. Familial peace and harmony seemed to be disturbed constantly by two particular conditions: first, grown girls were a perpetual source of anxiety for parents because the burden of a dowry or marriage gift was beyond their means. Second, the poor households recorded about a 25 percent rate of divorce/desertions. Unfortunately, neither the traditional local leadership was of any help in checking indiscriminate divorce/desertions, nor was there any effective legislation passed to protect the victimized married women.

Interestingly, most of the divorced/deserted women earned their own food. We also found instances where rich and powerful employers were having illicit sexual relationships with such working women.

Sons-in-law, on the other hand, enjoyed a somewhat privileged position. Sometimes their fathers-in-law lent or gave them money to do petty business. They also were presented with gifts from their fathers-in-law on special occasions. The primary concern of the girls' parents was to ensure that the marriages of their daughters survived. The weaker social position of women was clearly indicated. It is likely that the daily preoccupation with ceaseless efforts to find work and food changed the traditional mode of kinship relationships. Such relationships (both patrilineal and matrilineal) were limited to the exchange of visits at the most, and proximity was an important determinant. Relatives living in distant villages did not maintain connections with one another.

Status in the Community

Relationships with neighbors could be termed diffused. The pressure of outside laborers and the preference of some local employers to engage outside laborers at cheaper rates might have led to the ejection of a few of the working poor from the local employment market. But the majority were dependent on co-workers and poor neighbors for mutual support during emergencies or on rich and powerful neighbors for employment and other exigencies. There was a patron-client relationship between the rich and the poor, and the poor neighbors reciprocated by offering free services or supporting patrons in local elections (Khan, 1978). This dependence might have lowered their social position.

Their political awareness and participation seemed to be at the lowest ebb. Most adults voted in a ritualistic manner. The desire to achieve economic gains (e.g., relief goods) and the opinion and influence of the patrons acted as motivating factors. Local politics virtually became the monopoly of the local power elites.

Alternative opportunities for participation could be provided by voluntary social agencies and other programs that sprang up in the study community in recent years. Two voluntary organizations established to cater to the recreational needs of the local people had a very brief existence. At the time of research, two other organizations were working as cooperative saving societies.

Attitude

Almost everybody felt God had ordained their sufferings. The old, physically weak, and chronically sick were the most frustrated. Their sense of insecurity was obvious. Their ability to work and earn was their most valued possession and when that was threatened, their physical survival was endangered. Households with very young dependents or grown-up/divorced/deserted young girls were found to sulk in their pent-up frustrations.

Despite the fact that most of the poor were fatalistic, the majority were not content with their living conditions. They were unhappy because they failed to meet even the minimum food needs, let alone other basic necessities. The majority, however, did not give up and continued working hard for their basic survival. We agree with Gans (1970) in asserting that their reaction to present living conditions might be called fatalistic, "not because they were unable to conceive of alternative conditions but because they have been frustrated in the realization of alternatives."

Our observations did not support the prevalence of a so-called culture of poverty among our respondents.

IMPLICATIONS FOR SOCIAL POLICY

The study found survival by all the categories of the rural poor to be precarious. The problems of unemployment and lack of purchasing power appeared to have spread widely. The main problem is employment. It is, therefore, urgent that the nation adopt appropriate strategies of planned mobilization of our vast landless manpower through agro-based employment schemes, promotion of rural non-farm activities, and labor-intensive rural industrialization schemes. The traditional rural artisans should be incorporated into these schemes.

The productivity of small, marginal farmers should receive equal attention. Previous studies indicate that they were more productive than larger farms, provided they are given access to a regular flow of necessary credit, extension facilities, and inputs at the proper time (Hossain, 1974). The existing Integrated Rural Development Programme (IRDP) has failed to meet their needs because the cooperatives are dominated by the rural rich (Jones, 1979).

The deteriorating socioeconomic status of disadvantaged women is largely linked to the failure to make them economically independent. Those without any productive role in their families must be provided with one to supplement family income. Others should be taught alternative ways of performing household chores; the time saved may be used in undertaking additional income-producing activities. Moreover, the legislation enacted to protect their rights needs to be enforced.

To enable rootless people to derive the full worth of their work, their asset base has to be steadily created by suitable land and other asset reforms and by funnelling a substantial portion of the annual development funds to them. We found an unprecedented increase in the vulnerability of the old, infirm, and the young dependents who were previously supported by the joint family system. Society must introduce social security measures for them.

Health services were in disarray. The existing union level health care centers can be revitalized with essential medicines and equipment, and locally recruited paramedics may be trained to provide elementary health information as well as curative and preventive services. These centers could also serve as a nucleus for providing additional family welfare services.

In conclusion, we may emphasize two things. First, mass illiteracy reinforces the unemployment problem. The nation has to mobilize resources to introduce compulsory education in order to arrest illiteracy and raise the skill level of children and young adults. Second, organizations for the poor need to be turned into viable action groups by a gradual process of education and consciousness-raising. Existing poverty-focused programs and voluntary social agencies may be utilized as institutional bases for reaching and organizing them.

REFERENCES

Bangladesh Planning Commission (1980). *The second five year plan 1980–85.* Dacca: Bangladesh Government Press.

Gans, H. J. (1970). "Poverty and culture—Some basic questions about methods of studying life style of the poor," in P. Townsend (ed.), *The concept of poverty* (pp. 146–164). London: Heinemann.

Gil, D. G. (1973). *Unravelling social policy theory, analysis and political action towards social equality.* Massa: Schenkman.

Hossain, M. (1974). "Farm size and productivity in Bangladesh agriculture: A case study of Phulpur farms," *The Bangladesh Economic Review*, 2(1), 469–500.

Jones, S. (1979). "An evaluation of rural development programme in Bangladesh," *The Journal of Social Studies*, 6, 51–92.

Khan, F. R. (1978). "Problems and model of the study of elites in a district town in Bangladesh," *The Journal of the Institute of Bangladesh Studies*, 3, 149–172.

William Julius Wilson

THE BLACK UNDERCLASS
IN AMERICA

INTRODUCTION

This excerpt further explores the sources of poverty. The problem considered here is the persistence of poverty among the urban "underclass" in the United States.

The author finds that because affirmative action is aimed solely at reducing discrimination it has done little to help poor blacks. For although discrimination is certainly a problem, it is not what prevents most urban blacks from improving their economic situation. Wilson believes that the same factors promote poverty for white and African Americans alike. For example, in any population a high concentration of youth is a predictor of low incomes and high rates of unemployment and crime.

Urban American blacks have been particularly hard hit by the shift in the economy to services from manufacturing, the traditional sector of black employment. As in Canada, the problem poor people face is a drop in employment opportunities. Limited opportunities make it hard for black men to support their families, and in this way it erodes their self-esteem and sense of family responsibility.

Wilson notes that much of the research on black poverty has focused on the family for explanations. But recent research suggests that, even under slavery, black families were actually quite strong and stable. The high percentage of single-parent families we see today first appeared in the middle of the twentieth century, not during times of slavery. As we see in excerpt 5.1 on racial discrimination in Canada and Britain, the main problem visible minorities face in "white" countries like Canada is economic.

It is no secret that the social problems of urban life in the United States are, in great measure, associated with race.

While rising rates of crime, drug addiction, out-of-wedlock births, female-headed families, and welfare dependency have afflicted American society generally in recent years, the increases have been most dramatic among what has become a large and seemingly permanent black underclass inhabiting the cores of the nation's major cities.

And yet, liberal journalists, social scientists, policy-makers, and civil-rights leaders have for almost two decades been reluctant to face this fact. Often, analysts

Wilson, William Julius (1984). "The Black Underclass," *Wilson Quarterly*, Spring, 88–89. Copyright © 1984 by the Woodrow Wilson International Center for Scholars. Reprinted by permission.

of such issues as violent crime or teenage pregnancy deliberately make no refer-ence to race at all, unless perhaps to emphasize the deleterious consequences of racial discrimination or the institutionalized inequality of American society.

Some scholars, in an effort to avoid the appearance of "blaming the victim," or to protect their work from charges of racism, simply ignore patterns of behavior that might be construed as stigmatizing to particular racial minorities.

Such neglect is a relatively recent phenomenon. During the mid-1960s, social scientists such as Kenneth B. Clark (*Dark Ghetto*, 1965), Daniel Patrick Moynihan (*The Negro Family*, 1965), and Lee Rainwater (*Behind Ghetto Walls*, 1970) forthrightly examined the cumulative effects on inner-city blacks of racial isolation and class subordination. All of these studies attempted to show the connection between the economic and social environment into which many blacks are born and the cre-ation of patterns of behavior that, in Clark's words, frequently amounted to a "self-perpetuating pathology."

Why have scholars lately shied away from this line of research? One reason has to do with the vitriolic attacks by many black leaders against Moynihan upon publication of his report in 1965—denunciations that generally focused on the author's unflattering depiction of the black family in the urban ghetto. The harsh reception accorded to *The Negro Family* undoubtedly dissuaded many social scien-tists from following in Moynihan's footsteps.

The "black solidarity" movement was also emerging during the mid-1960s. A new emphasis by young black scholars and intellectuals on the positive aspects of the black experience tended to crowd out older concerns. Indeed, certain forms of ghetto behavior labeled pathological in the studies of Clark et al. were redefined by some during the early 1970s as "functional" because, it was argued, blacks were displaying the ability to survive and in some cases flourish in an economically depressed environment.

In the end, the promising efforts of the early 1960s—to distinguish the socioeco-nomic characteristics of different groups within the black community, and to identify the structural problems of the U.S. economy that affected minorities—were cut short by calls for "reparations" or for "black control of institutions serving the black com-munity." In his 1977 book, *Ethnic Chauvinism*, sociologist Orlando Patterson lamented that black ethnicity had become "a form of mystification, diverting attention from the correct kinds of solutions to the terrible economic condition of the group."

Meanwhile, throughout the 1970s, ghetto life across the nation continued to deteriorate. The situation is best seen against the backdrop of the family.

In 1965, when Moynihan pointed with alarm to the relative instability of the black family, one-quarter of all such families were headed by women; 15 years later, the figure was a staggering 42 percent. (By contrast, only 12 percent of white families and 22 percent of Hispanic families in 1980 were maintained by women.) Not surprisingly, the proportion of black children living with both their father and their mother declined from nearly two-thirds in 1970 to fewer than half in 1978.

In the inner city, the trend is more pronounced. For example, of the 27,178 families with children living in Chicago Housing Authority projects in 1980, only 2,982, or 11 percent, were husband-and-wife families.

TEENAGE MOTHERS

These figures are important because even if a woman is employed full-time, she almost always is paid less than a man. If she is not employed, or employed only part-time, and has children to support, the household's situation may be desperate. In 1980, the median income of families headed by black women ($7,425) was only 40 percent of that of black families with both parents present ($18,593). Today, roughly five out of 10 black children under the age of 18 live below the poverty level; the vast majority of these kids have only a mother to come home to.

The rise in the number of female-headed black families reflects, among other things, the increasing incidence of illegitimate births. Only 15 percent of all births to black women in 1959 were out of wedlock; the proportion today is well over one-half. In the cities, the figure is invariably higher: 67 percent in Chicago in 1978, for example. Black women today bear children out of wedlock at a rate nine times that for whites. Almost half of all illegitimate children born to blacks today will have a teenager for a mother.

The effect on the welfare rolls is not hard to imagine. A 1976 study by Kristin Moore and Steven B. Cardwell of Washington's Urban Institute estimated that, nationwide, about 60 percent of the children who are born outside of marriage and are not adopted receive welfare; furthermore, "more than half of all AFDC [Aid to Families with Dependent Children] assistance in 1975 was paid to women who were or had been teenage mothers." A 1979 study by the Department of City Planning in New York found that 75 percent of all children born out of wedlock in that city during the previous 18 years were recipients of AFDC.

WHY NO PROGRESS?

I have concentrated on young, female-headed families and out-of-wedlock births among blacks because these indices have become inextricably connected with poverty and welfare dependency, as well as with other forms of social dislocation (including joblessness and crime).

As James Q. Wilson observed in *Thinking About Crime* (1975), these problems are also associated with a "critical mass" of young people, often poorly supervised. When that mass is reached, or is increased suddenly and substantially, "a self-sustaining chain reaction is set off that creates an explosive increase in the amount of crime, addiction, and welfare dependency." The effect is magnified in densely populated ghetto neighborhoods, and further magnified in the massive public housing projects.

Consider Robert Taylor Homes, the largest such project in Chicago. In 1980, almost 20,000 people, all black, were officially registered there, but according to one report "there are an additional 5,000 to 7,000 who are not registered with the Housing Authority." Minors made up 72 percent of the population and the mother alone was present in 90 percent of the families with children. The unemployment rate was estimated at 47 percent in 1980, and some 70 percent of the project's 4,200 official households received AFDC. Although less than one-half of one percent of Chicago's population lived in Robert Taylor Homes, 11 percent of all the city's murders, nine percent of its rapes, and 10 percent of its aggravated assaults were committed in the project in 1980. Why have the social conditions of the black underclass deteriorated so rapidly?

Racial discrimination is the most frequently invoked explanation, and it is undeniable that discrimination continues to aggravate the social and economic problems of poor blacks. But is discrimination really greater today than it was in 1948, when black unemployment was less than half of what it is now, and when the gap between black and white jobless rates was narrower?

As for the black family, it apparently began to fall apart not before but after the mid-20th century. Until publication in 1976 of Herbert Gutman's *The Black Family in Slavery and Freedom*, most scholars had believed otherwise. "Stimulated by the bitter public and academic controversy over the Moynihan report," Gutman produced data demonstrating that the black family was not significantly disrupted during slavery or even during the early years of the first migration to the urban North, beginning after the turn of the century. The problems of the modern black family, he implied, were a product of modern forces.

Those who cite racial discrimination as the root cause of poverty often fail to make a distinction between the effects of *historic* discrimination (that is, discrimination prior to the mid-20th century) and the effects of *contemporary* discrimination. That is why they find it so hard to explain why the economic position of the black underclass started to worsen soon after Congress enacted, and the White House began to enforce, the most sweeping civil-rights legislation since Reconstruction.

MAKING COMPARISONS

My own view is that historic discrimination is far more important than contemporary discrimination in understanding the plight of the urban underclass; that, in any event, there is more to the story than discrimination (of whichever kind).

Historic discrimination certainly helped to create an impoverished urban black community in the first place. In *A Piece of the Pie: Black and White Immigrants since 1880* (1980), Stanley Lieberson shows how, in many areas of life, including the labor market, black newcomers from the rural South were far more severely discriminated against in Northern cities than were the new white immigrants from southern, central, and eastern Europe. Skin color was part of the problem, but it was not all of it.

The disadvantage of skin color—the fact that the dominant whites preferred whites over nonwhites—is one that blacks shared with Japanese, Chinese, and others. Yet the experience of the Asians, whose treatment by whites "was of the same violent and savage character in areas where they were concentrated," but who went on to prosper in their adopted land, suggests that skin color per se was not an "insurmountable obstacle." Indeed, Lieberson argues that the greater success enjoyed by Asians may well be explained largely by the different context of their contact with whites. Because changes in immigration policy cut off Asian migration to America in the late 19th century, the Japanese and Chinese populations did not reach large numbers and therefore did not pose as great a threat as did blacks.

Furthermore, the discontinuation of large-scale immigration from Japan and China enabled Chinese and Japanese to solidify networks of ethnic contacts and to occupy particular occupational niches in small, relatively stable communities. For blacks, the situation was different. The 1970 census recorded 22,580,000 blacks in the United States but only 435,000 Chinese and 591,000 Japanese. "Imagine," Lieberson exclaims, "22 million Japanese Americans trying to carve out initial niches through truck farming."

THE YOUTH EXPLOSION

Different population sizes also helped determine the dissimilar rates of progress of urban blacks and the new *European* arrivals. European immigration was curtailed during the 1920s, but black migration to the urban North continued through the 1960s. With each passing decade, Lieberson writes, there were many more blacks who were recent migrants to the North, whereas the immigrant component of the new Europeans dropped off over time. Eventually, other whites muffled their dislike of the Poles and Italians and Jews and saved their antagonism for blacks. As Lieberson notes, "The presence of blacks made it harder to discriminate against the new Europeans because the alternative was viewed less favorably."

The black migration to Northern cities—the continual replenishment of black populations there by poor newcomers—predictably skewed the age profile of the urban black community and kept it relatively young. The number of central-city black youths aged 16–19 increased by almost 75 percent from 1960 to 1969. Young black adults (ages 20–24) increased in number by two-thirds during the same period, three times the increase for young white adults. In the nation's inner cities in 1977, the median age for whites was 30.3, for blacks 23.9. The importance of this jump in the number of young minorities in the ghetto, many of them lacking one or more parent, cannot be overemphasized.

Age correlates with many things. For example, the higher the median age of a group, the higher its income; the lower the median age, the higher the unemployment rate and the higher the crime rate. (More than half of those arrested in 1980 for violent and property crimes in American cities were under 21.) The younger a woman is, the more likely she is to bear a child out of wedlock, head up a new household, and depend on welfare. In short, much of what has gone awry in the ghetto is due in part to the sheer increase in the number of black youths. As James Q. Wilson has argued, an abrupt rise in the proportion of young people in *any* community will have an "exponential effect on the rate of certain social problems."

The population explosion among minority youths occurred at a time when changes in the economy were beginning to pose serious problems for unskilled workers. Urban minorities have been particularly vulnerable to the structural economic changes of the past two decades: the shift from goods-producing to service-providing industries, the increasing polarization of the labor market into low-wage and high-wage sectors, technological innovations, and the relocation of manufacturing industries out of the central cities.

BEYOND RACE

Roughly 60 percent of the unemployed blacks in the United States reside within the central cities. Their situation continues to worsen. Not only are there more blacks without jobs every year; many, especially young males, are dropping out of the labor force entirely. The percentage of blacks who were in the labor force fell from 45.6 in 1960 to 30.8 in 1977 for those aged 16–17 and from 90.4 to 78.2 for those aged 20–24. (During the same period, the proportion of white teenagers in the labor force actually *increased*.)

More and more black youths, including many who are no longer in school, are obtaining no job experience at all. The proportion of black teenage males who have never held a job increased from 32.7 to 52.8 percent between 1966 and 1977; for black males under 24, the percentage grew from 9.9 to 23.3. Research shows, not surprisingly, that joblessness during youth has a harmful impact on one's future success in the job market.

There have been recent signs, though not many, that some of the inner city's ills may have begun to abate. For one, black migration to urban areas has been minimal in recent years; many cities have experienced net migration of blacks to the suburbs. For the first time in the 20th century, a heavy influx from the countryside no longer swells the ranks of blacks in the cities. Increases in the urban black population during the 1970s, as demographer Philip Hauser has pointed out, were mainly due to births. This means that one of the major obstacles to black advancement in the cities has been removed. Just as the Asian and European immigrants benefited from a cessation of migration, so too should urban blacks.

Even more significant is the slowing growth in the number of *young* blacks inhabiting the central cities. In metropolitan areas generally, there were six percent fewer blacks aged 13 or under in 1977 than there were in 1970; in the inner city, the figure was 13 percent. As the average age of the urban black community begins to rise, lawlessness, illegitimacy, and unemployment should begin to decline.

Even so, the problems of the urban black underclass will remain crippling for years to come. And I suspect that any significant reduction of joblessness, crime, welfare dependency, single-parent homes, and out-of-wedlock pregnancies would require far more comprehensive social and economic change than Americans have generally deemed appropriate or desirable.

The existence of a black underclass, as I have suggested, is due far more to historic discrimination and to broad demographic and economic trends than it is to racial discrimination in the present day. For that reason, the underclass has not benefited significantly from "race specific" antidiscrimination policies, such as affirmative action, that have aided so many trained and educated blacks. If inner-city blacks are to be helped, they will be helped not by policies addressed primarily to inner-city minorities but by policies designed to benefit all of the nation's poor.

I am reminded in this connection of Bayard Rustin's plea during the early 1960s that blacks recognize the importance of *fundamental* economic reform (including a system of national economic planning along with new education, manpower, and public works programs to help achieve full employment) and the need for a broad-based coalition to achieve it. Politicians and civil-rights leaders should, of course, continue to fight for an end to racial discrimination. But they must also recognize that poor minorities are profoundly affected by problems that affect other people in America as well, and that go beyond racial considerations. Unless those problems are addressed, the underclass will remain a reality of urban life.

QUESTIONS

DISCUSSION QUESTIONS

1. Would you expect to find that social inequality, in some form, is "universal," or found in all societies? Why or why not?

2. Compare and contrast the concepts of "social class" and "socio-economic status," and give examples drawn from the excerpts in this section.

3. Compare Sadeque's and Wilson's views on the causes of poverty in the cases they discuss.

4. Define and discuss the concept of "underclass" as Wilson uses it. Is there an "underclass" in your home community?

DATA COLLECTION EXERCISES

1. Recall the set of class categories used in the Black and Myles study. In what ways might they need to be changed in order to be useful in analyzing class structures of a wider spectrum of contemporary societies—for example, Russia, Mexico, or South Africa?

2. Study newspaper articles for information on the fact that poor people are less healthy, and die younger, than other people. Also, look for explanations of these patterns.

3. Suggest ways of measuring "relative" and "absolute" poverty in your community. How would they have to differ in order to be appropriate for the communities studied by Sadeque and Wilson?

4. Gather library data on the situation of social inequality of Canada's native peoples. Are they an "underclass" as Wilson uses this concept?

WRITING EXERCISES

1. Write a brief (500-word) essay in which you speculate on the ways that Black and Myles' results might have turned out if they had done their comparative study of Canada and the United States a hundred years ago.

2. Write a brief (500-word) essay on the role of class conflict in contemporary discussions of "exploding" health care and old-age pension costs.

3. Both Sadeque and Wilson see improved educational opportunities as a partial solution to the inequalities they studied. In about 500 words, write a critical assessment of this view.

4. Write a brief (500-word) letter to the Prime Minister listing ways in which inequalities in social class and socio-economic status may be lessened in Canada (or, if you prefer, in another society of your choice).

SUGGESTED READINGS

1. Laxer, Gordon (1982). *Open for Business.* Toronto: Oxford University Press. The author uses a comparative approach to examine the role of government and the state in shaping historical patterns of foreign ownership in the Canadian economy.

2. Rossi, Peter H. (1989). *Down and Out in America: The Origins of Homelessness.* Chicago: University of Chicago Press. A penetrating analysis of why homelessness and extreme economic hardship increased markedly in North America in the last decade. The author puts forward policy suggestions based on the analysis.

3. Sennett, Richard and Jonathan Cobb (1973). *The Hidden Injuries of Class.* New York: Vintage. An interview study, with provocative interpretations, on how people come to grips with the fact that they are situated towards the bottom of the community's class structure.

SECTION 5   RACE AND ETHNIC RELATIONS

Introduction

To discuss the relations between different racial (or ethnic) groups in Canada, we must begin by defining some concepts—ethnocentrism, discrimination, genocide, and multiculturalism—that are widely used in this subdiscipline of sociology.

Ethnocentrism is the tendency to use one's own culture as a basis for evaluating other cultures. One's own culture is taken to be the norm and considered superior to all other cultures that deviate from this norm. Ethnocentrism is natural enough, especially for people who have had little exposure to other cultures. But natural or not, ethnocentrism poses problems in a world filled with different values, languages, and cultural groups.

It is difficult to avoid ethnocentrism and to accept cultural variation as a fact of life. After all, ethnocentrism is not merely cultural short-sightedness; it is rooted in people's upbringing. Some North Americans, for example, hold the stereotypical view that Asian students are passive and overly methodical. Teachers may see these students as poor communicators, but the difference is mainly cultural—the result of a different style of communicating.

Discrimination, which usually grows out of ethnocentrism, refers to the actions people carry out against other people because of their race or ethnicity. In particular, discrimination is the denial of opportunities that people would otherwise grant to equally qualified members of their own group.

Discrimination takes a variety of forms, for example job segregation, unequal pay for equal work, and denial of promotion. It is hard to measure the direct effects of discrimination, as they are often subtle. However, we can usually show that the members of some ethnic and racial groups have advantages over the members of others. When people with the same qualifications receive different rewards for doing the same work, we can logically claim that discrimination exists.

It took field experiments by Frances Henry and Effie Ginzberg (*Who Gets the Work? A Test of Racial Discrimination in Employment*) to show the true extent of job discrimination in Canada. The researchers found that, in twenty calls, black applicants would be offered 13 interviews, yielding one job. By contrast, in twenty calls white applicants would be offered 17 interviews, yielding three jobs. In excerpt 5.1 below, Jeffrey Reitz compares these results with those obtained in Britain using the same method. The comparison tells us a great deal about the race relations problems that Canada may be facing in future.

Genocide, an extreme form of discrimination, is the attempted murder of an entire people. Methods of genocide have included slaughter with bombs, chemical weapons, starvation, and gas chambers. In modern history, societies have committed genocide against the Jews, Armenians, Kurds, and Gypsies (Romany), to name a few. In the former Yugoslavia, Bosnian Muslims are the recent victims of genocide by the Serbs. So are the Croats, although Serbs see this as revenge for genocide committed against them during the Second World War. Excerpt 5.2 below discusses the Yugoslavian genocide, and world reactions to it.

Historically, native peoples of North and South America have also died in large numbers from infectious diseases and mass starvation. But it is unclear whether the white explorers and colonizers intended mass murder.

Multiculturalism is at the opposite end of the continuum from discrimination and genocide. Originally, "multiculturalism" was nothing more than the name of a policy devised by the federal Liberal party (under Prime Minister Trudeau) in order to give importance to the ethnic concerns of minority Canadians. However, Canadians have found it increasingly useful to distinguish between traditional multiculturalism, or pluralism, and modern multiculturalism.

Traditional pluralism protects the rights of minority individuals through provincial human rights codes and other legislation. By contrast, modern multiculturalism sees each of us as a member of an ethnic or racial group—a representative of the groups to which we belong. Thus it is the group—not the individual—that is to be protected by law.

By its nature, traditional pluralism is concerned with civil liberties. It protects individual job-seekers against discrimination. It also forbids the publication of certain pre-trial information in criminal cases if this information threatens the right of the accused to a fair trial. Modern multiculturalism, on the other hand, supports blanket preferences—i.e., employment equity—in the hiring of groups that are traditionally discriminated against. It also categorically opposes the collection or publication of statistics on the ethnic or racial origins of criminals.

CANADIAN IMMIGRATION POLICY

Many issues connected to ethnocentrism, discrimination, and multiculturalism arise in discussions about immigration. In excerpt 5.3 below, sociologist Morton Weinfeld asks how many immigrants of which kinds should be admitted, and for what reasons; and how they should be assimilated into Canadian society. Canada has always had policies about these issues, and these policies have always protected the interests of Canadian citizens.

The history of Canada's settlement reflects the country's changing need for labour power. In periods when the country needed more farmers or workers, the Canadian government made more vigorous efforts to attract immigrants. In the country's early years, there was an ethnocentric preference for people much like the English and French: first for northern (Protestant) Europeans and secondarily for eastern and southern (Catholic) Europeans. After Confederation, the national government committed itself to strengthening the state against threats of an American invasion. It did this by building a railroad from coast to coast and bringing settlers to the sparsely populated Prairies.

Immigration to Canada slowed between 1914 and 1945 because of the two world wars, the Depression of the 1930s, and the decline in the demand for labour.

But after the Second World War, immigration entered a new phase. Throughout the 1950s, '60s, and '70s vastly increased numbers came from southern Europe: first Italy, then other Mediterranean countries (Greece, Portugal, and Spain). Most of them settled in the rapidly growing cities of central Canada. Over the last three decades, Canada has accepted immigrants who are unlike the Charter Groups in important ways. In doing so it has followed a "point system" guided by economic concerns. However, even so calculated a strategy has raised anxieties about the assimilability of the new immigrants.

Anxiety about culturally and racially different immigrants has long been a central feature of Canadian life. Historic discrimination against the Chinese in Canada was symptomatic of a general dislike of visible minorities, whether they were from China, India, Africa, the Pacific islands, or the Caribbean. But in the 1970s and '80s non-white immigrants began to pour into Canada. Many Chinese came from Hong Kong, a British colony since the nineteenth century. As well, for the first time many Asians came from other parts of the British Commonwealth, especially India and Pakistan. By 1980, the numbers of immigrants from Latin America, the Caribbean, and southeast Asia had also increased dramatically.

Many of these people were fleeing poverty, desperate postwar strife, or political upheaval. Yet entry into Canada has never been open to all. Canada's policies currently use a point system to grade applicants for immigration. Some immigrants have brought large amounts of capital, which has earned them a high priority with officials. Only recently have refugees, who are exempt from the point system, entered Canada in larger numbers than other immigrants.

We need reliable research on the consequences of immigration. What happens to immigrants once they come to Canada? Who benefits from high immigration rates and who loses? As well, how have immigrants historically helped the economy? the culture? the country's social life? Uncertainty about the answers to these questions is causing conflict in our race and ethnic relations, and has resulted in a lack of clear official policy. Many of these issues are discussed in excerpt 5.3. In that essay Professor Weinfeld calls for policies that would maintain a constant immigration level and help to guard against discrimination and racism.

Jeffrey G. Reitz

RACIAL DISCRIMINATION IN CANADA AND BRITAIN

INTRODUCTION

Canadians pride themselves on having avoided large-scale race riots of the kind that have occurred in the United States, Britain, and elsewhere. This success, along with the country's formal commitment to multiculturalism, has led many Canadians to suppose that a "race problem" does not exist in Canada.

But in this excerpt Jeffrey Reitz suggests another conclusion. There is, in fact, a race problem in Canada. Similar research on job discrimination in the two countries produces similar findings: there is no less job discrimination against black people in Canada than there is in the United Kingdom.

According to Reitz there are four factors that keep racial conflict from breaking out today, but these are likely to weaken in the future. We may be facing the creation of a black underclass of the kind described by W. J. Wilson in excerpt 4.3. This leaves Canada vulnerable to racial conflicts of the kind that Britain saw several decades ago, and perhaps even racial conflicts of the kind seen in the United States.

If this analysis is correct, we must stop being smug and complacent. Canadians need to take steps to overcome racial discrimination in the workplace and elsewhere. This may avert the disaster of violent racial conflict. And even if it doesn't, Canada loses nothing by opposing racism. It simply makes good on the promise of multicultural tolerance.

Credible comparative evidence on racial discrimination in Canada compared to Britain or the United States is sparse, but the evidence that exists runs counter to the usual assumption of less discrimination in Canada. Our interest here is specifically in discriminatory behaviour, that is to say, the denial of access to jobs and other significant resources in society, solely on the basis of race.

COMPARATIVE EVIDENCE ON RACIAL DISCRIMINATION: BRITAIN VS. CANADA

Generally, in Britain, racial minorities are less well off than they are in Canada. West Indian men in Britain are substantially less well-educated than whites, have

Reitz, Jeffrey G. (1988). "Less Racial Discrimination in Canada, or Simply Less Racial Conflict? Implications of Comparisons with Britain," *Canadian Public Policy/Analyse de Politiques*, XIV(4), 424–441. Reprinted by permission.

lower occupational status, earn less when employed full time, and have almost double the white unemployment rates. In Canada, West Indian men have comparatively high levels of education in relation to other groups. While their incomes are lower than the incomes of whites, their unemployment rates are only marginally higher than white unemployment rates. Thus West Indian men in Canada experience less economic disadvantage compared to West Indian men in Britain. In Britain, Asians, mainly Indians and Pakistanis, are relatively better situated than are West Indians, but so are Asians in Canada, including many Chinese and Indo-Chinese as well as Indo-Pakistanis.

The higher status for Canadian racial minorities does not necessarily reflect less discrimination. Higher status is expected because occupationally-selective Canadian immigration policies have brought more highly educated and employable immigrants to Canada, and because the buoyant Canadian economy provides opportunities for minorities, insulating them from the "last hired, first fired" syndrome.

Actual racial discrimination in employment in Britain and Canada can be compared in data gathered from experimental field trials. In Toronto, such discrimination field trials were conducted by the Social Planning Council (SPC) of Metropolitan Toronto. Because these studies were modelled closely on similar British studies in London and Birmingham (McIntosh and Smith, 1974), results can be directly compared.

The field trials, including telephone applications by actors with varying accents, and walk-in applications by black and white actors presenting comparable qualifications, produced remarkably similar results in the two countries. (See Table 1.) In both studies, whites more often received positive responses to telephone applications than did non-whites. (See panel A.) In Toronto, whites received positive responses in 86.9 percent of applications, whereas non-whites received positive responses in only 60.1 percent of applications, a difference of 26.8 percent.[1] In London and Birmingham, the corresponding percentages were 89.3 percent for whites and 73.9 percent for non-whites, a difference of 15.4 percent. These data do not support the hypothesis of less discrimination in Canada. In actual in-person job offers, whites in both countries had about a three-to-one advantage over non-whites.[2]

In other words, the data show the measured extent of direct racial discrimination in employment in Toronto is not less than its extent in London and Birmingham.

A follow-up SPC employer survey showed how little Toronto employers are aware of discrimination or other race-related problems within their organizations (Billingsley and Muszynski, 1985). Employers oppose government intervention in hiring decisions. These results, too, correspond closely to British findings (Carby and Thakur, 1977), and suggest that in both countries, major voluntary changes in employer behaviour will not occur soon.

Some comparative evidence relevant to racial discrimination in housing is also available. According to demographic analyses, residential concentration of racial minorities in Britain in the first years following their settlement was not significantly greater than current patterns in Canadian cities. Studies in Britain by Collison (1967:281) and Peach (1982:36) found that indexes of residential racial dissimilarity (the proportion of racial groups who would have to move to bring about a similar distribution across all groups) were between 0.3 and 0.6 in the 1960s. For Canadian cities, Balakrishnan and Kralt (1987:143–54) found index values between 0.4 and 0.6 in 1981. Residential concentrations evidently were comparable at comparable stages in the development of racial minority communities in the two countries.

TABLE 1 Comparison of Employment Discrimination Field Tests: Britain, 1974; Canada, 1985

	Canada[1] (Toronto)			Britain[2] (London, Birmingham)		
A. Telephone application results						
	Percent positive	Percent negative	(N)	Percent positive	Percent negative	(N)
White	86.9	13.1	(237)	89.3	10.7	(84)
Non-white	60.1	39.9	(474)	73.9	26.1	(69)
B. In-person application results						
	Number	Percent[3]		Number	Percent	
White offer	27	75.0		23	71.8	
Both offer	10	–		49	–	
Non-white offer	9	25.0		9[4]	28.1	
No offer	155	–		52	–	
Total	201	100.0		133	100.0	

[1]Source: Henry and Ginzberg (1985:27); study included newspaper advertised non-skilled jobs both white collar and blue collar; West Indian workers only.

[2]Source: McIntosh and Smith (1974:41-42); study included industrial non-skilled jobs only; West Indian and Asian blue collar workers only.

[3]Percentages are calculated based on cases in which jobs were offered to either a white or a non-white, but not to both.

[4]In the British study, it was noted that several of these jobs offered to non-whites were very low paying; the authors excluded them from some of the results they reported. In the Canadian study, no data on pay were provided.

SOCIAL FACTORS MODERATING RACIAL CONFLICT

The extent of overt racial conflict in Canada is quite plainly less than in Britain. In the British inner cities of London, Birmingham, Liverpool, and Bristol, hostility and violence have become the norm in relations between young, unemployed blacks and the police. In Canada, chronic violence is not nearly as visible a part of race relations. Furthermore, in Canada there is far less controversy about the status of minorities.

The favorable tone of racial politics in Canada is expressed in positive ways, too. Canadian policy-makers now repudiate past instances of racial bias, such as the incarceration of Japanese-Canadians during World War II.

There is no contradiction between the observation that racial conflict is less in Canada, and the evidence presented above that racial discrimination is not less. By racial conflict, I refer here primarily to minority group responses to discrimination and inequality: the extent to which discrimination is perceived, the extent to which it is thought to be unjust, and the extent to which it becomes the focus of social and political resistance.

What conditions may be operating to moderate racial conflict in Canada, independent of levels of racial discrimination? The following discussion will identify four specific factors, which seem to account for lack of racial conflict in Canada compared to Britain. These are: 1) the generational composition of racial minorities, 2) the economic status and position of racial minorities in relation to overall economic trends, 3) the structure of immigration institutions, and 4) multi-ethnic political structures and culture.

Generational Composition of Racial Minorities

The emergence of a native-born generation within immigrant groups has been crucial to the development of race politics in Britain. British-born blacks have a distinctive social experience, different from the immigrant experience. They often lack the clear economic niche of the immigrant generation, they have no return-migration option, their expectation for equality is greatly increased, and they have an increased identification with minority communities within the country. Increased racial conflict has resulted. Rex and Tomlinson (1979:212), in their study of racial minorities in Birmingham, were "very struck by the gap between the attitudes expressed by the parents on the one hand (which . . . were relatively conservative and complacent), and those expressed by young people . . . on the other. . . . Our data showed increasing militancy amongst this group."

In Canada, most racial minority group members are recent immigrants, and a major generational transition lies in the near future. Whereas in Britain, 43 percent of racial minority group members are British-born, in Canada only 23 percent are Canadian-born.

The British experience suggests that existing inequalities will be less acceptable to the large new Canadian-born generation, and will provoke a significantly stronger political reaction than we have seen from the immigrant generation.

However, the generational transition will not necessarily have the same outcome in Canada as in Britain. Racial tensions in Britain were greater than in Canada even when immigrants predominated in minority communities. There are other factors which may serve to moderate racial conflict in Canada.

Socio-Economic Position of Racial Minorities

As was mentioned above, racial minorities in Canada have higher entrance status than racial minorities in Britain. It is likely that the greater economic integration of racial minorities in Canada will produce lower potentials for conflict because higher status increases the sense of having a stake in society.

In the short term, any British-Canadian differences in levels of conflict resulting from higher entrance status in Canada probably will be small. In the first years following immigration, immigrants to both countries have jobs more or less as expected. West Indian, East Indian and Pakistani immigrants to Britain in the 1950s and 1960s settled in traditional industrial areas of London and the Midlands (Peach, 1966; 1967; 1968), so initially, unemployment rates were extremely low. Likewise in Canada, the racial minority population has settled mainly in the affluent cities of Toronto and Vancouver, and to a lesser extent in Montreal, cities of southern Ontario and the West.

Concentration of minorities in affluent regions helps to insulate them from the impact of recessions, despite racial discrimination. As time passes, however, racial minority groups cannot remain immune to impacts of economic trends. In a buoyant economy, expansion creates opportunities for minorities; in an economic downturn, privileged groups close ranks, carefully guarding their own interests against those of newcomers.

In Britain, the industries initially most attractive to immigrants were textiles and heavy manufacturing, and immigration boosted local economies (cf. Cohen and Jenner, 1968). These industries were precisely those most hard hit by the new international competition, and by the economic downturn in that country. The lower educational levels of the earliest immigrants to Britain reduced their capacity to adapt to changing economic circumstances.

For Canada the important economic trends lie in the future. No one knows what impact the current national and international economic restructuring will have on particular industries in which racial minorities are concentrated.

The Immigration and Citizenship Issue[3]

Historical British-Canadian differences in immigration and citizenship policy appear to have affected the levels of racial conflict in the two societies, again for reasons having little to do with predispositions toward racial tolerance. In Britain, controversy over immigration control and the creation of British citizenship clearly aggravated domestic race relations. Canada's immigration and citizenship policies, comparatively speaking, have enjoyed a political consensus.

The British immigration policy in place after World War II was, for Commonwealth members, essentially an open door. The policy, which provided for free movement within the UK, colonies, and independent Commonwealth, was defended as a cornerstone of non-racist international relations.

A changing world economic order in the post-war period resulted in unexpected numbers of black immigrants moving to Britain, and the open-door policy came under severe attack domestically. Because immigrants were being accepted as a Commonwealth obligation, with no controls over numbers or qualifications, they came to be perceived as a welfare problem with an open-ended price tag. The open-door policy was quickly abandoned by both parties. A series of highly controversial immigration and citizenship acts were passed, instituting skill-based selection criteria and a kind of retroactive citizenship status governing residence rights in Britain. Racial motivations behind these policies were clear. These events negatively affected the entire atmosphere of race relations in Britain.

Canada's immigration policy reflects its world-system location, which was different from that of Britain. Canada formulated a nation-building immigration policy directed at national social and economic goals (Hawkins, 1972; Parai, 1975). Toward such ends, Canada admitted immigrants selectively, based on social and economic needs, or "absorptive capacity." In the 1960s, in moves to end racial discrimination in immigration policy, geographic selection criteria were abolished, and economic and occupational selection criteria were formalized in a point system. While skill-graded selection criteria may have reduced the number of racial minority third world immigrants, this was never considered a racially-motivated policy because the legitimacy of selection criteria was well-established (cf. Kalbach and McVey, 1979).

The elimination of geographical selection rules produced, in the late 1960s and early 1970s, a shift in ethnic composition of immigration to those of predominantly non-European origins, and an increase in total immigration. An immigration "Green Paper" (Department of Manpower and Immigraton, 1974) was debated, and a new Immigration Act in 1976 empowered Parliament to set annual immigration targets. Total immigration declined to about 100,000 per year. Hong Kong and other Southeast Asian countries became more significant as source countries. In Canada there is popular confidence that immigration serves economic expansion, and this perception dampens controversy.

Canada's broad but selective program of immigration may have had other effects in reducing racial conflict. For one, Canada's policy has affected the higher socio-economic status of racial minorities in Canada. The potential effects of this in reducing racial conflict were outlined earlier. Canada's broader policy, which encourages immigration from all sources, probably also has increased the diversity of cultural origins among the racial minorities in Canada compared to Britain.[4] Ethnic boundaries among racial minorities impede group formation, including the formation of potential conflict groups. Rather than forming political alliances, diverse immigrant groups tend to remain distant from each other.

This factor could operate to reduce racial conflict in Canada compared to Britain, though its force would attenuate as homeland attachments fade over time and through generations.

Multiculturalism, Bilingualism, and Race

Canada's ethnic and linguistic diversity is the feature most often cited as a source of greater racial tolerance. It may, however, be much more important as a force deflecting minority group responses to inequality, thus moderating racial conflict.

Multicultural advisory structures in government are far more developed in Canada than in Britain, but such structures are concerned with cultural status, and not with economic status. Survey data show equity issues are relatively more important to disadvantaged ethnic groups including racial minorities (cf. Reitz, 1980:381).

Advisory structures specifically devoted to race issues are emerging mostly at the municipal level. These structures appear to have been responsible for more significant accomplishments in Britain than in Canada, at least in terms of promoting employment equity within municipal government itself (cf. Ouseley, 1981; 1984). They have had little independent clout, however, and have been ineffective in producing broader changes. Katznelson (1973) showed that race advisory groups, in Britain and the U.S., co-opt minority leaders, and marginalize racial politics. In the long run, co-optation reduces conflict, not inequality.

In the field of equal rights legislation Canada had a headstart over Britain, because of Canada's longer multicultural history. However, such legislation, while important and necessary, is unlikely to produce fundamental change in either country. The procedures are complaint-driven, individually-initiated, and conciliation-oriented. They cannot be used to initiate investigations of entrenched inequities affecting entire groups. Thus, they may make a greater contribution to the avoidance of racial conflict by providing a political safety valve, than to the reduction of underlying inequality. Smith (1977) showed perceptions of discrimination within minority communities in Britain declined following the passage of the first Race Relations Act, while actual discrimination did not decline.

The bilingual structure of Canadian society impedes the formation of a common political consciousness among racial minorities. Immigrants to Canada include both Anglophones and Francophones. Efforts to mobilize racial groups are impeded by the linguistic boundary. As time passes, the effect of this factor could increase, as each linguistic minority integrates within its respective linguistic majority.

SUMMARY

This discussion has examined evidence that the degree of racial discrimination in Canada compared to Britain is similar, while the degree of racial conflict in Canada has been much less. It is possible for social conditions and processes to moderate social conflict without necessarily ensuring that underlying issues and inequities are addressed. It is suggested that such conditions and processes may apply to race relations in Canada.

Racial conflict is likely to increase in the future with the generational transition. There are many unknowns, however, including economic trends in specific industries affecting the distribution of opportunities for minority group members. This analysis suggests that levels of racial conflict in Canada may remain comparatively low, even if levels of racial discrimination remain as high as in Britain.

ENDNOTES

[1] The procedure called for non-whites to make the approach first, to ensure that negative reactions are not a result of employers regarding the job as already committed to the white applicant.

² After the adjustment noted in Table 1, note 4, discrimination appears greater in Britain, but the difference is not significant. Other differences in Table 1 are contrary to the hypothesis of less discrimination in Canada.

³ The following section draws from Reitz (1988).

⁴ In both Britain and Canada, the proportion of the population which is of West Indian origin is approximately one percent. However, the other non-European origin groups in Canada are distributed differently and are more diverse than those in Britain. There are relatively few persons of Indian and Pakistani origins in Canada compared to Britain, and relatively more persons of various Asian origins in Canada.

REFERENCES

Balakrishnan, T. R. and John Kralt (1987). "Segregation of visible minorities in the Metropolitan areas of Montreal, Toronto and Vancouver." Pp. 138–57 in L. Driedger (ed.), *Ethnic Canada: Identities and Inequalities* (Toronto: Copp Clark Pitman).

Billingsley, B. and L. Muszynski (1985). *No Discrimination Here? Toronto Employers and the Multi-racial Workforce* (Toronto: Social Planning Council of Metropolitan Toronto and The Urban Alliance on Race Relations).

Carby, Keith and Manab Thakur (1977). *No Problems Here? Management and the Multiracial Workforce* (London: Institute of Personnel Management, in co-operation with the Commission on Racial Equality).

Cohen, B. G. and P. J. Jenner (1968). "The employment of immigrants: a case study within the wool industry," *Race*, 10:41–56.

Collison, P. (1967). "Immigrants and residence," *Sociology*, 1:277–92.

Department of Manpower and Immigration (1974). *Immigration Policy Perspectives*. Canadian Immigration and Population Study, volume 1 (Ottawa: Information Canada).

Government of Canada (1984). Response of the Government of Canada to "Equality Now!," the report of the Special Parliamentary Committee on Visible Minorities in Canadian Society (Ottawa: Supply and Services Canada).

Hawkins, Freda (1972). *Canada and Immigration: Public Policy and Public Concern* (Montreal: McGill-Queen's University Press).

Henry, Frances and Effie Ginzberg (1985). *Who Gets the Work? A Test of Racial Discrimination in Employment* (Toronto: The Urban Alliance on Race Relations and the Social Planning Council of Metropolitan Toronto).

Kalbach, Warren E. and Wayne W. McVey (1979). *The Demographic Bases of Canadian Society* (Toronto: McGraw-Hill Ryerson).

Katznelson, Ira (1973). *Black Men, White Cities* (London: Oxford University Press).

McIntosh, Neil and David J. Smith (1974). *The Extent of Racial Discrimination*, Vol. XL Broadsheet No. 547 (London: PEP, The Social Science Institute).

Ouseley, Herman (1981). *The System: a Study of Positive Action in the London Borough of Lambeth* (London: Runnymede Trust and The South London Equal Rights Consultancy).

——— (1984). "Local authority race initiatives." Pp. 133–59 in Martin Boddy and Colin Fudge (eds.), *Local Socialism? Labour Councils and New Left Alternatives* (London: Macmillan).

Parai, Louis (1975). "Canada's immigration policy, 1962–1974," *International Migration Review*, 9:4:449-77.

Peach, Ceri (1966). "Factors affecting the distribution of West Indians in Britain," *Transactions of the Institute of British Geographers*, 38:151–63.

———— (1967). "West Indians as a replacement population in England and Wales," *Social and Economic Studies*, 16:3:289-94.

———— (1968). *West Indian Migration to Britain* (London: Oxford University Press, for the Institute of Law Relations).

———— (1982). "The growth and distribution of the black population in Britain, 1945–1980." Pp. 23–42 in D. A. Coleman (ed.), *Demography of Immigrants and Minority Groups in the United Kingdom* (London: Academic Press).

Reitz, Jeffrey G. (1980). "Immigrants, their Descendants, and the Cohesion of Canada." Pp. 329–417 in Raymond Breton, Jeffrey G. Reitz and Victor Valentine, *Cultural Boundaries and the Cohesion of Canada* (Montreal: Institute for Research on Public Policy).

———— (1988). "The institutional structure of immigration as a determinant of interracial competition: a comparison of Britain and Canada," *International Migration Review*, 22:1:117–46.

Tomlinson, Rex, John, and Sally (1979). *Colonial Immigrants in a British City* (London: Routledge and Kegan Paul).

Smith, David J. (1977). Racial Disadvantage in Britain: the PEP Report (Harmondsworth, Middlesex: Penguin Books).

ARTICLE 5.2

Stejepan G. Mestrovic

POSTEMOTIONAL POLITICS IN THE BALKANS

INTRODUCTION

Fifty years have passed since the first clear revelations of the genocide that the Nazis perpetrated against the Jews, Gypsies, socialists, and other European peoples. Since then, many have sought explanations of this horrible episode in world history, and vowed that "never again" would such genocide be permitted.

Yet, as this excerpt shows, Canada and the rest of the world have stood by as genocide was perpetrated once again—this time, by Serbs against Croats and especially Muslims in Bosnia and other parts of the former Yugoslavia. Once again, journalists and social scientists struggle to understand the causes behind these mass murders carried out in the name of "ethnic cleansing." However, several things are different this time.

Mestrovic, Stejepan G. (1995). "Postemotional Politics in the Balkans," *Society*, January/February, 69–77.

First, the global public has been aware of this genocide as it has been carried out. This makes us all bystanders or even accomplices; such was not the case when the Nazis were doing their dirty work in the '30s and '40s. Second, analyses of the recent genocidal events in Bosnia have been shaped by a peculiar moral relativism marked by a reluctance to lay blame and a desire to speak about the events in roundabout or euphemistic ways. In effect, strenuous efforts have been made to blur the facts and "explain away" the guilt of the Serb killers.

This is due, in part, to a postmodern tendency to avoid emotionalism and the taking of sides. So great is the distrust of media- and elite-generated fictions that there is a general unwillingness to believe what is under our noses.

A curious, implicit formula seems to govern the Western media's presentation of the genocidal war in the Balkans: Belgrade-sponsored genocide is rationalized on the basis of alleged Serbian fears of Muslims that stem from a battle fought in 1389, and of Croats based on a Nazi quisling government established in Croatia during World War II. The West's actions vis-à-vis Belgrade are depicted as fumbling *inaction* in the face of alleged tribalism in the Balkans, and Europe's toleration of this instance of post-Holocaust genocide is explained away with the lame argument that the fighting is "contained" in the allegedly subcivilized, not-yet-European Balkans and therefore does not affect Europe or other Western democracies.

But such ostensibly safe and neat (albeit racist) categorization is defied by facts. Bosnia is about more than Bosnia, which is precisely why it has mesmerized the popular consciousness. The genocide is not affecting only a limited corner of Europe; at Friday prayer services all over the Islamic world the faithful are being told that Bosnia is the latest stage in the arrogant West's effort to wipe out Islam. Furthermore, it is not clear whether this Balkan War is being fought in the present or in the past. Huge chunks of history, European and non-European, are being invoked. For example, the suspected war criminal Radovan Karadzic is constantly and shamelessly telling the West that he is doing them a favor by persecuting the Muslims. Karadzic reminds us of the Crusades, as if they were a good thing and not an exercise in genocide. The Serbs hark back to the Battle of Kosovo in 1389 in which they lost their turf, and in many ways the ethnic cleansing directed against Bosnian Muslims is revenge for that event.

Serbian propagandists and their apologists often bring up the atrocities committed by Ante Pavelic and his Ustasha regime in World War II, but such discussions rarely mention the fact that many others in Europe also collaborated with the Nazis or the fact that Croatia had one of the largest antifascist movements in Europe during World War II. The mention of Croatia's Nazi quisling regime is gratuitous and serves as a ready-made excuse for Western journalists to justify contemporary Serbian aggression.

My encounters with anthropologists, sociologists, and other social scientists concerning the current Balkan War reveal that most of them reflect the opinions and prejudices of Western governments, media, and the masses in their assessments of current genocide in the Balkans. Holocaust studies continue in Western universities without cultural analysts making the connection to the fact that despite the refrain, "Never again," genocide is occurring in Europe, again.

It seems that postemotionalism holds more explanatory power than the now fashionable concept of postmodernism. The gist of my argument is that postmodernism refers to that broad intellectual movement that centers on nostalgia, the blurring of the distinction between fiction and reality, and other antimodern tendencies. But the phenomena described above involve more than nostalgia; rather, they involve the transference of "dead emotions" from the past into the living present. Instead of the circulation of fictions described by Baudrillard, it is more accurate to point to the coexistence of reality with emotionally charged "fictions," or what might be termed circulating emotions; for example, Helsinki Watch reports condemning Serbian aggression alongside sympathy for Serb fears of the Muslims and Croats. There appears to be a need to move beyond the parameters of postmodernism in cultural studies.

Let us return to Jean Baudrillard—frequently cited as the foremost postmodernist writer—and his observations that the Gulf War and the Vietnam War did not happen, that these and other postmodern wars are just fictions played out on the television screen. It is not enough to dismiss cruel genocidal wars of the present as fictions. The more interesting question becomes: Why is it that the world's postmodern audience treats wars—current as well as past—as if they were fictions, but fictions charged with emotionalism borrowed from the past? The Balkan War becomes, for the Americans, a "Vietnam quagmire"; for the Serbs, revenge against "the Turks" for 1389 and a quest for Greater Serbia; for the French and British, a revival of German expansionism; for the Russians, another instance of the West picking on their "little Slavic brothers," the Serbs. What is surprising is that these quasi-historical arguments are printed in a matter-of-fact fashion in Western newspapers despite all the loud rhetoric concerning the end of history.

How does one distinguish fiction from reality when it comes to the conceptualization of the current Balkan War? How has its "reality" been transformed by various metaphors, euphemisms, and fictions? Are these euphemisms really just "circulating fictions" (as opposed to what, reality?) without rhyme or reason, as Baudrillard argued, or do they make a kind of sense? The metaphors, euphemisms, and fictions that have been used to conceptualize the current Balkan War include these neo-Orwellian characterizations:

- the Bosnian Muslims as the new Palestinians
- the Bosnian Muslims as Native Americans on reservations or "safe havens"
- "safe havens" overrun by Serbs
- "making peace" in war zones merely by sending in unarmed "peacekeepers"
- the Croats as Nazis
- the social construction of "humanitarian aid": for example, sending the Bosnians war-rations left over from the Gulf War and other specific foods, but not cigarettes (which they request) and not psychiatric help for their rape victims
- "peace negotiations" versus terms of surrender
- "all sides are equally guilty"
- Germany as largely responsible for the current Balkan War because of its "premature recognition" of the sovereignties of Slovenia and Croatia

- the West as "not involved," despite the weapons embargo it imposed on Serbia's victims
- "tribes" in Europe
- the cultural imperialism discussed by Edward Said: "we" are "civilized" and "they" are "barbaric"
- the Balkan War as a natural disaster that requires bureaucratic (UN) assistance, but without any consideration of ending the suffering once and for all
- ethnic division as a problem in mathematics, proposed by the European Community (EC); that is, the EC told the "warring parties" to divide Bosnia into certain percentages of Croats (17 percent), Muslims (30 percent) and Serbs (53 percent). But what about mixed marriages and mixed parents? What about the millions of people who do not fit this neat, mathematical formula?
- former Secretary of State Lawrence Eagleburger's statement that the conflict will end when all the parties exhaust themselves. A wrestling match? A brawl?

These characterizations read like a list of class projects from an elementary marketing course, yet they are apparently treated very seriously by the culture industry. We point to a common pattern in all the euphemisms and metaphors (those mentioned above and others): In an ideally rational society that followed the principles of the Enlightenment, if respected fact-finding organizations determined that genocide was occurring, the world community would take action to stop it. This principle is enshrined in the UN charter, but Western politicians, diplomats, media, and laypeople are reacting on the basis of past emotionally charged events that obfuscate the present. A significant aspect of this reaction is that it does involve emotion, but the emotion is displaced. Hence Baudrillard and the postmodernists who follow his lead are wrong to claim that there is no pity in the dawning postmodern world, no compassion among postmodern mass societies. On the contrary, plenty of emotion is shown in the postmodern 1990s, and the term "compassion fatigue" is used; but the emotion always relates to some historical event and fails to address the situation at hand.

Thus, to repeat, German Nazism is invoked from World War II to "explain" Serbian fears of Croats, who are depicted as an essentially pro-Nazi genocidal people. Yet the collaboration with the Nazis by the rest of Europe is NOT invoked; Croatia's antifascist movement is never mentioned; the horrors committed by Communists are left out of the discourse completely; and no effort is made to contrast contemporary Germany with the prevalent image of Germany—left over from World War II—as an "expansionist" power. Why? What purposes do these charges serve? The answer is complex, but one can speculate on a number of purposes, including these: The demonization of Germany masks Britain's long-standing geopolitical strategy vis-à-vis Europe. The demonization of Croatia deflects the moral outrage that should be the response to Belgrade-sponsored genocide, and it continues the long-standing process of revisionism of Europe's extensive collaboration with the Nazis. Croatia becomes the scapegoat for

Europe's guilt for Nazism. The relative silence on the evils of communism masks the West's nostalgia for the "order" that tyrants wielding power from Moscow to Belgrade imposed on whole peoples who wanted to be free.

Similarly, the Bosnians are not like the Palestinians, because Bosnia is a duly recognized nation-state, and Bosnia's President Izetbegovic does not offer a program like Arafat's. Yet the contemporary crisis of the Bosnian nation-state is muffled in an incorrect transference to the long-standing, deeply emotional, yet completely different problem of Israeli-Palestinian relations.

Humanitarian aid bespeaks a nostalgic image that the West has of itself as a generous culture. Yet humanitarian aid is normally offered to victims of natural disasters, such as floods and hurricanes, not to the victims of an active and ongoing war of genocide. Moreover, nations and peoples on the margins of the West do not see the West as generous or compassionate; consider the general hostility shown by Russians to the cruel economic "shock therapy" being imposed upon them by the West in the name of Western humanitarian ideals.

UN "peacekeeping" harks back to the UN's Cold War mission to engage itself quickly in hot spots so that the former Soviet Union and the United States would not go to war. But clearly, sending in unarmed "peacekeepers" in the middle of a post-Cold War genocidal war fails to address the demands of the present situation.

These and other examples seem to point to a new and distinctive Orwellian newspeak that has been perfected by the culture industry with the aim of post-emotional displacement.

The modernists have depicted a reified, bounded, and fixed world of bloodless categories; the postmodernists seem to imply an abstract world of rootless fictions devoid of emotions; while I am here implying a concrete world of rooted fictions saturated with emotions that are *displaced*, misplaced, and manipulated by the culture industry. Emile Durkheim's notion of "collective effervescence" serves as an excellent basis for this elaboration. Durkheim argued that there exist times of rapid social change in which collective representations seem to explode as if they had been contained under tremendous pressure and then suddenly released. The key difference between Durkheim's and the postmodernists' versions of "fictions" is that for Durkheim, these representations can be traced to a cultural point of origin and involve *emotion*. They seem haphazard and misplaced only because of the tremendous release of pressure. The end of communism constitutes such a "release of pressure," and it has given rise to representations that have been repressed up to now, pertaining to the Holocaust, the Yugoslav civil war in the midst of World War II, the Vietnam syndrome, the quest for a Greater Serbia. But these centers of representationalism are by no means colliding into one another spontaneously; they are manipulated by *modernist* centers of the culture industry emanating from Belgrade, London, Paris, and Washington, among others.

Despite soothing talk from President Clinton, he and other Western leaders (primarily Britain's John Major and France's François Mitterrand) have kept the victims of the Balkan slaughter outgunned and unable to defend themselves. These leaders pretend to condemn "ethnic cleansing" but propose to keep the "peace" between a gulag of disarmed Muslim ghettos and the armed Serbian ethnic cleansers themselves. The postemotionalism concept enables one to expose the emotional discrepancies in how the West arrived at this point, pushing ethnic partition and division when its own cultural principles point to pluralism.

Let me review the situation: From 1991 to 1994, the president of Serbia, Slobodan Milosevic, used the Yugoslav People's Army directly to arm Radovan Karadzic and directly to help seize and cleanse one-third of Croatia and then 70 percent of Bosnia. He succeeded by convincing the West that the Serbian minority in Croatia was right to fear the Croats as an allegedly "genocidal people" because of the atrocities committed by World War II Ustasha. The Serbian line skillfully uses the emotionally charged and traditional concept of collective guilt, which runs contrary to principles derived from the Enlightenment, principles that hold only individuals responsible for crimes. But the important point is that this postemotional argument worked on the West. Collective guilt is an integral aspect of Euro-Christian culture, even though it is denied and despite the smoke screen of the Enlightenment. Euro-American politicians routinely punish whole peoples for the actions of a few: witness the trade sanctions against Iraq and Haiti, the British bombing of Dresden, the weapons embargo against Israel in 1947. Very few sociological and anthropological treatises have explored this ambiguity in the West regarding collective guilt.

Thus, people are led to believe that the peoples of the former Yugoslavia have succumbed to "tribal" hatred and that the West should not get involved. This is an interesting, seemingly postmodern mixing of metaphors: Nazism and primitive tribes. Yet the West is involved. For example, instead of standing up for a pluralistic society, which is a key Western ideal and, especially, a key component of American civil religion, the West is promoting a quasi-apartheid system of ethnic partition in Bosnia-Herzegovina, and the West is doing this ostensibly on the basis of a postemotional humanitarianism. It is ironic that the Bosnian government is trying to stand up for pluralism derived from an Islamic tradition dating back to the Ottoman Empire, whereas President Clinton seems to be supporting the ethnic partition, proposed by Lord David Owen and the Europeans, that is the central component of the so-called peace plan still being offered to victim and aggressor alike in the former Yugoslavia. President Clinton rebuffed President Izetbegovic's plea for military help and instructed him to cut the best deal that he could with those who seek to dismember his country along ethnic lines.

Instead of standing up for the Western principle of national and territorial sovereignty with regard to both Croatia and Bosnia-Herzegovina, the West is trying to rationalize away its diplomatic recognition of these countries. Moreover, diplomatic recognition was coupled to the maintenance of a weapons embargo—established at Serbia's request—that benefited Serbia and hurt Serbia's victims. The West continues to deprive Serbia's victims of their inviolable right to self-defense, as set forth in Article 51 of the UN Charter. Certain emotionally charged aspects of Western political culture seem to be violated here, most notably the principle of fair play. The United States and other democracies exercise their inherent right to self-defense without permission or even endorsement by the UN Secretary General. The UN Charter acknowledges an inherent right of individual and collective self-defense—that is, this right existed before there was a Charter or a UN—yet the Western rationalization for withholding weapons from Serbia's victims has been that more weapons would only prolong the fighting. Again, this explanation can be characterized as emotional, even compassionate (albeit paternalistic) but postemotional in that it fails to address the slaughter—as it is called by Bosnian Muslims—occurring in the present.

We need to guard against reifying the West here according to the ideals it sometimes espouses. We use these ideals in order to expose the inconsistency of Western actions relative to its postemotional rhetoric of concern and sympathy. But my real intent is to deconstruct this rhetoric and expose the Western penchant for ethnic partition, collective guilt, and acquiescence to genocide that is so very evident from a glance at European history.

If it is true that the Gulf War was a major war fought under the illusion (in the postmodern sense) that the West was standing up to aggression, then the current Balkan War is a watershed event in that it is a "major" war (symbolically) in the sense that the West is appeasing aggression under the guise of humanitarian and compassionate concern. Even here, the concept of postemotionalism adds a new dimension to discourses of this sort. But this postemotional complex has now blocked intelligent responses to Belgrade-sponsored aggression and is causing new problems on the world's political scene: Would-be dictators and extremist parties in the former Soviet Union are watching eagerly as the West fails to live up to its ideals. The West is fantasizing that Boris Yeltsin will succeed in a post-Cold War Disneyworld process of magical, instant democratization and "free-market reform" even though it is giving the green light to antidemocratic forces. On the threshold of the next century—which promises to be one of ethnic and religious violence dominated by propaganda images on the television—the West has apparently learned little from a bloody twentieth century. Is all this leading to a major European War for the third time in this century?

THE COMING CULTURAL FISSION

The keystone of my analysis is the new concept of postemotionalism, a term that captures, with more elegance than is currently the case, both the confusion, hypocrisies, hysteria, nostalgia, ironies, paradoxes, and other emotional excesses that surround Western policies toward the postcommunist Balkans, and the inability of Western cultural analysts and intellectuals to make the Balkan War intelligible to the masses. Postemotionalism has greater explanatory power than postmodernism because postmodernism holds that one should revel or feel comfortable in the face of the ironies, inconsistencies, and contradictions such as those uncovered here. But I hold that genocide and crimes against humanity are neither an occasion for revelry nor situations that make one feel comfortable. Thus, like the postmodernists, I debunk, demystify, and criticize the explanations given by the media and governments involved, but I go beyond the postmodernist argument that social life consists of a mental text made up of circulating fictions in which it does not make sense to include the emotions. And I point out that the postmodern goal of tolerance is not being achieved: Extreme intolerance seems to be the rule, not the exception, in the postcommunist world as the world heads for the end of the century.

Far from being an instance of Eurocentrism, the current Balkan War seems to be a watershed event in our fin de siècle that involves Islamic, European, and

American cultural interests. It seems to be foreshadowing ethnic violence that has already increased and will probably continue to increase in the coming century: in Rwanda, Angola, the southern fringes of the former Soviet Union. Critical theory was largely a response to the horrors of modernism exemplified by Stalin and Hitler; postmodernism was largely a foreshadowing of the collapse of the modernist system in communism and a reaction to the last stages of modernist capitalism; I propose that postemotionalism ought to be regarded as a new theoretical construct to capture the fission, Balkanization, ethnic violence, and other highly *emotional* phenomena of the late 1990s.

ARTICLE 5.3

Morton Weinfeld
IMMIGRATION AND DIVERSITY

INTRODUCTION

All answers to population questions—including the issue of how many immigrants should be admitted into Canada—are conditional on the kind of society we want to have, and the effort we are willing to make to have it. What changes are needed to accommodate twice or even ten times as many immigrants each year, and what would it take to make those changes? Can we afford to make them? Can we afford not to? How long could we put off making those changes before something bad happened? How bad would it be? These are some of the questions that must be answered in reaching a decision.

That the debate about immigration is so open-ended is no cause for despair, simply because it reflects the complexity of social policy-making in this area. All our actions carry a danger and a cost. Inaction also carries a danger and a cost. In this particular case, there is a danger that policy-makers will allow the support for multiculturalism to erode, and for anti-immigrant—even racist—sentiments to go unchallenged. As we saw in excerpt 5.1, discrimination against visible minorities in Canada is suffered mainly by immigrant minorities. If we are to admit immigrants to Canada, and we should continue to do so, then we must address the problems of ethnocentrism and discrimination as part of our immigration policy.

As the author of this excerpt shows, the job of the sociologist is not to obscure the reality of discrimination with pat answers. We will have done our job, as sociologists and citizens, if we treat the debate and the evidence fairly and with respect.

Weinfeld, Morton (1993). "Immigration and Diversity," *Policy Options*, July-August, 66–71.

Immigration policy over the next decade will become increasingly controversial. Some Canadians have always feared (incorrectly) that immigrants steal jobs or add disproportionately to welfare rolls. In the minds of many, immigration is linked with apprehension about the changing ethnic and racial makeup of the population. They fear the effects of immigration on Canadian values, institutions, and national unity.

In this paper, I shall briefly review current Canadian immigration data, analyze four sets of factors that condition the evolution of Canadian policy, and outline several recommendations.

Immigrants comprised about 16% of the Canadian population in 1991, a level constant since the 1960s but down from inter-war proportions of 22%–23%. Immigration from all sources in 1991 totalled 230,000, based on 206,000 landings and an additional number of backlogged refugee claimants. Estimates for 1992 suggest a total figure of around 250,000, of which about 220,000 would be actual landings. Current proposals are for 250,000 immigrants per year up to 1995. These numbers are up significantly from figures of under 90,000 in the mid 1980s.

Annual immigration as a percentage of our total population is now at just under 1%, slightly greater than the rates for the US and Australia, but lower than the high point of 4% for Canada in 1913. The proportion of immigrants from countries other than the USA and Europe has been increasing steadily, reaching 76% in 1991.

The key nation-building role of immigration in Canada dates back to the migration of First Nations people 12,000 years ago, and continues today. Policy makers must never forget two central facts. First, immigration and the resulting diversification of the population have almost always been associated with conflict, discrimination, and social strain. Second, and notwithstanding the first fact, Canada's ongoing experiment with immigration and diversity has been, in historical and comparative perspective, a resounding success, despite periodic episodes of racism and impatience with remaining inequalities.

The subtle impediments of Canadian systemic racism are a far cry from the horrors of ethnic cleansing. White European immigrants have "made it" in Canada. Even visible minorities are en route, though there is major variation in the degrees of racism and socio-economic inequalities experienced by different groups, with Asians doing relatively better and African Canadians faring worst. It is no coincidence that reformers from South Africa to Russia seek to learn from the Canadian experience.

Immigrants fall into three broad groups: independents, such as skilled workers, business immigrants and assisted relatives; family class; and refugees. In 1991 the immigrant intake broke down to 37%, 37% and 26% respectively, with projections through 1995 aimed at keeping a roughly similar mix. Recent legislation has reshuffled these categories into three streams: an "on demand" stream for immediate family, refugees landed in Canada, and investors, and two "limited" streams, one selected for human capital considerations and one with a mix of overseas refugees, parents and grandparents, and other categories.

Space limitations preclude a review of all possible consequences of the immigration changes in the new Bill C-86. However, four broad factors must be analyzed in any overview of immigration policy.

FIGURE 1 Immigration Planning Components 1991

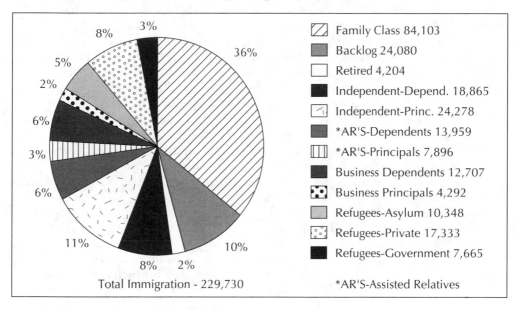

▨ Family Class 84,103	
■ Backlog 24,080	
□ Retired 4,204	
■ Independent-Depend. 18,865	
◤ Independent-Princ. 24,278	
▨ *AR'S-Dependents 13,959	
⦀ *AR'S-Principals 7,896	
■ Business Dependents 12,707	
⬤ Business Principals 4,292	
▨ Refugees-Asylum 10,348	
⬚ Refugees-Private 17,333	
■ Refugees-Government 7,665	

Total Immigration - 229,730   *AR'S-Assisted Relatives

ECONOMIC FACTORS

Recent studies by the Economic Council of Canada and the Demographic Review of Health and Welfare suggest that the overall macro effects of immigration are positive but very small, and that Canada's future economic well-being would likely be unchanged by fluctuations in immigration and population size.

So immigration is not associated with economic harm. But are there no benefits? Regression models may be unable to capture the multidimensional ways socio-demographic factors shape a country's economic development now and in the future. Since the 1870s Canada's population has increased about 11 times, and the per capita constant income rose by a factor of about 14. To be sure, this may be simply coincidence. But it is unlikely that Canadian prosperity today would be the same whether we had 27 million or 27 thousand inhabitants, or whether our population was all immigrant or all tenth generation Canadian born. Population also relates to benefits of international economic status: a levelling off of our population would affect our Gross Domestic Product, and thus our position as a G-7 member nation.

In the short term, it is undoubtedly true that hard times, like the recent recession, may increase levels of intolerance and make the economic integration of immigrants—and all new entrants to the labour market—more difficult. Vigilance is certainly required. But any accompanying increases in racist attitudes, if provable at all (and the trend from surveys over the past decade is not clear-cut) would likely be short lived.

Policy makers have historically tried to micro-manage immigration in the short term by tying it to the unemployment rate and to perceived specific shortages in the labour markets, or by favouring wealthy or skilled immigrants. But attempts to anticipate and deal with specific labour shortages and gluts in the Canadian economy remain more an art than a science.

Has the investor class really paid the expected dividends? The vitality of our labour force, past and present, has been strengthened by a broad mix of immigrants, some with educational credentials (which we often undervalue) and some not. They will contribute to our economic growth and quality of life in different ways. The over-representation of the foreign born in small business is well known; they and their children are also over-represented as students in science, math and engineering. Neither trend is a clear result of any fine tuning of the immigrant intake.

The large majority of family class and refugee migrants work and contribute economically. An illiterate grandmother who stays home to care for grandchildren while both parents are off to work, or the hardworking cook in an ethnic restaurant—perhaps unintegrated into the general labour market but paying taxes, raising well integrated children, consuming, and preparing food which Canadians enjoy—are both "economically" productive.

Immigration always involves short-term start up costs. But Canada benefits from adult immigrants who begin working immediately, since we have not had to bear the costs of creating the human capital. This makes immigration a good deal economically, an investment with a steady, long-run return.

SOCIAL FACTORS

To the extent new non-white immigrants exacerbate (or are thought to exacerbate) racism in the country, or add unique strains to our social, cultural and political systems, some Canadians call for a moderating of immigration. The policy maker's fear of racism may be as insidious as the bigot's racism itself.

The happy normalcy of Canadian ethnic and race relations does not capture popular attention, in the tradition of the newspaper headline "All planes land safely." For better or worse, the identities, languages, cultures, and organizations of minority groups are important primarily for the immigrant generation, and facilitate the process of adaptation. Acculturation is strong among the second and third generations, but not before the host Canadian culture itself is enriched by contributions from all groups.

Immigrants to Canada (particularly visible minorities) inevitably experience discrimination, and difficulties of adjustment to a new society. We should remember that adult immigrants generally have one foot in the old country; the ultimate test of integration is with the second or third generations.

Systemic and attitudinal racism exist. Racist radical right groups attempt to spread their bigotry. They should be watched carefully; one hopes the RCMP redirects its former anti-communist zeal to these groups.

But to decry racism as a fundamental and unyielding feature of Canadian society might be to serve the racist aim of curtailing (non-white) immigration, by perpetuating a fear of escalating racism. It would also be wrong. The evidence of racial inequality is far more nuanced, varying by outcome measure: education, income, social and political participation; by Canadian or foreign birth; and by the specific minority group. For example, while Canadian school systems are often labelled as racist, in fact Canadian-born visible minorities do as well or better than whites in terms of educational attainment, as seen in 1986 census data.

There is also no systematic evidence that the majority of recent immigrants actively challenge the basic values of Canadian society, as represented by western democratic liberalism and enshrined in our Constitution and criminal law. Moreover, the importance of sensitivity to minority concerns and respect for various cultural traditions should not lead Canadians to become timidly apologetic about those values.

People should not confuse the invigorating impact of immigration and diversity on many aspects of Canadian culture, from art to cuisine, with more fundamental challenges. Where some immigrants from traditional cultures may take exception to some proclaimed values such as full sexual equality, they are free to promote different values in their own homes, as are all Canadians. We must not blur the distinctions between the private and public spheres. But if immigrants cling too tenaciously to old-country patterns, they may encounter increasing inter-generational conflict with their children—again, nothing new in the immigrant saga.

In any case, what is remarkable is the degree to which the vast majority of immigrants and more particularly their children, share in Canadian core values, and indeed embrace the freedom and opportunity which so many other Canadians take for granted. One would certainly hope that such misperceptions would never colour Canadian immigration or refugee policy, for example, by leading to the favouring of east Europeans over Africans.

Progress toward equality and integration led by natural social forces may be derailed by well meaning policies to "manage diversity." The welcome fact of Canadian multicultural diversity need not require that every nook and cranny of Canadian public life be subject to "multicultural" policy scrutiny. Honest debate on these issues should not degenerate into guilt-tripping and name-calling; if everything is racist, then nothing is racist. Most Canadians would rather that Toronto, Montreal, and Vancouver escape the ethnic and racial tensions—economic, social, political, educational and cultural—that are now besetting New York, Los Angeles, and Miami. Policies that avoid entrenching entitlements based on ethnicity or race are the preferred route.

DEMOGRAPHY

Immigration policy can be used to maintain, if not increase, the population in the face of below-replacement fertility levels. Some have argued that priority be given to the immigration of children, to even out the missing curves of the age distribution caused by the baby bust, and help secure the solvency of pension plans. Immigration has also affected sex ratios. Historically, immigration has tended to favour males. Most recently immigration of women from the Caribbean and the Philippines without a corresponding number of men has created a potential for increasing the number of single-parent families. In fact, immigration can moderate some of the impact of population aging and stability, but its effect will be minimal.

A related issue concerns the concentration of Canada's immigrants, and the Canadian population generally, in Toronto, Vancouver, and Montreal. Efforts to direct immigrants prior to arrival to designated regions of the country as anticipated in Bill C-86, and in conformity with section 6 of the Charter, are important. But serious efforts at immigrant dispersion will require much greater policy initiatives than at present.

FIGURE 2 Immigrants as a Percentage of Census Metropolitan Areas, 1991

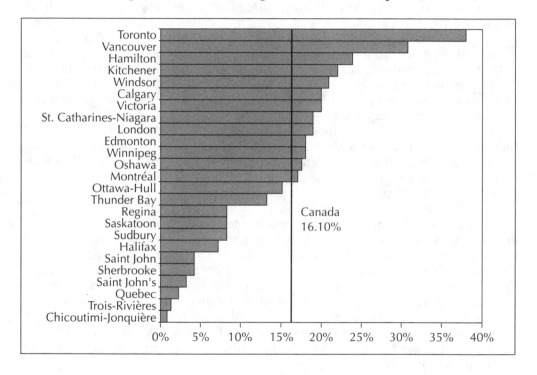

The pattern of immigrant settlement is of course affected by the attraction of new immigrants to pre-existing immigrant communities. So processes of integration may be more difficult in the more remote areas. Moreover, immigrants are not that dissimilar from other Canadians in their move toward large metropolitan centres. The solution must involve linking immigration to issues of regional development as part of a national population policy. In the future some provinces, like Saskatchewan, may decide to promote in-migration more vigorously, possibly further decentralizing Canadian immigration policy and complicating federal-provincial relations.

At a more micro level, immigrant/ethnic dispersion involves municipal governments. While immigration policy is set by the federal government in consultation with the provinces, major fiscal burdens of immigrant integration are felt by the larger municipalities and provinces. The move of the middle class to outlying suburbs may leave cities with an eroding tax base through which to meet these responsibilities. While some tripartite consultations have been undertaken, far more needs to be done.

The next decades will likely see enormous external population pressures on countries such as Canada, Australia, and the US. It remains to be seen how our adherence to the definition of refugee in the 1951 United Nations Convention Relating to the Status of Refugees, and to the policies in place, will withstand the future pressures associated with what policy makers euphemistically call "unchosen" or "irregular" immigrants—say, ten boatloads of refugee claimants sailing into Halifax harbour. While some tightening up of entry systems under C-86 is warranted, how would replays of the St. Louis or the Komagata Maru affect our image at home and abroad as a tolerant society? Our immigration and refugee policies are symbolic and real elements of our foreign policy.

Canada is in a privileged position: it has two oceans and the US as buffers against refugee claimants, and enjoys a land mass advantage which may grate on the less fortunate as the planet becomes more crowded. In the long run, population pressures, along with environmental concerns, the internationalization of human rights, and economic interdependence will act to erode traditional notions of sovereignty and constrain Canadian options. In the shorter run, immigration policy may become more concerned with protecting our borders from irregular migrants, through multilateral preventive interventions in or near source countries, and through recourse to greater foreign aid and trade as alternatives to increased immigration. The distinction between humanitarian concerns and national self-interest will become increasingly blurred. There will be greater pressure to expand the definition of Convention refugees to other persecuted social groups. The new administration and control measures of Bill C-86 may help "manage" the system, but will inevitably raise questions of civil liberties and national purpose.

In both 1991 and 1992 Canada undershot the target quota for government-assisted and privately sponsored refugees, by roughly 26,000. The explanations offered for this shortfall ring hollow, and pass the buck to the United Nations High Commissioner for Refugees. The undershooting is ostensibly due to the UNHCR's preference for voluntary repatriation and local (area) integration over "third country resettlement," to the easing of conditions in east bloc countries such as Poland, and the UNHCR's claim that "only 72,000 refugees worldwide were in need of resettlement in a country like Canada" (when there are at least 15 million Convention refugees in the world). This seems ridiculous, almost obscene. A more pro-active leadership refugee effort could enhance Canada's image in the world community and turn up the elusive 26,000.

Canadian immigration policy faces formidable internal and external challenges in the future. These will require creative tripartite approaches developed within a framework of a multidimensional population policy. But these challenges must be approached with confidence. Immigration will continue to play a major, positive role in Canadian nation-building, as it has so successfully in the past. Voices apprehensive about immigration and diversity are nothing new. But there are economic, cultural, demographic, geo-political and humanitarian reasons to carry on Canada's generous immigration traditions.

RECOMMENDATIONS

(1)   Canada needs a population policy in which immigration would play a key role. Such a policy should be developed in consultation with the provinces—Quebec is already elaborating its own—and interest groups. A modern population policy is not simply about boosting the birth rate. It focuses on the complex relation of size, age-sex composition, regional distribution and settlement patterns, and other socio-demographic features.

(2)   Overall immigration levels should be retained at a minimum of 1% of the population, pending sustained rises in fertility rates. The currently prevailing ratio should be maintained among the various components or streams, with any change favouring government-assisted and privately sponsored refugees.

(3)   More should be done to ensure that the educational qualifications of immigrants are assessed fairly. Large employers must assume a legal obligation to make sure that any devaluation of foreign credentials is warranted.

(4)   Canada should adopt a more proactive posture with regard to refugees. It remains to be seen if recent administrative changes will facilitate the meeting of these targets. The investor class program, when coupled with the recent refugee shortfalls, is a moral embarrassment. How about "requesting" that each investor class immigrant undertake to provide funds for private sponsorship of an overseas refugee?

(5)   The long awaited Race Relations Foundation should be established. Ideally the leadership of the Foundation should be drawn from among visible minority communities and white Canadians.

(6)   A Royal Commission, or at least a Commission of Inquiry, should be established to study the activities of overt hate groups, and recommend tough action along the lines of higher penalties for bias crimes.

(7)   Government policy and rhetoric dealing with systemic racism should be examined for unintended consequences. The more the discourse of racism predominates, the more immigration and diversity come to be seen as social problems. Moreover, the construct of "visible minority" is becoming less useful as a guide to policy, given the variability in the conditions of target groups. The use of census data detailing race and ethnicity to establish hiring goals is becoming problematic given the increasing numbers of Canadians who report multiple or "Canadian" ethnic categories, and the complex permutations of ethnic origin, religion, birthplace, and language that confound accurate ethnic designations. In this light, the government should review the principles and methods of employment equity, to see that those most in need are the ones who benefit most.

(8)   The Department of Multiculturalism has assumed importance far beyond its puny $27 million budget. Many immigrants/minorities see in it symbolic affirmation of their status. Racists see in multiculturalism the source of all evil. Any wholesale dismantling of multiculturalism would send a signal of triumph to the forces of extremism. One can tinker with the name, or repackage multiculturalism with immigration, with or without citizenship. But the infrastructure and objectives of promoting tolerance and valuing ethnic heritages should remain. Stay the course.

QUESTIONS

DISCUSSION QUESTIONS

1. Under what conditions are ethnic or racial tensions likely to escalate from discrimination to genocide?

2. Besides the reasons put forward in the excerpt on Yugoslavia, can you think of reasons why the mass media are "soft" on perpetrators of discrimination, racism, or even genocide?

3. In what respects is ethnic and racial diversity a good thing for Canadian society? In what respects, if any, is it a bad thing?

4. What kinds of characteristics should we look for in people applying to immigrate to Canada? Give reasons for your answer.

DATA COLLECTION EXERCISES

1. Collect information on one or more groups in the world—whether linguistic, religious, or racial—that favour ethnic or racial purity. What factors gave rise to this desire? What methods does this group use to achieve this goal?

2. Has the historic creation of non-white empires (e.g., by the Mongols, Chinese, Japanese, Persians, and Turks) had the same result as the creation of white empires, namely a colour hierarchy within (and later, outside) the empire? Collect historical data on one empire to answer this question.

3. How does the magnitude of the genocide—the number of killings—committed against Bosnian Muslims compare with other historic genocides? (For a reference point, also read excerpt 14.2 on "megamurders.")

4. Collect information on job discrimination against racial minorities in a developing society (e.g., India, Brazil, or Algeria). Would you predict an eventual increase in interracial conflict there? If not, what other conditions are necessary before conflict escalates?

WRITING EXERCISES

1. "The modern world has no place for cultural differences based on ethnic ancestry." Write 500 words explaining why you agree or disagree with this view.

2. "Racial and ethnic differences are wholly imaginary. That is why they are defended with such ferocity and, often, bloodshed." In 500 words, explain what you think this statement means and indicate why you agree or disagree.

3. "In theory, you can get different kinds of people working with one another to form a nation. In practice, they'll never really come together." Imagine that you are Jeffrey Reitz and write a brief (500-word) essay defending or opposing this point of view.

4. "Doctrines of nationalism and ethnic survival are often used to justify discrimination, exclusion, and even genocide." Imagine that you are the leader of an important ethnic community or nationalist movement and write a brief (500-word) letter replying to this charge.

SUGGESTED READINGS

1. Flere, Sergej (1991). "Explaining ethnic antagonism in Yugoslavia," *European Sociological Review,* 7(3), December, 183-193. Regional inequalities of wealth and power played a part in causing the bloody, genocidal civil war in the former Yugoslavia. The conflict exploded once the state could no longer regulate conflicts between contending ethnic groups.

2. Breton, Raymond et al. (1990). *National Survival in Dependent Societies: Social Change in Canada and Poland.* Ottawa: Carleton University Press. This volume focuses on policies adopted towards ethnicity and multiculturalism in Canada and Poland. Over time Canada has become more multicultural, while Poland has changed in the opposite direction. The authors explain why.

3. Sharma, S.S. (1986). "Untouchability, a myth or a reality: A study of interaction between scheduled castes and Brahmins in a Western U.P. Village," *Sociological Bulletin,* 35(1), March, 68-79. In India, different caste groups lead different lives. The status differences between these groups are age-old and protected by religion. Today the practice of "untouchability" persists, even though it is illegal.

SECTION 6   GENDER RELATIONS

Introduction

In Section 2 we described the learning of gender as a key aspect of socialization. "Learning gender" means internalizing rules of behaviour and learning to act in culturally approved ways as males or as females. Our experiences, the ways we learn to interact with other people, and the words we use to categorize reality all combine to reinforce these gender differences. But the process is so smooth, and the outcome so successful, that we grow up thinking of gender differences as natural. How does this happen?

THE REPRODUCTION OF GENDER

Canadian children are born into a social environment that emphasizes gender difference. From the beginning, most of their social encounters reinforce a particular set of understandings about gender and the gendered division of labour.

The mass media reinforce gender stereotypes particularly effectively. Advertisers, entertainers, and writers of television programs all present a consistent and stereotyped message that reinforces the ideal of female economic and social dependence. For example, they idealize romance, marriage, and motherhood. In this way, they encourage young women to see these events and relationships as natural, desirable, and even inevitable. They also idealize the show of aggression and dominance in men. By doing this they deny men the cultural right to express kindness and gentleness.

Early on, children learn to make distinctions between males and females and to categorize the world in these terms. By internalizing the social expectation of a gendered division of labour, children grow up believing that men and women are suited to different adult responsibilities. Their own sense of self and the expectations they have of others reflect and reinforce this early understanding. Later on, they make (largely conventional) education, career, and relationship choices that further reinforce gender distinctions. In the end, they have reproduced gender inequality by continuing to attach social importance to gender differentiation.

This cycle is called the "reproduction of gender." Because gender differentiation is so pervasive, it is hard to break the cycle. No matter how we encourage children to think otherwise, the world they see inevitably reflects gendered stereotypes. Most of the nurturers they encounter at home, on television, at day care, and at school are women; most of the decision-makers are men. For children, the exceptions do not disprove the rule. The reason gender differentiation is problematic is because men and women are not equal—in this, or any other society.

Gender Inequality

In every society, people expect different behaviour from boys and girls, and men and women. This is because much of what children are taught in primary socialization anticipates adult roles and responsibilities. Women's role in reproduction—their biological hold on motherhood—has led people to make a connection between women and domestic work that is hard to change.

The result is a split between the private, domestic world of women and the public world of men. We find this split reproduced with varying degrees of rigidity throughout the world. In Middle Eastern societies like Saudi Arabia (see excerpt 6.1), men and women live in more or less separate worlds. Women's participation in public life is limited, largely confined to gender-segregated institutions. Mexican women, on the other hand, are supposedly less restricted in their activities. But in practice Mexican husbands do not like their wives to take paid employment, and try to regulate their other actions as well (see excerpt 6.2).

Women throughout the world are saddled with most of the responsibility for housework and child care. Data for developing regions is sparse, but United Nations analysts offer two generalizations: "First, women everywhere have nearly total responsibility for housework. Second, men in developing regions generally do even fewer household chores than men in the developed regions."

Although the structure and organization of family life has changed dramatically in the second half of the twentieth century, the changes have been inconsistent. This inconsistency occurs in two ways. First, some social arrangements have changed significantly, and others have not. Most women are gainfully employed, but they still face discrimination and do most of the housework and child care. Work structures are not "family friendly." Second, different groups experience the changes differently. Professionally trained white women do not experience the constraints encountered by the countless thousands of women with "McJobs."

It is hard to determine precise rates of women's labour force participation throughout the world, since much of women's work is in the informal economy (see excerpt 6.2), and so is not officially counted. In 1990, the highest rates of economic activity for women were in the USSR (60%), eastern Asia (59%) and North America (50%). Lowest participation rates were found in Latin America and the Caribbean (32%), southern and western Asia (24% and 21%) and northern Africa (16%).

Like the domestic division of labour, occupational segregation is universal. In Western economies, women typically work in clerical, service, and sales jobs. In Africa and Asia, women work in agriculture. It is no accident that these "women's" jobs all have low status and provide few financial rewards.

Family changes and changes in the organization of paid work have had a more fundamental impact on women than on men. Women have entered the labour force in large numbers, but men have not made the parallel shift to assuming more responsibility for domestic work. One consequence is that women have less free time than men and feel overburdened. Such expressions as the "double day" or the "second shift" remind us that women continue to do (or organize) the largest share of housework and child care. Excerpt 6.3 focuses on the domestic division of labour in Canada. Not surprisingly, few couples actually share housework equally, although in some instances the male partner does most of the housework. Perhaps it will be a surprise to learn that couples who share housework are more likely to be happy.

FEMINISM

The feminist struggle has been an important force for change throughout the world. A first and crucial step was to draw public and academic attention to issues of sexual inequality. Working within formal political organizations and in grassroots community groups, women have effectively challenged the roots of gendered inequality.

A second wave of feminism, which began in the 1970s, has initiated truly revolutionary reforms. They include new educational and employment opportunities, protections for women's right to reproductive choice, and freedom from abuse. The goal of equality is elusive and the road is full of obstacles, as the world recession creates a climate of anti-feminist sentiment.

People's attitudes about men and women tend to resist change, despite legislative attempts to limit systemic discrimination. Among Western countries Sweden is perhaps the forerunner in legislative initiatives to ensure that women have reproductive control, equality in the workplace, and the equal participation of spouses in family duties. Gendered socialization practices and structured gender inequality are two sides of the same coin. One way to create change is through socialization, but this is a slow process, and will not work effectively if structural barriers remain.

Two effective ways of changing structured gender inequality are through economic independence and reproductive control for women. In advanced industrial economies, most women work for pay. The educational and occupational histories of young women increasingly resemble those of young men. Women and men now have more opportunities to exercise choice concerning their domestic arrangements—to remain single, cohabit, or marry. It is when women have children that the equality gap begins to widen. The conflicting demands of paid work and caring for young children are difficult to resolve, and become only more problematic in hard economic times.

Yakin Erturk

DIFFERENCES IN THE STATUS OF MOSLEM WOMEN IN TURKEY AND SAUDI ARABIA

INTRODUCTION

Men and women in Canada dress somewhat differently, though often very similarly. This similarity in dress indicates a general equivalence in the roles and status of men and women. But in many Middle Eastern countries gender inequality is maintained by a rigid system of gender segregation. For example, when leaving their homes, Middle Eastern women have traditionally worn the abayah, a heavy floor-length cloak that covers them completely. The supposed reason for the abayah is to protect women's sexual purity. Like many Middle Eastern customs, this practice owes more to entrenched cultural traditions than to Islamic religious principles.

This excerpt compares the status of Moslem women in Turkey and Saudi Arabia. Both are predominantly Moslem societies, but Turkey has been far more liberal regarding women's rights. The 1926 Civil Code outlawed polygamy and gave women the right to divorce and child custody. Turkish women have had the vote since 1930 and actively participate in the public realm.

Saudi Arabia, by contrast, is a far more traditional society. Like Bangladesh (described in excerpt 7.1) it is also a rigidly segregated society. Women have recently gained access to education and employment opportunities, but these are restricted to segregated institutions. Saudi women do not drive cars, although they have gained a measure of independence with the allocation of special women's sections on public buses. Reducing the proportion of foreign workers may create pressure to use the labour of skilled Saudi women and, in turn, create pressure for further emancipation.

This paper will explore points of divergence and convergence in two Muslim societies representing different models of national transformation and compare the impact of these experiences on the status of women. While the cultural and structural variability is illustrated by focusing on such seemingly contradictory examples it will also be argued that it is not Islam per se (i.e. the implementation of the Sharia) that accounts for the subordination of women but rather that it is the reli-

Erturk, Yakin (1991). "Convergence and Divergence in the Status of Moslem Women: The Cases of Turkey and Saudi Arabia," *International Sociology*, 6(3), September, 307–320. Reprinted by permission.

gious, political and social tradition which is so profoundly embedded in the intimate levels of consciousness and identity of gender roles. Therefore, it is necessary to approach the problem at two levels:

1. The *structural* level, where Islam as a way of life is interpreted and institutionalised within a concrete socio-political entity within which the status of women is determined. Analysis at the structural level will require us to examine the formal aspects of gender relations and ask, "Is the public domain accessible to women?" The emphasis will necessarily be the quantitative representation of women in the public sphere of life and the socio-political orientation of the state which organises this realm.

2. The *conscious* level, where Islam as an ideology is internalised into identities and personal structures of both men and women. As a result, gender inequalities become perceived as natural rather than social. At this level of analysis the concern is on the qualitative aspects of identity and gender relations. Therefore, here the question shifts to whether sex-role stereotyping is eliminated at all levels of social relations and consciousness, while at the same time creating alternative gender roles.

THE CASES OF TURKEY AND SAUDI ARABIA

A. *Turkey.* Turkey represents a secular approach in terms of the relationship between state and religion. Turkish secularism implies the subordination of the latter to the former rather than a complete divorce between the two. In the process of national transformation, modernising elites of Turkey chose to separate the two institutions and introduce reforms aimed at emancipating women from centuries of seclusion. It must be emphasised, however, that the actual seclusion of women under Ottoman rule was more of an urban upper-class phenomenon, just as the main impact of the secular emancipatory reforms that followed was on that group of women. The Civil Code of 1926 outlawed polygamy and gave women the right to divorce and child custody. Civil marriages replaced religious marriages. In 1930 women were granted their right to vote and to be elected to office. While the Turkish modernisers took measures to integrate women into the public domain, crucial aspects of gender relations (sexuality, domestic division of labour, and so on) and the sex bias of the public/private domains remained untouched.

After the 62 years since the reforms were initiated, in practice the situation is far from what might be expected. Women in the rural areas have faced more of a paradox than emancipation in the face of some of these changes.[1] The laws granting them rights are quite irrelevant to the objective conditions of their daily lives. Many especially in the Eastern provinces are still married by religious ceremony and some are still subject to polygamy. In both cases under the new secular/modern system, the conventional legitimacy of their marital status and the protective mechanisms it provided for women no longer hold. As a result these women are confronted with real hardship in cases where the husband abandons them or dies. Furthermore, they are unable to make any legal claim over their children or inheritance from their husbands. Since they lack the know-how and means by which to function within the modern external institutions (such as courts), they are left to the mercy of their men and the effectiveness of the traditional mechanisms by which rights and obligations were customarily arranged.

As for urban women, the situation varies significantly by social class. For the majority of lower- and middle-class women, the burden of having to contribute to the family budget has been added to the existing burden of domestic responsibilities. At the same time, the working woman had to assume a somewhat "Victorian modesty" to prove her worthiness of being admitted to the "club." They "voluntarily" accepted the ideology of the public domain for the sake of not only being accepted by it, but also for the greater cause of the new role granted to them in the modern nation-state. The first generation of Republican women in particular promoted emancipation as part and parcel of nationalism and the road to modernity. One positive outcome of the state-initiated reformist approach was that the indiscriminate recruitment of women during nation-building into many jobs avoided the emergence of sex stereotyping, especially in the professions.

In the light of recent developments, however, it is questionable whether this trend still holds. As the social transformation becomes more settled and the need for mobilising female labour becomes less urgent, women are being discretely discouraged from the more prestigious positions within the occupational hierarchy. The most obvious areas for such closure are the high administrative positions in state and private enterprises (Gülmez, 1972) and in the medical profession, where women are particularly discouraged from becoming surgeons. Often the ideological justification offered is that some positions are neither compatible with female psychology and a woman's innate qualities nor with their primary duties as mothers and wives. Despite these drawbacks, perhaps the most significant and irreversible outcome of women's entry into the occupational structure is the fact it provided new role models for the younger generations (Öncü, 1981). At the same time, however, the growing fundamentalist movement cannot be overlooked as a competing trend. There appears to be an increasing appeal of the Islamic ideology to young university students even in major urban centres. This has undermined the significance of the urban/rural-modern/traditional dichotomy which was believed to have characterised the women of the Republic of Turkey. Instead, a secular/Islamist differentiation among the educated urban women is gaining precedence.

Kemalist reforms paved the way for the emancipation of women, while at the same time undermining their motivation to struggle for change. In other words, the reforms had a co-opting effect. The average middle-class woman saw little need to struggle for her liberation since she faced no obvious formal barrier. However, this co-optation has not been free of contradictions for urban middle-class women. Pressures arising from the conflict within and between the traditional demands of the private domain and the public domain are forcing women to search for alternative ways of organising their lives and exerting their power to produce new gender roles at home and at work. In addition, the intensity of labour migration within the past two decades had an impact on traditional relations as this process left women with the responsibility of managing their household affairs. In some cases, women joined the labour force as the primary providers for their families. This change, in turn, has required new legislation to accommodate the emerging needs. For example, since 1981 women are allowed to pass citizenship rights to their offspring (a right previously obtained only through the father). Parallel to these changes is the emergence of a more radical women's "consciousness" along feminist and Islamist lines. The latter sees the ultimate liberation of women in a total submission to the will of Allah; the former regards all forms of submission as an obstacle to women's liberation.

B. *Saudi Arabia.* Saudi Arabia came into being as a result of the hegemony of one tribe over others. The power of the Al-Saud hegemony relied on: 1) the Wahhabi[2] connection, which provided the ideological legitimacy of the Saudi regime; and 2) strategic marriages, which allowed them to form alliances with other powerful tribes (Salameh, 1980). This process was supported by oil wealth which reinforced the political-religious alliances of the Al-Saud and Al-Shaikh families.[3] Thus, the material and ideological preconditions for the preservation of traditional institutions were secured. It became feasible for Saudi Arabia to "modernise" without having to restructure their society. Women could participate in the public domain only within private/segregated female institutions. Especially after 1960, the Saudi government extensively supported the education of women and created new employment opportunities in health, commerce and social services among others.[4] The import of sophisticated technology along with foreign domestic labour has freed women from household chores. Private drivers and special women's sections in public buses have given women some physical mobility and independence. These practices allow women to acquire a more diversified image of themselves and their abilities.

How much opportunity will be made available to Saudi women, however, is a contested issue. The contradictions confronting the regime manifest themselves in the constant loosening and tightening of "Islamic principles." It is therefore not possible that under the existing political order the public integration of Saudi women will improve.

Saudi society is literally divided into black and white, private and public, with little chance to deviate from the norm except in secrecy. This sex-divided society is most readily observable in the dress code, i.e. black *abaya* for women and white *deshdasha* (robe) for men. It is also reflected in the organisation of the urban physical environment. Even modest houses or apartments are designed with internal divisions to allow for the observance of the public/private domains.

Overemphasis on morality and strict control of public behaviour has created widespread hypocrisy in Saudi society. Taboos are broken behind the walls. The private domain, which is reserved for the observance of honour, purity and morality, in some cases serves also for "immorality." The by-products of the oil boom— supermarkets, videos, cars, telephones, foreign domestic help, and so on—have, on the one hand, increased the concern for morality, and, on the other, undermined control over individual behaviour. And the veil, in fact, provides a disguise for those women who indulge in the "forbidden."

While the contradictions produced by the concern to preserve segregation, on the one hand, and the need to educate Saudi women, on the other, is mounting, the system is responding with new ideologies of consumerism and "Saudi superiority." The former acts to keep women preoccupied with the consumer market; the latter emphasises the need to distinguish oneself as a Saudi in the face of an influx of expatriates. The veil and the *abaya* symbolically serve such distinctness. Even the more critical Saudi women carefully arrange their veil in the "proper" style so as not to be mistaken for a foreigner. The ideology of "Saudi superiority" works in two ways to preserve the status quo: 1) it assures the conformity of Saudi men and women, and 2) it makes self-appointed managers out of them as they keep an eye on the expatriates they work with. In other words, the Saudis in both state and private institutions act as *managers of the managers*. The native/foreign distinction is also supported by a higher pay scale for Saudis.

Beneath the black and white outer appearance, there is a quiet but persistent revolution. The risk involved in being rebellious bears a heavy price. Even those who are less challenging must put in much effort to gain very little. For example, in 1980 a group of Saudi women from King Saud University decided to attend a conference at the male campus. They observed the veil carefully so that their intentions would not be misinterpreted. The authorities were taken by surprise. They did not lose much time, however, in controlling the situation by confining the women to a separate room where they were allowed to listen to the speaker and submit their questions in writing. Subsequently the issue was never again brought up—as if it never happened.

In November 1990 about 50 women, completely veiled, were reported to have driven their cars in the streets of Riyadh to protest against the Saudi tradition which prevents women from driving. The protestors used the Gulf Crisis as a pretext. They claimed that in the event of war men would be away fighting and they would be left immobilised. This time, however, the response of the authorities was direct. Six protesters who were professors at King Saud University were suspended from their jobs. The reaction of other women in Saudi Arabia has been mixed. The fundamentalists charged the protesters with being infidels. Others from the professional community expressed concern that the act would have adverse consequences for women in the long run. Aside from such incidents there are a number of women writers who write regularly in local magazines and newspapers on women and oppression. Life for these women is not easy. They are constantly harassed by the authorities, their right to publish is periodically or permanently withdrawn, and pressure is brought to bear on their male guardians who are ultimately responsible for their conduct. Most of these women do not attribute the restrictions imposed on them to Islam, rather they see Islam as a political weapon used by the regime. The following quotation from a Saudi woman in the *Wall Street Journal* reflects a commonly held viewpoint. "The royal family is using religion like a lash on our backs to stay in power. They know it's all hypocrisy. The Koran doesn't require veils. We should be a model Islamic society and not accept the word of fanatics" (House, 1981).

Declining oil prices and a multitude of problems arising from the presence of a large foreign workforce is increasing the pressure on Saudi rulers to replace the expatriates with an indigenous workforce. This is a potential challenge to the existing balance which is allowing them to maintain the sex-segregated institutions of education, law, banking, and so on. The Saudisation of the labour force, which must rely on every skilled and experienced Saudi, will require the recruitment of those women who have already acquired these skills in the all-women institutions.[5] A drastic restructuring of society will follow. Within this process,

Saudi women, as double victims of oppression, are strategically placed to become a potential force in giving direction to change, more so than their male counterparts.

CONCLUDING REMARKS

In both societies the patriarchal-Islamic culture continues to impose standards by which the moral and structural positions of women are defined. Women's natural drives, individuality and independent participation in the public realm are seen as destructive of the institution of the family, and hence society. Therefore, the protection of the family and social order justifies the subordination of women to patriarchal institutions. These linkages are, no doubt, manifest in the Saudi society where male and female distinctiveness is emphasised in segregated but sometimes parallel spheres of activity. The situation is somewhat discrete in Turkey. The Saudi case further illustrates that women are the central targets of regimes which appeal to political-religious alliances for their legitimacy. Similar trends are making their way into the Turkish political life.

The Turkish experience shows that the problem of women in Moslem societies is not merely one of gaining entry rights to the public domain. As important as this is, it can only lead to piecemeal reforms and a few token women in high positions. This is only a precondition. Beyond this it requires alternative models of gender roles at all levels of social relations. This can only be achieved by a conscious effort for change—individually and collectively. In this respect, women in Moslem societies are in a more advantageous position vis-à-vis men. They have access, even under the veil, to the male world. They can observe and become acquainted with male gender roles. In contrast, men's familiarity with women is, in most cases, limited to the more subordinate and traditional female roles. As a result they are not equipped when confronted with women in an unfamiliar context. At the societal level this gap provides women with the opportunity to challenge conventional expectations and to impose an alternative image and self. Of course, the hard reality of political regimes, rising Islamic fundamentalism, and the brutal force men exercise over their wives and daughters cannot be dismissed. Hence, efforts for change must be directed towards both the external and internal obstacles embedded in identity as well as institutional structures.

ENDNOTES

[1]　While legal changes concerning the status of women and the family were being introduced, Turkey was also experiencing processes such as national integration, rural transformation and the internal contradictions created by Turkey's position within the world system. These latter processes have probably had a more profound impact on the role and status of rural women. Most studies reveal the changes have preserved traditional formations while modifying their form.

[2]　Wahhabism, a movement started in the eighteenth century by Abdul Wahhab, called for a return to the fundamentals of Islam as preached by the Prophet Mohammed. The association of Abdul Wahhab and the Al-Saud family formed the basis of Al-Saud's victory over other tribes and the unification of Arabia.

3   The members of the Al-Shaik family who hold religious power today are descendants of Abdul Wahhab.

4   Teaching, social work, and medicine were the first areas to open up for Saudi women. Positions in the service sector followed. With the exception of medicine, all jobs are carried out in segregated institutions. In the past ten years women have also been appearing on television as news readers or programme directors.

5   According to the Central Department of Statistics, the employment status of the Saudi population over 12 years of age shows that, while 59.3 percent of the men are in the labour force, this is true for only 4.8 percent of the women. Over 90 percent of the Saudi women in the workforce are secondary school and university graduates. It would not be wrong to assume that women in the labour force are employed in professional and administrative positions. These figures do not include the traditional informal sector. (Although the above data were published in 1977, women's participation in the labour force could not have increased significantly.)

REFERENCES

Gülmez, M. (1972). "Kamu Yönetiminde Feminizasyon Olayi" (Feminisation in Public Administration). *TODAIE Dergisi* 5(3):51–71.

House, K. E. (1981). "Modern Arabia: Saudi Women Get More Education, but Few Get Jobs," *The Wall Street Journal,* 4 June.

Kingdom of Saudi Arabia, Ministry of Finance and National Economy, Central Department of Statistics. *Labour Force in Saudi Arabia, 1397 A.H.–1977 A.D.* Riyadh: Central Department of Statistics.

Öncu, A. (1981). "Turkish Women in the Professions: Why so Many?" in Abadan-Unat, N. (ed.), *Women in Turkish Society.* Leiden: E.J. Brill. pp. 81–193.

Salameh, G. (1980). "Political Power and the Saudi State." *Merip Reports,* October: 5–22.

Sylvia Chant

FEMALE LABOUR IN QUERETARO, MEXICO

INTRODUCTION

Women's labour force participation rates in Latin America are low compared to other world regions, including Canada. One of the reasons for such low involvement is the strong resistance of men.

This excerpt is based on a study of households in three very poor areas of the Mexican city of Querétaro. The city is rapidly industrializing and the best job opportunities are in the industrial sector, but most women work in the informal (non-industrial) economy. The informal economy is unregulated, outside the law, labour-intensive, unskilled, and low paying. Women's most common job is making tortillas.

Expectations about the household division of labour and male authority are rigid in this society. Women are expected to do all of the domestic work; men are expected to be economic providers. Even male children do not help their mothers with domestic jobs. Furthermore, Mexican husbands strongly oppose their wives' employment. They are concerned that their wives might earn more money than they do, and that other people might think they were unable to support their wives. Husbands also fear that paid employment would give their wives an opportunity to be unfaithful.

In Mexico, female heads of families are financially better off than married women, having no husband to prevent them from working. Marriage gives women economic security through their husbands, but denies them economic independence. In Canada, conversely, women have economic independence but marriage is economically insecure. (For more on this, see excerpt 7.2 on the economic consequences of divorce.)

This chapter seeks to show the effects on female employment of household-related factors in three shanty towns in Querétaro, an industrializing city in Mexico. The data are derived from a 1983 survey of 244 low-income households selected randomly from lists of owner-occupiers. It is suggested in the present study that a non-nuclear family structure maximizes a woman's opportunities to participate in economic activities outside the home.

Chant, Sylvia (1987). "Family Structure and Female Labour in Querétaro, Mexico," in Janet H. Momsen and Janet Townsend (eds.), *Geography of Gender in the Third World*. Albany: State University of New York Press, pp. 277–293. Reprinted by permission.

THE LABOUR MARKET IN QUERETARO

Rapid industrialization, much of it due to the investment of foreign capital, has fundamentally altered Querétaro and in 1983 its population was about 350,000.

Querétaro has become a key centre for industrial location under a nationwide programme of economic decentralization. Industry employed 38 percent of the workforce in 1980 and an estimated one-quarter of the industrial labour force were women (Meza, 1982). However, women tend to figure more prominently in "informal" occupations than in industrial employment. "Informal" employment is a term used to describe economic activities which are small scale, which operate outside the law, which are labour intensive, which use rudimentary technology and which are characterized by low and irregular earnings (Bromley, 1982; Gugler, 1981; Lailson, 1980; LACWC, 1980; Moser, 1978, 1981). The "formal" sector is the converse of this, being distinguished by large-scale enterprises, foreign capital inputs, mechanized production and social and labour legislation. The informal sector itself is highly differentiated, and the term often acts as a catch-all for a variety of non-institutionalized employment; but it has often been seen as inferior to "formal" sector work.

EMPLOYMENT PATTERNS IN THE STUDY SETTLEMENTS

In the sample, if we discount the 169 (69 percent) who are full-time housewives, only six percent of the female household heads and spouses at work were in manufacturing, 32 percent are domestic servants and the overwhelming majority (55 percent) are in commerce or in the hotel and restaurant trade. Traditionally these occupations have been associated with informal employment. In Querétaro, two-thirds of the working male heads of household in the study settlements were in "protected" employment, but only one-quarter of female workers. Although factory work was considered desirable by both men and women in the interviews, it was not the main occupation of working-class females. While 27 percent of all employed male household heads in the study settlements worked in formal manufacturing enterprises, only two percent of employed female household heads and spouses do so. Additionally, men in factory employment earned an average of 3586 pesos a week as manual workers, whereas women earned half this amount.

In the study settlements, informal employment is most common in commerce and private services, in which women outnumbered men. The most common form of female commercial enterprise is the making and selling of *tortillas*, the Mexican staple foodstuff. In about one-third of these cases the wife makes them and the man sells them, otherwise women produce and sell direct to a specific clientele they have built up. Women also produce other types of cooked food, or engage in small-scale manufacture of plant pots, dolls and soft toys. Net income in informal commerce for men amounted to an average of 3232 *pesos* a week, whereas their wives and female heads of household make an average of 1741 *pesos*. This is probably because women spend more time producing items than trading and thus earn less. Furthermore, women are more restricted in their choice of market locations.

Women, therefore, are not only heavily involved in unprotected, non-unionized employment; they also rank low in the hierarchy of informal sector jobs, being in the worst paid activities with least status. Why do fewer women work than men, and why are they concentrated in different forms of economic activity?

Undoubtedly, this derives in part from the demand side. Querétaro industry is heavy, it produces many high-technology goods and parts for export, it is subject to state legislation, and it does not commonly employ home-based piece-workers. Thus there is little opportunity for women to work in manufacturing, so they take up informal employment. On the supply side, low levels of education, high fertility and a cultural formation emphasizing domesticity also decrease women's chances of getting out of the home.

HOUSEHOLD CONSTRAINTS ON FEMALE LABOUR

Age

In the study settlements, the correlations between age and female employment accord with the results of previous studies—among women of working age and under 25 a total of 49 percent are in paid work or self-employed; this is a much higher proportion than in any other age group. However, when these figures are controlled for marital status different results emerge: 66 percent of unmarried daughters of all ages are in paid work, but only 10 percent of married mothers. Among married mothers the highest rate of participation in the labour force is in the age group 40–44; about half the married women of that age work. The highest rate of employment for female heads of households is between the ages of 30 and 34, when children are probably too young to work and the mothers have no other option. So, age is interlinked with marital status: where there is a high frequency of marriage break-up, for example, women are far more likely to enter the labour force.

Family Size

It is generally thought that women with smaller families are less bound to the home and more likely to engage in paid work. However, in the Third World, the prevalence of part-time, informal, home-based jobs for women means frequently there is little connection between the two variables. In the study settlements in Querétaro, women working outside the home in paid employment had the largest average number of children (5.4), compared with full-time housewives (4.1), and female workers in small family businesses (3.4). Logically this would also be affected by the age of the children, but no significant differences between age groups were found.

Education

In Mexico, in 1980, only 16.7 percent of all men were recorded as illiterate compared with 21.3 percent of all women. In the study settlements in Querétaro the discrepancy seems even more marked. One-quarter of the 211 male household heads had no education whatsoever, and the proportion rose to more than half for the 33 female heads. Only three female heads had completed more than four years of primary education.

Educational requirements even for manual work in the formal sector, for example, exclude half the workforce from protected employment. In the study settlements, male and female factory workers had an average of six years' education (i.e., they had completed primary school). The men with the least education worked in construction and agriculture (average of two to three years' schooling), the women with least education in commerce and private services. Most domestic servants had no education whatsoever.

CULTURE AND THE SEXUAL DIVISION OF LABOUR

Fieldwork in Querétaro indicated men had three main reasons for not wishing their wives to work. First, the wife might earn more than her husband and "get ahead," though this is unlikely in practice. Second, it might suggest to other families that the husband is unable to fulfil his role as breadwinner and to other men that he is failing to exercise authority over his wife: in other words, that he is weak. And third, the greater freedom of movement accruing to working wives is viewed suspiciously by their husbands, who fear it may result in their spouses being unfaithful (Chant, 1984a). This last explanation means women are less likely to be allowed to apply for jobs where they will work alongside men, and it may account for the concentration of women in occupations noted for their isolation, such as domestic service.

THE EFFECT OF FAMILY STRUCTURE ON FEMALE EMPLOYMENT

Nuclear families represented 68 percent (167) of the sample households. Single-parent families (headed by women) represented nine percent (22) of the total. Extended families (families residing with kin) constituted 23 percent (55). Four-fifths (44) of this group were headed by males and one-fifth (11) by females. One interesting feature emerging from the Querétaro data is that the prevalence of the nuclear family may be related to male authority. In-depth interviews with a sub-sample of 47 families revealed many women would welcome the opportunity of introducing a relative into the house, but there was much male resistance to this. As many as four-fifths of the male heads of nuclear families were unwilling to share their homes with a relative, for fear of losing exclusive ownership of the family's property, or because they feared lack of privacy, or were jealous that another man, even a brother-in-law, would share the same house.

The structure of the nuclear family lends itself most easily to a strict sexual division of labour, the male partner earning a wage and the woman in the home doing the housework and looking after the children. That women bear children, and that men earn more in the Mexican labour market combine to favour the man's position as breadwinner, apart from cultural influences. This rigid division of male and female labour often results in a marked imbalance of power, with female subjugation to male authority reinforced by economic dependence. In as many as half the nuclear families in the Querétaro study, men regularly withheld half their wage packets from their wives and children. The amount and regularity of family privation varied according to the strength of the husband-father's commitment to his dependants.

The husband's economic support was often negligible, yet if his was the only wage in the family and he was opposed to his wife working, she was on weak ground if she wanted to earn a wage of her own and thus raise the level of household well-being. In single-parent families and in extended families where there may be several adults under one roof, the cultural norms may be sufficiently diluted to allow greater equality within the household and thus improve the women's status. The exigencies of life in low-income communities have been seen in the past as forcing certain families to seek alternative roles to survive (Nalven,1978; Lomnitz, 1977): this appears in Querétaro to apply most to non-nuclear families. In "unconventional" family structures, albeit often through economic necessity, women have more freedom both to enter the labour force and to choose the kinds of jobs they do.

Only one-third of the female spouses in nuclear families have paid work, compared with nearly half of the women in male-headed extended families and four-fifths of female heads. What explains this variation? Several authors assert the rise of the nuclear family in industrializing economies is accompanied by an improvement in the status of women. This is not borne out by the data from Querétaro. There it appears to be the women from non-nuclear households who gain access to work in urban areas, and not those nuclear families.

The organization of housework is one factor explaining why women in some families are more likely than others to take paid employment. Domestic work is often seen as women's main obstacle to entering the labour force. Nowhere is this truer than in the study settlements, which lack many basic urban services such as piped water, sewerage, rubbish collection and paved roads, and where housing is of poor quality. Deficient housing and servicing make the domestic workload much greater for women in shanty towns than for their counterparts in more consolidated neighborhoods, and it is therefore probably far more difficult for them to take up paid work in addition to their domestic chores.

Family structure may reduce some of these problems by allowing housework to be shared. In nuclear families the frequency and amount of help is considerably lower than in non-nuclear households, and often housework is done by the female spouse alone. The reasons are as follows. First, because the woman has no other role except her domestic one, it is assumed she can manage that labour in its entirety. Second, even where her husband encourages the children to help, they may be too young to do so. Third, there may only be male children, and in a culture which discourages male participation in "female spheres," boys should not be seen to help their mothers. In non-nuclear families the help of both sons and daughters in single-parent households (movitated by the fact their mothers have full-time jobs), and of female relations in extended families, means there are often two, if not three, people to shoulder the burden of housework.

Another factor influencing female work-roles is the relative need for women to work. In many single-parent families, women have to take up paid work, especially if their children are young. In extended households, because the housework is shared and because there are more people to support, there is less pressure on women to be in the home on a full-time basis and a greater need for them to earn money. In nuclear households women not only find it far more difficult to balance the two work-roles, especially if they have no daughters to whom they can delegate some of the domestic tasks and if they are rearing young children, but also, if the husband is earning, there is less apparent need for them to enter the labour force. They conform to a cultural pattern whereby the man alone provides for his wife and dependants.

In single-parent households, sons and daughters help financially because women's earnings need to be supplemented. In extended families, the greater number of adults allows more people to enter the labour market. A notable finding of the Querétaro study was that in families where wage-earning was divided between two or more people there was a greater tendency to pool all earnings in a collective family budget and to allocate finance more equitably among the dependants (Chant, 1984a). The built-in checks to egoism caused by sharing earnings could mean the family (and its male head where relevant) has a vested interest in sending as many members as possible out to work and maximizing potential income. In one in two of the nuclear households the husband-father does not share his earnings, and he feels he has nothing to gain if his wife goes out to work.

Male authority is modified in non-nuclear structures. In single-parent households the absence of the male leaves the woman the freedom to decide whether to take up paid work (though she often has to). In extended households, the presence of several earners means no man has the position of sole provider and arbiter of expenditure. Women who are not dependent on one wager-earner alone are in a stronger position to press for the right to employment outside the home. Furthermore, the sharing of workroles, both paid and unpaid, appears to spread an ethic of equal participation in the strategies and benefits of family life: it makes it less easy to justify the division of labour on the basis of sex. For example, if one adult woman in the family has paid employment, it is difficult to substantiate an argument that another woman may not.

A final influence on the entry of women into the labour force is the support gained through having other women resident in their homes. For example, there is often more than one adult woman in the home in male-headed extended families; this contributes to female solidarity and strength and helps women challenge male authority.

CONCLUSION

We have discussed the way household type and composition influence women's involvement in the labour force in Querétaro, Mexico. These "supply" constraints include cultural norms, age and fertility, and the predominance of the nuclear family, in which few women are allowed by their husbands to enter the labour market. The nuclear family is conducive to a strict segregation between male and female roles, whereas other family patterns not only make it functionally more feasible for women to work, but also allow a degree of deviation from the standard ideology that a woman's place is in the home.

Female heads have the freedom to determine how they will organize the family's earning strategies. Female spouses in male-headed extended families enjoy a reduction in their housework burdens if these are shared by other family members, they have greater support for their claim to work from other female members, and the sharing of decision-making and finance among several adults means the male head has less of a prerogative in dictating what his wife will do and more of a vested interest in maximizing the earning potential of the household.

REFERENCES

Bromley, R. (1982). "Working in the streets: survival strategy, necessity or unavoidable evil?" in Gilbert, A. in association with Hardoy, J. E. and Ramirez, R. (eds.), *Urbanisation in contemporary Latin America: critical approaches to the analysis of urban issues.* Chichester: John Wiley, 59–77.

Chant, S. (1984a). *Las Olvidadas: a study of women, housing and family structure in Querétaro, Mexico,* unpublished Ph.D. dissertation, University College, London.

Gugler, J. (1981). "The rural-urban interface and migration," in Gilbert, A. and Gugler, J., *Cities, poverty and development: urbanization in the Third World.* Oxford: Oxford University Press.

Lailson, S. (1980). "Expansion limitada y proliferacion horizontal. La industria de la ropa y el tejido de punto," *Relactiones del Colegio de Michoacán,* 1(3), 48–102.

Latin American and Caribbean Women's Collective (1980). *Slaves of slaves: the challenge of Latin American women.* London: Zed Press.

Lomnitz, L. A. de (1977). *Networks and marginality—life in a Mexican shanty town.* New York: Academic Press.

Moser, C. (1978). "Informal sector or petty commodity production: dualism or dependence in urban development?" *World Development,* 6(9–10), 1041–64.

—— (1981). "Surviving in the surburbios," *Bulletin of the Institute of Development Studies,* 12(3), 19–29.

Nalven, J. (1978). *The politics of urban growth: a case study of community formation in Cali, Colombia,* Ph.D. dissertation, University of California at San Diego, reprinted by Ann Arbor: Michigan.

Meza Vargas, M. A. (1982). *"Desarrollo industrial en el estado,"* in PRI, Consulta popular en las reuniones nacionales: Querétaro, 22–24, Mexico City, PRI.

Katherine Marshall

EMPLOYED PARENTS AND THE DIVISION OF HOUSEWORK

INTRODUCTION

The structure and organization of family life has changed dramatically in the second half of the twentieth century. This is true not only in Canada, but worldwide. However, the changes have had a universally greater impact on women than on men, because the domestic division of labour has not changed. Every year Statistics Canada collects data from a representative sample of Canadians about some aspect of their lives. This excerpt reports on data collected in the 1990 General Social Survey, which asked questions about the division of household work. Not surprisingly, in most households women do more housework than men. Also not surprisingly, men do relatively more housework in homes where both partners work.

The most equitable arrangements regarding housework are found among younger couples who are well educated. One of the most interesting findings in this study is the relationship between the sharing of household tasks and satisfaction. The more couples shared, the more likely they were to be satisfied. Do you suppose that equality has satisfying effects in social relations outside the family too?

While the division of labour in the paid workforce has been given much attention, the division of labour at home has received less scrutiny. This issue is of particular concern to women because they have traditionally been responsible for housework, and now the majority of them are also facing the demands of a job outside the home. One of the central questions is how, in the midst of employment and parenting responsibilities, families manage domestic chores.

Results of Statistics Canada's 1990 General Social Survey (GSS)[1] show that dual-earner couples employed full time outside the home are the most likely to share responsibility for housework. Yet even for them, the allocation of household chores is far from equal. Sharing tends to be most common among younger, well-educated couples with few children. The likelihood of shared responsibility increases as the wife's income level rises. As well, the partners' satisfaction with several dimensions of their lives seems to be related to the way they divide responsibility for housework.

Marshall, Kathy (1993). "Employed Parents and the Division of Housework," *Perspectives*, Autumn, 23–30.

MOST COUPLES ARE DUAL-EARNERS

The balancing of family and job obligations has become a challenge for more Canadian couples than ever before. In 1990, 71% of couples with children aged 18 or younger in the household were dual-earners (both partners had at least some employment outside the home); by contrast, just over 20 years ago, only 30% of such families were dual-earners.[2]

FIGURE 1 The Majority of Parents Worked Full Time

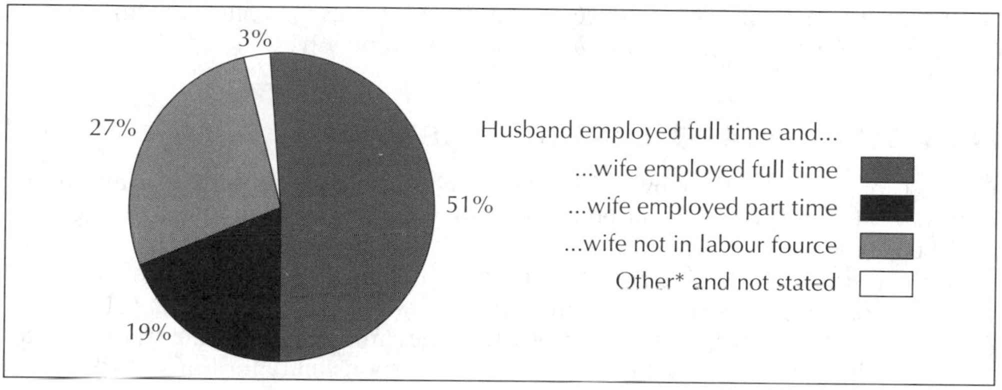

Source: General Social Survey, 1990

*Includes other work statuses of husbands and wives.

In 1990, both the wife and the husband were employed full time in 51% of two-parent families. In 19% of two-parent families, the husband worked full time, and the wife, part time (Figure 1). Single-earner families, in which the husband was employed full time and the wife was at home full time, accounted for 27%.[3]

TRADITIONAL DIVISION OF LABOUR

The 1990 GSS showed that the assignment of housework tends to follow traditional patterns. For the purposes of this paper, housework refers to meal preparation, meal clean-up, and cleaning and laundry. Women are likely to assume primary responsibility for these routine tasks, which must be performed on a regular basis and which account for 78% of all housework. On the other hand, men tend to be responsible for repairs, maintenance, and outside work, tasks that must be accomplished less frequently. Because the 1990 GSS did not ask direct questions about the responsibility for child care, this activity is not directly analysed in this article. However, the population studied consists only of couples with children at home, and it is generally accepted that children in a household increase the amount of housework.

The extent to which wives are responsible for housework varies with their employment status. As wives' involvement in the workforce increases, their responsibility for housework declines, but their husband's contribution does not increase enough to approach parity (Table 1). For example, 89% of wives who were not in the labour force were solely responsible for meal preparation; this compared with 86% of wives employed part time and 72% of those employed full time.

While husbands in full-time, dual-earner families were the most likely of all husbands to assume responsibility for domestic chores, the proportions who did so were relatively low. Meal clean-up was the task that these men most often shared (15%) or did on their own (16%). Slightly fewer shared (12%) or had sole responsibility (13%) for meal preparation. And although 13% of husbands shared the cleaning and laundry, these were the chores that they were least likely to do alone (7%).

There was almost no difference in the degree of responsibility for housework taken on by wives working part time and stay-at-home wives.

FULL-TIME, DUAL-EARNING PARENTS

The division of housework by full-time dual-earners deserves particular attention, since half of couples with children aged 18 or younger now fall into this category. These parents generally have less time to devote to domestic chores than do those with other employment patterns. By definition, full-time dual-earners deviate from traditional gender roles because both partners share responsibility for paid work. Therefore, it may be reasonable to expect that they might also deviate from the traditional division of household labour by sharing responsibility for housework.

TABLE 1 Primary Responsibility for Housework of Parents Under Age 65, by Employment Status of Couple, 1990

Household chore and employment status	Total*	Primary responsibility			
		Wife only	Husband only	Wife and husband share equally	Other**
		%			
Meal preparation					
Dual-earner, both working full time	100	72	13	12	2
Dual-earner, husband full time, wife part time	100	86	7	6	—
Single-earner, husband full time	100	89	5	5	—
Meal clean-up					
Dual-earner, both full time	100	59	16	15	6
Dual-earner, husband full time, wife part time	100	72	9	10	3
Single-earner, husband full time	100	78	7	8	3

TABLE 1 Cont'd

Household chore and employment status	Total*	Wife only	Husband only	Wife and husband share equally	Other**
		Primary responsibility			
Cleaning and laundry					
Dual-earner, both full time	100	74	7	13	3
Dual-earner, husband full time, wife part time	100	86	4	6	—
Single-earner, husband full time	100	86	4	7	—

Source: General Social Survey, 1990

* May not add to 100% due to exclusion of non-response.
** Someone other than the wife or husband had primary responsibility for the chore.

In reality, this was not the case. In most full-time, dual-earner families, the wife had primary responsibility for housework.[4] The majority (52%) of wives employed full time had all of the responsibility for daily housework, while 28% had most of this responsibility (Figure 2). Only 10% of dual-earning couples shared responsibility for housework equally; in the remaining 10% of couples, the husband had all or most of the responsibility.

FIGURE 2   Among Full-time Dual-Earner Couples, Wives Were Largely Responsible for Housework

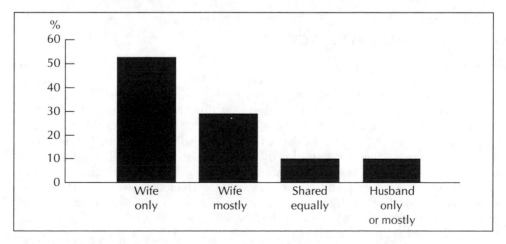

Source: General Social Survey, 1990

WHO SHARES . . . WHO DOESN'T?

Only a small minority of full-time, dual-earning couples had an egalitarian division of housework. What distinguishes these couples from those who do less sharing?

Several characteristics were associated with the likelihood that the husbands would assume greater responsibility for housework—or more precisely, that the wives would not be solely responsible. For example, the younger the partners, the less likely was the wife to be solely responsible for housework. The proportion of full-time, dual-earner wives under age 35 who were responsible for all daily housework was 47%, compared with 69% among those aged 45 to 64. The trend was similar according to the husband's age.

The number of children in the household also had some bearing on the allocation of domestic responsibilities. The percentage of dual-earner wives with all responsibility for housework increased from 44% of those with one child at home to 83% of those with four or more children. This suggests that when there is additional housework, as is the case with several children at home, women are more likely to do the extra work required.

As well, dual-earner women in common-law unions were somewhat less likely than those in marriages to do all the housework. The wife had sole responsibility for housework in 46% of common-law unions, compared with 52% of marriages.

The educational attainment of both partners was also associated with the allocation of housework: the more educated the couple, the less likely was the wife to assume full responsibility for domestic chores. For instance, in 58% of households where the wife had less than high school graduation, she alone was responsible for daily housework; if she was a university graduate, the corresponding figure was 45%. The trend was similar according to the husband's level of education.

The relationship between domestic responsibility and income differed for wives and husbands. As the wife's income rose, the likelihood that she alone would be responsible for housework declined. By contrast, the higher the husband's income, the greater was the proportion of wives with all responsibility for housework.

SHARING AND SATISFACTION

The way that full-time dual-earners divide housework appears to be associated with their satisfaction with several aspects of their lives: the allocation of household tasks, the time for other interests, and the balance between work and family.[5]

The majority of dual-earners indicated that they were satisfied with the allocation of housework in their homes. However, the most satisfaction was expressed by wives (98%) and husbands (97%) in households where housework was shared equally. Not surprisingly, spouses with little responsibility for housework also reported high levels of satisfaction (94% or more) with this allocation of duties. On the other hand, lower levels of satisfaction were expressed by spouses who did all the housework: 75% of wives who were responsible for all the domestic chores and 88% of husbands who had most of the responsibility were satisfied with the arrangement.

A sizeable proportion of all full-time dual-earners felt that they did not have sufficient time to pursue other interests. Dual-earners' satisfaction with this aspect of their life, however, was also related to their partner's responsibility for housework. The highest satisfaction levels (at least 70%) were reported by spouses with little responsibility for domestic chores. By contrast, just 58% of wives who managed all the housework and 54% of husbands who assumed most responsibility for these tasks were satisfied with the time they had for other activities. Dual-earners who shared housework responsibility also tended to feel pressed for time, as only 58% of wives and 63% of husbands expressed satisfaction with their time for other interests.

The distribution of responsibility for housework did not affect the way dual-earner couples felt about the balance between their job and their family. Regardless of how housework was divided, approximately eight out of ten wives and husbands were satisfied with the balance.

SUMMARY

According to the 1990 General Social Survey, women employed full time have somewhat less responsibility for housework than do women with part-time jobs or those at home full time. But while husbands tend to respond to their wife's working full time by taking a greater role in domestic chores, the division of housework is still far from equal. The majority of wives who are employed full time continue to have all or most of the responsibility for daily household tasks. These women face the double burden of paid work and unpaid housework.

ENDNOTES

[1] The General Social Survey (GSS) was established by Statistics Canada in 1985 to monitor changes in the living conditions and well-being of Canadians, and to provide information on various social issues of current or emerging interest. Data are collected annually from a random sample of households. Approximately 13,500 persons were interviewed in 1990. The target population consists of all persons aged 15 and over, except full-time residents of institutions and residents of the Yukon and the Northwest Territories. For further information, contact Douglas Norris at (613) 951-2572.

[2] The 1967 information is based on unpublished data from the Survey of Consumer Finances, which refer to families with children under age 16.

[3] The remaining 3% consisted of dual-earners with the wife working full time and the husband part time or both working part time, and single-earners with the wife employed full time and the husband at home full time. Those respondents who did not state their employment status were also included in this residual category.

[4] A point system was used to determine responsibility for housework. Individuals scored a point each time they were acknowledged as having primary responsibility for meal preparation, meal clean-up, and cleaning and laundry. If responsibility for a chore was shared equally, each partner scored a point. Since daily housework consisted of three chores, the maximum score was three points. For example, "wife mostly" comprises scores of W = 3 H = 2; W = 3 H = 1; and W = 2 H = 1.

5   Reports of satisfaction are difficult to interpret. Generally, it is more socially acceptable to be satisfied rather than dissatisfied with one's personal life. Therefore, reported levels of satisfaction may be exaggerated, depending on the nature of the question.

REFERENCES

Coverman, S. "Explaining husbands' participation in domestic labor." *The sociological quarterly* 26, no. 1 (1985): 81–97.

Haas, L. "Domestic role sharing in Sweden." *Journal of marriage and the family* 43 (November 1981): 957–967.

Statistics Canada. *Where does time go?* General Social Survey Analysis Series. Catalogue 11-612E, no. 4 (August 1991).

QUESTIONS

DISCUSSION QUESTIONS

1. Ask men and women in the class to consider their occupational choices in light of gender socialization. What (or who) has influenced their choices?

2. The attitudes of Mexican men (excerpt 6.2) to the employment of their wives reminds us of the opinions of North American men a half century ago. What brought about the changes in attitude in North America? Do you predict similar attitude change in Latin America?

3. Brainstorm a list of male-female differences. (Follow the most important rule of brainstorming: don't evaluate people's ideas until you have finished collecting and listing as many as you possibly can.) Then, try to reach a consensus on the list—which ideas should go and which should stay. Finally, discuss each trait on the list in order to decide whether it is determined by nature or nurture.

4. Is feminism passé in North America? Why or why not?

DATA COLLECTION EXERCISES

1. Research has shown that cohabiting couples are more likely to share housework than married couples. Interview people to find out if this holds for students at your institution.

2. Using the 1991 United Nations sourcebook *The World's Women 1970-1990: Trends and Statistics* (New York: United Nations Publications), create a table to compare political participation, labour force participation, fertility rates, and divorce rates for women in countries by region. What does this table show you?

3. Select representative questions from the Canadian Gallup Poll (look in the reference section of a university library) to evaluate changing attitudes to maternal employment over the last two or three decades.

4. Ask twenty men and women at your college or university what job they expect to be doing in ten years time. Then, using current labour force data, calculate the extent to which identified jobs are gender-typed. Also, try to find current income data for the jobs.

WRITING EXERCISES

1. Is gender inequality inevitable? Answer in a brief (500-word) essay.

2. Can women have it all: career, relationship, and children? Create a brief (500-word) dialogue between two women who take opposing sides in this question.

3. Write a brief (500-word) essay analyzing gender inequality in two developing countries. Be sure to compare rates of labour force participation, occupational segregation, and participation in political life, among other things.

4. Write a brief (500-word) essay about the anti-feminist backlash in North America. What is the basis of its appeal? Do you think it will gain or lose strength in the latter years of the 1990s?

SUGGESTED READINGS

1. Brettell, Caroline B. and Carolyn F. Sargent (1993). *Gender in Cross-Cultural Perspective*. Englewood Cliffs, New Jersey: Prentice-Hall. This book of readings, most of which are by anthropologists, gives a good flavour of the ways that gender differentiation is institutionalized in diverse cultural settings. It includes sections on domestic spheres, sexuality, the state, religion, and politics.

2. Nelson, E. D. and B. W. Robinson (1995). *Gender in the 90s: Images, Realities and Issues*. Toronto: Nelson Canada. This is an extensive collection of over forty readings including, but not limited to, articles on gender in Canada. It includes an interesting section on the future of gender relations and the feminist backlash.

3. Statistics Canada (1996). *Women in Canada: a Statistical Profile*, Third Edition. Ottawa: Minister of Supply and Services. This book is an excellent source of information about a number of aspects of Canadian women's lives, including family, education, health, labour force activity, and income.

SECTION 7   FAMILY

Introduction

North American family life has changed a great deal in the last half of the twentieth century. Compared to families in the 1950s, families today are smaller and much less stable. Divorce is more common and far more people live alone. The birth rate has dropped to below replacement level. Attitudes have also changed. For example, we are much more accepting of gay and lesbian relationships, and other kinds of unmarried cohabitation.

However, it is not only North American or Western families that are changing. Cross-cultural studies show that families everywhere are becoming more similar in structure. Research on families worldwide finds that an increasing number of marriages are monogamous, neolocal (i.e. the couple lives separately, not in an extended family household), love-based (rather than arranged) and (relatively) egalitarian.

Family wealth is increasingly derived from waged work, and women are active in the labour force. In this setting, children are an economic cost, not the asset they are in rural communities, so couples cannot afford to have large families. Excerpt 7.1 describes changes in marriage in Bangladesh, where modernization, increased education, and increased Westernization have all contributed to changing marriage norms.

CHANGES IN PARTNERING

Although most Canadians do marry, an increasing number of people choose to live singly or to cohabit. This change reflects our changing attitudes and increased affluence. A great many adults can now earn enough to live comfortably on their own. They may live alone because they have made a long-term commitment to single living, or because they have not yet married or remarried.

In Canada and the United States, (unmarried) cohabitation has become increasingly common. (Interestingly, these rates are far higher in Quebec than in any other province.) Rates of cohabitation have increased for all age groups, including once-married people. Nevertheless, North American rates are far lower than rates in Scandinavia, where it is rare for a couple to marry without living together first.

Attitudes towards cohabitation have changed as rates have increased. In 1981, 5.6% of couples were living common law. By 1986 that figure had increased to 7.2%, and it increased again to 9.9% by 1991. About one-third of men and women in Canada have ever cohabited. People live together for a variety of reasons. Some are opposed to the institution of marriage; others are unsure of their commitment to a particular relationship. Some are awaiting a divorce, or are legally married to someone else. Cohabitation is no longer simply a premarital step for young people.

The rise in divorce rates is a worldwide phenomenon, although the United States has one of the highest rates anywhere. While Canadian divorce rates are not as high as those in Sweden or the United States, they too have jumped since the 1968 Divorce Act changed the grounds for divorce. The crude divorce rate (the number of divorces per 100,000 married people in the population) was 54.8 in 1968. It rose to 124.2 in 1969 and 621.0 in 1970. Between 1970 and 1987 the divorce rate tripled. In Canada and a number of other countries, divorce rates declined slightly in the mid-1980s, suggesting that divorce had peaked. However, by 1986 rates again began to rise in Canada, so it is difficult to predict an upper limit.

One of the most important consequences of the higher divorce rate is the larger number of women and children who suffer financially as a result. Research in the United States found that at divorce women's standard of living decreases by about 50 percent, while men's standard of living actually increases. In excerpt 7.3 Canadian sociologist Ross Finnie found similar results for Canada. As Finnie argues, this amounts to a financial incentive for men to divorce and for women to stay married.

Why did divorce rates increase so dramatically and why have they remained so high? There are no simple answers. We seem to have developed extremely high expectations of marriage, and these expectations are not tied to a relationship with a particular spouse. As a result, a large fraction of adults divorce, but the majority of divorced people remarry.

CHANGES IN FERTILITY

In the industrial world, including Canada, fertility is now below replacement levels. Indeed, low levels of childbearing in the developed world have been consistent enough to have been termed "the second demographic transition" by van de Kaa (see excerpt 9.3). Without immigration the populations of most Western countries would shrink. Low fertility also ages the population, in the sense that the smaller the proportion of young people, the greater the proportion of elderly.

Canada's declining birth rate reflects a smaller average family size and the postponement of childbearing. However, about 90 percent of women in industrial countries have at least one child, and Canadian women conform to this trend.

One of the most significant recent changes in women's lives is increased control over reproduction. For the first time in history safe and reliable contraception is available to women. In Canada and the United States there is strong resistance to the use of abortion as a means of birth control. This is not so in China, where the dramatic success of the 1979 one-child policy has depended on a wide net of medical services that includes both contraception and abortion. In India, sex ratios that strongly favour males suggest that with increasing economic pressures some families have resorted to female infanticide, or selective abortion (to eliminate female fetuses).

The general availability of contraception has *not* reduced nonmarital pregnancy. Interestingly, the United States has the highest rates of teenage pregnancy in the developed world. Countries with liberal attitudes towards contraception and sex education have much lower rates of teenage pregnancy.

CHANGES IN LABOUR FORCE PARTICIPATION

One of the most significant recent changes in family living has been the increased labour force participation of married women. In 1941 only 4.5 percent of married Canadian women were in the labour force. By 1951 this figure had risen to 11.2 percent, and by 1961 to 20.8 percent. In 1991, 68 percent of women with children at home were working or looking for work—an increase of over half a million women since 1981. This increase can be attributed primarily to economic need. (In Section 2 we described the changes in preschool child care that have resulted from the decline of the single-earner family.)

Some people are tempted to draw a causal connection between increased rates of divorce and the increased labour force participation of married women. Indeed, the "new right" does just this. But clearly this is not a simple, one-way relationship. Women do not see their labour force participation as a frill or supplement. They work for the same reasons men work: economic necessity.

The decline in real wages means that families need more than one breadwinner. Often both parents are employed. But today's family instability, coupled with increasing economic instability marked by downsizing and layoffs, means that typical patterns can no longer be discerned. In some families husbands are unemployed, and wives and children are breadwinners. Wives earn more than husbands in over 20 pecent of dual-income families in Canada. So the vast majority of women can expect to juggle family responsibilities and paid employment for at least some, or all, of their lives. They will try to negotiate greater involvement by other family members, and will likely feel over-worked and underappreciated as a result.

As we saw in excerpt 6.3, few men share domestic work and child care. (On the other hand, the minority of couples who do share these responsibilities have been found to be more satisfied, with the fathers wanting to spend more time parenting.) It seems likely that conventional work structures will have to change to meet the needs of employed parents, but so far this change has not met with much enthusiasm in North America.

Ashraf Uddin Ahmed

THE TRANSITION FROM ARRANGED MARRIAGE IN BANGLADESH

INTRODUCTION

Sociologists have often found it useful to distinguish between Eastern and Western models of the family. Western families, of the kind found commonly in Canada, have typically been monogamous and love-based; households are small and nuclear; and couples live "neolocally," away from both sets of parents. By contrast, Eastern families of the kind we find in India have been based on arranged marriage, often contracted when brides are very young. Couples live with or very near extended family members; typically they bear many children, and sons are valued more highly than daughters. The wealthiest men in society often practise polygamy.

Over the last few decades Eastern marriage patterns have begun to change, and increasingly resemble the Western model. Now couples marry later, exercise more choice in marriage partners, and are more likely to live in newly established households.

The reasons for this change vary slightly from society to society. In China, for example, highly effective family planning policies initiated in the 1970s legislate a minimum age of marriage and limit family size to one child. In the Middle East, change was accelerated by a dramatic rise in the standard of living and a subsequent increase in women's education. In Bangladesh, as this excerpt shows, change was precipitated by a combination of economic factors along with increasing exposure to Western culture.

In South Asian countries, irrespective of cultural conditions, a transition is visible in the pattern of family formation, the mating process, divorce and remarriage. In the last few decades, Bangladesh has also experienced transition in these aspects. The deterioration of socio-economic conditions has resulted in changes in the marriage pattern. For example, a dowry system is supplanting the older bride price system, and family background is no longer given its former importance in marriage negotiations. This paper attempts to evaluate these changing patterns and their linkages with socio-economic factors in Bangladesh society.

MARRIAGE

Arranged marriage is dominant in most African and Asian countries. The proportion of marriages which are arranged nevertheless varies across nations. South

Ahmed, Ashraf Uddin (1986). "Marriage and its Transition in Bangladesh," *International Journal of Sociology of the Family,* 16(1), Spring, 49–59. Reprinted by permission.

Asian countries, except Sri Lanka, will probably be the highest in terms of the percentage of arranged marriages.

The arranged marriage performs the following functions: (1) it helps to maintain social stratification in general, (2) it affirms and strengthens parental power over the children, (3) it helps keep the family traditions and value systems intact, (4) it helps consolidate and extend family property, (5) it enhances the value of the kinship group, (6) it helps keep the tradition of endogamy if one desires (Goode, 1963; Chekki, 1968), and (7) it helps young people from getting into the uncertainty of searching for a mate.

Muslim Marriage

In Islam, marriage is a civil contract as opposed to a sacrament (Korsen, 1979). The Qu'ran encourages marriage. For those who do not have enough money to set up a separate house or to provide the basic necessities, however, it encourages abstinence until their condition improves. Besides this economic restriction, Islam has put restrictions on the eligibility of marriage partners such as uncle-niece, or aunt-nephew. Cross-cousin rather than parallel-cousin marriage is more common in Muslim societies, more so than any in other societies. For men to marry non-muslims is permissible, but for women it is not.

Hindu Marriage

From ancient times, marriage among Hindus has been considered as a ritual and a sacramental union. Marriage is an indispensable event of Hindu life, and the unmarried person is considered unholy. From the religious point of view, the unmarried person remains incomplete and is not eligible for participation in some social and religious activities. Except in a very few cases, the importance of marriage transcends not only the entire family but also the past ancestral line as well as future generations.

The Hindu religion has given great importance to progeny whereby fathers and their ancestors are assured a peaceful and happy afterlife. The customs and the rites of Hindu religion demand male children from each married couple. Parents want to make sure their sons marry and continue to have male children. Pointing to the tradition and custom of the Hindu religion, Basham said, "a father who did not give his daughter in marriage before the first menstruation incurred the guilt of procuring abortion (a very sin, worse than many kinds of murder) for every menstrual period in which she remained unmarried" (1963:167). These factors partly explain why marriage is universal and why child-marriage has been well accepted in the Indian sub-continent.

Child Marriage

The child-marriage system was started by the Hindus, and later adopted by the Muslims. In the mid-nineteenth century, this practice became more common among Muslims and lower-caste Hindus. The proportions used to vary by regions.

In some areas Muslims had a higher child-marriage rate, and in other areas, the Hindus did. After a long struggle, progressive Indian leaders with the help of the British government succeeded in 1929 in making a law on age at marriage, known as the Sarda Act. According to this act, the minimum age at marriage for girls was fifteen years. The law, however, has largely remained unenforced to this day.

Having a female child was considered by Hindus to be a sign of God's unhappiness with a girl's parents. If parents had a girl-baby, they were reluctant to mention it to friends and relatives. Girls are always an economic burden to the parents until their marriage because they cannot contribute to the household income like sons. This has been strengthened by the partial acceptance of the Muslim *purdah* system, which does not allow them to work outside the household. Besides, the society places a high value on the chastity or virginity of the girls before marriage. Girls are also a psychological burden to the parents. If it is known that a girl is no longer a virgin, it will be difficult for her parents to find a husband for her. All these fears and responsibilities induce the parents to marry off their daughters as soon as possible no matter how old they are. The situation is gradually changing, however.

Economically, child-marriage is profitable to the parents. The amount of dowry or bride price is usually significantly smaller when it is a child-marriage than a youth marriage. The overall cost of gifts is usually less. To minimize the ceremonial costs, parents sometimes try to arrange the marriage of two sons or daughters at a time, even if the younger one is not of marriageable age.

Besides the economic factors, child betrothal occurs in order to maintain social ties between families. In some cases, two couples who have been good friends commit to the marriage of their children even when their children are not yet born. For Hindus, this practice may occur among friends within the same caste or subcaste. Among Muslims, it occurs among brothers and sisters, and this extends to friends. As most of the marriages are arranged, parents take it for granted that these marriages will eventually take place without objection from their children.

MATE SELECTION AND SOCIAL MOBILITY

Most marriages in a traditional Muslim society are arranged by parents or guardians. Conventionally, parents of boys take the initiative. Sometimes they talk directly to the parents or propose through a *ghatak* (marriage broker) or through relatives and friends of either family. When parents of both families find the would be in-laws are suitable, the marriage takes place. Where marriage is arranged, the interests of the families get priority over the interests of the couple. Sometimes, the marriage partners do not get to see each other before the marriage. This is primarily a marriage between families and is termed a "blind marriage" by Parish and Whyte (1978).

Classical Islamic law sets two conditions—consent of the parties involved and a contract specifying the bride price (*mehr* [mahr]) to be given by the husband to his wife in the presence of witnesses. The consent sometimes is not free from the influence of parents.

Love marriage is thought to be disruptive to family ties, and is viewed as a children's transference of the loyalty from a family orientation to a single person, ignoring obligations to the family and kin group for personal goals. There is an old saying "love is blind." It overshadows the quality of spouses. It is a weak criterion for selection of a mate. People believe love after marriage is a heavenly or spiritual thing. God helps those who have sincere love for their spouses by giving them a peaceful life.

If parents are looking for a mate for their son, they first inquire about non-economical factors—beauty, age, family status, modesty, religiousness and literacy—and then economic factors—the amount of dowry and gift. Although dowry and gifts are important, there is no standard set for these. For daughters, parents inquire about the occupation, income, education and social status of the family of the would be son-in-law. The economic factors into which they inquire are the extent of land holding by his family if they are in rural areas, otherwise economic solvency or well-being of the family.

In Western societies, personal beauty of a girl is an important quality in the marriage market. A beautiful girl of low social class has a chance to marry a man at a much higher social class. She has a chance to trade her beauty at a higher price in the marriage market. Although this is true to some extent for every society, the chances of her upward mobility are much lower in a traditional society, where most of the marriages are arranged by guardians, so beauty does not get much importance in marriage negotiation.

Among the factors considered as important determinants in mating, education appears to have a stronger influence in the marriage market. Education increases the chances for hypergamy. If a man with a good education reduces his expectation for dowry and increases his willingness to make bridal gifts, he might be able to marry into a higher social class than his own, although this is forbidden in Islam. Education still has a strong influence in the marriage market, but it may not remain the same in the future if the employment situation in the non-agricultural sector does not improve. A business profession with some education is gradually overriding the value of an educated bridegroom.

Occupation, which has a strong relation with education, is another important factor for men. Employment in urban areas plus education has more demand in the marriage market. Of course, it depends on the type of occupation. Recently, men working in the Middle-East or in any foreign country have been preferred by the bride's parents. Parents think to marry off their daughters to economically solvent and socially well-placed mates. Economic solvency often gets the highest priority among the factors. On the other hand, when parents look for a mate for their sons, they place greater importance on the social status of the bride's family in addition to the economic factor. Marriage is therefore emerging as one way social mobility might take place. If the family status of a person is high, but achieved personal quality is low, the person has a chance either to marry in the same social class or one relatively lower than one's own. As a result, downward mobility takes place in one family and upward mobility in the other family. On the other hand, if the family status of a person is low but his achieved personal quality (or human capital) is high, the person has a chance to marry in a social class higher than one's own and thereby upward mobility takes place. Otherwise, most marriages occur within the same social class (homogamy).

Hindus practice endogamy. The first criterion is caste and sub caste identity. Within caste or sub caste, the factors of dowry and selection process are the same as discussed before. Cross-caste marriage does not occur unless it is love marriage. A negligible percentage of marriage can be found around the border line of sub-castes. Love marriage seldom occurs among Hindus. In Bangladesh, marriages between relatives appear to be declining. Three factors seem to have contributed to this fact. The first is the rise of dowry which resulted from the delay of men's marriages and a surplus of marriageable women. The second is the rise in men's spatial mobility resulting from increased literacy and non-agricultural occupations. The last factor is the diffusion of the Western belief that these marriages produce sickly children.

IS THERE A MARRIAGE SQUEEZE IN BANGLADESH?

A few decades back, there was a scarcity of potential wives in the area. This shortage of marriageable women may be regarded as one cause of child-marriage. The impact of the demographic transition, high fertility and declining mortality, has resulted in an age-distribution with a broader base. Although the sex-ratio at birth has been about 105 males per 100 females for a long time, this does not imply the number of potential husbands is higher than the number of potential wives. This is because the age of eligibility for marriage is not the same for men and women. Parents of girls, particularly in rural areas, consider their daughters marriageable at menarche. On the other hand, men are not usually considered marriageable until they have stable source of income either from a job or from their parents' property. This contributes to the age difference between spouses.

In urban areas, young men are deferring their marriages. Under present economic conditions, men are finding it difficult to marry because the amount of money they earn cannot buy the basic necessities for even two people, aside from the problem of housing. As a result, men's demand for dowry is becoming a dominating factor in the marriage market, although the government has officially banned the dowry system. If the job market for educated women were better, the situation would be somewhat better; their potential earnings would be a substitute for dowry.

In rural areas, the situation does not differ much. People who own cultivatable land and can earn their own living are more likely to get married earlier. The surplus of labor in rural areas has also affected the marriage pattern there. Besides these economic factors, the age distribution of a growing population demonstrates that the potential wives outnumber the potential husbands, since the population of the preceding age groups are often larger than the following age groups.

Another factor, labor migration to the Middle-East, has affected the marriage market. Most of these migrants appear to be single. This employment opportunity has delayed the marriages of some people. On the other hand, it has helped some people to afford to marry. In general, however, it has contributed to late marriage for most of the people involved.

Lastly, the liberation movement had some effect on the number of potential husbands, as the number of deaths of young men was much higher than other age groups.

These factors are working together for the creation of late marriage and for increasing the number of single people. This marriage squeeze has emerged in all the South Asian countries (Caldwell, Reddy and Caldwell, 1983) and in other parts of Asia.

DISCUSSION

Social development has made changes in Bangladesh. The concept of marriage might have not changed much, but the process of family formation and mating process has.

In mate selection, the persons involved in marriage are having more to say. Economic considerations are coming to have increasing importance, as are the achieved qualities of the marriage partners. In absence of other capital, human capital is becoming the strongest determinant in the selection since 90 percent of the population live below the poverty level in this country. As a result, transfer of assets among them is gradually declining due to their inability to produce a surplus. Human capital thus is becoming a dominant exchange commodity in marriage. The rationality of this consideration lies in the condition of the job market, which is to say on the demand for human capital.

The urbanites are gradually being highly exposed to Western culture. These people like to imitate the imported culture. Consequently, urban culture is not highly traditional. Also, the severity of economic pressures is making people less able to perform according to the demands of the traditional culture. Although this country is one of the least developed countries, nevertheless the society is experiencing a change in the pattern of family formation, family type and marriage decision. These changes are somewhat in the direction of the characteristics of the Western World, as limited by a poor economy.

Both demographic and socio-economic conditions have contributed to the marriage squeeze. The situation might improve if employment opportunities for women and the overall literacy rate increase. The concept of marriage as universal in the society may not remain as strong as it used to be. From the marriage squeeze, a positive effect, a reduction in population growth, is emerging.

REFERENCES

Basham, A. L. (1963). *The Wonder that Was India.* New York: Howthorn Books, Inc.

Caldwell, J. C., P. H. Reddy, and Pat Caldwell (1983). "The Causes of Marriage Change in South India." *Population Studies,* 37:343–361.

Chekki, D. A. (1968). "Mate Selection, Age at Marriage and Propinquity Among the Lingayats of India." *Journal of Marriage and the Family,* 30:707–711.

Goode, William J. (1963). *World Revolution and Family Patterns.* London: The Free Press.

Parish, William L. and Mortin L. Whyte (1978). *Village and Family in Contemporary China.* Chicago: The University of Chicago Press.

Ross Finnie

WOMEN, MEN, AND THE ECONOMIC CONSEQUENCES OF DIVORCE

INTRODUCTION

The phrase "feminization of poverty" was first used to describe the large number of divorced or widowed women who, because of little or intermittent work experience and the responsibility to care for young children, could not support themselves or their children adequately.

The impoverishment of divorced women was exacerbated by no-fault divorce, which was first introduced in the United States but is now in place throughout North America. With assets divided equally, and alimony limited, divorced women were expected to become self-sufficient soon after the end of the marriage. Responsibility for child care, unequal wages, and the failure of many ex-husbands to pay child support meant that self-sufficiency was elusive.

Ross Finnie's study tracks the economic well-being of divorced men and women. Finnie found that women's family income drops to about half while men's drops 25 percent. Women are worse off economically after divorce, while men (because they do not have dependents at home) are slightly better off.

Finnie suggests some interesting implications of this pattern. In the face of such a large financial penalty women who decide to leave their husbands must be very dissatisfied. Men, on the other hand, have far less to lose by moving on. This inequity means that within a marriage the wife has generally less bargaining power than the husband.

I INTRODUCTION

This paper presents the results of an empirical investigation of the economic consequences of divorce which uses the recently developed Longitudinal Administrative Database (LAD) constructed from Canadian tax files. This is the first study to use Canadian longitudinal data to investigate the economic consequences of divorce, while the massive nature of the LAD generates a sample of splits which is unequalled *anywhere* in terms of its size and representative nature. It thus provides a useful empirical foundation for understanding the effect of divorce on men's, women's, and children's economic well-being.

Existing empirical evidence suggests that the economic well-being of separated and divorced women is well below that of 1) men in the same situation (their ex-

Finnie, Ross (1993). "Women, Men, and the Economic Consequences of Divorce," *Canadian Review of Sociology and Anthropology*, 30, 2, 205–237.

partners in general), and 2) women (and men) in intact families. Further, many divorces involve children, and children in mother-only families (in particular) are, on average, much worse off than those in two-parent families. Finally, divorce is not only associated with *relatively* lower levels of well-being for women and their dependent children, but it is also characterized by *absolute* deprivation; for example, the poverty rate of mother-only families with children is around the 50 per cent mark, versus 10 per cent for two-parent families. Thus, marital splits are associated with 1) large *differences* in economic well-being between men and women, 2) low income *levels* for women, including a large proportion in poverty, and 3) associated relative and absolute economic deprivation of *children*. We might classify these issues as, first, one of equity between the man and the woman, and second, economic deprivation generally (and poverty in particular) for the woman and her dependent children.

Department of Justice Canada (henceforth 'Justice Department') (1990) is probably the best Canadian source concerning the divorce process in general, including the treatment of economic outcomes. The report is based on two phases of research conducted in the mid-1980s, thus bracketing the new *Divorce Act*, whose effects on divorce processes and outcomes the report was designed to evaluate. But this by no means represents a random sampling of Canadian divorces: records were selected from only four cities (Saskatoon, Montreal, St. John's, and Ottawa); there was an over-sampling of 'contested' cases and an under-sampling of childless divorces, and the interview samples were somewhat biased towards more affluent, better educated, and more 'responsible' individuals; follow-up interviews were performed only with those who could be located in the jurisdiction; all splits which passed outside of the legal divorce system were ignored (including all common-law divorces). Further, pre-divorce income data were mostly missing, so pre- versus post-divorce comparisons could not be made. The results should therefore again be considered as broad indicators, rather than tight estimates of Canadian divorce outcomes in general. The principal findings are that approximately one year after the legal divorce women's gross income was just over 60 per cent of men's, while poverty rates for women were 58 and 46 per cent respectively in the two periods, versus 11 and 13 per cent for men.

The LAD is a new and unique database, and therefore merits some general description.

At relatively low cost Statistics Canada has constructed a very large longitudinal sample containing useful tax-based information on individuals and their families, with the income data.

The matching of individuals into legal or common law marriages was accomplished using algorithms developed by Statistics Canada expressly for this purpose.

The data limit the analysis in many ways, but the identification of family structure and the excellent quality of the income data allow us to study the critical issue of how men's and women's economic well-being changes at divorce.

II THE ANALYSIS

This study looks at two types of outcome variables: those which directly measure economic *well-being* (income levels, income-to-needs ratios, poverty status) and others which capture economic *behaviour* (labour force participation, individuals' earnings levels, intra-family earnings shares). These are presented in two ways: 1) tracked over time for all years leading up to and through the divorce, and 2) direct comparisons of the post-divorce levels to the year preceding the breakup. The established conventions are followed by denoting the divorce year (i.e. the year during which marital status changes, as indicated by end-of-year status) as t_0, and referring to pre-divorce years as t_{-i} and post-divorce years as t_i. Thus with the first perspective we track variables over time, from t_{-4} to t_3; and with the second we obtain direct post- versus pre-divorce comparisons, for t_0 to t_3.

The principal measure of economic well-being used in this study is the income-to-needs ratio (INR), which is defined as the ratio of total family income to the poverty line for the family. INR values below one therefore indicate that the family is in poverty, while values greater than one reflect proportionately higher levels of well-being. Tracking this variable over time from t_{-4} to t_3 thus provides a useful index of the level of economic well-being in any given year, while the post-pre ratios given for t_0 through t_3 provide a direct measure of proportional changes in well-being, with values greater than one indicating improvements, and values less than one reflecting declines relative to the last year of marriage. Total family income (INC) is also analysed: tracked over time, the ratio of post-divorce to pre-divorce levels, and the absolute change from the pre- to post-divorce situation. Since these measures—in contrast to the INRs—are not adjusted for need, they are less appropriate as indicators of economic well-being, but are interesting nevertheless, and provide useful comparisons with other published work.

Poverty status constitutes the second principal measure of economic well-being employed in this study. Poverty incidence (POV) is tracked over time to assess general pre- versus post-divorce patterns, while actual poverty *dynamics* are revealed by looking at individuals' movements into and out of poverty relative to the pre-divorce situation (INTOPOV, OUTOFPOV). Poverty gaps are also tracked over time—for all individuals (POVGAP-ALL, which takes negative values for the non-poor), as well as for the poor only (POVGAP-POOR). Other outcome variables include labour market participation (LFPART), defined as earnings of at least $1,500 per year (in the absence of data on actual time worked); the individual's total labour market earnings (EARNI); total family earnings (EARNF); and the share of own to total family earnings (RIFEARN). Taken together, these measures of levels of and changes in INRs, family income, poverty status, labour market participation, and earnings provide a multi-faceted and dynamic view of the economic consequences of divorce.

III EMPIRICAL RESULTS

Both men and women experience significant drops in total family income. This is the expected result of a couple splitting apart: their incomes are no longer combined, and total family income falls on both sides. The initial decline is almost 2.5 times further for women (down to .57 the pre-divorce level on average) than men (a ratio of .82). And while men are almost back to their pre-divorce incomes three years later, women remain at only .76 the pre-split level.

These findings are paralleled by what we see with the poverty dynamics. Just over one-third of all women who were non-poor before the divorce fall into a low-income situation in the transition year, and the rate remains near 30 per cent in the later post-divorce years. The rate for men is around 10 per cent. On the other hand, a significant number of men are observed to leave poverty with divorce. Women's poverty escape rates are about one-half those of men in the transition year, and remain considerably below men's thereafter.

The comparisons of men's versus women's post-divorce *relative* well-being are very robust, and this holds throughout the entire post-divorce period. The INRs are shown in the upper portion of Figure 1.

FIGURE 1 Tracking INRs and Poverty Across Marital Splits

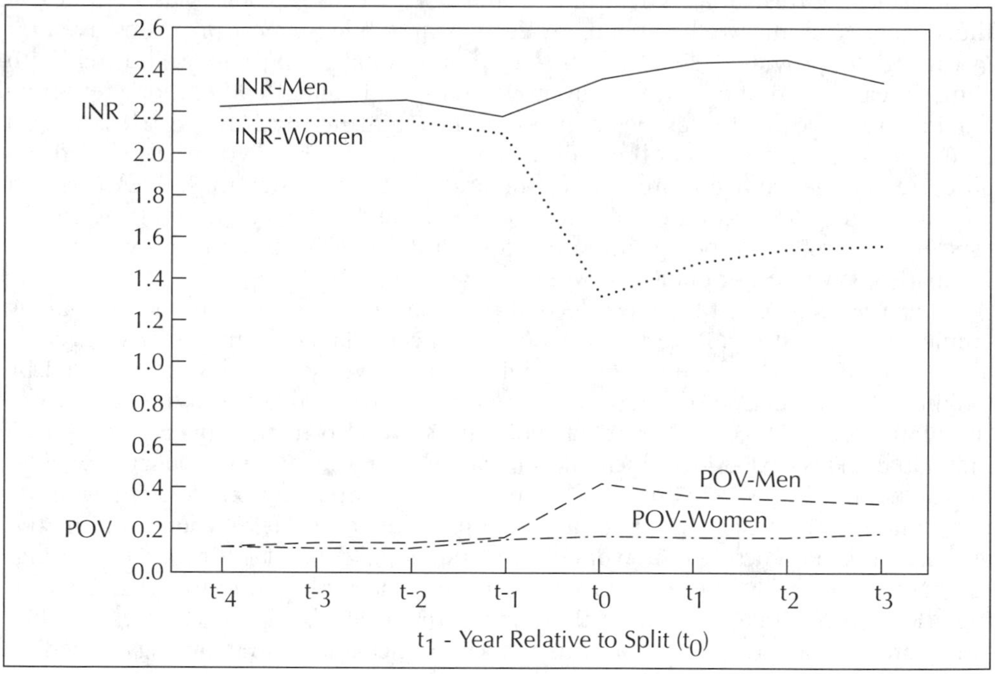

Note: The figures plot the income-to-needs ratios (INR) and poverty rates (POV) of men and women from 4 years previous to a split (t4) through the year of the split (t0) to 3 years after (t3).

The results are very robust in terms of the general magnitude of changes and the great divergence of men and women at the point of divorce. Women's family income drops roughly one-half, and men's declines about one-quarter in the first year of divorce, while the INRs indicate a smallish rise in economic well-being for men, versus drops of about 40 per cent for women. These initial changes are followed by moderate rises for both men and women in the following years. The measures of *relative* well-being are particularly robust across the entire set of estimates, with the INR measures indicating that women are initially at about .55 the level of men, and then rise to the .6–.7 range in the later post-divorce years.

The poverty rates show an initial moderate *increase* for men, from .14 to .17, which indicates that although men's *average* well-being improves slightly, the distribution apparently widens to leave more at the bottom end as well. For women there is no such ambiguity: poverty rates leap from .16 in t_{-1} to .43 in the year of the divorce, and then drop off slowly. There might be some reverse causality here, with poverty rates increasing slightly in the year prior to divorce and perhaps *causing* some splits, but the post-divorce divergence of men and women is again the dramatic story. These poverty trends are illustrated in the bottom portion of Figure 1. Men remain in families which are on average far above the poverty line after divorce, while on *average* women's families are not far out of poverty after divorce. Those men who *do* drop into poverty do not fall so very far into it, as the post-divorce average is smaller than the average pre-divorce gap. Women, on the other hand, when they fall into poverty at the time of divorce fall hard and stay down.

IV CONCLUSION AND DISCUSSION

These results paint a picture of divorce where, on average, women experience steep declines in economic well-being while men enjoy moderate increases. And while there is some recovery for women in the post-divorce years, three full years after the split they remain well below their pre-divorce levels, as well as the current levels of their ex-husbands. The gender earnings gap and low levels of spousal/child support payments are the key factors underlying these patterns. Women who face the greatest impoverishment upon divorce are less likely to split, and therefore the results probably under-estimate the negative effects of divorce which would hold for the general population of married Canadian women.

Some implications are now discussed. First, the patterns are interesting in terms of assessing incentives to divorce. To the degree the measures employed in this study truly represent economic well-being, men have a (small) positive economic incentive to divorce (on average), while women pay a substantial price in the form of a sharp decrease in their standard of living. It follows that—again, *'on average'*—women who initiate divorces must be sufficiently unhappy in their marriages to pay this high (economic) price of leaving, while men's gains from departing mean they are more likely to leave relationships which are not so desperately flawed. That is, divorce behaviour is likely to be very different for men and women—with the threshold level of discontent necessary to trigger a divorce lower for men than women due to the differential economic situations faced in the post-divorce situation. This is not to say that such narrow economic considerations are all-determining, but they probably often figure into decisions to *some* degree, and *can* undoubtedly be a crucial factor in many situations.

Second, there are associated implications for inter-spousal relations within marriage. Common sense, as well as formal economic modelling (e.g., Becker et al.,

1977), suggest there is compromise within marriage, and that sometimes this comes in the form of one partner trying to persuade the other not to end the union. The findings in this paper suggest that men have a fundamental advantage in terms of intra-marriage bargaining power, since 'walking out' is a much more (economically) attractive option to them, while women have stronger incentives to make the marriage continue. It follows that women will make more concessions within marriage than men.

One upshot of the above discussions is that we might expect still-married women to be, on average, less content in their marriages than still-married men. That is, there will be a group of women who are unhappy in their relationships but who have not yet passed the threshold which makes descending into the difficult economic situation of divorce worthwhile, while still-married men must be happy enough to not have been tempted to make the switch, which is so less costly—or even carries economic advantages.

While the LAD data do not reveal who initiates the divorce, Justice Department (1990) reports that through the mid-1980s women were petitioners in approximately 60 per cent of the divorce cases in their samples. There are probably many reasons for this pattern (including the weight of tradition), but to the degree that these women *were* actually initiating divorces they *wanted*, these figures taken together with the results reported here suggest that many divorce-initiating women were hoping to improve their overall situation even while accepting significant declines in their economic well-being. Therefore some of what we observe as desperate post-divorce economic situations are actually overall *improvements* in well-being relative to the failed marriages.

Justice Department (1990) also reports that 63–64 per cent of the divorced women in their study judged their standard of living to have remained unchanged or actually *improved* with the divorce, which would seem to be inconsistent with the results reported in this paper (as well as with the Justice Department's own findings in this regard). One possible explanation is that many women felt better-off in *other* ways, which caused them to give a more optimistic response concerning their economic situation than was objectively true. On the other hand, it might be that many of these women *were* better-off economically (or at least no worse-off) even as their *measured* well-being declined. For example, it could be that they gained more control over a smaller amount of family income.

The discussions of these last paragraphs 1) imply that some of the concern we feel towards the difficult position of women (and their children) in divorced situations should actually be directed towards women *still in marriages*, and 2) highlight the limitations of conventional measures of well-being based on measured family income, and draw attention to issues of intra-family distributions of income and well-being generally. It is especially important to keep in mind that these discussions are relevant not only to actual break-ups, but also to 'near divorces,' and within-marriage spousal relationships in general.

Some final musings concern 'interests'—in both the sense of inquisitiveness, and regarding consequences of actions. Why has there not been more research on the economic consequences of divorce, and why does divorce remain largely ignored in the standard models of individual economic behaviour (especially women's) and the economics of the family? Why do divorce court settlements so often result in great disparities in the economic well-being of men and women, and hardship for the children involved? Why have we not seen legal reform of spousal and child support payments? Obviously these questions cannot be answered here, but we might speculate in a querying manner. If it were men who suffered large declines in well-being with divorce, would there be more of a clamour for better documentation of the situation? If women economists were more numerous would there be more of a natural inclination to take the model of the family towards a more realistic treatment of the woman's situation, including a full treatment of divorce? If there were more female judges would there be a shift in decisions commensurate with an alternative perspective regarding inputs to marriages by those who specialize in home production, and to ensure a higher standard of living for the children involved? And if there were more politicians who were likely to personally gain—rather than lose—from reform of the spousal/child support system, would these individuals perhaps (to put it kindly) have better understanding of, and appreciation for, the need for such changes? (How many legislators have ex-spouses and noncustodial children for whom support payments would rise were serious reforms adopted in this direction?) This is part of a more general question: How gender-neutral is our system in terms of identifying and addressing important socio-economic problems? The results reported in this paper might cause one to reflect upon this general question in the specific context of divorce.

ARTICLE 7.3

Judith Stacey

BRAVE NEW FAMILIES IN THE SECOND NORTH AMERICAN FAMILY REVOLUTION

INTRODUCTION

Many North Americans are concerned about the effects of changes in family living, especially the effects on children. We worry particularly about whether or not children are neglected by the necessary employment of their parents. (Recall that excerpt 2.2 dealt with the issue of child care.) We also worry about increased family instability. Do higher rates of cohabitation and divorce mean that family life in general is less stable than in the past?

Stacey, J. (1993). "Brave New Families," *Transition*, September, 8–10.

Judith Stacey argues that current changes in family living are more than evolutionary; they amount to a second revolution in family life. The first revolution was the shift that accompanied industrialization, when the modern nuclear family became the norm. The second revolution is the change from the modern to the "postmodern" family. The nature of postmodern family life is so amorphous that we no longer agree about what family form is "normal."

Brave New Families *is the title of Judith Stacey's insightful book about recent changes in family living. Stacey's study focuses on a small cluster of working class families living in California's Silicon Valley. These families showed amazing resilience in the face of unemployment and family breakdown. Stacey argues that, although change may be stressful for individuals, it need not signal the demise of the family as an institution. And what Stacey writes about families in Silicon Valley USA applies just as well to families living in Burnaby, B.C.; Burlington, Ontario; or Bromont, Quebec.*

This is not the first period of family crisis or redefinition of family in modern history. Fears of family decline have always been with us. What I call the first North American family revolution was the shift from the *premodern* to *modern* family. Premodern families inhabited the patriarchal, integrated family economy of agrarian society. The "modern" family arose with industrial society. This unit, featuring the male breadwinner, the full-time female homemaker, plus dependent children, is often mistakenly called "the *traditional* family."

The first family revolution was spearheaded by the middle class and took a century to consolidate. It came to fruition in the Victorian era, the late 19th century, and evolved into the companionate version of the first half of the 20th century— the Ozzie and Harriet ideal.

The second family revolution moves us from the modern family to what I call "the *postmodern* family." It is postmodern in multiple senses. It comes *after* the demise of modern family system. It includes a pastiche of old and new elements. This family form is recombinant and fluid. Most especially, this is a period of doubt, uncertainty, ambivalence, and a collapse of consensus about what constitutes a normal family. There is no longer a single family form, like the modern family, that the majority inhabit and most of the rest desire.

Instead, Americans and Canadians today uneasily inhabit and frequently reconstitute a wide diversity of family and household arrangements. This diversity harkens back to the premodern family, but with very different causes and consequences. The postmodern family is not a new model of family life, and not the next stage in an orderly progression of family history. Instead, it is the historical stage in which belief in an orderly progression of stages breaks down.

From a historical perspective, the modern family is an aberration, but an important one. It achieved cultural and statistical dominance. But in both our countries, most working-class people attained their economic passport to modern family status—the male family wage—very late, if at all, maybe in the late 1960s. By the time the white working class got there, another family revolution was well underway.

In this revolution too, middle-class families appeared to be in the vanguard— white feminists especially. But it turns out, ironically, that Betty Friedan and other middle-class feminists were flailing a crippled horse. Frustrated middle-class home-makers and their more militant daughters subjected modern domesticity to a sustained critique. At times, that critique showed little sensitivity to the effects that its ideology might have on women who had rarely been able to achieve the modern family ideal of full-time domesticity. Thus, feminist family reform came to be regarded widely as a middle-class agenda. White, working-class families were its most resistant adversaries.

Consequently, many, like me, came to view white working-class families as the most "traditional" (i.e. modern—like TV's Archie Bunker). My field research between 1984 and 1987 in California's Silicon Valley has, however, convinced me that white, middle-class families are less the innovators than the propagandists and principal beneficiaries of contemporary family change.

My book *Brave New Families* is a product of this research. Its main characters are Pam, a feminist, I'd thought, and an unexpected recent Born-Again Christian; and Dotty, a formerly-abused wife in a long-term, intact marriage, who held views I found surprisingly feminist.

SHORT SHELF LIFE FOR BENEFITS OF FAMILY WAGE

Pam, Dotty and their friends whom I came to know are members of Betty Friedan's "feminine mystique" generation, but not of her social class. Unlike more affluent members of Friedan's audience, Pam and Dotty were "beneficiaries" of the late achievement of a male family wage won by privileged sectors of the working class. This was a Pyrrhic victory, as it turned out. It allowed this population a brief period of access to the modern family system just as it was decomposing. However, their experiences with the modern family were always more tenuous than those of the women to and for whom Friedan spoke.

Because their husbands' earnings were insecure and inadequate, each had to work periodically in low-wage jobs. Their wage labour was both necessary and resented by their husbands. Feminism provided analysis and rhetoric for their discontent, and helped each develop the self-esteem to exit or reform her unhappy modern marriage. Both left their husbands. Pam was divorced. Dotty and Lou separated, but later reunited on much better, and nonabusive terms.

EVANGELISM AND FEMINISM CONVERGE

By the time I met Pam and Dotty, a decade later (1984), national and local feminist ardor had cooled. Pam was a recent convert to evangelical Christianity, receiving Christian marriage counselling to buttress a second marriage to construction worker Al. Certainly this was a retreat from feminist family ideology, but as I was to learn, it was far less dramatic a retreat than I imagined. Like many other women in the contemporary evangelical Christian revival, Pam made creative use of her religion's surprisingly flexible patriarchal ideology to reform her husband in her own image.

Nor did conversion return Pam to a "modern" family pattern. Instead, she collaborated with the live-in lover of Pam's first husband. Together, they built a congenial and inclusive divorce-extended network of kin related by marriage, common-law and otherwise, blood, and other ties. The households swapped resources, labour and lodgers in response to shifting family circumstances and needs.

Between them, Pam and Dotty have five daughters, and three sons—children of modern families disrupted by post-industrial developments and feminist challenges. All five daughters distanced themselves from feminist identity and ideology. At the same time, all also selectively incorporated feminist principles into gender and kin expectations and practices. They took for granted, and at times rejected, gains in women's work opportunities, sexual agency, and male participation in childrearing and domestic work for which feminists of their mothers' generation struggled. They are ignorant or disdainful of political efforts by feminists to secure such gains, and they are preoccupied coping with the expanded opportunities and burdens that postmodern working-class women encounter. All but one of the daughters of successful white working-class fathers absorbed what I think of as post-feminist family expectations—to combine marriage to a communicative, egalitarian man with motherhood and an engaging, rewarding career. None has attained such a pattern.

One explicitly rejected it. Pam's younger daughter Katie, at 14, joined the Christian revival. In it she found an effective refuge from the disruptions of parental divorce and adolescent drug culture. Ironically, her total immersion in Pentecostal ministry led her to practice the most alternative family arrangement of all, living as part of a sectarian community. Its communal living arrangements included joint households, multiracial families, "accordian" family structures that repeatedly expanded and contracted, shared childrearing and resources, and religious work.

At the outset of my fieldwork, none of the five daughters inhabited a modern family. During the next few years, however, discouraging experiences with available work led three of them to retreat temporarily from paid work and attempt a modified modern family strategy. All three demanded, and two received, significant male involvement in child care and domestic work.

Only one, however, had a fair chance at succeeding in this "modern" gender strategy, and only because of the unacknowledged benefits feminism helped her to enjoy. Legalized abortion, liberalized sexual norms, and expanded blue-collar work opportunities allowed Dotty's second daughter Polly to be sexually active and defer marriage and childbearing until she could negotiate a marriage on better terms than her mother had in the 50s. [But I later learned that Polly returned to the work force part-time, even though she had two children under the age of four.]

POSTMODERN MEN A MYSTERY

I have less to say about the postmodern family strategies among men in Pam's and Dotty's kin groups. Despite my best efforts, the men remained comparatively marginal to my research. This is not just a problem of access. Rather, it accurately reflects men's more marginal participation in contemporary family life in North America. Economic pressures have always encouraged working-class women to form strong kin networks, while often weakening men's family ties.

My study suggests a masculinity crisis among blue-collar men. The decline of the family wage and escalation of female labour force participation are generating profound ambivalence about the eroding breadwinner ethic. Male kin are uncertain whether a man who provides sole support to a family is a hero or a chump. Too many of those I met expressed masculinity in antisocial, self-destructive and violent forms. At the same time, due to demands from women, more men are now involved in child care and domestic work than were "modern" husbands.

Hence, one of my research punch lines: "farewell to Archie Bunker." The research shattered my own false stereotype of the white working-class as the last repository of the old-fashioned "modern" North American family. Postmodern family arrangements among blue-collar families in Silicon Valley proved to be at least as diverse and innovative as within the middle class. Pam and Dotty each managed to transform divorce from a rupture to a kinship resource—cooperative, ex-familial relationships that are being imitated by some in the middle class. Accordian households and kin ties crafted by Dotty and Pam and by Katie's Christian ministry draw more on the "domestic network" traditions of poor African-Americans and on matrifocal strategies of working-class whites than on family reform innovations by the white middle-class. Ironically, sociologists are identifying a new middle-class "social problem"—crowded nests filled with "incompletely-launched young adults." This phenomenon is long familiar to the less-privileged, like Dotty.

The massive reorganization of work, class and gender since the 50s has turned family life into a contested terrain. Ironically, just when women are becoming the new working class, the postmodern family is becoming an increasingly female domain. There is hair-raising data in the U.S. that indicates a 43% decline between 1960 and 1980 in the duration of male residence with young children. Yet widespread lament over the family crisis is framed as women's abandonment of domesticity.

If there is a family crisis in my country, it's primarily a *male* family crisis, as large numbers of men either abandon their families entirely or absent themselves through long work weeks and male pursuits. Increasingly, people are coming to realize that it is impossible to restore the modern family system. Despite nostalgia, there is little evidence that most folks wish that gender order. The vast majority, like Pam, Dotty and kin, are actively remaking family life.

The second North American revolution—the overthrow of Ozzie and Harriet—is by now far advanced, and in my view, irreversible. However, it is also incomplete, ragged, and, in a historical sense, still raw. It also has had the historical misfortune of coinciding with the major decline of the American dream, readily symbolized by independent hearth and home, and with the racial diversification of our populations.

The greatest divergence in family patterns and resources today is actually between families with two steady earners and single-mother families. These divide fairly cleanly along racial, class, and ethnic lines. Marriage and male bread-winning increasingly are becoming a new form of race and class privilege.

"Family values" talk takes the focus off the social failings and shifts to the individual. It will never solve our national family problems.

The first North American family revolution replaced the diversity of premodern families with a uniform model that promised equality and justice, but couldn't deliver within its own terms. The second North American family revolution displaces the false uniformity of the modern family with postmodern diversity. It too holds promise for greater justice, but thus far only a privileged minority is reaping the full benefits. To distribute these more broadly might require not a family revolution, but a second North American social revolution.

QUESTIONS

DISCUSSION QUESTIONS

1. Rags to riches is a popular theme in fiction, from fairy tales to modern soaps to pulp fiction. Is marriage still a vehicle of upward mobility for women? Is marriage a source of economic security, if not mobility?

2. Surprisingly, young people do not seem to put a greater emphasis on chastity in the face of the AIDS virus. Indeed there is some resistance among young people to practising safe sex. How can we explain this seeming anomaly?

3. Describe and compare your early experiences of child care (parental care, relatives, private day care, public day care, nanny or housekeeper, and so on) with those of your classmates. What are the pros and cons of each method? Which method do you and your classmates recommend?

4. One frequently encounters "doom and gloom" references to changes in family living. Are these justified? Arbitrarily assign students to take one side or another in this debate, then as a class decide which side makes the stronger case.

DATA COLLECTION EXERCISES

1. A Canadian study of university students published in 1993 found that approximately 30 percent of the female college students had been victims of physical abuse while dating. Interview students to determine the extent of the problem at your campus.

2. One of the signals of family change is the increased number of people who cohabit. Using census data, look at the changes in cohabitation in Canada. Why do you think Quebec has much higher rates of cohabitation than any other region in Canada?

3. Given the current sexual permissiveness in our society, it may be hard to believe that before the 1960s strong stigmas prevailed in Canada against "divorcées," "living in sin," and "illegitimate" children. Sample magazines or newspapers from the '50s and the '70s to track the change in society's attitudes.

4. Investigate and compare old age security benefits provided by four countries of your choice. How does Canada rank in comparison to these other countries?

WRITING EXERCISES

1. Write your own ideal marriage contract, in 500 words or less.

2. Sweden has an extensive net of social services to support its citizens. Write a brief (500-word) essay describing how far you think the Canadian government should go in assuming responsibility for the care of dependent Canadians.

3. Script a brief (500-word) discussion between two friends, with one arguing that family life would be incomplete without children, and the other describing the benefits of childlessness.

4. Does pornography contribute to violence against women? In a brief (500-word) essay, evaluate the arguments on both sides and draw your own conclusion.

SUGGESTED READINGS

1. Baker, Maureen (1995). *Families: Changing Trends in Canada.* Toronto: McGraw-Hill Ryerson. This multi-authored text focuses on changing families in Canada. Topics covered include the origins of the family, mate selection, economic conditions and family structures, alternatives to traditional marriage, marital dissolution, family law, and patterns of family violence.

2. Mandell, N. and A. Duffy (1995). *Canadian Families: Diversity, Conflict and Change.* Toronto: Harcourt Brace. This reader focuses on family diversity, and includes chapters on gay and lesbian families, and the family life of Native Canadians. It also includes a section on the pressures of change, including poverty and violence.

3. Wilson, S. J. (1995). *Women, Families and Work,* Fourth Edition. Toronto: McGraw-Hill Ryerson. This brief overview of family change in Canada from the perspective of women includes historical sections on family change and housework.

SECTION 8   WORK

Introduction

A people's vocabulary can be a good indicator of what's important to them. And the rich vocabulary relating to the word "work" in a modern industrial society like ours confirms what a centrally important topic this is to us. As part of our cultural training we all learn to distinguish between concepts such as work and play, jobs and careers, professions and trades, labour and management, keeners and slackers, blue collar and white collar, sweatshops and gravy trains, vocations and vacations, time servers and go-getters, layoffs and dismissals, straight-time and over-time, and so on.

Most of us take no great pride in our ability to grasp these distinctions. But a sophisticated understanding of work doesn't mean that a consensus always exists on its meaning. The question of how to evaluate a job's worth is often in dispute. Guy Oakes' excerpt, for example, is about the battle endlessly raging within the hearts and minds of life insurance salespeople as they grapple with their occupation's status. Life insurance companies are always trying to get their salespeople to think highly of themselves as professionals, but it's hard for the salespeople to believe this knowing what little respect is accorded them by the general public.

Oakes' excerpt deals with one specific kind of job. But some of the earliest sociological debates on the meaning of work took a much broader, ambitiously macro, focus. In fact Marx, Durkheim, and Weber all wrote extensively about such Big Questions as the social and historical significance of changing work patterns. They all saw that, as industrial work supplanted agricultural work within their own lifetimes, Europe was becoming a new and different "modern society."

All three saw benefits in the emerging work structures and none romanticized the old structures that were being supplanted. But all three also warned of some chillingly inhumane aspects to the new modes of production.

MARX'S CONCERNS ABOUT INDUSTRIALIZATION

For Marx, the new capitalist industrialist production was inhumane because it alienated workers from their own humanity by thwarting their natural desire to see the creative act of making a product through from beginning to end. Under the new industrial system, workers were not allowed to perform multiple or complex tasks since it was more efficient to have them do only a few simple, repetitive actions that required endurance but not skill. The only "ability" valued in the new production mode was a capacity to suppress one's own natural and individualistic work rhythms in order to conform to the rhythms set by the machines. In the new system, it was the machine or the production process that set the pace of work, thereby inverting the traditional relationship between man and machine.

According to Marx, the new system also led to a dehumanizing of social relationships, mainly by upsetting the power balance between the social classes. The new system vastly increased the wealth and power of the factory owners, and sent the workers' fortunes in the opposite direction. The system's very efficiency meant that fewer workers were needed now, since the low skill requirements meant there would be more than enough qualified applicants for every job.

Marx held that as workers lost bargaining power vis-à-vis their employers they would suffer the fate that any suddenly weakened competitor suffers in any adversarial system. Their lives would get bleaker and nastier as more and more interpersonal relationships became poisoned by the new economic order. Employers would begin to see workers not as people but as "production costs" and as exploitable resources. Workers would start to view one another not as friends and neighbours but as competitors for scarce jobs.

Harry J. Van Buren III's excerpt shows that the exploitation of workers that Marx talked about is not something confined to the annals of history. It is a phenomenon recurring in the sweatshops of many newly industrializing countries.

DURKHEIM'S CONCERNS ABOUT SPECIALIZATION

Durkheim also worried about alienation resulting from the modern practice of breaking work up into narrowly specialized tasks. But he framed the issue differently. He too focused on how people can become alienated from one another, but he was also interested in "anomie"—the problem of modern individuals feeling alienated from the traditions and values of their culture. And for Durkheim, the main problem of alienation was not so much that it fuelled social conflicts but that it left people feeling rootless, disoriented, and disconnected.

Durkheim's premise was that a society's work provides the solidarity—the glue—that binds its people together. He believed that small, agricultural, pre-modern societies were held together by "mechanical solidarity." That was his term for the cohesiveness that results from people working together in close proximity, doing similar jobs that result in a similar standard of living for all of them. Their similar experiences provided a natural basis, Durkheim believed, for a shared culture.

Durkheim contrasted this image with the situation in modern industrial societies, where people do a wide variety of work in a wide variety of workplaces for widely varying rewards. In modern societies people don't usually work with or near their neighbours. It is common not to even know the names of one's neighbours, let alone their occupations.

In short, there is less common ground in a modern society because people share fewer life experiences. We have a harder time relating to one another and so misunderstandings and mistrust are more frequent. As a result society tends to fragment as individuals opt to stick to their own familiar and comfortable group. Traditional cultural beliefs and customs that used to provide a common cultural identity for all are replaced by numerous subcultures with their own unique and exclusionary beliefs. In other words, society becomes "unglued."

Counteracting this, according to Durkheim, was a new form of social glue called "organic solidarity." It was based on an intellectual recognition that the division of labour makes us mutually dependent on one another. We may not know, like, or understand our neighbours any more. But at least we know that we need them to keep making their unique contribution to society. And they know they need us. We can only hope that this abstract knowledge is strong enough to hold a society together.

WEBER'S WORRIES ABOUT BUREAUCRACY

Weber's worries about the human costs of the division of labour grew out of his analysis of bureaucracies. He believed that modern bureaucratic organizations are the most rational and efficient forms of organization ever devised. But their rational and efficient structures also caused Weber to write of "the iron cage of bureaucracy." Like Marx, he saw workers in a bureaucracy subordinating their own work rhythms and styles to those of the system. Reason and efficiency are intolerant masters; there is only one way—the best way—of doing things.

Like Durkheim, Weber knew that modern interpersonal relationships were more reserved and impersonal than relationships used to be. But Weber's analysis suggests that this too could be blamed on the bureaucratic values of rational efficiency. As Ester Reiter's excerpt on Canadian fast food workers shows, even interpersonal relationships can become part of a production process. The decision to react towards a customer in a spontaneous manner governed by one's mood becomes irrational and indefensible once it has been established that smiles, whether phoney or genuine, tend to produce higher hamburger sales.

FINAL THOUGHTS: ON THE OTHER HAND

But despite all of the above, sociology's founding fathers, much like today's commentators on post-industrialism, were ambivalent about the changes they saw. For Marx, modern production methods brought more than just alienation and misery for workers. It also brought them class consciousness, made socialism inevitable, and vastly increased the size of the economic pie to be divided up. Similarly, the fragmentation that Durkheim worried about is also the basis for the pluralism and tolerance of modern society. And Weber knew that the same lack of sentiment that rationalism creates also excludes such irrational feelings as bigotry, chauvinism, and favouritism.

Harry Van Buren III

THE EXPLOITATION OF
MEXICAN WORKERS

INTRODUCTION

Among the most basic questions that can be asked about any work is: what value does it have? What's a proper level of remuneration for a person doing this or that job?

In traditional economics, the theoretical free market answer is that employees will receive whatever the job market will bear. When labour is scarce workers will have strong bargaining leverage with their employers and so win pay raises. When labour is plentiful the power balance tips in the employers' favour and wages fall.

At best, this answer is amoral. It's about power balances rather than fairness. It says only that either side will take what it can because it can. To the extent that economists ever defend the morality of free markets, they usually argue that such markets promote economic efficiency, which in the long run leads to greater productivity and greater prosperity for the society as a whole.

Because economics is not much concerned with moral questions the issue of exploitation is usually raised only by non-economists. This leads to a lot of apples versus oranges arguments that pit efficiency against compassion, prosperity against equality, employers' interests against employee interests, and so on.

This excerpt tries to reconcile some of these conflicts with reference to Mexican workers by arguing that exploitation is a bad business practice in both economic and moral terms. The same analysis can be applied to increasingly market-driven economies, and governments, in Canada.

Workers in many low-income countries are invisible to the developed world. Whereas many manufactured goods consumed in the United States during the late nineteenth and early twentieth centuries were made in inner-city sweatshops, now many manufactured products are made in poor countries and imported into the United States. Labor rights such as a living wage and workplace safety are frequently ignored in many nations that export to this country. Companies rationalize low wage levels by stating that they pay more than the market-clearing rate—without thinking about whether their workers can afford even the necessities of life. Shoppers in the United States often overlook the conditions in which imported goods are produced.

Van Buren III, Harry J. (1995). "The Exploitation of Mexican Workers," *Business and Society Review*, Winter, *29-33*.

WAGES AND LABOR

In modern economic theory, wages are roughly a function of labor demand, labor supply, and skill levels required for particular jobs. In the United States wages are high and (at least partially) correlated with skill levels. Design, marketing, finance, and administration are all high-skill, high-wage occupational areas. U.S. manufacturing companies therefore will do most of their administrative and product development work in the United States.

Suppose a U.S. company develops a product that requires a low level of skill to assemble—a child's toy, for example. It would make certain economic sense to employ a relatively low-wage, low-skill work force to do the product assembly (assume in this example that the parts are manufactured in a U.S. plastics factory). U.S. wages are quite high, even for such mundane work.

A U.S. company in this situation can build a maquiladora factory in Mexico—a country where wage rates are much lower, the work force is usually nonunionized, and labor and environmental standards are not as stringent as those in the United States. The toys would be assembled in Mexico and shipped back to the United States for sale. The U.S. company only pays import tariffs on the value added in Mexico, not the full cost of the product.

This analysis guided the first maquiladora operations as U.S. companies moved unskilled jobs to Mexico during the 1980s. But now maquiladoras also exist in relatively high-wage, high-skill industries such as automobiles, chemicals, and electronics. In low- and high-skill occupations alike, Mexican workers only receive a small fraction of the wealth they create. Citizens in Mexico deserve a living wage in return for their labor. Unfortunately, a vast majority of maquiladora employees live in poverty and squalor.

Although other countries are building manufacturing facilities in Mexico, a vast majority of maquiladoras are owned by U.S. corporations: approximately 90 percent of the more than 2,000 plants. Conditions in these facilities are often horrific:

- In 1993 a lawsuit was filed against 88 maquila owners alleging that pollution from plants in the Matamoros area had caused at least 16 cases of anencephaly—a neural tube defect where the brain or part of it is missing. The rate of such births in Matamoros is four times that of the U.S. average. Several families settled their suits with some, but not all, of the defendants the following year.

- Workers protesting an allegedly fraudulent union election at a Nuevo Laredo Sony plant were attacked by police. The company's tactics were designed to force employees to work weekend shifts—the only time available for family and religious activities. The elections were not secret. Employees were required to line up in public on the side of either the union-prepared or the company slate.

- Several workers were fired at a Zenith plant in Reynosa after a positive pregnancy test.

- At another Zenith plant in Matamoros an annex not subject to the collective bargaining agreement with the main plant's employees has been built. Workers complain that the entrance to the plant is too narrow and a fire would lead to disaster.

Companies moving to Mexico from the United States can avoid labor regulations taken for granted by U.S. workers. But relatively low wage and benefit levels offer the most important incentive for maquila operators—wage levels that barely support a Mexican family's basic needs. For many years, there was anecdotal evidence of economic deprivation among Mexican workers. But a recent study concerning the standard of living that maquiladora wages will buy in Mexico has quantified the tremendous human need now being experienced by employees and their families.

PURCHASING POWER PARITY

To compare income levels between countries, it is useful to differentiate between money income and income at purchasing power parity (PPP income).

For the purposes of analyzing consumption patterns, money income is an employee's take-home pay (gross pay less any workplace deductions less taxes). PPP income measures what a worker can actually purchase for consumption. PPP income is a more accurate way to compare wages and consumption levels between countries because it adjusts for price differences.

Getting at the issue of how much a maquila worker is paid, however, is not easy. The current gross minimum wage, as set by Mexican law, is approximately 110 new pesos per 48-hour week. The unionized plants of Matamoros earn a higher wage, averaging $2.45 per hour. Calculating average PPP income (most important for analyzing living standards) is unfortunately quite difficult.

There is, however, a methodology that helps clarify this issue. The methodology starts by identifying a market basket of nonluxury goods such as food, over-the-counter medicines, and cleaning supplies. After determining how much a worker makes per hour, a simple calculation translates hourly take-home pay into a measure of how many minutes an employee must work to purchase a particular item. Differences in compensation and market prices between countries are therefore collapsed into a uniform comparative measure.

To address the issue of how much maquiladora wages would buy in Mexico, F.L. Putnam Securities Company developed a "market basket survey" comparing wages paid to United Auto Workers union members working for General Motors in the United States and to maquiladora employees in Mexico. GM was selected for the survey because it operates more maquilas in Mexico than any other U.S. corporation, and also because it has closed many plants in the U.S. and opened similar facilities in Mexico. It can be argued that Mexican workers are therefore being substituted for U.S. employees, to the detriment of workers in both countries. The UAW-GM contract book specified a first-quarter 1994 gross wage of $18.03 per hour. Using 65 percent as the average take-home portion of gross wages (deducting 35 percent for taxes), the net hourly wage was calculated to be $11.72 per hour. The average hourly take-home pay for Mexican maquiladora workers averages $1.06 per hour.

GOODS FOR FAMILY SURVIVAL

Survey volunteers shopped for a basket of goods that would be needed for family survival. After averaging both wages and prices in the U.S. and Mexico, a chart comparing the minutes of work necessary to purchase different items was compiled.

TABLE 1

Item	Amount	Work Minutes Mexico	Work Minutes U.S.
		Mexico	U.S.
Apple	1 lb.	32.3	4.3
Aspirin	100	250.0	22.1
Bacon	1 lb.	60.0	10.7
Bread, white	20 oz.	45.1	4.1
Butter	1 lb.	315.8	7.3
Carrots	1 lb.	11.9	1.5
Cheese (Amer.)	1 lb.	214.3	12.6
Chicken, whole	1 lb.	87.0	4.5
Coffee, ground	13 oz.	117.6	8.4
Corn flakes	1 lb.	111.1	9.3
Flour, white	5 lb.	11.9	5.9
Ham, fresh	1 lb.	176.5	11.9
Jelly	18 oz.	84.5	7.0
Juice, orange	64 oz.	136.4	3.1
Ketchup	28 oz.	127.7	7.3
Macaroni	1 lb.	32.3	4.2
Milk, whole	1 gal.	142.9	12.2
Paper towels	1 roll	51.7	3.0
Peanut butter	16 oz.	166.7	8.4
Razor blades	5	150.0	8.2
Rice	5 lbs.	69.0	13.5
Salt	26 oz.	20.4	1.8
Sugar	5 lbs.	96.8	8.4
Tomatoes, fresh	1 lb.	20.4	5.7

Several points should be noted:

- Although prices in Mexico are somewhat lower than those in the United States, such differentials are not so great that they make up for lower Mexican wages.

- Purchasing power for UAW workers is obviously much greater than that of the average maquiladora worker. Even the higher Matamoros take-home wage of $2.45 provides only a survival standard of living.

- The survey humanizes the issue of income for maquila workers. One could take the market basket survey and his or her personal grocery list for a week and determine if they could maintain their standard of living on a 40- or 48-hour work week.

When plants move from high-wage to low-wage geographic areas, capital owners generally benefit at the expense of labor providers. Are the interests of labor suppliers and capital owners inevitably at odds? This question lies at the heart of business-society relationships.

LABOR VS. CAPITAL

Holders of capital have more market power than suppliers of labor. It is inevitable that the latter will be abused by the former. It is not difficult to find examples of such exploitation. Our own country's history, for example, is replete with horror stories of child laborers, long workdays with no benefits, of people used up by greedy factory owners and then summarily discarded. A similar dynamic can currently be observed in Mexico—a country that only now is developing (albeit tentatively) a tradition of democracy, human rights, and an impersonal rule of law.

The ownership of capital does not confer an inalienable right to deny workers a fair wage, mistreat them, or subject them to unsafe working conditions. Unfortunately, macroeconomic policy often harms the interests of workers. For most of the last half century in both the United States and Mexico, governmental policy has promoted the interests of capital owners at the expense of labor suppliers. Most of what has been called supply-side economics in the United States—lower marginal tax rates, higher defense spending, reduced spending on social welfare programs, regulatory "reform" (read: gutting enforcement of labor and safety laws)—was instituted during the Reagan presidency. Supply-side economic policies were designed to generate aggregate wealth creation, but instead contributed to economic inequality.

But there have also been voices in the economic wilderness that have made a connection between equity and economic efficiency. Alan Blinder, the current vice chairman of the U.S. Federal Reserve System, wrote that:

> We must marry the hard head to the soft heart, join the calculating accountant to the caring social worker. Conservatives must accept the principle of equity and realize that intelligently designed policies need not interfere unduly with efficiency. Liberals must gain greater respect for efficiency and learn that conservative ends can be harnessed to liberal means.

Justice and efficiency are complementary goals—one cannot exist in an economic system without the other. There is, fortunately, a theory as old as modern economics that can help analyze the issue of Mexican poverty-level wages—with surprising results.

Critics of capitalism (Marx et al.) have long alleged that workers do not receive wages that reflect their contribution to production. Both domestically and internationally, wage structures and differentials have served to create economic polarization. Social discord and poverty often have been the unhappy result. It is perhaps time to apply the labor theory of value concept to an analysis of Mexican wage levels—the idea that the price of a good or service should depend on its labor content. This theory is associated with Karl Marx, but Adam Smith (the father of modern economics) also gave it great credence:

> The real value of all the different component parts of price, it must be observed, is measured by the quantity of labour which they can, each of them, purchase or command. Labour measures the value not only of that part of price which resolves itself into labour, but of that which resolves itself into rent [of land or physical capital] and that which resolves itself into profit.

In Smith's conception, labor serves as the unit of account—a function in modern economics ascribed to money (as a proxy for land, labor, and capital). If labor serves as the unit of account for economic production (as suggested by Smith), then it follows that capital exists for the benefit of labor, rather than the other way around. This is not to say that capital formation is not important in a capitalist economy—quite the contrary. Without aggregations of capital that are called companies or corporations, it would be difficult to employ everyone in a society. The Industrial Revolution in the United States and Europe was sustained by the fact that industrial production was more efficient than production by individual artisans, making possible (eventually) a higher standard of living for everyone in those societies except the very poor.

But only eventually did the Industrial Revolution lead to higher standards of living for the vast majority of citizens. As previously mentioned, governmental policy in this country and others during the Revolution's early years (c. 1870–1920) was heavily tilted in favor of capital owners. Child labor laws, unionization, worker safety regulations—all of these mechanisms that allowed workers to achieve the standard of living they deserved did not manifest themselves until much later in the Industrial Revolution. As Henry Ford understood, giving workers a living wage and treating them fairly was in the best long-term interests of the employer—something that was as true then as it is now. Work therefore exists not singularly for the benefit of either the individual or society but rather both simultaneously.

CUSTODIANS OF CAPITAL

The main focus of economic theory should be the creation of systems that will provide for the well-being of all citizens. Perhaps one good starting place for the creation of a more equitable social contract between capital owners and laborers is a recognition that people (and institutions) who own productive wealth should do so as custodians of capital. As custodians of capital, capital owners have a duty to use it wisely for the public good—and especially for the good of workers, without whom capital owners would be unable to produce anything of value. Speaking about the need for philanthropy (albeit from a strongly capitalist framework), Andrew Carnegie wrote:

The only point required by the gospel of wealth is that the surplus which accrues from time to time in the hands of a man should be administered by him in his own lifetime for that purpose which is seen by him, as a trustee, to be the best for the good of the people.

Carnegie's point can be equally applied to the ownership of capital.

To speak of the labor theory of value as a guiding principle for society means that people and machines exist in a symbiotic relationship, but the needs of people are paramount. Far from being a social/Marxist utopian vision for the world where everyone earns the same wages, the labor theory of value provides a theoretical connection between economics and social justice. It would also help alleviate poverty among people who are economically productive but not receiving a fair wage for their work. The economic value created by maquiladora workers, for example, must be shared with them as a matter of both social justice and economic efficiency.

Policies that promote income equality in the short run boost economic growth in the long run. The problem is that the returns to capital are greater than those of labor in the initial stages of economic development—because capital is scarce while labor is plentiful.

When policies to improve returns to labor (minimum wages, labor standards) are proposed, they are often opposed by capital owners. Balancing the interests of the two groups can be understood only as a long-term phenomenon—if capital owners are willing to pay higher (than market-clearing) wages in the short run commensurate with the economic output generated by workers, income growth will be higher in the long run than it would have been in the absence of egalitarian policies.

Capital owners are not to be despised or eliminated—but they do have a duty to act for the common good. Mexico illustrates what can happen when people serve an economy instead of the economy serving a people. It is a highly stratified society, but it can potentially become prosperous and just—although it cannot be either prosperous or just. In the long run, economic inequality is inefficient.

Guy Oakes

THE AMERICAN LIFE INSURANCE SALESMAN: A SECULAR THEODICY

INTRODUCTION

The comedian Woody Allen used to joke that one way to commit suicide would be to inhale next to a life insurance salesman. Such nasty humour is funny stuff, unless of course you actually happen to be a life insurance salesman.

The following excerpt examines how life insurance salespeople cope with doing a job that is widely conceded to be legitimate, but which is also viewed as annoying, boring, and vaguely depressing. In many ways, life insurance salespeople have a fairly unique public relations problem. Even though their product is necessary and worthwhile, potential customers are rarely eager to see them.

As Oakes' excerpt shows, the life insurance salesperson's lot is to be shunned, ignored, postponed, rescheduled, rejected, ejected, and often insulted. Only the thick-skinned survive. Only a very few persevere to prosper and thrive.

In part, salespeople cope by trying to see themselves as professionals in a potentially lucrative business offering a legitimate product. The insurance companies reinforce this kind of positive thinking with morale-boosting training sessions and sales conventions. But ultimately, Oakes suggests, the salespeople who persevere best are the ones who learn to take pride in their ability to handle adversity. It's a coarser version of the old "when the world hands you lemons, make lemonade" motto.

As you read the excerpt, see if you can relate it to Max Weber's famous analyses of rationality and a secular Protestant work ethic. For Oakes is exploring the evolution of this work ethic in a hostile and grudging business environment.

Professional sales personnel have an obligation to see to it that clients treat their joint relationship in a purely professional fashion. In the life insurance industry, the social mechanisms necessary to establish and legitimize professional status are not in place. This is why training manuals instruct agents—inelegantly, bluntly, and with brutal candor—that it is crucial for them to "sell the prospect on their professionalism." Why should this be necessary? It is due to the fact that, in important respects and for a number of evident reasons, life insurance agents are not acknowledged professionals at all.

Oakes, Guy (1990). "The Life Insurance Salesman: A Secular Theodicy" *International Journal of Politics, Culture and Society*, 4, 1, 95–112.

From the standpoint of the cognitive dimension of professionalism, agents receive no training comparable to the education of the physician, the attorney, or even the dentist or the accountant. From the standpoint of the status dimension, the agent is notoriously lacking in prestige. Even in the industry there is considerable ambivalence concerning the prestige of agents and their work. On the one hand, industry managers know that agents want to believe in their prestige. Indeed, this belief is regarded as a condition for their effective performance. On the other hand, industry managers themselves are responsible for commissioning LIMRA research that documents the virtually universal disdain in which the agent is held by the public. The conclusions established by this research confirm what Woody Allen told us some years ago at the end of *Love and Death*: If you have spent an evening with a life insurance agent, you know there are some things worse than death itself.

The contempt in which they are held is a theme that appears repeatedly in interviews with agents. General terms such as professional status or prestige rarely appear in these accounts. Two complaints are especially frequent: the hours wasted in waiting for prospects who do not keep appointments, which is said to exhibit prospects' disrespect for agents, and the ill-mannered and insolent treatment agents receive at the hands of employees near the lower end of organizational charts—gatekeepers whose job is to isolate the prospect from the agent. As regards the latter complaint, one agent reports as follows.

> There's something I often notice when I go into an office—a lot of my friends have this, in fact. There is a sign in a lot of these places. You walk in and it says: "Absolutely No Solicitors!" You know, it's the first thing you see. Really, what they're saying is: "No goddamn salesmen, no insurance salesmen, no pharmaceutical salesmen. We don't want any of you jerk-offs here without seeing so-and-so." And so-and-so is the lowest paid, lowest-rung person, who now has a chance to assert his or her authority over you. These are the people you have to deal with, who just can't wait to shit all over you. It's very frustrating.

How do agents carry on in spite of these frustrations? How do they take it? This agent claims that there are no satisfactory solutions to this problem.

> How do I take it? You really get shit on in this business. Car salesmen, aluminum siding salesmen, insurance salesmen—you're really garbage. The insurance industry, of course, is aware of this, but they don't want the agent to think of himself that way. For obvious reasons. But believe me, you're really treated shitily. For me, it's very difficult. I'm not able to wash it off. I'm always going to these office complexes where there are doctors, accountants, and lawyers. You go in there and you start knocking on doors. Sometimes the secretaries will let you in. I'll be sitting there, and there'll be a secretary younger than my daughter, right? Who may or may not have graduated high school. She's painting her finger nails, watching a soap opera on a little tv set. And she treats you like you're lower than an asshole. She'll sit there and let people come in ahead of you. Even if you've made an appointment to see somebody. You're on the bottom of the barrel, the last guy anybody's gonna see. So you make an eleven o'clock appointment. You get there at eleven o'clock. At eleven-thirty, you finally ask this girl, and she just says: "Well, you'll have to wait. He's very busy." And just ignores you. You know? And you ask yourself: What am I doing here? Why am I in this business? You're just so unimportant to these people.

Industry managers do not assume that agents are so obtuse as to believe what everyone knows to be false. This is why industry claims about the prestige of the agent are often framed in an equivocal and oblique fashion. Prestige is said to be something that agents must earn. It is a value they produce in their work as sales personnel. No one gains prestige merely by virtue of becoming an insurance agent. In fact, given the derision, scorn, and sheer bad manners that must be borne by those who have chosen this occupation, precisely the contrary seems to be the case.[1]

Finally, from the standpoint of the normative dimension, the conduct of the agent is not subject to a guild ethic enforced by gatekeeper organizations. Agents who commit moral or legal lapses in their work at one company may have no difficulty moving to another company, or even transferring to another agency within the same organization. Consider the following account of the arrangements made to retain rogue agents.

> If you get caught doing something that's really hideous or really embarrassing to the company, they'll fire you outright, ostensibly for "breaking regulations." Otherwise, it doesn't happen. There was one guy who left Covenant Life to work for Verity who was supposedly keeping premiums instead of sending them up to the company. Can you imagine that? Now you're entering the grounds of fraud, felony, you know, stealing. Verity supposedly let him go. But I later found out that they basically suspended him for ninety days and let him do business. At my agency, there is somebody who committed outright criminal fraud. He's still working there. No problem. They licensed somebody else to sign all his applications. Of course the reason is the numbers. This guy is a great salesman, and they wanted to keep him. They worked something out. This happens a lot. A first-rate agent doesn't truly get fired from an insurance company unless he's going to jail. Or unless he becomes a total embarrassment. We might close this little vignette by saying that if you're a really successful agent, it's almost impossible to get fired. Arrangements get made.

Another agent offers the following remarks on the kinds of arrangements that are made in such cases.

> Here's a possible scenario. I come to general agent Joe Blow and say: "Look, I can supply you with one $30,000 premium every June. But my past record is a little spotty. I went bankrupt. I embezzled money from my previous employer. I did three months in Allenwood [minimum security federal penitentiary in Pennsylvania]. You know, I'm not gonna get a license! All the general agents I've ever worked with would say: "Fine. Call the prospect up every June. Call me up, and we'll go see the prospect together. We'll take the application, and I'll sign it. We'll take the case, and when the commission comes to me, there are various ways we can cut you in. Straight cash. Or we make you a consultant of some sort and pay you a finder's fee." All above board and legitimate. In other words, there are ways these things get worked out if I, an ex-con, have business to bring into the agency.

In sum, the life insurance industry expects agents to appear to be what they are not: namely, professionals. This means that agents must endeavor to act as if they were professionals and prove their professionalism to the prospect. How does the life insurance industry respond to the discrepancies between the ideal of professional service inculcated in training programs and the realities encountered by the sales force in the field? The answer to this question lies in three quite different strategies. The first is based on a philosophy of financial security that enables the agent to endure the psychic stress and metaphysical emptiness of life in personal sales. The second is based on the role of sales conventions, which are carefully staged productions designed by the industry as rituals of recognition that celebrate the virtues of the service ideal, reinforce a commitment to its principles, and reward agents who measure up to its requirements. The third is based on a sales force ethic of toughness, imperturbability, and nonchalance that endows agents with the iron-clad defenses and hardened sensibilities required to perform their sales tracks with poise and bland affability in the face of insult and humiliation.

THE SALES CONVENTION

In the personal sales industry, the ideal of professional service is powerfully reinforced by the rites to which the agent is subjected at company sales conventions. From the standpoint of the care and feeding of the sales force, the convention functions essentially as a legitimation ritual.[2] Conventions are generally held either in a major city, featuring tourist attractions and prime shopping opportunities for the daytime amusement of spouses and children, or at a "mega-resort." New and promising agents as well as experienced high achievers are celebrated in reward ceremonies and cheered on by motivational speakers. Both agents and their families are showered with prizes, perquisites, and entertainments that testify to their success. Successful performers and their families receive spacious and impressively appointed quarters. Luxurious "theme suites" with fresh flowers, imported champagnes, and other accessories are reserved for higher achievers. The top performers may be diverted with even more exotic accommodations and perquisites: a flight to Tangier, Bangkok, or Hong Kong; extravagant suites with marble bathrooms; daily fashion shows; and lavish gifts such as porcelain tea sets and silk robes.[3]

The main purpose of the convention is to recharge the energies and pump up the egos of sales personnel, to inspire the sales force to ever higher levels of achievement. Short blocks of time in business meetings are reserved for brief speeches by upper-level managers from the home office. These remarks are intended to increase the self-esteem of sales personnel, a part of their equipment likely to be severely battered after a year of rough treatment at the hands of boorish and recalcitrant prospects. In documenting the size and traditions of the company, its impressively diversified holdings and carefully managed portfolio of investments, company officers encourage sales personnel to identify themselves with the prestige claimed by the company and link their fate with what is represented as a major growth industry. These exquisitely choreographed presentations are served up with an assortment of company-commissioned videos, often of commercial television quality and set against the background of upbeat but unobtrusive white-disco music. Final scenes are generally devoted to a few select members of the sales force: unusually successful performers of recent years together with their families, captured in some "world-class" resort playground enjoying the fruits of their commissions.

Agents who devote themselves systematically and unremittingly to the disciplines of the sales process are congratulated at the convention for performing in precisely the ways that are responsible for their presence there. The ethos of the convention presupposes that success and prestige are tied to the demands of the professional ideal. Agents who fail to measure up to these demands are not charged with weakness and defeatism. At the convention, they are not even mentioned. It is as if they did not exist, a wordless condemnation to the social hell reserved for those whose identity has been forgotten. In the end, it is hard work and training in the basics that produce success. Prime-time on the speaker's platform at the convention is reserved for inspirational talks by super salesmen who reinforce the doctrine that even the highest paid performers achieve their results by applying the simplest principles of sales training programs: setting goals that are challenging but not unreasonable; fashioning the plans required to reach these goals; and acquiring the training and practicing the skills essential to the execution of these plans. Thus the message of the convention—pounded into the agent in a heady emotional atmosphere that combines elements of televangelism, Las Vegas lounge acts, the Miss America Pageant, and television game shows—produces powerful sanctions that reconfirm the industry theory of the sales process as a seamless synthesis of commerce and professional service.

DEGRADATION CEREMONIES

In the interest of closing sales, agents are expected to endure repeated rejections and suffer veiled, and occasionally even open, attacks on their honesty. They must master their own emotions, which could threaten to explode into a dispute with the prospect that would be virtually certain to terminate the possibility of a sale. And they must absorb repeated rebuffs to their pride and self-respect and learn to live with the knowledge that they are regarded as crass, deceitful, and mendacious. Consider the position of the novice agent.

> In the beginning, I had to learn how to use the phone—phone solicitation. That's when I had to use these sales tracks [company produced scripts]. Cold calling, which is a very bad experience. Every Tuesday and Thursday, I had to stay at the office at night. Because what you do is call these people at dinner time. You know how you hate getting calls at dinner time? Well, I was one of these people. They would just hang up on you and treat you like shit all the time. That's the way I felt. This is a problem with being a good insurance agent. The problem is not to feel this way. I assume this is what they were treating me like. But my manager said: "Look, that's your own imagination. Just hit em, one after the other. Just forget about who they are. Don't personalize it. Don't become emotional about any of these things." But it was very tough.

Or consider the everyday degradation ceremonies to which an agent is subjected.

> My partner and I went to see an officer of some big company near Philly. This guy was extremely impolite. In fact, he treated us like shit. He said he was interested in an estate plan. The thing is, we saw this guy three times. Each time was more embarrassing than the last. It became clear in the end that this guy was only using us for information, picking our brains with regard to different kinds of proposals we had. He probably had an in-house person to take care of this and just wanted to

check up on him. I guess the key here is that as a trainee, I was introduced to this idea that you can't be concerned with being embarrassed or treated like shit.

In order to survive in the trenches where the dirty war for the commitment of prospects is fought, agents must steel themselves to withstand the constant stress, the attacks on their integrity and their metier, and the routine experience of conflict, fear, and uncertainty. The life insurance industry attempts to limit the damage to the professional identity of the agent with the underpinnings provided by the philosophy of financial security and the reaffirmation and legitimation rituals celebrated at sales conventions. However, agents themselves respond to the conflicts between the ideal of professional service and the exigencies of personal sales in ways that are not sanctioned by the training programs in which they are socialized. The most important protective mechanism developed by agents is a sales force ethic of cynical toughness. The ethic at stake here seems to approximate much more closely a pathos of masculine anti-heroism: being able to take it, having the endurance to stand up under indignities, degradations, even catastrophes that are prepared for the agent by the fates that govern the world of personal sales. In view of the demands of life insurance sales, it is difficult to see how agents could withstand the rigors of everyday life in the industry without developing protective insensitivities and a defiant pride in their ability to keep going, regardless of the humiliations they face. The agent who is respected by his fellows—and it is clearly a male agent that this ethic envisions—is precisely someone who "can take it," who can hold his professional posture intact and maintain an appearance of insouciance and savoir faire in spite of the shocks he must absorb.

Agents frequently express the sort of fortitude they respect by using a crude metaphor of defecation and consumption, the prospect doing the former, the agent the latter. The seasoned agent is said to be capable of eating immense quantities of shit. Such an agent, who has endured weeks or months of failure, rejection, and denigration at the hands of prospects, is said to be able to respond to this treatment with the defiant provocation "Shit on me again!"—a strangely perverse expression of hauteur and insolence in the face of adversity. This is not primarily a way of contending that the agent can retain his self-respect and dignity in spite of the abominations that are heaped upon him. It is rather a coarse reaffirmation of his determination to keep going, regardless of what he must suffer, until he closes the sale.

CONCLUSION

It may be the case that the ideal of professional service enunciated in sales training programs conflicts with the realities of the sales process that agents encounter in the field. However both the life insurance industry and agents themselves respond to these conflicts in ways that diminish their force and obscure their import.

By means of quite different strategies, the philosophy of financial security, the legitimation ceremonies performed at sales conventions, and the agent ethic of cynical toughness maintain the fiction of a basic consistency between the ideal of professional service and the exigencies of the sales process. This fiction requires that even if the sales process is a struggle for power over who controls the terms, logic, and direction of the interaction between agent and prospect, the agent can prevail in this struggle only by gaining the trust of the prospect. The realities of the sales process may compel agents to engage in sales as a form of urban guerilla warfare in which success requires an aggressive, take-no-prisoners attitude, and this attitude may be driven by the narrowest conception of self-interest imaginable. However, agents can succeed often enough to return and do battle again only if they consistently meet certain expectations of the prospect. Thus the vulgar utilitarian ethic of pure self-interest must be tempered by a fiduciary ethic of professional responsibility. In the long run, success is possible only for agents whose self-interested motives include an interest in putting the prospect first. Paradoxically, agents can exploit all their opportunities for sales only if they restrain their own opportunistic motives. This means that agents can master the commercial demands of the sales process only if they also respect the requirements of the ideal of professional service.

ENDNOTES

[1] On the ambivalence of industry literature concerning the esteem in which agents and their work are held, see *New England Life Associate's Career Track*, unit I, module 1 (Boston: New England Life, 1983). On the low occupational prestige and "occupational stigma" that attach to life insurance sales, see Zelizer, *Morals and Markets*, pp. 134–140. Zelizer borrows Erving Goffman's concept of stigma to elucidate the sense in which life insurance agents are contaminated by the "dirty work" of profiting from death. See Erving Goffman, *Stigma* (Englewood Cliffs, NJ: Prentice-Hall, 1963). On the low prestige of personal sales in general, see Prus, *Making Sales*, pp. 262–263.

[2] On the company conventions held by direct selling organizations as legitimization rituals, see Nicole Woolsey Biggart, *Charismatic Capitalism: Direct Selling Organizations in America* (Chicago: University of Chicago Press, 1989), pp. 126–127.

[3] See Leslie Aldridge Westoff, "As Incentive, Anything Goes," *The Business World: The New York Times Magazine*, April 2, 1989, p. 81.

Ester Reiter

WORK IN A CANADIAN FAST-FOOD FACTORY

INTRODUCTION

Picture yourself working in a "post-industrial information age economy." Chances are you're seeing a futuristic-looking office filled with computers, fax machines, and other high-tech equipment. It's less likely that you've pictured yourself in a high-tech restaurant, wearing a uniform and giving people their burgers, fries, shakes, and change. But in fact both kinds of workplaces are common in a post-industrial economy.

In this excerpt Ester Reiter describes this second kind of post-industrial workplace by showing us the work that goes on in a Toronto Burger King. In some ways her description makes us wonder if the term "post-industrial" isn't a misnomer. Apparently industrial-age assembly line work procedures haven't died out after all. They've just been moved out of the factories and into the fast food restaurants.

Fast food workers, like factory workers, use expensive pieces of machinery to perform simple repetitive tasks under close supervision in an assembly line environment. Like factory workers, they have little scope for individual innovation and find their work pace set by the machines they tend. Any deviation from the routine prescribed by head office is forbidden since it would likely reduce efficiency.

But fast food employees face an added burden that factory workers don't. As service workers meeting the public they become part of the "package" being sold. They are on display and so must submit to having their personal appearance, speech, and demeanour monitored, moulded and, as much as possible, standardized. An irregular personality, it seems, is as unacceptable to the system as an underdone french fry or a burnt burger.

This paper focuses on the technology and the labour process in the fast-food industry. Using Marx's description of the transitions from craft to manufacture to large-scale industry, it considers the changes in the restaurant industry brought about by the development of fast-food chains. The description of life in a fast-food factory is based on my experience working in a Burger King outlet in 1980/1.

Founded in 1954 by James McLamore and David Edgerton, Burger King became a wholly-owned subsidiary of Pillsbury in 1967. The company grew from 257 restaurants at the time of the merger to 3,022 by May 1981. About 130,000 people are employed in Burger Kings all over the world. By November 1982, there were 87 Burger King stores in Canada, 40 of them company owned.[1]

Reiter, Ester (1986). "Life in a Fast-Food Factory," pp. 309–326 in Craig Heron and Robert Storey (eds.), *On the Job: Confronting the Labour Process in Canada*. Kingston and Montreal: McGill-Queen's University Press. Reprinted by permission.

TRANSFORMING THE OPERATIONS OF A KITCHEN

Until approximately 25 years ago, all restaurant work involved an extensive division of labour: a complex hierarchy within the kitchen required workers with varying levels of skill and training. For a restaurant to be successful, all workers' had to co-ordinate their efforts. A supervisor's function was not only to ensure that the work was done, but to see that the various parts of the operation were synchronized.

This production arrangement resembles what Marx called "manufacture." The skill of the worker remains central to the production process. The commodity created (the meal served to the customer) is the social product of many workers' efforts. Human beings, using tools to assist them in their work, remain the organs of the productive mechanism.

In the fast-food industry, the machines, or the instruments of labour, assume a central place. Instead of assisting workers, the machines are dominant. Marx described this as the transition from "manufacture" to "large-scale industry."[2] Since the motion of the factory proceeds from the machinery and not from the worker, working personnel can continually be replaced. Frequent change in workers will not disrupt the labour process—a shift in organization applauded by Harvard Business Review contributor, Theodore Levitt.[3] According to Levitt, this new model is intended to replace the "humanistic concept of service" with the kind of technocratic thinking that in other fields has replaced "the high cost and erratic elegance of the artisan with the low-cost munificence of the manufacturer."

The labour process admired by Levitt has been adopted by many of the large fast-food companies including Burger King.

MANAGING A STORE

The brain centre of all Burger King outlets lies in Burger King headquarters in Miami, Florida. There the Burger King bible, the *Manual of Operating Data*, is prepared. The procedures laid down in the manual must be followed to the letter by all Burger King stores. To ensure procedures are followed, each outlet is investigated and graded twice yearly by a team from regional headquarters.

In order to maximize volume and minimize labour costs, there is tremendous emphasis on what Burger King management calls speed of service. Demand is at its peak during the lunch hour, which accounts for about 20 percent of sales for the day; the more people served during the hour twelve to one, the higher the sales volume in the store.

Ideally, service time should never exceed three minutes.[4] Labour costs are also kept down by minimizing the use of full-time workers and by hiring minimum-wage part-time workers. Workers fill out an availability sheet when they are hired, indicating the hours they can work. Particularly when students are involved, management pressures them to make themselves as available as possible, though no guarantees are provided for how many hours a week work they will be given, or on which days they will be asked to work.

Scheduling is done each week for the coming week and workers are expected to check the schedule each week to see when they are supposed to show up. The

Manual of Operating Data recommends as many short shifts as possible be assigned, so that few breaks will be required.

Food and paper costs make up about 40 percent of the cost of sales in Burger King outlets. These costs are essentially fixed, owing to company requirements that all Burger King outlets buy their stock from approved distributors. In effect, individual stores have control over food costs in only two areas—"waste" of food and meals provided to employees. Both together make up less than four percent of the cost of sales.

Store operations are designed from head office in Miami. By late 1981, it was possible to provide store managers not only with a staffing chart for hourly sales—indicating how many people should be on the floor given the predicted volume of business for that hour—but also where they should be positioned, based on the type of kitchen design. Thus, what discretion managers formerly had in assigning and utilizing workers has been eliminated.

Having determined precisely what workers are supposed to be doing and how quickly they should be doing it, the only remaining issue is getting them to perform to specifications. "Burger King University," located at headquarters in Miami was set up to achieve this goal. Burger King trains its staff to do things "not well, but right," the Burger King way.[5] Tight control over Burger King restaurants throughout the world rests on standardizing operations—doing things the "right" way—so that outcomes are predictable.

WORKING AT BURGER KING

I did fieldwork at a Burger King outlet in suburban Toronto in 1980/1. The Burger King at which I worked was opened in 1979, and by 1981 was the highest volume store in Canada with annual sales of over one million dollars.

Workers use the back entrance at Burger King when reporting for work. Once inside, they go to a small room (about seven by twelve feet), which is almost completely occupied by an oblong table where crew members have their meals. Built-in benches stretch along both sides of the wall, with hooks above for coats. Homemade signs, put up by management, decorate the walls.

The crew room is usually a lively place. An AM/FM radio is tuned to a rock station while the teenage workers coming off or on shift talk about school and weekend activities or flirt with each other. Children and weddings are favourite topics of conversation for the older workers. Each worker must punch a time card at the start of a shift. A positioning chart, posted near the time clock, lists the crew members who are to work each meal, and indicates where in the kitchen they are to be stationed.

There are no pots and pans in the Burger King kitchen. As almost all foods enter the store ready for the final cooking process, pots and pans are not necessary. The major kitchen equipment consists of the broiler/toaster, the fry vats, the milkshake and coke machines, and the microwave ovens. In the near future, new drink machines will be installed in all Burger King outlets that will automatically portion the drinks. At Burger King, hamburgers are cooked as they pass through the broiler on a conveyor belt at a rate of 835 patties per hour. Furnished with a pair of tongs, the worker picks up the burgers as they drop off the belt, puts each on a toasted bun, and places the hamburgers and buns in a steamer.

The more interesting part of the procedure lies in applying condiments and microwaving the hamburgers. The popularity of this task among employees rests on the fact that it is unmechanized and allows some discretion to the worker. However, management is aware of this area of worker freedom and makes efforts to eliminate it by outlining exactly how this job is to be performed.

Despite such directives, the "Burger and Whopper Board" positions continue to hold their attraction for the workers, for this station requires two people to work side by side, and thus allows the opportunity for conversation. During busy times, as well, employees at this station also derive some work satisfaction from their ability to "keep up." At peak times, the challenge is to not leave the cashiers waiting for their orders.

As with the production of hamburgers, the cooking of french fries involves virtually no worker discretion. The worker, following directions laid out in the *Manual of Operating Data*, empties the frozen, pre-cut, bagged fries into fry baskets about two hours before they will be needed. When cooked fries are needed, the worker takes a fry basket from the rack and places it on a raised arm above the hot oil, and presses the "on" button. The arm holding the fry basket descends into the oil, and emerges two minutes and twenty seconds later; a buzzer goes off and the worker dumps the fries into the fry station tray where they are kept warm by an overhead light. To ensure the proper portions are placed into bags, a specially designed tool is used to scoop the fries up from the warming table.

Even at this station, though, management is concerned about limiting worker discretion. Despite the use of a specially designed scoop to control the portions each customer is given, a sign placed in the crew room for a few weeks admonished crew about being too generous with fry portions.

At the cash register, the "counter hostess" takes the order and rings it up on the computerized register. The "documentor" contains 88 colour coded items, ensuring that all variations of an order are automatically priced. As a menu item is punched in at the counter, it will appear on printers in the appropriate location in the kitchen. In this manner, the worker at sandwiches, for example, can look up at the printer and check what kind of sandwich is required. When the customer hands over the money, the cashier rings in "amount tendered" and the correct amount of change to be returned to the customer is rung up. Thus, cashiers need only remember to smile and ask customers to come again.

The computerized cash register not only simplifies ordering and payment, but is used to monitor sales and thus assist in staffing. If sales are running lower than expected, some workers will be asked to leave early. Output at each station is also monitored through the cash register. Finally, the computer at all company stores is linked through a modem to the head office in Miami. Top management has access to information on the performance of each store on a daily basis, and this information is routed back to the Canadian division headquarters in Mississauga.

Skill levels required in a Burger King have been reduced to a common denominator. The goal is to reduce all skills to a common, easily learned level and to provide for cross-training. At the completion of the ten-hour training program, each worker is able to work at a few stations. Skills for any of the stations can be learned in a matter of hours; the simplest jobs, such as filling cups with drinks, or placing the hamburgers and buns on the conveyor belt, can be learned in minutes. As a result, although labour turnover cuts into the pace of making hamburgers, adequate functioning of the restaurant is never threatened by people leaving. However, if workers are to be as replaceable as possible, they must be taught not only to perform their jobs in the same way, but also to resemble each other in attitudes, disposition, and appearance. Thus, workers are also drilled on personal hygiene, dress (shoes should be brown leather or vinyl, not suede), coiffure (hair tied up for girls and not too long for boys), and personality. Rule 17 of the handout to new employees underlines the importance of smiling: "Smile at all times, your smile is the key to our success."

While management seeks to make workers into interchangeable tools, workers themselves are expected to make a strong commitment to the store. If they wish to keep jobs at Burger King, they must abide by the labour schedule. Workers, especially teenagers, are expected to adjust their activities to the requirements of Burger King.

THE WORKERS

One of the results of the transformation of the labour process from one of "manufacture" to that of "large-scale industry" is the emerging market importance of the young worker. While artisans require long training to achieve their skills, a machine-tender's primary characteristics are swiftness and endurance. Thus, young workers become ideal commodities: they are cheap, energetic, and plentiful. As well, they can be used as a marketing tool for the industry: the mass produced, smiling teenager, serving up the symbols of the good life in North America—hamburgers, cokes and fries.

Making up about 75 percent of the Burger King work force, the youngsters who worked after school, on weekends, and on holidays were called "part-timers." The teenager workers (about half of them boys, half girls) seemed to vary considerably in background. Some were college-bound youngsters who discussed their latest physics exam while piling on the pickles. Others were marking time until they reached age 16 and could leave school.

The daytime workers—the remaining 25 percent of the workforce—were primarily married women of mixed economic backgrounds. Consistent with a recent study of part-time workers in Canada, most of these women contributed their wages to the family budget.[6] Although they were all working primarily because their families needed the money, a few expressed their relief at getting out of the house, even to come to Burger King. One woman said: "At least when I come here, I'm appreciated. If I do a good job, a manager will say something to me. Here, I feel like a person. I'm sociable and I like being amongst people. At home, I'm always cleaning up after everybody and nobody ever notices!"[7]

Common to both the teenagers and the housewives was the view that working at Burger King was peripheral to their major commitments and responsibilities; the part-time nature of the work contributed to this attitude. Workers saw the alternative available to them as putting up with the demands of Burger King or leaving; in fact, leaving seemed to be the dominant form of protest. During my period in the store, on average, eleven people out of ninety-four hourly employees quit at each two-week pay period. While a few workers had stayed at Burger King for a few years, many did not last through the first two weeks. The need for workers is constant.

Burger King's ability to cope with high staff turnover means virtually no concessions are offered to workers to entice them to remain at Burger King. In fact, more attention is paid to the maintenance of the machinery than to "maintaining" the workers; time is regularly scheduled for cleaning and servicing the equipment, but workers may not leave the kitchen to take a drink or use the bathroom during the lunch and dinner rushes.

The dominant form—in the circumstances, the only easily accessible form—of opposition to the Burger King labour process is, then, the act of quitting. Management attempts to head off any other form of protest by insisting on an appropriate "attitude" on the part of the workers. Crew members must constantly demonstrate their satisfaction with working at Burger King by smiling at all times. However, as one worker remarked, "Why should I smile? There's nothing funny around here. I do my job and that should be good enough for them." It was not, however, and this worker soon quit. Another woman who had worked in the store for over a year also left. A crew member informed me that she had been fired for having a "poor attitude."

Management control and lack of worker opposition is further explained by the fact that other jobs open to teenagers are no better, and in some cases are worse, than the jobs at Burger King. The workers all agreed that any job that paid the full rather than the student minimum wage would be preferable to a job at Burger King; but they also recognized that their real alternatives would often be worse. Work at a donut shop, for example, also paid student minimum wage, under conditions of greater social isolation; baby sitting was paid poorly; and the hours for a paper route were terrible. Work at Burger King was a first job for many of the teenagers, and they enjoyed their first experience of earning their own money. And at Burger King, these young men and women were in the position of meeting the public, even if the forms of contact were limited by a vocabulary developed in Burger King headquarters: "Hello. Welcome to Burger King. May I take your order?" Interaction with customers had some intrinsic interest.

In sum, workers at Burger King are confronted with a labour process that puts management in complete control. Furnished with state-of-the-art restaurant technology, Burger King outlets employ vast numbers of teenagers and married women—a population with few skills and little commitment to working at Burger King. In part, this lack of commitment is understood through reference to a labour process that offers little room for work satisfaction. Most jobs can be learned in a very short time (a matter of minutes for some) and workers are required to learn every job, a fact that underlines the interchangeable nature of the jobs and the workers who do them. The work is most interesting when the store is busy. Paradoxically, work intensity, Burger King's main form of assault on labour costs, remains the only aspect of the job that can provide any challenge for the worker. Workers would remark with pride how they "didn't fall behind at all," despite a busy lunch or dinner hour.

It would be reassuring to dismiss the fast-food industry as an anomaly in the workplace; teenagers will eventually finish school and become "real workers," while housewives with families are actually domestic workers, also not to be compared with adult males in more skilled jobs. Unfortunately, there are indications that the teenagers and women who work in this type of job represent an increasingly typical kind of worker, in the one area of the economy that continues to grow—the service sector. The fast-food industry represents a model for other industries in which the introduction of technology will permit the employment of low-skilled, cheap, and plentiful workers. In this sense, it is easy to be pessimistic and agree with Andre Gorz's depressing formulation of the idea of work:

> The terms "work" and "job" have become interchangeable: work is no longer something that one does but something that one has. Workers no longer "produce" society through the mediation of the relations of production; instead, the machinery of social production as a whole produces "work" and imposes it in a random way upon random, interchangeable individuals.[8]

The Burger King system represents a major triumph for capital. However, the reduction of the worker to a simple component of capital requires more than the introduction of a technology; workers' autonomous culture must be eliminated as well, including the relationships among workers, their skills, and their loyalties to one another. The smiling, willing, homogeneous worker must be produced and placed on the Burger King assembly line.

While working at Burger King, I saw the extent to which Burger King has succeeded in reducing its work force to a set of interchangeable pieces. However, I also saw how insistently the liveliness and decency of the workers emerged in the informal interaction that occurred. Open resistance is made virtually impossible by the difficulty of identifying who is responsible for the rules that govern the workplace: the workers know that managers follow orders from higher up. The very high turnover of employees indicates workers understand that their interests and Burger King's are not the same. As young people and women realize that their jobs in the fast-food industry are not waystations en route to more fulfilling work, they will perhaps blow the whistle on the Burger King "team." The mould for the creation of the homogeneous worker assembling the standardized meal for the homogeneous consumer is not quite perfected.

ENDNOTES

1   Promotional material from Burger King Canada head office in Mississauga, Ontario.

2   Karl Marx, *Capital*, vol. 1 ([1867]; New York 1977), ch. xv.

3   Theodore Levitt, "Production Line Approach to Service," *Harvard Business Review* 50, no. 1 (Sept.-Oct. 1972): 51–2.

4   A "Shape Up" campaign instituted at the beginning of 1982 attempted to set a new goal of a 2 1/2-minute service time.

5   Personal communication, Burger King "professor," 4 January 1982.

6   Labour Canada, Commission of *Inquiry into Part-Time Work* (Ottawa 1983) [Wallace commission].

7   Personal communication, Burger King worker, 8 August 1981.

8   Andre Gorz, *Farewell to the Working Class* (Boston 1982), 71.

QUESTIONS

DISCUSSION QUESTIONS

1. What does someone's job say about him or her as a person? Are we defined by the work we do? Are we accurately defined?

2. "De-industrialization" was a term formerly used to describe what happens when an economy loses a big share of its manufacturing jobs. The term once had negative connotations because it was associated with economic recession and depression and with rising unemployment. Today the term "post-industrial" is used to describe an economy that has seen its manufacturing sector shrink. Is the difference between these two terms merely semantic or real and substantial?

3. Durkheim didn't think modern societies would have just one unified culture because people's life experiences would be too varied and dissimilar. Yet Ester Reiter's excerpt shows a modern corporation doing its utmost to ensure that one experience—eating a Big Whopper—will be the same no matter where it happens. Can the standardized products and practices of corporate consumer capitalism provide the basis for a common culture?

4. One way to create jobs would be to reduce the hours people work and to reduce their pay accordingly. This would free up some work for the unemployed. Discuss why you think a substantial proportion of working people would (or wouldn't) be willing to trade more leisure for less pay.

DATA COLLECTION EXERCISES

1. Compile a list of Canada's ten most dangerous occupations by gathering statistics on on-the-job injuries and on-the-job fatalities. Are there any surprises on your list?

2. One of the rewards of hard work is supposed to be economic success. And one of the rewards of economic success is that you no longer have to work so hard. Gather data on the length of the work week in nine countries. Randomly choose three poor countries, three affluent ones, and three that are rapidly becoming affluent. Do people work less as their nation's wealth increases?

3. Find 20 students who say they have made a definite decision to pursue a specific career. Ask them how they came to choose the career they did. After comparing their answers, try to generate a hypothesis on which factors are most important in the career selection process.

4. Agricultural workers make up less than 4 percent of Canada's labour force. With this in mind, find out how many people have agricultural jobs in China, India, and Indonesia. What percentage of their labour forces work in agriculture? Now calculate how many people in those countries would have to give up farm work if agriculture were as small a sector of the job market as it is in Canada. Where would such large numbers of people seek work if they were no longer needed as farmers?

WRITING EXERCISES

1. Choose one occupation in which either women or men are severely under-represented. Write a brief (500-word) essay accounting for this under-representation.

2. Studies show that the average person will change jobs several times during his or her working life. In light of this fact, write a brief (500-word) essay describing some ways to maximize one's chances of remaining happily employed at all times.

3. Under global free trade some Canadian jobs will be re-located in other countries. Write a brief (500-word) essay describing the kinds of jobs that are mostly likely to stay in Canada. Explain why Canada is a particularly suitable location for these types of jobs.

4. Write a brief (500-word) essay about a place where you have worked. Describe how the workplace culture (or working atmosphere) was influenced by the kind of work done there.

SUGGESTED READINGS

1. Armstrong, Pat and Hugh Armstrong (1978). *The Double Ghetto*. Toronto: McClelland and Stewart. This book, which contains much Canadian as well as international data, demonstrates that the double burden is not simply a problem of women having too much work to do. It's also an issue of "women's work" not being highly valued in either the marketplace or the domestic sphere.

2. Bell, Daniel (1973). *The Coming of Postindustrial Society*. New York: Basic Books. This was the book that launched the debate on the nature of post-industrial societies. Twenty years later it can also be read as an interesting case study in the field of social forecasting.

3. Hamper, Ben (1992). *Rivethead: Tales from the Assembly Line*. New York: Warner Books. This lively, gritty, and often funny book is written by a man who spent several years working on a General Motors assembly line. He offers an insider's perspective on why this kind of work can at different times be boring, challenging, ridiculous, and tragic.

SECTION 9   EDUCATION

Introduction

In complex societies such as our own, the recent historical trend has been for formal education to take up an increasing proportion of the individual's life span. Two basic theoretical perspectives—the functionalist and conflict approaches—have been developed to account for the growth of formal education in society.

THE FUNCTIONALIST PERSPECTIVE

The functionalists view formal higher education in industrial societies as resulting from the extensive economic and professional specialization that has taken place over time. Because the family cannot transmit all of the important specialized technical knowledge that has been accumulated, formal education has been developed as the most efficient device for transmitting such knowledge.

The functionalist perspective looks at education in terms of the functions it fulfils for society. The development of mass secondary and higher education is seen as a response to shifts in the occupational structure as society moved from an agrarian to an industrial economy. In his essay entitled "Education" (in *Sociology*, Fourth Edition, edited by Robert Hagedorn), Jos Lennards has summarized the premises of this perspective as follows: (1) the skills requirements of occupations in our society are constantly increasing; (2) people need to be recruited to fill the more highly skilled jobs; (3) the educational system is the place where the selection and training of talent occurs; and 4) rising skill requirements for occupations therefore require an expansion of the educational system.

Excerpt 9.1 on "shadow education" shows how in Japan formal education and education that is over and above (or outside) the normal hours have become the key route to upward mobility in this highly industrialized society. Nowhere is it clearer that formal education is the means by which people are recruited into elite educational and occupational channels.

However, we may question the validity of the functionalist theory of educational development on several grounds. First, educational requirements for jobs in industrial societies have not increased primarily because of an increase in jobs requiring a great deal of skill and a decrease in jobs requiring little skill. For the most part, as Randall Collins argues in his 1979 book *The Credential Society: An Historical Sociology of Education and Stratification,* well-educated people are currently doing the same kind of work that less educated people used to do.

Second, the functionalist theory of education assumes that formal education provides training in actual job skills. However, most skilled manual workers acquire their skills on the job or as part of apprenticeships. Also, vocational education for manual positions is not strongly predictive of occupational attainment.

Third, formal education seems to be more of a status-achieving mechanism than a mechanism for imparting new knowledge. For example, the professional occupational associations of teaching, social work, and nursing have consistently tried to make educational qualifications a legal necessity for practice; this restriction of entrance to a select group of people helps improve the group's position in the labour market.

Last, beyond the stage of mass literacy, formal education does not necessarily contribute to economic development. Time-lag correlations between education and economic development show that mass secondary education has not preceded industrialization; usually it has followed it.

THE CONFLICT PERSPECTIVE

Randall Collins provides what can be called a conflict model of education. According to this model, society is made up of status groups. Such groups are social classes, gender, religious groups, races, and ethnic communities.

In general, members of a status group share a common lifestyle or culture that defines particular patterns of social behaviour. Individuals in all societies derive their social identity through membership in these groups. Individuals may identify themselves in certain ways that reflect their status group. For example, upper-class or even middle-class individuals often identify themselves as having "breeding" or "respectability," and individuals with less income may identify themselves as "just plain folks."

The social basis for these status groups is the system of stratification itself: individuals have different lifestyles because they hold different economic positions, and have affiliations with different ethnic, religious, educational, and cultural groups.

People struggle to obtain what is highly valued and scarce—namely property, power, and prestige. Most of the conflict concerning access to valuable goods is actually conflict between status groups. For example, in large organizations status groups may hire individuals on the basis of their status-group affiliation, and not merely on the basis of their ability or acquired skills. Educational requirements for jobs serve a dual purpose: they limit applicants for higher level positions to those who share a particular subculture and are more likely to be from some status groups rather than others, and they secure the respect of lower-level employees who do not have the requisite formal training.

Viewed from the perspective of conflict theory, the increase in secondary and higher education and in educational requirements for jobs results more from the desire of status groups to maintain their positions in the occupational hierarchy than from the need for more formal training. Advanced-level schools, then, are seen as vehicles of social inequality. They help create and maintain inequality in access to occupations, and in this way they are the link between certain status groups and occupational prestige.

The functionalist view of education fits the fact that there is a growth of formal education in all industrial and industrializing societies. However, the conflict perspective offers alternative interpretations for why the pattern has occurred. One interpretation stresses the role of education in teaching people to accept supervision and control in the workplace.

By attending school year after year students acquire a conception of social structure and their place in it, which helps support the status quo. By learning to passively take notes and directions from teachers, they learn a way of submitting to authority that they will continue to uphold in the workplace. They learn to work for grades, certificates, degrees, and the approval of their teachers. In so doing, they learn to work for extrinsic reasons and rewards, rather than for such intrinsic rewards as the joy of learning.

Excerpt 9.2, based on ethnographic research in a Quebec fourth grade classroom, illustrates a related principle: namely, the teaching of order in the service of nationalism and religious belief. In this classroom, order itself is being taught—though students may think they are studying arithmetic or history. The chilling question that arises from this is, to what end will such training in passive conformity be put by employers or the state?

EDUCATION AND SOCIAL INEQUALITY

Despite the proliferation of secondary and post-secondary schools, people's social origins—their social class backgrounds, ethnic and racial backgrounds, and genders—tend to determine their educational attainment levels. One of the best recent studies of social inequality in educational attainment is entitled "Who Benefits from Higher Education? Differences by Sex, Social Class and Ethnic Background," by Neil Guppy and A. Bruce Arai (in *Social Inequality in Canada: Patterns, Problems and Policies* edited by James Curtis, Edward Grabb and Neil Guppy). They found that "the likelihood of attending college or university is higher if you come from white-collar origins, with parents who have already attended post-secondary institutions. Study at college or university is also more likely if you are English-speaking as opposed to French-speaking . . . [and] more women than men . . . [are now] earning diplomas and degrees."

Women's growing participation in higher education has had the unintended consequence of widening the educational gap between social classes. Overall, the results suggest that coming from the "wrong" social class origins is a stronger obstacle to attainment of higher education that being of the "wrong" gender or from the "wrong" linguistic group. In excerpt 9.3 below, the authors suggest strategies for moving towards "educational equity" across genders and racial and ethnic groups. Until such equity is achieved, we cannot suppose that either educational or occupational statuses are based (mainly) on merit.

David Lee Stevenson and David P. Baker

SHADOW EDUCATION IN FORMAL SCHOOLING IN JAPAN

INTRODUCTION

Not all education occurs within the formal school system, as evidenced by the prevalence of "shadow education" in Japan. This activity is designed to give the student an advantage over, or at least be competitive with, other students in the pursuit of marks and advancement in the formal education system.

The authors report results from a study of students who were interviewed near the end of high school and again later on. The study shows that families of different socio-economic backgrounds vary in how effectively they use shadow education. As is often the case, higher status families are better able to take advantage; they use shadow education more than other families. The authors show that shadow education does pay off for students, giving them better success in getting into the highly competitive university system in Japan.

Do you think this type of activity is very widespread in Canada? There is certainly a lot of tutoring and extra training in special skills—including computing, language, math, music, and sport training programmes—available in this country. A quick review of the Yellow Pages for any urban area will attest to this. But if the "economic miracle" achieved by the Japanese is anything to judge by, perhaps more rapid economic growth will demand more and better education in Canada—and especially an increase in shadow education.

The capacity of formal schooling to differentiate students is central to allocation theories of education (Bourdieu and Passeron 1977; Bowles and Gintis 1976). Allocation processes, however, vary across educational systems in terms of the criteria by which allocation decisions are made, in the timing of such decisions, and in the factors that influence those decisions (Eckstein and Noah 1989). Allocation processes also can have institutional effects on schooling itself (Meyer 1977).

An example of such an institutional effect is the way allocation processes encourage the development of shadow education, a set of educational activities outside formal schooling that are designed to improve a student's chances of successfully moving through the allocation process.

Certain characteristics of the educational allocation process foster the development of shadow education. First, and most important, is the use of formal examina-

Stevenson, David Lee and David P. Baker (1992). "Shadow Education and Allocation in Formal Schooling in Japan," *American Journal of Sociology;* 97(6), May, 1639–1657.

tions—particularly centrally administered examinations. Second, shadow education flourishes if schooling uses "contest rules" instead of "sponsorship rules" (Turner 1960). And third, shadow education is prevalent when there are tight linkages between the outcomes of educational allocation in elementary and secondary schooling and future educational opportunities, occupations, or general social status.

When these qualities occur together, extensive shadow education can be observed. For example, in Taiwan, graduates of elite universities have significant advantages in the labor market, and there is extensive shadow education to prepare students for university entrance examinations (Lin 1983). In Hong Kong, graduates' hiring and pay rates are partly dependent on their performance on secondary-school-certificate examinations, and shadow education takes the form of tutoring and after-school classes to prepare students for the examinations (Mitchell 1968; Sweeting 1983). In Greece, because admission to an elite secondary school is considered critical for acceptance at a prestigious university, students use tutors and attend special after-school classes to prepare for the national entrance examination for secondary school (Katsillis and Rubinson 1990).

The timing, use, and forms of shadow education are shaped by allocation rules. We use the term "shadow" to denote the strong connection between allocation rules and nonformal schooling; we do not imply that these activities are hidden. Indeed, in systems such as Japan's, these activities make up a large, open enterprise.

SHADOW EDUCATION AND CONTESTED SPONSORSHIP IN JAPAN

Educational allocation in Japan is organized around the institutional qualities that foster the development of shadow education. First and foremost is the use of formal examinations in the educational allocation process, particularly since the examinations are central to the allocation process, the weight of nonexamination criteria in the selection process is minimal, and there are few critical school-to-career transition points (U.S. Department of Education 1987; Amano 1990). Second is the clear and immutable connections between the outcomes of the educational allocation process and future occupational positions or general social status (Brinton 1988; Rosenbaum and Kariya 1989). The Japanese combination of meritocratic examinations and rich educational rewards shapes an allocation process that can be described as "contested sponsorship." Contested sponsorship arises from the organization of Japanese education that shifts from more compulsory and nonselective schooling in the lower grades to increasing levels of selectivity by the end of high school.

Increasingly larger numbers of students attempt to enter college, in part because the potential prize is entrance to one of the most prestigious universities, which leads to recruitment into a sponsored elite. As elsewhere, universities in Japan have social characters: the ability "to define people as graduates and as therefore possessing distinctive rights and capacities in society" (Meyer 1970, p. 59). But the clear hierarchy of Japanese universities has produced a set of "narrow" charters so that *which* university one attends affects one's occupational career and general social status (Amano 1986; U.S. Department of Education 1987).

University graduates are recruited by firms directly from university and many spend their entire work career with their first employer (Brinton 1988). Recruitment by employers begins in November and, within a five-day period, almost 80% of the spring graduates have selected an employer (Ushiogi 1986). Major companies and elite departments of the civil service only recruit graduates of certain departments in the most prestigious universities. Graduates employed by major companies have life-long advantages over graduates employed by small firms in terms of salaries, promotion opportunities, benefits, job stability, and yearly bonuses (Ushiogi 1986).

The tight linkages between education and work and the narrow charters of Japanese universities produce intense competition for admission to the most prestigious universities. In 1980, for example, 13,000 applicants competed for 3,077 places at Tokyo University (Rohlen 1983). For admission to the prestigious departments of law, economics, and medicine, the ratio of applicants to places may reach 7:1.

It is clear, then, why Japanese students with college aspirations arduously prepare for the entrance examinations. The importance of this transition point is heavily emphasized in the name "examination hell" (*juken jigoku*). The intensity of the competition is captured in the popular phrase, "four pass, five fail," which admonishes students that those who sleep four hours pass their entrance examinations but those who sleep five hours fail.

The contested sponsorship process in Japan is ripe for the development of shadow education. The dominance of examinations, the social and financial rewards for success, and the concentration of allocation at one time point intensify the growth of shadow education.

There are two sets of Japanese shadow-education activities: one used primarily during secondary school and the other used immediately after high school. During the secondary school years, students participate in after-school and weekend preparation activities such as private cram schools, correspondence courses, and practice examinations. If high school graduates do not earn admission to the university of their choice, they may spend one or more additional years preparing. Such students are known as *ronin*, a word that was used to describe lordless samurai. Ronin do not legitimately belong to either the world of formal schooling or the world of work. They spend their time engaged in preparation for the university entrance examinations, often in intensive preparation schools (*yobiko*).[1]

Shadow education encompasses a large set of varied educational activities that are firmly rooted within the private sector. Students and their families pay tuition for private schools to prepare them for examinations, purchase workbooks with questions from previous examinations, and pay for practice tests that are administered and graded by private companies. Since there are millions of students competing for university entrance examinations, shadow education is a vast market representing an industry worth 870 billion yen (in U.S. currency, approximately $7 billion) in 1986 (Katsuki 1988).

1. Practice examinations (*mogi shiken*), provided and graded by private firms, assess a student's chances of being admitted to university. Students receive a report comparing their performance with national norms, are notified of subject areas that require greater study, and are given an estimate of their chances of being admitted to a particular university.

2. Correspondence courses (*tsuchin tensaku*), purchased from mail-order companies, provide exercises for entrance examinations that are mailed back and then returned graded.

3. Private tutors (*katei kyoshi*) are primarily used for staying abreast of regular schoolwork and used less for examination preparation.

4. Private after-school classes (*juku*) come in two types: *gakushu juku,* which are remedial classes, and *shingaku juku,* for preparation for the university entrance examinations. *Juku* vary in the size of the classes from small classes that may meet in the home of the tutor to large classes in a school. Students in primary school may participate in *juku* to develop academic abilities in coordination with the curriculum of the formal school, while secondary students in *juku* prepare for university entrance examinations. There is a great deal of variation in the atmosphere and demands of *jukes* but there is a general opinion that participation in a *juku* is an important part of a student's school career (Cummings 1980; White 1987).

5. Full-time preparation following high school (ronin) is a strategy used by students who do not gain admission to any university or by those who do not gain admission to the university they wish to attend. Ronin take a year or more to prepare solely for university entrance examinations and often attend *yobiko,* a private examination preparation school (Tsukada 1988).

PREVALENCE OF SHADOW EDUCATION

Because shadow education is both a large industry and is publicly defined as useful for educational advancement in Japan, we would expect to find high proportions of students using these educational practices, particularly among those students who definitely plan to attend a university. Table 1 presents the percentage of students who participate in shadow education activities during high school and the percentage who are willing to become ronin after high school. The first column shows the participation of all base-year students and the second column shows the participation of only those base-year students who have college plans (about 74% of the base-year sample).

Japanese students are voracious consumers of shadow-education activities. Eighty-eight percent of those students with college plans participated in at least one activity during high school and 60% participated in two or more of these activities. Almost a third of the seniors were willing to become ronin after graduating if they needed additional preparation for the university examinations.

We have argued that the use of shadow education is related to its perceived educational benefit. If that is so, we should find that students' participation varies with their plans for postsecondary education. The last four columns in Table 1 show that participation is related to the age at which students stated they planned to attend a university. Students who had college plans early in elementary school were most likely to use shadow education, while the rates of participation declined among late planners.

TABLE 1 Participation in Shadow Education by Japanese Students during High School (Base-Year Sample)

Shadow-Education Activity	Total Sample of Students (%)	Students with College Plans* (%)	School Period when Student Began to Plan for College				x^2 (%)
			Early Elementary School (%)	Late Elementary School (%)	Junior High School (%)	1st-2nd Year, High School (%)	
Practice examination (*mogi shiken*)	54	68	72	69	68	60	40.0†
Correspondence course (*tsushin tensaku*)	30	43	45	41	35	26	99.2†
Private tutor (*katei kyoshi*)	8	11	15	12	8	7	66.9†
After-school class (*juku*)	35	46	52	43	38	29	144.4†
Plans to be a ronin after high school	29	32	41	33	26	19	123.0†
N	7,240	5,352	1,740	826	1,924	862	

Note: Fifty-four percent of all students took a practice examination; 46% did not.
*Students with college plans represent 74% of base-year sample.
†$P < .00001$, $df = 3$.

DETERMINANTS OF PARTICIPATION IN SHADOW EDUCATION

Although shadow education is pervasive, participation may not be equally spread across all students. The transition to university offers significant benefits, and many students engage in extraordinary preparation activities, but, because these educational activities are expensive and time-consuming, we expect children from families with more resources to participate more in shadow education than children from poorer families. Differential investments in shadow education also can occur within families. For example, because of the better job prospects for Japanese males and perceptions about gender and social opportunity (Brinton 1988, 1989), families may tend to invest their resources in the education of sons rather than daughters. Or families may invest in shadow education for only their most promising child or do so only when they live in areas, such as cities, in which these activities are most available.

To examine this we estimated logistic regression equations in which the dependent variable is whether or not the student ever participated in a particular shadow-education activity. We find that investment in shadow education for students is associated with three measures of family's SES, even after student and school characteristics are controlled for. Students from wealthier families and families in which the parents have higher levels of education are more likely to purchase shadow education. These effects are moderate, generally adding only 4%–5% to the likelihood of participating in a form of shadow education, but taken together they increase the probability of undertaking shadow education by 12%–15%. For the majority of activities, all three indicators of family SES increase the likelihood of shadow participation.

There are moderate to large gender differences in participation for every activity except after-school classes. Compared with females, males participate more in practice examinations, correspondence courses, and are more willing (54% more) to become ronin after high school. Almost one-half of the male seniors had plans to become ronin if not admitted to university, while only one-tenth of the female students had similar plans.

Scholastic characteristics also influence participation; students with better grades (academic standing) and students in academic curriculum tracks purchase shadow education. The latter effect is large as students in the academic track are 22%–68% more likely than other students to use shadow education, while the largest effect of grades increases participation by only 7%. The curriculum-track effect indicates the strength of the connection between shadow education and educational allocation.

High school reputation has a mixed effect; students from high schools that are successful in university placement use shadow education, except for *juku* (after-school classes). Among these students *juku* is not used because in many prestigious high schools examination preparation activities are now incorporated into an extracurricular schedule, by creating within-school, after-school classes. This shows how pervasive systems of shadow education can in turn influence the instruction and organization of formal schooling.

Finally, living in an urban area moderately increases the use of shadow education, except for the purchase of correspondence courses, the only form of participation not restricted by proximity.

We examine one final issue of participation in shadow education. Some students, who are either not admitted to any university or are admitted but decide to continue to prepare for the examination of a more prestigious university the following year, undertake perhaps the most extensive form of shadow education—the ronin year. Since no limit exists as to the number of times a student can participate in the annual examinations, up to 25% of examination takers in any one year are ronin. While ronin activities can keep the student preparing and competing for the prestigious positions, the financial, social, and emotional costs can be quite high. The average tuition for *yobiko* (private cram school for ronin) ranges from the equivalent of $2,000 to $2,800 per year, but can go as high as $20,000 for *yobiko* designed for entrance to special programs, such as medicine. For some there are additional room and board costs. Other costs for ronin come in the form of emotional stress from constant pressure to prepare, damaged social and peer affiliations, and anxiety about uncertain futures (Tsukada 1988).

To assess which students become ronin, we analyzed those students in the follow-up who, as seniors, had had college plans (69% of the follow-up sample) since this is the pool from which ronin will come. Of this group 27% became ronin the year immediately after high school.

We find that, as is true of participation in shadow education during the high school years, family resources have a modest influence on becoming a ronin after high school. Students whose families have more money and whose parents have more education are more likely to continue in the most extensive forms of shadow education. These effects are small however, adding only about 5%–6% to the likelihood that a student undertakes the ronin year. Family expenditure and student sacrifice for the ronin year is far more motivated by the gender of the student. Males dominate the ranks of ronin, and we find that, even after we control for a number of other factors, when we compare males with females, the former are 49% more likely to become ronin if this is necessary for continuance in the allocation process. Naturally students who failed examinations during the first year are more likely to become ronin and students from rural areas less likely to, because of the higher costs of sending a student to live in the city to attend a *yobiko*. Finally, students from prestigious high schools tend to become ronin, most likely because they are taking the most competitive entrance examinations.

CONSEQUENCES OF SHADOW EDUCATION

We examine the consequences of participation in shadow education for university attendance at two points in time: (1) the first year out of high school and (2) the second year out of high school. The first point includes all base-year students with university plans and the second point includes only those follow-up-year students with university plans who did not attend university after high school.

Because we have no measure of the quality of the shadow-education experience, our analysis provides a limited assessment of the effect of participation in shadow-education activities on university attendance. We can, nevertheless, determine whether participation in shadow education increases the student's chances of attending university, in addition to including various control variables, such as student, family, and school characteristics, in order to assess the relative contribution of shadow education to allocation outcomes in Japan.

We find that among students two years out of high school with college plans, high school shadow education had a diminishing effect on attending university, but the effect of being a ronin is dramatic because it increases university attendance by 80%. There is a strong association between the ronin year and continued competition in the race for university; among this part of the follow-up sample 86% became ronin and of these 72% entered college compared with only 6% of the non-ronin from this group. This is particularly true among the males, who are much more likely than females to become ronin. A further 19% of the original ronin continued for a second year to prepare for another round of university examinations. Even though the dominant effect in this model is that of the ronin, shadow education as a group of activities still adds significantly to the background model.

DISCUSSION

As we have seen, many Japanese high school students participate in preparation activities that are not offered in formal schooling, and many high school graduates continue such preparation activities during the two years after high school.

Although rates of participation in various forms of shadow education are uniformly high, there are different patterns of participation. The likelihood of participation increases if the student is male, or has good grades in high school, or is from a higher SES family. These patterns of participation in shadow education reflect broader patterns of stratification by gender, secondary schooling, and SES. Such evidence suggests that participation in shadow education is not a remedial strategy used primarily by students who have difficulty meeting the academic standards of a formal school setting, but is instead a proactive strategy used primarily by students who have already accumulated significant advantages in the formal educational system. Shadow education provides an avenue for parents to enhance their children's chances in the educational allocation contest.

Consequences of participation are modest for some forms of shadow education and large for others. Becoming a ronin is an institutionalized way for one-time losers to stay in the educational allocation contest, and staying in the contest seems to have its pay-offs. Forms of shadow education are designed to help students increase their knowledge in order to improve their performances on the entrance examinations. Gaining admission to a Japanese university is, however, not merely a transfer of family background through investment in shadow education. The meritocratic contest of university admission in Japan emphasizes the academic ability of the student and measures of previous academic performance have large, direct effects on university attendance.

Shadow education is designed to enhance the school careers of students. Its content and existence is tightly coupled to the organization of transitions both within schooling and from school to the workplace. For some societies, the study of shadow education will enhance our understanding of the process by which students are allocated within formal schooling and how social advantages are transferred across generations.

ENDNOTES

[1]   There was a similar status of intensive preparation for aspiring feudal Chinese literati *(shen-shih)* whose existence was referred to as an "examination life" (Franke 1963).

REFERENCES

Amano, I. 1986. "Educational Crisis in Japan." pp. 23–43 in *Educational Policies in Crisis*, edited by W. K. Cummings, E. R. Beauchamp, S. Ichikawa, V. N. Kobayashi, and M. Ushiogi. New York: Praeger.

———. 1990. *Education and Examination in Modern Japan.* Tokyo: University of Tokyo Press.

Bowles, S., and H. Gintis. 1976. *Schooling in Capitalist America*. New York: Basic.

Bourdieu, P., and J. Passeron. 1977. *Reproduction in Education, Society, and Culture*. Beverly Hills, Calif.: Sage.

Brinton, M. 1988. "The Social-Institutional Bases of Gender Stratification: Japan as an Illustrative Case." *American Journal of Sociology* 94:300–334.

———. 1989. "Gender Stratification in Contemporary Urban Japan." *American Sociological Review* 54:549–64.

Cummings, W. 1980. *Education and Equality in Japan*. Princeton, N.J.: Princeton University Press.

Eckstein, M., and H. Noah. 1989. "Forms and Functions of Secondary-School-Leaving Examinations." *Comparative Education Review* 33:295–316.

Katsillis, J., and R. Rubinson. 1990. "Cultural Capital, Student Achievement, and Educational Reproduction in Greece." *American Sociological Review* 55:270–79.

Katsuki, N. 1988. "The Learning Business." *Tokyo Business Today* (January), pp. 34–36.

Lin, C. 1983. "The Republic of China (Taiwan)." Pp. 104–35 in *Schooling in East Asia: Forces of Change*, edited by R. M. Thomas and T. W. Postlethwaite. New York: Pergamon.

Meyer, J. 1970. "The Charter: Conditions of Diffuse Socialization in Schools." Pp. 564–78 in *Social Processes and Social Structures*, edited by W. R. Scott. New York: Holt, Rinehart & Winston.

———. 1977. "The Effects of Education as an Institution." *American Journal of Sociology* 83:55–77.

Mitchell, R. 1968. *Pupil, Parent and School: A Hong Kong Study*. Taipei: Orient Cultural Service.

Rohlen, T. 1983. *Japan's High Schools*. Berkeley and Los Angeles: University of California Press.

Rosenbaum, J., and T. Kariya. 1989. "From High School to Work: Market and Institutional Mechanisms in Japan." *American Journal of Sociology* 94:1334–65.

Sweeting, A. 1983. "Hong Kong." Pp. 272–97 in *Schooling in East Asia: Forces of Change*, edited by R. M. Thomas and T. W. Postlethwaite. New York: Pergamon.

———. 1988. "The *Yobiko:* The Institutionalized Supplementary Educational Institution in Japan: A Study of the Social Stratification Process." Ph.D. dissertation. University of Hawaii, Department of Sociology.

Turner, R. 1960. "Sponsored and Contest Mobility in the School System." *American Sociological Review* 25:855–67.

U.S. Department of Education. 1987. *Japanese Education Today*. Washington, D.C.: Government Printing Office.

Ushiogi, M. 1986. "Transition from School to Work: The Japanese Case." Pp. 197–209 in *Educational Policies in Crisis*, edited by W. K. Cummings, E. R. Beauchamp, S. Ichikawa, V. N. Kobayashi and M. Ushiogi. New York: Praeger.

White, M. 1987. *The Japanese Educational Challenge*. New York: Free Press.

Jacques Zylberberg and Yuki Shiose

JESUS SAYS, "ORDER CHILDREN!": ETHNOGRAPHY OF A CATHOLIC CLASSROOM

INTRODUCTION

Schools, or the teachers in them, teach students more than the content of traditional subjects such as writing and reading skills, literature, math, and science. The following excerpt illustrates this, using the results of an ethnographic study of a fourth grade classroom in a small Quebec Catholic school.

The study shows that "order" or good behaviour is the subject of much instruction in the classroom, even though "order" is not one of the subjects on the formal curriculum. Students are not only taught what is deemed to be good behaviour; they are also taught that those who misbehave are morally inferior. Religious piety, and even patriotism, are associated with good behaviour in the classroom; misbehaviour is associated with evil and "the foreign."

Using value- and feeling-laden content, children are taught simultaneously to value norms of good behaviour, nationalism, and religiosity. They are also implicitly taught to mistrust "foreigners," people who misbehave, and the irrreligious. Try relating this to the socialization of the Oneida children—another highly ideological group (excerpt 2.1); the influence of religion on moral judgments in Kuwait (excerpt 3.2); the politics of religious fundamentalism (excerpt 11.2); and ideologies that delegitimize the opposition (excerpt 15.1). What elements do you think are similar to the indoctrination of this fourth grade classroom? What elements are different?

SETTING THE SCENE

A small state school in French Canada is presented as a matrix through which young human beings create their world, by which they are initiated to the world, and in which they become *socialized*.[1]

We selected a fourth grade class in a state primary school and spent two terms with the teaching staff and the pupils. The fieldwork consisted of: participating in and observation of the schooling from September 1987 to June 1988; open-ended interviews with the actors in the class; and document-based research.

Zylberberg, Jacques and Yuki Shiose (1991). "Jesus Says, "Order, Children!" Ethnography of a Catholic Classroom," *Social Compass* 38(4), 417–431.

The class does not exist in a vacuum. It is situated in the complex and most of the time contradictory context of the outer world. The 24 pupils and the teacher are the main characters of the forum; they also are components of a larger whole, while constructing their own worlds in face-to-face contact. As such, the class becomes a singular world where a macrocosm collides with a microcosm, where an individual belief system encounters a larger order.[2]

THE PROCESS OF KEEPING ORDER IN THE CLASSROOM

Classroom life was systematically organized. The teacher regulated everything, from when and how to go to the bathroom to how to dress, talk, move and play. The orders were given each time with plenty of rationalization. It is for the good of the children that they must not walk freely during the break hour (everybody *must* be either out in the playground playing under surveillance or, on rainy days, in the classroom doing homework); it is not permitted to take textbooks home, or to bring the wrong kind of notebooks. Daily school life was under the total control of the teacher who tried to diminish all the ambiguity of the child's existence by reducing his margin of choice to the minimum.[3]

As Piaget states, the children's complex world(s) were completely reorganized by the teacher in the "one and only correct" order.[4] But this order is at the same time a function and a means. *The teacher is involved more in transmission of order than transmission of knowledge.* Religious iconography on the wall silently endorsed the commands given by the teacher.

At the entrance to the school and in each classroom there was a cross with the figure of suffering Jesus. Our classroom had, besides this symbol, a large coloured poster of Pope Jean-Paul II with his hands spread out, pinned to the side wall. There was also a calender printed with the phrase "God loves you" just by the door. But it would take months for the children to grasp the relations between daily rules and religious ornaments.

The utmost emphasis was placed upon the learning of *savoir-vivre* or proper behaviour. Life was about order and obedience. The good life was a peaceful life filled with order, discipline and commandments.

The teacher signalled docile behaviour as the best. Every Friday, at the end of the day, the most obedient child was picked from the class by the teacher and presented to the director of the school. The director later announced the best behaved children of the week, chosen from the names received by each class. The names of those children would be on the roll of honour on the public blackboard (just at the entrance of the school) during the next week. The children who were chosen gleamed with pride and all the others were encouraged to praise the prize winners by clapping their hands. These were the only moments within the school year where an overt competitive element was introduced in the class. Thus, the most important thing to learn in the class was not to excel in the three Rs ("reading, writing and 'rithmetic") but to be docile. Docility in the classroom was equated with order. Order was explicitly equated with peace . . . and war. Peace was the ultimate objective of life laid down by Jesus himself. Disobedience thus meant an outrageous war against Jesus, against mankind. The teacher was the representative of good and right (Jesus), in the classroom. His war was "legitimately" waged against the offenders, the troublemakers, the warriors.

Religious and political metaphors were used constantly and explicitly to "demonize" the behavior of the disobedient children.

REWARDS

The general atmosphere of the classroom was saturated with religious metaphors, evoked by the authoritative figure of the teacher. The teacher, as friendly as Jesus, emphasized peace. As Jesus did, the teacher separated the disobedient from the obedient if the former did not understand the spirituality of peace, consensus and obedience. Further, the non-docile behaviour of a pupil was presented as uncatholic.

The children, even those who asked for exemption from the Catholic religion class and chose civic education, were irradiated constantly with the message of God: they were to remember the absolute negativity of war, violence and disagreement. On the other hand, harmony, friendship and peace were the words most used to describe a positive atmosphere. However, tranquillity was maintained by the teacher through threats of punishment and fear. The children were emotionally and physically at the complete mercy of "symbolic violence."[5] Coercion was never physically violent, but when the children disobeyed him, the teacher employed several methods of punishment which were highly feared and thus effective. For example, a noisy child was placed in front of the class, facing the wall, throughout the period. He or she was not permitted to turn around in order to participate in the class activities; as such, the child became a humiliating and humiliated object of the class. The child who did not listen and obey the dogma of the prophet of the class (teacher) was an outrage because he was refusing Jesus' message of peace. Thus he needed to be cast out, for as long as the teacher saw fit.

If someone tried to communicate with the ostracized, he or she also risked becoming an object of shame, so the ostracism was achieved with the complete cooperation of the child's "peace-loving friends."

When the teacher decided that the entire class was too disorderly, he simply withdrew the children's most cherished liberty, the recreation period; and ordered all of them to sit silently for the entire period. This punishment, called *"faire du calme"* (sic), which consisted of closing the eyes and crossing the arms upon the desk, was frequently used whenever the teacher felt it was necessary. He also made use of the lighting of the classroom, switching the light off when he required better concentration from the children. The children very quickly grasped that their comfort, benefit and success depended solely on their ability to appease the teacher.[6]

THE CURRICULUM

The class met 5 days a week from 8.45 am to 3.30 pm. There were three breaks: two 15-minute breaks (morning and afternoon) and a 90-minute break for lunch when the children must be out of the school, eating lunch at home.

The basic unit of the classes was 45 minutes, and there were thirty units. Officially, we had eight units of French, five units of mathematics, three units of religion/civic education, two units of English, two units of physical education, two units of music and dramatic arts, two units of natural science, two units of social science, one unit each of nutrition and plastic arts, and two more units for revisions of the week. However, in practice only the classes which involved other teachers (music, drama, physical education and English) and the religious class, which was given at same time as the civic class, followed the fixed schedule. The other subjects were changed quite freely according to the decision of the teacher. Most of the French units were thus utilized for administrative communication, paperwork, cleaning the desks of the children, and finishing ongoing projects from the other courses.

Social science or natural science could totally take up the time of French for weeks in a row. The official five units of mathematics, too, could be diminished when the teacher decided there were other priorities. Thursdays and Fridays were the most hectic days. Within these 2 days, the teacher gave out several different kinds of printouts to the children for their weekly conduct reports and several written communications to the parents. The children must, within the 2 days, answer a list of questions concerning their weekly behaviour and each time wait in rows to have their personal evaluations confirmed by the teacher. These routines were not intellectual but took up a tremendous amount of time, and the teacher was always anxious to finish them by the end of Friday.

Consequently, the activities in the classroom were much more centred upon the establishment of routine for the sake of order than on the transmission of academic knowledge. Among these activities, the religious course was considered fundamental to this process of socialization.

THE CATHOLIC RELIGIOUS COURSES

The religious course was the subject the teacher considered the most central and important. The teacher required far more concentration from the children here than in the other subjects. These units were never jeopardized to accommodate other subjects. He used three printed books, which was already unusual by the standard. Other courses rarely required books; instead the children received handouts of texts or problems one week ahead. By contrast, the religious class had the formal aids of a New Testament, a guide book to the Bible and a work book accompanying the guide book. These materials used much more sophisticated language than the children were learning in the usual French class. We often heard children from the religious class complain: "It is not fair, the civic class lets the children draw, and does not make them memorize complicated phrases nor write long sentences." The Bible was, however, read less than the guide book. It was the work book that was mostly used in the class.

The Vatican Council II had little influence upon our small class. The Jewish part of the Bible was not mentioned, and even the New Testament received limited attention.

The guide book was written in more formal French, in contrast with the colloquial version of the teacher's speech. In it, Jesus was depicted as a presence transcending any particular historical period, except in His connection with historical groups and activities. He was a spiritual presence, of friendship and especially of peace. This peace was localized in Palestine, but the land was troubled by the opposition between the true family—the followers of Jesus—and the false family—the relatives who do not listen to the word of Jesus—the Jews and the Romans. The Holy Land was thus torn between Jesus and the nonbelievers.7

After the dichotomization of the different religions and institutions in Palestine in the time of Jesus, the texts dealt with contemporary situations. They did not make explicit the existence of other religions but stated casually the necessity of respecting different groups.

Jesus the friend was Jesus the "Big Brother," who expected good behaviour from the children: children with no hidden, contradictory thoughts. Jesus was never shown as a suffering individual who contradicted the status quo, but a demure organizer of the children's entire lives. With Saint John the Baptist, Quebec's patron saint, Jesus made up the teacher's ideal world, untroubled and obedient. To the teacher, the actual world, with the exception of Quebec, did not follow God's message of submission. It was unruly, chaotic and thus excluded, except as the destination of tourism.

THE GHETTO: CIVIC CLASS

In contrast to the well-structured Catholic class, the civic class had neither a manual nor a work book. The teacher, who gathered these children from different grades, improvised with the help of loosely organized printed matter. The atmosphere of the class was much less of study than of amusement. The children drew and conversed rather freely in the class, and learned about "the rights and the duties of everybody," the main theme of the year in the class. The civic class, in contrast with the religious class, had many characteristics of a ghetto, or a group of marginalized people.[8]

1. As we have noted, the teacher in charge of the non-religious course was the most ardent Catholic of the school, and her teaching tacitly presented the Catholic way of life as the model for everybody who wanted to live decently. The children thus received a diluted version of Catholic education despite making an explicit choice to follow the non-religious course.

2. The children had fewer materials to learn from; the teacher, fewer expectations. When the teacher recapitulated the weekly activities of the children on Fridays, the religious course was mentioned first, the civic course the last.

3. Whenever a religious ceremony was held during the period for the Catholic children with the participation of the vicar or priest, the civic children were left alone "to play" and the civic teacher assisted the Catholic ceremony.

4. The civic children could not stay in the classroom with their own classmates but were gathered with the children of other grades, in another classroom, wherever vacant.

RELIGIOUS TEACHING IN THE OTHER COURSES

The "profane" courses were structured by the metaphors of "Jesus," "Quebec" and "Peace." This holy trinity was implanted in the following manner. The main subjects of the natural sciences and social sciences were always based on Quebec; even the mammals, the principal object of study of the natural science course, were divided in two: "There were Quebecker wolves and non-Quebecker wolves and we study only the Quebecker ones. It is the same with all the other mammals. If you study an animal which is not Quebecker, you won't earn your point!", the teacher told the pupils. Simultaneously, the children learned in the social science course that Quebec is different from the rest of Canada and the United States. The teacher asked "Why is Quebec different from the rest of the continent and the world?" The children who responded "Because we speak French," were encouraged to go further in search of the reason. Finally, the teacher wrote on the blackboard (below the crucifix) the word "Paix" and ordered the class to look at the wall which was covered with photographs of war in other parts of the world. He encouraged the children to appreciate their luck in living in the land of harmony, and asked the children whether they went to church. Not seeing enough hands raised, he expressed his dissatisfaction by telling them that they were "even less Catholic than the foreigners!" and should be ashamed of themselves.

The teacher's constant association of positiveness with "peace," "Quebec," and "Jesus" were gradually assimilated by the children. When the teacher allowed the children to draw during the art class, they often sketched a cross (never Jesus himself), and the figure of the teacher, with words such as "peace" and "love." However, when we later asked the pupils whether they or their family went to church, the overwhelming majority of the children (nineteen out of twenty-one) did not, and were not interested in attending weekly mass in the future. Ironically, the two who did go to mass were from the marginalized group of children: the slow girl and the Salvador-born boy.

The non-religious curriculum, then, was saturated with Roman Catholic-based religious messages; peace was legitimized by the concept of Jesus and localized in the province of Quebec. The teacher encouraged the children to "be" as they should be, which is docile, authority-fearing little conformists. The teacher often invited a young priest of the neighbouring church to the class, informally, to talk to the children as a friend. The teacher also addressed the children as "friends." However, despite this superficial familiarity and equality between the teacher and the children, he never let the children forget that he had the upper hand.[9]

Our teacher often preached about war and peace in the world. The teacher asked the children to bring newspaper articles about war and peace. During the first term, the teacher distributed pictures of Jean-Paul II, Mother Teresa and the local bishop as notable examples of peace-loving citizens of the world. Jean-Paul II's address to Quebec youth, about the mission of young Quebeckers to preserve peace, was photocopied and used as a text in the French language class.[10] Quebec was presented in the geography class as a peaceful and peace-loving country which was consistently opposed to any kind of violence. The teacher divided one of the walls into two and named them "peace" and "war." The children put their newspaper articles under the appropriate section and the teacher commented on them. He equated peace with love and with the presence of God on earth and, by contrast, war meant violence, trouble and evil. All wars were considered equally extremely negative—as an antipode of the love of Jesus—but the historical failure of peace in the Middle East was often the subject of especially lengthy comments: Jesus tried to bring love and peace to Palestine but the Jews and the Romans refused to listen to the sweet message. Several times the teacher produced large posters of peaceful pastoral scenes of Palestine and explained to the children that these images depicted how it had been before the war.

In the French class the children used as texts the prayers of Jean-Paul II and of Saint Francis. The teacher distributed the texts, explaining that these men were model citizens. The children were to copy these texts without error in their notebooks. This was one of the rare occasions when the teacher actually told the children to write down texts. Usually, oral practice was preferred. The teacher emphasized the importance of understanding the content of those prayers; because they were about peace, the youth of Quebec should be interested in them. He also used an editorial of a women's magazine (*Châtelaine*)[11] in the course. The text spoke of the privilege of living in peaceful Quebec. The writer mentioned that, coming back from a world trip, she almost kissed the ground of the airport as the Pope did. The teacher read this article aloud and pinned it up on the wall.

An annual school trip to see the exhibition of Christmas cribs in the nearby museum was integrated into the ordinary curriculum. The outing obliged not only the Catholic class children but also the non-religious course children to observe more than one hundred models of the holy family with baby Jesus in the crib. Throughout the school year, the children had no occasion to learn about other religious movements. After the trip, the teacher instructed the children to make their own enlarged model of the scene, with extensive detail. This model was made during ordinary lesson-time (French, maths, etc.), and was displayed in the classroom for weeks.

Even in the maths class, the teacher found a way to introduce the holy trinity "peace-Jesus-Quebec." During the Christmas season, which started at the beginning of November, the children learned addition and subtraction by using Christmas gift catalogues. The children were to bring several cutouts from their choices of toy catalogues and learn to calculate by combining these toys according to an imaginary budget. The teacher ordered the children not to bring any cutouts of violent, war-related, "foreign" toys. He made several children throw away their pictures of Rambo dolls, which were very popular at that time.

CONCLUSION

In spite of repeated emphasis on "Quebec," at the end of the school year seventeen out of twenty-one children could not draw correctly the provincial boundary of Quebec. The children learned the dichotomy of the world between Quebec and non-Quebec, without actually learning the geography. Our case study demonstrated that the children, without actually comprehending the geographic meaning of the word "Quebec," associated the word with positive religious qualities cherished by the teacher.

Life in the class as organized by the teacher-prophet conveyed two religious messages. One was the creation of a sacred order—cosmos—based on the symbolic realm of Quebec, and the other, the damnation of chaos, was conversely associated with the outer world.

Last but not least, "Jesus" legitimized all the teacher's classroom rules: disciplined by Jesus, the children learned to act out the beliefs of the teacher's image of "children" in the classroom.

ENDNOTES

[1]   Jean Rémy and Marcel St-Jacques, "L'Ecole comme modalité de transaction sociale," in *Recherches sociologiques* XVII(3), 1986, pp. 309–25.

[2]   See, for example, Erving Goffman, *Les moments et leurs hommes*, Y. Winkin (ed.) p. 214. Paris, Minuit, 1988.

[3]   It is interesting to note the discrepancy between the superficial image of the public or state school being free for all and its actual atmosphere of control and obedience.

[4]   Jean Piaget, *Le jugement et le raisonnement chez les enfants*, pp. 135–6. Neuchâtel, Delachaux et Niestlé, 1971.

[5]   Pierre Bourdieu and Jean-Claude Passeron, *La Reproduction*, Paris, Minuit, 1970, p. 75.

[6]   Thus, for example, a child who was not baptized, whose parents sent her to the non-religious course, often drew a scene of the teacher with flowers and a cross and gave these drawings as a gift to the teacher. She was the best in the class, but was always afraid of disappointing the teacher.

[7]   Interestingly, the guide book showed the Maoist doctor Norman Bethune as a pacifist, and as a contemporary model of Christian behavior.

[8]   The non-religious courses have been more organized in recent years. See, for example: Direction générale du développement pédagogique, *Programme de formation morale*, Government of Quebec, June 1977.

[9]   This, in spite of the fact that the children were encouraged to call the teacher by his first name, and to use the familiar form, not the polite form when conversing with him.

[10] Jean-Paul II, *Paroles d'un pèlerin. Tous les discours du Pape Jean-Paul II au Canada*, Ste-Foy, Anne Sigier, 1984.

[11] Editorial, *Châtelaine*, February 1987.

Edward B. Harvey and John W. P. Veugelers

PURSUING CANADIAN EDUCATIONAL EQUITY: THE NEXT STEPS

INTRODUCTION

In Canada, as in many other societies, people with post-secondary education have major advantages over others with less education. These advantages include higher occupational prestige, higher incomes, and greater job security.

The following excerpt spells out these advantages, as well as the ways that women, visible minorities, aboriginal people, and disabled people are disadvantaged in their ability to gain access to higher education. Women have increased their proportionate participation in post-secondary education to the extent that they now exceed the rates for men, but women remain under-represented in fields of study that lead to particularly high levels of income. (Coming from the lower class also hinders one's access to higher education, but this is not considered in this excerpt.)

The authors point out that the success of the employment equity programs now in place in much of the labour force depends on the educational system's ability to supply large numbers of people with minority status who have the requisite educational training. For this reason—and because education is both an important benefit for society and the individual—the authors argue that we should strive to achieve equal opportunity for educational attainment.

Post-secondary education confers important social and economic benefits. Canada's highest average incomes, best chances of being in the labour force, and lowest likelihoods of being unemployed belong to men and women who have graduated from a post-secondary institution. Recent data (1987–1992) from Statistics Canada illustrate these points:

- compared to male full-time employees with a high school education, average income is 9% higher for men with some post-secondary education, 12% higher for those with a post-secondary certificate or diploma, and 58% higher for university graduates;

Harvey, Edward B. and John W. P. Veugelers (1993). "Pursuing Canadian Educational Equity," *Policy Options*, November, 19–23.

- compared to female full-time employees with a high school education, average income is 11% higher for women with some post-secondary education, 21% higher for those with a post-secondary certificate or diploma, and 73% higher for university graduates;

- the labour force participation rate is 81% for men who have graduated from high school, 77% for those with some post-secondary education, 84% for those with a post-secondary certificate or diploma, and 87% for those with a university degree;

- the labour force participation rate is 64% for women who have graduated from high school, 68% for those with some post-secondary education, 73% for those with a post-secondary certificate or diploma, and 80% for those with a university degree;

- the unemployment rate is 12% for men who have graduated from high school or have some post-secondary education, 10% for those with a post-secondary certificate or diploma, and 6% for those with a university degree;

- the unemployment rate is 10% for women who have graduated from high school, 11% for those with some post-secondary education, 8% for those with a post-secondary certificate or diploma, and 5% for those with a university degree.

Moreover, post-secondary education has retained its value in the face of high unemployment levels. Statistics Canada reports an increasing shift toward higher education in the labour market, noting that between 1991–92 employment fell for all groups except post-secondary graduates. In sum, post-secondary education remains a key pathway to upward social and economic mobility in Canada.

ACCESS TO POST-SECONDARY EDUCATION

The tuition fees paid by post-secondary students represent a relatively small proportion of the total cost of their education. In fact, post-secondary education is heavily subsidized from the taxes paid by all working Canadians. Despite this broad base of financial support, inequality of access has long marked the history of post-secondary education in Canada.

In the 1950s and 1960s, the growing debate over the accessibility and benefits of post-secondary education centered on social class. Specifically, substantial evidence showed that persons from less advantaged socioeconomic backgrounds were much less likely to enroll in post-secondary educational programs than their counterparts from more advantaged socioeconomic backgrounds.

During the 1960s, government policy fostered the rapid expansion of post-secondary education in Canada. Several factors supported this thrust, including changing demographics, a growing need for a more educated workforce, and higher public expectations. As public expenditures on post-secondary education grew, the accessibility issue came into sharper focus. The Canada Student Loans Plan of 1964 represented a major policy initiative to ease the financial burden that placed post-secondary education beyond the reach of many qualified students.

In terms of socioeconomic background, has accessibility to post-secondary education improved over time? The available evidence suggests the answer is "yes," although people from more advantaged socioeconomic backgrounds continue to be over-represented in the universities.

CHANGING CONCEPTIONS OF EDUCATIONAL EQUITY

In 1986, after almost two decades of voluntary programs, Canada entered the era of mandated employment equity with the proclamation of the federal Employment Equity Act and the parallel implementation of the Federal Contractors Program for Employment Equity. The movement toward employment equity continues. Ontario, for example, has recently introduced comprehensive legislation at the provincial level.

These regulatory initiatives require employers to do several things, including: (1) survey their workforce to determine the representation level (by job and salary level) of the designated groups (women, visible minorities, persons with disabilities, persons of aboriginal origin); (2) compare internal workforce representation levels with representation levels in the larger labour market (or markets) in which the employer recruits; (3) set numerical goals and timetables for the hiring and promotion of designated group members; (4) review all employment systems and change any practices having an adverse effect on the employment and promotion opportunities of designated group members. The March 1993 issue of *Policy Options* was dedicated to employment equity and explores these and related issues in much greater detail.

The success of employment equity partly depends on the educational system's ability to supply designated group members to the labour market. We will explore this issue by examining the under-representation and segregation of designated group members in post-secondary education. Under-representation exists when a group's proportion of full-time post-secondary enrolments falls significantly below its share of high school graduates who are qualified for post-secondary studies. Segregation occurs when a group's distribution across the different fields of post-secondary study deviates significantly from the distribution for the corresponding comparison group. An example of gender-based segregation would be a situation in which 16% of male undergraduates but only 2% of female undergraduates study engineering.

Post-secondary under-representation and segregation may be analyzed at a number of levels, including the provincial and the institutional. We focus on national patterns, although a comprehensive assessment of the situation is hindered by the paucity of appropriate data. Unfortunately, Statistics Canada regularly surveys the enrolments and fields of study of men and women only. However, other types of information give a preliminary view of the barriers to post-secondary access for aboriginal persons, visible minorities, and persons with disabilities. The situation will be examined on a group-by-group basis.

WOMEN

Female representation in post-secondary education has grown considerably since the 1970s. Between 1970–71 and 1987–88, full-time community college enrolment (as an average of Canadians aged 18–21) increased from 10.0% to 22.1% for women, compared with 10.6 to 18.7% for men. Similarly, full-time university enrolment increased from 13.0% to 27.9% for women, compared with 22.2% to 26.6% for men.

Yet, pockets of female under-representation persist, notably at the doctoral level. While the proportion of female full-time graduate students has risen considerably over the past two decades, in 1987–88 it stood at 3.4% of Canadians aged 22–24, in contrast with 5.0% for men. Further, while women received 56% of all bachelor's and 47% of all master's degrees granted in 1990, they received only 32% of all doctoral degrees.

Gender-based segregation by field of study remains high. In the community colleges, men predominate in the natural and applied sciences (including engineering and computer science), whereas women are over-represented in the humanities, the health sciences (especially nursing), the social sciences and services and business and commerce (especially secretarial science). In most university fields of study, segregation actually increased between 1971 and 1987. Undergraduate women are over-represented in education and nursing, and under-represented in dentistry, applied science (including engineering), mathematics and the physical sciences. Segregation is even stronger among the eight major fields of graduate studies: women are clearly under-represented in three fields at the master's level, and four at the doctoral level.

ABORIGINAL PERSONS

Given the lack of data on aboriginal enrolment patterns in Canada, differences in access for aboriginal and non-aboriginal persons must be inferred from patterns of educational attainment. The most recent data available from Statistics Canada (1986) show that among aboriginal persons 15 years of age and over, 16.9% have a non-university post-secondary education and 1.2% hold a university degree. By contrast, 24.4% of the non-aboriginal population have a non-university post-secondary education, and 9.7% hold a university degree. Given these wide disparities, there can be little doubt that aboriginal peoples are under-represented in post-secondary education.

PERSONS WITH DISABILITIES

Patterns of educational attainment also point to differences in post-secondary access between disabled and non-disabled Canadians. The most recent data available from Statistics Canada (1986) show that among disabled persons 15 years of age and over, 13.6% have some post-secondary education, 8.3% hold a post-secondary certificate or diploma and 4.3% hold a university degree. By contrast, 18.7% of the non-disabled population in this age group have some post-secondary education, 13.5% hold a post-secondary certificate or diploma, and 10.2% hold a university degree. Clearly, disabled persons are also under-represented in post-secondary education.

VISIBLE MINORITIES

Unlike most aboriginal and disabled persons, many members of visible minority groups completed their schooling outside Canada. According to Statistics Canada (1986), people who were at least 20 years old when they immigrated to Canada constitute 43% of the visible minority population. Like most adult immigrants, they usually have higher levels of schooling than the Canadian-born population. Including those born and educated abroad, the proportion of visible minorities aged 15 years and over with some post-secondary education is 19.7%, compared with 15.7% for the total Canadian population of this age; the proportion of visible minorities with a post-secondary certificate or diploma is 14.3%, compared with 17.6% for Canada as a whole; and the proportion of visible minorities with a university degree is 16.8%, compared with 9.6% for Canada.

However, these figures strongly reflect the preference for highly qualified candidates under our immigration selection system. They say little about patterns of post-secondary representation among Canada's visible minorities of school age; neither do they tell us about segregation by field of study, or levels of post-secondary access for the different minority groups.

THE CASE FOR EDUCATIONAL EQUITY

The following general patterns emerge from this group-by-group analysis. Though women have overcome many traditional barriers, they remain under-represented in graduate studies. It is also highly likely that aboriginal peoples and the disabled are under-represented, especially in the universities. Little is known about the educational participation of visible minorities. Segregation along gender lines is particularly strong in mathematics and the sciences, but next to nothing is known about the fields of study of aboriginal peoples, visible minorities or the disabled.

As our earlier comments imply, the absence of adequate data is a persistent problem in the analysis of designated groups' participation in post-secondary education. Two databases maintained by Statistics Canada contain information on post-secondary enrolment and graduation patterns, broken down by institution and field of study. The University Student Information System (USIS) contains annual data collected from all degree-granting institutions in Canada, and the Community College Student Information System (CCSIS) contains parallel information for the non-degree-granting institutions. Unfortunately, apart from women, these data do not contain breakdowns for the designated groups.

Data problems aside, why should active consideration be given to developing educational-equity programs to complement existing employment-equity regulation?

While post-secondary education confers clear benefits to individuals, its costs are heavily subsidized by general tax dollars. As a public good, subsidized education is defensible as an investment in human resources which benefits the country. However, absence of discrimination is also a public good, and thus there is a contradiction when the state indirectly subsidizes institutional practices which perpetuate discrimination.

Educational equity is also defensible from an economic point of view. Assuming that intellectual capacities are distributed irrespective of sex, ethno-racial background, or physical disability, the systemic exclusion of people from these groups represents an under-utilization of Canada's human capital.

Finally, educational equity makes sense from a sociological point of view. Research shows that designated groups have traditionally experienced segregation and disadvantage in employment. These considerations drove the Abella Commission on Equality in Employment and subsequent federal legislation. By requiring employers to set goals and timetables for the representation of designated group members, mandatory employment equity seeks to reduce occupational segregation and exert a pull effect in the labour market. However, we also need a push effect. This can be achieved by policies designed to increase designated group representation (and desegregation) in post-secondary education—in short, educational equity.

Moreover, employment-equity programs alone will not correct discrimination in Canadian society, for discrimination begins outside the labour market. An understanding of discrimination calls for a comprehensive or systemic view of societal processes. From this perspective, it is clear that post-secondary education has an important effect on the labour market. Employers can reasonably be asked to hire and promote designated group members in a manner consistent with or reflecting the availability of qualified designated group members; employers should not be asked to compensate for the failures of post-secondary education. We might add that post-secondary institutions cannot be reasonably asked to compensate for the failures of primary and secondary institutions. The issue is not to pass the buck to ever earlier stages of preparation for life and work, but to define the fair responsibility of each institutional sector involved in the perpetuation of discriminatory inequities.

Why bother? Won't things change with time? This was the argument used to support voluntary affirmative action. The fact is, mandates work, voluntarism doesn't.

Already, some initiatives have been taken. The federal government provides financial assistance to aboriginal students enrolled in eligible post-secondary programs and the Legal Studies for Aboriginal People Program provides support to aboriginal people studying law. At the provincial level, Manitoba has a set of comprehensive programs targeting aboriginal and inner-city students. Known as ACCESS, these programs help students to negotiate the different phases of university education, and include counselling and special instruction. At the institutional level, the College of Arts and Science at the University of Saskatchewan has increased the representation of aboriginal students by lowering the minimum entrance requirement for this group.

NEXT STEPS

Looking to the future, two broad options—each with its own strengths and weaknesses—present themselves.

The first option gives priority to immediate action. As soon as possible, educational-equity programs would be elaborated, legislated, and put in place for areas where there is documented under-representation or segregation. In practical terms, this would translate into immediate initiatives on behalf of women. Beginning with women does not reflect a bias against the other designated groups. Rather, it reflects the fact that right now proper data are only available on gender differences in post-secondary access. When other barriers to post-secondary access are documented, other groups would become designated for the purposes of educational equity.

A drawback of the immediate action option might be the fragmentation of educational-equity policy. If fragmentation is accompanied by a weakening of political will, groups which ought to be targeted for educational equity may be forgotten. Alternatively, latecomer designated groups may find the institutional resources and energies needed to achieve educational equity are already spoken for.

Under the second option, comprehensive educational-equity programs would be implemented only after the proper information for all designated groups had been collected, analyzed, and interpreted. A unified approach might enjoy broader societal support, and could result in a fairer allocation of the institutional resources needed to promote equity for all designated groups. The main drawback arises from the difficulty of waiting until all the information comes in, especially when there can be no doubt that delay only adds to the under-representation and segregation of designated group members in post-secondary education.

Whichever option for educational equity is followed, the data on post-secondary enrolments collected by Statistics Canada should include new breakdowns. In the area of employment equity, the collection of detailed information at different points in time has made it possible to confidently assess the extent to which designated groups are represented in the workplace. Experience shows the availability of such information is of crucial importance. It gives a reliable picture of the employment-equity situation, identifies areas where progress has or has not been made, and strengthens program planning and evaluation. Similarly, a good understanding of educational equity will require appropriate data. Both the USIS and CCSIS databases maintained by Statistics Canada contain a wide range of useful information. The value of this information—particularly from the point of view of educational equity—would be greatly enhanced if breakdowns were obtained for all designated groups, not just women.

QUESTIONS

DISCUSSION QUESTIONS

1. Would you expect that education, in some form, is "universal"; that is, found in all societies? Why or why not? Discuss.

2. What is "educational equity" according to the excerpt by Harvey and Veugelers? Define and discuss.

3. What is "shadow education" according to the Stevenson and Baker selection? Define and discuss.

4. What is meant by the statement that schools are one of the vehicles of "social control" in society?

DATA COLLECTION EXERCISES

1. Check the gender distributions (the proportion of females and males, respectively) in each of your college or university classes. Which gender is over-represented, if any? Do you think the gender proportions in your classes are representative of gender proportions in your school as a whole? Why or why not?

2. Check the Yellow Pages in your local telephone book for examples of ads for "shadow education." Which types of shadow education predominate? Do you think the availability of shadow education in your community has changed over time? If so, in what way?

3. Through informal observations, assess whether "order" is an issue in the classrooms you are attending this year. Draw comparisons with the findings in excerpt 9.2.

4. What roles of higher education do you find mentioned most by your student colleagues in casual conversation? What are their particular goals for their current participation in school?

WRITING EXERCISES

1. Write a brief (500-word) essay on what you think would be the best way to achieve greater educational equity across social classes in Canada.

2. Write a brief (500-word) essay on the ways that Canada's shadow education likely differs from that of Japan, and why.

3. Write a brief (500-word) essay on your recollections of how order was maintained in your classrooms when you were in grade school. Did your teachers differ in their approaches? Do you suppose these differences were caused by the teachers' different personalities or teaching styles, or were they caused by differences in grade level?

4. Write a brief (500-word) essay on the important social consequences of schooling, both for individual students and for society.

SUGGESTED READINGS

1. Illich, Ivan. *Deschooling Society* (1972). New York: Harper and Row. This is a classic, controversial attack on schooling, emphasizing the negative consequences of anything approximating what we understand as formal education.

2. Murphy, Raymond (1979). *Sociological Theories of Education*. Toronto: McGraw-Hill Ryerson. This book presents a very readable and comprehensive discussion of the different sociological theories of how education operates in Canada and other similar societies.

3. Wotherspoon, Terry (1991). *Hitting the Books: The Political Economy of Retrenchment*. Toronto: Garamond. This volume contains a collection of articles on how education is currently organized in Canada, and how changes in the economy and public policy are affecting our schools. Also featured are analyses of the way the Canadian education system affects inequalities in social class, gender, and race.

SECTION 10   COMMUNICATIONS MEDIA

Introduction

As a group, sociologists react to communications media much like other people react to Rorschach ink blots—they look at the same data but see it in vastly different ways. Sociologists differ widely about which aspects of the communication process are the most important. Some focus on the messengers—who controls the flow of communications. Others focus on the media itself, the actual methods of communicating. Still others focus on the message, or media content. And finally, others focus on the receivers of the message, or the effects of media on people.

Scholars also differ in their attitudes towards the mass media, with theoretical perspectives that range from the highly critical to the fairly complacent.

VARYING INTERESTS IN THE MEDIA

The Interest in Messengers

The interest in messengers stems from the fact that access to the mass media is controlled. Editors decide what news stories to run or what books to publish. Filmmakers decide which scripts to film. Television managers decide what shows to air. Radio stations decide what music to play. Government censors decide what material is or isn't obscene, and so on.

In media theories, people who control access to the media are called "gatekeepers" because they decide whether or not to open the gate and let some information through. Gatekeepers range from the day-to-day decision-makers like news reporters to the owners of giant mass media corporations.

An interest in gatekeeping has led media scholars to study such issues as the concentration of media ownership, and the socio-economic backgrounds of such gatekeeping groups as reporters and editors. It has also led to an interest in the criteria that gatekeepers use in making decisions. Gatekeeping is especially important to groups who have been "marginalized" in the media. To be marginalized means that your group is rarely portrayed; and that your views, ideas, and concerns are rarely conveyed.

The Interest in the Medium

An interest in the medium of expression itself occurs because communications messages are never sent from one person's brain directly into another's. There is always a medium or vehicle that carries that message—even if the vehicles are just spoken words.

This fact raises all sorts of interesting questions about how the media vary in their means of, and capacity for, conveying certain kinds of messages. For example, the joy or sadness, sincerity or sarcasm, that can be easily expressed by a tone of voice has to be conveyed in a different way in the soundless medium of print. And a relatively simple written message will acquire a lot of additional visual messages if it is converted into a video form. The video as messenger becomes part of the message. The audience assesses not only a person's words, but also his or her body language, dress, physical features, and physical setting.

The fact that each medium that is chosen to convey a message will add and/or subtract something from that message means that the media don't just convey messages. The media actually become part of the message being conveyed. This is what media theorist Marshall McLuhan was emphasizing with his famous, though somewhat overstated, aphorism that "the medium is the message."

The Interest in Media Content and Media Effects

While scholars who are interested in media content all agree that audiences are affected by what they watch, how they are affected is much debated. Some scholars have studied how effective the media are at directly influencing public behaviour through education, advertising, or propaganda. Others have studied the ability of the media to influence popular behaviour through role modelling, stereotyping, trend setting, and "desensitization." A commonly alleged example of desensitization is when people who watch a lot of violent movies or television shows cease to be horrified by such images and may come to enjoy them.

Another way that media content affects popular behaviour is through "agenda setting." In deciding what to show or publish, media gatekeepers help establish what's new, meaning what constitutes an interesting topic for small talk or serious conversation whenever people meet at work or play. Equally important, the gatekeepers help set what *won't* be on most people's conversation agenda. Among the alleged effects of agenda setting is that the public has become excessively concerned with consumerism and such trivial diversions as sports and television entertainment.

SIX METAPHORS FOR THE MASS MEDIA

Different metaphors have been suggested for understanding the mass media. Each of the following six metaphors suggests a different way of interpreting what the mass media are, who controls them, and how and to what purpose they are used.

1. *The media as tools for socialization.* This perspective stresses that the mainstream media are controlled by society's ruling classes. The goal of the media is seen as being to present entertainment and information that supports and reinforces status quo attitudes, ideas, and opinions.

2. *The media as corporations.* The privately owned media corporations are seen as being controlled by business people whose chief interest is in making a profit. They reap these profits by designing products that attract large audiences and then selling access to those audiences to advertisers.

3. *The media as cultural mirrors.* Media content is considered to be a reflection of reality and therefore controlled by reality. Mirrors not only don't lie, they can't lie. The goal of the media is to show society to society. Cultural critics, includ-

ing Mary Vipond in this section, argue that a society's arts and entertainment reveal the essence of that society. The mass media should thus ensure that they reflect Canadian culture back to Canadians.

4. *The media as technology.* This is the perspective favoured by the medium-is-the-message theorists. It emphasizes that each medium has its own strengths, weaknesses, and rules of rhetoric and grammar that dictate how it will be used and what kinds of effects it will have on people. The medium itself, rather than its human controllers, determines much of the message content. The newspaper managers described in Deborah Cameron's excerpt would also seem to believe in this perspective. As Cameron points out, newspapers' language style policies create the impression that clear writing can guarantee honest, accurate reporting.

5. *The media as a debating forum.* Like the "media as socialization" perspective, this one stresses the media's ability to efficiently convey information, although in a way that is considered neutral or beneficial to the audience. The media are not seen as having any bias or interest in the outcome of any particular issue. Rather they provide a public service by seeking out and showcasing (rather than passively reflecting, as in the mirror metaphor) all legitimate viewpoints and ideas.

6. *The media as watchdogs.* Here the media are seen as going even further in protecting the public interest. The media's goal is to expose lies and injustices and provide the information the public needs in order to make democracy work. It's this perspective that informs Francis Kasoma's excerpt on the need for privately owned media in African countries.

ARTICLE 10.1

Deborah Cameron

STYLE POLICY AND THE LANGUAGE OF THE NEWS

INTRODUCTION

In a complex, busy world most of us rely on journalists to keep us informed about what important or interesting things are happening. In effect, we need them to be our eyes and ears. We want them to find out about topics that interest us and to report back in a clear, accurate, and unbiased way. We don't want them censoring information or slanting their reports to suit their own biases or the biases of any pressure group.

Cameron, Deborah "Style Policy and Style Politics: A Neglected Aspect of the Language of the News," *Media, Culture and Society* © 1996 (SAGE, London, Thousand Oaks and New Delhi), Vol. 18:315–333.

Deborah Cameron argues that one way newspapers appear to provide the whole, unvarnished truth is through enforcing rules about writing style. She argues that the policy of insisting on a simple, concise, factual style achieves more than just communications goals. In her words, it also "does ideological work." This is because our prevailing political ideology considers simplicity and clarity to be the virtues of straight-talking democrats. Conversely, only totalitarians and liars resort to convoluted, long-winded rhetoric that obfuscates rather than illuminates.

Cameron warns against equating simplicity and clarity with objective truthfulness. She reminds us that editorial choices about what's fit to print are necessarily subjective. So it's a bit ironic that some journalists vigorously refuse to bow to the stylistic wishes of the "politically correct" movement, yet uncritically accept the "journalistically correct" writing style imposed by the policies of their employers.

INTRODUCTION

Little attention has been paid by analysts to the fact that media institutions typically have explicit policies on language-use. Rules about usage are commonly codified in a 'style sheet' or 'style book' whose prescriptions journalists are expected to observe and editors to enforce, and there is also a more general notion of 'good style', which is meant to inform reporting and editing practice. Becoming familiar with the principles of journalistic style, and with the rules that follow from them, is part of the socialization of professional journalists.

The existence of style policies is relevant to a critical analysis of the language of news media for two main reasons. First, when analysts look for ideological effects resulting from lexical and syntactic patterning in news discourse, it needs to be acknowledged that some textual regularities may be the outcome of explicit style rules rather than implicit assumptions about the matter at hand. That does not mean ideological factors are irrelevant, but it does mean certain choices have been made in advance of any particular story or subject-matter.

The second, more important reason why style policies are of interest is that they are ideological themselves. Though they are framed as purely functional or aesthetic judgements, and the commonest criteria offered are 'apolitical' ones such as clarity, brevity, consistency, liveliness and vigour, as well as linguistic 'correctness' and (occasionally) 'purity', on examination it turns out that these stylistic values are not timeless and neutral, but have a history and a politics. They play a role in constructing a relationship with a specific imagined audience, and also in sustaining a particular ideology of news reporting.

Below I will develop these points by examining specific examples of stylistic regulation in news media.

MATERIALS FOR A CASE STUDY OF NEWSPAPER STYLE

The following analysis is based on a number of sources, among which the most important (and voluminous) are materials relating to *The Times* which are held in the archive of News International plc. The archive contains copies of successive *Times* style guides since the first edition of 1913 (revised editions were produced in

1928, 1936, 1939, 1953, 1960, 1970, 1984 and 1990). There is also a file containing internal correspondence in which *Times* style policy was discussed and amended between the Second World War and the 1980s. In addition, I had access to both draft and final versions of the current style book, compiled by Simon Jenkins during his tenure as editor and issued in 1992.

I was also able to consult the style sheet used at another News International title, *Today;* in addition I consulted those style texts which are in the public domain because they, or versions of them, have been published for a general readership: *The Economist Pocket Style Book* (*Economist*, 1986) and *Daily Mirror Style* (Waterhouse, 1981).

THE TONE OF *THE TIMES:* PLAIN LANGUAGE AND THE IDEOLOGY OF NEWS REPORTING

Many general stylistic precepts are regularly commended by newspapers across the social and political spectrum. In his foreword to the 1970 *Times* style book, William Rees-Mogg offered a summary of his stylistic goals that expresses the ideals of most English language newspapers in the 20th century:

> The style in which *The Times* itself should be written is based on the traditional plain style of English prose. It should be simple and clear. It should not sound affected, and should be neither archaic nor exaggeratedly contemporary in tone. . . . The tone of *The Times* has always been calm and judicious. It is this professional tone—clear, to the point, impartial and sensible—which is one of the essential virtues of the prose style of this newspaper. (*The Times*, 1970)

Here Rees-Mogg is making an explicit connection between certain formal qualities of language—clarity, simplicity, plainness and freedom from affectation—and a set of professional values that are not primarily linguistic, such as impartiality, judiciousness, cogency and good sense. The virtues of 'the traditional plain style of English prose' are congruent, it appears, with the values that ideally underpin news reporting in democratic societies. This connection between linguistic values and journalistic ones is a piece of received wisdom, by now so familiar and obvious as to be wholly unremarkable, certainly among journalists themselves. Yet, like most received wisdom or common sense, it rests on implicit, ideologically non-neutral propositions.

The arch-apostle of the 'plain style of English prose' was George Orwell, whose 1946 essay 'Politics and the English Language' is frequently cited in style guides (Orwell, 1968). Among the stylistic precepts recommended in the essay are to choose shorter words and phrases over longer ones, simpler over more complicated expressions and native over foreign ones, to prefer concrete formulations over abstractions, and to avoid jargon, euphemisms, clichés and dead metaphors. These precepts collectively represent an ideal of 'plain' language whose virtues lie in its accuracy and accessibility.

A 'plain' representation is idealized as a transparent form of communication (a point Orwell underlined when he compared good writing to a pane of glass): plain language is both an exact evocation of things in the world, and an unobtrusive representation that does not draw attention to itself as representation. Just as one can see through a pane of glass the undistorted image of whatever lies on the other

side, the ideal informing the 'plain style of English prose' is that nothing percepti-
ble should stand between the reader and the subject matter.

Orwell's thinking on this issue had an explicit political edge. In 'Politics and the
English Language' he argued that deviations from plainness and transparency in
public discourse could be exploited to manipulate public opinion. The questionable
actions of politicians could be buried under a mountain of impenetrable jargon,
glossed over in words too imprecise to yield a meaning or clichés too familiar to
engage the mind's eye, and rendered palatable by being smothered in a cloud of
euphemisms. Orwell suggested these were deliberate techniques of totalitarian pro-
paganda-making.

Orwell made plainness into a political as opposed to merely social or aesthetic
symbol, and as a result, newspapers' insistence on 'the traditional plain style of
English prose' could come to signify their commitment to the fearless truth-telling
which is the unique contribution of the press to upholding democratic values and
liberties—the implicit contrast being with what goes on in totalitarian states. This
idea echoes through William Rees-Mogg's foreword to *The Times*'s style guide of
1970, the plain style is the outward and visible sign of the sterling inner qualities of
a free press in a free society—objective, calm and sensible, impartial, judicious.

The argument I wish to make here parallels arguments made by critical discourse analysts with respect to the alleged 'impartiality' of news media; in this case,
however, I want to extend the argument that the language of the news is not
value-free. The celebration of 'plainness' does ideological work.

In an article on his new style guide published in *The Times* in 1990, Simon
Jenkins provides a good illustration of what that work might be, remarking: 'The
mirror that a newspaper holds up to the world is constantly smudged with jargon,
bad usage and verbosity. A style guide is a periodic cleansing of that mirror' (*The
Times*, 12 June 1990). Here once again is the image of the mirror, the pane of glass:
and the point is to impress upon us that the mirror, though it needs to be periodically 'cleansed', can in principle provide an undistorted reflection of reality.

The plain and transparent style recommended by Orwell is particularly well
suited to the prevailing ideology of modern news reporting as simply 'holding up a
mirror to the world'. The use of a plain, terse, concrete language in news items—a
language that deliberately aims not to draw attention to itself as language—is a
code, not unlike the code of realism in fiction, and what it conventionally signifies
is unmediated access to the objective facts of a story. It conveys that what we are
reading is not a representation: it is the simple truth.

That the idea of reportage as a 'mirror' is widely accepted may be demonstrated
by examining the way media producers trade on it. In 1993, for example, *Life* magazine mounted a billboard advertising campaign in Manhattan whose slogan was '*Life*.
For those who appreciate the difference between a view and an opinion'. Initially I
found myself unable to decide which alternative was supposed to be the positive
term; then I saw another poster with the slogan 'The last thing New Yorkers need is
another opinion'. It was also explained to me that 'view' in the first slogan was a play
on words, meant to evoke *Life*'s reputation for the quantity and quality of its photographs. The magazine, then, was selling the idea of 'views without opinions', the
prototypical 'view' being the one you get through a camera lens. This, I suggest, is

also the idea behind the norm of plain language in news reporting: it is the linguistic analogue of the camera that never lies, and should be treated with similar suspicion.

Linguistic representations, like visual ones, always embody a point of view; as critical analysts of the media have taken pains to show, even the most 'natural' and seemingly artless discourse is not free, and in principle cannot be free, from ideological presuppositions. The politics of discourse are, precisely, about convincing people otherwise: about persuading them that one way of representing a state of affairs is neutral, natural, obvious and true, while another way of representing it is ludicrous, loaded and perverse.

Orwell himself was less an incisive analyst of this kind of politics than a brilliant exponent of it. He excoriated the kind of political discourse that talked about 'the elimination of undesirable elements' instead of 'murdering your political opponents'; and most commentators have been too busy agreeing with Orwell's judgement on the first expression to notice the proposed substitute is not neutral either; it may use 'plainer' words, but it is equally a political intervention embodying a moral judgement.

Recently, those who make style rules for journalism have been forced to confront the issues raised by the argument that there is no neutral language in the phenomenon glossed as 'political correctness'.

POLITICAL CORRECTNESS: BEYOND THE PANE OF GLASS

Arbiters of news style have an abiding concern with the question, 'what is the correct way to refer to such-and-such a group or individual?'. The 'PC' controversy faces them with a proliferation of variants to choose from, and with the additional problem that choice itself has been politicized: none of the possibilities will any longer be apprehended as 'neutral' by the entire speech community. Should they prefer black or African-American/Afro-Caribbean, actor or actress, the old or the elderly? Since meaning works by contrast, any of these alternatives, even the most traditional, will be taken to express an attitude. I can say 'Ms X is our chair' and convey one attitude, or 'Miss X is our chairman' and convey another: the one thing I cannot do any more is utter either sentence and hope to convey by it only that a certain woman holds a certain office. Editors are right to see this development as a real and deliberate challenge to their assumptions about language and style.

Both the draft and final versions of the current *Times English Style and Usage Guide* contain entries under the heading of 'political correctness', but there is an interesting difference between the two versions. The draft entry reads:

> The English language, especially in the USA, has become infested by a stylish authoritarianism, designed to use style to make political statements—often on the pretext that style does that already. Since there is some validity in the pretext, every newspaper needs to be careful of all normative or emotional phrases, especially those referring to women and race. A story should not cause offence.

In the final version (pp. 116–17) the clause 'since there is some validity in the pretext' has been deleted. Instead the following sentence is prefaced with 'That said . . .'.

I find it interesting that this clause was 'pruned'. The acknowledgement that 'there is some validity in the pretext' that style makes political statements would, in the context of a style book, be remarkably radical; it might call into question the objectivity emphasized elsewhere in the guide, and pose awkward questions about why the prescriptions of editors like Mr Jenkins are legitimate whereas those of the 'PC' lobby are 'stylish authoritarianism'.

In choosing between linguistic variants, arbiters like Simon Jenkins are choosing between values that are not merely linguistic. Unable to fall back on the idea of neutral terms that simply 'tell it like it is' without conveying any particular attitude, how are they to justify their decisions?

In fact, the idea of plainness or transparency continues to be invoked to disparage 'PC' terms by contrast with traditional ones. African-American, for instance, has been condemned in Orwellian terms as a euphemism; but this begs the question, for what 'neutral' expression is it a euphemism? If the term critics have in mind is black, and the implicit argument is therefore that African-American coyly conceals the skin colour of the group it designates, it must be asked why the designation of this ethnic group (but not others) by skin colour should strike people as neutral and natural. What opposition to new nomenclature really signifies is a reluctance to call subaltern groups by names they choose for themselves, and by implication to accept their own criteria for identity (history/geography rather than race/colour in the case of African-American, for instance).

An alternative argument licensing the selective acceptance of new terms has found favour recently: the argument for 'civility' or 'sensitivity'. As Simon Jenkins suggests in the passage from the *Times* guide quoted above, one might choose to be careful about naming certain people, even if this meant deviating from plain terminology, on the grounds that 'a story should not give offence'. This is not unproblematic, because the tendency of 'PC' interventions to politicize all terms, especially in the domains of race and gender, means that all available usages are likely to be offensive to somebody. In practice, therefore, style arbiters are faced with deciding which usages will give least offence to a particular readership.

The 'civility' argument acknowledges that language does not just directly and neutrally refer to reality, but it denies the broader implications of that point, suggesting the problem is not so much how one represents the world at large as how one accommodates the 'sensitivities' of certain social groups. The argument implies that if an audience were made up entirely of conservative white men there would be no reason to be 'sensitive' to issues of sexism and racism.

Sometimes, the 'civility' argument is coupled with a return to the Orwellian position that language should above all represent facts accurately. In an *Observer* piece on so-called 'political correctness' (11 July 1993), Simon Hoggart offers a qualified defence in these terms of the 'sensitivity' section of the BBC guidelines. Referring specifically to the gender-neutral term firefighter, he suggests that 'now fire brigades are hiring women, firefighter isn't PC but just accurate.'

Linguistic innovations now placed under the heading of 'political correctness' are most likely to get past the media gatekeepers and be accepted or even prescribed in style books if they can be defended using arguments about neutrality, civility or accuracy. For example, the liberal feminist argument for gender-neutral terminology appeals to all three of these criteria: it suggests that acknowledging the existence of two gender groups rather than one is less biased, more accurate and generally less likely to offend. The principle has been widely accepted in the media. On the other hand, innovations are most likely to be rejected or ridiculed if they concern groups to whom the mainstream media feel no need to be civil, or if they represent some phenomenon in a way that is intended overtly to counter mainstream perceptions of it, thus transgressing mainstream understandings of 'accuracy'.

A good illustration of both these considerations is provided by Simon Hoggart in the article I have quoted already, where he discusses the term sex worker, a so-called 'politically correct' alternative to prostitute. Hoggart objects to sex worker on the grounds that: 'it does not merely spare feelings but makes a moral judgement—or rather, pointedly fails to make one by implying that "the sex industry" is on a par with hairdressing or engineering'. This is an accurate reading of the intention behind the term sex worker, which seeks to avoid the disapproving moral connotations of prostitute and to foreground the idea that providing sexual services for money is a job, just as cutting hair or making widgets for money is a job. The point is not to conceal unpleasant facts in the manner of a euphemism, but to present the same facts from a different angle.

By showing he understands this, but nevertheless objects to it, Hoggart reverses the argument about avoiding 'loaded' terms. In this case it is the traditional term that makes a moral judgement and the innovation that 'pointedly fails to make one'. Hoggart is therefore in the position of arguing that in some cases it is right for words to embody an a priori judgement and objectionable for them not to. His objection to sex worker is not that it conveys some attitude instead of no attitude, but that it conveys the 'wrong' attitude—which here, paradoxically, is moral neutrality itself. This suggests that when journalists talk about 'neutrality' and 'accuracy' in language, what they really mean is a language whose meanings and connotations coincide with prevailing common sense.

REFERENCES

The Economist (1986) *The Economist Pocket Style Book.* London: Economist Publications.

Hoggart, S. (1993) 'Silly Shibboleth of the Sex Workers'. *Observer* 11 July.

Jenkins, S. (1990) 'A Change of Style to Suit The Times', *Times* 12 June.

Jenkins, S. (ed.) (1992) *The Times Guide to English Style and Usage.* London: Times Books.

Orwell, G. (1968) 'Politics and the English Language', in S. Orwell and I. Lang (eds) *Collected Essays, Letters and Journalism of George Orwell,* Vol. 4. Harmondsworth: Penguin.

The Times (1990) *The Times English Style and Usage Guide.* London: Times Ltd. Today (1985) Stylebook. London.

Waterhouse, K. (1981) *Daily Mirror Style.* London: Mirror.

Francis P. Kasoma

THE ROLE OF THE INDEPENDENT MEDIA IN AFRICA'S CHANGE TO DEMOCRACY

INTRODUCTION

In many highly industrialized Western democracies, one hotly debated topic concerning mass media is the concentration of ownership. In Canada, for example, a handful of extremely wealthy people such as Conrad Black, Ken Thomson, Pierre Peladeau, and Ted Rogers now control the vast majority of daily newspapers sold in our country. Critics contend that concentration of ownership of the press is bad for democracy because it makes the information gatekeepers (i.e., the owners) too powerful.

Francis Kasoma reminds us that democracy isn't just threatened when the privately owned media become too powerful. In Africa democracy is palpably suffering because the privately owned media are too weak, under too much government control, or simply non-existent.

Certain conditions need to exist if the media are to perform their vital roles as sources of reliable information, debating forums, and watchdogs of government. They need to be profitable enough to pay the costs of responsible journalism—and most African economies are too poor to support a strong media sector.

More importantly, the media need the rule of law to protect free speech. And they need a political climate in which people believe that a "loyal opposition" is not an oxymoron. But African countries are often multi-ethnic states, with one-party political systems that are rationalized by the need to include all ethnic groups in government. So in many African countries, anything that divides people—be it a multi-party political system or a multi-viewpoint mass media—is viewed as potentially dangerous.

The role the independent media in Africa have played in resuscitating and maintaining democratic governance lost during three decades of dictatorship has, in the early 1990s, suddenly come to the fore. Two questions are being asked. First, could Africa's democratic rebirth have been possible without pressure from the independent media? Second, can the newly acquired multiparty political system and democratic governance last without the support of virile, independent media?

Kasoma, Francis P. (1995). "The Role of the Independent Media in Africa's Change to Democracy," *Media, Culture and Society* (SAGE, London, Thousand Oaks and New Delhi), Vol. 17, 537–555.

At independence in the early 1960s, most African governments came to power through democratic elections. For the first few years, they ruled in compliance with the democratic requirement of allowing opposition parties and other bodies to criticize the administration. They were also, by and large, accountable to the electorate. But dictatorship soon crept in. Opposition political parties and other critical groups and associations were silenced and one-party or military rule was adopted. The 1990s, however, have, once again, seen a return to democracy with the re-emergence of multiparty politics in most African countries.

This article discusses in perspective the role the independent media have played in bringing about the fall of one-party or military-ruled states and the realization of democratic governance. It also discusses the role the independent media should continue to play to keep the banner of democracy flying in a continent that is still, in 1995, largely being served by media which are both owned and controlled by governments.

In this article, by independent media, is meant newspapers as well as radio and television stations not subject to governmental, political and economic control or control of materials and infrastructure essential for the production and dissemination of newspapers, magazines and periodicals (adapted from Unesco, 1991). Under this term are excluded partisan media such as government-owned newspapers and broadcast stations as well as political party organs.

CONTRADICTORY VIEWS ON THE POWER OF INDEPENDENT MEDIA

When all has been said, there has not been much of an independent press in Africa to sing about. In Francophone Africa, the independent press only started in the 1990s, 30 years after the independence of various states was won (Duteil and Duteil, 1991). Official government newspapers or those belonging to the sole ruling parties or military regimes dominated the newspaper industry in nearly all sub-Saharan Africa. Even the so-called community media and rural newspapers were almost totally established and maintained by government (Unesco, 1989: 196–8). In Anglophone Africa, apart from a few countries like Botswana, Nigeria, South Africa and Kenya, which had a sizable number of independent newspapers prior to 1990, in most countries there were hardly any independent newspapers to speak of. Nearly all broadcast stations on the continent have, until the last couple of years, been owned and controlled by government (Kasoma, 1988). Moreover, the few independent newspapers that have been published in Africa have concentrated on urban people, both in terms of circulation and content, leaving the rural people, who constitute the majority of the population, untouched. And even in the urban areas, the independent press has been accessible only to a few relatively rich people who can afford to buy and read them. Millions of marginalized people in peri-urban shanty townships have been left out.

There are two contradictory views by media analysts, therefore, which this article seeks to reconcile, regarding the role of the independent media in Africa in enhancing democracy. On one hand, there are those who hold that African mass media are autocratic rather than democratic. The views, activities, trials and triumphs of the vast majority who are peasants, labourers, farmers, shepherds and market traders are usually excluded from them (Domatob, 1991).

Concurring about the dominance of an urban press on the continent, Fergusson (1993: 32) as well as Kpudeh and Riley (1992: 269) have stated that in the clamour for democracy sweeping across Africa, it is the urban professional's voice which is often heard and his or her demands appeased while the needs and perspective of the rural majority remain neglected. Fergusson (1993: 32) has further submitted that it is precisely to limit the participation of rural citizens that African states have been reluctant to extend modern telecommunication infrastructure outside main urban areas. The protagonists of this view are saying that the independent press in Africa has been so small in terms of reach and so elitist in terms of content that it cannot be much of a driving force towards bringing about democracy.

On the other hand, other media analysts do not agree. For Imanyara, the independent press, which he sometimes refers to as the alternative press, has been decisive in democratization.

> Generally, the role of the press in democratisation has been that of an independent forum and mouthpiece of crusaders of change. The openness of the alternative press to the public and its bold approach to sensitive and critical political issues, has had the cumulative effect of inciting the general public to wake up to their democratic rights and demand change. (Imanyara, 1992: 21)

Writing about the Kenyan experience before the coming of multiparty politics, Imanyara states that the alternative press had provoked the people to debate their political destiny at a time when the integrity of parliament was smothered by an overweening and predatory executive (Imanyara, 1992: 21).

Although in terms of size and reach the independent media in Africa have been generally small, particularly before the 1990s, they have tended to reach the most politically influential people. It is precisely the better educated urban dwellers, who the independent media have tended to reach, who can reasonably be expected to be receptive to the political views they may present and not the less educated and less politically aware rural and marginalized people who have been largely ignored by the independent press.

After being politically charged by the independent press, the urban elite start politicizing the rural and marginalized people with ideas largely borrowed from the agenda set by the independent media.

Africa's independent media can specifically be credited for contributing to political change in two significant ways. First, the independent press has broken the myth that African dictatorial presidents were invincible and could not be criticized. The once idolized presidents are no longer untouchable and, for the first time, have become subjects of severe criticism. The once so-called dissidents have found a voice in the independent press to express their recalcitrant views against the establishment to the disgust of the demythologized presidents, who have been quick to try and silence the unwelcome opposition.

An example was in Kenya where the incarceration of *Nairobi Law Monthly* editor Gitobu Imanyara by the government of Daniel arap Moi did little to stop the barrage of independent press criticism against the official one-party rule. Moi eventually had to capitulate and allow multiparty politics in Kenya.

The second significant contribution of the independent press to democratic, political change in Africa has been that some of the few readers who have been the most fervent supporters of independent newspapers have themselves been political aspirants of the new order and have used the newspapers to propel their ideas of dissent against government and call for a new political order.

INDEPENDENT MEDIA AS CO-REQUISITES FOR DEMOCRACY

The information that government media publish in most African countries gives the people mainly the government side of issues. When editors of government newspapers try to be objective by giving a semblance of criticism of government, they have been threatened with dismissal. Zambia's minister of information Kelly Walubita, for example, has constantly threatened editors of the government-owned *Times of Zambia* and *Zambia Daily Mail*, the country's only two dailies, with dismissal if they continued to criticize government (*Times of Zambia*, 18 March 1995).

Views from Africa's opposition parties have been, and are still, often censored out of government media amid protests from lovers of democratic politics. This is particularly more visible during electioneering, when the governing party marshalls all the government media to campaign for it at the exclusion of election messages from the opposition. In Zambia, for example, the state-owned Zambia National Broadcasting Corporation, the only radio and television broadcasting station in the country, even refused, during the transition to multiparty politics in 1990–91, to carry paid advertisements of the opposition Movement for Multiparty Democracy, until the court ordered it to do so. When the government media did publish news about the opposition, it usually painted the opposition parties in an unfavourable light.

In the new multiparty situation, political parties are too numerous and too weak to own and maintain their own party media which would give people alternative information. Even in some of the few cases where opposition parties are financially strong enough to have their own media, the governments do everything within their power to ensure that the media from the opposition are either not there, or do not operate effectively. Methods used include refusing to grant opposition parties licences to operate their own media. In Zambia in 1994, for example, the United National Independence Party (UNIP), the official opposition party, was denied a licence to operate a radio broadcasting station, in spite of the fact that the government has been granting licences to anybody who applies.

African governments are also known to refuse opposition party newspapers the use of their printing presses. Since in most countries the only printing presses are owned by the government, this effectively means that no opposition party newspapers can appear even if the parties had the money to publish them. Where privately-owned printing presses are available to opposition parties, the surcharge on newsprint and other printing requisites is so high that the newspapers, which hardly earn any money from advertising, are forced to close down.

To compound the situation even further, in some of the few countries where opposition party media have thrived, the information they publicise is as biased against government as government media information is against opposition parties. The result is that people are left wondering which of the two types of media are telling the truth. To compound the situation even further, some of the so-called independent newspapers in Africa are independent only by name. They sometimes publish blatant lies about government hoping to get away with it in the name of the freedom of the press.

TRANSPARENCY AND ACCOUNTABILITY

Apart from providing people with alternative information, the independent press in a democracy has a duty to promote transparency, accountability and good governance by revealing to the citizenry what government is doing or not doing that deserves public scrutiny. Government owes it to the people to explain its actions or the lack of them and does this mainly through the media of public communication (Kasoma, 1994b). The 'pressphobia' that many African leaders have that the press would destroy them politically unless they win it to their side does not augur well for democracy.

Of course, there is sometimes the possibility that independent newspapers conduct unethical journalism to put those in power on the spot (Kasoma, 1993). An instance of unethical journalism is when reporting is based on hatred of those in power rather than on an honest desire to make them answerable to the electorate. Some of the so-called independent newspapers in Africa today are guilty of this unprofessional conduct.

An independent and critical press acts as a safety valve of the steam boiler of the body politic. In a situation where people cannot speak freely because government agents are watching them, emotions start building up until they cannot be held back any longer. In the end, the people vent their anger and frustration through violent means such as riots. Violence is undemocratic because democracy is about the exchange of ideas and not about exchanging blows.

The problem in Africa has been that of partisan, usually government media, fanning the fire in conflicts to a point where one of the sides thinks it has no choice but to reply by starting a fight. As the fighting rages on, more fuel is poured on the political fire by a partisan press, resulting in a full-scale war. Evidence coming from Rwanda, for example, indicates that the media of that country played a big part in fanning the genocide. In November 1994, a press freedom watchdog based in Paris, Reporters Without Borders (RSF), accused Rwandan journalists of crimes against humanity for their part in the ethnic massacres which claimed hundreds of thousands of victims. The report, sponsored by the European Union and entitled 'Rwanda: Media of Hatred or a Democratic Press?', accused several journalists of playing a significant part in both preparing and carrying out the massacres. It named 27 journalists who worked for the nominally independent Radio-Television Libre des Mille Collines (RTLM), and said the radio station urged its listeners to exterminate the 'rats'. The channel would often name opponents and tell its audience to flush them out (*Zambia Daily Mail*, 4 November 1994: 1).

The study by Reporters Without Borders on the role of RTLM in fanning the genocide in Rwanda is corroborated by another study by Richard Carver and Adewale Maja-Pearce (1995), who provide chilling transcripts of the station's broadcasts inciting the Hutu population to genocide against the Tutsi minority. Carver and Maja-Pearce conclude that the role of RTLM in the genocide in Rwanda provides an instance of a growing trend in the region—from the Rift Valley in Kenya to the townships in Natal—of what might be termed the 'privatization' of violence, in which governments give covert assistance to 'tribal' militias whose subsequent activities can then be disowned by the authorities. The two researchers claim that after the state-owned Radio Rwanda had been forced to desist from inciting anti-Tutsi hatred following the massacres at Bugesera in March 1992, it simply switched to the nominally independent RTLM (Carver and Maja-Pearce, 1995: 207).

A partisan press is often capable of starting but not stopping a war. Where there is war, there is no democracy. Africa has a better chance of preserving its democracy if independent media brought all ideas to the marketplace for open discussions rather than letting the partisan government or party media present greatly biased information which raises tempers on the other side and causes fighting to flare up.

It is the view of this writer that even the so-called sensitive issues like tribal quarrels should be brought in the public arena by the independent media rather than be smothered, as they often are in Africa. There have been countries in Africa, including Kaunda's Zambia, which have taken the attitude that media should not publicize disagreements and quarrels among tribes because they are divisive and do not promote national unity. Supporters of such a view interpret national unity in a very narrow sense, as meaning complete unison and agreement among the various tribes in a nation. Disagreements and quarrels do not, however, necessarily negate national unity. People can disagree and still retain allegiance to one nation. Sometimes greater unity among the various people of a nation results from resolving a disagreement or conflict amicably.

THE FUTURE

If the concept of independent media excludes government-owned media, and if the current trend of the new governments of the multiparty state era continue resisting pressure to privatize government media, then the future of democracy on the continent is really bleak. Governments would still continue to manipulate the main media of public communication to their selfish advantage. The free flow of ideas that is a *conditio sine qua non* for democracy would continue to be curtailed in most of the African countries, as has largely been the case to date.

The independent newspapers and broadcast stations that would be there would not be financially strong enough to withstand pressure from the publicly-funded media, which would continue to get favourable treatment from government. In the meantime, governments would continue to proclaim that the media within their borders are free just because of the presence of a number of financially weak independent newspapers which hardly circulate beyond the borders of the towns in which they are published.

It is this author's prediction that the continued presence of government-controlled main media of public communication will make Africa revert back to dictatorship since there will be little public means of checking bad governance and misuse of power.

The demise of Africa's fledgling independent press is likely to be caused by two factors. First, it may, with the assistance of politicians in power, simply be strangled economically since it would be, so the people in government think, in their political interest to do so. At the moment, the economies of scale are against independent newspapers surviving as viable businesses. Most of them are surviving on subsidies, some of which are from foreign donors who are interested in seeing Africa's democratic experiment succeed; such subsidies cannot go on forever.

Second, the independent press could die by government legislation. There are two possibilities. Laws may be passed that would make it impossible for private media to continue operating, so that they are forced to close down. Alternatively, laws may be passed that would make the critical role of the independent media unattainable so that they would still be there physically but without the teeth to act as watchdogs against government.

REFERENCES

Carver, Richard and Adewale Maja-Pearce (1995) 'Making Waves', *Index on Censorship* 24(1): 205–29.

Domatob, Jerry Komia (1991) 'Serious Problems Face Media Education in Sub-Saharan Africa', *Media Development* 27(1): 31–4.

Duteil, Michel and Mireille Duteil (1991) 'The Press in Francophone Africa', paper commissioned by the International Federation of Newspaper Publishers on behalf of the United Nations and UNESCO for the Seminar on Promoting an Independent and Pluralistic African Press, Windhoek, Namibia, 29 April–3 May.

Fergusson, Philip (1993) 'The Links Between Democracy, Communications and Human Rights', *Media Development* 40(4): 31–4.

Imanyara, Gitobu (1992) 'Kenya: Indecent Exposure', *Index on Censorship* 21(4): 21–2.

Kasoma, Francis P. (1988) 'The State of the Media in the SADCC Countries: Overview of the Media in Angola, Botswana, Lesotho, Mozambique, Swaziland, Tanzania, Zambia and Zimbabwe', pp. 17–33 in *NORDIC/SADCC Media Seminar Proceedings, Harare, Zimbabwe, 16–19 September.* Tampere: University of Tampere, Department of Journalism and Mass Communication.

Kasoma, Francis P. (1993) 'Ethical Journalism and the New Political Liberalisation in Africa: The Case of South Africa and Zambia', paper presented at the Conference on Making Media Work for Southern Africa's Development organized by the Department of Journalism, Rhodes University, Grahamstown, South Africa, 27–9 April.

Kasoma, Francis P. (1994b) 'Adversarial Role of the Press in Zambia: Ethical Perspectives', paper presented at the seminar on Ethics, the Media and the Law, sponsored by the (Zambian) Ministry of Legal Affairs, Leisure Bay Lodge, Siavonga, 28–9 October.

Kpudeh, Sahr J. and Stephen P. Riley (1992) 'Political Choice and the New Democratic Politics in Africa', *The Round Table* 323: 263–71.

UNESCO (1989) 'Africa', pp. 196–8 in *World Communication Report.* Paris: UNESCO.

Mary Vipond

THE PROS AND CONS OF CANADIAN CULTURAL NATIONALISM

INTRODUCTION

Canadians live next door to the country with the strongest popular culture and most powerful mass media industry in the world. People the world over enjoy American movies, music, and television, and Canadians are no different. In fact Canadians are especially receptive, since we have so many cultural similarities with Americans.

Given the attractiveness and availability of the American alternative, preserving and encouraging an independent and uniquely Canadian culture is difficult. Mary Vipond examines whether or not the effort of trying to create and sustain a Canadian culture is worth making.

The value one sees or doesn't see in Canadian culture raises a kind of chicken or egg question about national identity and national culture. Having a strong sense of ourselves as a people with a distinct identity may be a prerequisite for caring about Canadian culture. But on the other hand, a strong national culture may be a prerequisite for developing a sense of our own uniqueness. So which comes first, a distinct identity or a strong nationalistic culture?

The objective fact is that Canadian culture is in some ways unique. Even critics of Canadian culture acknowledge this fact, although they may claim that "unique" is merely a euphemism for "second-rate." That Canadians have such divergent reactions to their own uniqueness suggests that the French-English split may not be the only great divide in Canadian culture. The other great schism is between those who can and those who can't appreciate the value of what makes us different from our neighbours in the U.S.

Let us examine the various positions taken over the years by the device of a mock debate.

Resolved: "Government intervention is necessary to preserve Canadian culture endangered by the Americanization of our mass media."

Affirmative:

A nation must have control of its own mass media, to facilitate the formation and expression of its own culture. Without that binding culture, the nation will disappear. As the Report of the O'Leary Royal Commission on Publications put it:

Vipond, Mary (1992). "The Pros and Cons of Canadian Cultural Nationalism," from *The Mass Media in Canada*, Rev. Ed., Toronto: James Lorimer.

Socrates' saying that the unexamined life is unfit to be lived is applicable to a nation as to an individual. A society or community, deprived of searching criticism of its own, among its own and by its own, has within it seeds of decay. . . . It may be claimed—claimed without much challenge—that the communications of a nation are as vital to its life as its defences, and should receive at least as great a measure of national protection.[1]

The economic realities, however, dictate that as long as our media remain private enterprises driven by market forces, they will be filled with American material or actually owned by Americans. But every hour or page devoted to foreign content on our mass media is one less available for Canadians to speak to each other. When Canadian voices are heard, they do say different things in different ways than American voices. Various studies show that there is an identifiable cultural difference between English-Canadian and American media content, not only in the selection of different subjects for news and entertainment, but in the tone and values conveyed.[2] The only possible protection of this unique expression is government regulation to require Canadian ownership and content of our media, or even actual government ownership, run on the principle of public service rather than profit. Canadian historian A.R.M. Lower wrote in 1953:

There is no doubt in my mind that if we Canadians allow television to pass under American control and with American programs providing the determinative element in the items offered, we may as well sooner or later shut up shop: our future will be American. Persons who deny this are blind when they are not worse. They were characterized in Parliament as "virtually traitors." With this description I agree. It is not a matter of public vs. private ownership—at least that is a secondary aspect of the controversy. The point is that private ownership means American control. No amount of subterfuge can whittle that statement away.[3]

There are also some very practical reasons why we should encourage a more Canadianized mass media. Canadian creative artists need opportunities to express themselves. They also need employment. Being labour intensive, the cultural industries create a disproportionate number of jobs and enhance tax revenues. Canadian companies also require Canadian media on which to place advertisements for their products. Both the cultural and the manufactured goods of Canada need protection from the economic might of the United States.

The only way to preserve our independence as a nation is to retain control of our communications sector, so we can continue to form bonds with one another rather than with Americans. That is why it was so important that cultural industries be left out of the free-trade negotiations. We run the risk of our values and beliefs and attitudes becoming indistinguishable from the American.

While Quebec is somewhat protected from American culture by language, even in that province there are reasons for great alarm about the penetration of American television, popular music and films. Not even a different language is strong enough to act as a natural barrier against the mass-media giant of the world—our next-door neighbour.

It is essential that Canada practise "defensive expansionism" by using the government to restrain and counteract the American presence in order to preserve and promote the cultural expression of our distinct sovereignty.

Negative:

The large presence of American popular culture in Canadian society, and particularly on our mass media, is the product of historical development; it is a natural phenomenon. The first large group of English-speaking Canadians, the Loyalists, were Americans, and they founded in English Canada a North American culture that is common to both countries. Since the nineteenth century most Canadians have largely adhered to American values such as individualism and free enterprise; our society is basically American in its shape and outlook, and therefore our culture is too. "The popular arts in Canada have always been foreign, never alien."[4] The border is imaginary.

The evidence is overwhelming that Canadians not only enjoy but actually prefer American popular culture. Recently a Montreal newspaper columnist put the point colourfully:

> Politicians take note: If we wanted Canadian content, dammit, we'd watch the *Beachcombers*. Will you clowns please stop forcing us to watch boring drivel made by your greedy and clamorous friends in the "cultural community"! Go away and leave us in peace to watch *Miami Vice!*[5]

When Canadian content rules were imposed on television and radio stations Canadians complained loudly—especially those who lived too far from the border to be able to receive American TV. The general desire for direct access to American television is the principal reason for the fact that Canada has one of the highest rates of cable penetration in the world. As well, a number of polls have shown that Canadians consistently believe that American TV programs are superior to their own.[6] No one forces American television, magazines, movies, newspaper comic strips or popular music on Canadians—they have shown how much they want these products by their willingness to purchase them in large numbers.

The issue is really one of freedom: first, freedom of expression and free access to the marketplace for all producers of cultural products no matter what their nationality, and secondly, freedom for all Canadian consumers to purchase what they want without censorship. Any interference in the natural functioning of the marketplace for cultural products, whether by regulation or by public ownership, is an interference not only with the most efficient and productive economic system but with the principle of freedom of speech fundamental to democracy. The consumer must be sovereign; the wishes of ordinary Canadians must not be ignored.

Most of the measures introduced so far by the Canadian government to counteract the natural desires of ordinary Canadians have been undertaken in the self-interest of a small élite that will benefit personally from rules and regulations imposing Canadian culture. If their products were truly valued by Canadians, they would be purchased. Instead, Canadian cultural producers have disdained anything "popular" as "American" and have lost touch with their own audiences. Because this élite is articulate and has access to the media, however, it has managed to convince Canadians that its interests are theirs. It claims the authority to define Canadian cultural goods as morally superior without addressing the issue of quality or admitting that other Canadians have the right to different cultural tastes. Attempts to interfere with the marketplace are thus unpopular and self-serving.

One extremely negative result of the nationalist approach to culture has been the centralization of media control in Toronto and Montreal and the consequent destruction of regional and ethnic identities. Far from creating national unity, these endeavours have exacerbated tensions within Canada. Many people in many regions, and especially those in Quebec, believe that the excessive focus on creating nationalism through federal cultural institutions has ignored their points of view. The emphasis on a national struggle against American culture has diverted attention from the fact that what Canada really needs is more inter-regional and inter-language communication.[7] Canada is becoming more, not less, decentralized, and media regulations that force "pan-Canadianism" are simply out of step with reality. To make the point from a slightly different angle, as Marc Raboy does in his recently published *Missed Opportunities*, "official" Canadian culture as defined in broadcasting policy has become an instrument of the state; it serves the needs of the state, not the diverse needs of Canada's many peoples. The *public* interest has been submerged by the drive to sustain the *national* interest.[8]

Finally, Canada is totally misguided to adopt policies that close it off from the rest of the world in any way. We live in a global village, and should take advantage of the ability of our media to offer us a window on the world. Ideas and information are too important to be stopped at borders. Protection just encourages the development of inferior materials; our audiences must be given the chance to see the best quality cultural products available in the world and our producers the opportunity and incentive to seek global markets.

Rebuttal by Negative Side:

Far from harming Canada's national interests, American culture in fact helps bind Canadians together. It gives us myths, heroes, and guides for living that Canadians from coast to coast can share. Most particularly, we are united by the model of the affluent society in which we can all participate.[9] In a very profound sense, then, American culture is also Canadian culture. It has been the basis of the national unity we have maintained to date—a popular national unity, not one dictated from Toronto or Ottawa. Indeed, American culture is one of the great common factors between English and French Canadians; both groups would rather consume American culture than each other's.

Clear proof that American culture is not damaging to the Canadian identity is the fact that Canada still exists, although it has been flooded by Americanized mass media for at least the past one hundred years. Many strands, both material and spiritual, hold this country together; *Time* and "America's Funniest Home Videos" cannot destroy it. As Richard Collins put it in his recent book on Canadian television, the assumption that political sovereignty depends on cultural sovereignty is not only mistaken but inappropriate to the present global circumstances. Culture is becoming transnational, appealing across national boundaries horizontally; Canada demonstrates to the world the possibilities of this more integrated, non-national, future.[10] Moreover, Canadians are quite capable of intelligent selectivity. In fact, our access to American cultural products probably makes us less rather than more receptive to the American way of life. We have a unique view of both the best and worst of our neighbour; we can choose to adopt and adapt the best and discard the rest. We can be and are critical; we know who we are and what we want.

In 1985 the federal government commissioned a private poll on public attitudes to foreign ownership in the cultural industries. Although they were well aware of its extent, only 37 per cent of those polled considered foreign content a serious threat to Canada's national culture. The report given to the Department of Communication by the pollster Decima Research concluded: "Many Canadians feel comfortable enough about their own identities to believe exposure to American culture will not undermine their own sense of Canadian identity."[11]

Rebuttal by Affirmative Side:

The large Canadian consumption of American mass media culture is not a natural phenomenon at all. It is the product of a complete misconception—that culture is a commodity. But culture is not a product like any other, it is a social good. It should not be sold in the marketplace by profit-seeking enterprises but should be developed as a public and national service. To some extent, in fact, American involvement in our cultural sector has not been "natural" at all but quite a deliberate part of U.S. government policy. For example, for many years the United States kept its postal rates for international second-class mail very low in order to stimulate the export of newspapers and magazines displaying the American world view.[12] It also allowed cartels like the Motion Picture Export Association of America to act in collusive ways contrary to domestic American law in the world market. The American government also fought long and hard to prevent Canada in the 1920s from getting a larger share of the radio spectrum allocation for North America, as it has more recently fought against developing countries at the international level. These are only a few instances of deliberate rather than natural factors lying behind our large consumption of American cultural products.

It has been argued that all the evidence indicates that Canadians prefer American popular culture. This may well be untrue. Figures gathered by the Caplan-Sauvageau Task Force indicate that Canadian television shows, when available, have audiences just as large as American shows. In 1984, Canadian-origin material constituted 28 per cent of the programming available on English-language TV, and 29 per cent of the viewing; it comprised 57 per cent of the programming on French-language TV and 68 per cent of the viewing.[13] More recent figures show that on the CBC, 67 per cent of the viewing is of Canadian material, and only 64 per cent of the offerings.[14] *Maclean's* and *Saturday Night* outsell their American equivalents in Canada handily, despite having much smaller editorial budgets. That Canadians watch so much American TV, buy so many American magazines and so on is a product solely of the availability of these products. This is not a choice made by the viewer or reader, it is the profit-driven choice of the owner, distributor or advertiser. The low Canadian demand for some specific indigenous products such as English-language TV drama and films is not "natural" at all, but the result of the fact that for many years Canadians were not offered anything else; they became conditioned to like American products because they lacked any alternative. "Tastes in viewing and listening are not innate qualities of the human species but are acquired by exposure and are shaped by what is available."[15]

Canadians have also indicated in many polls that they support government intervention in the cultural sector. For example, a 1980 Gallup poll indicated 67 per cent support for CRTC Canadian content rules, and a CROP survey the same year showed that 60 per cent favoured rules requiring movie theatres to schedule Canadian films 10 per cent of the time.[16]

We need government intervention in the mass media sector in order to make Canadian culture available to Canadians. No one wants to exclude foreign voices entirely, only to make more room for Canadian ones. Government intervention does not prevent choice, it enhances choice. It gives Canadians the freedom to choose Canadian that they would otherwise lack. Freedom of the press is indeed important, but it is not an end in itself. The press is only one part of the whole community, and does not have the right to injure that community in the name of a principle that often is simply a cover for profit-making.

ENDNOTES

[1] Royal Commission on Publications (O'Leary), *Report* (Ottawa: Queen's Printer, 1961), p. 4.

[2] See, for example, D. Hall and A. Siegel, "The Impact of Social Forces on the Canadian Media," in Singer, p. 66 and Morris Wolfe, *Jolts: The TV Wasteland and the Canadian Oasis* (Toronto: James Lorimer, 1985).

[3] Quoted in Frank Peers, *The Public Eye* (Toronto: University of Toronto Press, 1979), p. 42.

[4] Paul Rutherford, *The Making of the Canadian Media* (Toronto: McGraw-Hill Ryerson, 1978), p. 102.

[5] Doug Camilli, Montreal *Gazette*, Sept. 25, 1986, p. D-8.

[6] For example, see those of 1970 and 1980 cited in Collins, pp. 86, 234, and those of the late 1980s cited in David Ellis, *Networking* (Toronto: Friends of Canadian Broadcasting, 1991), p. 163.

[7] Arthur Siegel, *Politics and the Media in Canada* (Toronto: McGraw-Hill Ryerson, 1983), p. 178.

[8] Marc Raboy, *Missed Opportunities: The Story of Canada's Broadcasting Policy* (Montreal: McGill-Queen's University Press, 1990), pp. xii, 339.

[9] Rutherford, *Making of Canadian Media*, p. 103.

[10] Richard Collins, *Culture, Communication and National Identity* (Toronto: University of Toronto Press, 1990), pp. 4, 13.

[11] Montreal *Gazette*, Oct. 21, 1986, p. A2.

[12] I. Litvak and C. Maule, *Cultural Sovereignty: The Time and Reader's Digest Case in Canada* (New York: Praeger, 1974), p. 34.

[13] Report of the Task Force on Broadcasting Policy (Caplan-Sauvageau Report) (Ottawa: Minister of Supply and Services, 1986), p. 91.

[14] Ellis, p. 63.

[15] J. Meisel, "Stroking the Airwaves: The Regulation of Broadcasting by the CRTC," in B.D. Singer, ed., *Communications in Canadian Society*, 3rd ed. (Toronto: Nelson, 1991), p. 227.

[16] P. Audley, *Canada's Cultural Industries* (Toronto: James Lorimer, 1983), pp. xxv, xxvi. See also the table of poll results from the 1960s and 1970s in S. Bashevkin, *True Patriot Love* (Toronto: Oxford University Press, 1991), p. 73.

QUESTIONS

DISCUSSION QUESTIONS

1. Canada's music industry is arguably the strongest of our cultural industries. Do superstars such as Bryan Adams or The Tragically Hip owe much of their success to the Canadian content regulations that have forced Canadian radio to play the songs of Canadian artists?

2. Sometimes the media's desire to mirror reality will conflict with the desire to maximize profits. For example, the makers of a made-for-TV movie that is based on a true story may conclude that their product would be more appealing if they alter some of the facts. What kinds of fact changing, if any, are ethically justified if the story is to remain basically true?

3. Kasoma suggests that a privately owned media independent of government control is necessary to democracy. Discuss whether the "gatekeepers" in privately owned media would be more democratic than gatekeepers in government-owned media.

4. Discuss the media coverage of a recent major event. What biases, if any, did you detect in the coverage?

DATA COLLECTION EXERCISES

1. The mass media can both report and distort facts. Choose one impression of social reality that you believe to be true (e.g., that some kind of crime is more prevalent than it used to be). Then use library resources to see if the data tell the same story as the media.

2. Why do Canadian television stations air so many American-made programs? One reason may be economic. Compare the costs of producing a Canadian show and importing an American-made one.

3. Do a content analysis of a newspaper for one week. Record which kinds of people (in terms of age, gender, ethnicity, and occupation) are and are not considered newsworthy.

4. Find out what the major media corporations are and what percentage of each industry they own.

WRITING EXERCISES

1. Some messages are better suited to some media than others. Choose a musical artist whom you think wouldn't have been as successful before videos became prevalent, and explain why you think this in a brief (500-word) essay.

2. Write a 500-word editorial on why tax dollars should (or shouldn't) be used to support public broadcasting in Canada.

3. Write a brief (500-word) essay on why you agree or disagree with the proposition that the amount of violence on television and in the movies is excessive and ought to be curtailed.

4. Choose a group of people who you think have been either unduly ignored or stereotyped in the media. Give some examples.

SUGGESTED READINGS

1. Herman, Edward S. and Noam Chomsky (1988). *Manufacturing Consent*. New York: Pantheon Books. The authors subscribe to the "media as tools of socialization" model. They challenge the belief that the privately owned media are open to a variety of viewpoints. The book analyzes the news coverage of several major events, and documents how in each case the media portrayals propagandize the issues in order to win people over to the corporate establishment's viewpoint.

2. McLuhan, Marshall (1964). *Understanding Media*. New York: McGraw Hill. McLuhan is an eclectic and often cryptic writer. In this seminal book he gives numerous historical examples of how each communication innovation transmits much more than just content. He argues that by changing our capacity to express and understand information, each new medium changes the nature of being human.

3. Postman, Neil (1985). *Amusing Ourselves to Death*. New York: Viking. In this book media critic Postman argues that the electronic media have disrupted people's capacity to use and appreciate linear logic, which he associates with the print medium. What's worse, Postman says, the main function of the electronic media has been to divert us with entertaining but superficial images and trivial amusements.

SECTION 11   RELIGION

Introduction

Some sociologists define religion as "a set of beliefs, symbols, and practices (for example rituals) which is based on the idea of the sacred, and which unites believers into a socio-religious community. The sacred is contrasted with the profane because it involves feelings of awe" (*The Concise Oxford Dictionary of Sociology*). This approach to religion follows in the steps of Emile Durkheim, who focused on the functions of belief and ritual in binding people together in social groups.

Other sociologists, following in the steps of Max Weber, view religion as "any set of coherent answers to human existential dilemmas—birth, sickness, death—which make the world meaningful. In this sense, religion is the human response to those things which concern us ultimately" (*The Penguin Dictionary of Sociology*). Here, the concern is less with social cohesion and more with the role that religion plays in interpreting the world for us.

In both definitions, religion includes all of the thoughts and practices that put people in touch with the "transcendent." The followers of some religions believe the transcendent lives in natural objects like the ocean and in natural forces like the wind. Others think of distinct creatures—gods, goddesses, nymphs, devils, and so on. Some religions have many gods, others have only one, while some religions—like Buddhism—have none. Some believe in an afterlife or in reincarnation, while others do not. Differences in ideas of good and evil, and in ritual practices, also distinguish the religions of the world.

THE SOCIOLOGY OF RELIGION

Since there are two main approaches to religion in sociology, there are at least two sociologies of religion and they tend to move in different directions.

The sociology of religion that grows out of Durkheim's work tends to include all beliefs and rituals that create intense social bonding and/or involve the use of ritual objects. For many, this includes nationalism as a form of "civil religion," complete with flags, patriotic songs, and historic heroes. For some, it even includes such activities as watching rival teams play soccer or following a TV series like Star Trek. Both activities excite intense emotion, encourage loyalty, and come complete with ritual objects (e.g., team scarves, Trekkie memorabilia). Excerpt 11.1 discusses some aspects of the Star Trek "religious" phenomenon.

Such inclusions make the study of religion a little too broad for many sociologists. However they also raise interesting questions: How is a soccer championship game, or the final Star Trek voyage, like a religious experience? How is the Catholic Mass, or a Jewish circumcision, like a mass sporting or entertainment event? Why do people spend so much money on NBA team shirts? On Elvis memorabilia? On crucifixes and trips to the Holy Land?

On the other hand, we know there is something essentially different between the meaning of a "sacred" object and one that is "profane"—even if the profane object (e.g., John F. Kennedy's armchair) also excites strong sentiment and awe. This is the difference between something that is ultimately important and something that is ultimately trivial.

In the Weberian tradition, religion is concerned with questions of ultimate importance: Am I saved or damned? What is the moral way to live? How will I know if I am doing the right thing? and so on. From this standpoint, religion is a cultural or philosophical system that confers meaning and interprets reality.

In some cases, these religious interpretations can have an important influence on political behaviour. In the last few decades, fundamentalist religions have been especially important in this way. Excerpt 11.2 illustrates the way that the "religious right" has attempted to mobilize support for a new political party.

Religious systems of interpretation are also important for economic life, as Weber showed in his study of the Protestant Ethic. Recall that Weber linked the rise of capitalism—a new style of economic thinking—with the rise of Protestantism, a new form of Christianity. In particular, he tied capitalism to Calvinism, a form of Protestantism that developed in western Europe in the sixteenth century.

What Weber called the "Protestant Ethic" is a doctrine formulated by Protestant reformer Martin Luther, who believed that everyone should work very hard for the glory of God. Later Protestants, called Calvinists, took this doctrine of Luther's, combined it with a belief in predestination, and unwittingly helped to create the new economic system of capitalism. Weber explained the connection as follows: Calvinists believe that all people are predestined to go to either Heaven or Hell. Precisely who is going to Heaven and who is going to Hell is already decided. Nothing that people can do will change the outcome, and (strangely) this is what makes people free. As a result, Calvinist religion strongly emphasizes the freedom of the individual, and reduces people's dependence on the Church, priesthood, and ritual. Such autonomy and independence played a key role in the historic rise of capitalism.

Both approaches to the sociology of religion—Weber's and Durkheim's—converge in the study of charismatic social movements. Here we see social bonding occur, with important political consequences, around new conceptions of the world and an inspiring new leader.

CHARISMATIC MOVEMENTS

Social movements typically form around a set of common interests or grievances—and even ultimate concerns about life, death, virtue, and justice. In some cases, however, the goals of a social movement become secondary to its leadership. The followers develop a commitment to their leader that may become more important to them than their particular interests.

Max Weber identified such a movement as one centred on a "charismatic," inspiring leader. "Charismatic authority" is based on the belief that the leader possesses extraordinary personal qualities that should be admired and deferred to, independent of any bureaucratic office the leader may or may not hold.

The history of a charismatic social movement is, largely, the history of its leader and the successes or failures of that leader. The leader of a movement is charismatic when he or she inspires loyalty and enthusiasm among followers, despite the cost or danger this affiliation poses to them.

Charismatic leaders hold unshakeable beliefs about the rightness of their cause. They exert a powerful hold over their followers, who believe the leaders' qualities of personality are transcendent, superhuman, or inaccessible to common people. Such powers, which often include the gift of prophecy, make it easier for leaders to control the masses—particularly in new or developing societies.

However, charismatic social movements are also self-limiting. Because the followers' attachment to their leader is intensely emotional these social movements are unpredictable and operate at a fever pitch. They can be loving one minute and violent the next. Paradoxically, the movement becomes more stable and predictable after the leader dies or retires. Then the movement enters a process of routinization. A bureaucratic structure emerges, patterns of authority develop, and day-to-day duties replace spontaneous acts. The group relies less on inspiration and more on tradition than it once did. This transition was particularly marked in the rule of Ayatollah Khomeini, described in excerpt 11.3.

Routinization creates institutions—for example, churches and trained clergy—that draw on people's deepest faith in the movement. Rational and well-organized, these institutions are strong enough to withstand the tests of faith that people suffer in everyday life. Through routinization, the movement achieves a measure of permanence. Movements that routinize charisma provide their members with friendship and help, maintaining their involvement with the group. Failure to routinize almost ensures that the movement will die out.

As we see in the following excerpts, there is no easy way to separate religion, politics, and the concerns of everyday life.

Michael Jindra

STAR TREK FANDOM AS A RELIGIOUS PHENOMENON

INTRODUCTION

Some scholars believe that religion is on the decline in Western society, and that people's views have become more "secular" (or this-worldly) and less "sacred" (or other-worldly). Others argue that religion remains a central part of people's lives, but that forms of religious involvement are changing. This second set of scholars argue that traditional religion is now sometimes replaced by "emergent forms" of religion, or quasi-religions. Examples of these new forms are Alcoholics Anonymous, or "New Age" groups.

These groups have no churches or church services. But like traditional religions, they have regular meetings and are socially organized, albeit in a less stable and hierarchical manner. They espouse particular beliefs and provide people with explanations of their lives in the context of ideas about ultimate and universal reality.

The author of this excerpt argues that the fans of Star Trek—the science fiction TV series and the movie spinoffs—constitute one such quasi-religious group. He shows that Star Trek fandom involves sacred beliefs and shared views about the future and the meaning of life. As well, there are communities of fans with regular practices and rituals. Like members of other new religions, Star Trek fans are sometimes stigmatized by "outsiders," making for feelings of persecution and creating a shared identity among them.

So, is Star Trek fandom a new religion? Or is it more like the hockey fandom discussed in excerpt 1.3—a mere form of North American popular culture? And how can you tell the difference between popular culture and a modern religion?

INTRODUCTION

Star Trek (ST) fandom is a phenomenon unlike any other. Now over 25 years old, it originated when the original *Star Trek* television series was threatened with cancellation after its first year. Fans immediately sprang into action with a letter-writing campaign to keep it going. When it finally was canceled after its third year, the show went into syndication, and ironically, that is when the "fandom" phenomenon really started to take off. The first convention was in New York in 1972. A centralized fan clearinghouse organization, the Welcommittee, was established in 1972 to introduce fans to ST fandom. At this time, noncommercial

Jindra, Michael (1994). "Star Trek Fandom as a Religious Phenomenon," *Sociology of Religion*, 55, 1, 27–51.

fan magazines ("fanzines") were already being written; and books, manuals, and novels were published.

Efforts to revive ST broadcasts in some form continued. An animated series was produced from 1973–1974, and in 1979 the first of the six (at present) ST movies was released. In 1987 *Star Trek: The Next Generation* (TNG) was produced by Paramount for first-run syndication. Going into its seventh season in Fall 1993, it has achieved its highest ratings yet, often making it the top hour-long show among males 18–49 years of age, and also a top-rated show among other viewer categories, including females.

No other popular culture phenomenon has shown the depth and breadth of "creations" or "productions" (in the broad sense of "cultural productions") that Star Trek has, both officially and unofficially. The numbers are staggering: over $500 million in merchandise sold over the last 25 years (Paikert 1991), over 4 million novels sold *every year* (often bestsellers), dictionaries of ST alien languages, institutes that study them, "fanzines" numbering in the thousands, hundreds of fan clubs, conventions, on-line computer discussion groups, and tourist sites, plus of course the endless reruns, broadcast in over 100 countries. Captain Kirk and Mr. Spock, the two main characters on the original series (TOS), are household names not only in the United States but in other English-speaking countries, as is the spaceship on which they travel, the *Enterprise.* Other popular culture fads have come and gone over the years, but ST recently celebrated its twenty-fifth anniversary and shows no sign of letting up.

STAR TREK AS A RELIGIOUS PHENOMENON?

When I undertook this research, my first intention was to focus on how ST draws a picture of the future that is attractive to many Americans. But early on I realized I was dealing with something much bigger and more complex than I had anticipated. Star Trek was not limited to science fiction fans, nor was it just a pop culture phenomenon created for corporate profit, as will be made clear by this essay.

Star Trek fandom seemed akin to some kind of *movement.* It certainly was not a political movement, but it had political aspects. It was something broader than that, more like a religious movement. At first thought this seems rather ludicrous, for *ST is a TV show.* And yet as I looked at it further, it had features that paralleled a religious-type movement: an origin myth, a set of beliefs, an organization, and some of the most active and creative members to be found anywhere.

SOMETHING TO "BELIEVE" IN:
THE WORLD VIEW OF STAR TREK

ST, of course, is to a certain extent a subset of the larger category of science fiction. Frederick Kreuziger calls science fiction a religion in America, with its "central myth" of progress "which helps people live in or into the future" (1986:84). It is a universalizing faith, meant for all people everywhere. Much science fiction does not allow for the possibility that people may opt out of the type of society envisioned by writers, for it is assumed all will happily participate in it. Science and technology are the vehicles by which this future will be brought into existence, "and should be understood in religious terms" as that which "breathes new life into humankind" (1986:15).

There have been two main genres of science fiction, the utopian and the apocalyptic (1986:100). ST falls solidly into the utopian category. ST history shows that war on Earth eventually stopped, and nations and planets joined together in a "United Federation of Planets" for which the *Enterprise* is an ambassador, explorer and defender. This "positive view of the future" is one of the most popular reasons fans like the show, as they often state themselves. William Tyre (1977) sees in ST the mythic theme of paradise, one that links past and present, or that disguises the past as present. ST embodies the symbols, ideas and ways of feeling or arguments about the meaning of the destiny its members share, one that is uniformly positive. April Selley (1990) sees in ST:TNG an Emersonian type transcendentalism that is a sort of "naturalism" based on the power of science and humanity's manipulation of it. Faith is placed in the power of the human mind, in humankind, and in science. On ST, threats are normally from alien forces, as problems such as poverty and war and disease on Earth have been eliminated.

Even Star Trek writer and director Nicholas Meyer states that "ST has evolved into a sort of secular parallel to the Catholic Mass. The words of the Mass remain constant, but heaven knows, the music keeps changing. . . . Its humanism remains a buoyant constant. Religion without theology. The program's karma routinely runs over its dogma" (1991:50).

Star Trek is part of American mythology, similar to the frontier myth and the TV show "Westerns" that exemplified it.

This mythic element of ST is explored more fully in *The American Monomyth*. The authors examine how the Star Trek mythology of progress, discovery, science and egalitarianism is deeply ingrained in our culture, and it is these notions we seek to transmit to others through the world (Dolgin and Magdoff 1976; Kottak 1990). ST exemplifies this on a literally universal scale.

One cannot talk of central American values, religion or myths, without seeing "progress" at the center of them. Progress underlies our economic policy ("development") and is central in our politics, especially in election years, when the political rhetoric extols the great "potential" of the American people.

ST mixes the scientific and technical ideals of America with its egalitarian ideology to produce a progressive world where people from all races work together in a vast endeavor to expand knowledge. The following was written by a fan about the first public viewing of ST, at a World Science Fiction convention in 1966: "We noticed people of various races, genders and planetary origins working together. Here was a future it did not hurt to imagine. Here was a constructive tomorrow for mankind, emphasizing exploration and expansion" (Asherman 1989:2).

Religion often points us to another world; ST does the same. As we will see below, this world is ambiguously real to many ST fans. In this way it is not different from the tradition of Christian eschatology that sees, in the context of a linear history, a future perfection. Variations on this theme have been adapted by many other Western philosophies, such as orthodox Marxism.

STAR TREK FANDOM

ST as a religious phenomenon can be understood as a set of beliefs, but the activities of its fans gives us a much fuller picture of its religious potential. To see the origins of the vast activities of ST fans, let us look briefly at the history of science fiction fandom, the precursor of today's widespread ST fandom movement.

ST fandom is in part the culmination of a phenomenon that began in the post World War I era, when science fiction pulp magazines had a small but loyal readership. From the beginning it had the makings of a group set apart from the rest of society.

> The central fact about the science-fiction community, writers and readers alike, was that it was a family. The members shared interests and outlooks that the rest of the world disdained. They thought in terms of science and the future, and when they weren't reading or writing about those things, what they wanted most was to talk about them. In so doing, they gave birth to that unique cultural phenomenon, science-fiction "fandom."

> It is very difficult to explain science-fiction to anyone who has never experienced it. The closest analogy, perhaps, might be to the "cellar Christians" of pagan Rome, small, furtive groups of believers, meeting in secret, shunned or even attacked by outsiders, or as fans came to call them, the "mundanes" (Pohl 1984:47).

> These fans formed a community, at first exclusively male, with females entering later: "fans married fans and raised their children to be fans; there are third- and even fourth-generation fans beginning to show up these days at the 'cons'—a short term for science-fiction conventions" (Pohl 1989:47).

So a precedent was set for ST fandom, and it was out of science fiction fandom that the first ST fans came. The story of the origin and growth of ST fandom has itself attained a level of mythology, as a kind of origin myth of the movement. One of the first showings of ST, at a science fiction convention in 1966, is recounted in the following manner in the *Star Trek Compendium*. The author talks of the event almost in terms of a conversion experience:

> After the film was over we were unable to leave our seats. We just nodded at each other and smiled, and began to whisper. We came close to lifting the man (Roddenberry) upon our shoulders and carrying him out of the room. . . . [H]e smiled, and we returned the smile before we converged on him (Asherman 1982:2).

From then on, according to the author, the convention was divided into two factions, the "enlightened" (who saw the preview) and the "unenlightened."

ST's exposure to a prime time television audience, however, began to give it a wider audience than science fiction ever had. The letter-writing campaigns to save the series are now legendary, as is the leader of this movement, Bjo Trimble, who later published her memoirs (1983). In it she details the organization of the campaign and the massive numbers of letters that were sent to NBC, which saved the show from being canceled after its first year. The movement became even stronger after the series was finally canceled (largely due to a bad time slot) in 1969 after three seasons. Here is how ST fandom is described by one of its earliest fans:

All in all, fans literally starved for new information, new material, more fuel for their fiery obsession—for their almost-religion of a more-than-promising future. Because of a lack of material to placate a mind hungry for ST, fans had to be creative. . . . [E]very fan of ST was family—a distant friend we had not met. Conventions were like stepping through an enchanted doorway into another world. The force of fandom was palpable and we longed for rebirth. We believed we could make it a reality so we wrote letters and scripts and reviews and novels. We wished. We dreamt. We burned with inspiration.

The author goes on to speak of "suffering," which made the revival all the sweeter. ST "brought hope." It also brought "intolerance and prejudice" against fans. Why? "Probably because Trek somehow threatens their perfect little microcosm of existence." The writer then speaks about the "cultural acceptance" of ST. "ST and its fans still have the powerful magic to make an impact on society; even to manipulate the future. That ability has been proven" (Van Hise 1990:11–12).

LINKING THE STAR TREK UNIVERSE TO THE PRESENT

In various ways, the Star Trek universe is "linked" with the contemporary world. The lead-in to every TNG episode ("Space: the final frontier. These are the voyages of the Starship Enterprise . . .") begins with a shot of the Earth from close in, and then a gradual "tour" through the other planets of the solar system until it finally focuses on the Enterprise. This sequence orients the viewer to envision the events as taking place in his own universe.

Other "linkage" is accomplished by some of the Trek manuals and novels. The recently published *Star Trek Chronology: A History of the Future* (Okuda and Okuda 1993), compiles a history of the world from the present to the time of the latest *Enterprise* in the twenty-fourth century.

This world is a direct projection into the future from the present, for the show continually refers to historical events from the twentieth century and before. Through time travel, many plots actually take place in pre-twenty-first century time. Episodes that have done this are frequently among the most popular. One fan I talked to focused on how space and time are manipulated in the plots, especially through time travel, which allows one "a second chance, . . . to set things right again." Time travel allows us this ritualistic recourse, much the same way healing rituals or rituals based on origin myths do.

It has been suggested that ST is ahistoric. It relates not to any specific time and place but is meant for all time (Amesley 1989:336–37). William Tyre argues the same thing:

Myths no longer link us to the past, since we know the past is gone and is of historical, not immediate, relevance to the present. Bicentennialism recalls the past. On the other hand, any science fiction can link us to the future. . . . ST, by disguising our past as our future, puts us in it, not the historical past but the mythic past of our first beginnings. . . . [T]he series (ST) itself mediates the tension between the past and the present by establishing a third time, that of first beginnings. It is a time with the anticipation and wonder of the future without the anxieties of the present, with the glory and security of the past without its remoteness. By transcending in an ultimately inexplicable way the sum of message and medium STAR TREK puts the fan-become-believer in that time (1977:713, 717).

ST has also affected the fans' lives. Actors often relate how they get letters from fans telling them how the show inspired them to become engineers or doctors, or to do well in school (also see Lichtenberg *et al.* 1975). ST has given people hope for the future, inspiring them to take control of their lives in the same way many self-help and quasi-religions do (Greil and Rudy 1990).

Fans also want to bring ST into the present time, to order things along the lines of the ST universe. ST fans have had an impact on the United States space program, supporting increased funding and specific space programs involving manned and exploratory space missions. Science fiction becomes science fact (Asherman 1989:151) as "fans actively engineer events to make it true" (Van Hise 1990:14), such as naming the first space shuttle the USS *Enterprise*.

CONCLUSION

Is Star Trek fandom a religion, or at least a religious phenomenon? Recently, academics have been exploring different definitions of religion, prompted by the growth of new religions and "quasi-religions." ST fandom does not seem to fit the more restrictive, substantive definition of religion that posits belief in a deity or in the supernatural. It does, however, have some commonalties with broader definitions of religion that come under the rubric "quasi-religions," such as Alcoholics Anonymous and New Age groups. These organizations "ride the fence between the sacred and secular" (Greil and Rudy 1990:221), between religion and nonreligion. The religious content varies according to whom in the movement one talks, and how involved they are.

These new religions often have "no stable organization, canonized dogmas, recruitment system, or disciplining apparatus" (Luckmann 1991: 178). They tend to be more therapeutically-oriented, qualifying as "Identity Transformation Organizations" (ITOs), which "encourage adherents to undergo radical shifts in worldview and identity" (Greil and Rudy 1990:226–27). This element is less explicit in ST fandom, but it is there. George Takei (who played Sulu in TOS), one of the more popular convention speakers, usually gives an inspirational-type speech detailing the history of ST and fandom, how they both show the potential of humankind and help inspire people to get their lives together and make career decisions. "For the believer 'Star Trek Lives' is more than a slogan of a TV show that would not die. It is the ritual cry to a world where he belongs, where he has it all together. STAR TREK offers the comfort of religion" (Tyre 1977:717).

ST fandom, however, differs in some significant ways from the quasi-religions described above. It is more organized than many of these other groups. ST fandom may not have a disciplining apparatus (outside of "flaming" someone on the computer nets), but it does have an organization, dogmas, a low-key recruitment system, and a "canon." The appeal of many of the above groups tends to be limited to certain segments of society. ST fandom cuts across class, gender, and ethnicity more than many other quasi-religions. Fans come both from working-class and academic and professional backgrounds (though what they like about the show often differs). Even though there is a stigma associated with serious fandom, ST does provide a certain commonality and unity of purpose for a wide variety of people.

Indeed, I would argue that ST fandom has strong elements of a "civil religion." Robert Bellah, who popularized the notion of a civil religion, calls it "an understanding of the American experience in the light of ultimate and universal reality" (1974:40) that seeks to become a world civil religion, which is exactly what we seem to have in the assimilationist, homogeneous Earth of twenty-fourth century Star Trek. The generalized beliefs involved in ST fandom consist, as detailed above, in putting faith in science, humanity and a positive future.

For many fans of popular culture, organized religion seemingly has less relevance, partially because they perceive it not as forward looking but as backward looking. Americans are traditionally forward looking, and it is events like the space race that animate them. ST fandom embodies this idealism and offers fans reasons to hope.

ST fandom does not have the thoroughgoing seriousness of established religions, but it is also not mere entertainment. This interplay of seriousness and entertainment, I argue, is a sign of its vitality. The communities, both symbolic and geographic, that are formed by ST fandom are evidence of the ongoing sacralization of elements of our modernist culture that express hope in the future. It is a phenomenon that relates to deep-seated American beliefs about the nature of humankind, the world and its future, and encourages the practices that parallel religious processes of codifying, forming a community and developing institutions to guide its practices.

REFERENCES

Amesley, C. 1989. "How to watch Star Trek." *Cultural Studies* 3:323–39.

Asherman, A. 1989. *The Star Trek Compendium* (updated). New York: Pocket Books.

Bellah, R. 1974 [1967]. "Civil religion in America," pp. 21–44 in R. Richey and D. Jones (eds.), *American Civil Religion*. New York: Harper & Row.

Dolgin, J. and J. Magdoff. 1977. "The invisible event," pp. 351–63 in J. Dolgin, D. Kemnitzer, and D. Schneider. (eds.), *Symbolic Anthropology*. New York: Columbia University Press.

Greil, A. and D. Rudy. 1990. "On the margins of the sacred," pp. 219–32 in T. Robbins and D. Anthony (eds.), *In Gods We Trust*. New Brunswick, NJ: Transaction.

Jenkins, H. 1988. "*Star Trek* rerun, reread, rewritten." *Critical Studies in Mass Communication* 5(2):85–107.

Kreuziger, F. 1986. *The Religion of Science Fiction*. Bowling Green, OH: Popular Press.

Lichtenberg, J., S. Marshak, and J. Winston. 1975. *Star Trek Lives!* New York: Bantam.

Luckmann, T. 1991. "Religion old and new," pp. 167–82 in P. Bourdieu and J. Coleman (eds.), *Social Theory in a Changing Society*. Boulder, CO: Westview.

Meyer, N. 1991. "Star Trek." *Omni* 14 (3):48–51.

Okuda, M. and D. Okuda. 1993. *Star Trek Chronology*. New York: Pocket Books.

Paikert, C. 1991. "Special report on *Star Trek*." *Variety* (Dec. 2):49ff.

Pohl, F. 1989. "Astounding story." *American Heritage* 40 (Sept./Oct.):42–54.

Selley, A. 1990. "Transcendentalism in *Star Trek: The Next Generation.*" *Journal of American Culture* 13:31–34

Trimble, B. 1983. *On the Good Ship Enterprise.* Norfolk, VA: Donning.

Tyre, W. B. 1977. "Star Trek as myth and television as myth maker." *Journal of Popular Culture* 10:711–19.

Van Hise, J. 1990. *The Trek Fan's Handbook.* Las Vegas: Pioneer Books.

A R T I C L E   1 1 . 2

Scott Grills

TOMORROW FOR SALE: POLITICS AND RELIGIOUS FUNDAMENTALISM

INTRODUCTION

Their stock may go up or down across elections, but most political parties are relatively long-standing. Rarely are we able to see first-hand how a new political movement develops itself into a genuine party. The author of this excerpt has watched the emergence of the Christian Heritage Party in Canada. He has interviewed party promoters, and attended many public meetings aimed at acquiring new party members. In this excerpt, he focuses on the procedures used to "sell" the party to potential members.

Scott Grills points out the many similarities between the Heritage Party's activities and the behaviour of salespersons in the marketplace. Familiar techniques that are used to sell goods and services are also evidenced in the attempts to "sell" the party. They involve procedures for establishing credibility of the product, promoting the involvement of the customer, and closing the sale. (Compare this with excerpt 8.2 on life insurance sales.)

However, there is one major difference: for this party, not just any willing customer will do. Because of the centrality of the party's religious beliefs to the political ideology and public policies it supports, party promoters look for particular kinds of members. Everyone joining the party must sign a statement indicating that they hold specified religious and political beliefs. So in this case the social institutions of religion and politics are closely connected. Historically, is this connection between politics and religion common or rare?

Grills, Scott. "Tomorrow for Sale: Politics and Religious Fundamentalism." By permission of the author.

Fledgling political parties with aspirations for electoral success must promote the initial involvements of members and adherents. Through an extension of the marketplace analogy (Prus, 1989a; 1989b), this essay examines the recruitment activities of one such party—the Christian Heritage Party of Canada (C.H.P.). While party promoters may utilize a variety of strategies to encourage the involvements of others, here I examine the process of recruitment in the context of the "public information meeting." Focusing on party promoters' efforts to recruit others, this article examines the processes of establishing credibility, promoting involvements, and closing the "sale." It is through such recruitment-directed activities that party promoters attempt to move audience members from onlookers to party members and through such organizational advances alter the direction and agenda of Canadian federal politics.

SETTING THE STAGE

The public information meeting is often the first extended effort made by the C.H.P. to establish a membership base in a riding. The meeting is organized, promoted and chaired by members of the local community previously brought "on side." Party membership is not required of these initial organizers, rather they are sold on the idea of the appropriateness of Christian political action. If these people become members, all the better, but the aim of the provincial organizers is generating a local team within a riding whose responsibilities begin and end with the public information meeting. Once such a meeting is held, the party will have generated a contact base within a riding from which to launch a recruitment drive and organize subsequent meetings if required.

This paper draws on a range of ethnographically derived data, obtained as a part of a much larger study over three and a half years (Grills, 1989), from observations of 42 public meetings and 73 in-depth unstructured interviews with 52 respondents. Attendance at these meetings has ranged from 7 to over 1300, with a typical meeting attracting between 28 and 35 people.

Conversations with those attending the meetings make clear the "church dependent" nature of the networks utilized by the C.H.P. in this initial building process (Grills, 1994). Meetings may be held in the sanctuary of church buildings themselves, sometimes scheduled to coincide with a regularly held service of fellowship. This combination of political recruitment and religious observance occurred exclusively within evangelical assemblies. Meetings were more commonly held on theologically "neutral" ground. However, the church affiliation of those in attendance tended to parallel those involved with the local organization of the event. While the party keeps no official records of the church affiliation of its members, the executive have a clear indication of where its support is to be found:

> Without a doubt the strength of this organization is within the Reform community, the Canadian Reformed and the Free Reformed. Next I guess would come the evangelical churches, the pentecostal assemblies of Canada and then third would be the Roman Catholics. They are quite a diverse group. We saw it the other night where the one priest was with us and the other was against us. But we are going to

get more support from these people down the road when we make clear that we are the only national party with a clear statement on the protection of the unborn. (provincial executive)

The following discussion is organized relative to the central processes of promotion and recruitment which accompany the "selling" of the C.H.P. in public settings. My central concern is an examination of the processes by which party promoters encourage others to undertake party membership—a commitment which requires the acceptance of the following statement of belief:

> We believe in one creator God and the Lordship of Jesus Christ, and the inerrancy of the Holy Bible as the inspired word of God.
>
> We believe that the major functions of government are to uphold law and order, to maintain justice in the land, and to ensure for each individual:
>
> i) the sanctity of life from conception to natural death
>
> ii) the privilege to own property
>
> iii) freedom of religion, speech, and assembly
>
> iv) the freedom to live one's life according to Biblical principles.
>
> We believe that any legislative decision or plebiscite to be held must not contravene any Biblical principles.
>
> I/we support the above principles and wish to become (a) Christian Heritage Party Member(s). (membership application)

ESTABLISHING CREDIBILITY

C.H.P. spokespersons seek to legitimize their enterprise through staging competent and creditable performances before their audiences. The message they offer is one which combines an interpretation of Christian theology and a rather specific political-moralistic program. As Garfinkel (1956) has demonstrated, "degradations" on the basis of a shared morality require the empowerment of the denouncer to speak on behalf of the principles held by the collective. Reflecting such collective empowerment, public information meetings begin with an attempt to establish the subservience of those gathered to a shared understanding of "God's will," while at the same time demonstrating that the C.H.P. is a viable and/or necessary political entity.

> Oh heavenly Father, we give our thanks for this country that You've given us to live in. We give You our thanks for the freedom that we have to assemble together to build the Christian Heritage Party. We pray for parts of the world where it means prison or death to assemble as we are tonight. Give us hearts that we never forget the blessings which You have provided in multitudes too great to count. We ask Your blessing for those who rest in authority over us. We pray that You will keep them in the way of wisdom and understanding. Bless our time together this evening. We ask that it be a time of fruitful fellowship. We commit ourselves now and forevermore to Your service, through Jesus Christ our Lord and Saviour. Amen. (local clergy)

The symbolic importance of a time of common prayer extended beyond the expression of and political subservience to a common set of beliefs. For party promoters "prayer time," while respected, was a precursor to the message which they delivered. To "open in prayer" was deemed essential as it grounded the activities to follow in a common understanding of purpose and intention. As representatives for the local community often led participants in prayer, "prayer time" was a dimension of the meeting outside party promoters' immediate control and thus was not without risk. The hope was that the prayer would not prove divisive by reflecting the theology of one tradition to the exclusion or degradation of others present.

Credibility may be initially established through a clear demarcation of the shared aspects of Christian belief, yet the search for audience support also includes the demonstration that this fledgling party was worthy of consideration seriously in the world of electoral politics. Given the party's limited success by any traditional measures of political influence, the organizational accomplishments of the party were emphasized. Key aspects brought forward included the quick momentum accompanying the growth of the party and its "truly national" character. A year and a half after its founding, the C.H.P. had 6500 members and offices across Canada.

The message of party growth served to establish legitimacy and promote subsequent involvements. It also provided promoters with a context within which to imply that the party was in one way or another "God-sanctioned." Credibility was established by drawing a link between the party's organizational successes and the demonstration of God's favour. Party promoters may refer to this dynamic to suggest that this "success" is an indication of the divine sanction of the party's activities.

PROMOTING INVOLVEMENTS

Party spokespersons promote involvements by supplying techniques of neutralization for anticipated lines of resistance (Sykes and Matza, 1957). Party promoters speak of their work as the "awakening of a sleeping giant." The social scientist might choose to describe this process as the politicization of an extended religious community. Phraseology aside, both speak to a central aspect of the work carried out by the C.H.P. and its supporters.

The religious communities represented at C.H.P. meetings reflect a range of perspectives, yet all tend to refer to the scriptures as "the truth" of human existence and to identify themselves as "Bible-believing" Christians. Within this tradition, there is a clear endorsement of the separation of the church and state, and a tendency for community members to include activities in their lives which can be seen as contributing to a Christian life style. As such, C.H.P. meetings include some people who do not own a television or a radio, who have never been a member of a political party in their lives, and who have never cast a ballot in a federal election.

> Who would I vote for? None of them are Christians in what they do. If I were to try and vote for one my wife might pick the other and we'd cancel out each other's vote. Better to stay at home and let others with the stomach for such things to go about their business than vote for what we have. (audience member)

The task of the party promoter involves politicizing an audience which has, in part, formed some objections to blending church and state—of "dirtying one's hands" or "lending the Lord's name" to an exclusively secular affair. To be sure, some audience members are veterans of the political process, who have had careers of involvement in alternative political enterprises. However, these other political organizations have not been so clearly tied to a Christian world view.

The following discussion focuses on techniques used by party promoters to neutralize objections which they perceive to deter Christian participation in the political process. Specifically, I examine efforts to overcome audience resistances through cleansing the enterprise, stabilizing the enterprise, and creating a moral imperative of involvement in the enterprise.

Cleansing the Enterprise

Party organizers refer to the difficulty they face in promoting involvements due to the more or less negative public images attributed to those engaged in political work. Typified notions of politicians as "untrustworthy," "two-faced," and "evasive" promote audience resistance and serve to further distance the "Christian community" from the political enterprise. In much the same fashion as used car salespersons may try to distance their performance from the discreditable images of their role (Swan and Ortinau, 1988), party promoters attempt to distance the Christian political enterprise from the field of party politics more generally.

> For the past twenty years people in this country have gotten used to their politicians lying to them. Remember Trudeau in '80 vs. Clark. Clark said there would be an increase in gas taxes, Trudeau said no way, he wins the election and before you know it the taxes are up. He tries to excuse it away but people say we were lied to. This is what we are up against. People say we know politicians and they are liars, so if you are a politician you must be a liar too. I have to agree with them, they have been lied to. But we have to show them that this is a sorry state when you cannot trust your Prime Minister, we have to get across that we are honest and open and trustworthy. (party promoter)

Party promoters may attempt to distance their activities from the perceived disrespectable nature of politics by engaging in the "Christianization" of the political process. By asking "what does it mean to be a Christian in politics today?", party enthusiasts attempt to neutralize objections which focus on the perceived corrupting influence of politics and political power. By maintaining that the C.H.P. involves Christians first and politicians second, promoters attempt to establish their enterprise as a form of political expression qualitatively distinct from the mainstream.

In practical terms, this is done by reformulating the political message. The goals of other parties—of winning elections, forming governments and courting the favour of the press—are criticized as "unprincipled government by consensus and public opinion poll." Party promoters put forward an alternative "blueprint" for political action whereby the standard for evaluation is "obedience to God's word." The accompanying view of the political enterprise is one which stresses honesty, the permanency of moral precepts, the praise of opponents, and the rejection of populist notions of success.

Stabilizing the Enterprise

Recruitment to the party is, in part, contingent on party promoters' ability to neutralize concerns about the future "moral fibre" of the C.H.P.'s membership and leadership. The name "Christian" brings with it varying audience expectations of the nature of the political enterprise and invites comparison with others united under the extended banner of Christianity. These comparisons may do little to ease the task of party promoters. The record of Christian political enterprises in Ireland, South Africa, the Netherlands, Germany, and the United States may detract from the image of this Canadian endeavour.

> One of the toughest questions that I know is out there is how can we be sure that this party won't go like the others. The European Christian parties that have continued to slide to the left to the point that their policies cannot be defended biblically. I don't have a clear response to that. . . . Ultimately it comes down to a belief, in a faith that God will continue in his support of our efforts and not allow us to go astray. (party promoter)

With an awareness of this audience concern and its potential hindrance of recruitment efforts, party promoters attempt to assure audiences of the long term stability of the collective. Specific strategies utilized in an attempt to neutralize audience resistances involve grounding policy in a set of unalterable principles based on the "immutable word of God," and restricting membership to those who sign a statement of faith.

An Obligation to the Enterprise

The activities of party promoters tend to encourage the audience to become comfortable with the idea of political involvement. As discussed, this includes attempts to neutralize common objections to the political enterprise held by audience members. Efforts here focus on demonstrating that political involvement does not inherently contradict theological commitment, nor need it necessarily involve a compromise of religious beliefs. Presentations vary across party promoters, based upon their impression of their audience and local issues in the community. Promoters may take an opportunity to stress the importance of Christians "getting involved" in the political process. The message often is not so much "join with us" as it is that people have an obligation to "do something":

> The Bible commands us to be salt and light. You cannot spread light by hiding it under a bushel. How do you shed light in a world where so many important decisions are in the hands of the politicians? You have to go where they are. We have to stand up at the all candidates meetings and ask each candidate what they are doing to protect the unborn. It means supporting your local right to life groups. It means doing what we can for [like-minded provincial parties]. (party promoter)

While such arguments may encourage involvements in the C.H.P., they are something more than a recruitment strategy for party promoters. Unlike merchants who may have little or no personal involvement with the products they sell, party promoters are deeply committed to the principles which they put forward. When asked about the implications of promoting involvements in issues important to the Christian community and their place in the "sales pitch" for the C.H.P., a member of a provincial executive reminded me:

> I suppose you're right. We do do some of that. We do say you have an obligation to get involved. I think it is their duty as Christians to become involved. And I do want them with us, to help fight the next election. But remember, I would rather have the C.H.P. fold right now, than have the abortion situation continue as it is. Sometimes we make political mileage out of issues, out of ideas. But I'd give up everything we have accomplished to stop the murder of 65,000 Canadians. (party promoter)

CLOSING THE SALE: CREATING MORAL CLOSURE

Much like any sales performance, the C.H.P. performance hinges on the close—the attempt to generate the involvements of those assembled. Much of the earlier C.H.P. presentation contributes to establishing a sense of moral closure (Lemert, 1953). Through the promotion of involvements, party representatives attempt to demonstrate the appropriateness and necessity of Christian involvement in the political enterprise. While political involvements are encouraged, promoters attempt to discredit mainline political parties as representative of the policies and programs which Christians need to unite to oppose. The intent is to effectively restrict the alternatives for political involvement by audience members. Through earlier attempts at establishing party credibility, promoters have presented their organization as a "truly Christian" political alternative. To close the sale, promoters argue that the C.H.P. is the place for Christians to put forward the political voice which they have a duty to express.

Like Prus' (1989a) vendors, party promoters may be relatively inattentive to the use of closing techniques, or may shun this aspect of the sales analogy:

> I am there to openly and honestly tell them about our party, to answer their questions as truthfully as I can. I do see myself as a salesman for the party at times, but (some of the others) they go for a big finish. They try to leave the people they are talking to no other choice but to join. Personally I'd rather leave them with a way out. If they are going to go out that door without becoming a member after hearing what we stand for, then I'm not sure that we needed them as a member anyway. (party promoter)

This quotation also suggests a striking difference between vendors and the work of party promoters. While vendors may have a "personal stake" in the goods they offer for sale and have an interest in the qualities of the consumer, most consumer exchange is relatively impersonal and is oriented towards the completion of the sale. C.H.P. promoters do not seek to sell a membership to anyone with the ability to purchase. The "pitch" is directed to "Bible-believing" Christians, and so too is the close. Specifically, promoters attempt to create a moral closure through: (1) an appeal to history, (2) an appeal for the victims and, (3) an appeal for the facilitation of Christian expression.

Appeal to History

Party promoters resurrect the images of the original "Dominion of Canada," the participants of the Charlottetown Conference, and their dependence on scripture as a personal guide in the formation of the nation state of Canada.

> And who will deny that we in Canada have a Christian heritage. If someone asks you, is this country Christian, ask him what is it? Is it Buddhist, is it Muslim, is it Hindu? Of course not, it is Christian. Evidences of that are abounding. Look at our constitution. What does it say? The very opening premise, "Whereas Canada is based on the supremacy of God, and the rule of law", our original name, Dominion of Canada, has its roots at the Charlottetown Conference of 1864, when Sir Leonard Tilly stood up and read Psalm 72, "And He shall have Dominion from sea even unto sea and from the rivers unto the ends of the earth." . . . There is a Christian heritage that our forefathers saw fit to pass on to us, and it is this heritage that is under attack. (party promoter)

Thus, party promoters argue that Canada has a Christian heritage, and that audience members have an obligation to this heritage to continue the work undertaken by their predecessors. What begins as a historical treatise becomes a personal admonishment. Moral closure here takes the form of placing before the audience an implicit dilemma: either they support the Christian Heritage Party and the precepts upon which "this great nation was founded," or they endorse alternative involvements which constitute an abandonment of the labour of founding peoples and the sacrifices of a nation's martyrs. Alternative political involvements have been discounted as non-Christian. Through claims on behalf of objectified predecessors, party promoters solicit audience involvements out of loyalty to those who have gone before.

Appeal for the Victims

Party promoters may also attempt to close the sale by soliciting participation on behalf of those members of the community who are seen as "victims" of current government policy. Audience members find their involvements encouraged on behalf of "the weakest members of our society." The message is comparatively simple, albeit based on a complex web of shared definitions. Individuals have a duty to protect the helpless, be they the "unborn", the A.I.D.S. patient, or the "indebted grandchild." The C.H.P. casts its policies and programs as protective of the weak. It calls on those who share an interest in the protection of the "victims of secular humanism" to join with them.

While audience members may differ in their definitions of "victims" worthy of protection (Elias, 1986: 28–34), party promoters utilize typified notions that those who attend their meeting are united on the abortion issue. Audience members are encouraged to see their involvement in this campaign as having the potential to "save lives" in the "protection of the unborn." Further, the medical act of abortion is cast as a victim-producing encounter with consequences for the everyday lives of those it touches. Audience members are encouraged to join together to "prevent ongoing victimization."

In my community there was a lovely couple. They were living together and she got pregnant. And he said, "I love you baby, I want to marry you but not right now. Have an abortion. There's nothing to it." So she went to the doctors. They said it would be quick and simple and would be over with. Time passed and they got married and were blessed with a child. She looked at that little baby and said to her husband, "What was the one like that you made me kill?" Their marriage broke up, both grandparents are upset. One abortion has had a terrible impact on seven lives. When the pro-abortionists say that it is only a woman's affair they are lying my friends. (party promoter)

Attentive to potentially discrediting aspects of party policy and its portrayal within the media, party promoters may selectively disclose information in an effort to distance the party from "undesirable" designations. Of particular concern is the possibility of being defined by audience members as representative of the radical or hate right.

We have to be careful to mix our condemnations with compassion. That sounds funny. What I mean is that we say that homosexuality is wrong, it is sodomy. I will make no apology for that. But we can't come across as the anti-homosexual party. We'd be murdered in the press come election time. (party promoter)

One strategy which party promoters have utilized to mitigate against such portrayals has focused on the designation of A.I.D.S. patients as victims. Through an appeal to the sanctity of human life and a depiction of the threat of euthanasia, party promoters encourage individual involvement on behalf of "the weak." Party spokespersons tend to engage in the "condemnation of the sin and not the sinner," and by so doing promote membership out of an obligation to those constructed as victims.

Appeal for Christian Expression

Party promoters also encourage involvement by emphasizing the need to facilitate Christian expression within the Canadian federal political system. Audiences are encouraged to consider personal activity within the party on behalf of the extended Christian community within their riding. Party promoters attempt to demonstrate a moral imperative of action by arguing that Christians are, for all practical purposes, disenfranchised. Previous efforts to discount opponents are recalled. Audiences are encouraged to reach the conclusion that without a C.H.P. candidate in their riding, "Christians of conscience" will have no candidate for whom they can vote. Involvement is encouraged relative to a shared Christianity—a shared basis of expression.

I ask you tonight, ladies and gentlemen. Does this riding . . . deserve a Christian Heritage Party candidate in the next election? Do Christians here deserve an opportunity to cast a vote for a man or woman of integrity—who stands forthrightly on Christian principles? That is the decision you will have to make tonight. Are you willing to help make this happen? Do you want to help us send out a clear message that Christians will be silent no longer? (party promoter)

The activities of establishing credibility, promoting involvements, and closing the sale are central features of the recruitment work of C.H.P. party promoters. The strategies utilized by party advocates to create moral closure are specifically directed at promoting party membership. These efforts are grounded within typified notions of who the audience is and how they tend to see the world (Schutz, 1964). Unlike the attempt to generate broad based public support within a general election, the recruitment process addressed in this essay is directed towards a comparatively homogeneous audience—an audience which shares the qualities desired of party members.

REFERENCES

Elias, Robert (1986). *The Politics of Victimization*. New York: Oxford University Press.

Garfinkel, Harold (1956). "Conditions of Successful Degradation Ceremonies." *American Journal of Sociology* 61 (March): 420–424.

Grills, Scott (1989). Designating Deviance: Championing Definitions of the Appropriate and Inappropriate Through a Christian Political Voice. Doctoral Dissertation, McMaster University (Sociology).

Grills, Scott (1994). "Recruitment Practices of the Christian Heritage Party" pp. 96–108 in *Doing Everyday Life*. Mary Lorenz Dietz, Robert Prus and William Shaffir (eds.) Mississauga: Copp Clark Longman.

Lemert, Edwin (1953). "An Isolation and Closure Theory of Naive Check Forgery." *Journal of Criminal Law, Criminology and Police Science* 44: 296–307.

Prus, Robert C. (1989a). *Making Sales: Influence as Interpersonal Accomplishment*. Newbury Park, CA.: Sage.

Prus, Robert C. (1989b). *Pursuing Customers: An Ethnography of Marketing Activities*. Newbury Park, CA.: Sage.

Schutz, Alfred (1964). *Collected Papers II: Studies in Social Theory*. The Hague: Martinus Nijhoff.

Swan, John E. and David J. Ortinau (1988). "Customer Trust Versus Suspicion Based on Interpretations of Automobile Salespeople's Actions." Paper presented at Qualitative Research Conference, May 16–18, University of Windsor, Windsor, Ont.

Sykes, Gresham and David Matza (1957). "Techniques of Neutralization." *American Sociological Review* 22 (December): 664–679.

ARTICLE 11.3

Ahmad Ashraf

CHARISMA AND STATE POWER IN IRAN

INTRODUCTION

The closest Canada ever came to a charismatic political leader was Prime Minister Pierre Elliott Trudeau. During some periods of Trudeau's career writers described the popular response as "Trudeaumania." Trudeau drew large crowds wherever he spoke, and became a trend-setter in style and thinking.

In many ways, Iran reacted similarly to Ayatollah Khomeini, who took power in 1979 through the revolutionary overthrow of the Shah and his government. Khomeini ruled until his death in 1989. In this excerpt, Ahmad Ashraf emphasizes that Khomeini's power and authority were very much of the "charismatic" type. But once in power, Khomeini also exercised strong bureaucratic or "rational-legal" control of the state.

Ashraf argues that the economic interests of the state required that Khomeini modify his anti-economic and anti-bureaucratic views. Nonetheless, because of his charisma and near-absolute authority the Ayatollah's views carried great force and had integrative consequences for Iran. Since Khomeini's death it has been difficult for the new leadership to rule with the same effect.

The current leadership of the state lacks the charismatic authority of Khomeini, but this should not be surprising. Because charismatic authority is rooted in the leader, it generally cannot be passed on to others. The new men of power (they are all men in Iran) must rely even more heavily than Khomeini did on bureaucratic control of the state, economy, and religion.

Ayatollah Ruhollah Khomeini's prophetic mien, the manner of his rise to power, the overwhelming commemoration of his death, and the edifice of a shrine which was erected over his graveyard leave little doubt that his leadership warrants the attribution, "charismatic." Genuine charisma is a rare historical circumstance, deriving from a conviction that an individual possesses a mysterious and supernatural gift of grace—a belief which the person and his disciples share collectively. Even though the phenomenon of pure charisma is universal, it is often most evident in the religious realm, and it thrives with particular abundance in the fertile soil of the Shi'ite culture.

Ashraf, Ahmad (1990). "Theocracy and Charisma: New Men of Power in Iran," *International Journal of Politics, Culture and Society*, 4(1), 113–153. Reprinted by permission of Human Sciences Press, Inc.

Television has rarely shown more astonishing sights than the crowds in Tehran literally ripping the shroud from Ayatollah Khomeini. It was a scene from the Age of Belief: mourners flagellating themselves and crushing one another as they grabbed at a helicopter bearing aloft the Imam's coffin. What may also have fed the crowd's awesome grief was awareness that the Ayatollah's authority was unique, that this was the last act of drama expiring with its dominating character (NYT, editorial, June 8, 1989:A30).

Khomeini exemplified in his own person the presence of a multiple charisma in the course of his ascendance, first, to the position of the highest Shi'ite authority and, later, to the theocratic position of the national political leadership. Both positions were achieved through his leadership of rebellious movements. Khomeini's multiple charisma led to the creation of a number of contradictory positions.

First, and above all else, he was the most emotional and inventive charismatic leader of recent times; the radius of his charisma spread beyond the boundaries of Iran to reach millions of Muslims all over the world. Khomeini was endowed with a number of character traits that could easily appeal to the hearts and minds of Muslims in the times of crisis, including the will to power, cunning, an innovating orientation, youthfulness, asceticism, militancy, and radicalism. Khomeini gave the masses a sense of personal integrity, collective identity, historical rootedness, and feelings of pride and superiority.

Second, Khomeini acquired an "office charisma," a religious office with traditional charismatic authority, i.e., the well-established traditional office of the Shi'ite source of emulation which granted him the religious authority and entitled him to receive religious charities and financial obligations, including the tithe as the share of the Hidden Imam. Third, Khomeini introduced the new theocratic institution of the divine commission of the jurisconsult to assume political authority and sovereignty as the vicegerent of the Hidden Imam. Fourth, Khomeini assumed the position of the supreme leader and commander in chief of the armed forces of a modernizing state apparatus, while as a supreme theocratic ruler he transcended the constitutional constraints of an apparently legal-rational order. Finally, Khomeini assumed the title of the Imam, the position exclusively reserved in the Iranian Shi'ite community for the twelve infallible Imams.

For Weber (1968:1115) the prototype of the charismatic leader is a person who "in a revolutionary and sovereign manner . . . transforms all values and breaks all traditional and rational norms." Such a person says to his disciples, "It is written . . . , but I say onto you . . ."—a claim that clearly challenges the authority of the established order, without regard for whether it is traditional or legal-rational. He is not bound by administrative organs, rules of conduct or legal wisdom oriented to judicial precedent. Charismatic leadership is prophetic; the leader demands obedience from his disciples and followers on the basis of the mission he feels called upon to perform. The genuine prophet, Weber (1968:243) says, "demands new obligations—most typically by virtue of revelation, oracle, inspiration, or of his own will."

KHOMEINI'S CHARISMA AND POWER

Khomeini's rise to the theocratic leadership of the bureaucratic apparatus of a modern state with a sizable "surplus producing" economic sector confronted him with a very complex situation in the period of 1979–89. He found himself caught between the pressures coming from the major conflicting forces in the state and civil society. He had to modify his personal and traditional arenas of leadership and adapt himself to the new situation. In doing so he had to cope with three basic challenges: (1) to modify his antibureaucratic orientation; (2) to alter his antieconomic stance; and (3) to adopt a radical stand that deviated significantly from conservative Islamic jurisprudence.

Genuine charisma is antibureaucratic—it does not get along with officials. Khomeini, therefore, was faced with a number of problems in the process of transforming his inexperienced clerical and lay disciples into the officials of the bureaucratic state: of bringing under his control a large number of modernized officials and state managers; of leading a huge and complicated state apparatus; and of bridging the hiatus between the two inherently contradictory political entities of theocracy and modern republican democracy.

The men of power who emerged had to learn through trial and error and a sort of an in-service-training how to run the modern state. The confidants of the leader were superimposed upon major revolutionary and ordinary bureaucratic agencies. A mode of democratic centralism was developed in which the elected representatives, councilmen, and officials of the state could express their views and even stand against the will of the leader, but the final voice in the key decisions was that of the leader. At the same time the constitution gave the supreme charismatic leader the authority to appoint the members of the Council of Guardians of the Constitution who had veto power over legislations passed by the Majlis. When he became dissatisfied with the conservative and traditional stance of the guardianship Council in vetoing several radical bills, Khomeini did not hesitate to institute a Discretionary Council to overrule the veto power of the former council.

Economic factors were even more significant and pressing in shaping the behavior of the new men of power and privilege than were the workings of the bureaucracy. The economics of charismatic revolution, as an independent variable, directs the process of transformation (Weber, 1968:254).

Khomeini was fairly successful in revolutionizing Shi'ite world views but he was limited by the requirements of the modern state and its economic base. Thus, he succeeded in making a revolution in Qom because in "traditionalistic periods charisma is the great revolutionary force," but he was forced to modify his attitude and assume an adaptive orientation in Tehran because of overwhelming bureaucratic and economic constraints. In the end, Khomeini became an ardent advocate of the central state and its superordination over the civil society. He also accepted the principles of rationality, efficiency and profitability in administering the public bureaucracy and state owned capitalist enterprises.

Khomeini exemplified, apparently, a rare case of a genuine charisma in the modern time. Most modern charismatic figures, including Lenin, Mao, Castro, and Nkrumah, argue Bensman and Givani (1975:599–604), do not have genuine charisma. They are at best pseudocharismatics. Their charisma is non-personal and rational, it was fabricated by rational planning, by mediation of the impersonal mass media, by the propaganda machine of a bureaucratic mass society. By operating in the modern world, Khomeini's genuine charisma was thus contaminated by rationality, by impersonality, and by accommodation to the modern bureaucratic and economic order.

He combined, however, tradition and modernity, personal relation of gemeinschaft with impersonal relations of gesellschaft. He increasingly used the mass media, particularly television, for communicating with the masses. As a matter of fact, the mass appeal of his charisma emerged at this stage through the use of newspapers, cassettes, radio, and later, television. Furthermore, tens of thousands of believers who were seduced by the regime's propaganda officers and the mass media were brain-washed and dispatched to the war front for suicide missions and martyrdom.

Most observers of modern charisma recognize the central role of the mass media in the making of modern charismatic politics. Bendix (1971:172) notes that "modern means of publicity can give such leadership all the appearance of charisma." Loewenstein (1966:86) observed that "mass media can produce a reinforcement and deepening of an originally spurious but artificially promoted charisma attributed to the ruler." Bensman and Givani (1975:604,606) say that

> Modern charisma . . . rests upon the conscious selection of themes, appeals, slogans, and imagery that is based upon the systematic study of audiences, target populations, constituencies, and strategic public. . . . Modern charismatic leaders may rationally select irrational themes, motifs, and values to personify those themes and values and a sense of pseudo Gemeinschaft to distant publics.

Khomeini's charisma, as a typical case, was also a dramaturgical phenomenon. It was created by symbolic representations in the Shi'ite community and involved selective and purposive activities in terms of mobilization of human, physical, and financial resources as well as manipulation of tools and strategies of a rhetorical nature. The drama and the passion play of Hossein, the commemoration of his death, and the notion of martyrdom in Shi'ite culture were manipulated for the purpose of political mobilization of the masses. These rhetorical symbols served as significant cultural resources for the purpose of mass mobilization.

Furthermore to appeal to the intelligentsia, Khomeini's disciples adopted an innovative modern political discourse as early as 1960. By mastering three contradictory discourses of the traditional elitist language of Islamic law, the popular rhetorical sermons and passion plays focused on the drama of Hossein, and the modern political discourse of the intellectuals, Khomeini's group succeeded in manipulating and deceiving individuals from all walks of life.

Khomeini's charismatic revolution in Iran was the culmination of the recent Islamic revivalist movements and provided them with a new perspective and hope. Khomeini's movement was, at the same time, an Iranian national movement. It was a religious revolution which served, though tragically and at a great human cost, the arena of political development and nation building. It has led to an expansion of national identity which goes beyond loyalty to small groups. The Protestant reformation occurred in the West much earlier than the processes of industrialization and nation building began. All these three major processes of our time have occurred, argues Ernest Gellner (1985:1–3), simultaneously in the Islamic society

in the recent time. The combination of these giant processes has profoundly affected and complicated the processes and goals of the Islamic movements; it has constituted the heart of "the Islamic dilemmas."

A significant consequence of Khomeini's charismatic revolution has been the
process of further integration of the state through mass participation in the course
of rebellious activities and particularly via the mass mobilization of hundreds of
thousands of villagers, tribesmen, and urbanites to fight in the eight-year war.
Even though the motives for fighting in the war were a mixture of patriotism and a
religious duty to wage a holy war, it led to the intensification of feelings of both
national identity and political participation.

Unintended consequences of what Ali Banuazizi (1988) has called the
"democratization of martyrdom" may lead to further the national identity and
even to enhance democratic processes. A shift in the primary loyalty of individuals
from their village, tribe, clan, neighborhood, status group, class or profession to
that of the Islamic state seems to have taken place. Furthermore, the revolution
had advanced the level of political awareness and the political maturity of major
social classes and groups and brought them to the arena of national politics. Thus,
it is fair to say that the charismatic revolution has led to further political integration and that the process of national integration has, to some extent, reduced the
intra-societal tensions and led to further cultural-ideological consensus.

Khomeini's charismatic revolution was, however, a double-edged sword. It also
led to the exacerbation of a number of salient internal tensions, which could
potentially lead to instability of the regime and deter the progressive integration of
the state. One major area of tension and conflict is the genuine arational charismatic pursuit of a futile war abroad and an oppressive policy at home with grave
human cost and destructive physical effects. Almost all major leaders of the regime
spelled out their grievances due to the directives of the supreme leader on major
issues on the occasion of the commemoration of the tenth anniversary of the revolution on February 11, 1989. They believe, for example, that they "had to make an
effort to prevent war to break out," from the beginning or at least "to refrain from
prolonging the war after the retreat of Iraqi forces from Khorramshahr" (Iran
Times, 17 February, 1989).

A major event with disintegrative effects has been the mass exodus of hundreds of thousands of well-educated and prosperous members of the new middle
classes. This has created a brain drain at home and a sizable hostile Iranian community in exile of about two million abroad. Together with those members of the middle classes who still reside in Iran, they constitute a threat to political integration
and the stability of the regime.

Another source of conflict is the status of religious minorities in a predominantly Shi'ite theocratic state. Armenians, Jews, Zoroastrians, and Baha'is have
been increasingly excluded from the public domain, alienated from the society,
purged from offices, persecuted and even executed in postrevolutionary Iran.

A more severe area of strife and antagonism is the problem of ethnolinguistic
groups that may cost the very geographical integrity of the nation state. The
ambivalent attitude of the theocratic regime toward the question of Iranian nation-

alism and Islamic internationalism has, ironically, fanned the nationalist feelings of both Persian speaking Iranians as well as other ethnolinguistic groups. The intelligentsia of the former group have increasingly resorted to their pre-Islamic historical roots and mythologies. Azaris, Kurds, Turkomans, Baluchis, and Arabs who have been alienated from the Islamic state have been encouraged by the Islamic internationalist ideology to denounce the overarching Iranian nationalism, on the one hand, and to resort to their own secessionist local chauvinism under the oppressive measures and ambiguous signals of nationalism/internationalism of the Islamic state, on the other. This tendency has been particularly enhanced as they have become the targets of mounting propaganda campaigns by neighboring states with claims over these groups.

Above all, the major disintegrative legacies of Khomeini's charisma are the exacerbation of internal strife within the religious hierarchy, the factional politics within the regime, and increasing antagonism between the state and the civil society. The split and antagonism between the state and the Shi'ite establishment emerged from the beginning of the post-Khomeini era; the regime is separated from the source of emulation and thus its theocratic basis of legitimation is under question.

The split among the followers of Khomeini in supporting two sources of emulation, the Grand Ayatollah Mohammad Reza Golpayegani and the prominent Ayatollah Mohammad Ali Araki, marks the beginning of a long road of strife and antagonism within the regime. This conflict is exacerbated by the antagonism between the state and the bazaar-mosque alliance. The core elements within the regime have supported Ayatollah Araki, whereas the traditional marginal force of the bazaar-mosque alliance has supported Ayatollah Golpayegani. The roots of some of these tensions, with disintegrative potential, could be traced into the very politics of Khomeini's charismatic revolution and the symbolic manipulation of the rhetoric of the Shi'ite movement on the one hand and the canopy of his leadership that temporarily united conflicting social forces against the old regime on the other.

In this way, Khomeini's charismatic revolution has had both integrative and disintegrative effects, both constructive and immensely destructive consequences on modern state building in Iran. Thus it seems premature to overestimate the integrative effects of the revolution or to characterize the charismatic movement of Khomeini as simply "the turban for the crown."

Both international and internal developments which have occurred in the late 1980s and at the turn of 1990s are likely to lead to a more moderate regime in Iran. The sweeping changes which have rolled the socialist world and the new relations which have developed between the West and the Eastern block have drastically altered the old geopolitical role of Iran as a buffer state. Iran has already lost most of its capability for playing a militant role in the region and is likely to follow a more moderate foreign policy in the future. Furthermore, the failure of state socialism will lead to demoralization of the radical groups within the regime—the groups who have preached an Islamic variant of state socialism for Iran—and will strengthen the position of more moderate groups.

As a result, those who are succeeding Khomeini are far less preoccupied with his charismatic mission. They are men who are concerned mainly with the day-to-day problems of the country. Their goal is not to change the world, but to accommodate themselves to it. As Weber (1968:1120) noted:

> Every charisma is on the road from a turbulently emotional life that knows no economic rationality to slow death by suffocation under the weight of material interests: every hour of its existence brings it nearer to its end.

CONCLUSION

Yet, the shadow of Khomeini's charismatic revolution and the bolstering of the sense of self-esteem, collective identity, and historical rootedness that it gave to the masses, with all its productive and destructive repercussions, seems to remain in Iran and the world of Islam in the future.

REFERENCES

Banuazizi, A. (1988). "Martyrdom in Revolutionary Iran," a lecture delivered at the Iranian Studies Seminar, Columbia University.

Bendix, R. (1977). *Max Weber: An Intellectual Portrait*. Berkeley: University of California Press.

Bendix, R. and G. Roth (1971). *Scholarship and Partisanship: Essays on Max Weber*. Berkeley: University of California Press.

Bensman, J. and M. Givani. "Charisma and Modernity: The Use and Abuse of a Concept," in *Social Research*, Vol. 2, No. 4, pp. 570–614.

Gelner, E. (1985). "Introduction," in *The Islamic Dilemma*. Berlin: Mouton Publishers.

Loewenstein, K. (1966). Max Weber: *Political Ideas in the Perspective of Our Time*. Amherst: The University of Massachusetts Press.

Weber, M. (1968). *Economy and Society*. Translated by G. Roth and C. Wittich. New York: Bedminister Press.

QUESTIONS

DISCUSSION QUESTIONS

1. Grills uses the idea of creating "moral closure" to describe how a sale is closed. What does he mean by this phrase? Are all religious institutions concerned with creating "moral closure"?

2. Some would argue that the most crucial defining characteristic of religion is its explanation of the meaning of death, and the comfort that this sense of meaning provides. How well do you think Star Trek meets this definition of religion?

3. "Charismatic leadership is a selling job, whether it is done in a religious or political framework." Do you agree or disagree? Give your reasons.

4. If the Christian Heritage Party were a typical religious movement rather than a true political party, how would it be likely to evolve?

DATA COLLECTION EXERCISES

1. Using several issues of a daily newspaper, study the policy positions and supporting arguments put forward by political leaders. Are these politicians involved in "selling" ideas? Selling themselves? What aspects of selling behaviour can you discern in these newspaper accounts?

2. Khomeini exercised charismatic authority within the bureaucratic state organizations in Iran. Gather some data from library sources on one or two other examples of a religious-political leader who had strong charismatic authority in a country of your choice. Say a few words to defend your way of measuring charisma.

3. In his research the author of the Star Trek excerpt combined several data sources, including online materials. ("Electronic ethnography" is the label he gives to this approach.) Discuss the advantages and disadvantages of using several types of data for this kind of research.

4. Watch two or more episodes of Star Trek re-runs on TV, or rent them from a video store. (Or, rent one of the movie versions instead.) Analyze these to determine whether you agree with the author about the religious content of this science fiction show. Explain why you do or do not agree.

WRITING EXERCISES

1. Think back to a major purchase that you or a family member or friend made recently, where you had a chance to watch a salesperson in action over a reasonably long period of time. Write a 500-word essay detailing how this selling process was similar to, or different from, the process described in Grills' excerpt.

2. Choose another example of a quasi-religion (besides Star Trek fandom) with which you are familiar. In a 500-word essay, indicate how this example is similar to and different from traditional religion.

3. Imagine that you are the Ayatollah Khomeini. Write a 500-word letter to your followers explaining why you do not think that bureaucratization will undermine the religious beliefs of your government.

4. "A religion can contain just about any set of beliefs, just so long as people can be persuaded to believe in them." Write 500 words indicating whether you agree or disagree with this statement, explaining the reasons for your view.

SUGGESTED READINGS

1. Bellah, Robert et al. (1985). *Habits of the Heart: Individualism and Commitment in American Life*. Berkeley, CA: University of California Press. This fascinating analysis of modern America examines how individualism, as a philosophy of private life, correlates with an involvement in public life. From the standpoint of sociology of religion, it shows that Weber's understanding of personal "meanings" can be combined with Durkheim's insight into social cohesion in order to better understand the difficulties in the American pursuit of happiness.

2. Bibby, Reginald (1987). *Fragmented Gods: The Poverty and Potential of Religion in Canada*. Toronto: Irwin Publishing. Perhaps the best sociological book on religion in Canada, Bibby shows how survey research can be used to examine the vast variety of religion "con-

sumers": their varied religious needs, the reasons why many have deserted traditional denominations, and what people will want to get from religion in the next century.

3. Weber, Max (1964 [1922]). *The Sociology of Religion*. Boston: Beacon Press. This masterful study of religion ranges widely across societies and historical periods to show the relationships between religion and social stratification, politics, economics, and even sexuality and art. The book discusses both the meanings of religion (e.g., asceticism, mysticism, and salvation) and its practitioners (e.g., magicians, priests, and prophets).

SECTION 12   HEALTH AND ILLNESS

Introduction

One of the most highly valued characteristics of being Canadian is our commitment to universal health care. Medical sociologists study the social aspects of health and illness, and view medicine as a social institution. Although medical sociology is an important subdiscipline of sociology if measured in terms of the number of practitioners and the amount of money committed to research funds, it developed far later than did the subdisciplines that focus on the institutions of education, politics, religion, or law. Indeed, medical sociology is largely a post-war phenomenon in North America.

HISTORY AND PERSPECTIVE

Medical sociology has two origins. These have been labelled sociology *in* medicine and sociology *of* medicine. Sociology in medicine is an applied sociology that tries to answer medical or health questions using sociological theory and methods. Sociology of medicine, on the other hand, is university-based and grounded in sociological rather than medical questions. However, these differences have increasingly diminished, with most current work now having an applied focus. A second shift—from sociology of *medicine* to sociology of *health*—is indicative of a broadening focus and a movement away from a medical definition of illness.

   One of the first theoretical works in the field of medical sociology was Talcott Parsons' 1951 book *The Social System*. Parsons described the "sick role"—the social expectations that are related to being sick or caring for a sick person. Parsons' concept of the sick role has been described by many people as the most important theoretical contribution to the field of medical sociology. It has been widely used, even by those who are otherwise critical of Parsons' work.

   The sick role is based on four major components: (1) the sick person is exempt from "normal" social roles, (2) the sick person is not responsible for his or her condition, (3) the sick person should try to get well, and (4) the sick person should seek technically competent help. Excerpt 12.1 is about how individuals and families cope with chronic illness. As we see in that excerpt, one common strategy is to define one's life as "normal" while not denying the existence of the illness. The entire family plays a part in building and enacting this "story."

SOCIAL FACTORS AFFECTING HEALTH

Social epidemiology, a field whose origins lie in the study of epidemics, is the study of the patterning of disease. What is revealed by analyzing patterns in rates of morbidity and mortality? What social variables explain the patterns? In other words, what do sick and dying people have in common that is not shared by those who are unaffected? Sociologists, of course, are fundamentally interested in how *social* factors affect health and illness. How do class, gender, and race affect health outcomes?

A fundamental and consistent finding of the sociology of health is the connection between socioeconomic status and mortality and morbidity rates. Lower socioeconomic status is associated with lower life expectancy, higher overall mortality rates, higher rates of infant and perinatal mortality, and higher rates of disability. Class is also associated with other indicators of mental and physical health. Although these relationships are well established, the causal direction is not always clear. Does poverty cause poor health, or does poor health lead to downward mobility or poverty?

Poor people are less likely to use medical services. The study outlined in excerpt 12.2 finds that while the needs of poorer Canadians have increased their health care use has not. For class differences in health go beyond access to care. Quality of life—including fundamental differences in nutrition, housing, and so on—is a significant factor in the relationship between class and health status.

A second consistent pattern is the morbidity and mortality differences between men and women. While women are not as healthy as men, at all ages men have higher mortality rates. Women suffer more from frequent illness and have higher rates of depression and anxiety, but men have more serious diseases and are more apt to die from them. How can this morbidity puzzle be explained? Is it a question of biological difference, life circumstances, or some aspect of sickness or caregiving behaviour?

Women are more likely to seek medical advice, and consequently more likely to assume a sick role. Women also have less control over their lives, and have far less leisure, and so they feel greater stress. On the other hand, men are more apt to engage in such risky behaviours as driving too fast or consuming excess alcohol.

As we saw in Section 6, gender differences have declined in many areas of social life. One wonders how greater gender equality will affect differences in health and mortality. Will women's increased labour force participation contribute to an equalizing of mortality rates? Will exposure to similar "opportunities" equalize morbidity? Among adolescents, for example, the proportion of male smokers is now about the same as female smokers. Presumably this will mean more equal rates of lung cancer forty years from now.

Race is another important predictor of health status. In the United States, black Americans have higher overall rates of mortality, including infant mortality, renal failure, and strokes; but lower rates of coronary heart disease. In Canada, native peoples have the poorest access to health care, as reflected in their higher mortality rates at all ages.

In Canada, the principle of universality is designed to minimize the financial barrier to access to health care. But will rising costs and declining levels of federal funding undermine this expectation? As the proportion of older people in the population increases, and as baby boomers age, Canadians have begun to worry about the ability of the system to sustain itself. Will universality be sacrificed to a two-tiered system such as that of the United States? It is ironic that these concerns about maintaining universal access are raised in Canada at the same time as our American neighbours look with envy at the principles of our system.

THE MEDICALIZATION OF HEALTH CARE

In our society health care is dominated by hospitals and doctors. As Parsons' definition of the sick role suggests, when we are sick we are expected to seek technically competent help. Doctors have a very high status in our society, and are well paid for their expertise. While no one would argue that we are not better off with available, expert medical care, one might wonder what is lost when something as fundamental as our own health is largely taken out of our hands. Along similar lines, excerpt 12.3 looks at the adoption of Western scientific medical practices by industrializing countries, and the effect this transition has on traditional medical practices.

Medicalization is the process whereby non-medical problems become defined as medical problems. Childbirth is a classic example. Until the early twentieth century, it was uncommon for children to be born in hospitals or to be attended by doctors. In Britain, midwives still assist at most deliveries, although most babies are born in maternity hospitals. For several decades in North America childbirth was highly managed by doctors, in hospitals. Women were typically anaesthetized for the birth, while fathers waited in the wings. In the 1970s, advocates of natural childbirth challenged the medicalization of childbirth, and women argued for more control over delivery, birthing rooms, and the involvement of midwives rather than doctors. While this movement succeeded in some ways, childbirth still remains largely medicalized in North America.

Despite the negative effects of medicalization, the wider adoption of scientific medical practices has produced significant reductions in death rates. Although Canadians worry about the erosion of our health care system, there have been great improvements in our health status over the years. The life expectancy of Canadians has increased 33 years for men and 36 years for women in this century. And according to the 1994 Statistics Canada National Population Health Survey, most Canadians consider themselves to be healthy.

Carole Robinson

MANAGING LIFE WITH A CHRONIC CONDITION: THE STORY OF NORMALIZATION

INTRODUCTION

Most people and most families have to deal with illness or death. But medical advances mean that people will live for long periods with conditions that once meant certain, often immediate demise. How do people with chronic illnesses and their families manage? This is the question raised in the following excerpt.

The answer: Families develop paradigms for organizing the world around them. One aspect of the family's "definition of the situation" is their definition of health and illness. When a chronic illness is first identified it is important for the individual and the family to maintain a sense of control over the illness. Many people experience illness as a betrayal of the body. In order to maintain control and counter the sense of betrayal, a common coping strategy is to develop a family narrative, or "story line," about the illness.

Carole Robinson shows how respondents go about developing a story of life as normal, and how they maintain this story over time. As life goes on the story is altered to account for changes in health. These stories—in effect, definitions of the situation—give meaning to the lives of the chronically ill and to their relationships with others. Illness is an ever-present biological fact, but as this excerpt shows it is also a socially defined process.

Like religion, a family narrative that encompasses pain and suffering as a part of everyday life provides "a set of coherent answers to human existential dilemmas which make the world meaningful . . . a human response to those things which concern us ultimately."

Nurses are interested in understanding how families manage a member's chronic condition, and normalization has proven to be both a theoretically and clinically pertinent concept in this regard (Anderson, 1981; Anderson, Elfert, & Lai, 1989; Deatrick & Knafl, 1990; Dewis, 1989; Holaday, 1984; Knafl & Deatrick, 1986, 1990; Krulik, 1980; Rechner, 1990; Robinson, 1984). This article attempts to address the process by which family members come to define their ill member and their family life "as normal."

Robinson, Carole (1993). "Managing Life with a Chronic Condition: The Story of Normalization," *Qualitative Health Research*, Vol. 3 No. 1, February 1993 6–28. © 1993 Sage Publications, Inc.

THE STUDY

The data are taken from 62 accounts constructed with 40 Caucasian informants during the course of repeated in-depth interviews. Thirty informants were female and 10 were male. Nine informants were parents speaking about their experience with a child's chronic illness; the other 31 were adults managing chronic conditions for themselves, their spouses, their parents, or their siblings. The chronic conditions represented in the sample are varied and include spina bifida, muscular dystrophy, asthma, allergies, multiple sclerosis, arthritis, back problems, heart disease, and inflammatory bowel disease.

CONSTRUCTING THE STORY OF LIFE "AS NORMAL"

The study participants were clear that when they first began to manage life with a chronic condition the story was not "Our life is normal, we just have a few problems." Instead, the informants reported that life was problem saturated—there was little life beyond the problem. The story at that time was characterized by despair; however, at some point, it began to shift. A problem existed, but there was clearly life beyond the problem. As Knafl and Deatrick (1986) point out, the story began to acknowledge the chronic condition while minimizing its personal and social significance. The story of normalization sounds like this:

> It's just treating things that occur in your life as things that occur in your life and not as things that are major determinants of who you are. That they're facts of life and you deal with them. . . . You cope with things as you go along. . . . [You're] just trying to make it part of your everyday life. Normal to me is psychologically healthy more than ... physically.... Here you got this physical illness, but let's try to deal with it just like you got brown hair and brown eyes—it's part of you. You're not going to look so good in light blue as I do, and you're not going to do so good at soccer but you'll do better at swimming. So it's keeping things in perspective—that's normalcy.

Initiating the Story of Life "as Normal"

Sometimes, the shift from the problem-saturated story toward the alternate story occurred in the absence of any further life experience that could be used to support normalization. In these instances, it was a conscious leap of faith based on firmly held beliefs that resulted in a reorientation of the story. For example, one mother talked about her despair after her child was born with spina bifida and her concentration on all the things he would never do. The baby had been flown to a tertiary care center. At some point in the 2-week separation this mother consciously pulled herself together based on the belief that the only way she could be helpful to her son was to be strong. At this time she said,

> We have to be strong for him, and we have to show him that he can do things himself that other kids can do but he has to work harder at it. . . . I had him going to university 2 weeks after he was born. . . . He was going to be a doctor. . . . He could take any path he wanted to, and I know there are so many things he can do. . .

They're capable of anything—whatever they set their mind out to do, but they may have to work a little harder for it.

Some informants revealed that important personal information was the key to initiating the new story of life "as normal." This information was always about the individual experiencing the chronic condition and was clearly contradictory to the story of deviance, difficulty, and despair. Thus the information illuminated abilities or attributes that were salient to a deep sense of essentially being normal, such as being able to continue caring for one's husband by managing the house despite the presence of a chronic condition.

In other instances, when personal experience did not appear to support the possibility of normalization, the shift occurred in response to important outside information, which presented the possibility of a radical shift in perspective. For example, another mother talked about seeing a television program about very normal young adults who had been born with extremely damaged brains. She applied this to her situation, saying, "You just never know."

Thus the change to a new story involved reframing:

> To reframe, then, means to change the conceptual and/or emotional setting or viewpoint in relation to which a situation is experienced and to place it in another frame which fits the "facts" of the same concrete situation equally well or even better, and thereby changes its entire meaning. (Watzlawick, Weakland, & Fisch, 1974, p. 95)

The reality we experience is always a subjective construction. It involves making choices or discriminating between data that are to be included in the construction and data that are not to be included. What permitted these persons with chronic conditions and their family members to choose pieces of information that supported the story of life "as normal" rather than the multitude of pieces that were oriented toward a story of difficulty, despair, and deviance? The author can only speculate that a fundamental, underlying belief in the importance or "goodness" of living life "as normal" was the impetus.

The Evolving Story of Life "as Normal"

The shift in perspective that occurred through reframing resulted in a particular focus being set such that the story could grow and develop. Focusing, as part of the continued construction of this story of normalization, can be likened to the focusing of a camera lens. It permits one to see part of a scene while rendering other parts invisible or blurry. Thus the choice of a normalization lens determined a focus on those aspects of life experience that supported the premise of life as normal. Events that do not fit with the evolving story are placed in the background where they do not intrude on the dominant story. The accounts contain evidence that, to an outside observer or reader, support a conclusion of abnormal family life. However, it appears that in relation to the story of the informant this evidence is simply disregarded. For example, one mother who emphasized the normalcy of family life also reported that her 6-year-old daughter had been taught to catheterize her brother when baby-sitters would not participate in this necessary aspect of care. Thus, although the "abnormal" piece was acknowledged, it did not count as important in the construction of a story of normal family life.

Focusing supported the continuation of the story by permitting the significance of the problem to be minimized. When the focus was on their own situations, some participants talked about the comfort that was engendered by a sense of familiarity. In these instances, fear of the unknown was replaced with a sense of competence— "I've been through this and I can manage." When the focus was on others, a form of mirroring was used such that a favorable comparison of one's own situation with that of an often less fortunate other resulted—"There's always somebody worse off than us." As one woman who was confined to a wheelchair stated, "Everyone has problems. I don't think I have any problems that are different from everybody else's. So I don't get around like everybody else—you just have to carry on with what you have."

Family members often chose a narrowed or constricted focus in order to encapsulate the problem. Here, minimization of the problems associated with the chronic condition was accomplished by reducing the issues and concerns to a single element and thus the wide-reaching effects of the chronic condition were contained. Reduction involved choosing one aspect of a multifaceted situation to represent the problem. For example, a father whose son had spent 14 of his 16 months in the hospital with eating problems, life-threatening allergies, and asthma stated it this way: "He's normal—it's just that his throat—that is his only one problem really." In response to a question about living life as normally as possible, a woman with multiple sclerosis replied, "The only thing that's not normal, I don't do anything. The odd time I put the dishes in the dishwasher and take them out. I can't take out the glasses 'cause I can't reach. But I never cook a meal or make a sandwich. My husband does all that. That's what isn't normal."

The elements of lived experience that encompassed recognizably normal occurrences were important subjects for the "camera." When normal occurrences were brought into clear focus, problems could be pushed into the background. What is critical here is that the normal occurrences had significance to the families and individuals involved. For example, going to work was important to some but unimportant to others who focused on participation in physical activities. The mother who began her shift toward normalization based on faith engendered by the television program gathered evidence of her daughter's normality and reported, "She's just like a normal baby—doing everything a normal baby does. And now, the last two days, she is even smiling." Thus once the story is initiated it is self-generating by virtue of its determination of what may be counted as data. This is the essence of focusing.

For many participants, the chronic conditions were associated with particularly intrusive experiences that were contradictory to the story of life "as normal" but were difficult to minimize. These experiences included repeated hospitalizations, frequent diarrhea, and chronic pain. To support the continuation of the story, these experiences were realigned so that they agreed rather than disagreed with the story. Thus frequent hospitalization became a "normal" part of some families' lives and was managed as a "normal" event (Robinson, 1984). In the same way, a certain level of pain or a certain frequency of diarrhea was reconstrued as "normal" for the individual with the experience and was accepted as a given within the story. Thus there appear to be two ways that the evolution of the story of life "as normal" is supported. The first is by minimizing the significance of problems associated with the chronic condition through selective focusing of attention. This enables people to "look on the bright side" of their experiences. The second is by reconstructing the reference points by which the experience is judged. For example, informants reported being normal now but anticipating being "not normal" when an anticipated change occurred, such as not being able to walk any longer. However, when the change did occur, then not walking became reconstrued as normal.

The construction of the story of life "as normal" with a chronic condition was a balancing act. The chronic condition and its associated problems of living were both recognized and acknowledged. However, they were acknowledged in such a way that deficits and difficulties were minimized while abilities were emphasized. The acknowledgment usually included only key aspects, such as visible differences: for example, "He can do things that other kids can't do [ride horses] and of course he can't do things like run around." It is interesting to note that the "and of course" part serves almost as a postscript.

LIVING THE STORY OF LIFE "AS NORMAL"

Once the story gains life, how is it used? The story is performed and "with every performance, persons are reauthoring their lives" (White & Epston, 1990, p. 13). Thus the construction of the story and the living of the story are interactive processes. Again, as Knafl and Deatrick (1986) argue, a key element of the process is conveying to others the truth of essential normalcy. The story acts as a guiding light or beacon that can be shone to illuminate the past, present, or future. Thus the past is given meaning in relation to normalization and is judged in terms of its contribution to the story. One mother was reviewing the past, which included multiple hospitalizations and major surgeries, with student nurses. The nursing students' response was "poor little girl," but the mother said, "Look at her—she bounces right back. . . . I don't sympathize with her. I give her credit for having stamina and being able to bounce back after any of her letdowns." Her evaluation of the past was positive: "As far as I'm concerned, going through this so she can walk and lead a fairly normal life later—it's been worth it."

In the present, the story orders daily life. White and Epston (1990) point out that different "readers" of particular events will have different perspectives. Thus there is a degree of ambiguity to every text or story that permits a "spectrum of actualizations" (p. 13). Different families will perform the story of normalization in different ways and the performance will be seen as practice or management. The whole may be termed a family management style, and the "discrete behavioral accommodations that family members use to manage on a daily basis" may be termed management behaviors (Knafl & Deatrick, 1990, p. 9; see also Deatrick & Knafl, 1990). As already stated, the story does not encompass all of life; therefore, practice may not be entirely congruent with the story of life "as normal," but those pieces that do not fit will not be counted as data. The practices that are directed by the story of normalization are covering up, doing normal things, desensitization, and making trade-offs. These practices comprise the final criterion identified by Knafl and Deatrick (1986) for defining and recognizing the concept of normalization.

COVERING UP

Covering up (see also Wiener, 1975) is related to visibility of difference and conveying to others the truth of essential normalcy. Successful covering up renders problems less visible to others and is accomplished through three strategies: pushing, pacing, and controlling information. This practice is similar to the behavior identified by Knafl and Deatrick (1986) of making the child appear as normal as possible. For some informants, actual invisibility of the difference was achieved through covering up; however, for others, this practice served to make differences less visible or dominant and was used to convey the significant message of normalcy despite visible difference.

Pushing was the strategy most often chosen by parents of children with chronic conditions and by many adults who were early in the experience of managing a chronic condition. This is similar to the strategy described by Wiener (1975) as keeping up. It had the additional intent, beyond rendering differences less visible, of promoting independence and self-reliance. One mother described it this way:

> We have never sympathized with him—never felt sorry for him. People have thought I was mean because I make him do things for himself, but if I'm going to make things easier for him, then he's not going to learn to do things for himself.

For a child with eating problems, pushing meant giving him a wide variety of food by mouth rather than relying on a gastrostomy tube. Pacing (see also Wiener, 1975) was the strategy chosen by ill adults and children when lack of energy was a problem. Many of the informants were explicit about this approach. For example:

> It all has to do with pacing yourself when you have multiple sclerosis. I plan everything—I can't push myself anymore. I monitor myself so closely. I budget my energy, like people budget their money. I won't allow myself, for example, to leave the house more than once a day. If I have to take my kids to the doctor in the morning, I cancel my meeting at night.

Pushing and pacing serve to control the availability or dominance of visual information. That is, the self that is presented for outsiders to see is a normal self with limitations or differences masked. A parallel strategy was used to control the availability of verbal information. The verbal sharing of information was very selective, with only certain individuals having access to selected information. For example, one mother did not talk to her friends or family about what was happening with her child but did choose to talk with other parents in the hospital because "you probably wouldn't see them again." Other informants withheld information about such things as pain or fatigue or difficulties managing family life with an ill member from co-workers and health care professionals. Yet other informants actively manipulated information through lying. All of the covering-up strategies created an appearance of life as "normal" and facilitated the practice of doing normal things.

DOING NORMAL THINGS

Doing normal things was critical to the performance of the story of normalization. Three strategies supported the practice: maintaining a routine, letting go, and filling in. Having and adhering to a routine proved to be an important aspect of doing normal things and was a particularly useful way of normalizing such aspects of the experience as hospitalization. As with all the practices, the actualization of this part of the story was an individual family matter. Parents typically focused on discipline and the importance of treating the ill child like any other child (see also Knafl & Deatrick, 1986). One mother with two children who were severely affected by muscular dystrophy explained, "We've tried to bring them up so that they don't expect [pity], and just like normal kids they need getting after. Okay, we'll lay down the law to both of them. If it's no, it's no." Doing normal things included working full- or part-time either inside or outside the home, going to school, taking vacations, going on field trips, or going shopping. It encompassed the doing of normal things by all family members, whether ill or well, young or old.

Letting go was a parental strategy that facilitated doing normal things. Over time, the parents had carried a great deal of responsibility for protecting their children from experiences that would bring them harm or would falsify the story of normalization. However, at some point, protection was inappropriate to the story of normalization, and the parents had to let the children go to do normal things on their own. Letting go was difficult for the parents because of the fear that the children's differences would dominate their experiences. As one mother said, "This will be the toughest part I'm gonna have to live through. I can't shield him." Another mother emphasized the difficulty, saying, "I just about grew grey hairs overnight." Family members and ill individuals also engaged in a process of letting go of unattainable expectations in order to maintain the story of living life as normal. This was an ongoing process that occurred in response to the changing experience of illness.

Family members of individuals with chronic conditions engaged in an additional strategy of filling in. For example, siblings often took a more adult role in relation to their ill brother or sister and actively participated in caretaking. Again, this facilitated the doing of normal things by both the affected child and the family. In one family, a well sibling carried his wheelchair-bound brother up and down stairs between classes so that he could attend a normal school and the parents could work. Filling in meant that a family member would take on part of a task so that the ill member could complete the task. For example, in another situation, a husband prepared all the apples so that his ill wife, who was renowned for her baking, could make him a pie again. By necessity, the doing of normal things was a balancing act between all family members.

DESENSITIZATION

Desensitization was used to normalize interactions with others when visible differences could not be covered up. One mother took her son out shopping so he could see people and people could see him. She did this in the hopes "that he can get adjusted to people staring" and people can get adjusted to him. Another mother explained right away about her daughter to people so they would feel comfortable and be able to talk with her. Some adult participants reported making jokes in order to convey the message that they were just like everyone else and so that the person they were communicating with could relax.

MAKING TRADE-OFFS

A final way that life was ordered to support the story of normalization was through making trade-offs. This entailed giving something up in order to gain something else that was of greater value to the story. For example, a woman with multiple sclerosis who was still able to walk short distances requested a wheelchair so that she could go to the mall to shop with her teenaged daughter.

SUMMARY

To summarize, persons give meaning to their lives and relationships by storying their experience and, in interacting with others in the performance of these stories, they are active in shaping their lives and relationships. Knafl and Deatrick (1986) identified five common strategies used by parents of children with chronic conditions to enact the story of normalization. Three of these strategies—engaging in usual parenting activities, making the child appear normal, and controlling information—are apparent above. However, the other two strategies—limiting contacts with similarly situated others and avoiding embarrassing situations—were not explicit in these informants' stories.

REFERENCES

Anderson, J. M. (1981). The social construction of illness experience: Families with a chronically-ill child. *Journal of Advanced Nursing, 6*, 427–434.

Anderson, J. M., Elfert, H., & Lai, M. (1989). Ideology in the clinical context: Chronic illness, ethnicity and the discourse on normalisation. *Sociology of Health & Illness*, 11(3), 253–278.

Charmaz, K. (1990). "Discovering" chronic illness: Using grounded theory. *Social Science and Medicine*, 11, 1161–1172.

Deatrick, J. A., & Knafl, K. A. (1990). Management behaviors: Day-to-day adjustments to childhood chronic conditions. *Journal of Pediatric Nursing*, 5(1), 15–22.

Dewis, M. E. (1989). Spinal cord injured adolescents and young adults: The meaning of body changes. *Journal of Advanced Nursing*, 14, 389–396.

Featherstone, H. (1980). *A difference in the family: Life with a disabled child*. New York: Basic Books, Inc.

Glaser, B. G., & Strauss, A. L. (1967). *The discovery of grounded theory: Strategies for qualitative research*. Chicago: Aldine.

Goffman, E. (1963). *Stigma: Notes on the management of spoiled identity*. Englewood Cliffs, NJ: Prentice-Hall.

Holaday, B. (1984). Challenges of rearing a chronically ill child. *Nursing Clinics of North America*, 19(2), 361–368.

Knafl, K. A., & Deatrick, J. A. (1986). How families manage chronic conditions: An analysis of the concept of normalization. *Research in Nursing and Health*, 9, 215–222.

Knafl, K. A., & Deatrick, J. A. (1990). Family management style: Concept analysis and development. *Journal of Pediatric Nursing*, 1, 4–14.

Krulik, T. (1980). Successful "normalizing" tactics of parents of chronically-ill children. *Journal of Advanced Nursing*, 5, 573–578.

Rechner, M. (1990). Adolescents with cancer: Getting on with life. *Journal of Pediatric Oncology Nursing*, 7(4), 139–144.

Robinson, C. A. (1984). When hospitalization becomes an "everyday thing." *Issues in Comprehensive Pediatric Nursing*, 7, 363–370.

Robinson, C. A. (1985). Parents of hospitalized chronically ill children: Competency in question. *Nursing Papers*, 17(2), 59–68.

Sandelowski, M. (1991). Telling stories: Narrative approaches in qualitative research. *Image*, 23(3), 161–166.

Seligman, M. & Darling, R. B. (1989). *Ordinary families: Special children*. New York: Guilford.

Strauss, A., & Corbin, J. (1990). *Basics of qualitative research: Grounded theory procedures and techniques*. Newbury Park, CA: Sage.

Thorne, S. E., & Robinson, C. A. (1988). Health care relationships: The chronic illness perspective. *Research in Nursing and Health*, 11, 293–300.

Throne, S. E., & Robinson, C. A. (1989). Guarded alliance: Health care relationships in chronic illness. *Image: The Journal of Nursing Scholarship*, 21(3), 153–157.

Watzlawick, P., Weakland, J. H., & Fisch, R. (1974). *Change: Principles of problem formation and problem resolution*. New York: Norton.

White, M., & Epston, D. (1990). *Narrative means to therapeutic ends*. New York: Norton.

Weiner, C. L. (1975). The burden of rheumatoid arthritis: Tolerating the uncertainty. *Social Science and Medicine*, 9, 97–104.

John Eyles, Stephen Birch, and K. Bruce Newbold

ACCESS TO FAMILY PHYSICIAN SERVICES IN CANADA

INTRODUCTION

As Canadians we are justifiably proud of our health care system. As a Queen's University professor observed, health care has become the symbolic railway of the twenty-first century (Maclean's July 31, 1995, p. 10). Universal medical insurance was first proposed in Canada in the early years of this century, but it was not introduced into legislation until the Medical Care Act was implemented in 1972. While the cost is shared by the provinces and the federal government, the plan is administered by the provinces. But for the last decade concern has risen as costs rise and transfer payments shrink. This study looks at shifts in care as a result of recent cutbacks.

The data used by the authors is from the General Social Surveys (GSS) of 1985 and 1991. These surveys were conducted annually during the 1980s, and will be done every other year in future. These surveys are based on large representative samples of Canadians, and focus on questions of wide social interest. Question sets are repeated periodically to enable researchers to analyze change. The 1985 and 1991 surveys asked questions about health care access.

This study explains the assumptions behind the 1984 Canadian Health Act (CHA) and the funding of health care in Canada. A key objective of the CHA is to ensure that all Canadians have reasonable access to health care. Have funding cutbacks created barriers to reasonable access?

The GSS data analyzed in this study show that (1) Canadians of all income groups are equally likely to visit a physician, and (2) poorer Canadians have significantly more health problems. Thus, improved access to doctors has not yet brought about an equalization in people's health.

INTRODUCTION

The focus of this paper is the performance of the Canadian system of universal publicly funded health care during changing economic circumstances. In particular, has the burden of policies of cost containment generated by the fiscal crises of the late 1980s and early 1990s been shared among the population? Considerable international interest has been shown in the Canadian health care system in recent years, largely

Eyles, John, Stephen Birch, Bruce Newbold (1995). "Access to Family Physician Services in Canada," *Journal of Health and Social Behavior*, Vol. 36 (December):322–332.

because of the universal public funding of medical services. The Canadian model of single payer has been presented by some as a way of restraining the rate of growth of health care expenditures in the face of aging populations, technological developments and increasing expectations of populations, while maintaining comprehensive coverage of medical services for all the population without recourse to any form of user payment (Barer, Evans, and Labelle 1988; Evans et al. 1989; Evans, Barer, and Hertzman 1991; Danzon 1992). Table 1 presents comparative data on the percentage of Gross Domestic Product absorbed by health care expenditures over the period 1975–1991 in Canada and the United States, a period in which Canada introduced legislation, the Canada Health Act (1984) (CHA), that effectively mandated the principles of universal coverage of the population without use of user charges.

TABLE 1 Percentage of GDP Expended on Health Care, 1975–1991

	Canada	U.S.
1975	7.2	8.5
1985	8.5	10.5
1991	9.9	13.0

Source: Health and Welfare Canada, 1993

In the Canadian model, the use of sole source funding was seen as a way of guiding the distribution of health care resources in accordance with social goals. In particular, acknowledging that all needs for health care could never be met, the model was aimed at allocating whatever resources were made available for health care services in accordance with medical necessity (or the principle of 'reasonable access' to services). Several studies of the distribution of health care services in the Canadian population have shown that income is no longer a barrier to health care use.

However, most of these studies involved data sets collected in the mid-1980s immediately following the introduction of the CHA. Possibly based on these findings, policy-makers have tended to assume that reasonable access is a natural consequence of, or is caused by, sole source public funding. Attention has become increasingly focused on the challenge of cost containment as part of an overall policy direction of government deficit reduction brought on by the sluggish economy and consequent fiscal crises of the early 1990s.

It could be argued that, in the absence of any structural changes in the health care system over the last ten years, there is no reason why reasonable access would be threatened. The purpose of this paper is to consider whether this focus on cost containment has been associated with any erosion in the achievements of reasonable access. In other words, has the burden of cost containment considerations been allocated equitably across the population, or have particular groups 'shouldered' a greater share of this burden than others in ways which indicate that access to care in 1991 is less reasonable (or less in accordance with needs) than in 1985?

The next section presents a brief description of the recent developments in and main features of Canadian policy on the funding of health care services. The results are then reported, followed by discussion of the implications for universal public funding for health care.

PAYING FOR HEALTH CARE IN CANADA

Health care in Canada is a provincial responsibility with each of the ten provinces administering a public health insurance program. Each of these programs is funded through provincial tax revenues and federal government transfers. Under the Canada Health Act (1984), which covers the arrangements for the funding and delivery of specified 'insured services,'[1] the federal transfers are paid to provinces only where the provincial insurance program complies with the five stated principles of the Act—namely, universal coverage of the population, portability of insurance coverage across provincial boundaries, comprehensive coverage of services, reasonable access to those services without direct payment, and public administration of the insurance plan.

Under these arrangements, provinces which choose to impose or permit forms of patient copayment for the provision of these insured services risk losing these federal funds. As a consequence, each province introduced legislation to prohibit direct charges to patients. Although this protected the continuation of federal funding of provincial programs, the level of these funds is determined solely by the federal government and has been gradually reduced in real terms over recent years as part of a broader federal deficit reduction policy. But this means that provincial governments cannot turn to copayment policies as a means of compensating for these federal reductions or for raising additional funds. Health care policy at the provincial level has therefore focused, out of necessity, on reducing and controlling costs.

Under the CHA, the policy objective was stated clearly to be:

> . . . [T]o protect, promote, and restore the physical and mental well-being of residents of Canada and to facilitate reasonable access to health care services without financial or other barriers. (Canada 1984)

Although reasonable access is not defined in the legislation in ways that are meaningful for policy purposes, the federal government has stated elsewhere that ". . . medical necessity is the overriding determinant of reasonable access" (Health and Welfare Canada 1989), and others have noted that ". . . it is generally agreed that 'access' means not the provision of all services imaginable for everyone but services according to need (Evans 1992)."

The findings of studies concerning the distribution of health care services among the Canadian population have led to a general sense that this objective has been achieved. For example, federal and provincial government reports have noted that the inequities that remain represent needs for health improvements but not needs for health care, and are primarily issues of population—as distinct from patient—health (e.g., Canada 1986; Ontario Health Review Panel 1987; Ontario 1991). These concerns are matters for social policy rather than health care policy with the non-health care determinants of health such as occupation, lifestyle, environment, and so on being the focus of attention. As such, the health care system comes out with a glowing report card with claims that the system ". . . has been very successful in equalizing access to health care" (Evans 1992) and having ". . . eliminated the preexisting inequalities in the provision of health care" (Badgley 1991) (see also Birch and Abelson 1993).

Recent research has challenged the basis of some of these claims. In particular, Manga (1987), Birch, Eyles, and Newbold (1993), and Eyles, Birch, and Newbold (1994) have argued that, if needs for health care are inversely associated with income, then a health care system which allocates services equally across all income groups is hardly achieving reasonable access in the terms of the CHA. In an analysis of utilization of family physician services among the population, Birch and his associates (1993) found that the additional prosperity of the more prosperous groups in the population was associated with no advantage in terms of greater use of these services, even after controlling for levels of health status; but utilization rates within groups of the population with similar levels of health status were associated with other non-price barriers such as education.

At this stage it is unclear to what extent the health care system's achievements to date as well as its ability to meet the remaining challenges result from the presence of universal public funding or are conditional upon the level of funding of the system. In order to inform this issue we present a model for explaining variations in the incidence and use of family physician services, which we estimate separately for 1985 and 1991. We then use the findings of these analyses to explore whether (a) need variables are more or less helpful in explaining variations in utilization in 1991 than in 1985 and (b) the effect of particular socioeconomic variables on the relationship between utilization and need changes over the same period. The particular hypotheses to be tested are:

H1: The explanatory power of the need variables in explaining variations in the incidence and quantity of use is no less in 1991 than in 1985;

H2: Within groups of the population with similar needs, the level of correlation between particular socioeconomic variables and the incidence and quantity of utilization of family physician services is no greater in 1991 than in 1985.

DATA AND METHODS

Each stage of analysis is performed using data from both the 1985 and 1991 General Social Surveys (GSS) (Statistics Canada 1987, 1993). There are weighted random samples of the Canadian population which include data on individuals' self-assessed health status, self-reported use of family physician services in the past 12 months, and personal and behavioral attributes, as well as various socioeconomic indicators for the adult population (age $\geq$ 15).

RESULTS

Table 2 records the probabilities of use and need by family income for 1985 and 1991. In both years the probability of having visited a family physician is the same across income groups, but the incidence of activity limitation from a health problem is greater among poorer groups. Relative to the most prosperous quintile, activity limitation in the lowest quintile was greater in 1991 by almost 50 percent. Although equal likelihood of use has been maintained across income groups over time, the differences in need between the most and least prosperous groups has widened. In other words, not only does the incidence of use fail to reflect differences in need, but it has failed to respond appropriately to changes in the differences in need among these groups over time.

TABLE 2 Relative Probability[1] of Family Physician Use and Need for Health Care in the Last Year, by Household Income Quintiles, 1985 and 1991

	Income Quintile[2]				
1985	I	II	III	IV	V
Visited Physician in Previous Year	1.04	.98	1.04	1.00	1.00
Had Activity-Limiting Health Problem[3]	2.48	1.81	1.48	1.10	1.00
1991					
Visited Physician in Previous Year	1.05	1.04	.98	1.01	1.00
Had Activity-Limiting Health Problem[3]	3.50	2.33	1.67	1.50	1.00

Source: Data from Statistics Canada 1987, 1993.

[1]Probabilities expressed in relation to highest income quintile.

[2]Approximate quintiles in income distributions with I being the lowest and V the highest.

[3]Activity limitation used as need variable in order to provide a dichotomous variable for comparison. Construction of a dichotomous variable from self-assessed health status variable produced similar observations.

Tables 3 and 4 show the results of estimating the equations for quantity of use for groups in the same level of need for both years of observation; that is, partitioning the sample by need group. Because of the small sample sizes in some of the need groups, we combined the groups into two: a healthy group (excellent, very good, or good self-assessed health) and a sick group (fair or poor self-assessed health).[2] The results for 1985 and 1991 are similar for the healthy group. The consistent regional effects may be explained by persistent differences in supply among the regions. Neither income nor education is significantly associated with quantity of use, but the changing signs in the age-quantity relationship should be noted. The youngest two age groups as well as the 65 to 74-year-olds use more services than the over-75-year-olds. For the 'sick,' patterns of utilization by education and income group change over the period, but the changes are not significant. However, younger age groups and non-divorced are all significantly greater users of service. This implies that certain non-need factors become instrumental in explaining use among the sick over the period of comparison.

TABLE 3 Two-Stage Estimation: Quantity of Family Physician Utilization Among 'Healthy' Individuals, 1985 and 1991

Explanatory Variables		1985 B	1991 B
Sex	Male	−1.576*	−2.1*
Age	15–19	−1.972*	1.416*
	20–24	−.637	1.101*
	25–44	−1.266*	−.412
	45–64	−1.003	−.322
	65–74	−.489	1.258*
Marital Status	Married	.525	1.557*
	Single	.382	1.438*
	Widow	.896	2.505*
Region	Quebec	−.589	−.644
	Ontario	1.066*	1.520*
	Prairies	1.143*	.571
	B.C.	1.407*	1.758*
Employment[1]	Working	−.356	−.113
	Sick	2.684*	.430
	Looking	.582	
Household Income	II	−.328	.212
Quintile	III	.412	−.396
	IV	−.240	−.135
	V	−.340	−.219
Education[2]	SSGD	−.271	−.135
	Some	.061	−.269
	Post	.151	−.098
Constant		7.18*	9.38*
Adjusted R-Squared		.045	.055
F		8.5*	14.8*
N		4,209	6,213

*$p < .05$.

[1]In 1991 data 'Sick' and 'Looking' combined as 'Unemployed.'

[2]Post = Post-secondary school education with degree; Some = Some post-secondary school education but no degree; SSGD = Secondary School Graduation Diploma.

TABLE 4 Two-Stage Estimation: Quantity of Family Physician Utilization Among 'Sick' Individuals, 1985 and 1991

Explanatory Variables		1985 B	1991 B
Sex	Male	−1.489*	−.532*
Age	15–19	−6.728*	9.063*
	20–24	.832	8.274*
	25–44	.889	4.210*
	45–64	.626	4.574*
	65–74	.295	2.130*
Marital Status	Married	−.243	3.928*
	Single	−.662	4.809*
	Widow	1.691	5.323*
Region	Quebec	1.092	−1.674
	Ontario	3.992*	2.078*
	Prairies	3.354*	1.067
	B.C.	4.398*	1.816
Employment[1]	Working	−4.013*	−4.099*
	Sick	2.115*	−2.674*
	Looking	1.725	
Household Income	15–25	−.067	−.855
Quintile	25–35	−.615	−1.178
	35–50	−1.233	1.448
	50+	−.742	−.063
Education[2]	SSGD	1.292	−1.550
	Some	.331	−.071
	Post	.120	−.009
Constant		10.817*	10.348*
Adjusted R-Squared		.110	.042
F		6.9*	3.102*
N		1,296	1,256

*$p < .05$.

[1] In 1991 data 'Sick' and 'Looking' combined as 'Unemployed.'

[2] Post = Post-secondary school education with degree; Some = Some post-secondary school education but no degree; SSGD = Secondary School Graduation Diploma.

DISCUSSION

Our comparisons of use and need among the population in these two years indicate that, although the needs of the poorer income groups have increased relative to richer groups between 1985 and 1991, the position for relative use was largely the same. There are some indications that it may have worsened. In other words, there is little indication that this system of service provision with sole source public funding has responded to the changing distribution of needs in the population. Moreover the multivariate analyses suggest that demographic variables are more important in explaining variations of use in 1991 than in 1985. The changes in estimated coefficients between 1985 and 1991 were consistent with this finding. Moreover, the subgroup estimates indicated that any such increases in the role of demographic factors in explaining variations in use were not paralleled by an erosion of the achievements of the system in apparently removing income as a barrier to 'reasonable access.'

Our findings draw a distinction between open (or universal) access to services and reasonable access where use is determined by who needs the service most. Systems that adopt 'reasonable access' as a way of achieving collective (or social) goals may require public programs directed at those with the poorest health status. Programs designed solely around universal coverage that is free at the point of delivery may increase use among the target groups—but at the 'price' of subsidizing (and increasing by greater amounts) use by the rest of society.

Our comparative analysis 'tells a story' of health care system performance in Canada, and provides some support for arguing that the nature of inequalities in use (or unreasonable access) in family physician utilization may have changed between 1985 and 1991. Although there have been no significant structural changes in the health care system during this period, predisposing factors such as age and sex seem to have become more important characteristics in explaining the variations in utilization.

The implication is that policymakers should be wary of assuming that the continued reliance on universal public funding alone is sufficient to ensure a distribution of services unrelated to income. As cost-containment policies continue to dominate and health care reforms arising from these policies are introduced, there is the potential for the narrower goals of these particular policies to be achieved at the cost of the erosion of the income-free basis of access to services.

ENDNOTES

[1]   These are mainly inpatient hospital care and physician services—other services such as dental care, ambulatory care, drugs, health promotion, and community health services are not covered by the federal legislation with the funding and provision of these determined provincially.

[2]   In 1985, respondents could choose between 'excellent' and 'good' responses; in 1991, between 'excellent,' 'very good,' and 'good.' So the 1985 'excellent' group combines two categories; the 1991, three.

REFERENCES

Aday, Lou-Ann and Robert Andersen. 1974. "A Framework for the Study of Access to Medical Care." *Health Services Research* 9:208–20.

Arling, Greg. 1985. "Interaction Effects in a Multivariate Model of Physician Visits by Older People." *Medical Care* 23:361–71.

Badgley, Robin. 1991. "Social and Economic Disparities Under Canadian Health Care." *International Journal of Health Services* 21:659–71.

Barer, Morris L., Robert G. Evans, and Roberta J. Labelle. 1988. "Fee Controls as Cost Controls: Takes from the Frozen North." *Milbank Quarterly* 66:1–64.

Barnow, Burt, Glen Caine, and Arthur Goldberge. 1981. "Issues in the Analysis of Selectivity Bias." Pp. 43–49 in *Evaluation Studies Review Annual*, vol. 5, edited by W. Stormsdorfer and G. Farke. Beverly Hills, CA: Sage.

Birch, Stephen and Julia Abelson. 1993. "Is Reasonable Access What We Want?" *International Journal of Health Services* 23:629–53.

Birch, Stephen, John Eyles, and K. Bruce Newbold. 1993. "Equitable Access to Health Care: Methodological Extensions to the Analysis of Physician Utilization in Canada." *Health Economics* 2:87–101.

Blaxter, Mildred. 1990. *Health and Lifestyles*. London, England: Routledge.

Canada. 1986. *Achieving Health for All*. Ottawa, Ontario: Ministry of Supplies and Services.

Canada. House of Commons. 1984. *Canada Health Act*. Ottawa, Ontario: Queen's Printer.

Collins, Elizabeth and Rudolf Klein. 1980. "Equity in the NHS." *British Medical Journal* 281:1111–15.

Danzon, Patricia M. 1992. "Hidden Overhead Costs: Is Canada's System Less Expensive?" *Health Affairs* 11(1):21–43.

Duan, Naihua, Willard G. Manning, Colin N. Morris, and John P. Newhouse. 1984. "Choosing Between the Sample Selection Model and the Multi-part Model." *Journal of Business and Economic Statistics* 2:283–89.

Evans, Robert G. 1993. "The Canadian Health Care Financing and Delivery System: Its Experiences and Lessons for Other Nations." *Yale Law Policy Review* 10:362–96.

Evans, Robert G., Morris L. Barer, and Clyde Hertzman. 1991. "The 20-Year Experiment: Accounting for, Explaining, and Evaluating Health Care Cost Containment in Canada and the United States." *Annual Review of Public Health* 12:481–518.

Evans, Robert G., Jonathan Lomas, and Morris L. Barer. 1989. "Controlling Health Expenditures: The Canadian Reality." *New England Journal of Medicine* 320:571–77.

Eyles, John, Stephen Birch, and K. Bruce Newbold. 1994. "Equity and Health Care: Analysis of the Relationship Between Need for Care and Utilization of Nursing Services in Canada." *Canadian Journal of Nursing Research* 25(4):27–46.

Health and Welfare Canada. 1989. *Health and Welfare in Canada*. Ottawa, Ontario: Ministry of Supplies and Services.

Health and Welfare Canada. 1993. *Health Expenditures in Canada: Fact Sheets*. Ottawa, Ontario: Health and Welfare Canada.

Heckman, James. 1979. "Sample Bias as a Specification Error." *Econometrica* 47:153–62.

Jones, Andrew M. 1994. "Health, Addiction, Social Interaction, and the Decision to Quit Smoking." *Journal of Health Economics* 13(1):93–110.

Kmenta, Jan. 1988. *Elements of Econometrics*. New York: Macmillan.

Le Grand, Julia. 1982. *The Strategy of Equality*. London, England: Allen and Unwin.

Maddala, Gangaddharrao. 1983. *Limited Dependent and Qualitative Variables in Econometrics*. Cambridge, MA: Cambridge University Press.

Manga, Pran. 1978. *The Income Distribution Effect of Medical Insurance in Ontario*. Toronto, Ontario: Ontario Economic Council.

———. 1987. "Equity of Access and Inequalities in Health Status." Pp. 637–48 in *Health and Canadian Society*, edited by D. Coburn. Markham, Ontario: Fitzhenry and Whiteside.

Manning, Willard G., Joseph P. Newhouse, Naihua Duan, Emmett B. Keeler, Arleen Leibowitz, and M. Susan Marquis. 1987. "Health Insurance and the Demand for Medical Care." *American Economic Review* 77:251–77.

McFadden, Daniel. 1974. "Conditional Logit Analysis of Qualitative Choice Behavior." Pp. 105–42 in *Frontiers in Econometrics*, edited by D. Zarembka. Cambridge, MA: Cambridge University Press.

Newacheck, Paul. 1988. "Access to Ambulatory Care for Poor Persons." *Health Services Research* 23:401–19.

O'Donnell, Owen and Carol Propper. 1991. "Equity and the Distribution of UK National Health Service Resources." *Journal of Health Economics* 10:1–20.

Ontario. 1991. *Nurturing Health*. Toronto, Ontario: Premier's Council on Health Strategy.

Ontario Health Review Panel. 1987. *Towards a Shared Direction for Health in Ontario*. Toronto, Ontario: Ontario Ministry of Health.

Schieber, George J., Pierre Poullier, and Leslie M. Greenwald. 1993. "Health Spending, Delivery, and Outcomes in OECD Countries." *Health Affairs* 12(2):120–29.

Starr, Paul and Walter A. Zelman. 1993. "A Bridge to Compromise: Competition Under a Budget." *Health Affairs* 12(Suppl.): 7–23.

Statistics Canada. 1987. *Health and Social Support 1985*. Ottawa, Ontario: Ministry of Supplies and Services.

———. 1993. *Health and Social Support 1991*. Ottawa, Ontario: Ministry of Supplies and Services.

Van Doorslaer, Eddy, Adam Wagstaff, and Frans Rutten. 1993. *Equity in the Finance and Delivery of Health Care*. New York: Oxford University Press.

Zelman, Walter A. 1994. "The Rationale Behind the Clinton Health Reforms." *Health Affairs* 13(1):9–29.

R. Alan Hedley

INDUSTRIALIZATION AND THE PRACTICE OF MEDICINE: MOVEMENT AND COUNTERMOVEMENT

INTRODUCTION

This study looks at two issues: the relationship between industrialization and the provision of scientific health care, and the renewed interest in alternative health care practices as a means of personal empowerment.

In preindustrial Canada, folk medicines (including whisky, brandy, and opium) were widely used. The first medical practitioners were barbers, who had some training in surgery, and apothecaries, who dispensed both advice and medicine. There has recently been increasing interest in what we currently call alternative medical practices—some of which have deep roots in folk medicine. Herbal medicine, for example, is one of the fastest growing alternate treatments. Another example is acupuncture, an ancient Chinese treatment based on the belief that there are several distinct energy channels in the body. The insertion of thin needles at strategic points in these channels is intended to promote healing and reduce pain.

No less important than the specific remedies of traditional medicine is its emphasis on holism. Traditional medicine respects the integrity of the patient, and the interdependence of body, mind, and spirit in causing (or curing) illness. Much of this has been lost in today's highly specialized and "empirical" medical practice.

The thesis of cultural convergence predicts that as a result of the common technological and organizational elements involved in the process of industrialization, other common features also necessarily appear within societies regardless of any initial differences that served to make these societies culturally distinct (see Kerr et al., 1964). Among these consequences of industrialization are trends toward secularization, bureaucratization, and the increasing importance of scientific inquiry. Moreover, these features are extended universally throughout society (see Form,

Hedley, R. Alan (1992). "Industrialization and the Practice of Medicine: Movement and Countermovement," *International Journal of Comparative Sociology* XXXIII, 3-4.

1979). As Max Weber observed, the overall result is one of "cumulative technologi-cal rationalization" in all endeavors (Gerth and Mills, 1958: 51).

Nowhere have these secondary effects of industrialization been more apparent than in the practice of medicine. From its origins in diverse folk belief systems throughout the world, it has evolved into a relatively unified body of medical sci-ence that can be systematically applied wherever common ailments and diseases present themselves. Modern allopathic medicine is the embodiment of the rational, scientific, and bureaucratic approach to problem solving that is characteristic of industrial societies.

The purpose of this paper is twofold: 1) to demonstrate the direct relationship between industrialization and the provision of organized, scientific health care throughout society; and 2) to determine what happens to the traditional and folk medical practices that modern scientific medicine seeks to replace.

INDUSTRIALIZATION AND SCIENTIFIC MEDICINE

On the basis of three commonly accepted measures of the multidimensional concept of industrialization (percent of labor force in industry; percent of professional and technical workers in the labor force; and commercial energy consumption per capi-ta), an overall index was constructed (see Hedley, 1992: 38–41; 128–33). The index was formed by adding the rank orders of all countries for which data existed on each of the three separate measures of industrialization.[1] This exercise was complet-ed for 50 countries for which data existed; they adequately represent the complete range of industrialization present in the world today (Table 1). The correlations between the rankings of these countries on each measure of industrialization ranged between .71 and .85. Consequently, there is a relatively high degree of similarity among countries on all three measures.

TABLE 1 Countries Ranked by Three Measures of Industrialization

Rank	Country	Rank	Country
1	Sweden	11	Austria
2	Finland	12	New Zealand
3	West Germany	13	United Kingdom
4	Norway	14	Trinidad & Tobago
5	France	15	Singapore
6	Belgium	16	Japan
7	United States	17	Libya
8	Australia	18	Venezuela
9	Canada	19	Greece
10	Kuwait	20	Jordan

TABLE 1 Cont'd

Rank	Country	Rank	Country
21	Mexico	36	Zimbabwe
22	South Africa	37	Sri Lanka
23	Panama	38	Ghana
24	South Korea	39	Honduras
25	Ecuador	40	Pakistan
26	Tunisia	41	Indonesia
27	Peru	42	India
28	Morocco	43	Thailand
29	Paraguay	44	North Yemen
30	Turkey	45	Sudan
31	Dominican Republic	46	Cameroon
32	Colombia	47	Nepal
33	Philippines	48	Bangladesh
34	Nicaragua	49	Mali
35	El Salvador	50	Rwanda

Data source: See Note 1 for a list of measure and data sources.

In order to represent the presence of an organized medical establishment in each country, four measures were used: 1) population per physician; 2) percentage of population with access to health services; 3) population per hospital bed; and 4) public health expenditures per capita.[2] Together these four measures reflect the degree to which scientific medicine is organizationally established and supported in the infrastructure of each country, and also how extensive its impact is. While obviously the development of a sophisticated medical infrastructure is dependent upon adequate funding, money by itself does not necessarily ensure it. For example, Kuwait has the fourth highest GNP per capita of the countries represented (World Bank, 1987), yet it ranks between 14th and 18th on the medical presence measures. Its rank on the industrialization index (10th) is more closely related to these medical indicators than its per-capita income.

Table 2 presents the correlations between the industrialization index and each of the four organized medical presence measures. They range in value between .83 and .91, thus demonstrating that, indeed, one of the consequences of industrialization is the appearance of a scientific medical infrastructure available to all. While this fact was never in dispute, a more interesting set of questions revolves around what happens to the traditional health-care system upon the introduction and endorsement of scientific medicine. It is to these questions that we now turn our attention.

TABLE 2 Correlations of Industrialization Index to Four Measures of Organized Scientific Health Care (N = 50 countries)

Pearson's r	Measures of Organized Health Care
−.91	Population per physician
.90	Percentage of population with access to health services
−.83	Population per hospital bed
.91	Public health expenditure per capita

Data sources: See Notes 1 & 2. Correlations are based on data collected between 1980 and 1987.

INDUSTRIALIZATION AND ALTERNATIVE HEALTH CARE

In an article that examines the broad processes of social change involved in industrialization and modernization, Gusfield (1967: 362) argues strongly against "pitting tradition and modernity against each other as paired opposites." The two poles can and very often do coexist in mutually supportive ways. Old traditions are not necessarily weakened or replaced by new changes. Traditional and modern forms are not always in conflict; they are not mutually exclusive systems.

While it is true, for example, that modern scientific medicine is a product of industrialization and is, therefore, extensively available in all developed countries (see Table 1), it is also true that "the bulk of all care is self-care" (Dean, 1989: 118). According to one American study, "79% of all illnesses are managed completely by the individual/family without any sort of professional advice or attention" (DeFriese et al., 1989: 202). In other words, notwithstanding the truly phenomenal accomplishments of modern medicine, traditional methods of health care are the methods of choice in virtually all but the most extreme of medical symptoms. According to Dean (1986: 275), "lay care continues to be viewed as residual and supplemental to professional care in spite of the well-documented fact that professional care is the supplemental form of health care."

Not only are traditional methods of health care generally preferred over professional consultation, there are indications that their frequency of use has increased in recent times. Arising out of the human potential movement of the 1960s (Alster, 1989), the feminist movement of the 1970s (Butter and Kay, 1990), and the "wellness" movement of the 1980s (Whorton, 1988), there is renewed concern for self-reliance and taking charge of one's own life. As Naisbitt (1982) explains, the tremendous technological rationalization that we have experienced during the past three decades has produced a countervailing drive toward personal empowerment. This is particularly apparent in the resurgence of the holistic health movement as an antidote to the excesses of the highly specialized and mechanistic invasion by modern medicine into that most intimate of all domains—our own bodies (see Alster, 1989).

Also contributing to the move toward self-responsibility for health is the fact that Western scientific medicine has reached an impasse of sorts. While it has largely eradicated the infections and diseases of the previous century to the point where life expectancy begins to approximate life span, it has not had as much success with diseases associated with ageing (heart disease, cancer, and other degenerative ailments). These are diseases that are not cured by intrusive therapies; rather, their resolution lies in prevention through changes in lifestyle. As a result, the responsibility for health has shifted from doctor to patient. Only through a daily regimen that involves the whole person (e.g., diet, exercise, habits, and state of mind) can "wellness" be attained (see Whorton, 1988).

Consequently, subsequent gains by medical science in reducing death rates are likely to be marginal at best and will only be achieved at what are now becoming intolerable costs. Furthermore, conventional medical practice in which standardized treatment is dispensed in 13 minute allotments per patient (Alster, 1989: 169) is increasingly being rejected by a populace that is more intent on assuming control of its own health care.

Another part of the explanation for the increase in "alternative" health-care practices is the fact that the definition of sickness itself has expanded to include social problems not hitherto defined as "medical" (see Crawford, 1980). The "medicalization" of the human condition has resulted in a burgeoning industry of therapists, both orthodox and unorthodox, who have responded to the growing demand for "treatment."

As an illustration of this new array of health-care practitioners, Table 3 presents those listed in the "yellow pages" of a Los Angeles-area telephone book. They are divided into two groups. The "allied practitioners" consist of therapists who are generally considered to be part of the mainstream of health-care. While they do offer "alternatives" to conventional allopathic medicine, in most cases their services are part of the expanding network of orthodox health-care. In some cases, however, individual practitioners may not be appropriately licensed or they may not operate in accordance with "acceptable procedure." On the other hand, the "alternative practitioners" represent unorthodox approaches to health care. Whether it is because their techniques have evolved from different cultural traditions, or because they rely on "nondemonstrable" methods, or simply because they are defined as quacks, these alternative practitioners are generally not part of the mainstream of health-care in America.

TABLE 3 "Allied" and "Alternative" Practitioners of Health Care

Allied Practitioners	Alternative Practitioners
Audiologists	Acupressure practitioners
Behavioral science consultants	Acupuncture practitioners
Chiropractors	Art therapists
Community & home-care workers	Biofeedback therapists
Dieticians & nutritionists	Chelatian therapists
Educational therapists	Christian science practitioners
Health & fitness consultants	Drugless practitioners
Holistic practitioners	Feldenkraisian practitioners

TABLE 3 Cont'd

Allied Practitioners	Alternative Practitioners
Homeopaths	Herbalists
Human relations counselors	Hypnotherapists
Kinesiologists	Iridologists
Learning disability therapists	Massage practitioners
Mental-health workers	Metaphysicians
Midwives	Naturopathic physicians
Nurse practitioners	Parapsychologists
Occupational therapists	Pastorial counselors
Opticians & optometrists	Psychic arts & science instructors
Orthoptists	Reflexologists
Orthotists & prosthetists	Respiratory therapists
Osteopathic physicians	Spiritual healers
Pharmaceutical consultants	Structural integrationists
Physical therapists	Tai chi chuan instructors
Psychologists	Transactional analysts
Social workers	Yoga instructors

Data source: Adapted from Pacific Bell, Beverly Hills & Westside Yellow Pages. February 1989–1990.

In addition to standard medical conditions, the practitioners listed in Table 3 have become responsible for a whole host of other problems. These can be grouped into three main areas:

1) Birth and death (e.g., family planning, birth control, abortion, abortion alternatives, type and location of childbirth, care of the elderly, terminal patients, ethical limits of medical technology, and death and dying);

2) Life cycle (e.g., child development, marriage, family and human relations, "wellness," adult education and training, and social support services); and

3) Social problems (e.g., alcoholism, drug abuse and addiction, tobacco addiction, eating disorders and weight control, sleep disorders, sexual problems, stress and burnout, mental and emotional disorders, violence, abuse and neglect, and suicide prevention).

The inclusion of this broad array of problems into the health-care field has resulted in a tremendous expansion of both orthodox "allied" and unorthodox "alternative" practitioners. Thus, Table 3 provides further evidence for the existence of alternate systems of health-care despite the fact that conventional medicine is available to all.

Finally, it is important to point out that in addition to these formal avenues of alternative health-care, there are also many informal networks and support services. Basically, these are of two kinds: 1) personal networks that have long been responsible for the transmission of health-care information and treatment; and 2) self-help groups that "address problems which are either neglected or not helped by the professional services directed toward particular conditions" (Dean, 1986: 280). Prominent among these self-help groups are women's organizations who are critical of the dominant health system "for denying women autonomy and decision-making power" (Butter and Kay, 1990: 1331). Others include seniors advocacy groups as well as groups seeking social and emotional support and information for problems currently insoluble by medical science (e.g., AIDS, Alzheimers disease, and cancer). Indications are that these self-help groups have also expanded during recent years (Dean, 1986).

Consequently, the alternatives to conventional medical care are many and well used. From self-care to informal networks to a wide variety of professional services, "alternative" health-care methods are predominant. While Western scientific medicine has been most successful in virtually eliminating many diseases and in extending life beyond seemingly impossible limits, nevertheless, most of us most of the time continue to attend to our health needs much as we have always done.

SUMMARY AND CONCLUSIONS

While this paper provides support for the convergence thesis by demonstrating a strong direct relationship between industrialization and the provision of organized scientific health care, this does not mean that indigenous medical practices are thereby superseded. Despite tremendous financial and organizational support, the scientific medical establishment remains supplementary to traditional medical and health-care practices. "The bulk of all care in illness is self-care" (Dean, 1989: 118), which, in turn, is reinforced by personal health-care networks and support groups. Only rarely do people use the facilities and services provided by organized medicine.

It may be concluded that while individual health is precious and, therefore, should be preserved at all costs, it is also a very personal matter. Consequently, before submitting oneself to all manner of medical experts, and thereby losing control over self, individuals will rely on less intrusive, but nevertheless reliable methods. Only when their health is beyond their perceived ability to control will they then relinquish that control to others.

ENDNOTES

1   Data on percentage of labor force in industry and commercial energy consumption per capita were taken from the World Bank, 1987: 264–265; 218–219. Data on professional and technical workers in the labor force came from Muller, 1988.

2   Data sources for these measures are as follows: population per physician (World Bank, 1987: 260–261); percent population with access to health services (UNICEF, 1989: 98–99) and population per hospital bed and public health expenditures per capita (Kurian, 1984: 334–335; 344–345).

REFERENCES

Alster, Kristine Beyerman (1989). *The Holistic Health Movement.* Tuscaloosa, Ala.: University of Alabama Press.

Butter, Irene H. and Bonnie J. Kay (1990). "Self-certification in lay midwives' organizations: A vehicle for professional autonomy." *Social Science and Medicine* 30(12): 1329–1339.

Crawford, R. (1980). "Healthism and the medicalization of everyday life." *International Journal of Health Issues* 10(3): 365–388.

Dean, Kathryn (1986). "Lay care in illness." *Social Science and Medicine* 22(2): 275–284.

Dean, Kathryn (1989). "Conceptual, theoretical, and methodological issues in self-care research." *Social Science and Medicine* 29(2): 117–123.

DeFriese, Gordon et al. (1989). "From activated patient to pacified activist: A study of the self-care movement in the United States." *Social Science and Medicine* 29(2): 195–204.

Form, William (1979). "Comparative industrial sociology and the convergence hypothesis." *Annual Review of Sociology* 5: 1–25.

Gerth, H.H. and C.W. Mills (eds.) (1958). From *Max Weber: Essays in Sociology*. New York: Oxford University Press.

Gusfield, Joseph R. (1967). "Tradition and modernity: Misplaced polarities in the study of social change." *American Journal of Sociology* 72(4): 351–362.

Hedley, R. Alan (1992). *Making a Living: Technology and Change*. New York: Harper Collins.

Kerr, Clark et al. (1964). *Industrialism and Industrial Man*. New York: Oxford University Press.

Kurian, George T. (1984). *The New Book of World Rankings*. New York: Facts on File.

Muller, George P. (1988). *Comparative World Data: A Statistical Handbook for Social Science*. Baltimore: Johns Hopkins University Press.

Naisbitt, John (1982). *Megatrends: Ten New Directions Transforming Our Lives*. New York: Warner.

UNICEF (1989). *The State of the World's Children 1989*. Oxford: Oxford University Press.

Whorton, James C. (1988). "Patient, heal thyself: Popular health reform movements as unorthodox medicine." In Norman Gevitz (ed.), *Other Healers: Unorthodox Medicine in America*. pp. 52–81, Baltimore: Johns Hopkins University Press.

World Bank (1987). *World Development Report 1987*. New York: Oxford University Press.

QUESTIONS

DISCUSSION QUESTIONS

1. Hedley (excerpt 12.3) raises an interesting question about the loss of individual control inherent in modern medical practice. Do you agree that we lose control over our own health care when we seek help from the mainstream medical profession? Is this loss inevitable?

2. In the kinds of cases that make journalists ecstatic, PMS (pre-menstrual syndrome) has been used as a murder defence. Do you consider PMS to be a medical condition, or is it simply medicalization carried to an extreme?

3. Should Canadians be expected to take greater personal responsibility for their health? What about people who engage in such dangerous behaviours as drinking or smoking to excess? What about those who fail to live healthy lifestyles by ignoring good nutrition, etc.?

4. Should health care professionals denounce such alternate health practices as homeopathy, reflexology, and therapeutic touch? Or do you think these practices are valid treatments?

DATA COLLECTION EXERCISES

1. Using data from the Statistics Canada publication *National Population Health Survey Overview 1994-95* (Catalogue 82-567) or the quarterly journal *Health Reports* (Statistics Canada Catalogue 82-003), test two or three hypotheses concerning the social basis of health outcomes.

2. Working in pairs or groups, interview a number of people about their conception of health. What does "health" mean to them? How would they define "good health"? Make your sample large enough to allow for comparisons by gender, age, occupation, etc.

3. Feminists are critical of the media image of women, particularly the use of fashion models with extremely slim bodies. Men too are objectified in print advertisements. Has the ideal body shape and style (for men, women, or both) changed over time? Do a content analysis of a selected magazine to document changes. What does your analysis imply about the relationship between health and the way bodies are idealized?

4. Interview several people who practice or use alternative health therapies. Why did they turn to these alternatives? Are these therapies best used in conjunction with mainstream practices?

WRITING EXERCISES

1. Select one alternative medical practice (for example, chiropractic, acupuncture, therapeutic touch, homeopathy, herbal medicine, reflexology, naturopathy, or aromatherapy) and write a 500-word essay following the history of the adoption of the treatment in Canada.

2. In Canada most medical doctors are men and most nurses are women. Analyze this structure from the gender inequality point of view.

3. Why did Canada wholeheartedly adopt the principle of universal health care while the United States continues to resist it? Write an essay trying to answer this question by exploring cultural differences between the two societies.

4. Is universal health care in jeopardy in Canada, or is the crisis manufactured to protect special interests? Answer this question in a 500-word essay.

SUGGESTED READINGS

1. Armstrong, Pat and Hugh Armstrong, J. Choiniere, G. Feldberg and Jerry White (1994). *Take Care: Warning Signs for Canada's Health System*. Toronto: Garamond Press. This book critically evaluates the notion that Canada's health care system is in crisis. The authors show how consequent cutbacks have negative effects on patients and caregivers, most of whom are women.

2. Bolaria, B. Singh and Harley D. Dickenson (eds) (1994). *Health, Illness and Health Care in Canada* (Second Edition). Toronto: Harcourt Brace and Company, Ltd. This is a useful and extensive collection of articles related to health care and the health care professions in Canada.

3. Coburn, D. and J. Eakin (1993). "The Sociology of Health in Canada: First Impressions." *Health and Canadian Society* Vol. 1, No. 1, pp. 83-110. An overview of three threads in the sociology of health in Canada: the social determinants of health status, health and illness behaviour, and the health care system. An extensive bibliography makes this a particularly useful resource for students.

SECTION 13   POPULATION

Introduction

A population is a set of people in a particular territory. It changes size through births, deaths, and migrations. But of these three, only births and deaths affect the population of the world as a whole. The world's population increases through an excess of births over deaths, and this excess is called natural increase. Today, the world's annual birth rate is about 2 percent higher than its death rate, which means that the world's population is growing at a rate of 2 percent each year. If the population continues to grow at this speed, it will double in less than 35 years. And if that happens, the world will contain more than 8 billion people early in the next century.

Sooner or later, population growth must stop. But when and how will growth end? Will the decline be sudden or gradual, chosen or forced upon us? Will it be accomplished by a drastic drop in childbearing, a sudden rise in the number of deaths, a lower fertility rate, or a higher mortality rate?

MALTHUSIAN THEORY

This question has been the subject of close analysis for two hundred years. The first to study it systematically was Thomas Malthus (1766-1834), an English clergyman and economist. Malthus theorized that a population will always outgrow its food supply. According to Malthus the food supply can increase only arithmetically, as in the series 1, 2, 3, 4, 5. However population will always increase geometrically, as in the series 1, 2, 4, 8, 16. Over time the gap between these two series widens, and the amount of food available per person becomes smaller and smaller. Finally a disaster occurs.

To illustrate this, consider a population of 1000 girls and 1000 boys. Now, assume that every girl survives to adulthood, marries, has four children, and dies. If all of these children survive to adulthood and bear four children each, in the next generation there will be 2000 women and 2000 men. If all of these children survive and bear four children, in the next generation there will be 4000 women and 4000 men; in the generation after that, 8000 women and 8000 men; and so on.

With a constant four births per woman, the population doubles every generation (roughly thirty years). In four generations (a mere 120 years), the population grows from 2000 people to 16,000 people: an 8-fold increase. This is the power of exponential growth. Populations really can grow this quickly; look at southern and southeastern Asia, where 1.5 billion people live today. The same thing is happening in Latin America, where another half-billion people live. So these kinds of calculations are realistic and important.

Malthus doubted that food supplies could also increase 8-fold in 120 years. Increases in the food supply are only "additive" or "arithmetic," he said. And in

1800, when Malthus was writing, the growth of the food supply was severely limit-ed by poor soil, the amount of land available, and the level of agricultural technol-ogy. In Malthus's time, increases in the food supply were arithmetic and fairly slow. That's what led Malthus to believe there was a strong chance that population growth would outstrip increases in the food supply, and that the human race would starve.

Malthus saw several ways out of the trap. In short, people had to settle for "preventive" or "positive" checks on population. Positive checks limit population growth by increasing the death rate. They include war, famine, pestilence, and dis-ease. Preventive checks limit population growth by limiting the numbers of births. They include abortion, contraception, sexual abstinence, and delayed marriage.

Of these two options, Malthus preferred preventive checks, especially delayed marriage. So, in his view, people had a choice to make: either delay marrying or face starvation, war, and epidemic disease.

Malthus painted a grim picture of the world's future; and in some respects, he was right to do so. Throughout the nineteenth and twentieth centuries famines and epidemics have occurred around the world. They usually occur where the pop-ulation is poor, people marry young, and the birth rate is high. Yet, amazingly, the human race still exists. One reason for our survival is the opening of new land for food production in the nineteenth and twentieth centuries. Another is the improvement of agricultural methods, which are better today than they were two centuries ago. The third reason is industrialization. Most economies have shifted from an agricultural to an industrial base, and industrial economies produce more food and consumer goods.

In the less developed countries many people still lack enough food to eat. But many of the famines that have recently plagued Africa, for example, are due to primitive technology and desertification resulting from broader economic and polit-ical pressures and inequities. Sometimes they are a result of civil war and other political factors. Rarely are they a simple result of overpopulation.

Since Malthus' time the world's food supply has increased more than arithmeti-cally. As well, people have slowed down their birth rates by using a preventive check that Malthus couldn't support: contraception. As England entered the twentieth cen-tury, the "Malthusian problem" of too many people seemed to take care of itself. The standard of living rose, and people began to bear fewer children. This represented the full flowering of what has been called the (first) "demographic transition."

Once mortality rates were under control, people began to feel that they could plan and control the number of children they produced. Declines in infant and childhood mortality rates meant that most of the children they did produce would live to adulthood. Thus, they needed to produce fewer babies in order to end up with the desired number of adult children two or three decades later.

NEW WAYS OF LIVING REDUCE FERTILITY

Cheap, safe, and easy contraception helps women avoid childbearing as much as they wish. And new individualistic values lead people to want fewer children as they become more prosperous. And contrary to what Malthus feared, new individualistic values encourage people to enjoy their prosperity and leisure, not bear and raise a larger number of children. Throughout Europe and North America, what van de Kaa in excerpt 13.1 calls the "second demographic transition" is producing lower fertility rates. Marriage and childbearing have become lifestyle choices. As we see in excerpt 13.2, the decision to bear children is personal, but it is also cultural. In a world full of competing opportunities, average Canadians—along with Belgians, Germans, Italians, and other Europeans—share similar notions about what it means to marry (or not) and have children (or not).

Other factors also play a part in lowering fertility. For example, greater educational and work opportunities lead women to limit their childbearing. Conversely, when women lack such opportunities or aspirations—even in industrial societies—they are more likely to become mothers early and often. This goes a long way towards explaining the large number of teenage pregnancies among women who have little real hope of a higher education or a career.

Low Fertility and Population Aging

In industrial, low-fertility countries there is now concern about an "aging population" and the shortage of young people. The rising number of old people means more public spending on health and old-age pensions. Decreases in the relative number of young people means that less youthful energy, labour power, and creativity are invested in the economy. And in some societies like China's, a rapid decline in fertility has rapidly produced a crisis in care for the aged, as we see in excerpt 13.3 below. No longer is it possible to leave the care of the elderly to the family alone, since families are getting smaller and ties of obligation are becoming weaker.

In order for people to worry less about having children who will provide for them in their old age, the state must provide pensions. And for people to worry less about their children dying before they reach adulthood, medical care must improve. When these changes do take place—and in most industrialized countries they already have—people will stop equating large families and rapid population growth with wealth and personal security. But as we enter the twenty-first century the most pressing population problems are the growing disparity between rich and poor nations, environmental degradation in the poor and rapidly growing societies, and care for the aged in (older) industrialized societies.

These are problems Malthus could not have foreseen two centuries ago.

Dirk van de Kaa

EUROPE'S SECOND DEMOGRAPHIC TRANSITION

INTRODUCTION

When your grandparents were young, Canada—like most of the Western world—had higher rates of childbearing and a stricter moral code. Cohabitation was unusual and disapproved of, divorce was rare, and unwed pregnancy was hidden. Today morals have changed, and so has demographic behaviour.

Interestingly, what has been called "sexual liberation"—more sexual activity outside of (and perhaps inside) marriage—has coincided with falling fertility rates. Indeed, in many countries, birth rates have plunged below the level needed to replace the population. Some European countries have already seen their populations decline; others will experience the same declines soon. What happened? Why are sexually active European women having so few babies?

In this excerpt Dirk van de Kaa explains the "second demographic transition" in terms of a shift in values. He shows that in the last thirty years more and more Europeans have become concerned with the "opportunity costs" of having children. People today are more likely to think that children crimp their lifestyle and strain their marriage. In short, parents (and potential parents) are no longer as willing to sacrifice their own enjoyment for the sake of children.

A second factor in the dropping birth rates, according to van de Kaa, is that today's Europeans feel freer to use contraceptives, have abortions, or remain childless. And they are exercising this freedom to choose. As a result, unwanted babies are far less likely to be born in Europe now than in the past.

According to current United Nations medium projections, Europe's population will increase a scant six percent between 1985 and 2025, from 492 to 524 million, while the world's population nearly doubles, from 4.5 to 8.2 billion, and nearly one in every five Europeans in 2025 will be pensioners aged 65 and over.

The new stage in Europe's demographic history might be called its "second demographic transition." Europe's first demographic transition began with a gradual decline in death rates dating from the early 19th century, followed by fertility decline beginning around 1880 in most countries, though earlier in France. By the 1930s, both birth and death rates were at low levels.

van de Kaa, Dirk (1987). "Europe's Second Demographic Transition," *Population Bulletin*, 42(1), March, 1–57. (Washington, D.C., Population Reference Bureau, Inc.) Reprinted by permission.

The start of the second transition can arbitrarily be set at 1965. In the interim had come World War II and the baby boom that followed it. The principal demographic feature of the second transition is the decline in fertility from somewhat above the "replacement" level of 2.1 births per woman, which ensures that births and deaths will stay in balance and population remain stationary over the long run, to a level well below replacement.

If fertility stabilizes below replacement, as seems likely in Europe, and barring immigration, population numbers will sooner or later decline, as had begun already by 1985 in four countries (Austria, Denmark, the Federal Republic of Germany, and Hungary). Changes in mortality and migration—the other two variables that shape changes in population numbers—have had relatively little impact in the second transition.

Early theories about the demographic transition, based on Europe's experience to the 1930s, usually ended with the stage of "zero" population growth. The stage of long-term population decline, now imminent in Europe, has since been called "beyond the demographic transition," but its special features in Europe seem to merit the label "second demographic transition." This *Bulletin* describes the broad features of this second demographic transition as it has evolved among Europe's some 30 heterogeneous countries.

SECOND DEMOGRAPHIC TRANSITION: THE BACKGROUND

Two keywords characterize the norms and attitudes behind the first and second demographic transitions and highlight the contrasts between them: *altruistic* and *individualistic.* The first transition to low fertility was dominated by concerns for family and offspring, but the second emphasizes the rights and self-fulfillment of individuals. Demographers Ron Lesthaeghe and Christopher Wilson argue convincingly that industrialization, urbanization, and secularization were the indirect determinants of the first transition.[1] The shift from family-based production to wage-paid labor that accompanied industrialization and urbanization reduced the economic utility of children. Moreover, a large number of children could mean the dissipation of family assets like land after the parents' death, so birth control became a sound strategy. Secularization reduced the influence of the churches and increased couples' willingness to practice family planning.

Demographically, the first transition reflected the disappearance of the Malthusian pattern of family formation. Couples no longer had to delay marriage until they acquired a separate means of existence by succeeding their parents. The age at marriage declined and so did the number of people who remained permanently single. Within marriage, the number of children was controlled; quality replaced quantity.

The indirect determinants of the second transition cannot be summed up so neatly.

In these societies, one's standard of living is largely determined by one's level and quality of education, degree of commitment to societal goals, and motivation to develop and use one's talents. This holds for women as well as men; both sexes tend to strive to earn a personal income. Getting married and/or having children may involve considerable opportunity costs.

For a couple, children involve not only direct expenditures, but also their utility has declined even further. They are no longer either expected or legally required to support their parents in old age or help with family finances. The emotional satisfactions of parenthood can be achieved most economically by having one or perhaps two children.

Beyond the simple calculation of economic utilities, social and cultural changes play a role in people's move away from marriage and parenthood in postindustrial societies. The forces behind these changes have been described in various ways.

I have argued that most European societies have shifted remarkably toward greater progressiveness in the postwar period and this helps explain many demographic changes. Philosophically, "progressiveness" characterizes a tendency to embrace the new, look critically at the present, and largely disregard the past.

A SEQUENCE OF EVENTS IN FAMILY FORMATION

An interesting perspective on recent population change in Europe is to see the changes that have occurred in factors bearing on family formation as a sequence through which all countries pass. The timing and speed of the sequence have differed substantially between Eastern and Western Europe and within these regions, but there is strong evidence of a logical ordering. Each step taken seems to have led to the next; each option chosen made a further choice possible. Looking back, the sequence of events that led to today's low fertility seems both logical and understandable. One wonders why it was not predicted! Reflecting the shift to progressiveness and individualism, the sequence involves shifts from marriage toward cohabitation, from children to the adult couple as the focus of a family, from contraception to prevent unwanted births to deliberate, self-fulfilling choices whether and when to conceive a child, and from uniform to widely diversified families and households. Let us sketch the sequence as it has progressed to completion in a "standard" European country.

To trace the story, one must begin with the great impact of World War II. Virtually all European countries were involved in the fighting, suffered from occupation and shortages, and experienced the uncertainties and sorrows that war brings. Many young men saw military service and became familiar with techniques to prevent conception and venereal disease. Retrospective surveys document a steady increase from cohort to cohort in the proportions of adults who have experienced premarital intercourse and a sharp postwar decline in the age at which such sexual relations begin. Geeraert, citing a long list of research in Western European countries since 1900, concludes that among young women in particular, both students and working women, premarital intercourse is increasingly common.[2]

Social attitudes regarding premarital or extramarital sexual relations did not change so rapidly. Most couples therefore sought official sanction through marriage. This was also the solution in the case of an out-of-wedlock pregnancy.

Besides official sanction to live together, most couples who married in the early 1950s also wanted and were economically ready to start a family. The average age at first marriage declined, the interval between marriage and the first birth remained short, and birth rates for lower-order births began to rise. The increase in fertility in the early childbearing ages more than made up for the decline in higher-order births, so that the total fertility rate increased—at least to the mid-1960s.

The decline in higher-order births reflected general acceptance of birth control as a means to limit family size. This was the tail end of the first demographic transition in which birth control was used not for spacing but to bring completed family size down from seven or eight children in the 1880s to two or three some 50–60 years later. But the contraceptives available before the mid-1960s were not very effective or suitable for inexperienced couples and many "unwanted" children were no doubt born.

The decline in age at first marriage loosened the link between marriage and the start of childbearing. Marriage was still desired to earn official approval of sexual relations (certainly by a couple's parents), but for many young couples it no longer marked a readiness to have children. Parents anxious to help their just-married children avoid the burdens of an immediate birth may well have introduced them to family planning. Family planning organization enrollments soared. Membership in the Dutch organization (Netherlands Association for Sexual Reform, NVSH) more than doubled from 97,000 in 1955 to a peak of 206,000 in 1965 (and now has almost evaporated). As contraception became more popular for avoiding births early in married life, the age at marriage could decline further. Young married couples could accumulate assets together before deciding to take on the care of children.

Just about that time, in the mid-1960s, the effective, as well as safe, pills and IUDs came on the market. They were readily adopted. First and second birth intervals lengthened, and there were somewhat fewer lower-order births. Doubtless due also to further reductions in family-size norms, fertility above age 30 plummeted and the birth of fourth, fifth, and later children became an exception. The proportion of unwanted births—conceived out of marriage or too late in marriage—declined.

By the early 1970s, changes in abortion law made it possible to terminate unintended premarital pregnancies safely, so the frequency of unwanted first births declined further. The gradual disappearance of "forced marriages" slowed the decline in age at first marriage and this age began to climb.

Abortion could, of course, also be used to avert unwanted births among married women—high-order births, risky and socially unacceptable births to older women, and, if so desired, births conceived extramaritally. Increased adoption of sterilization to control fertility after couples had all the children they wanted further cut the number of higher-order births in the early 1970s. Fertility fell below replacement level.

Once it was generally accepted that sexual relations in marriage were not solely or primarily aimed at procreation and contraceptives of high quality had become available, a further step was taken. Law changes had already increased the frequency of divorce and legal separation. Divorce and separation were also occurring at earlier ages and sooner after marriage. Since young people now married with the intention of delaying childbearing for several years, it is understandable that the need to seek a seal of approval for such an arrangement was questioned. Why not start living together and marry only when children were wanted or on the way? Stable unions were formed, differing from early marriage mainly in that they were "paperless." The first marriage rate began to decline and the age at first marriage went up.

The proportions ever-marrying declined markedly; age at first marriage rose further. Remarriages became much less common. A rise in out-of-wedlock fertility became noticeable, particularly among somewhat older women. Some of these women deliberately chose to bear a child without having a stable relationship with a male partner. The proportions of out-of-wedlock births legitimated by marriage or the male partner declined. In addition, voluntary childlessness was no longer solely an option for men and women who elected not to marry. Being married or living in a stable union no longer differentiated people strongly with regard either to having children or desired family size. Fertility seemed to stabilize well below replacement level.

This "standard" sequence of changes in family formation is obviously impossible to trace in detail for all 30 of Europe's heterogeneous countries and the sequence itself is likely to be different as it evolves among them. However, the countries can be grouped roughly according to their place in the sequence as it has evolved so far and fairly simple period data available for a reasonable number of the countries demonstrate the basic features of the second transition to low fertility. These features involve four related shifts:

1. Shift from the *golden age of marriage* to the *dawn of cohabitation*;
2. Shift from the era of the *king-child with parents* to that of the *king-pair with a child*;
3. Shift from *preventive contraception* to *self-fulfilling conception*;
4. Shift from *uniform* to *pluralistic* families and households.

WHERE COUNTRIES ARE IN THE SEQUENCE

Only two European countries appear to have experienced the full sequence of changes in family formation that have led to very low fertility—Denmark and Sweden. Even here there have been deviations from the "standard" sequence described above. However, in these two countries the proportion of out-of-wedlock births has risen from about 10 percent in 1956–60 to well over 40 percent currently. And the tremendously changed social significance of the "married" status probably best demonstrates the transition toward greater individualism.

The following four groups indicate where European countries now are in the standard sequence.

First Group. In addition to Denmark and Sweden, this group includes the Northern and Western European countries which appear to be following close in their tracks. The birth rates of these countries as of the mid-1980s generally fall between 10 and 12 per 1,000 population and the rate of natural increase (births minus deaths) is no more than 0.4 percentage points above zero or actually negative. Finland, Norway, the United Kingdom, Austria, Belgium, France, the Federal Republic of Germany, the Netherlands, Switzerland, and

Italy (in Southern Europe) all qualify for this group. Here the second demographic transition is well advanced.

Second Group. This group includes Greece, Malta, Portugal, Spain, and Yugoslavia in Southern Europe. The fertility decline has been less marked in these countries; they follow the first group at a distance. Current birth rates range from 12 to 16 per 1,000 population and the rate of natural increase usually exceeds 0.4 percent. The second transition is late, but there is little doubt that it has begun and will be completed.

Third Group. The six Eastern European countries make up this group: Bulgaria, Czechoslovakia, the German Democratic Republic, Hungary, Poland, and Romania. Here the postwar trend toward greater sexual freedom appears to be less pronounced. In reaction to forcible attempts to change the structure and norms of society after the political change, many people have clung tenaciously to traditional mores in their personal lives. On the other hand, legal abortion became available in these countries earlier than in most other European countries, while government intervention to raise birth rates has had some impact on fertility trends. Current birth rates are close to 14 per 1,000 population, except for Hungary (12.2 in 1985) and Poland (18.2).

Fourth Group. This group covers the remaining countries which, for a variety of cultural and historical reasons, are all late in completing the *first* demographic transition. It includes Iceland and Ireland in Northern Europe and Albania and Turkey in Southern Europe. Even parts of the USSR belong to this group. Whether or when they will begin the second demographic transition is not easy to predict. Their current birth rates tend to be high by European standards and rates of natural increase range from about 0.9 percent in Iceland and Ireland to 2.1 percent in Turkey.

MAKING THE GIFT OF A BABY TO THE PENSION FUNDS?

In 1986 the influential Germany weekly Der Spiegel ran a series of articles under the heading *Den Alterskassen ein Baby schenken?,* which translates roughly as above. It sums up Europe's demographic dilemma well. Collective and individual interests do not seem to coincide. The transition to individualism appears to have led to an extended period of below-replacement-level fertility, population decline, and an age structure that will in the long run make full funding of old-age pensions virtually impossible. Yet it is difficult to imagine people having babies to please the pension funds, and economic incentives, even at the level offered in France and some Eastern European countries, appear incapable of overcoming individualistic desires and raising fertility to replacement level. Relying on immigration to adjust age structures is practically out of the question. All countries of immigration have taken effective measures to end the influx and increasingly aim at rapid integration of the current minorities.

What then is the answer to the predicament? Most countries will probably follow the old maxim: If in doubt, do nothing; wait and see.

Another approach is to try out new, more imaginative measures to raise fertility and have them ready when needed. Thinking in this direction is developing rapidly. So far no serious proposal seems to be compatible with the shift to individualistic values. But a recent proposition by demographer Paul Demeny is certainly imaginative.[3] He proposes to relink fertility behavior and economic security in old age. The pronatalist institution he sees would "earmark a socially agreed-upon fraction of the compulsory contribution from earnings that flow into the common pool from which pay-as-you-go national social security schemes are now financed and transfer that fraction to individual contributors' live parents as an additional entitlement."

It is easy to make a long list of reasons why this proposal has no chance in the world of being implemented. But then, in demographic matters the unexpected sometimes happens.

ENDNOTES

[1]   Lesthaeghe, R. and C. Wilson. *Modes of Production, Secularisation, and the Pace of the Fertility Decline in Western Europe, 1870–1930,* working paper, Brussels, 1978.

[2]   Geeraert, A. *Sexualiteit bij jongeren* (Sexuality among Young People) (Brussels: De Sikkel, 1977), p. 27.

[3]   Demeny, P. Population Note No. 57 (New York: The Population Council, December 1, 1986).

A R T I C L E   1 3 . 2

Roderic Beaujot

HOW CANADIANS MAKE MARRIAGE AND CHILDBEARING DECISIONS

INTRODUCTION

In and around London, Ontario, where this research was carried out, most people lead lives that are very different from those of their parents and grandparents. Most of them marry later, start bearing children later, produce fewer children, and are more likely than their ancestors to divorce. As we saw in excerpt 13.1, this package of behaviours is found in

Beaujot, Roderic (1992). "Rationales Used in Marriage and Childbearing Decisions," *The Peopling of the Americas,* Proceedings of the International Union for the Scientific Study of Population Conference, Veracruz, Vol. II, pp. 173–154.

most highly developed societies today, and is responsible for the low population growth in the developed world.

Roderic Beaujot set out to discover what ideas about marriage and parenthood support modern demographic behaviours: to find the cultural bases of modern marriage and fertility. Surprisingly, what he discovered is startlingly familiar, even banal. In the voices of his respondents we can hear our own friends, workmates, and parents chanting "Marriage is good if you're ready for it," "Marriage is nothing without children," "A good family life is the key to happiness," and so on.

But how do these familiar, traditional views correspond to the non-traditional behaviours we see around us? The fact is, they don't. Our real lives are complicated and full of contradictions; many of us want everything—families, careers, children, leisure, and so on—and that's simply impossible. In the end, our culture does not provide a strict set of decision-rules about marriage and parenting. Rather it ends up justifying several alternatives: whether marrying or not marrying, having many or few children, and so on.

Where are the clues to our real motives?

While much is known about the proximate factors and differentials in Canadian childbearing behaviour, existing analyses based on census and survey data can provide only speculative suggestions regarding some of the underlying economic and socio-cultural dynamics. It is proposed here that some of these fundamental questions can be studied by asking actors themselves to explain the rationales of behaviour: Why do people get married, what are the advantages of being married and of not being married, when is it best to marry, why do people have children, what are the advantages and disadvantages of having or not having children, what is the ideal number of children to have, why not more, why not less. The purpose is not to predict individual behaviour, that would be redundant, but rather to attempt to uncover the "cultural content of the decision making calculus" (Handwerker, 1986). To use Caldwell's language, cultures set limits to the kinds of cost-benefit analyses that individuals can make. In particular, we wished to identify what people invoke as legitimate considerations in making these decisions, and thus the cultural parameters. We need not assume that people make fully conscious rational decisions after having explored the advantages and disadvantages of the various alternatives. Instead, we would assume that the culture influences behaviour by presenting a "logic of behaviour," or ready-made rationales in terms of which actors can justify their behaviour. The "content" that is brought forward in these rationalizations would therefore tell us important things about the legitimate bases for behaviour, in a given cultural context.

MARRIAGE

Asked "why do people get married" and the "advantages of being married," the most common response refers to companionship, love, social support, or the emotional aspect of life. Marriage was seen as providing stability, having someone to come home to, share happiness and problems with, someone to lean on in good times and bad times, someone who is there for you, providing the experience of being needed, or working together on common goals. It is often seen as natural to get married, it is largely taken for granted, a base for a family, to bring children into the world. Marriage is the norm: people are made to be together, to have a partner in life. There are also family related reasons: marriage is a good foundation for a family, it is better for children to be raised in a family. A few mention practical aspects like tax breaks, security, sharing finances or economic benefits. Others mention a healthy sexual relationship without fear of AIDS.

The advantages of being single relate largely to the freedom to do what you want, when you want, as you want. Many seem to ignore the constraints that single people still have, for instance those related to responsibilities at work. They speak of single people being able to pick up and go as they please. Being single provides independence, no need to compromise with anyone. Being single allows one to make career and other decisions without having to take into account anyone else. A few, especially younger respondents, say that by being single you can keep your money, car, etc. for yourself, not having to share it with anyone. Others mentioned being able to date a number of partners. Some 4.9 percent of respondents said there were no real advantages of being single, some older respondents cannot see how anyone would possibly want to go through life single, they think that such people simply did not find the right partner.

Asked to compare the advantages of being married or single, the overwhelming majority (85.1 percent) say that marriage provides more advantages. Some say they are happy to be single now but prefer marriage for the life course. The few (5.1 percent) who say being single is preferable includes persons who have separated from a marriage and had no intention of being married any more, or women who refer to the fact that the work load is greater in marriage, being single means not having someone to dominate your life, to have to answer to him.

Asked what they would guess a man or woman was like if all they knew about them was that they did not want to get married, many found the question difficult to answer without further circumstances. They thought people would know best what is best for themselves, it is their choice. Some thought they may have strong goals, know what they want, independent, while others spoke of being self-centred, not willing to take responsibility, fancy free or party goer. They may have made a conscious decision and are not interested in having children, or women may be facing the difficulty of combining career pursuits and a family.

How is a man's life changed by being married? He becomes more responsible, marriage provides a stabilizing function, he has more responsibilities. Even if negatives were mentioned, such as limitations on what he can do, having to compromise in making decisions, the overall change was typically thought of as being positive for the man, he becomes more devoted to the family and the welfare of his family, it is good to have to take another person into account in making decisions. A man settles down, he is more family and home oriented, goes out with the boys less. Most see this as a positive thing: getting to understand himself, a growing experience which may be more important for men who are less mature. There are also more responsibilities, especially financial.

The responses on how a woman's life is changed were similar. Marriage gives stability, women become more responsible, devoted to the family, more secure.

Some spoke of the extra domestic work load especially if she has children. Some women said that a man's life is not much changed but for women there is more work, they do not think there is such a thing as an egalitarian marriage, women need to do the majority of the housework, to put themselves second, to make more compromises. These still see marriage positively. Some men thought women's career prospects are more likely to be hindered, they do more household chores, even if there is ideally a 50-50 sharing of chores. Interestingly, 72.3 percent of the men said these changes were positive compared to 65.3 percent of women.

The ideal age for a man to get married is considered to be in the mid to late 20's, after having achieved a certain maturity and stability in life, having had the freedom to do things as a single person first, and achieved a certain "state of mind" appropriate for marriage. They should have completed their education and have a sense of direction in life. Many said that a man should have lived on his own first, be independent, learn to take care of himself, had his opportunity to ride motorcycles or whatever he needed to do as a single person, find himself, had time "between families." The ages stated were largely minimum ages, with marriage at older ages being considered acceptable. Some said that if they wait too long they may become too established, unwilling to make sacrifices, hard to make compromises together.

For women, the responses were similar, possibly a year or two younger. They also need a certain level of maturity, be able to handle the responsibilities of marriage, have the education necessary to get a job. Many said that women mature faster and are ready for marriage sooner, they can handle the responsibilities sooner, men take longer to settle down. At the same time, most do not support a large age gap at marriage.

CHILDBEARING

Asked "why do you think people have children" and the advantages of having children, most refer to love, companionship, the joy of watching them grow and achieve things in life. Many spoke of the joy of teaching children in a fundamental way, watching them develop into responsible human beings. Some spoke of a deeply personal experience, or referred to intangible things, the little smiles when they are babies, the enduring love of children, things that are hard to put into words, "the true joys in life" so that the hard parts do not mean that much. Some spoke simply of enjoying children, it is a learning experience, get to know yourself, the joy of doing things as a family and the comfort of having people around when you are older, of being part of an extended family. Some spoke of carrying on the family name or of regeneration in the broad sense: reproducing yourself, seeing yourself in the children, someone to pass things to. Others mentioned creating a bond within the family, healthy for a marriage, the need for families to have children.

A number of people found it difficult to say why people have children, it was not consciously figured out: people want children, it is the natural thing to do, tradition, they had not thought much about it. Many, especially older respondents, did not know why people have children. Having had children, they enjoyed raising them, older people mentioned friendships with children, which were not the reasons for having children initially, these reasons came later.

The disadvantages of having children, or what is problematic about having children, relate especially to financial costs and emotional costs. Children involve personal costs, you have to give a lot of yourself, they represent constraints on your time and on the decisions you can make. Some spoke of the worry when they are sick or in trouble, or worrying about how they will turn out (given the condition the world is in). The worry focuses especially on the teenage years. Others spoke of the work load. In effect, some see lots of disadvantages: children are so expensive, they are now at home for a longer time through school and college, they are so much work, you have to make so many sacrifices for them from being up in the night to steering them through all the stress and worry of the teenage years. But they note that all this disappears once the children are adults. Many said they would not consider these things to be disadvantages, you have to expect this. Sometimes, children can be a real disappointment, if they do not turn out to meet your expectations.

Asked if there were more benefits or disadvantages to having children, the vast majority (86.2 percent) said there were more advantages. Those who said there were more disadvantages (4.8 percent) simply did not care too much for children. Or these were single mothers who were referring to the disadvantages at the stage of life when children are dependent. Some 15.2 percent specifically said there were no real disadvantages.

Regarding the best age for women to start having children, most thought it was around the mid to late 20's. They should first get their lives in order, but not wait until it is too late to have the children they want. Those who said after 30 referred to having careers in order, then taking time out for children and back to the career. Persons who suggested younger ages, say early 20's, referred to being more flexible at this age, and that it was more difficult later. Some suggested a gap of some two years after marriage. Women should be mature enough to handle the responsibility, be physically ready, and have some financial security. That is, they should first develop themselves, be married a few years, be secure in their job or career. Some referred to the difficulty of doing so many things by a given age: education, be on your own, career, marriage, children. In effect, the ideal age varied considerably, between 20 and 35.

Asked why they think there is an increase in the number of women having their first child after age 30, most referred to career questions, higher education and financial stability. Some saw this very positively, for instance in terms of careers for women, orienting family and marriage questions in terms of women's interests. Slightly less than half of respondents were basically positive about the change. Others saw negative aspects, it could be too late, it may be hazardous to wait too long, health questions, not fair to children to have older parents, or being physically too tired by that time. Some referred to making choices, not following the set patterns, choosing marriage, the time to marry and to have children. Older respondents were more likely to see the negative side, possibly considering it more appropriate for women to stay home and raise a family. Younger women sometimes spoke of it being safe to have children later, when one is more financially secure and can give the children the things they need.

FAMILY SIZE

The majority (73.7 percent) of respondents say that the ideal number of children is two or three. Asked why not more, most refer to costs, hard to afford more, hard to manage, time and emotional costs, the need to give a certain amount of time to each child each day. The world is built for smaller families: number of bedrooms in houses, seats in cars, etc. There are also population and environmental problems with larger families. Asked why not less, most say that a child should have at least one sibling or that one child does not make for a real family.

Asked what they think of couples who deliberately choose not to have children, most would say that this acceptable if that is what the couple wants: fine, their decision, their choice. Some, especially older people, would wonder why people bothered to get married if they did not want to have children. Some refer to the couple being selfish, but if they do not want the responsibility then they should not have children. Having no children can be justified for health or career reasons. A few say that if people marry they should have children.

What do you think of couples who only have one child? Most responses were somewhat negative: having one child is not good for the child, they need sibling interaction to really develop as individuals. One child is seen to be lonely, selfish and spoilt, gets too much attention, does not have to share, lacks the companionship of other children. It was acceptable if it was due to medical reasons or if the couple could not afford to have more (mentally or financially). Some said it was fine to have one child, it was their choice, better to take care of one properly, yet it is not that great. Some realize they were not suited to take care of children, then it is best to stop at one.

Having large families, say five or more children, was generally not seen as realistic. Quite a few value a large family, but there are constraints making it difficult if not impossible. Some would say that they prefer two or three but people can have as many as they want if they like children, are happy with more and have the resources. Large families can mean more fun at Christmas, birthdays and family gatherings, it is a joy, and as you get older the joy of the large extended family grows. While a few say it is great if the couple can manage, most say that it is very hard in this day and age, or that it is not a possibility in their own life. Some say they are crazy to have a large family, they cannot understand someone doing this, there is simply no need, you have to struggle more, why do it? Some say they know some large families, especially from olden days and things were great, but most say that it is not practical today.

In the hypothetical situation that a husband wants more children than his wife, most say that these things should be discussed, negotiated, reach a compromise, joint decision, make these decisions before they marry, have equal say. Pressed further, most would say that the wife should have the last word or that they should not have an extra child unless both want it, settle for the lower number. If there is disagreement they should not have the child because one of them will resent the child and it will cause tension in the family. Some said that if he really wants the extra child he should do more around the house, or coach a hockey team to get it out of his system. The wife should have more say since the pain of childbirth and much of the responsibility falls on her, it is the woman's decision, her body.

If it is the wife who wants more than the husband, the responses are largely the same, ultimately not to have a child that only one wants, both should want it. They should discuss the reasons why he does not want more children, how strong are his opinions. Some say that the wife should have the final word since it affects her more.

DISCUSSION

Contrary to the view that marriage and children may be "out of favour," this survey finds respondents largely speaking rather eloquently of the importance of these questions to their lives. Asked at the end what contributed most to their sense of happiness in life, 76 percent specifically referred to marriage or family questions. While those who refused to take part in the survey may well have included a higher proportion for whom marriage and children are viewed less favourably, the results correspond to those obtained in other surveys. In a sample of Canadian college students in 1978, Hobart (1984) finds average ideal and expected family sizes of 2.6 to 2.7 children. In a sample of American high school seniors in 1986, Crimmins et al. (1990) find 78 percent indicating that they are likely to get married and 82 percent likely to have children, only 13 percent said they questioned marriage as a way of life. Among the various goals in life, "a good marriage and family life" ranked at the top of the list, considerably higher than "having lots of money." Similarly, Thornton (1989) finds little evidence for growth in preferences for remaining single or for not having children.

Following Thornton further, while there is little active embracement of such behaviour, there is considerable expression of tolerance toward those who might decide not to marry or not to have children. It would appear that the culture is not imposing rigid requirements. If anything, it would seem that persons who have large families and those who have one child are seen as deviating from expected behaviour. Although it is not supported by research results (Blake, 1981), people expect that only children will be rather disadvantaged.

While marriage and children are placed high in people's priorities, the main difficulty may be in finding room for everything that people want to achieve in life. It is seen as important for both men and women to pursue education, to have a period of independence before marriage, to get established and to be married at least a short while before having children. At the same time, preference is generally expressed to begin childbearing before age 30. That is a lot to fit into a decade of life, and it assumes that all will happen as planned. If the marriage is further delayed looking for the ideal partner, and if children are delayed until one is better established, the real life options may become more limited. While 38 percent expressed preference for three or more children, these real life situations may make it difficult even to have two children. In addition, there is the ambivalence about the appropriateness of day care, and the often expressed preference to have one parent at home or working only part-time while the children are young. This confronts the interest in maintaining one's employment prospects and in preventing an entrenchment of gender based divisions of labour. All these circumstances would appear to make it difficult for couples to achieve their goals, especially if these goals include more than two children.

Goals may be further thwarted if unanticipated events like unemployment or marriage breakdown intervene.

It may be suggested that these responses, including the high degree of consensus expressed, indicate ways in which the culture sets limits to the options available to individuals at a given point in time. Particularly telling may be the contradictions inherent in the expectations around marriage, gender roles, childbearing and childrearing. Included here are the contradictions between two models of the family to which people ascribe. People seem to be subscribing to both the breadwinner and the dual-earner family, be it to a varying extent.

REFERENCES

Ariès, Philippe, 1980, Two Successive Motivations for the Declining Birth Rate in the West. *Population and Development Review of* 6(4): 645–650.

Balakrishnan, T.R. and Jiajian Chen, 1990, Religiosity, Nuptiality and Reproduction in Canada. *Canadian Review of Sociology and Anthropology* 27(3): 316–340.

Beaujot, Roderic, 1988, Attitudes among Tunisians toward Family Formation. *International Family Planning Perspectives* 14(2): 54–61.

Bernstam, Mikhail S., 1986, Competitive Human Markets, Interfamily Transfers, and Below-replacement Fertility. *Population and Development Review* 12(suppl.): 111–137.

Blake, Judith, 1981, The Only Child in America: Prejudice vs Performance. *Population and Development Review* 7(1): 43–54.

Burch, Thomas K., 1987, Babel Revisited: The Role of Ideas in Explanations of Human Behaviour. London: Population Studies Centre Discussion Paper No. 1.

Caldwell, John C., 1985, Strengths and Limitations of the Survey Approach for Measuring and Understanding Fertility Change: Alternate Possibilities. Pp. 45–63 in J. Cleland and J. Hobcraft, *Reproductive Changes in Developing Countries,* Oxford: Oxford University Press.

Caldwell, John and Allan G. Hill, 1985, Recent Developments in Micro-approaches to Demographic Research. *International Population Conference, Florence,* Liège: International Union for the Scientific Study of Population, Vol. 4: 235–248.

Chesnais, Jean-Claude, 1989, L'inversion de la pyramide des âges en Europe: perspectives et problèmes. *International Population Conference, New Delhi,* Liège: International Union for the Scientific Study of Population, Vol 3: 53–68.

Cicourel, Aaron V., 1974, *Theory and Method in a Study of Argentine Fertility.* New York: Wiley.

Cleland, John, 1985, Marital Fertility Decline in Developing Countries: Theories and the Evidence. Pp. 223–252 in J. Cleland and J. Hobcraft, *Reproductive Changes in Developing Countries,* Oxford: Oxford University Press.

Crimmins, Eileen M., Richard A. Easterlin and Yasuhiko Saito, 1990, Preference Changes among American Youth: Family, Work and Gender Aspirations, 1976–1986. Paper presented at the meetings of the Population Association of America, Toronto, May 1990.

David, Paul A., 1986, Comment. *Population and Development Review* 12(suppl.): 77–86.

Davis, Kingsley, 1986, Low Fertility in Evolutionary Perspective. *Population and Development Review* 12(suppl.): 48–67.

Easterlin, Richard, 1978, What Will 1984 Be Like? Socioeconomic Implications of Recent Twists in Age Structure. *Demography* 15(4): 397–432.

Fort, Alfredo L., 1989, The use of Focus Group Interviews in the Investigation of Fertility in Peru. Paper presented at the meetings of the International Union for the Scientific Study of Population, New Delhi, October 1989.

Handwerker, W. Penn, 1986, *Culture and Reproduction*. Boulder: Westview Press.

Henripin, Jacques, 1974, *Immigration and Language Imbalance*. Ottawa: Manpower and Immigration.

Henripin, Jacques et al., 1981, *Les enfants qu'on n'a plus au Québec*. Montreal: Presses de l'Université de Montréal.

Hobart, Charles W., 1984, Interest in Parenthood among Young Anglophone and Francophone Canadians. *Canadian Studies in Population* 11(2): 111–133.

Kamuzora, C.L., 1989, In-depth Interview Approaches to Demographic Data Collection. *International Population Conference, New Delhi*, Liège: International Union for the Scientific Study of Population, Vol. 2: 17–32.

Kettle, John, 1980, *The Big Generation*. Toronto: McClelland and Stewart.

Keyfitz, Nathan, 1986, The Family That Does Not Reproduce Itself. *Population and Development Review* 12(suppl.): 139–154.

Lesthaeghe, Ron, 1983, A Century of Demographic and Cultural Change in Western Europe. *Population and Development Review* 9(3): 411–435.

Lesthaeghe, Ron and Johan Surkyn, 1988, Cultural Dynamics and Economic Theories of Fertility Change. *Population and Development Review* 14(1): 1–45.

McQuillan, Kevin, 1989, Discussion. Pp. 377–381 in J. Légaré, T.R. Balakrishnan and R. Beaujot, *The Family in Crisis: A Population Crisis?*, Ottawa: Royal Society of Canada.

Preston, Samuel H., 1984, Children and the Elderly: Divergent Paths for America's Dependents. *Demography* 21: 435–458.

Preston, Samuel H., 1986, Changing Values and Falling Birth Rates. *Population and Development Review* 12(suppl.): 176–195.

Rainwater, Lee, 1960, *And the Poor Get Children*. Chicago: Quadrangus Books.

Roussel, Louis, 1989, Les changements démographiques des vingt dernières années: quelques hypothèses sociologiques. Pp. 399–416 in J. Légaré, T.R. Balakrishnan and R. Beaujot, *The Family in Crisis: A Population Crisis?*, Ottawa: Royal Society of Canada.

Ryder, Norman B., 1983, Fertility and Family Structure. *Population Bulletin of the United Nations* 15: 15–34.

Stone, Lawrence, 1982, *The Family, Sex and Marriage in England 1500–1800*. London: Peregrine Books.

Thornton, Arland, 1989, Changing Attitudes toward Family Issues in the United States. *Journal of Marriage and the Family* 51(4): 873–893.

Ursel, Jane, 1986, The State and the Maintenance of Patriarchy: A Case Study of Family, Labour and Welfare Legislation in Canada. Pp. 150–191 in J. Dickinson and B. Russell, *Family, Economy and State*. Toronto: Garamond.

van de Walle, Etienne and John Knodel, 1980, Europe's Fertility Transition: New Evidence and Lessons for Today's Developing World. *Population Bulletin* 34(6).

Watkins, Susan Cotts, 1990, From Local to National Communities: The Transformation of Demographic Regimes in Western Europe, 1870–1960. *Population and Development Review* 16(2): 241–272.

A. Goldstein and S. Goldstein

THE CHALLENGE OF AN AGING POPULATION IN CHINA

INTRODUCTION

In the West, fertility began to fall and longevity to rise in the early 1800s; the transition lasted more than a century. Mainly as a result of the fall in fertility the West's population has gradually "aged." In other words, the proportion of older people in the population has increased over time.

During the twentieth century life expectancy in Canada has increased by about 25 or 30 years. In 1900 only 5 percent of the population was over 65; today it is over 10 percent and by 2020 it will be closer to 20 percent. As well, the older population itself is aging as more and more Canadians live well into their 80s and 90s.

Compared to Canada, China is demographically quite young, with a much smaller fraction of the population being over 65. But China's huge population means that the absolute number of old people is very large.

Arranging for the care of so many old people is a challenge, particularly because China does not have a system of old-age security like Canada's. Such a provision was unnecessary in the past when life was short, people lived in extended family households, and there was a strong tradition of filial piety. However, the success of the one-child policy instituted in 1979 means that most children born now are only children. Fewer people will be available to care for the aged in the next century. This will spell the beginning of the end for an ancient, distinctive Chinese cultural pattern of filial piety—or children's obligation to honour and care for their parents.

China's current population policy envisages an eventual stable population of about 700 million. Before then, if the one-child family policy is fully successful, the population is expected to reach a peak of 1.2 billion by 2010. It is projected to fall below 1.2 billion only by 2040. Until then, the large cohorts already born will move through the age hierarchy to swell the absolute number of aged persons. Because of concurrent reductions in the number of births, the aged proportion of the total will also rise.

THE TRADITIONAL AND LEGAL POSITIONS OF THE AGED

The aging of China's population must be considered within the context of the traditional position of the elderly in Chinese society, a position that in many respects

Goldstein, A. and S. Goldstein (1986). "The Challenge of an Aging Population: The Case of the People's Republic of China," *Research on Aging*, 8(2), June, 179–199. Reprinted by permission.

remains today. In the traditional Chinese family the aged held particularly high status (Yang, 1965). Such a position is understandable in a primarily illiterate society where experience rather than formal education is the main source of knowledge.

The communist ideology promulgated since 1949 has had considerable influence on these traditional attitudes. Because the young formed a dynamic element in the establishment of the new regime and in spreading its doctrines and policies, young people assumed roles of political importance. Furthermore, a stress on the capacity of all Chinese to be productive implies the young are to be as respected as the old. This attitude was emphasized by the restructuring of the work unit in rural areas under the commune system, which deemphasized the family as the basic unit of production and thereby also weakened the position of its older members. In urban areas, where education and modern technology became widespread, the young also held an advantage. Nonetheless, although they no longer exercise authoritarian power within the family, the elderly continue to command a high degree of respect (Tien, 1977), and the traditional patterns of interdependence between generations have been largely maintained (Davis-Friedmann, 1983).

Legally, the position of the aged is defined by the Constitution of 1982 (Chinese Documents, 1983:27): "Children who have come of age have the duty to support and assist their parents." The Marriage Law of 1980 goes further to stipulate, "When children fail to perform the duty of supporting their parents, parents who have lost the ability to work or have difficulties in providing for themselves have the right to demand that their children pay for their support" (Beijing Review, 1981a). The Marriage Law even carries the burden of support to the next generation; grandchildren are also enjoined to support grandparents if the parents have died. Failure to meet these obligations is punishable under China's Criminal Code (Beijing Review, 1981b:23).

China is clearly attempting to reinforce and take advantage of the traditional obligations of children toward their parents. In the absence of any national social security system, such support is undoubtedly seen as especially essential in rural areas, where 80 percent of China's population lives. The provisions therefore shift the primary burden of support onto the family rather than onto the government, the commune, or the work unit.

POLICIES INDIRECTLY AFFECTING THE AGED

The One-Child Family Policy

China's one-child family policy not only subverts traditional values favoring large families, but jeopardizes the system of social security that depends on children's support of elderly parents. The problem is exacerbated by the still widespread custom of patrilocal residence after marriage. A couple, especially in rural areas, whose one child is a daughter can likely look forward to an old age without grandchildren or a child close by.

The one-child policy is also eroding one of the traditional roles of the elderly, that of child care. Even if grandparents live in the same place with their offspring, they will have few grandchildren to care for.

Moreover, although children are supposed to care for their parents, it is difficult to assess either how adequate such care is or how much of a strain it places on
the younger persons. If one couple must support four elderly people the costs may
be excessive (Du, 1984).

Job Assignment Policies

Upon graduation from secondary schools or universities, students are assigned jobs
wherever the government believes they are needed. Although a majority may be
placed close to their family homes, many are not. The situation may be particularly
acute if rural-born youth are given urban job assignments as China's strict policies
to control urban growth generally preclude other family members from joining the
urban resident. Therefore, even if an aging couple has children, these children may
be in distant places and unable to provide the physical or psychological support
older persons need.

The New Economic Responsibility System

In rural areas, the individual responsibility system has placed a premium on intensive labor in the fields, so as to produce surplus crops that individual families can
sell. Such hard work is likely to bypass the aged who no longer have the stamina to
spend long hours in the field. In addition, the proliferation of small-scale light
industry, which is also part of the new economic development, is geared to the
absorption of the younger segments of the rural population.

A third aspect of the responsibility system does, however, offer opportunities
for the elderly. The system encourages the cultivation of private plots and private
raising of livestock. Produce from such enterprise can be sold in the free markets.
Such enterprise has traditionally occupied elderly peasants and has helped to contribute to household income (Davis-Friedmann, 1983:16–22).

PROGRAMS FOR THE ELDERLY

Retirement Policies

China's retirement policies, although designed to apply to the rural as well as
urban population, are adhered to more in urban places. As a result, relatively more
individuals fall into the "aged" category in cities and towns than in the countryside.
Male factory workers and cadres retire at age 60; female workers and cadres at age
55, unless they are engaged in heavy work, in which case they retire at 50.
Intellectuals and cadres may work up to age 65.

Among nonagricultural workers, a child may take over the job of a parent upon
the parent's retirement. With about 4 million urban young people entering the labor
force ages annually, a labor surplus exists. Most young people can expect to wait a
year after graduating before receiving an assigned job. They can avoid such a delay if
a parent retires and the child thereby "inherits" the job. Considerable pressure may,

as a result, be exerted by the young on parents in their early 50s to retire earlier than necessary under law. The pressure is especially great for mothers to do so.

The Childless Elderly

The childless elderly have been promised "Five Guarantees": food, clothing, medical care, housing, and burial expenses (*Beijing Review*, 1984). Rural brigades that are developing retirement policies may provide extra services to the childless. Such policies are designed not only in recognition of the particular needs of the childless aged, but to prove that having only one child need not lead to misery in old age. The press now often reports how young people organize themselves to help the childless elderly—doing household chores, shopping, running errands, or just visiting (e.g., *Beijing Review*, 1982b; Jian, 1983). In addition, some administrative units (such as municipalities or provinces) now provide old age homes for those without children or close relatives.

Pension Systems

Formal retirement programs or facilities specifically for the rural aged are rare, but a few brigades have rudimentary pension systems.

Moreover, production-team-sponsored retirement plans are likely to undergo change because of the institution of the responsibility system. Under this new system, individual families negotiate directly with the brigade for the amount of cultivation to be undertaken and are responsible directly to the brigade for delivery of their crop quotas. The production team has thereby had its functions and sources of income curtailed, and programs for social welfare are becoming the responsibility of the brigade or commune. (See *Beijing Review*, 1982b.)

For urban residents, a more widespread pension system is in place. According to the Constitution, "The state prescribes by law the system of retirement for workers and staff in enterprises and undertakings and for functionaries of organs of state. The livelihood of retired personnel is ensured by the state and society" (Chinese Documents, 1983:26). This provision translates, in part, into pension systems developed and administered by individual factories or work units.

Other Programs for the Aged

The urban aged who are not eligible for pensions fall primarily into two groups: (1) those who left the labor force before a pension system was instituted by their work units or after having worked for less than 10 years in a unit with a pension system; and (2) those—mainly women—who never were members of the labor force. As indicated above in principle, and as mandated by the Constitution, these aged are to be cared for by their children. Only the childless aged become the state's responsibility. Figures released by the State Labor Bureau (Beijing Review, 1981b) suggest only about 45 percent of urbanites above retirement age are covered by pension systems.

The state also recognizes the need to supplement income for persons not eligible for pensions and allows such individuals to engage in small-scale private enterprise. This most often involves setting up a stand for the sale of clothing or small dry goods.

Licenses for such stalls are typically issued by the city's Industrial and Commercial Bureau for a one-time fee of Y5. Only persons without employment in the formal sector, or support from that sector in the form of pensions, can apply.

With the advent of springtime in China, still another segment of the elderly population enters the informal sector, as ice cream (popsicle) vendors appear on almost every street corner. Most commonly older women, the vendors are licensed by the city and buy their products from state shops.

Such economic avenues for older people with no direct, official support have met several important needs. Not only do they provide some income for the elderly, but the variety of merchandise made available thereby to the masses also fills a need for more color and variety in consumer goods.

Several other ways have been found to utilize the elderly population. Older men may direct traffic in congested neighborhoods. Men and women help enforce regulations in free markets. Older persons sit on the Neighborhood Committees, help to ensure neighborhood sanitation, help enforce family planning regulations, and generally see that the neighborhood functions properly. Others may act as mediators in disputes or as after-school counselors (Wu, 1984).

Because highly skilled workers are at a premium in China, the elderly skilled are used to teach others. Thus, a factory may ask a technician to stay on after retirement to help train younger workers. Other retired workers may go "on loan" to factories in other cities or towns, and such a sojourn may last 2–3 years.

Despite all these efforts, however, large numbers of older people are left with essentially nothing to do. As one Chinese social researcher interested in the problems of his nation's aged commented, "Many are just waiting to die."

CHALLENGES FOR THE FUTURE

In many respects, the elderly in China are better off today than in the past. Family solidarity continues to provide a support system for the aged, whereas at the same time government policies are beginning to provide economic security independent of the family's role.

In rural areas, the welfare of the aged is closely tied to the economic well-being of the communes but, increasingly, also to the ability of individual households to realize higher incomes under the responsibility system. As the rural population ages dramatically over the next 50 years, the changing balance between labor force participants in their prime productive ages and the aged may have a serious negative impact on the well-being of the aged. A key determinant of continued agricultural productivity will be the extent to which China will by then have been able to modernize agriculture.

In urban areas, wherever larger proportions of the retired population are covered by pension systems, the oldest segment of the aged are the most disadvantaged as they are in large part not covered by retirement benefits. This disparity should disappear as the aged segment of the urban population comes to be constituted almost entirely by persons who have worked most of their lives in state enterprises.

The welfare of the aged is thus inextricably related to the degree to which China is able to modernize and to continue to increase its output value of agricultural and industrial products. Such development is, in turn, predicated on achieving success in the nation's overall population control programs, including family planning and rural-to-urban migration.

Traditional values about family solidarity are likely to be put under considerable strain as family size and residential patterns change. New ways of expressing and maintaining family ties will have to be found. The programs beginning to be developed for the aged will have to be greatly expanded in the future, and their cost is likely to be high. The very decentralized mechanisms by which they are currently being funded will likely also require alteration. In addition, other social welfare programs will need to be instituted both to meet the social needs of the elderly and to utilize their energies and expertise to the fullest extent possible.

REFERENCES

Beijing Review (1981a). "China's Marriage Law." March 16: 24, 24–27. (1981b). "Growing old in China." October 16: 24, 22–28. (1982a). "Five-guarantees households in the countryside." March 1: 25, 9. (1982b). "Support and respect the elderly." May 3: 25. (1984). "Old people—a new problem for society." January 23: 27, 10.

Chinese Documents (1983). Fifth Session of the Fifth National People's Congress. Beijing: Foreign Language Press.

Davis-Friedmann, D. (1983). *Long Lives: Chinese Elderly and the Communist Revolution.* Cambridge, MA: Harvard Univ. Press.

Du, R. (1984). "Old people in China: hopes and problems." *Beijing Review* 27 (April 16): 31–34.

Jian, C. (1983). "Volunteer service shows improving social mores." *Beijing Review* 26 (December 12): 24–25.

Tien, H. Y. (1977). "How China treats its old people." *Asian Profile* 5 (February): 1–7.

Wu, Y. (1984). "A new look in gerontology." *Beijing Review* 27 (April 16): 34–35.

Yang, C. K. (1965). *Chinese Communist Society: The Family and the Village.* Cambridge: MIT Press.

QUESTIONS

DISCUSSION QUESTIONS

1. London, Ontario (and the surrounding Oxford and Middlesex counties) is a more homogenous community—in class and ethnic terms—than many others. How would Beaujot's findings differ if this research were carried out in your own community?

2. Is there likely to be a "third demographic transition," and if so, what will it look like?

3. Beaujot's research assumes that people (a) know why they act as they do, and (b) are able and willing to explain their motives. In social research, are these assumptions generally warranted? Are they warranted where marriage and childbearing are concerned?

4. How would you explain the survival in London, Ontario of '50s sentiments in the context of '90s behaviours? Do sentiments (i.e., attitudes, ideas, and values) generally change very slowly?

DATA COLLECTION EXERCISES

1. Has the aging of the Canadian population caused some of the same problems as the Goldsteins (excerpt 13.3) foresee in China? Collect some statistics on the living conditions and social lives of Canadians over the age of 75.

2. Through interviews, collect data in your own community (or school) to determine (a) how conscious people are of their desired family size, (b) how many children they want to have, and (c) what they expect their children to do for them when they are old. What correlations do you find?

3. Collect information in the library to find out whether, in the ten years since van de Kaa collected his data, any new countries have entered the highest stage of the second demographic transition.

4. Interview your grandparents, or two other old people you know well. In various direct and indirect ways, find out (a) who took care of their grandparents in old age, (b) what kinds of support they expect from their own children and grandchildren, and (c) whether they believe that state support for the aged is preferable to family support.

WRITING EXERCISES

1. Write a brief (500-word) essay discussing the shift from a pre-industrial society focused on old people to an industrial society focused on young people.

2. "Changing traditions of child bearing is the most important, and difficult, thing a demographer can help to do." Write a brief (500-word) essay evaluating this statement.

3. Interview at least six of your friends, then write 500 words on the topic of "What my generation hopes to get out of marriage."

4. Do you believe there is "population problem" in the world today? Write a 500-word essay arguing forcefully in support of the view that you do not personally hold.

SUGGESTED READINGS

1. Chen, P. (1984). "China's Other Revolution: Findings from the One in 1,000 Fertility Survey," *International Family Planning Perspectives*, 10, 2, June, 48-57. This survey of Chinese women documents the amazing reductions in fertility that followed from the official state policy to promote the idea of one child per woman. (The resultant aging of the Chinese population is covered in excerpt 13.3.)

2. Huth, Mary Jo (1986). "Population Prospects for Sub-Saharan Africa: Determinants, Consequences and Policy," *Journal of Contemporary African Studies*, Vol. 5, No. 1/2, (April/October), 167-181. A comprehensive report on the state of fertility planning and fertility behaviour in sub-Saharan Africa, where many women still desire (and achieve) the world's highest levels of recorded childbearing.

3. McNeill, W.H. (1976) *Plagues and Peoples*. Garden City, New York: Anchor Books. Written by a prize-winning author, this book shows how human history has been shaped by shifting "disease balances" and "disease pools." It will make you wonder whether people make their own history, or if it's being made for them by germs and microbes.

SECTION 14   THE STATE AND GOVERNMENT

Introduction

Who makes the decisions that most shape the histories of countries and influence their futures? Do different societies have similar patterns of power distribution? Such questions have been central to sociology since its beginnings in the works of Karl Marx, Max Weber, and other scholars.

Sociologists have put forward two main theories to answer the above questions for modern societies like Canada's. One theory emphasizes the role of various elites who hold top positions in society's major institutions. This was the approach Max Weber took, among others. The other theory looks for answers in the class structure (see Section 4). It locates power in the upper economic class, whose members typically inherited their wealth and influence from their parents.

THE ROLE OF ELITES

Elites and the State

Let's begin with a few key definitions. An *elite* is a small group that holds power in society as a whole, or in a particular segment. The elite has legitimate authority to make decisions that affect the lives and work of others; its right to make decisions is seen as proper by society members. We find elite positions in economic organizations (e.g., the highest ranking executive officers of the largest corporations), in government (e.g., elected prime ministers or appointed deputy ministers), and in a variety of other organizations such as labour unions, universities, and the church.

The state is a set of organizations concerned with maintaining and enforcing decisions in a society. These organizations make decisions that are binding upon all members of a particular society. Thus, the state includes the government and public bureaucracy, courts, police, and military. It follows, then, that the *state elite* includes the highest ranking members of state organizations.

Accommodating Elites

According to the *accommodating elite theory*, elites in different sectors of society struggle to promote the goals of their own organizations. Each sector and each organization has some power in this struggle; but no sector or organization usually has enough power to prevail over all the others against their wishes. For that reason, elites must usually work together with other elites. In the long run this will further their organization's interests. So elites, whatever their locus of power, are fundamentally committed to keeping things as they are. They want to avoid upsetting the social order, which works to their advantage.

Elites interact with one another and share a common set of values. They are members of the same social class, with similar socialization experiences in the family and at school. Many of these people are acquaintances, friends, and even kin. But despite these similarites and ties, elites nonetheless fight to further their own organizations' interests.

Economic Elite Control of the State

Economic elite control theory also assumes that dominant organizations are more likely to cooperate than they are to compete and conflict with one another. However, this theory argues that the people in a capitalist society who control its largest and wealthiest organizations—i.e., banks and other financial institutions—will control all other sectors of the economy. By controlling the economy they control all other elites, including the state's elected and appointed officials. They are able to do all this because they control access to capital—the ultimate source of power.

THE CANADIAN CASE

John Porter's work has given the most sustained attention to the accommodating elite view as it applies to Canada. In *The Vertical Mosaic* (1965), Porter concludes that continuity and change in society are the product of acts, or failures to act, on the part of various elites. The average person has little chance to bring about social change except by working through organizations that may ultimately influence the behaviours of elites. Thus, organizations such as unions and lobby groups are essential weapons that average people must use if they are to effect change.

In Porter's view, Canada is ruled by five collaborating elite groups. They consist of people in the top positions of each of five broad areas of Canadian society: the major economic corporations, political organizations, government bureaucracies, labour organizations, and ideological (i.e., church, educational, and media) organizations. Power is dispersed among elites because elite people are responsible to different large organizations, each with their own wealth, power, and goals.

Porter saw a plural set of elites, with two being more powerful than the others. The economic (or "corporate") elite, according to Porter, has probably been the most successful of all in ensuring that its interests are served. In second place, by the same criterion, is the bureaucratic elite, made up of high-ranking civil servants—the so-called "mandarins" of government. Federal bureaucrats are the most powerful civil servants, but high-ranking personnel of provincial bureaucracies may also be members of this elite. Coupled with the political elite, they make up what others call the "state elite."

Why are the corporate and bureaucratic elites so powerful? Each of these two sectors commands enormous economic resources, and each employs large fractions of the Canadian working population. They also provide better-paying and more stable careers than politicians and labour leaders typically enjoy. That's why the corporate and bureaucratic sectors are able to recruit the most talented people for membership in their bureaucracies.

Despite some conflict between elites, Porter concluded that accommodation often holds sway. Cooperation between elites is facilitated by a sharing of values and interests, as we noted earlier. Each of the elites, Porter felt, has many members who subscribe to the idea that corporate capitalism is "for the common good," and who share in the "Western" values of democracy, nationalism, and Christianity. They come to these common views from similar social experiences: training in upper-class schools, interaction on boards of directors, memberships in the same clubs, and so on.

The accommodating elites theory rests on the assumption that in society there exists some equivalent of democratic political participation. Labour organizations and other lobby groups are thus free to pursue their members' interests, which are often opposed to the interests of the economic, state, and other elites. Sometimes these citizens' groups are modestly successful as the elites accommodate and compromise in their decision-making.

Three Excerpts about State Elites

The excerpts that follow can only begin to suggest how elite power is arranged in other societies. Excerpt 14.1 is a study that looks at how elite control in Haiti varied over time. It is the state elite that controls Haiti, and that gives priority to economic elite interests. The state and business elites are in turn highly reliant on the military elite, who from time to time directly seize power. Thus, Haiti's military elite wields an influence over the state that is far beyond what we have ever seen in Canada.

Excerpt 14.2 is a cross-national comparative study showing that the extent to which state control prevails—i.e., the extent to which it is more or less absolute—varies across societies. A high level of state control has serious consequences for the level of violence against individuals in the society. The more absolute the power, the more violence is likely to go unchecked. Highly democratic societies, and societies with countervailing power among the elites, are the safest for citizens and outsiders. This observation is entirely congruent with the findings of the first excerpt on Haiti.

Excerpt 14.3 looks at the ability of the Canadian state elite to virtually control the lives of the poor in this society. The analysis shows that people who are poor, and dependent on the state for their security, are under tight control of the state in a way that most of us are not. This violation of their privacy and dignity again reminds us that unchecked power, even without physical violence, can do a great deal of harm.

Yolaine Armand

THE LEGACY OF ANTI-DEMOCRATIC TRADITIONS IN HAITI

INTRODUCTION

In this excerpt Yolaine Armand provides a historical overview of the shifting composition of Haiti's state elite. Over a long sweep of time various changes have taken place, but the poor have benefited very little.

When the French ruled Haiti whites held absolute power. After the French left a ruling class of lighter-skinned, racially mixed people—the mulattoes—took over, and continued to exclude people from the elite on the basis of race. Many black Haitians actually became poorer under mulatto rule.

However, a black middle class eventually developed. Its climb to political power in the 1940s brought hope that things might improve for the masses of Haitian poor. This hope culminated in the election of a black president, Francois Duvalier, in 1957. But Duvalier became a ruthless dictator, and was succeeded by his son Jean-Claude, who was equally corrupt. Things continued to get worse for the poor.

Duvalier was ousted in 1986, renewing hope of improvement in Haiti. But experiments with democracy and more equitable power sharing have all been short-lived. The black middle class oppresses the poor as much as the upper-class mulattoes did—and the poor have too little power and organizational support to do anything about it.

We learn several important things from this study. First, an anti-democratic, racist legacy continues to bear bitter fruit for a long time (see also excerpt 1.2). Second, white capitalists are not the only source of oppression in today's world.

This paper examines Haiti's enduring political instability in terms of cultural and socio-historical variables. It examines the legacy of Haiti's political and economic past and an assortment of other obstructions that seriously impede the establishment of democracy in Haiti.

Armand, Yolaine (1989). "Democracy in Haiti: The Legacy of Anti-Democratic Political and Social Traditions," *International Journal of Politics, Culture and Society*, 2(4), Summer, 537–56. Reprinted by permission of Human Sciences Press, Inc.

POLITICAL OBSTACLES

A Tradition of Political Autocracy

Political power in Haiti is highly centralized in a chief of state with lesser power delegated to a handful of friends. The latter in turn, control all other legal or political apparatus, including the Executive Branch, the Legislative, the Judiciary, the Armed Forces, all of which are rubber stamping institutions expressing the will of the supreme ruler. Once political power has been taken, most often by force or fraud, it becomes legitimized by its mere existence. The way it is usually challenged is again by violence.

For the Haitian people, it is so much easier to follow a familiar, undemocratic process. Attempts at changes are met with resistance, denials, skepticism, and a great deal of reticence. For example, when General Namphy regained political control last June 20 by ousting President Manigat, it was reported that people met the event with indifference. They went about their daily activities as if nothing significant had happened. The old pattern of favoritism and paternalism was so familiar that people seemed ready to fall back into it matter-of-factly. By the same token, General Avril's successful coup three months later seemed no less expected. A number of Haitians polled in New York reported only two general concerns: that the new ruler be "a good guy" and that he satisfy the demands set forth by the people after Duvalier's departure.

THE DIRECT LEGACY OF 29 YEARS OF DICTATORSHIP

The long-awaited departure of former President Jean-Claude Duvalier in 1986 was greeted with elation among Haitians both in Haiti and abroad. The first few weeks after the overthrow saw a tremendous surge of relief and hope for a brighter future. People visiting the country reported seeing Haitians sweeping the sidewalks, disposing of long-accumulated garbage that defaced city streets and painting tree trunks with bright colors. Neighborhood community councils were spontaneously created to channel the ideas, needs, and suggestions of the people. All Haitians seemed willing to work together to defend their newly won freedom and to participate in the creation of a truly democratic system.

This euphoria was short-lived, however, for it soon became evident that twenty-nine years of absolute power had left the country with a burdensome political legacy that would impede the establishment of a democratic system.

The Remnants of an Anti-Democratic Political Structure

The Duvaliers created some peculiar institutions whose influences ran strongly counter to the democratic process:

A unique party system akin to a "political mafia." For many years, the only recognized (i.e., openly functioning) political party was the one represented by the ruling dictatorship. It is perhaps a misnomer to even call it a political party since it possessed neither a political platform open to discussion, nor any other democratic mechanisms responsive to the public. Adherents held membership cards identifying them as "Volunteers for National Security" (VSN), the official designation of the dreaded "Tontons Macoutes."[1]

An army dominated by Duvalier sympathizers. High army echelons and most officers were compelled by fear of reprisal to display loyalty to the system or at least to not demonstrate open opposition against it. Officers who were critical of the regime would be "retired" or went into exile. The rank and file expressed a similar loyalty for fear of denunciation by other soldiers or by the "tontons macoutes."

A cadre of undisciplined para-militaries (the "macoutes"). Some estimates place the number of "macoutes" as high as 100,000 at the time of Duvalier's departure. Since their purpose was to guarantee the security of the regime, the "macoutes" were left in disarray, with no recognized leadership. Many were armed, but afraid of popular vengeance.[2] Moreover, the upper to middle echelons were divided between the "old guard" attached to Francois Duvalier's rigid doctrine and the more liberal followers of Jean-Claude Duvalier.

An Inadequate Political Process

Although classifying itself as a "republic," Haiti has never had a tradition of institutions that could ensure the democratic process. The recent years of dictatorship have simply eliminated whatever embryo of democracy may have once existed in the country. Following are three major political obstacles left by the former regime.

Non-existence of key political institutions. No political institutions are sufficiently established to channel the demands and articulate the needs of the people. The Congress which traditionally rubber stamped presidential wishes had been abolished by Francois Duvalier. The press was heavily censored and local news of any significance was unilaterally broadcast by the biased government-owned media. The Constitution itself had no real weight since it had been routinely amended to reflect the many whims of ruling regimes.

Lack of alternatives in political leadership. Because it stifled all dissenting voices, the dictatorship left no real political leadership. Of those few opponents who managed to remain in the country, the most outspoken were in hiding most of the time and the remainder voiced only occasional timid protests. Except for the amorphous leadership of the Church, no effective political opposition existed. Shortly after Duvalier's departure, however, a flock of presidential candidates and political activists surged to the fore, several from abroad. As many as 20 odd political parties were created or came to action, many with undefined programs of government. The sudden surge of politicians caused people to divide their allegiance.

The controversial role of the Church in political leadership. When all dissenting voices were silenced, the Church-owned radio stations became the public voice, serving as the link both among the people and between the people and the government. Individuals and groups went to "Radio Soleil"[3] and "Radio Lumiere"[4] to report police brutality, riots, illegal arrests, murders, missing persons, and so forth. They used the Church sponsored radio stations to report hardships and to complain about poor public services.

ECONOMIC OBSTACLES

Widespread Poverty Hampering the Political Process

Haiti is among the poorest nations of the hemisphere, with a net per capita income currently at around $360 per year. The steady deterioration of rural farms due to years of unchecked land erosion, frequent hurricanes, the absence of governmental agricultural policy, the land workers' ignorance and lack of resources, and the dispossession of the farmers due to the corrupt political system all contributed to the steady impoverishment of the peasants and their exodus to urban areas.

This situation had worsened considerably during the Duvalier dictatorship. The last 30 years witnessed the neglect of the secondary towns, called "provinces." Under Duvalier, military—and therefore political—control was more easily maintained when all significant economic activities were centralized in the "Republic of Port-au-Prince." As a result, an estimated 20 percent of the total Haitian population (of about six million) is concentrated in the capital city of Port-au-Prince. As is usually the case in under-developed countries, there is a wide socio-economic gap between the few haves and the vast majority of have-nots.

The Political Elites

Political power has usually been seen as one means for gaining access to everything that can lead to the good life such as education, employment, and the countless lucrative forms of favoritism. Throughout Haitian history, each new political regime was expected to fire as many public employees as possible in order to replace them by a new hungry crowd. People pledged allegiance not to a political philosophy but solely to individuals who assured them of political favor, most often in the form of a salaried government position or other lucrative benefits.

Public political fund raising is not generally practiced. As a tradition, the financially well-to-do are able to "buy" potential voters by spending lavishly on food, money gifts, advertising, and anything else that will impress the public. By the same token, poor candidates are easily bought by private interest groups or wealthy industrialists who will finance their campaign in return for personal favors when elected. As a result, successful candidates for political power are often members of a privileged class bound by their own class interests, or have their hands tied by a powerful group whose interests they have pledged to support.

The Electorate

Haitians' widespread poverty is reinforced by a 75 percent rate of illiteracy. Illiteracy is another impediment to democracy. Ignorance of the political process and misconceptions about political issues, goals, and objectives make it easier for demagogy, intimidation, and sheer violence to take hold.

SOCIO-CULTURAL OBSTACLES

Political Implications of Class and Status in Haiti

The last three decades have brought significant changes in the social structure of Haiti. The previous two-class society in which income, education, occupation, skin color, and status were positively correlated has been modified. Research done by the author between 1981 and 1986 (Armand, 1988) found two patterns of social organization in Haitian cities: a system of class inequalities determined by the distribution of income, education, and occupation, and one of status inequalities based on such subjective factors as prestige, honor, and social recognition of worth.

A person's class, in turn, determines ownership of goods, patterns of consumption, areas and types of residence and general lifestyle.

Honor and prestige, which are more characteristic of *families* than of *individuals*, are based on such inherited attributes as family name, skin color, and wealth and occupation passed on by the family, as well as by such acquired distinctions as money, education, refined manners and tastes, and a mastery of the French language. The inherited or achieved sources of status further subdivides Haitian society into six status layers. These layers can be represented in descending order as follows:

- *White foreigners* who work with foreign or international agencies in Haiti.
- *The Higher Positive Status Group*, designated as "Elite," "Haute Bourgeoisie," or "bourgeoisie Traditionnelle." Consisting of upper class elites and a few black families, this group has some of the characteristics of a caste since membership is assigned at birth. Moreover, members retain their high prestige even if they lose (or fail to acquire) one or several of its identifying characteristics, such as education or occupation.
- *The Lower Positive Status Group*, known as "Bourgeoisie Noire," "Nouvelle Bourgeoisie," or "Nouveaux Riches."
- *The Neutral Status Group*, referred to as "Gens de Bien," "Honnetes Gens," "Bons Mounes" (Creole for "Good Folks").
- *The Negative Status Group*, identified as "La Masse" "Gens du Peuple," "Pitit So Yette," "Vagabonds," "Mounes Mone," "Gros Zoteye" (Creole for "Mountains Folks, Peasants").
- *The Lowest Negative Status Group*, considered as "Vauriens," or "Sans Zave" ("Good for Nothings, Trash").

Class, Status and Politics in Haiti

The dual pattern of class and status differentiation affects Haitian politics. Throughout the history of the country, the upper and middle classes have taken turns as the dominant political groups and have used politics as a means to strengthen their class positions, obtain new socio-economic gains, and acquire status. In the ongoing class and status competition, politics has become another battlefield.

For well over a century after independence, the economic upper class of mainly lighter skinned people entered politics as a way of sustaining or enhancing their status rather than to gain material privileges. The few well-educated dark-skinned persons of lesser economic rank also saw in politics a way to acquire status. The exercise of politics seemed to reflect the status conferred upon it by the upperclass, high-status group.

With President Magloire[5] and, to a greater extent, with the two Duvalier presidents, politics became the best avenue to intra-generational class mobility. Under the Duvalier regime, well-paid positions and all sorts of financial advantages could be obtained by allying oneself with the government. One entered politics not to espouse an ideology but to obtain power and material advantages. This helped to organize political practices and define political culture in a way that is antithetical to the principles of democracy.

As the traditional high status group was pushed out of politics by the black majority, they used their economic advantages to gain control of the business and industrial sector. The exercise of political power ceased to be a status symbol since it now belonged to those of lower status, but it remained the surest avenue of intragenerational class mobility. While the dark-skinned middle and lower classes used politics as a way of making status distinctions among themselves, the upper class now denied all such claims, regarding it as more prestigious to acquire wealth outside the arena of "dirty" and "shifty" politics.

Status and Political Leadership

The prevalence of status distinctions led to a tradition of political autocracy in Haiti. The authority of the president has been similar to that of a Patriarch. His authority was as undisputed as that of the old-fashioned husband and father over his family. The president expected to receive and was generally given respect and obedience, if not love and admiration. He centralized and epitomized the exercise of final authority, and was accepted as a legitimate ruler by a majority of people.

This authoritarian, paternalistic pattern has made the delegation of authority difficult in the country, imposed a heavy burden on higher-level administrators, and aroused temptations to abuse authority. Its consequence has been twofold: autocracy by those who hold power and dependency by those who do not.

Preeminence of Status as an Impediment to Democracy

Because of the predominance of status inequalities in Haitian society, the concept of equality that is inherent in democracy will be difficult to implement. The acceptance of inequality seems an integral part of Haitian culture and it conditions relationships among all groups and individuals. It is evident in the way people refer to and treat each other.

It is therefore not surprising that Haitians at different status levels attach different meanings to the idea of democracy. Both the upper class and the middle class welcome guarantees of human rights and freedom of expression, but are fearful of misinterpretations which could lead to "encroachment" and "invasion" by the lower class masses. With widespread illiteracy among the poor, it is assumed the latter will see democracy as unrestrained freedom to do and say what they please, with no self-restraint or respect for others. At the bottom levels of the society, even illiterate Haitians in Port-au-Prince understand democracy to mean the absence of arbitrary physical abuse and the freedom to vote without coercion or intimidation.

CONCLUSION

This paper has attempted to place Haiti's effort at democratization in its proper socio-cultural context. The Haitian case challenges the notion that in third-world countries with unstable political regimes, democracy needs only to be given a chance (i.e., to remove a dictator or a corrupt ruler) in order to be on its way. In their desperate efforts to survive and initiate socio-economic development, the less developed countries must often overcome age-old traditions and overwhelming internal constraints when political options are presented to them. As a case in point, Haiti's struggle for democracy is hampered by several serious obstacles whose origins are deep in the country's history. Besides widespread poverty and illiteracy, the country faces a tradition of autocracy and a pervasive acceptance of social inequalities which run counter the basic egalitarian principles of democracy. Class and status inequalities which permeate Haiti's social and political cultures and institutions, may prove to be one of the most serious roadblocks to the institution-alization of Haitian democracy.

ENDNOTES

[1]   The term "Tontons Macoutes" refers to members of a civilian force appointed by Francois Duvalier to maintain his dictatorship. They often fulfilled their mission by threatening, intimidating, beating, jailing, torturing, and physically eliminating known opponents or people suspected to be non-sympathizers of the regime.

[2]   There were widely publicized documented reports of a handful of incidents where angry mobs lynched or burned to death former Duvalier tortionaires in Port-au-Prince and in the countryside.

[3]   "Radio Soleil," a regular broadcasting station sponsored by the Catholic clergy.

[4]   "Radio Lumiere," the regular broadcasting station of the Protestant faith.

[5]   Dumarsais Estime, a black politician, was elected President by a two-house Congress in 1946, and overthrown four years later, before the end of his six-year term, by Army General Paul Magloire who then became President from 1950 to his overthrow in 1956.

R. J. Rummel

STATE POWER AND MEGAMURDERS

INTRODUCTION

This excerpt emphasizes that the power of the state is often absolute and arbitrary, and that this can have hideous consequences. R. J. Rummel looks at the relationship between the type of state regime and the practice of "megamurders"—the killing of large numbers of citizens and/or people from other countries.

Rummel shows, for example, that eleven governments have murdered in cold blood 143 million people in this century. He believes that the patterns in megamurders, across nations around the world, suggest the following principle: power kills, and absolute power kills absolutely.

This principle applies not only to genocide and mass murder, but also to wars and other forms of collective violence. The more power a government has, the more it can act arbitrarily according to the wishes of the state elite, and the more likely it will be to murder its citizens and make war on others.

Rummel believes that the way to end wars and genocides is to restrict the power of the state elite. The best way of doing this, he argues, is through an open democratic system with checks and balances provided by a relatively free flow of information, lobby groups, and regular elections. Also important is competition and countervailing power among elites. This conclusion—particularly the need for a flow of information—agrees with the findings presented in excerpt 5.2 on the Balkan genocides, and in excerpt 10.2 on the need for an independent media in Africa.

Power kills, absolute Power kills absolutely. This power principle—a variant of Lord Acton's dictum "Power tends to corrupt; absolute power corrupts absolutely"—is the message of my work on the causes of war and current, comparative study of genocide, politicide, and mass murder—what I call democide—in this century. The more power a government has, the more it can act arbitrarily according to the whims and desires of the elite, the more likely will it make war on others and murder its foreign and domestic subjects.

Power in the sense used here encompasses political power and its holders, as well as the agencies (government departments and bureaucracies) and the instruments (armies, concentration camps, and propaganda) at their disposal. Therefore, the more constrained the Power of governments, the more diffused, checked, and balanced it is, the less will it aggress against others and commit democide. At the

Rummel, R.J. (1992). "State Power and Megamurders," *Society*, 29, 6(200), September–October, 47–52.

extremes of Power, totalitarian communist governments have slaughtered their people by the tens of millions, while many democracies can barely bring themselves to execute even serial murderers.

These assertions may be extreme and categorical, but so is the evidence. Consider first war. There is no case of war involving violent military action between stable democracies, although democracies have fought non-democracies. The exception may be democratic Finland which joined Nazi Germany in its war against the Soviet Union during the Second World War. Although Great Britain declared war on Finland as a result, no military action took place between the two countries. Most wars have been fought between non-democracies. This general principle is gaining acceptance among students of international relations and war: democracies do not make war on each other. The less democratic two states are, the more likely they will fight each other.

This belligerence of unrestrained Power is not an artifact of either a small number of democracies nor of our era. The number of democracies in the world now number around sixty-five containing about 39 percent of the world's population. Yet we have had no war among them. Nor is there any threat of war. Democracies create an oasis of peace.

This is true historically as well. If one relaxes the definition of democracy to mean simply the restraint on Power by the participation of middle and lower classes in the determinations of Power holders and policy making, then there have been many democracies throughout history. Whether one considers the classical Greek democracies, the democratic forest states of Switzerland, or modern democracies since 1787, one will find that they have not fought each other—depending on how war and democracy is defined, some might prefer to say that they rarely fought each other. Once states that had been mortal enemies and had frequently gone to war (as have France and Germany in recent centuries) became democratic, war ceased between them. Paradigmatic of this is Western Europe since 1945. The cauldron of our most disastrous wars for many centuries, in 1945 one would not find an expert so foolhardy as to predict not only forty-five years of peace, but that at the end of that time there would be a European community with central government institutions, moves toward a joint European military force by France and Germany, and no expectation of violence between any of these formerly hostile states. Yet such has happened. All because they are all democracies. Even among primitive tribes, it seems, where Power is divided and limited, war is less likely.

Were all that could be said about absolute and arbitrary Power that it causes war and the attendant slaughter of the young and most capable of our species, this would be enough. But much worse is that even in the absence of combat, Power massacres in cold blood the helpless people it controls. Several times more of them. The eleven megamurderers of the twentieth century—states that have killed in cold blood, aside from warfare, 1,000,000 or more men, women, and children—have wiped out 142,583,000 people between them. This is almost four times the battle dead in all of this century's international and civil wars. States with absolute Power, that is the former Soviet Union, Communist China, Nazi Germany, Khmer Rouge Cambodia, Communist Vietnam, and Communist Yugoslavia account for 122,535,000 or 86 percent.

Among these megamurderers, by their annual percent democide rates [=100 democide/population/(the number of years that the type of regime was in Power)], none comes even close to the lethality of the communist Khmer Rouge in Cambodia during 1975 to 1978. They exterminated near 28 percent of the country's men, women, and children; the odds of any Cambodian surviving these four long years was only 2.5 to 1.

Then there are the kilomurderers, or states that have killed innocent citizens by the tens or hundreds of thousands, such as Communist Afghanistan, Angola, Laos, Ethiopia, North Korea, and Rumania, as well as authoritarian Argentina, Burundi, Chile, Croatia (1941 to 1944), Czechoslovakia (1945 to 1946), Indonesia, Iran, Rwanda, Spain, Sudan, and Uganda. All these, and other kilomurderers, add another 8,361,000 people killed to the democide for this century. The total global democide from 1900 to 1987 probably amounts to 150,944,000 people killed. This figure is the most reasonable and prudent mid-estimate within a low to high range. The overall, absolute highest estimate of democide may be around an almost inconceivable 335,000,000 killed; the absolute low near a hardly less horrible 70,000,000 killed. None of the conclusions would change, however, if we only dealt with the rock bottom total.

Putting the human cost of war and democide together Power has killed some 187,797,100 people in this century.

Democracies too are responsible for some of these democides. Preliminary estimates show that some 1,000,000 foreigners have been killed in cold blood by democracies. This includes those killed in indiscriminate or civilian targeted city bombings, like Germany and Japan in the Second World War. (Deliberate targeting of civilians with explosive and incendiary bombs simply because they happen to be under the command and control of an enemy Power is no better than lining them up and machine gunning them—a clear atrocity.) It also includes large scale massacres of Filipinos during the American colonization of the Philippines at the beginning of this century, deaths in British concentration camps in South Africa during the Boer War, civilian deaths due to starvation during the British blockade of Germany in and after the First World War, the rape and murder of Chinese in and around Peking in 1900, the atrocities committed by Americans in Vietnam, the murder of Algerians by the French, and the deaths of German prisoners of war in French and American prisoner of war camps after the Second World War.

All these acts of killing by democracies may seem to violate the Power principle, but actually they underline it. For in each case, the killing was carried out in secret, behind a conscious cover of lies and deceit by those agencies and Power holders involved. All were shielded by tight censorship of the press and control of journalists. Even the indiscriminate bombing of German cities was disguised before the British House of Commons and in press releases as attacks on German military targets. That the general strategic bombing policy was to attack workingmen's homes was kept secret still long after the war.

The upshot is that even democracies, where Power can take root in particular institutions, remain unchecked and undisciplined, and hide its activities, are capable of murder en masse. Such Power usually flourishes during wartime, for then the military are often given their head, democratic controls over civilian leaders are weak, and the press labors under strict reigns. Democracies too then become garrison states, Power is freed from many institutional restraints (note how easy it was to put tens of thousands of Japanese Americans in concentration camps during the Second World War for nothing more than their Japanese ancestry), and where it can become absolute, as in the military, it may kill absolutely. Witness Hiroshima and Nagasaki.

War and democide can be understood within a common framework as part of a social process, a balancing of Powers, where Power is supreme. It is not clear, however, why among states in which Power is limited and accountable, war and significant democide do not take place. Two concepts explain this: cross pressures and the associated political culture. Where Power is diffuse, checked, and made to be accountable, society is riven by myriad independent groups, disparate institutions, and multiple interests. These forces overlap and contend with each other; they section loyalties and divide desires and wants. Churches, unions, corporations, government bureaucracies, political parties, the media, special interest groups, and such, fight for and protect their interests.

Individuals and elites are pushed and pulled by their membership in several groups and institutions making it difficult for any one driving interest to form. They are divided, weak, ambivalent; they are cross-pressured. For elites to coalesce sufficiently to commit itself to murdering its own citizens, there must be a near fanatical, driving interest. But even if such an interest were present among a few, the diversity of interests across the political elite and associated bureaucracies, the freedom of the media to uncover what is being planned or done, and the ever-present potential leaks and fear of such leaks of disaffected members of the elite to the media brake such tendencies.

As for the possibility of war between democracies, diversity and resulting cross-pressures operate as well. Not only is it very difficult for the elite to unify public interests and opinion sufficiently to make war, but the diverse, economic, social, and political bonds between democracies that tie them together usually prevent the outbreak of violence.

Cross pressures are a social force that operates wherever individual and group freedom predominates. It is natural to a spontaneous social field. But human behavior is not only a matter of social forces, it also depends on meanings, values and norms—that is, a democratic culture is also essential. When Power is checked and accountable, when cross pressures limit the operation of Power, a particular democratic culture develops. This culture involves debate, demonstrations, protests, but also negotiation, compromise, and tolerance. It involves the art of conflict resolution and the acceptance of democratic procedures at all levels of society. The ballot replaces the bullet, and particularly, people and groups come to accept a loss on this or that interest as only an unfortunate outcome of the way the legitimate game is played. "Lose today, win tomorrow."

That democratic political elites should kill opponents or commit genocide for some public policy is unthinkable—although such may occur in the isolated and secret corners of government where Power can still lurk. Even in modern democracies, public defining and dehumanizing of out-groups has become a social and political evil. Witness the current potency of such allegations as "racism" or "sexism." Of course, the culture of democracy operates between democracies as well.

Diplomacy, negotiating a middle way, seeking common interests, is part of the operating medium among democracies. A detailed political history of the growth of the European Community would well display this. Since each democracy takes the legitimacy of the other and their interests for granted, conflict is only a process of nonviolent learning and adjustment. Conferences, not war, should be the instrumentality for settling disputes.

Where absolute Power exists, interests are polarized, a culture of violence develops, and war and democide follow. In this century alone, by current count, Power has killed near 187,797,000 people. Where among states Power is limited and accountable, interests are cross-pressured and a culture of nonviolence develops. No wars have occurred and comparatively very few citizens have been murdered by the governing elite—perhaps no more than one hundred or so in this century.

Our appreciation of the incredible scale of this century's genocide, politicide, and mass murder has been stultified by a lack of concepts. Democide is committed by absolute Power, its agency is government. The discipline for studying and analyzing Power and government and associated genocide and mass murder is political science. But except for a few specific cases, such as the Holocaust and Armenian genocide, and a precious few more general works, one is hard put to find political science research specifically on this subject.

The concepts and views promoted in political science text books are grossly unrealistic. They just do not fit in or explain, and are even contradictory to, the existence of a hell state like Pol Pot's Cambodia, a Gulag state like Stalin's Soviet Union, or a genocide state like Hitler's Germany. One textbook, for instance, spends a chapter on describing the functions of government as law and order, individual security, cultural maintenance, and social welfare. Political scientists are still writing this stuff, when we have numerous examples of governments that kill millions of their own citizens, enslave the rest, and abolish traditional culture. It took only about a year for the Khmer Rouge to completely uproot and extinguish Buddhism, which had been the heart and soul of Cambodian culture.

A systems approach to politics still dominates the field. Seen through this lens, politics is a matter of inputs and outputs, of citizen inputs, aggregation by political parties, government determining policy, and bureaucracies implementing it. Then there is the common and fundamental justification of government that it exists to protect citizens against the anarchic jungle that would otherwise threaten their lives and property. Such archaic, sterile views show no appreciation of democide and related horrors and suffering. They are inconsistent with a regime that stands astride society like a gang of thugs over hikers they have captured in the woods, robbing all, raping some, torturing others for fun, murdering those they do not like, and terrorizing the rest into servile obedience. This characterization of many past and present governments, such as Idi Amin's Uganda, hardly squares with conventional political science.

Consider also that library stacks have been filled on the possible nature and consequences of nuclear war and how it might be avoided. Yet, the toll from democide (and related destruction and misery among the survivors) is equivalent to a nuclear war, especially at the high 300 million end of the estimates. It is as though one had already occurred! Yet to my knowledge, there is only one book dealing with the human cost of this "nuclear war"—Gil Elliot's *Twentieth Century Book of the Dead*. And to my knowledge he is not a political scientist.

What is needed is a reconceptualization of government and politics consistent with what we now know about democide and related misery. New concepts have to be invented, old ones realigned to correct our perception of Power. We need to invent concepts for governments that turn their states into concentration camps, purposely starve millions of their citizens, set up quotas for those who should be killed. Although murder by quota was carried out by the Soviets, Chinese communists, and Vietnamese, the general political science literature does not give recognition to this incredible inhumaneness of certain governments. We have no concept for murder as an aim of public policy, determined by discussion among the governing elite in the highest councils and imposed through government bureaucracy. There is virtually no index in any general book on politics and government that makes reference to official genocide and murder, to the number of those killed, executed, or massacred, not even in books on the Soviet Union or China. Most indexes omit references to concentration or labor camps or gulags, even if a book contains a paragraph or two on the subject.

The preeminent fact about government is that some murder millions in cold blood. This is where absolute Power reigns. The second fact is that some, usually the same governments, murder tens of thousands more through foreign aggression and intervention. Absolute Power again. These two facts alone must be the basis of a reconceptualization and of taxonomies of states. These must be based, not only on whether a state is developed or not, third world or not, powerful or not, large or not, but also and more importantly, on whether Power in a state is absolute and has engaged in genocide, politicide, and mass murder.

The empirical and theoretical conclusion—still more work on comparative democide in this century remains to be done—is this: the way to end war and virtually eliminate the conditions for democide appears to be through restricting and checking Power. This means the fostering of democratic freedom.

Margaret Hillgard Little

THE POLITICAL REGULATION OF SINGLE MOTHERS

INTRODUCTION

The state helps to determine what constitutes morality in a society by defining which behaviours are good and bad. It also has the power to make its definitions of bad behaviour stick! Where necessary, government officials can ask their agencies of social control—e.g., the courts and police—to help ensure that laws are followed. However, this is often unnecessary. Most people obey the rules, either because they believe these represent the right ways to behave, or because they fear painful sanctions.

This excerpt shows how the government regulates moral behaviour by scrutinizing the activities of single mothers on welfare. The data, based on interviews with a sample of these women, show that single mothers face a welfare system that continually judges their "deservedness" and their "moral worth." The mothers must show their social workers, neighbours, and the teachers of their children that they are worthy enough to deserve monthly welfare payments. Each of these groups is encouraged to examine and report on the behaviour of welfare recipients. The state and its agents closely monitor the sexual behaviour of the mothers (e.g., do they have men living with them?), their housekeeping and child-rearing skills, and even whether they win money at bingo. Almost any report of misconduct can lead to an intrusive investigation, and the investigators have broad discretionary powers that they can use to disqualify individuals from social assistance.

MORAL REGULATION AND ITS APPLICATION

Ontario Mothers' Allowance (OMA), enacted in 1920, was one of the first pillars of welfare state legislation in Canada, and helped to lay the groundwork for the state's involvement in the moral scrutiny of the poor. This moral investigation of welfare recipients has not been adequately explored by most welfare scholars. Moral concerns about the poor are generally associated with charity work prior to the twentieth century. Many assume that this type of moral scrutiny withered with the emergence of the post-World War II welfare state (Guest, 1980; Splane, 1965). But the history of OMA or Family Benefits suggests that moral questions continue to dominate some areas of welfare legislation.

Little, Margaret H. (1994). "The Political Regulation of Single Mothers," *Canadian Journal of Sociology*, 19, 2, 233–247.

In a number of ways the concept of moral regulation helps to emphasize certain aspects of this seventy-three-year-old policy which have long been neglected or minimized by other welfare scholars. It is true that there were clear social and economic interests behind the enactment of OMA. There was a deep concern about the growing number of unemployed soldiers; there was also a desire to replace the losses on the battlefield with healthy future citizens, particularly of Anglo-Saxon stock. The gender politics of this era also played a role in the formation of this policy. Women had increased their role in the public arena. They had participated in the job market during the war and were encouraged to return to the home following the war, losing these jobs to men. They had also demanded and achieved the federal vote in 1918. Mothers' allowance provided a neat solution to these social, economic, and gender problems. It could persuade women to leave the paid work to the men, reducing the unemployment problem. It granted public value to the role of motherhood, to the delight of newly enfranchised maternal feminists. At the same time it ensured the continuance of healthy male workers and healthy future workers. As such this policy encouraged women into an economic, social, and sexual dependent relationship within the family.

But these economic interests do not explain the intrusive features of this policy. Charity women played a pivotal role in the introduction of mothers' allowance and consequently the formation of the Canadian welfare state. At the turn of the century a wide range of charity leaders had become anxious about the growing poverty caused by rapid industrialization. These philanthropists believed economic deprivations were at least partly due to drinking, promiscuity, and insanitary habits. In order to curb these tendencies these social leaders played an intrusive role in the lives of the impoverished. Women performed a pivotal role in these charity organizations and were active in both the naming of the problem and the creation of a solution. As middle-class white women they naturally defined the issue in their own terms. Ensconced in maternal feminist ideals, they condoned mothers who were forced to work outside the home. Through charity organizations they participated in an international campaign which urged the state to recognize the value of childbearing and alleviate the need for mothers to work by introducing mothers' allowance legislation (Strong-Boag, 1979).

In many ways Ontario Mothers' Allowance closely resembled charity work. First enacted to support poor widows, the Act stipulated that recipients must be "fit and proper persons" (OMA Act, 1920). This allowed for both intrusive scrutiny of the women's lives and enormous discretion on the part of the OMA administrators. Investigators, as the early social workers were called, were encouraged to conduct extremely thorough investigations. In some "particularly difficult" cases it was noted that investigators visited "daily to advise on everything from bedding, care of children, sleeping arrangements, etc." (OMA, 1921–22:30).

Over time this policy was expanded to include a variety of single mothers. Each category was placed upon a hierarchy of worthiness. Widows were considered most deserving and received the least scrutiny. Women with incapacitated husbands were the second group to receive the allowance and were generally approved provided a medical certificate could prove that their husband was "totally and permanently incapacitated." Deserted wives, on the other hand, were considerably less worthy according to the OMA administrators. Originally the deserted mother had to swear that she had not seen or heard from her husband in seven years. This time restriction was a barrier for many impoverished women and children; after considerable protest the period was reduced but it was not finally removed until October 1991. Similar to deserted women, divorcees were treated with suspicion and were not eligible until 1951. In 1955 the policy expanded to include unemployable single fathers, mothers whose husbands were imprisoned and unwed mothers. The latter was one of the most controversial groups to receive the allowance. Initially a two-year waiting period was enforced to ensure that these mothers were "fit" to care for their children and that they did not continue their "improper" sexual practices. Eventually this was reduced to three months, but only in October 1991 was this time restriction removed. Separated mothers became eligible in 1979, single able-bodied fathers in 1983 and mothers who cohabit with a man in 1987. The latter amendment was highly contentious and several stipulations were attached to this group. These women can receive the allowance for three years provided the man they live with is not the father to any of the children. After three years of cohabitation they are no longer eligible and the allowance is cut off. Each of these amendments has resulted in both a more inclusive policy but also new methods for morally regulating the lives of poor single mothers.

THE VOICES OF POOR SINGLE MOTHERS

Throughout the history of this policy poor single mothers had to prove themselves both financially and morally deserving of the allowance. Based on interviews with groups of poor single mothers this section will focus on their contemporary experiences of the policy. Most of the single mothers interviewed requested that pseudonyms be used to protect their anonymity. Their experiences suggest that they, like single mothers before them, must continually prove their worthiness.

Financial Matters

The boundaries between financial and moral worthiness for a poor single mother have often been blurred. Throughout the history of this policy single mothers were forced to meet the contradictory expectations of both raising and providing for their children. The allowance has always been below subsistence, forcing these mothers to work at least part-time. But paid work always interfered with their other prescribed role as mothers dedicating their lives to domestic duties. Thus poor single mothers have had to juggle two incompatible responsibilities and have often been criticized when they were not up to the task.

In the 1990s financial concerns dominate many poor single mothers' lives. As government budgets are squeezed single mothers experience increased financial scrutiny of their lives. One single mother in Kitchener said her bank book is constantly examined. "Every time they [the social workers] come, they see your bank book. They have a release form, so [they] have access to your bank account at any time" (Mothers and Others Making Change or MOMC, 1991; Hannah, 1991).

Others recalled "interrogations" because they had received a gift of furniture, groceries, or clothing from a friend or relative. Still others have their cheques withheld if they are not home when the social worker makes a surprise visit (di Salle, 1991).

Because the monthly benefit remains woefully inadequate, many single mothers spoke about the many ways they survive. Food is one of the few non-fixed items in a single mothers' monthly budget and therefore the one sacrificed to meet rent, hydro, and phone payments. Given the inadequacy of the Family Benefits cheque most mothers do not have enough money to meet the basic Canada's Food Guide requirements. Everyone agreed that the last ten days of the month are the toughest. "That's when I hear the rumble in my stomach. That's when there's no milk in the fridge and I have to give my kids dry cereal to eat," said one Kitchener mother (MOMC, 1991). "Those last ten days are really bad for groceries," remembered another mother from North Bay. "I would be counting the slices in a loaf of bread to make sure my son had at least two slices a day but I just couldn't make it" (Low Income People Involvement or LIPI, 1991). Many women said they had to use their food money to pay the rent and then visited the local food bank to make up the difference. Many food banks, however, have placed conditions on the use of their services. In North Bay single mothers on OMA are only permitted to visit twice a month and then they can only receive enough food for three days. In Belleville "you have to show your stub of assistance and [explain] where the money went and if your reasons don't meet with their satisfaction, they say no," explained one single mother (Hannah, 1991). And at least one Salvation Army food bank in downtown Toronto has told FBA recipients that they should only attend once every three months. "They've told us that their food is really for those who are newly unemployed—not for us," said one single mother (Fight Back Metro Coalition, 1992).

Other single mothers find alternative ways to make ends meet between FBA cheques. For some, bingo provides a way to make a little extra money and socialize at the same time (Ross, 1984: 212). But bingo participation is often heavily scrutinized. Single mothers in North Bay have to beware of the "bingo police" or social workers who attend bingo events, take account of the winners and then automatically subtract the amount from the Family Benefits cheque (LIPI, 1991). In Elgin County, neighbours, referred to as "bingo blabs," are encouraged to tell the Family Benefits office who attended the game (D'Arcy, 1991).

Some single mothers work "under the table" in the underground economy. They baby-sit, sell items from mail order catalogues, collect empty beer bottles, whatever they can to survive. Some set up extra bank accounts or give money to a relative or friend for safe keeping. "That's called abuse but we don't call it abuse, we call it survival," explains Jennifer Myers, a long-time anti-poverty activist from Kitchener (MOMC, 1991). A few single mothers said that their social workers have helped them hide money (MOMC, 1991; Women's Weekly, 1991b).

Retraining and employment are other arenas for financial scrutiny. Until recently Family Benefits' recipients were only permitted to work part-time. But welfare programs have experienced enormous pressure to reduce costs as a result of the federal government cuts in Canada Assistance Plan funding, the push towards global economic competitiveness and the popular demand for a reduced and privatized state.

Consequently, the provincial government has initiated a number of full-time employment schemes for single mothers and has produced several reports calling for more action in this area. The 1993 White Paper on social reform recommends a form of partial workfare which includes increased scrutiny of recipients and differentiated payments based on retraining and employment (Evans and McIntyre, 1987; Ontario, 1988; 1993). If implemented this plan will exacerbate a growing distinction between the deserving and undeserving, blaming the victims of this devastating recession.

Single mothers have voiced a number of concerns regarding these employment initiatives. Many women said they were unable to participate in such training programs because they could not find subsidized child care and those who had daycare considered themselves exceptionally lucky (LIPI, 1991). Carole Silliker, a long-time anti-poverty activist from Kitchener, is a strong opponent of retraining programs:

> Retraining is a farce. It is [a] band-aid solution. . . . You learn to be things that the market is saturated with—it makes no sense at all. And they think they're doing us a favour—and it's our fault when there is no job out there at the end. It's a big scam to make them look good. (MOMC, 1991)

There are many other single mothers from rural areas or one-industry towns like Carole who are discouraged by the lack of jobs available.

Those fortunate enough to find paid work have discovered that their new job does not make them more financially secure. Because of their job they have lost their drug benefits, housing subsidy, and childcare subsidy. Most of the single mothers who have jobs work for minimum wage with few, if any, fringe benefits to offset the FBA services they have lost. Since 1975 the purchasing power of minimum wage has declined by 22 percent, leaving a single mother with less ability to make ends meet (Ontario, 1988: 289). One mother explained her frustration during the SARC hearings.

> Even though I'm working I'm making less than if I'd be on Mothers' Allowance which is very discouraging to me. I'm trying to raise four teenagers on a very small budget and I feel I'm sinking lower and lower all the time. (Ontario, 1988: 291)

Single mothers who have found jobs have moved from the unemployed poor to the working poor. They are no longer scrutinized by their social workers or neighbours, but they do continue to live below the poverty line.

While poor single mothers have always had to juggle the incompatible responsibilities of caring and providing for their children, this contradiction will in all likelihood become more profound in the near future. With the increase in unemployment and the reduction in child-care spaces and other support services it is unlikely that most FBA recipients will find jobs. But this emphasis on retraining and employment may encourage the public to blame single mothers who do not find full-time work. This may also result in reduced welfare payments to those who, for whatever reason, remain on Family Benefits.

The Persistence of Moral Regulation

This financial scrutiny of poor single mothers' lives is intertwined with moral issues. It is the visits by the workers and the whispers from the neighbours about how they talk, dress, manage their homes and their children which most irritate and humiliate the FBA recipients interviewed. Even those who now have fulltime paid work will never forget the scrutiny they experienced during their years on FBA. At the end of the interview with Sally she said, "This has left such a scar. It's ten years later and just talking to you—I want to go and cry. It's brought up such terrible memories" (LIPI, 1991).

The blurring of financial and moral scrutiny is most obvious in the case of women with absent male partners. Whereas widows are considered deserving other mothers experience more intensive investigations to prove their worthiness. In keeping with the male breadwinner ideology, the state demonstrates its reluctance to financially support single mothers when fathers could do so.

In the case of desertion, mothers who know the whereabouts of their husbands are now eligible for the allowance but experience considerable difficulty from the social workers. Deserted mothers complained about social workers pressuring recipients to pursue the man through the Court system. "There's nothing in this battle for me. When I charge him he gets mad and comes after me. And even if he agrees to pay me support I have to claim it as income so I'm no further ahead," explained one mother (Women's Weekly, 1991a). Another recipient remembered the court procedure as both lengthy and emotionally exhausting.

Other mothers try to arrange under-the-table support payments from their husbands but these agreements are also difficult as one mother described.

> My Ex pays $100 a month under the table and says he'll stop paying this if I tell Mothers' Allowance—and if I tell Mothers' Allowance they'll go after me for fraud. He gets off. I get the blame. (Women's Weekly, 1991a)

The women at one single mothers' group agreed it was best to tell the social worker you did not know the husband's whereabouts. "You're better off saying you got drunk and got raped by several guys than to say there was one," claimed one recipient (Women's Weekly, 1991a).

Unwed mothers also experience intense scrutiny from social workers. One single mother, Dorothy, recounted her story of the social worker's attempt to discover the name of the father.

> The social worker asked, "Well did you actually go out with him [the father]?"
>
> I said, "No, I screwed him on the bar stool—what the hell do you think."
>
> Then the worker asks, "Do you know his name?" I said I only have his first name, Frank. So she writes that down on her form: F-R-A-N-K. Then she says, "Well have you gone looking for him?" Well yeah, like I'm going to run across the country yelling. "Frank, Frank." (Women's Weekly, 1991b)

Another group which is carefully watched by social workers is women who live with men. The 1987 amendment which permitted cohabitation for a three-year period has done little to reduce home investigations. According to the FBA manual, workers are expected to investigate every complaint. "This is an open warrant to investigate a recipient's home at any time, over and over again if they wish," said John Clarke, provincial organizer for Ontario Coalition Against Poverty (Clarke, 1991). And the definition of cohabitation is so broad that it includes eating meals together, baby-sitting, washing dishes together, going anywhere together (D'Arcy, 1991). This definition provided for FBA workers is not generally made available to FBA applicants and promotes confusion and fear. As one mother said, "I was frightened to have my brother to stay over the night. . . . No one told me I could" (Women's Weekly, 1991b).

Most of the women interviewed had their own experience of what some call the "manhunt." The bathroom investigation was the most common.

> One worker looked behind the shower. . . . He [the worker] was looking at absolutely everything. They ask to use your washroom, they go through your shaving cream, razors, three toothbrushes. Those are the things they looked for. (Women's Weekly, 1991b)

Another mother recalled a boot investigation at her home.

> I had to try on my boots in front of them [social workers] because I took size 11. I had cougar winter boots which could be unisex. It was so humiliating. (LIPI, 1991)

Social workers have also been known to check for tire tracks in the snow, examine fridge notes, search for hunting equipment and evidence of dogs, stake out parking lots at night, throw sand on the doorstep in order to trace footprints—all in an effort to confirm that a man is living in the home (Clarke, 1991; LIPI, 1991; Gunness, 1991).

Many community workers and anti-poverty activists expect these home investigations to escalate as more and more FBA recipients reach the three-year limit for cohabitation. As one legal aid worker warned, "We'd better get used to it because now they're going to start enforcing the three year stuff. I had a meeting with FB workers who hated the new rule, they couldn't wait to get these single moms" (LIPI, 1991).

As well as direct supervision of a woman's intimate relationships, there are also indirect forms of scrutiny. The current FBA regulations in regard to a single mother's sexual practices are contradictory at best. The cohabitation amendment would suggest that the policy now allows a mother to be sexually active, provided it is not with the father of her children. The three-year cohabitation limit encourages short-term rather than long-term relationships yet the drug plan does not allow for the purchase of a variety of reproductive products. The birth control pill is the only reproductive device permitted by the drug plan. In the era of the AIDS epidemic, condoms are not covered by the drug plan. Binkie, an FBA recipient, is exasperated by this regulation.

> I'm 36 years and they would give me the pill but I had to pay for my own diaphragm and gel. Even though I had a doctor's certificate saying I need a diaphragm they still won't pay for it. (Women's Weekly, 1991b)

Concerns about cleanliness, which dominated charity work at the turn of the century, still persist in FBA administration today. As one mother stated,

> Children's Aid Society, cops, society—everyone judges you on cleanliness. The teachers in the school system. How they see them [the children] dressed. . . . (Women's Weekly, 1991b)

Another single mother believes social workers expect your house to be especially spotless if you do not have paid work (LIPI, 1991). Ontario anti-poverty

activists and single mothers interviewed acknowledged that social workers continue to comment on a recipient's cleanliness or lack thereof (di Salle, 1991;
Women's Weekly, 1991b; Mott, 1991). A recent case involving the regulation of
poor mothers' cleanliness has occurred in subsidized New Brunswick housing.
Poor women, predominantly single mothers, living in this housing are forced to
take lessons in cleaning which involve childlike picture lessons and include a
twelve-step quiz on the cleaning of toilets. These lessons include a surprise investigation of the resident's home to ensure that she is following the prescribed regulations. If residents do not take these lessons or do not pass the class they can be
denied subsidized housing (New Brunswick Housing Corporation, 1992).

Attitude was very important to early charity workers and still remains significant. Several mothers interviewed agreed that a humble, grateful attitude was
essential when dealing with the social workers. As one mother explained, "I'm not
human to them, and I have to be subservient, or they just won't even talk to me"
(Ontario, 1992).

CONCLUSION

Throughout the history of this policy, poor single mothers have had to prove, time
and again, their worthiness. Although the policy has expanded over its seventy-
three-year history to now include a variety of single mothers, with these amendments have come new types of regulations. This is not to deny that change has
occurred in this policy, but what is perhaps most remarkable is how Ontario
Mothers' Allowance or Family Benefits continues to be intrusive and moralistic,
based on discretionary criteria which allow social workers to separate the worthy
from the unworthy. These regulations and the relationship between the regulator
and the regulated help to reinforce dominant race, class, and gender interests in
society at large. Through mothers' allowance both the state and other social organizations have been involved in a lengthy process of normalizing the stigmatization
and intense scrutiny of poor single mothers.

REFERENCES

Clarke, John (1991). Ontario Coalition Against Poverty, Toronto, Ontario, November 18.

D'Arcy, Richard (1991). Community legal worker. Community Outreach Programs of Elgin
County, St. Thomas, Ontario, November 22.

di Salle, Nick (1991). Former FBA worker, Toronto, Ontario, November 22.

Evans, Patricia and Eilene McIntyre (1987). "Welfare work incentives and the single mother:
An interprovincial comparison." In Jacqueline Ismael, ed., *The Canadian Welfare State:
Evolution and Transition*, pp. 101–25. Edmonton: University of Alberta Press.

Fight Back Metro Coalition (1992). Single Mothers' Workshop, Toronto, Ontario, April 11.

Guest, Dennis (1980). *The Emergence of Social Security in Canada*. Vancouver: University of
British Columbia Press.

Gunness, Patty (1991). Neighbourhood legal workers. Neighbourhood Legal Services,
London and Middlesex County, London, Ontario, November 19.

Hannah, Laurie (1991). Chair of Citizens for Action. Belleville, Ontario, December 10.

Low Income People Involvement (LIPI) (1991). North Bay, Ontario, November 28.

Mothers and Others Making Change (MOMC) (1991). Kitchener, Ontario, November 19.

Mott, Ruth (1991). Women for Economic Justice, Toronto, Ontario, December 3.

New Brunswick Housing Corporation (1992). *Home Orientation and Management Program*. Fredericton, New Brunswick.

Ontario (1920). "Ontario Mothers' Allowance Act." *Statutes of Ontario*, First Session of the 15th Legislature, Chapter 89.

Ontario (1921–22). "Second annual report of the Ontario Mothers' Allowance Commission." *Ontario Sessional Papers*, Vol. LV, Part VIII.

Ontario (1988). *Transitions: Report of the Social Assistance Review Committee*. Toronto: Queen's Printer.

——————— (1992). *Consumer Focus Group Project*. Advisory Group on New Social Assistance Legislation, Final Report. Toronto: Queen's Printer.

——————— (1993). *Turning Point: New Support Programs for People with Low Incomes*. White Paper, Ministry of Community and Social Services, Toronto: Queen's Printer.

Ross, Becki (1984). "A feminist reconceptualization of women's work and leisure: A study of Kingston mother workers." Unpublished M.A. thesis, Kingston: Queen's University.

Splane, Richard (1965). *Social Welfare in Ontario*. Toronto: University of Toronto.

Strong-Boag, Veronica (1979). "Wages for housework: Mothers' Allowances and the beginning of social security in Canada." *Journal of Canadian Studies* 14(1): 21–34.

Women's Weekly, discussion group for low-income women (1990). Toronto, Ontario, May; (1991a). Toronto, Ontario, June 19; (1991b). Toronto, Ontario, December 11.

Wright, Carolann (1991). Women for Economic Justice, Toronto, Ontario, December 3.

QUESTIONS

DISCUSSION QUESTIONS

1. "Elites" and "upper classes" (see also the discussions in Section 4) are related, but they are also quite different. Contrast the two and think of some good examples that show the importance of distinguishing between them.

2. In your view, who, or what group(s), has the most power in Canada? Indicate why you think so.

3. As used by Little, what does the term "moral regulation" refer to?

4. Some scholars argue that because males predominate in the making of laws (males are more likely to be politicians, lawyers, and judges—members of the state elite), the interests of women are rarely well served. Discuss three or four examples of laws in Canada that favour men over women. Can you find any that favour women over men?

DATA COLLECTION EXERCISES

1. Armand describes the role of race in conflicts over power and leadership in Haiti. Gather some library information on the role of race or ethnicity in power and leadership in Canada.

2. Study the regulations that apply to the behaviour of a social category of people—for example, university or college students—in your educational institution and in the broader community. Compare their situation to that of the single mothers on welfare described in excerpt 14.3.

3. For Canada or another society of your choice, find out the number of job vacancies and the number of unemployed people in some recent period. Discuss the results of your research and whether the elites and their behaviour help to account for the results.

4. Using newspaper accounts, study how the responses to single mothers on welfare may have changed over the past ten years.

WRITING EXERCISES

1. "The patterns of power in society seldom change very much." Write a brief (500-word) essay agreeing or disagreeing with this view, drawing on the excerpts in this section where appropriate.

2. Write a 500-word essay on whether Canada has had "megamurders" in its history.

3. Write a 500-word essay speculating on the ways Canadians may differ in their responses to single fathers on assistance and single mothers on assistance. What differences would you expect to find, if any, and why?

4. Prepare a 500-word essay in which you spell out what the average citizen can learn about decision-making from the excerpts in this section.

SUGGESTED READINGS

1. Michels, Robert (1962). *Political Parties*. New York: Harcourt Brace. A classic study arguing that for any organization (political or otherwise) to be successful as it grows in size and complexity it must become bureaucratized. As a result, even democratically inclined leaders of democratic parties come to focus their attention on maintaining power.

2. Porter, John (1965). *The Vertical Mosaic*. Toronto: University of Toronto Press. A classic of Canadian sociology. As we have already noted in the introductions to this section and Section 5, the book has much to say about ethnic groups and elites. But it also has a lot to say about class structure, the importance of education, and the value of democracy.

3. Wolf, Eric (1982). *Europe and the People Without History*. Berkeley: University of California Press. A sweeping, worldwide perspective on the ways that expanding European capitalism and colonialism affected pre-capitalist societies—including their structures of class and stratification.

SECTION 15   IDEOLOGY AND PROTEST

Introduction

Ideologies are emotionally charged values and beliefs that "explain" how society is organized. Sometimes they explain why society should be organized in a different way. In acquiring ideologies individuals are often unaware of the learning process, or that they have "acquired" anything at all. Over our lifetimes we are exposed to ideological beliefs and values in many subtle ways. We begin to learn ideology through family socialization, where we are taught the values and beliefs of our parents. This learning extends to socialization through the formal education system (as we saw in Section 9), in the community, and at work. Since the media disseminate the prevailing values and beliefs of government and business, they too are central to the teaching of ideology.

One main ideological element of North American culture is the explanation of the disparity between the rich and poor. Most people think along the lines discovered in a study by Smith and Stone ("Rags, Riches and Bootstraps: Beliefs about the Causes of Wealth and Poverty," *Sociology Quarterly*, 30 (1), pp. 103-107). They asked 200 Texan adults to answer a set of questions about the reasons some people are poor and other people are rich. They found people's answers fell into two main groupings, or clusters, which Smith and Stone called "individualism" and "structuralism."

A respondent with *individualistic views* about poverty thinks poor people are not motivated to succeed. Poor people can get welfare without any trouble, lack drive and perseverance, have loose morals, abuse drugs and alcohol, are not thrifty, and are lazy. A respondent with individualistic views sees rich people as having more drive and perseverance than other people, more willingness to take risks, and as hard-working and thrifty. These are "individualistic" views because they explain success and failure in terms of the personal characteristics of the rich or poor individual.

A respondent with *structuralist views*, on the other hand, focuses not on the individual but on the situation in which an individual finds him- or herself. So a structuralist explains poverty by saying that poor people lack contacts or pull; are victims of discrimination in hiring, promotions, and wages; are taken advantage of by the rich; are forced to attend inferior schools; and are ignored by an insensitive government. A structuralist explanation of wealth notes that rich people, on the other hand, have a lot of pull or contacts; attend good schools; inherit lots of money; are favoured in hiring, wages, and promotions; receive special treatment from the federal government; sacrifice their families for their careers; and take advantage of the poor.

Smith and Stone found the most common outlook in Texas was "individualism," especially in explaining poverty. Perhaps most interesting of all, the researchers found no connection between the respondent's own characteristics—gender, race, age, income, or educational attainment—and his or her explanation of wealth and poverty. This means that poor people are just as ready to attribute poverty to personal failure, and wealth to personal virtue, as rich people are. This state of mind—self-blame, even self-hatred on the part of the poor, and self-congratulation on the part of the rich—creates a powerful force against changes in the direction of more equality.

But this is not the sum total of ideology in our society. Questions of ideology arise in widely varying areas of life, for example in debates about whether Canada should admit more refugees; whether Crown corporations should be privatized; if a fetus is really a person entitled to legal rights; if Canada owes a moral, legal and economic debt to its native peoples; whether we need affirmative action to correct past inequalities.

IDEOLOGIES AS VEHICLES OF CONTROL AND PROTEST

We must distinguish between two broad types of ideology. *Reformist* and *radical ideologies* rally the forces of change, while *dominant ideologies* support existing social arrangements, or the status quo.

Reformist ideologies call for changes without challenging the basic ground rules. This is what happened when medicare, welfare, and unemployment insurance were established in Canada. These programs helped people, but failed to eliminate the unequal distribution of wealth between owners of capital and workers, or to challenge the principle of private property that underlies our economic order.

By contrast, *radical ideologies* call for a fundamental restructuring of society or one of its institutions. This is what the Co-operative Commonwealth Federation (CCF, the predecessor of today's New Democratic Party) did at the time of its founding in the 1930s. The Regina Manifesto, adopted by the CCF at its founding convention in 1933, declared that "no CCF government will rest content until it has eradicated capitalism and put into operation the full programme of socialized planning which will lead to the establishment in Canada of the co-operative commonwealth." Another radical ideology is the proposed reform of medicare, which would eliminate its universal coverage on the grounds that universal health care is too costly for taxpayers. Underlying this belief is the view that people should assume more of the cost of their own care, as they once did.

A second type of ideology is called *dominant ideology*. Ideologies can be "dominant" in the sense that most people endorse them, or in the sense that they reflect the way society is run, and are thus sponsored by the most powerful groups in society whether or not most people agree.

The "belief in private property" is an example of an ideology that is dominant in both respects in our society. Other dominant ideologies include sexism, which justifies the unequal treatment of women and men, and racism, which justifies the unequal treatment of visible minorities. Excerpt 15.1 shows how ideologies of racial or ethnic inferiority are used to delegitimize enemies or minorities through the use of stereotypes and discrimination. Delegitimization provides justification for attacking the enemy and, most important, viewing the enemy as less than human.

This is typically accomplished in support of the dominant group in society and its dominant ideology.

The reform and radical ideologies we find in any society are *counter-ideologies*. They are "counter" in the sense that they challenge the assumptions and beliefs of dominant ideologies. The purpose of counter-ideology is to expose the interests that dominant ideologies serve and to offer an alternative vision of society. Counter-ideologies are often responses to people's experiences with unequal treatment. Counter-ideologies call the status quo to account and, at least to some extent, threaten to delegitimize customary ways of treating people.

Feminism is an example of a counter-ideology that undermines sexist ideology and traditional ways of treating men and women. The anti-feminist counter movements discussed in excerpt 15.2 can be analyzed as a form of dominant ideology, or as a backlash against feminist ideology—and therefore as a counter-counter-ideology.

Ideology and Empowerment

Sometimes ideology has the effect of empowering people in subordinate positions in society. "Empowerment" refers to an ideology's effect on people's self-esteem, sense of power, and understanding of their position in the social structure. Once they have gained knowledge and confidence they willingly express their views and argue for them. People who have not attained such knowledge and confidence are not likely to pursue their interests.

For example, counter-ideologies equip members of racial minorities to question what happens to them, to understand changes in race relations, and perhaps even to anticipate significant changes in their social status. As we have said, counter-ideology is a source of self-esteem, as in "black is beautiful." It motivates members of minority groups to push for their own personal and collective advancement.

Consciousness-raising refers to a process of empowerment that occurs as people come to understand both their own subordination and the "deceptions" that dominant ideologies use to mask that subordination. This empowerment helps minority people to survive in the face of unequal treatment. Excerpt 15.3 on People's Kitchens in Lima, Peru illustrates how, by organizing to feed the poor, Peruvian women gained a foothold in local politics and found that they were more capable at organizing than they had imagined. Their sense of competence gradually became the basis for a more conscious feminism and for radical political action.

Daniel Bart-Tal

DELEGITIMIZATION: IDEOLOGIES OF CONFLICT AND ETHNOCENTRISM

INTRODUCTION

Stereotyping and discrimination are commonplace when groups interact. They are in fact among the most basic strategies that powerful groups use to undermine the less powerful. For this reason, disadvantaged groups often must discredit the lies behind stereotypes and discrimination in order to make their case for a better lot in life.

Daniel Bar-Tal drives home these points by analyzing a wide international array of examples of extreme stereotyping and discrimination. Bar-Tal shows how powerful groups use a process of "delegitimization" against others. Through this process the powerful ingroup comes to see the outgroup as less than fully human, and thus deserving of social exclusion and even aggressive attack. This is what the outgroup is up against in its efforts to protest and promote change.

Drawing on theories of conflict and ethnocentrism, Bart-Tal shows that when an ingroup perceives an outgroup's aspirations as threatening, it responds by delegitimizing the outgroup. But this delegitimization tends to intensify this sense of threat, rather than weaken it. That is because, as Durkheim has argued, any act that strengthens group cohesion by drawing clearer group boundaries also strengthens the sense of distance and separation from other groups.

Put another way, those who search for spies, witches, or devils in their midst will certainly find and punish these enemies, however imaginary. And it is their status as enemies that serves to justify these acts. This is no less true in modern, "rational," secular Canadian society than it is in strife-torn Bosnia (excerpt 5.2) or anti-democratic Haiti (excerpt 14.1).

The concept, *delegitimization*, describes *categorization of a group or groups into extremely negative social categories that are excluded from the realm of acceptable norms and/or values* (Bar-Tal, 1988, 1989a). Delegitimization permits moral exclusion. The most common means of delegitimization, which are not mutually exclusive, are:

1. *Dehumanization:* labeling a group as inhuman by characterizing members as different from the human race—using either categories of subhuman creatures,

Bart-Tal, Daniel (1990). "Causes and Consequences of Delegitimization: Models of Conflict and Ethnocentrism," *Journal of Social Issues,* 46(1), 65–81. Reprinted by permission.

such as "inferior races" and animals, or categories of negatively valued superhuman creatures, such as demons, monsters, and satans.

2. *Trait characterization:* describing a group as possessing extremely negative traits such as aggressors, idiots, or parasites.

3. *Outcasting:* categorizing members of a group as transgressors of such pivotal social norms that they should be excluded from society and/or institutionalized—e.g., murderers, thieves, psychopaths, or maniacs.

4. *Use of political labels:* describing a group as a political entity that threatens the basic values of the given society—e.g., Nazis, fascists, communists, or imperialists.

5. *Group comparison:* labeling with the name of a group that is negatively perceived, such as "Vandals" or "Huns."

Delegitimization (a) utilizes extremely negative, salient, and atypical bases for categorization, (b) denies the humanity of the delegitimized group, (c) is accompanied by intense, negative emotions of rejection, (d) implies the delegitimized group has the potential to endanger one's own group, and (e) implies the delegitimized group does not deserve human treatment and therefore harming it is justified.

The present paper explores the phenomenon of delegitimization by analyzing its causes and consequences. Two models are described—the conflict model and the ethnocentric model.

THE CONFLICT MODEL

Every intergroup conflict begins with the perception that one group's goals are incompatible with the goals of another group (Bar-Tal, Kruglanski, and Klar, 1989; Pruitt and Rubin, 1986). The perception that a conflict exists means a group finds itself blocked because the attainment of its goal or goals is precluded by another group.

FIGURE 1 Conflict Model: Far-Reaching Incompatibility of Goals

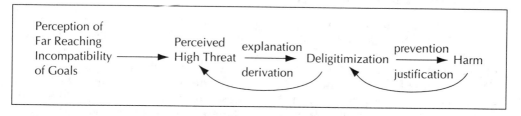

Two conditions in a conflict most frequently incite delegitimization: perception of the outgroup's goals as contradictory, far-reaching, and sinister; and the occurrence of extreme violence.

Threat and Delegitimization

An ingroup experiences threat when it perceives it cannot easily achieve its goals because of outgroup opposition. (See Figure 1.) The crucial questions in explaining the appearance of delegitimization in the early phase of conflict are: (a) How are the goals of the opponent perceived? (b) What is the nature of one's own goals that are perceived as blocked?

The first proposition is that *when a group perceives that the negating goal(s) of an outgroup is (are) far-reaching, especially unjustified, and threatening to the basic goals of the ingroup, then the ingroup uses delegitimization to explain the conflict.* These aspects are linked; when the goals of the outgroup are perceived as outrageous, farfetched, irrational, and malevolent, they are also seen as negating fundamental ingroup goals and therefore as threatening.

Usually this is a zero-sum type of conflict. The perception that the outgroup will achieve its goals poses a danger to the very existence of the ingroup. The danger can be economic, political, or military.

Threat perception in general is accompanied by stress, uncertainty, vulnerability, and fear. These feelings arouse the need to understand and structure the situation quickly, thus allowing explanation and prediction (Y. Bar-Tal, 1989). Delegitimization fulfills this function. It explains why the other group threatens and predicts what the other group will do in the future. (See Figure 1.)

Figure 1 illustrates this situation where the ingroup uses delegitimization to explain the outgroup's enraging aspirations and demands. As examples, delegitimizing labels provide an explanation to Poles about why German Nazis decided to occupy their country, or to Americans about why the Soviet Union strives to dominate the world. Who else would do such things other than a group that is imperialistic, satanic, or fascistic?

Once employed, delegitimization leads to inferences of threat from the delegitimizing category. (See Figure 1.) Thus, the labels "aggressive," "ruthless," "devious," or "oppressive" indicate the outgroup is capable of destruction, violence, or brutality, and this further disrupts the ingroup's sense of security. In this way, the perception of severe threat and delegitimization feed each other.

Delegitimization and Harm

In most serious conflicts, delegitimization leads to harm. Once the ingroup delegitimizes the outgroup with labels that imply threat and evil—"imperialists," "fascists," "terrorists"—acts for preventing danger usually follow. Because the outgroup is delegitimized, preventive measures can be severe, for delegitimized groups are perceived as not deserving human treatment. Deportations, destruction, and mass killings of civil populations are not unusual in these cases. An example of this phenomenon was provided in an insightful statement by an American soldier in the Vietnam War:

> When you go into basic training you are taught that the Vietnamese are not people. You are taught they are gooks, and all you hear is "gook, gook, gook, gook. . . ." The Asian serviceman in Vietnam is the brunt of the same racism because the GIs

over there do not distinguish one Asian from another. . . . You are trained "gook, gook, gook" and once the military has got the idea implanted in your mind that these people are not humans, they are subhuman, it makes it a little bit easier to kill 'em. (Boyle, 1972, p. 141)

Exceptionally violent and harmful actions by the ingroup augment the delegitimization because they seem to justify further actions that exceed normative behavior. (See Figure 1.) The more violent the behavior, the more delegitimization occurs because more justification is needed to explain the harm done. In addition, violent acts of the delegitimized group during confrontation reinforce delegitimization because they explain the deviant and extreme behavior of the delegitimizing group. Thus, the second proposition states that *a violent conflict leads to delegitimization to justify and explain it.*

A current example of delegitimization based on far-reaching incompatibility of goals exists in the Middle East. Israeli Jews and Palestinians persistently delegitimize each other to explain the threat that each group poses to the other and to justify the harm they inflict on each other (Bar-Tal, 1988, in press a). Both groups have struggled for the same land over the present century, and today, despite attempts to bridge the irreconcilable goals, the conflict continues.

The protracted conflict intensified the perception of threat and caused mutual attempts to exclude the other group from the community of nations through delegitimization. The continuing mutual harm and violence has strengthened the delegitimization process. The Palestinians label Israeli Jews as "colonialists," "racists," "aggressors," "Nazis," "imperialists," "fascists," and "oppressors." They call them "Zionists," and consider Zionism a "colonialist movement in its inception, aggressive and expansionist in its goals, racist and segregationist in its configurations, and fascist in its means and aims" (Article 19 in the National Covenant of the Palestine Liberation Organization (PLO)—Harkabi, 1979).

The Israeli Jews, from the beginning of their encounters with Palestinians, viewed them as primitive, bandits, cruel mobs, and failed to recognize their national identity. Later, with the eruption of violence, they delegitimized Palestinians with labels such as "robbers," "criminals," "gangs," "anti-Semites," "terrorists," and "neo-Nazis." In the last decades, special efforts have been made to delegitimize members and sympathizers of the PLO, which represents the national aspirations of the Palestinians. On September 1, 1977, the Knesset of Israel adopted a resolution by a vote of 92–4 saying

> The organization called the PLO aspires, as stated in its Covenant, to destroy and exterminate the State of Israel. The murder of women and children, and terror, are part of this organization's ideology, which it is implementing in practice.

Not all conflicts begin with far-reaching incompatibility between the goals of the parties involved. Conflicts may also begin with less incompatibility that does not involve a high level of threat. Although such a situation can continue as a stalemate for a long time, this can also escalate into violent confrontation.

As Figure 2 shows, delegitimization emerges from violence because an ingroup needs to justify and explain harm perpetrated by its members, as well as explain similar acts performed by the members of the outgroup.

FIGURE 2 Conflict Model: Deterioration

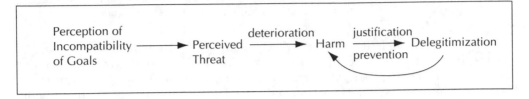

THE ETHNOCENTRIC MODEL

Delegitimization does not occur only in conflict. A group may also attribute delegitimizing labels to another group as a result of ethnocentrism. Ethnocentrism, a term introduced by Sumner (1906), denotes a tendency to accept the ingroup and reject outgroups. Delegitimization can serve this tendency. Using delegitimization, ingroup members see themselves as virtuous and superior, and the outgroup as contemptible and inferior (LeVine and Campbell, 1972).

Figure 3 illustrates how the ethnocentric tendency can foster delegitimization. Nevertheless, a necessary mediating condition for delegitimization is fear and/or contempt toward the outgroup. Subsequently, delegitimization can engender harm when the ingroup attempts to prevent the danger implied by the delegitimizing label, or to treat the outgroup inhumanely, "as deserved."

FIGURE 3 Ethnocentric Model

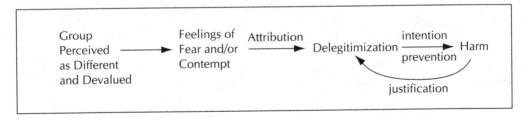

Ethnocentrism and Delegitimization

Delegitimization is used in extreme cases of ethnocentrism because it maximizes intergroup differences and totally excludes the delegitimized group from commonly accepted groups, implying a total superiority of the ingroup. It denies the humanity of the outgroup.

A mere perception of difference and devaluation does not lead necessarily to exclusion, for arousal of fear and/or contempt for the outgroup is also necessary. (See Figure 3.) The third proposition states *delegitimization is used when a group perceives another group as different and devalued, and feels fear of it and/or contempt for it.*

The more the two groups differ, the easier it is to delegitimize. The most salient differences are based on physical appearance because they enable a clear distinction and an easy identification. Thus, skin color, physiognomic features, hair color, body structure, or even dress permit unmistakable differentiation between groups. Throughout history, these differences were most often the bases for differentiation and delegitimization. People also differentiate and delegitimize on the basis of religion or ideology. In these cases, however, external identification may be impossible.

In addition to intergroup differences, devaluation is necessary for delegitimization to occur. Devaluation results from the ethnocentric tendency (Brewer and Campbell, 1976) for ingroup members to feel positive about their own group and attribute favorable characteristics to it, while feeling antipathy toward outgroups and attributing unfavorable characteristics to them. (See Adorno, Frenkel-Brunswik, Levinson, and Sanford, 1950.)

The final necessary condition, which not only evokes delegitimization but causes it, is fear and/or contempt. Fear is elicited when the different and devalued group presents a threat or a mysterious aspect. In this case, the ingroup uses delegitimization to explain their fear. (See Figure 3.) Feelings of contempt emerge when the outgroup is perceived as absolutely inferior, based on perceived cultural, economic, military, scientific, and/or political achievements.

There are two main reasons for ethnocentric delegitimization: first, the desire to completely differentiate the outgroup from the ingroup in order to exclude it from humanity; second, the desire to exploit the outgroup. These two reasons do not necessarily appear together.

A prime example of delegitimization used to rationalize exploitation is the enslavement of black people by white people. Delegitimization was, perhaps, the most important justification for slavery. Otherwise, how could the moral, deeply religious, and gallant Southerners have treated these people so inhumanely? Black people differed from whites in physical appearance, folkways and mores, religion, language, and culture, and these characteristics were also greatly devalued, so that black people were a perfect target for exploitation.

Stampp (1956) pointed to three beliefs that undergirded slavery: (a) the "all wise Creator" had designed black people for labor in the South; (b) being inferior in intellect and having a particular temperament, blacks were the natural slaves of white people; and (c) black people were barbarians who needed rigid discipline and control. These perceptions legitimized slavery in the Southern states.

The Intention and Justification of Harm

Once invoked, delegitimization can open the way to harm. Delegitimizing labels may indicate either that the delegitimized group is inhuman and therefore harming it is allowed, or that it is threatening and therefore, to prevent the danger, harm should be carried out. In addition, delegitimization may lead to intergroup conflicts. The goals of the ingroup and the outgroup may clash because of the superior and imperialistic feelings of the ingroup. Then, when harms are committed, delegitimization serves to justify inhumane treatment of the outgroup. (See Figure 3.)

The delegitimization of the American Indians facilitated cruel behavior toward them. Once they were labeled "savages," "inferior," or "animals," it was but a short distance to harm. Because "inferior" and "savage" men do not deserve human treatment, Europeans did not hesitate to destroy, to enslave, to drive them away, or to kill them.

The strengthening of delegitimization after harming others is illustrated in the development of defenses by white people to justify their enslavement of black people. Doctors, scientists, and phrenologists in the South searched for physiological differences to substantiate the assumed temperamental and intellectual differences:

> Dr. Samuel W. Cartwright of Louisiana argued that the visible difference in skin pigmentation is also extended to "the membranes, the muscles, the tendons, and . . . [to] all the fluids and secretions. Even the negro's brain and nerves, the chyle and all the humors, are tinctured with a shade of the pervading darkness," and Dr. Josiah C. Nott of Mobile proposed that negroes and whites do not belong to the same species. (Stampp, 1956, p. 8)

One striking case of ethnocentric delegitimization that led to tragic consequences is the treatment of Jews in Germany between 1933–1945.

Between 1933 and 1945, Jews in Europe were subjected to exclusion, deportation, expropriation, expulsion, pogroms, mass killings, and ultimately genocide. During 1939–1945, about six million Jews perished as a consequence of starvation, deadly epidemics, mass executions, and systematic gassing. There is little doubt that as these actions were carried out, Germans justified them with delegitimizing beliefs, which first encouraged the atrocities and later supported and reinforced them.

CONCLUSION

Delegitimization, the exclusion of an outgroup and denial of its humanity, is a phenomenon with cognitive, affective, and behavioral aspects. On the cognitive level, delegitimization organizes "reality" by providing an explanation for the perceived characteristics and behaviors of the outgroup and a prediction of potential future events. On the emotional level, delegitimization is a reaction to feelings of fear, threat, or contempt stimulated by another group. Its occurrence not only strengthens these feelings, but also may provoke new negative emotions. On the behavioral level, delegitimization leads to an array of behaviors including malevolent treatment and preventive steps to avert potential danger to the ingroup. Delegitimization is also a consequence of brutal and cruel behavior because it serves as a justification mechanism.

Delegitimization, as an extreme case of stereotyping and prejudice, is a widespread phenomenon. Two related models of the process have focused on situations that elicit delegitimization: conflict and ethnocentrism. Delegitimization occurs in conflicts that involve a perception of far-reaching, outrageous, and incompatible goals between groups and/or a high level of brutal violence. Delegitimization occurs in ethnocentrism when an outgroup is perceived as very different and is devalued.

REFERENCES

Adorno, W., E. Frenkel-Brunswik, D. J. Levinson, and R. N. Sanford (1950). *The authoritarian personality.* New York: Harper & Row.

Bar-Tal, D. (1988). "Delegitimizing relations between Israeli Jews and Palestinians: A social psychological analysis," in J. Hofman (Ed.), *Arab-Jewish relations in Israel: A quest in human understanding* (pp. 217–248). Bristol, IN: Wyndham Hall.

———— (1989a). "Delegitimization: The extreme case of stereotyping and prejudice," in D. Bar-Tal, C. Graumann, A. W. Kruglanski, and W. Stroebe (Eds.), *Stereotyping and prejudice: Changing conceptions* (pp. 169–188). New York: Springer-Verlag.

———— (1991). "Israeli-Palestinian conflict: A cognitive analysis," *International Journal of Intercultural Relations*.

Bar-Tal, D., A. W. Kruglanski, and Y. Klar, (1989). "Conflict termination: An epistemological analysis of international cases," *Political Psychology,* 10, 233–255.

Boyle, R. (1972). *The flower of the dragon: The breakdown of the U.S. Army in Vietnam.* San Francisco: Ramparts.

Brewer, M. B. and D. T. Campbell (1976). *Ethnocentrism and intergroup attitudes: East African evidence.* New York: Halsted.

LeVine, R. A. and D. T. Campbell (1972). *Ethnocentrism: Theories of conflict, ethnic attitudes and group behavior.* New York: Wiley.

Lieberman, E. J. (1964). "Threat and assurance in the conduct of conflict," in R. Fisher (Ed.), *International conflict and behavioral science* (pp. 110–122). New York: Basic Books.

Pruitt, D. G. and J. Z. Rubin (1986). *Social conflict.* New York: Random House.

Stampp, K. M. (1956). *The peculiar institution: Slavery in the ante-bellum South.* New York: Vintage.

Sumner, W. G. (1906). *Folkways.* New York: Ginn.

ARTICLE 15.2

Erin Steuter

ANTI-FEMINIST COUNTERMOVEMENTS

INTRODUCTION

Social movements are organizations—often just loose collectivities of people—that call for change in some of the ways of doing things in society. They ask us to commit to new goals, and to follow rules and regulations, that have never been successfully pursued in society. An example is the feminist movement demanding that society be changed in such a way as to

Steuter, Erin (1992). "Anti-Feminist Counter Movements," *Canadian Review of Sociology and Anthropology,* 29, 3, 1992, 288–306.

bring about gender equality. Social movements may also urge people to return to old ways of doing things that have been set aside or rejected over time. Or, they may argue that current ways of doing things should be forcefully protected against threats of change.

Social movements calling for change often prompt the emergence of "anti-movements" that try to resist these proposed changes. In this excerpt Erin Steuter describes the emergence and activities of the pro-family countermovement, and in particular the R.E.A.L. Women organization, which opposes many of the goals of the contemporary feminist movement.

A dialectical relationship exists between social movements and their anti-movements, as is evident in the case of the feminist movement and women organized against feminism. What goes on in a social movement is very much a function of what goes on in the oppositional movement; the two influence each other. This being so, we must focus our research on both forces in order to gain a full understanding of social movements and the ways they change over time.

INTRODUCTION

There is a new interest emerging within feminism in anti-feminist women. It is difficult for feminists to understand how a woman who is intelligent, articulate and strong, as many ardent anti-feminists are, can ignore the vast number of oppressive acts against women and instead fight the very changes which would end that oppression. Women's resistance to a movement which identifies itself as for women is not new. This paper examines the current role played by the pro-family movement in Canada, especially R.E.A.L. Women in opposing contemporary feminist goals.

THE PRO-FAMILY MOVEMENT IN CANADA

Margrit Eichler (1985: 1) has stated that the pro-family movement in Canada consists of a conglomeration of organizations which are united in their defence of the 'beleaguered' institution of the family.

The largest and best-known of the women's pro-family groups in Canada is R.E.A.L. Women (Realistic, Equal and Active for Life). It was founded in Toronto in 1983 and has affiliates in each province and a self reported membership of 45,000 (Erwin, 1988: 268). While the pro-family movement has male members and includes men's associations it is predominantly a movement which is made up of women. R.E.A.L. Women claims to speak for the heretofore silent majority and takes as its motto: 'Women's rights, but not at the expense of human rights'. There are also two pro-family political parties in Canada: the Christian Heritage Party, which operates at the federal level; and, in Ontario, the Family Coalition Party which won 4 per cent of the overall vote in the 1987 Ontario provincial election.

As in the case of the American pro-family movement, religion has played a key role not only in the lives of the constituents of the pro-family movement but also in the mobilization of pro-family forces in Canada. Lorna Erwin's study reveals that the pro-family network is located in the fundamentalist and Catholic churches which provide some important advantages including: a large potential support base of sympathetic, like-minded people, as well as financial support, office space, equipment and free advertising in religious publications.

Not surprisingly, the pro-family movement has its roots in the anti-abortion movement. Erwin (1988: 268) states that her national survey of 1,200 rank and file members of the pro-family movement revealed that 85 per cent of respondents involved in R.E.A.L. Women also belong to 'Right to Life' groups. Eichler (1985) notes that R.E.A.L. Women members are opposed to all forms of birth control other than abstinence and the 'rhythm method' as well as any form of sex eduction. A R.E.A.L. Women pamphlet states that 'there is probably a relation between the pill and the suppression of maternal instincts and child battering' (cited in Amer, 1987: 8). Eichler (1985: 17) notes that the movement's view of sexuality also explains their abhorrence of homosexuality, which represents 'non-marital, non-procreative sexuality in its purest form'. The movement also rejects explicitly and consistently the notion of sex equality as expressed in the *Charter of Rights and Freedoms.* Even male violence is not seen by some as sufficient grounds for marital breakup. In one of their more horrifying blaming-the-victim statements, one of their leaders has insisted that 'too often a woman is sexually attracted to a man and rushes into marriage within six months. If she had waited a couple of years, she would have realized that he was the type to beat her up' (cited in Dubinsky, 1987: 5). The pro-family movement does not support the concept of universally available, government-subsidized day care. Finally, the movement is opposed to the concept of equal pay for work of equal value and rejects the concept of affirmative action. In a speech at the first annual meeting of R.E.A.L. Women Canada, Anne de Vos argued that women are not equal to men, and hiring quotas were therefore unfair (cited in Eichler, 1985: 23).

Thus, it becomes apparent that the pro-family movement in Canada is virulently anti-feminist and in fact explicitly juxtaposes itself against feminism. Eichler cites as an example a statement made by the Alberta Federation of Women United for Families (A.F.W.U.F.),

> A.F.W.U.F. exists to provide a Pro-Family, Pro-Life voice for Alberta women. We are an alternative to the many groups which claim to represent 'the Women's Movement' and yet which are Pro-Abortion and which fail to appreciate the beauty in the career of wife and mother (Cited in Eichler, 1985: 2).

Eichler (1985: 4) states that according to the spokespeople of the 'so-called pro-family movement,'

> Feminism and feminists are not only responsible for destroying the family, but also the basic fabric of society, and the well being and health of individual women, men and children. Feminists are, according to this view, responsible for generating those problems feminists have struggled most with, such as abuse, violence, incest, rape and pornography.

Perhaps more important than these verbal attacks on feminism, is the pro-family movement's increased militancy on the issue of abortion. These groups have embarked on an intensive media campaign, lobbied government officials, and physically blocked the entrance to abortion clinics throughout Canada and the U.S. They have defied court orders banning them from the vicinity of the clinics, continued to harass women entering and exiting the clinics and have even been known to copy down the licence plate numbers of cars in the area of the clinic, acquire (by whatever means) the name and telephone number of the car owner and then make a call to the house informing the person answering the phone that someone of that address has had an abortion today!

The efforts of the pro-family movement to lobby for the supposed 'rights of the fetus' proved victorious in 1989 when provincial judges granted and upheld injunctions preventing two Canadian women from seeking abortions. The injunctions were requested by former boyfriends of the women and in both cases the judges stated that their rulings were made in order to 'protect the rights of the fetus'. The women were warned that any attempt to defy the injunctions could result in contempt-of-court charges involving a fine and/or jail sentence, and in one case the woman's boyfriend threatened to sue her for murder if she sought an abortion with or without the injunction. Both injunctions were eventually struck down by the ruling of higher courts and no charges were laid but not until after these women were exposed to public harassment and extensive delays that greatly increased the possible health risks that accompany late term abortions. The injunctions were doubly problematic in that they occurred just 18 months after the Supreme Court of Canada struck down the abortion section of the Criminal Code on the basis that the existing legislation subjected women to unnecessary and arbitrary delays when seeking an abortion through the Therapeutic Abortion Committee system.

Yet in spite of the victory that the 1988 Supreme Court ruling and the 1991 Senate veto of yet another restrictive abortion bill represented for pro-choice forces, the accessibility to abortion continues to be threatened. The U.S. Supreme Court recently challenged its own 1973 landmark ruling (Roe vs Wade) which effectively legalized abortions in the U.S. The clock was turned back on July 3, 1989 when the U.S. Supreme Court strengthened the rights of states to restrict access to abortion. While women with the access and means to go to private clinics will still be able to procure abortions, the new ruling severely restricts the accessibility of poor women by granting states the right to prohibit public hospitals from performing abortions. In both Canada and the U.S. pro-family groups have claimed credit for the courts' reversals of previous decisions. In Canada the anti-abortion group Campaign Life has three full-time lobbyists at work in Ottawa persuading politicians to support their cause. The group claims that they have 100 M.P.s solidly behind them and another 50 who are leaning in their direction.

In addition to the pro-family movement's anti-abortion lobby, groups such as R.E.A.L. Women have also been successfully pressuring the federal government for a share in the scarce resources of the Secretary of State's Women's Program. Traditionally this money has gone to organizations such as the National Action Committee on the Status of Women (N.A.C.), which is an umbrella group representing about 500 feminist-oriented women's organizations throughout the country. Of the approximately $13 million 1987 annual budget of the Women's Program, which was set up in 1973 to implement the recommendations of the Royal Commission on the Status of Women, N.A.C. receives an annual operating grant of between $400,000 and $500,000. While R.E.A.L. Women applied and were turned down three times in their request for funding, in March 1989 they received a federal grant totalling $21,212 to help fund their annual meeting in Ottawa. While their previous applications were denied because their proposals were 'not within the spirit of the objectives of the program' (spokesperson for the

Secretary of State cited in *Alberta Report* (A.R.), 1987a: 9), their organization now appears to have the formal recognition of the Secretary of State. According to the mandate of the Women's Program only projects promoting equality as defined under the *Charter of Rights* are to be funded. Yet R.E.A.L. Women have been criticized for failing to demonstrate that their activities will advance the cause of women in Canada. In response to previous funding requests, a spokesperson for the Secretary of State has said:

> We give funds to organizations whose objective is to promote the advancement of women. Most of their activities are directed against the women's movement (A.R., 1986: 17).

The pro-family movement claim to have the support of the majority of the Conservative Party caucus and have sought backing from them in their efforts to acquire Secretary of State funding. A Task Force Report on Government Spending submitted in 1986 by then-Deputy Prime Minister Erik Nielsen seems to lend some truth to this claim. 'We are particularly concerned,' it states, 'that the Women's Program as it has evolved may be addressing the needs of upwardly mobile, middle-class professional women which do not necessarily coincide with the concerns and problems of the majority of the women in Canada' (A.R., 1987a: 12). Gwen Landolt claims that Tory M.P.s tell her that 90 per cent of Conservative M.P.s are behind her. Tory M.P. Sidney Fraleigh said that 'more than 75 per cent of Conservative M.P.s, excluding cabinet ministers,' think the government should fund R.E.A.L. Women. 'There is no group I know,' he says, 'that represents the family better than R.E.A.L. Women' (A.R., 1987b: 12).

Thus, it is now possible to see the positions promoted by the pro-family movement appearing in government policy-making and in the press. Karen Dubinsky (1987b: 5) states that it is common to see R.E.A.L. Women comment included in press reports with a focus on women. She points to the C.B.C.'s 'Morningside' as an example, which began a R.E.A.L. Women panel to 'balance' their regular feminist panel. R.E.A.L. Women have frequently lobbied federal M.P.s and their 1987 'gift' of homemade muffins with pink icing earned national headlines. Dubinsky also points out the way in which the government has used the pro-family opposition as an excuse for inaction. The pro-family movement claimed a great victory when the federal government opted for a tax-credit system for childcare—a policy R.E.A.L. Women had been pressing—rather than direct funding for childcare. In addition, recent press reports have quoted several unnamed feminists in government complaining that more and more of their time is taken up justifying actions or decisions the pro-family movement might get angry about (Dubinsky, 1987a: 7).

It is very interesting to note that in recent years the pro-family movement has been more careful in its public policy statements than it had been in the past. Past president of R.E.A.L. Women Grace Petrasek's unequivocal statement at their first press conference that a woman's prime responsibility is her family, has been replaced in a recent brief with more flexible and reasonable comments, such as:

> To support homemaking as an option is not to say that we believe every woman should be in the home. We believe every woman should have the option to remain in the home if she chooses. Neither motherhood or a master's degree is for everyone (cited in Dubinsky, 1987a:5).

The social movements literature suggests that this does not represent a major ideological shift in the organization; rather it is characteristic practice of a countermovement at this stage in its relationship with the social movement.

Social movements theorists Ralph Turner and Lewis Killian (1972: 310) state that when the battle between a countermovement and social movement is not quickly won but instead results in an on-going conflict, a pattern of interdependence results. This pattern of interdependence is one in which programs, ideologies, and strategies on each side are continuously adjusted so as to deal with the programs, ideologies, and strategies on the other side and with the changes in ascendance between the two groups. They also note that the effort to defeat or wrest power from the initial movement soon begins to transcend the original program and ideology of the countermovement. The most important determinant of changes in the ideology of a countermovement is the increasing success or failure of the initial social movement. The countermovement begins to adopt popular elements of the initial movement's ideology as its own, attempting thereby to satisfy some of the discontent and also to get the opposed movement identified with only the most extreme portions of its whole program. Where movement and countermovement are of long standing, it is not infrequent for the countermovement eventually to promote everything the early adherents of the initial movement sought. As an example, Ralph Turner and Lewis Killian (1972: 312) cite the case of an American countermovement opposing socialized medicine that also lobbied against health insurance and prepayment medical plans, which they saw as a fundamental part of socialized medicine. The authors note that later these same programs were espoused by the countermovement as the free enterprise answer to socialized medicine.

In the case of the pro-family movement in both Canada and the United States, the countermovement has developed into an aggressive and politically astute organization that is successfully parrying the feminist movement. It has become an adept public relations machine that is now striving not to appear too hysterical or overly fervent, and is successfully styling itself as a viable alternative to the feminist movement. As seen in the turnabout of R.E.A.L. Women's language concerning women's place in the home, the pro-family movement have co-opted feminism's use of the term 'choice,' and used it for their own ideological agenda. Feminist Susan Cole, who debated Gwen Landolt in a university lecture series notes that it became very difficult to pin a political label on Landolt.

> Never once did she say women were naturally suited to the role of housewife and men born to run the world. She never sided with God. Her vision, at least the one she revealed on the podium, did not have any of the fundamentalist fervour we tend to associate with the right wing (Cole, 1987: 35).

Not surprisingly, feminists have reacted with a great deal of concern over the attacks by the pro-family movement and against the growing publicity that surrounds them. Norma Scarborough, former President of the Canadian Abortion Rights Action League (C.A.R.A.L.), spoke for many feminists when she said that R.E.A.L. Women represent 'a real threat to the gains we have made and to our future progress.' Ottawa lawyer and past N.A.C. President Louise Dulude stated that 'there will always be some females who will join groups like R.E.A.L. Women, which espouses traditional, conservative views. What worries us,' she says, 'is their influence with members of parliament. They are not trying to advance the status of women,' says Dulude, 'it is just one of their fronts when they say they are promoting the rights of homemakers' (cited in A.R., 1986: 11). In 1986 the annual N.A.C. convention at Carleton University in Ottawa held a workshop on the 'New Right' which observers say turned into a 90-minute debate on how to cope with the problem of R.E.A.L. Women. The workshop was the first in the history of the N.A.C. to be devoted to 'the other side,' and demonstrates the rising credibility and influence of the pro-family movement.

CONCLUSION

In light of these concerns, what can feminists learn about the nature of anti-feminist countermovements and their relationship to feminist social movements? The historical record shows that the two groups have remained firm in their commitment to their policies and strategies over time, yet in recent years, the countermovements have shown increased political and strategic acumen in their relationship with the feminist social movement, and this may in fact account for some of their recent successes.

The suffrage debate showed that the countermovement could launch a daunting challenge to the momentum of a feminist social movement by focussing public attention on perceived threats to the traditional role and status of women that feminism represented. While the American anti-suffrage movement did not succeed in their goal to prevent the vote for women, popular support for the maintenance of women's traditional roles was popular enough that Canadian maternal feminists incorporated these claims into their own policies and thus successfully avoided serious opposition to their cause. The lessons of the E.R.A. also showed that when countermovement advocates linked feminism to the disruption and decline of the family, opposition to feminism increased. Feminists have expressed concern that the countermovement forces are winning the public relations battle because of this kind of pro-family rhetoric. This has caused some feminists to consider reinforcing support for the family in their program. Others point out that this would only alienate the single, divorced and lesbian supporters of the movement. But perhaps, the most persuasive argument is made by feminists who respond that it is important not to fall into an 'us-versus-them' trap, in which the countermovement defines itself in opposition to the feminist social movement and thereby defines the image of the feminist movement. Feminists argue that there is an urgent need to clarify who and what they are and not become or accept the caricature that the other side paints. Dubinsky (1987a: 5) states that the image of feminism that these groups are trying to exploit must be challenged.

This us-versus-them trap becomes dangerous when it puts feminists in the position of being seen as being against homemakers. Feminists have noted that this is exactly the kind of affirmation that the countermovement forces need in order to claim a legitimate representation of women's interests. Eichler (1985: 5) points out that while feminists' critique of the patriarchal family may lead some to conclude that feminists are against the family, it is important to make clear that it is feminist organizations and individuals who have drawn attention to such things as unpaid work performed by women in the home. Feminists are the ones who have identified this work as socially necessary and important work that should be recognized as such. Indeed, upgrading the status of housewives, wives, and mothers have been feminist concerns from the very beginning of the movement.

Eichler states that it is important for feminists to make clear that they are critical of the patriarchal family and not all kinds of families. She states that it is time for the feminist movement to come to terms with its own ambiguity towards families by making clear distinctions between what types of families are seen as unacceptable (where there is exploitation, violence, abuse, incest, stifling of growth) and which ones are not only acceptable but indeed deserving of social support (where there is mutual caring, support, respect, commitment and growth)—irrespective of their structure and composition (Eichler, 1985: 29).

A final challenge raised by the countermovement is the strategy of modification of political rhetoric. As has been clearly illustrated by the case of R.E.A.L. Women, the countermovement has tried to occupy the 'middle ground' of the debate between themselves and feminists, thus forcing the feminist social movement into occupying the politically more marginal space. This is an important point to note, for just as the countermovement shifts and adapts its ideology and goals to the activities of the social movement, the social movement is also equally vulnerable to modification of its programs and policies. Social movements theorists have pointed out that sustained contention between a social movement and a countermovement often transforms the initial movement in the direction of moderation (Turner and Killian, 1972: 312). Feminists must be aware of this and make a conscious decision if they will in any way lessen their demands and apologize for or temper their desire for radical social change.

REFERENCES

Alberta Report (1986a). 'Feminists aim at R.E.A.L. foes,' 13(7): 11–12.

———— (1986b). 'Not REAL enough,' 13(12): 17.

———— (1987a). 'REALists versus feminists,' 14(13): 8–13.

———— (1987b) 'A Tory slap to R.E.A.L. Women,' 14(7): 12–13.

Amer, Elizabeth (1987). 'Muffin Lobby Goes Home Empty-Handed.' *This Magazine* 21(1): 7–8.

Bacchi, Carol Lee (1983). Liberation Deferred: The Ideas of the English-Canadian Suffragists 1877–1918. Toronto: University of Toronto Press.

Chafetz, Janet Saltzman and Anthony Gary Dworkin (1986). *Female Revolt*. Totowa, NJ: Rowman and Allenheld.

———— (1987). 'In the Face of Threat: Organized Antifeminism in Comparative Perspective.' *Gender and Society* 1: 33–60.

Cole, Susan G. (1987). 'On Muffins and Misogyny: R.E.A.L. Women get Real.' *This Magazine* 21(4): 33–36.

Conover, Pamela J., and Virginia Gray (1983). *Feminism and the New Right Conflict Over the American Family.* New York: Praeger.

Dubinsky, Karen (1987a). 'Really Dangerous: The Challenge of R.E.A.L. Women.' *Canadian Dimension* 21(6): 4–7.

———— (1987b). 'Forces of Opposition.' *Broadside* 8(6): 5–6.

DuBois, Ellen (1979). 'The Nineteenth-Century Woman Suffrage Movement and the Analysis of Women's Oppression,' Pp. 137–50 in Zillah Eisenstein (ed.), *Capitalist Patriarchy and the Case for Socialist Feminism.* New York: Monthly Review Press.

Eichler, Margrit (1985). 'The Pro-Family Movement: Are They For or Against Families?' C.R.I.A.W. working paper, pp. 1–37.

Erwin, Lorna K. (1988). 'What Feminists Should Know About the "Pro-Family" Movement in Canada: A Report On a Recent Survey of Rank and File Members.' Pp. 266–78 in Peta Tancred-Sheriff (ed.), *Feminist Research: Prospect and Retrospect.* Montreal: McGill-Queens University Press.

Gale, Richard (1986). 'Social Movements and the State: The Environmental Movement, Countermovements, and Government Agencies.' *Sociological Perspectives* 29:202–40.

Howard, Jeanne (1982). 'Our Own Worst Enemies: Women Opposed to Woman Suffrage.' *Journal of Sociology and Social Welfare* 9:463–74.

Killian, Lewis M. (1964). 'Social Movements.' In Robert E.L. Faris (ed.), *Handbook of Modern Sociology.* Chicago: Rand McNally and Co.

Mansbridge, Jane (1986). *Why We Lost the E.R.A.* Chicago: University of Chicago Press.

Marshall, Susan (1985). 'Ladies Against Women: Mobilization Dilemmas of Anti-feminist Movements.' *Social Problems* 32:348–62.

Marshall, Susan, and Anthony Orum (1986). 'Opposition Then and Now: Countering Feminism in the Twentieth Century.' In G. Moore and G. Spitze (eds.), *Research in Politics and Society.* Vol. 2, Greenwich, CT: JAI Press.

Mottl, Tahi L. (1980). 'The Analysis of Countermovements.' *Social Problems* 27:620–35.

Petchesky, Rosalind (1981). 'Antiabortion, Antifeminism and the Rise of the New Right.' *Feminist Studies* 7:206–46.

Turner, Ralph, and Lewis Killian (1972). *Collective Behaviour.* Englewood Cliffs, NJ: Prentice-Hall.

Wilson, John (1973). *Introduction to Social Movements.* New York: Basic Books.

Carol Andreas

PEOPLE'S KITCHENS AND RADICAL ORGANIZING IN PERU

INTRODUCTION

The People's Kitchens of Lima described by Carol Andreas are "cooperative kitchens," operated and supplied by some twenty to twenty-five households. Families contribute labour and money and receive meals in return.

These kitchens are a collective response by the urban poor to the hunger caused by severe and unpredictable economic conditions. The realization that working together can make a difference has given the people (mainly women) who manage the kitchens more self-esteem and a new sense of power. For example, women who work in the cooperatives can leave their houses without their husbands asking where they are going. This is a significant step forward for some Peruvian women.

People's Kitchens are vehicles for counter ideology in Peru and function as centres of protest by the disadvantaged. They show poor people that they can overcome the obstacles to community organization. The success of the People's Kitchens also legitimizes women's critique of public policies relating to reproductive rights, marital issues, and violence against women.

Finally, they serve as an interesting contrast to a type of "people's kitchens" we have in North America: namely, fast-food restaurants (discussed in excerpt 8.3). In both the North American and Peruvian cases not-rich women serve food to not-rich customers. But there the similarity ends. So far, Burger King is no source of communal cohesion or centre for radical politics.

There seems to be a breaking point in semi-colonial situations where unemployed or underemployed poor outnumber the employed so much that new conditions for class struggle come into existence. Distribution of goods and services becomes such an acute problem that issues of exploitation per se take second place to issues of survival or reproduction. The crisis in the family and community reaches a point of no return. Those who are excluded from regular wage work play an increasingly important role in defining political agendas, paving the way for the revolutionary transformation of daily life, not only in the production of goods and services, but also in the relations among women, men, and children in their communities.

Andreas, Carol (1989). "People's Kitchens and Radical Organizing in Lima, Peru," *Monthly Review*, November, 12–21. Copyright © 1989 by Monthly Review Inc. Reprinted by permission of Monthly Review Foundation.

Issues such as sanitation, public health, transportation, childcare, education, food, and housing are essentially reproductive concerns that are particularly acute in cities where massive migration from the countryside occurs. New community structures generated out of these concerns prepare the poor to take collective responsibility for their lives.

A decade of economic crisis in Peru has spawned many such structures. The most notable of these are the People's Kitchens established by the urban poor. At least 1500 existed in Lima alone by the end of 1988. In each of these some 20 to 25 families pool resources and work cooperatively to help maintain family members and others who may be temporarily or permanently without a stable source of income.

Because most of those involved in the administration of People's Kitchens are women, the growing importance of these organizations has given women a new source of political power, a new sense of self-esteem, and the experience of radical praxis in political struggle against the state.

BACKGROUND AND DEVELOPMENT

The People's Kitchens in Lima have their roots in the *olla común* (common pot), prepared during fiestas and community work projects in native communities in the countryside. The *olla común* is also traditionally prepared in support of striking workers in mines and factories, especially when families accompany workers on *marchas de sacrificio*, in which workers walk for days or weeks to confront government officials with their demands.

Another antecedent of the People's Kitchens can be found in the Mothers' Clubs established by the government and the Catholic Church (using surplus commodities from the United States). Some of these date from the 1950s and the 1960s. The Clubs were established to gain the political support of women and to establish a relationship of what Peruvians call *asistencialismo*—welfare clientelism. These programs "corraled" women with the enticement of individual allotments of basic food supplies such as cooking oil and flour, as well as certain sought-after items such as nylon hose, plastic kitchenware, and sewing supplies. In the 1970s, some Mothers' Clubs escaped the bounds of *asistencialismo* and became centers for grassroots organizing efforts aided by progressive nuns influenced by the Popular Church movement and feminism.

The first People's Kitchens in the *barriada* of Comas (Lima) were organized in 1979. Some women were able to utilize food allotments provided by Caritas, a Catholic relief service, even though collective utilization of Caritas' assistance was prohibited in other places by conservative church officials. Since the husbands of many women were hostile to the idea at first, and mothers were reluctant to be away from their homes for extended periods, the program operated out of individual homes. Families donated big cooking pots and other supplies, and women prepared meals for each neighborhood entirely on the basis of rotating labor. Those who were *socios*, or members of the program, came by to receive prepared food and carry it to their own homes.

Weekly meetings of those responsible for the planning, shopping, and cooking for People's Kitchens, and less frequent meetings of the entire membership, determined how much labor and/or money participants owed and on what basis free food and other assistance could be provided to the elderly, orphans, or others who couldn't contribute to the program for whatever reason. As the program expanded and became more centralized at the district level, and eventually at the city-wide level, those who planned menus were required to attend seminars in nutrition given by local health professionals. Savings were also effected, where possible, by organizing *almacenes* or food warehouses so that extra costs due to price speculation by individual businesses or market vendors could be avoided.

THE ORGANIZATION AND POLITICS OF PEOPLE'S KITCHENS

People's Kitchens are often organized in buildings or rooms that previously served some other purpose, such as a clinic or school. Several women serve as "permanent staff" for a period of time and receive four or five portions of free meals for their families each day in return for their efforts. Others pay either by the meal or in advance. In some cases, outsiders such as workers from nearby factories come to eat at the People's Kitchen regularly and pay a higher price than *socios*. On weekends the locale is used by individuals or groups to serve meals to the general public as a way of earning money for neighborhood causes or personal needs.

Young people support the People's Kitchens through volunteer labor and through helping connect the organization with other neighborhood programs such as literacy classes and political education.

While in most cases leaders of the People's Kitchens bring to these organizations years of neighborhood organizing experience and a certain amount of political sophistication, many *socios* are shy at first about speaking at meetings or taking initiative or responsibility. Over the years, such women have been transformed by their participation in the People's Kitchens. Not only have they come to be outspoken and self-confident, they are critical of those who used the Kitchens for personal profit and of those who attempted to manipulate the community's neediness to promote outside interests.

Fernando Belaúnde, who preceded Alán García as president of Peru, received U.S. government support in setting up official versions of the People's Kitchens, where inexpensive meals would be provided under government auspices. There was much fanfare over the establishment of several government-sponsored *comedores* (eating places). However, this token effort did not undermine the People's Kitchen movement but instead encouraged the women to demand government support of their own efforts.

The existence of People's Kitchens that were not subservient to the central government was important in the success of another *barriada* program, initiated by the Left Unity mayor of Lima in 1984. Alfonso Barrantes secured foreign assistance (but not from the United States) in order to provide a glass of milk daily for children and nursing mothers in the *barriadas*. Local women's committees were set up to administer the program, which was centralized in an overall Emergency Plan. This caused chaos in the *barriadas*, as many party men resisted turning local power over to the women's committees, which were thought to be insufficiently loyal to Left Unity. In many cases, committee membership overlapped with that of the *comedores populares* or People's Kitchens. When Barrantes was no longer mayor, the Glass of Milk Committees struggled to retain autonomy from the ruling APRA party and still receive powdered milk allotments.

More often than not, food assistance from the Church and/or the government has been cut off whenever People's Kitchens begin to show solidarity with other causes by sheltering political refugees or organizing marches to make demands on the government. It is this process, more than anything else, that radicalized many members. In the end, most Kitchens have been forced to "go it alone." In Villa El Salvador, 156 such *comedores* became the core of the Popular Women's Federation of the *barriada*. Nearly half the *socios* were the sole support of their families (that is, single mothers). The People's Kitchens helped free these women to work outside their homes.

In 1985, when the female-based organizations of Villa El Salvador and other *barriadas* of Lima attempted to get official recognition from the city-wide Federation of New Towns (*barriadas*), organized primarily by the Left Unity electoral coalition, they were told to go home.[1] The women persisted, however, and female political party members eventually found it necessary to work within the People's Kitchens in order to legitimize themselves as political leaders. The myriad of political parties of the left attempting to win support among the *socios* of the People's Kitchens gave rise to political debates about the function of these Kitchens beyond the provision of low-cost food for the families who benefited from them. Thus, the process of centralization further radicalized some of the women who were involved in organizing People's Kitchens, even as it gave rise to internal conflicts.

By 1987, the People's Kitchens were experiencing a leadership crisis. Centralization of the movement was resulting in disputes over who were the legitimate representatives of the coordinating bodies. Some were accused of being "terrorists" (in this case, Shining Path guerrillas). Others were accused of being conciliatory with APRA. Women sympathetic to Shining Path had been slow to involve themselves in the People's Kitchen movement. However, as Church and government participation became marginal or nonexistent within the movement, women who had been influenced by Shining Path began to take part in the organizations and to work to redirect them away from any remaining forms of *asistencialismo*.

Feminists were active in seeing the People's Kitchen movement through its initial political crises. Their involvement has been most effective when feminists are *pobladores* themselves, which is not as unusual in Peru today as it would have been even six or eight years ago. Feminists began to see the People's Kitchen movement as a potential springboard for women's agendas, ranging from a critique of public policies relating to reproductive rights, marital issues, and issues of violence toward women, to the legitimizing of collective domestic work.

In August 1988, the Peruvian government reinitiated a temporary work program that had been forced to close down earlier because of scandalous misappropriation of funds. Critics had also charged that workers were used to break unions and to engage in activities specifically in support of APRA. The recreated temporary work program is modeled after OFASA, a work-relief program for *barriada* women administered by the Seventh-Day Adventist Church. (As in the case of Caritas, this program enjoys the support of the U.S. government.) According to grassroots leaders in the *barriadas*, these programs are aimed primarily at disrupting non-governmental programs such as the People's Kitchen movement. Over 80 percent of those employed by the government work programs are female. Because these women work mainly cleaning up garbage dumps in the *barriadas*, they are unusually susceptible to bacterial infections. *Socios* of the Kitchens complain that by the time women have finished working in government programs they are so sick they can't help with the work in the *comedores populares*, yet are in need of the services these provide.

During the past two years the coordinating bodies of the People's Kitchens, Glass of Milk Committees, and Mothers' Clubs in Lima have waged periodic campaigns to demand that their programs be financed, at least in part, directly from government coffers. The demands were at first met with defiance and repression on the part of the government. However, a new National Program for Food Assistance has been implemented. It is based in part on the issuance of food stamps for the "truly needy." Thousands of other women have also been attracted to newly-established *comedores* sponsored directly by APRA, and *apristas* have taken over many *comedores* which used to be considered autonomous.

Electoral politics in 1989 has turned many People's Kitchens into centers for the organization of conservative forces. Welfare clientelism is rampant. But other forces are also at work.

As the food crisis continues in the cities, some urban migrants are returning to rural areas. Noncommercial avenues of food distribution and the "requisitioning" of trucks carrying food products to urban markets are reportedly increasing.

Organizations born in the *barriadas* are more than a reflection of workplace struggles. I think it is more useful to view them as direct expressions of popular discontent over issues of reproduction rather than production. These expressions bring into the political arena new social forces, predominantly female rather than male, and a new kind of revolutionary vision, not necessarily less radical than that of the urban work force.

It has often been assumed that the primary locus for revolutionary change is at the point of production, among those who work for wages in strategic industries. Political economists have also tended to take as given an ever-increasing demand for labor in an expanding economy.

The inexorable expansion of industry provides the main basis for working-class political power, even as periodic recessions are necessary for economic readjustment in capitalist societies. But conditions in debt-ridden "developing" countries are quite different. While workers on strike are a constant threat to stability, both government repression and efforts at "pacification" are often centered in working-class neighborhoods rather than at the workplace. In the neighborhoods, popular organization is facilitated by geographic concentration of the poor. Students, housewives, and unemployed workers are more active politically on a regular basis than are those employed in urban industries. The interests of these groups are also identified more closely with the interests of the rural poor. This is especially true in countries like Peru, where recent arrivals to the city are discriminated against as Indians. All these factors are important in assessing the significance of People's Kitchens in Peru and elsewhere.

It should be emphasized that the development of People's Kitchens in Peru has not been "spontaneous." Obstacles encountered by the women involved—from husbands, from political parties of both the left and the right, and even from within their own ranks as charges of opportunism and betrayal threatened to destroy their movement—have been at times overwhelming. However, many leaders have been able to resist cooptation and repression. Where women have succumbed to external or internal pressures, or retired from active involvement, often others have emerged to replace them.

CONCLUSION

In Peru, as People's Kitchens have assumed an ever more visible role in maintaining the physical well-being and promoting the collective strength of *pobladores*, the recognition of women's importance as political actors has been immeasurably advanced. And the possibility of a democratically-based revolution encompassing the larger concerns of families in their homes and communities as well as workers in the wage economy has also come into clearer focus.

ENDNOTES

[1] Cecelia Blondet, *Muchas Vidas Construyendo una Identidad: Mujeres Pobladoras de un Barrio Limeño*, Documento de Trabajo No. 9 (Lima: Instituto de Estudios Peruanos (IEP), January, 1986), p. 61.

QUESTIONS

DISCUSSION QUESTIONS
1. Compare "dominant ideologies" and "counter ideologies" using examples chosen from the excerpts in this section. Can you find any other examples in earlier sections?
2. By what means do you suppose counter-ideologies sometimes succeed in replacing dominant ideologies? Can you think of any examples?
3. Looking back to the material in Section 1, show how ideologies are aspects of "culture," but not identical to culture. What are the main differences between "culture" and "ideology"? Discuss, using specific examples.
4. Define and discuss "delegitimization," following Bar-Tal's use of the term. Under what conditions might this strategy be used against alien life forms from outer space, and under what conditions might it not be used?

DATA COLLECTION EXERCISES
1. Using newspaper articles, identify some particular aspect of "counter ideology" in society and indicate how the counter ideology calls for changes from existing ways of doing

things. Show how the ideology is presented in the articles; for example, is the treatment by the newspaper a fair and balanced one? Are any of the main ideas distorted in the articles?

2. Do the same exercise as in question 1, but for a "dominant ideology." Indicate how these ideas, and newspaper presentations of them, help to support existing social arrangements.

3. Interview some of the administrators of any organization serving the poor in your community or region. Identify how the organization "empowers" the poor, if it does. Indicate ways of increasing this empowerment.

4. Choose any social movement—countermovement or otherwise—and obtain some of its printed material for public circulation. Describe the ideological positions that are conveyed in this material.

WRITING EXERCISES

1. "People's kitchens" are not at all common in Canada and the United States. Write a brief (500-word) essay speculating on the reasons why this form of social organization has not developed in North America.

2. "Sustained contention between a social movement and a counter-movement often transforms the initial movement in the direction of moderation." Write a 500-word essay discussing this observation.

3. Choose any disadvantaged group in your society (e.g., the poor or lower classes, women, a minority racial or ethnic group, or the aged). Write a 500-word essay on whether or not this group has been "delegitimized."

4. Choose a political protest movement from Canada or elsewhere. In a 500-word essay describe the social sources or explanations for this movement.

SUGGESTED READINGS

1. Abercrombie, Nicholas, Stephen Hill, and Bryan S. Turner (1980). *The Dominant Ideology Thesis*. London: Allen and Unwin. A detailed analysis of theories of the role of ideology in supporting social inequalities and in promoting social change.

2. Curtis, James, Edward Grabb and Neil Guppy, eds. (1993). *Social Inequality in Canada: Patterns, Problems and Policies*, Second Edition. Scarborough: Prentice-Hall. Contains a series of articles that show how patterns of social inequality are rooted in ideological supports (including the law), and how changes in an egalitarian direction have usually required political struggles between haves and have-nots.

3. Marchak, Patricia M. (1988). *Ideological Perspectives on Canada*, Third Edition. Toronto: McGraw-Hill Ryerson. Provides discussions of various ideologies in Canada and their relation to elites, class protests, and nationalism.

SECTION 16   SOCIAL CHANGE

Introduction

As the twentieth century wanes, and for the first time in history, social change has become a conspicuous fact of life all around the world. Everywhere, it seems, the barriers to change are crumbling, albeit at differing rates and in differing ways and in response to differing pressures. Because social change is so widespread (and so important) sociologists have taken pains to try to understand it.

Social change obviously has many dimensions—ideological, cultural, economic, technological, political, and demographic. So one question sociologists are interested in is this: how do these different dimensions interact with one another? How, for example, does technological change influence economic change? How does ideological change affect culture, and vice versa? How do cultural changes lead to demographic changes? And so on.

The fact that these different aspects of social change are interrelated raises a tantalizing possibility in the minds of many would-be social reformers—that social change can be consciously manipulated by altering just a few "key" characteristics of the social structure. If change occurs in a chain reaction, then maybe big improvements can be sparked by relatively small, initial efforts.

INITIATING SOCIAL CHANGE

This kind of thinking prompted the American economist W. I. Rostow to theorize in 1960 that economic development consists of "five stages of growth." These are a traditional stage, followed by a pre-takeoff stage, a take-off stage, a maturing stage, and finally a stage of high mass consumption. Western societies such as Canada are in the last stage.

Rostow's advice was clear: to achieve affluence, first establish the pre-conditions necessary for economic take-off and then let economic forces do the rest. Part of the appeal of theories like Rostow's was that they made the task of development seem suddenly less daunting. Such optimism fit the can-do mood of 1960, which was a time when many Third World countries were just embarking on their independence. If Rostow was right it would no longer be necessary to contemplate closing the huge gap between affluent societies and poor ones overnight. The immediate task was just to get the process started in order to reach the next stage of growth. And once take-off had occurred (at a relatively low level of affluence) eventual success (i.e. a high consumption economy) was only a matter of time.

Theories such as Rostow's that look for the keys, the catalysts, or the levers of social change abound, but there is little consensus on whether a single prescription for producing social change in all (or most) societies even exists. Is the engine of economic growth started by different types of keys in different types of societies, or do all

economies respond pretty much alike to the same treatment? This debate often sur-
faces when, for example, the International Monetary Fund sends its experts in to
advise a financially strapped nation on how to get its finances back in order. The IMF
experts prescribe economic remedies that have worked elsewhere, while the host
countries seek more individualized remedies that are "sensitive to local conditions."

Nathan Keyfitz's excerpt in this section lends some support to the idea that
there are keys to social change that work essentially the same way everywhere. He
argues that one key factor in economic development is the universal desire for
more and more, better and better material possessions. Keyfitz believes that once
people anywhere have had even a little taste of middle class affluence, they will
undoubtedly hunger for more and ever more. And so this endless desire for more
material wealth becomes the fuel that drives an economy, transforming it from a
traditional society to a modern, mass consumption society.

Since material affluence is universally sought, the best indicator of development (or progress) in theories like Keyfitz's is the amount of material wealth
already amassed. The more cars, stereos, telephones, and refrigerators, the further
along the development process a society has moved. There is a problem though.

CONTROLLING SOCIAL CHANGE

The desire for material things is a key to stimulating economic growth, but it is not,
according to Keyfitz, an easily manipulated key. Once it is turned unexpected
things can happen. Sometimes, for example, the desire for material goods generates
unrealistic attitudes and an impatience and greed that are not conducive to sound
economic decision-making. The desire for middle class affluence is only the key
that turns on the economic engine. It doesn't guarantee that the economy will be
driven in the right direction.

Willem Vanderburg's excerpt in this section illustrates another reason why
social change is often difficult to direct and control. Vanderburg discusses how a
technical problem-solving approach has been increasingly applied to ever more
areas of daily life in modern societies. The technicization phenomenon introduces
two different forms of uncertainty into social change. On the one hand, the timing
of social change based on technical breakthroughs is always unpredictable. No one
can impose a timetable on the discovery of a cure for some disease, or the overcoming of some technical hurdle. It just happens when and if the technical experts
figure out how to make it happen.

Secondly, Vanderburg suggests that technicization has become a major social
force with deep historical roots. It is a familiar, pervasive, accepted, firmly established and often welcome part of modern life. It has far exceeded mere manufacturing applications and now influences even such personal decisions as finding
another person to date. This raises the issue of "technological determinism," which
is the idea that technologically driven change can gather such momentum that it
becomes irresistible and essentially uncontrollable. In short, the worry is that social
change can become a juggernaut without a steering wheel, without brakes, and
whose gas pedal is stuck to the floor.

Finding Brakes and Steering Wheels

There is also a range of theories among those who believe that we can control the speed and direction of social change. If one is optimistic about reason and the power of ideas, then the way to control social change is by making one's ideas known in the political and cultural arenas. Others think that the very forces that fuel social change also enhance our ability to control it. They argue, for example, that the economic growth and technological innovation that causes pollution also creates the wealth and know-how that are able to clean it up.

Still others believe that even if social change can't be controlled it will sooner or later run out of gas on its own. Marxists, for example, argue that capitalism is inherently unsustainable because it will gradually turn the vast majority of people into impoverished workers who will have no stake in, or love for, capitalism. And many environmentalists believe that the current rate of the world's economic and population growth can't be sustained because the world's resources are finite.

As we saw in the introduction to Section 13, the original pessimistic environmentalist may have been Thomas Malthus. In his 1798 book *The Principles of Population* he argued that human populations react to resources much like other kinds of animal populations do. That is, human population levels will keep rising unless nature stops them from doing so through, say, starvation or disease. The result is that human populations are doomed to periodically exceed their resources and suffer a mass die-off.

Two hundred years later the jury is still out on the validity of Malthus' theory. On the one hand, scientific advances have so far kept at bay any imminent mass die-off. But on the other hand, humanity has used this increased control over nature to do exactly what Malthus predicted we would do. We've increased our numbers more than sixfold since his day, and our numbers are still rising rapidly.

The result is that environmentalists remain nervous about the press of human populations on their environments. Ndalahwa Faustin Madulu's excerpt in this section provides a front-line glimpse of how population growth is leading to environmental degradation in Tanzania.

Nathan Keyfitz

DEVELOPMENT AND THE ELIMINATION OF POVERTY

INTRODUCTION

The consumer society is often criticized for being wasteful and harmful to the environment and for promoting shallow, materialistic values. Such criticisms are often heard in affluent Western societies. But how does consumerism look to people living in poorer countries?

According to Nathan Keyfitz, the consumer society still looks pretty appealing to them. Keyfitz argues that the desire for a middle class lifestyle and standard of living is becoming universal. People everywhere, he says, want cars, refrigerators, and the other comforts associated with affluence. This desire for material possessions has begun to fuel economic development. To get the money to buy such goods, people work harder or borrow money. Both activities stimulate the economy and expand the middle class. The bigger the middle class gets, the more entrenched middle class values become.

Keyfitz thinks that people's desire for a middle class lifestyle and standard of living can also have counter-productive consequences. For example, the civil service might be expanded simply to increase the supply of desirable white-collar jobs. But those jobs aren't productive and are therefore a drain on the public purse. Similarly, the middle class tends to be urban and to have little interest in agriculture or rural development. So the agricultural sector might suffer from neglect if middle class priorities start unduly influencing government policies.

What one sometimes forgets is that Canada went through the very same process of urbanization and rural migration earlier in this century.

The influence of the middle class in determining the course and type of development is strong even in those countries in which there is full democracy and in which the peasants are by far the largest part of the electorate.

The middle class has access to education and can understand the issues, is aware of its interests and able to act politically to further them. Schooling and influence enable it to pass its status to its young, and so it tends to be hereditary. It recruits from the peasantry through the process of urbanization, in highly selective fashion. Its initial task is to break the rural landholding class; once that is accomplished its influence is decisive, for the dispersed, uneducated peasantry are no match for it.

Keyfitz, Nathan (1982). "Development and the Elimination of Poverty," *Economic Development and Cultural Change*, 30(3), 649–670. Reprinted by permission of the University of Chicago Press and Nathan Keyfitz.

DIFFUSION OF THE MODERN CULTURE

Development may be seen as the diffusion of a certain culture and the dominance of a new class that carries that culture. This article is complementary to, rather than inconsistent with, the view of development as rising average income per head; it attempts to place the economics of development in a social and cultural framework.

THE MODERN WAY OF LIFE

The middle-class style has been taught to the Third World by the United States and Europe. It consists of centrally heated and cooled homes equipped with television sets and refrigerators, transport by automobile, and procurement of foodstuffs and other supplies in self-service supermarkets. It is found typically in cities with paved streets, the countryside between those cities being laced with a network of paved roads and another network of air transport. Literacy is essential to it, and the daily press and monthly magazines are conspicuous, along with television. The content of its media has remarkable similarity worldwide: local, national, and world politics; urban crime; and the cost of living.

Economists have written on one aspect of this modern conception of how to live and work, calling it the demonstration effect. People learn from films and other media to want a level of consumption that is for the moment beyond the capacity of their national productive apparatus to support. Such wishes cause premature spending and impedes the saving and investment that would bring such benefits within the scope of national production and trade. But in fact the demonstration effect has not had a large impact on economics. It should be taken seriously, both in its negative aspects, and positively as the motor of development.

MEASURING THE POOR AND THE MIDDLE CLASS

In the United States it is easier to measure poverty and take the middle class as a residual; in other countries it is on the whole easier to measure the middle class, the minority, and take the poor as the residual.

The U.S. Department of Agriculture designed a 1961 Economy Food Plan that forms the basis for the calculation of poverty income thresholds, recognizing family size, sex, and age of the family head, number of children under 18, and farm-nonfarm residence. Annual adjustments are made on the basis of the Consumer Price Index, but the consumption levels continue to be those established for the base year 1963.[1] The number of families that fall below the poverty line in the United States was just under 40 million in the late 1950s, and had dropped to 25 million by 1977.[2]

The figures, extrapolated to 1980, show 24 million poor, 196 million middle class, for a total population of 220 million. Our task is to find how this can be extended to the world.

The middle class can be traced broadly through statistics of ownership of certain artifacts. An automobile is one indicator, and we have statistics of automobile ownership for 75 countries. Counting two persons per automobile, the American standard, is a first approximation.

The *United Nations Statistical Yearbook* gives 271,620,000 passenger vehicles in the world in 1976, of which 109,003,000 were in the United States. Using this ratio to bring the U.S. middle class of 196 million to a world total gives us 196 x 271,620/109,003 = 488 million. But because automobiles are less used elsewhere by people who could afford them than they are in the United States, this is a low figure. It is also low insofar as families elsewhere are larger than in the United States. A figure of 2.5 or 3 middle-class persons per vehicle would bring us closer.

Energy consumed is one indicator. The total in million tons of coal equivalent for the world in 1976 was 8,318, and for the United States it was 2,485.[3] This ratio would bring us to 656 million middle-class people in the world. Better than automobiles, but still probably too low; the American burns more energy than middle-class people elsewhere.

The problem is distribution is not the same in all countries and is difficult to measure. We note the total for the market economies of the world in 1976 at 5,426 billion, and the United States in that year at 1,695 billion.[4] The ratio used crudely gives us 627 million people above the poverty line. To it would have to be added the middle class in nonmarket economies—on the order of 150 million. (The United Nations calculates for the centrally planned a weight of 0.196 in the world economy.)[5]

On the basis of such evidence, the number of middle class in the world in 1980 might be 700–800 million.

A similar calculation gives 200 million for the middle class of 1950. The entry of Europe and Japan, plus some progress in the Third World, brought the total to 800 million by 1980.[6]

PRODUCTION

Being middle class is not a matter of consumption alone; certain kinds of work are middle class and other kinds are not. Office work at a salary that permits owning a car and an adequately equipped house is the ideal; if the salary does not permit buying a car, then obtaining one as a perquisite of office will do. The boundary of the middle class does not coincide with that of nonmanual workers. Wages converge so that all can aspire to middle-class style.

Middle-class workers seek to avoid the hazards of entrepreneurship. Much better is the job of senior administrator, working according to fixed rules within a framework of law, with no personal capital at stake. Next in desirability to a job in government, and paying better, is being hired by a multinational corporation. The multinationals have access nearly everywhere, partly because their kind of operation is understandable and gratifying.

The entry of such cultural preferences into the work world creates a difficulty. The kind of work people like to do, and which they get jobs doing, diverges from the kind of work that produces the goods on which collectively they want to spend their salaries. The government employee may be engaged in the collection of taxes, or the organization of cooperatives, or the country's foreign policy. These activities make little contribution to producing the groceries he seeks to buy at the supermarket or the plumbing fixtures for his new house.

RELIEF OF POVERTY VERSUS A NEW CULTURE

Growth in the form of an expanding middle class is consistent with an increasing number of poor. Of course the middle-class way by itself is relief of poverty for some. Yet this relief of poverty seems incidental. For if adequate food and clothing, basic medical services, and literacy were the main objectives of development it would go on in a very different way from that now pursued. Brazil's national income per capita of $1,400 could provide these amenities for every one of its inhabitants. Yet in fact, the majority of its inhabitants lack these altogether, while others have them and much more. After 30 years of formal development effort in 75 countries, we can infer the objective of the process from actual observation. As much as anything it is the diffusion of the artifacts that support a certain way of life, and in a poor country only a minority can benefit.

While the particular culture of the middle class belongs to the second half of the twentieth century, the idea of an urban industrial group with incomes far higher than their rural contemporaries goes back much farther. Adam Smith saw development as taking place in the measure in which material capital accumulated in cities. With each increment of city capital some jobs would be created. A new factory or mill could offer wages high enough to attract people from the countryside. Until the call to city employment came, the peasant would remain in his ancestral village.

INCENTIVES TO RURAL-URBAN MIGRATION

Whatever expands city facilities, or lowers the price of foodstuffs, increases the size of the city. We can even suggest a positive feedback that results from legislation and administrative action. The price of rice is, in many countries, fixed well below the world market, and a law requires peasants to deliver part of their crop at this price. Officials go into the countryside to execute the procurement. The unpleasantness and actual loss contribute to causing some peasants to leave and go to the city. That increases the need for foodstuffs in the city, so the procurement activity is intensified.

One might think there would be an equilibrium point in migration. When enough have left, the living should be equal to what migrants could get by going to the city, and at that point migration should stop. One reason it does not, as Alfred Marshall pointed out (quoted by Lipton), is that there is selection on who comes to the city; on the whole those who come are better educated, and have more initiative.[7] Thus their departure does not make things better but worse.

We can imagine policies that would discourage internal migration. For one, taxes to provide urban services could be levied on urban real estate rather than coming out of the national budget. Inputs to agriculture could be subsidized. An effect similar to subsidies would be obtained by better prices for farm outputs.

The elite cannot make the city better for themselves without making it better for the newcomers, and so encouraging further newcomers. They could forcibly prevent migration, or expel existing migrants, and this has been tried in Moscow, Jakarta, and elsewhere, but by and large has not been successful.

The masses in the capital city are physically close enough to the government to communicate their wishes, as those of Cairo did two years ago when they forced the government to cancel its increase of food prices. Such an increase would have helped the peasant and discouraged migration, but the political forces did not permit it. Governments cannot always resist the reasonable demands of the protected segment of the labor force for decent places to live. Government often builds houses with funds that could have gone to rural investment.

Local transport within the city is often government run. The costs of the buses it imports, and the fares it charges, are public matters, and very much the business of administrators and legislators. They do not always set the fares high enough for even their low-cost imported buses, and when the bus operations make a loss it is covered from general revenues, which means in some part from the rural sector.

Other public utilities run by government at a loss even more clearly favor the middle class. Electricity is largely used by them. The view has been that industry needs protection more than agriculture, that manufactured exports are better than farm exports, that agriculture's decreasing returns justify removing resources to help industries giving increasing returns.

The need for food supplies to permit the town people to engage in manufacturing was accepted by all the classics: thus Smith says, "it is the surplus produce of the country only, or what is over and above the maintenance of the cultivators, that constitutes the subsistence of the town, which can therefore increase only with the increase of the surplus produce."[8]

Holding the price of grain down is not the way to increase the supply. Investment in agriculture is called for. Szcaepanik shows that the gross marginal capital/output ratios for 1960–65 are much higher for nonagricultural than for agricultural investment. On the whole the capital required to produce a given amount of income is more than double in industry what it is in agriculture.

Some of these points are now being recognized, and efforts are being made on behalf of agricultural output. The Mexican government is investing in modernization and stressing the use of machinery. The man with the bullock is to be replaced by a tractor operator, with backing by soil chemists, agronomists, irrigation specialists, and bankers ready to advance rural credit. All this will indeed provide employment, but for specialists and not for the masses in the countryside. Indeed, it could accelerate the move to the city.

Here much depends on the patterns of consumption and residence of the new classes in the rural areas. If the tractor operator and the soil chemist live in the city and commute to the rural area, or if they live in the village but use their new incomes on city goods, then unemployment in the countryside will be greater than ever, and cityward migration will continue and even accelerate.

In few fields does the middle-class urban bias reveal itself as clearly as in education. Most schools above the primary level are in cities, and the ordinary peasant's children stand little chance of attending. The disparity in numbers of secondary schools between rural and urban areas is matched by some disparity in the quality of instruction. Moreover, the primary schools that are now attended at least long enough for most peasant children to learn to read and write, have little to do with peasant life. Rather than being planned to make better farmers, they serve as a selection device, by which ability is discovered and sent to secondary school, usually in the city.

EXPLANATION RATHER THAN POLICY GUIDANCE

The present paper stands back from development and refrains from offering policy advice, at the same time that it tries to look at it from a point of view of the citizen undergoing the process. The citizen of poor countries sees development as the advent of goods that make possible a modern style of life. The goods are above all symbols that one has attained a certain status.

This wish for middle-class status is an engine of development—it can induce acceptance of the hard work and abstinence that development requires. Yet it is not a readily manipulated policy variable, like a tariff or the rate of interest. The object of this paper is not to reveal some easy way by which development can be brought about but to make it look as difficult on paper as it is in reality. I have tried to show why excellent policy advice is disregarded. Thus, reaching for middle-class status is an explanatory rather than a policy variable. It tells us why government has grown, why cities have expanded, why poor countries aim to produce automobiles rather than bicycles, why the import of consumption goods is everywhere so large an element in the balance of payments.

Within each of the poor countries is an expanding middle-class enclave. We need to observe more closely the social mechanisms that cause the spread of the middle class to take precedence over the alleviation of poverty.

ENDNOTES

[1]   U.S. Bureau of the Census, *Statistical Abstract* (Washington, D.C.: Government Printing Office, 1978), p. 438.

[2]   Ibid., p. 465.

[3]   United Nations, *United Nations Statistical Handbook* (New York: United Nations Department of International Economic and Social Affairs, 1978), p. 389.

[4]   Ibid., p. 748.

[5]   Ibid., p. 10.

[6]   Ibid.

[7]   Michael Lipton, *Why Poor People Stay Poor: Urban Bias in World Development* (Cambridge, Mass.: Harvard University Press, 1977), p. 376.

[8]   Lipton, p. 94.

Willem Vanderburg

THE TECHNICIZATION
OF SOCIETY

INTRODUCTION

Many of the social effects of technological innovation are obvious. It's hard to miss the dramatic impact made on people's lives by the introduction of specific inventions such as electric lights, telephones, automobiles, televisions, computers, or wonder drugs. But the impact of these individual gadgets and gizmos tell only part of the story.

Constant and continual social change due to technological innovation has also had a cumulative effect on our cultural values and preferences. We have come to accept, expect, and want "new and improved" products and ways of doing things in virtually every aspect of our lives. We actively seek such improvements through what Willem Vanderburg calls "the technicization of society." Technicization involves applying analytic reasoning to the design of experimental techniques for everything from paint manufacturing to romantic matchmaking.

In embracing technicization we tacitly embrace the idea of progress through technology and other related values. For example, we may learn to value "reasonable facsimiles" and "virtual realities" and to devalue real things. We may come to value quick convenience over time-consuming self-reliance. And we may learn to mistrust our own amateurish thoughts and feelings and to increasingly defer to professional experts in more and more areas of our own lives.

We may also resist these impulses. But as Vanderburg shows, technicization already has a long history behind it—and it's far from over. (For a discussion of related themes in health care, see excerpt 12.3 on the practice of medicine.)

Until the late nineteenth century, the development and application of techniques was largely empirical. They were passed on from one generation to the next by apprenticeship arrangements. Formal education played an almost insignificant role until the end of the nineteenth century. Take technology. The increasing precision and complexity of machines, as well as the growing pressure from competition to eliminate inefficiency, required a technological knowledge base that was scientifically founded.

This was the beginning of a transformation of the way technological knowledge is transmitted, developed and applied. There is a discontinuity between knowledge acquired from experience and knowledge acquired by formal educa-

Vanderburg, Willem H. (1986). "The Technicization of Society," from *The Social World*, First Edition, chapter 23. Toronto: McGraw-Hill Ryerson.

tion. No amount of experience can lead to a knowledge of the applied sciences. These can only be learned in the classroom. As a result, knowers and doers are more and more frequently different people.

Consider a welder with many years of experience erecting high-rise buildings. One day, as the crane is bringing up another beam for the twenty-sixth floor structure, the welder may alert the crane operator and the foreman by saying, "I've never seen such a light beam being used on this large a span. Are you sure we aren't making a mistake?" The foreman may then call the engineer to check the calculations. On the basis of experience, the welder has obtained a knowledge of the strength of beams. Yet he will never learn to calculate the strength of a beam by means of stress analysis, because this is not learned from experience but from books or classroom instruction.

The changes in the knowledge base of technology were accompanied by changes in other areas. A greater precision of one technique necessitates similar developments in other techniques. By the end of World War II, changes in the technical knowledge base had necessitated the restructuring of a variety of institutions in society. Galbraith (1978) has examined the restructuring of large corporations after World War II. We will briefly reinterpret his findings.

At the core of the large, modern corporation, we find what Galbraith has called its *technostructure*, essentially the brain of the enterprise, in which most activities are based on knowledge acquired by the formal education of its members. Together they have an expertise in the techniques necessary for running the corporation. Since the expertise of each member of the technostructure is highly specialized, each task must be so subdivided that every part is coterminous with a particular body of specialized technical knowledge.

The technostructure is surrounded by the body of the corporation, in which most tasks can be performed without advanced formal education. In these tasks, knowledge acquired from experience plays an essential role.

The gradual restructuring of large corporations during the second half of the twentieth century was, therefore, in part a response to the emergence of the new technical knowledge base. Without this restructuring, large corporations would not be able to take advantage of the latest developments in the sciences. All corporate operations became extremely efficient. The development of any new product, for example, now required the collaboration of a great many people with complementary types of expertise relevant to the task. Since these people must be paid, provided with support staff, have offices and so on, the capital investment needed to bring any new product to market skyrocketed. A competitively priced product could be produced only if this investment could be written off over a large number of units manufactured. In other words, restructuring the technical knowledge base necessitated a further acceleration in the trend toward mass production. This trend, in turn, required highly specialized production facilities.

All these factors greatly increased the risk involved in developing a new product. During the time it took to develop a new product and prepare the production facilities, market conditions could change. If sales fell far below the projected figures, however, the investment in the new product could not be transferred to another product. In order to protect themselves from such risks, companies diversified, so that the losses in one division could be offset by profits in another.

The corporations that exploited the new technical base, therefore, required a much greater concentration of capital than did the entrepreneurial firms of the nineteenth century. This made it virtually impossible for a family or a small group of shareholders to own these new firms. A modern corporation is usually owned by a large number of shareholders, who each own only a small part of the corporation. Shareholders tend to approve the plans put forward and prepared by the technostructure, which essentially controls the operation of the firm. The greatly weakened link between ownership and control also affects the economic behavior of the large corporation, whose goals are now much more complex than a simple profit maximization. Its relationship with the market also undergoes a profound transformation. No longer can it rely on the market to supply the specialized materials and machines that may be unique to one of its products. On the output side, the corporation attempts to manage consumer demand through a variety of techniques, including advertising. It relies on the state to create the educational institutions necessary to graduate specialists for its technostructure.

The development of the new technical knowledge base required an expansion in the role of the state. It alone could create the educational system necessary to produce specialists in the various areas of technical expertise.

To provide the large corporation with a stable economic environment in which it could plan new products, the state had to regulate the economy. It did so by creating a large public sector that it expanded or contracted to offset the fluctuations in the private sector. To ensure the development of the new technical knowledge base, the state also became involved in scientific and technical research. To efficiently carry out its new tasks, as well as to improve its effectiveness in more traditional domains, the state began to depend on experts. They brought their expertise to bear on these tasks, using patterns of collaboration very similar to the ones found in the technostructures of large corporations.

Developing the new technical knowledge base and the techniques derived from it did not only affect large corporations and the state, however. A growing number of activities in society were increasingly restructured in accordance with the latest technical knowledge. In fact, all the characteristics of "postindustrialism" derive from the proliferation of techniques throughout society.

THE PHENOMENON OF TECHNIQUE[1]

One thing that sets modern societies apart from all others is that a wide range of activities is no longer based on custom or tradition grounded in a culture. They systematically research virtually every sphere of human activity in order to render it more effective, rational and efficient or to eliminate problems. They do this on the assumption that life can be improved by making all facets of our existence more efficient. Research takes the form of what we will call the *technical operation,* which is constituted of four stages.

The first stage involves studying some area of human life for a particular purpose. The study's results are used next to build a model that can range from a precise mathematical theory to a theory that is largely qualitative. In the third stage, the model is examined to determine what happens when its parameters are altered, in order to discover when it functions optimally. The technical operation concludes with the reorganization of the area of human life studied originally, to achieve the highest efficiency and rationality demonstrated to be possible by the model. By this pattern modern societies seek to improve the productivity of a plant, the running of a hospital, the performance of a hockey team, and even the satisfaction derived from a sexual relationship. As a result, the technical operation permeates the fabric of technologies or techniques.

Increasingly in modern societies, almost every sphere of human activity is organized on the basis of techniques that ensure that everything is done as effectively as possible. Technology is only one part of the phenomenon of technique.

The reason the "industrially advanced" nations began to generate a mass of information at a certain point is now evident. When techniques began to replace tradition as the basis of human activities, much information was generated. New technologies or techniques became necessary to deal with the mass of information. The computer and associated techniques were developed to meet this challenge and immediately found a wide range of applications. This in turn accelerated the development described above.

The information economy, the proliferation of theoretical services, the rise of new intellectual techniques, the emergence of a new class of technical experts, the growth of the service sector and other phenomena taken to be signs of the "post-industrial age" (Bell, 1973) are simply the result of the proliferation of techniques in society.

THE CONSEQUENCES OF THE TECHNICIZATION OF LIFE

Techniques are not neutral; they do not merely make an activity more effective. An area of human life is studied not holistically but for a specific purpose. As a result, certain aspects of the situation will be externalized (i.e., excluded from consideration) in the technical operation. Consider a simple example.

Around the turn of the century, as machines in factories became increasingly efficient, the operations carried out by human beings caused a bottleneck. In this context, studies were done on how to rationalize human work to make it more efficient. Some famous studies were done by Gilbreth (Giedion, 1969: 102–105). By fastening a small electric light bulb to the wrist of a worker performing some task, it was possible to record the trajectory traced out by the bulb with three cameras. From the photographic records, wire models were constructed that showed how the worker moved. By analysing these models, it was possible to optimize the movements, and once this was accomplished, the worker was taught to perform the task more efficiently.

Gilbreth's technique illustrates the technical operation. As expected, rationalizing traditional work creates an important externality. It can readily be identified when we compare traditional with technicized work. If we observe a traditional craftsperson at work, the gestures reflect a variety of things, such as the person's state of mind, personality, previous experience (including apprenticeship training) and culture. Once the "one best way" was determined by means of the technical operation, all this had to be suppressed.

When workers are taught the one best way of moving their hands, they are being asked to suppress as much as possible their personality, state of mind, past experience and culture.

Technique as Milieu

There is a long tradition of thinking about technology as a means to accomplish human ends. Technology and techniques also mediate relationships between human beings or between human beings and their environment. Consider the telephone. It mediates between people who may never meet face-to-face. This transforms the relationship, since many sociocultural dimensions of a face-to-face relationship are stripped away. The culture's facial expressions, gestures and body language (Hall, 1977) are not transmitted by the telephone.

What is true for the telephone is equally true for television. It mediates between producer and consumer, between the politician and the voter, and so on. These mediated relations are also transformed in a non-neutral way. A politician may come across well in person but may have to rely on a media consultant to ensure that she projects the right image. Advertising is not a neutral diffusion of information about products. By linking a product to certain symbols alive in the minds of people, it affects them on the level where these symbols have become a part of their being, thus partly displacing the culturally mediated and conscious process of choice.

Many relationships are technically mediated with devices playing little or no essential part. Take a large office, for example. Here organization theory is applied to large numbers of people collectively performing tasks. Here again, organizational techniques have been developed to find the best way of identifying, executing and interconnecting the functions of the organization. People no longer primarily behave spontaneously. The relationships have been transformed. We are not suggesting that mediation on the basis of culture is eliminated in a modern office, but technically mediated relationships predominate.

A society changes fundamentally once most of the relationships in which its members are engaged become technically mediated. At this point, technique becomes the primary milieu for its members. It is in relation to this milieu that life evolves. This means much more than that the members of these societies live in an urban technical environment. Human existence has known only three primary milieus: nature in prehistory, society during much of our history and technique for the "industrially advanced" nations during the past two decades.

In prehistory, human beings lived in small groups totally dominated by nature. The natural milieu provided them with everything necessary for life, but it also posed the most serious threats in the form of droughts, wild beasts or storms, for example. Nature permeated almost every experience producing a unique type of consciousness characterized by a certain kind of mental map.

When human beings began to live in societies at the dawn of history the importance of the natural milieu became overshadowed by the social milieu. The latter interposed itself between the individual and nature. This made it possible for a society to better defend itself against natural dangers, but the new primary milieu also introduced new dangers, such as war and economic or political instability. Once the social milieu became the primary and nature the secondary milieu, a new type of consciousness emerged with correspondingly different mental maps.

When the phenomenon of technique began to transform society, the first steps toward another transition commenced. Technically mediated relationships eventually dominated culturally mediated ones, and technique displaced society as the primary milieu. Society now constituted the secondary milieu and nature moved to third place. Life in a modern society is impossible without a variety of technical support systems.

The separation of knowing from doing and knowledge from experience causes us to depend on experts in almost every domain of life. Since we have devalued daily life knowledge that is embedded in experience, we need to turn to experts who supposedly know more about the various aspects of our lives than we can know ourselves.

We are not saying that in the past, people did not rely on experts, we are saying that the phenomenon was on a completely different scale. We have created a society in which all of us, including the experts, must rely on others in important matters to the point that we have become spectators of much of our own lives. This phenomenon is taking on new proportions as a result of the proliferation of information services accessed through personal computers. It is fundamentally alienating, whether we are exploited or not. The fact that the control over one's own life has become largely external is a threat to human freedom, and it is also very stressful. The difficulty of participating in technicized relationships and the loss of control over one's life leads to the reification of the human subject—a fact powerfully portrayed in modern abstract art, which developed as the phenomenon of technique began to manifest itself. The human subject disappeared from art.

The technicization of life produces a new kind of alienation that is superimposed on economic alienation.

During its initial phases, the web of techniques was built up in the self-interest of a specific social class. As more and more techniques linked together during the technical revolution, they became increasingly difficult to control, due to the technical alienation produced. Such alienation was experienced even by the powerful and wealthy.

The patterns of development of the "industrially advanced" world are those of the growth of technique. Many of the problems faced by present-day societies derive from these very patterns of development. Yet, because of the way technique as milieu influences human consciousness, societal values and myths, we continue to turn to technique to solve the problems created by it. There can, however, be no security in evermore powerful weapons, and no real solution to our economic problems without addressing the challenge technique poses to human life and society. We need to create a civilization that includes technique but is based on a culture not permeated by it. This will determine the kind of world we will leave for future generations.

ENDNOTE

[1]   The following is largely based on W.H. Vanderburg, "Some Implications of Modern Technology for Culture and Knowledge," presented at the 1983 AAAS annual meeting in Detroit, later published under the same title in *Man-Environment Systems,* Vol. 13, no. 5, Sept. 1983.

REFERENCES

Galbraith, J.K. *The New Industrial State.* 3d rev. ed. New York: Mentor, 1978.

Giedion, S. *Mechanization Takes Command.* New York: Norton, 1969.

Hall, Edward T. *Beyond Culture.* New York: Anchor Books, 1977.

Vanderburg, W.H. *Culture and Technique: I—The Growth of Minds and Cultures.* Toronto: University of Toronto Press, 1985.

ARTICLE 16.3

Ndalahwa Faustin Madulu

POPULATION GROWTH AND ENVIRONMENTAL DEGRADATION IN TANZANIA

INTRODUCTION

Many of us in the West tend to contemplate the future with a Eurocentric bias. We assume that whatever big changes are coming will be launched from somewhere in the West. So we look to our governments, our giant corporations, and our advanced scientific institutes for clues as to what the future may hold. But it may be that the most salient clues to our world's future lie in the relatively poor, powerless, and low-tech regions of the globe.

*   The vast majority of the earth's people live in such regions, and that's where populations are growing fastest. That's also where the environmental problems of deforestation, desertification, and water shortages are most acute. And there too is where some of the world's fastest growing, energy- and resource-hungry economies are. In short, it is the developing world that*

Madulu, Ndalahwa Faustin (1995). "Population Growth, Agrarian Peasant Economy and Environmental Degradation in Tanzania," *International Sociology* 10(1), March, pp. 35-50.

is most likely to determine whether Thomas Malthus was right or wrong to be so pessimistic about the dangers in human procreation.

Ndalahwa Faustin Madulu examines the situation in Tanzania, an East African country with a relatively sparse but rapidly growing population. Madulu points out that many of the environmental problems there are exacerbated by the fact that a large proportion of the population remains rural and agrarian. Madulu's portrait of Tanzania is ominous—comparable, perhaps, to the portrait of abject poverty in a Bangladesh village described in excerpt 4.2. But, so far at least, the Malthusian nightmare of mass starvation has not begun.

This paper examines the population, economy and environment causal relationships in Tanzania.

THE POPULATION OF TANZANIA

Population size and growth. The population of Tanzania has been growing at a rapid rate, exceeding 2.5 per cent per annum since 1957. Census data shows the population increased more than threefold from 7.4 million in 1948 to 23.2 million in 1988 (Tanzania 1968, 1989). Table 1 shows the population size, growth rates and the estimated doubling periods between 1948 and 1988.

TABLE 1 Population Size and Growth Rates for Tanzania (1948–1988)

Years	Population	Growth Rates	Doubling Period
1948	7,410,269	—	
1957	8,665,336	1.8	39 years
1967	12,313,469	3.0	23 years
1978	17,512,610	3.2	22 years
1988	23,174,336	2.8	25 years

Based on the 1978–88 intercensal growth rate, the population is projected to reach 32.5 million people in the year 2000 and 43 million in 2010 (Tanzania 1991). As the population growth rate increases, the doubling period of the population declines. Given the recent slow-down of the population growth rate, the estimated doubling period of the population has risen from 22 years in 1978 to 25 years. However, it is too early to speculate that this decline in population growth will continue.

While projected death rates show a continued decline, fertility rates stagnated at higher levels above 50 births per thousand population between 1950 and 1990. The consequence is the widening gap between the stagnant high birth rate and the rapidly declining death rate leading to higher rates of natural increase. According to these projections, birth rates were expected to start declining in the 1990–95 period, reaching the lowest level of 30 births per thousand population in 2020–25 (UN 1991). It is not yet clear whether the decline in birth rates will actually follow the projected trend. The observed decline in growth rate in the 1978–88 intercensal period may be a signal of the start of a downward fertility trend.

However, the national level projections conceal the variations at regional and district levels.

The regional growth rates ranged between 1.7 per cent and 7.8 per cent in 1967–78 and between 1.4 per cent and 4.8 per cent in 1978–88. Population growth differentials were also observed within regions. Such differences reflect variations in culture, the rates of natural increase, intensity of internal and international migration, climatic conditions, and the availability of resources (Tanzania 1983).

The age distribution of the population shows a predominance of young ages. The 1978 and 1988 census data revealed that 46 per cent of the population was under 15 years, 50 per cent was aged 15–64 years and 4 per cent was 65 years or above (UN 1989; Tanzania 1991). This type of age structure illustrates a high fertility situation where many children form a broad base in the population pyramid. The consequence is a high child dependency ratio.

Population distribution and density. The national population density increased from around 9 persons per square kilometre in 1967 to 20 and 26 persons per square kilometre in 1978 and 1988, respectively. These figures give the impression that Tanzania is sparsely populated.

However, high rates of population growth put pressure and produce harmful effects on resources and the environment (Barke and Sowden 1992). Some 5.2 and 5.7 million people were added to the population in the 1967–78 and 1978–88 intercensal periods, respectively. These people need more food, land, firewood, water and other essential commodities as well as social services.

In almost all regions the population density increased, suggesting that there were significant absolute increases in the regional populations. The increasing population density is reflected in the declining per capita land from 11.8 hectares in 1948 to 3.8 hectares in 1988 (Tanzania 1989). The proportion of landless people in the population has been growing at all levels. Increasing distances to farms and declining productivity are becoming common phenomena as the population continues to increase. Moreover, land use conflicts and excessive land degradation characterise most of the densely populated areas. Increasing population pressure causes excessive environmental damage, especially in the arid and semi-arid areas of Tanzania.

CAUSES OF HIGH POPULATION GROWTH IN TANZANIA

Stagnant high fertility. High fertility is among the most significant causes of high population growth in Tanzania. The crude birth rate (CBR) and total fertility rate (TFR) are comparatively high. The recorded TFRs were 6.9 children per woman in 1978 and 6.5 children in 1988 (Tanzania 1991; Barke and Sowden 1992). The 1991–92 Tanzania Demographic and Health Survey (TDHS) observed a TFR of 6.1 children per woman (Robey et al. 1992; Ngallaba et al. 1993). There is an indication that the level of fertility has been declining. However, the current fertility decline is not conclusive because the rate is still far beyond the replacement level of the population.

Many factors influence high rates of reproduction in Tanzania. These include early and almost universal marriage, low contraceptive use, declining lactation periods and high mortality rates (UN 1989). High fertility is also influenced positively by the persistence of old customs and traditions favouring high reproductive rates and the continuing high labour and economic value of children, especially in peasant societies. Children provide the much needed labour on the farm, in the household and for the care of livestock. In most cases, children specialise in time-consuming and labour-intensive activities, such as fetching water, firewood collection, care of the young, milling and cooking (Kamuzora 1984). Moreover, old people are traditionally cared for by their children and relatives in the extended family kinship system. A decline in the value and need for such support from children may increase the desire for smaller families. To achieve this decline, a radical economic and socio-cultural transformation is necessary.

High but rapidly declining mortality. Mortality levels are high in Tanzania, although they are rapidly declining. The decline is from 24–25 deaths per 1,000 population in 1957 (Egerö and Henin 1973) to 15 deaths in 1988 (Tanzania 1991). Declines are also observed in infant mortality rates (UN 1989; Tanzania 1991). Table 2 shows the trends in mortality rates between 1957 and 1988.

TABLE 2 Mortality Estimates from Censuses of 1957–1988

Mortality Measures	Census Years			
	1957	1967	1978	1988
Crude Death Rates (CMR)	24–25	21–23	19	15
Infant Mortality Rates (1q0)	190	160	137	115
Life Expectancy at Birth	35–40	41	44	49
Survival Rate at Age Five (15)	–	740	808	810

Source: United Nations (1989:15), Tanzania (1991:8–11).

The declining mortality may reflect the progress made towards a policy of rural development which aimed at improving the living standard of the rural population. Further, improvements in the health services provided and a reduction in illiteracy levels may have contributed to mortality reduction.

Within the country, variations in mortality rates exist between and within regions. Mortality rates are comparatively higher in rural areas than in urban areas. Such differentials signal an unequal distribution of resources and health services. Urban areas are favoured at the expense of rural areas. Consequently, rural life is often characterised by poor living conditions, poor education, lack of transport, lack of water and poor sanitary services. Such inadequacies generate high levels of poverty and morbidity. The poor living conditions in rural areas stimulate a greater demand for large families. A sustained decline in mortality under high fertility conditions would enable many children to survive, thus causing high natural increases.

Low education level and socio-cultural reproduction. The impact of education on demographic behaviour is dependent on the type of education provided, its accessibility, and on the length of the schooling period. In Tanzania, most women of the older generation had acquired minimal or no formal education at all. The situation among the younger generation is not much better. Universal education extends only for seven years, and more than 90 per cent of the primary school leavers are unable to find a place in further education. This means that the time spent in school is too short to bring about major socio-cultural and behavioural changes. Many of the primary school leavers are forced by circumstances to start their *'reproductive career'* very early in life.

The fertility of women with some education in all age groups declined consistently with increasing educational attainment. The differences in CEB by the level of education of women suggest that low-level education for women can even lead to higher fertility. Given the low level of education among many rural women, high fertility and the resultant high population growth may continue for a long period.

Division of labour by age and sex. In most rural areas in Tanzania, the family has remained a joint economic unit, united in production and consumption. The family structure encourages high rates of reproduction and provides no incentive for fertility limitation. The organisation and division of labour within the family are carried on along gender and age lines. This encourages high reproductive behaviour because all age and sex groups have a role to play in the family labour force. Discussing the division of labour in the family, Bernhard et al. (1991: 53) argued that:

> Since the division of labour is linked to certain expectations, one has to consider that women might feel uncomfortable with admitting that they suffer under too great a labour burden, which would mean that they are not able to fulfil the socially and culturally defined roles.

Traditionally, women shoulder a disproportionate burden of work because they are responsible for almost all the domestic work and spend more hours on the farm than men. Even where hired labour is used, it is largely the men's labour which is replaced, not the women's. Given such labour burdens, women rely on their children as the most easily accessible source of help. Thus, the delayed fertility decline among rural women is often linked to the labour constraints that peasants, and especially women, are subjected to. The labour contribution of women and children provides a further motivation for early marriage and high fertility.

Use of contraception. In Tanzania, the rate of contraceptive prevalence is low. The 1991–92 TDHS data revealed that, although 74 per cent, 72 per cent and 44 per cent of the married women of reproductive age knew about some method, modern methods and traditional methods of contraception, respectively, only 10 per cent were using a method of contraception and 7 per cent a modern method (Ngallaba et al. 1993; Robey et al. 1992). These observations suggest that higher levels of contraceptive awareness do not necessarily lead to higher contraceptive use.

The lower contraceptive prevalence may be a result of the dominance of traditional norms and values which favour high rates of reproduction, and the low level of education among women. Moreover, the distribution system of services also hinders extensive use of contraceptives. Most services are distributed in urban areas, leaving rural women unaware and inaccessible to them. Similarly, the distribution of services is primarily done in public hospitals, dispensaries and clinics. These health facilities are not easily accessible to the majority of the rural population who have to walk longer distances to obtain them.

THE PEASANT AGRARIAN ECONOMY

Agricultural sector. The economy of Tanzania is predominantly oriented to agriculture. Agriculture provides a livelihood for over 80 per cent of the rural population which largely depends on small-scale agriculture. Subsistence farming is labour-intensive because only traditional technologies are employed (i.e., manual tools). A large labour force therefore seems to be a necessary precondition for higher agricultural production. According to Kamuzora (1984), children are considered the cheapest and most easily accessible source of labour. The use of modern agricultural technology could reduce the demand for human labour and indirectly the demand for large families. However, such technologies are rarely used because of high prices, lack of know-how and lack of capital.

The extensive rather than intensive agricultural system predominates. The more one expands the cultivated area, the higher the chances of having a sufficiently high output from the farm. Given the level of technology, extensive agriculture may succeed only with the availability of a large labour force. The accumulation of a labour pool consisting of parents, children, relatives and neighbours, enables peasant families to expand their agricultural activities. Whenever family labour is insufficient, many peasants opt for working parties as a way of accumulating labour input. Such a situation makes large families a necessity that can only be acquired through high fertility. Women engaging in cultivation have higher fertility than women engaged in other economic activities (Tanzania 1983; UN 1989). Thus, the introduction of other, non-agricultural, employment opportunities may reduce the size of the population depending on cultivation for survival, and hence the demand for large families and child labour in the long run.

The livestock sector. Livestock is also important to the peasants' socio-economic development and to the national economy. There are around 12 million cattle in Tanzania. About 60 per cent of the livestock population is concentrated on only 10 per cent of the total land area (Tanzania 1986). The consequence of such concentration of livestock is excessive overgrazing in the less favourable environments, which in turn leads to severe land degradation (Darkoh 1982). The dominance of small-scale livestock farming is a common characteristic in almost all livestock farming regions. The Ministry of Agriculture estimated that 99 per cent of all livestock in Tanzania is kept by small-scale livestock farmers (Tanzania 1986). Due to the population growth, the practice of transitory grazing has been abandoned. In many regions, the increase in population and the expansion of cultivation into grazing areas have driven herders into the less fertile and more fragile areas caus-ing serious environmental destruction.

POPULATION GROWTH AND ENVIRONMENTAL DEGRADATION

Population growth affects the environment in many ways. Many environmental problems are the result of taking something away from the environment: deforesta-tion, soil erosion, loss of species and loss of land. An increasing number of people causes increased demand for food, water and arable land. Agricultural expansion encourages deforestation which contributes to climatic change in turn. The steady increase in Tanzania's population has been accompanied by a decline in food produc-tion, which has been caused by land degradation and harsh climatic conditions among other things. This situation affects the environment in terms of soil erosion, desertification, famine, regular floods and recurring droughts. Darkoh (1982) esti-mated that between 45 and 75 per cent of the areas receiving a mean annual rainfall of 200–800 millimetres in Tanzania are susceptible to desertification. In addition to high population growth, these areas suffer from unreliable rainfall, repeated water shortages, periodic famines, rapid deforestation, cultivation in the marginal areas and concentrations of large herds of livestock. Generally, these outcomes are products of people's activities as they continue to extract resources from the environment. As the population increases, the arid and semi-arid marginal areas are becoming the last great frontiers into which people can expand (Barke and Sowden 1992).

Population growth also stimulates high demand for firewood and charcoal. Firewood meets the energy needs of virtually all the rural population and a large proportion of urban residents. FAO (1993) estimated that firewood and charcoal consumption in Tanzania increased from around 12.6 million cubic metres in 1980 to around 33.5 million cubic metres in 1991. The increase in consumption results in the excessive deforestation of many areas, especially around the urban areas. This effect is aggravated further by periodic burning of forests and grasslands. Bush fires are frequently lit for different purposes, such as the regeneration of new pastures for grazing, smoking bees, clearing farms, eradication of tsetse flies and wild animals, and for trapping game. Fire burns the vegetation cover and organic matter, which makes the top soil easily erodible. It also encourages overgrazing because the pas-tures available are reduced and livestock concentrates in the few unburnt areas.

Land use conflicts and competition between cultivators and herders are becom-ing common due to population growth. A high population growth in the highland areas around Mount Meru and Kilimanjaro has caused serious deforestation and influenced migrations of peasant groups into the adjacent drier marginal plains. The destructive effects of such population pressure are also evident in the Usambara and Pare mountains, in the southern highlands and in the Kondoa Irangi highlands. In almost all these examples, inappropriate agronomic practices, over-cultivation without adequate conservation measures and excessive tree-felling have accelerated the pace of environmental degradation.

CONCLUSION

To reduce the rate of environmental destruction, we need to seriously consider the population factor. The high rate of population growth which causes a rapid increase in population density and resource exploitation needs to be reduced. In some areas of Tanzania the ecological damage has already reached an irreversible stage. The semi-arid and arid areas of central and northern Tanzania in general, and Dodoma region in particular, contain the most degraded environments. However, merely fighting against the rapid population growth without considering improvements in the environments under which high growth rates are generated cannot be successful. The higher the population growth and the higher the dependency on subsistence agriculture, the higher the rate of environmental destruction. The socio-economic and technological aspects of the rural population need to be improved. Development policies and programmes need to be ecologically sound and should aim at both economic and social improvements. Both the population and the environment should be placed at the centre of the planning process. Action needs to be taken now before it is too late.

REFERENCES

Barke, M. and Sowden, C. 1992. 'Population Change in Tanzania 1978–88: A Preliminary Analysis'. *Scottish Geographical Magazine* 108 (1): 9–16.

Bernhard, H. et al. 1991. 'Crop Diversification and Food Security on Household Level with Special Reference to the Cultivation of Vegetables and Fruit Trees: The Case of Ufipa Plateau, Rukwa, Tanzania'. Centre for Advanced Training in Agricultural Development, Report No. 139; Technical University, Berlin.

Darkoh, M.B.K. 1982. 'Desertification in Tanzania'. *Geography* 67: 320–331.

Egerö, B. and Henin, R.A. eds. 1973. *The Population of Tanzania: An Analysis of the 1967 Population Census*, Vol. 6. Dar es Salaam: BRALUP/Bureau of Statistics.

Fao. 1993. *FAO Yearbook: Forest Products, 1991*. Rome: Food and Agricultural Organization of the United Nations. pp. 16–29.

Kamuzora, C.L. 1984. 'High Fertility and Demand for Labor in Peasant Economies'. *Development and Change* 15 (1): 105–124.

Ngallaba, S., Kapiga, S.H., Ruyobya, I. and Boerman, J.T. 1993. *Tanzania Demographic and Health Survey 1991/1992*. Dar es Salaam: Bureau of Statistics/Columbia: Macro International Inc.

Robey, B., Rutestein, S.O., Morris, L. and Blackburn, R. 1992. *The Reproductive Revolution*. Population Reports. Series M, No. 11. Baltimore, MD: Johns Hopkins University.

Tanzania, United Republic of. 1968. *Recorded Population Changes, 1948–1967*. Dar es Salaam: Central Bureau of Statistics.

Tanzania, United Republic of. 1983. *Population of Tanzania: 1978; Population Census. Vol. 8*. Dar es Salaam: Bureau of Statistics, Ministry of Finance and Economic Planning.

Tanzania, United Republic of. 1989. *1988 Population Census; Preliminary Report*. Dar es Salaam: Bureau of Statistics, Ministry of Finance and Economic Planning.

Tanzania, United Republic of. 1991. *Population Census; National Profile—Summary; 1988 Census Reports, Takwimu*. Dar es Salaam: Bureau of Statistics, President's Office, Planning Commission.

United Nations. 1991. *World Population Prospects 1990.* Population Studies, No. 120. New York: United Nations, Department of International Economic and Social Affairs (ST/ESA/SER.A/120).

QUESTIONS

DISCUSSION QUESTIONS

1. Does the history of the way the West developed serve as a useful and relevant guide for understanding and planning the development of today's poorest countries?

2. Many social problems are talked about more openly now than in the past (for example, incest or wife battering). Do societies have significantly more (or worse) problems today, or do we just talk about them more?

3. What does "sustainable development" mean? Is it a realistic goal? Why or why not?

4. The term "progress" is sometimes used to mean change that is positive or desirable. Discuss some recent social trends, and see whether your group reaches any consensus about which trends are "progressive."

DATA COLLECTION EXERCISES

1. Find out which jobs that were common in Canada 50 years ago have become rare today. Try to account for why these jobs disappeared.

2. Interview a small sample of people who are enthusiastic about one form of social innovation. For example, they might be computer hackers or trend setters in fashion. Try to determine whether they tend to be interested in innovation in general or just within their own narrow field.

3. The rate of increase in urbanization can be used as one measure of how fast social change is occurring. Find out what percentage of the world's population lived in urban areas in 1950 and what percentage lives in such areas now. If urbanization continues to rise at the same rate as in the past, how many years will it take before the world as a whole reaches Canada's current level of urbanization?

4. Traditionally, each generation of Canadians has been financially better off than their parents' generation. Is this still true today? What would be the best empirical way of answering this question?

WRITING EXERCISES

1. Some groups in modern society (such as the Amish) have successfully resisted the temptation to adopt modern lifestyles. Do some research on one such group and write a brief (500-word) essay explaining why the group opposes modern lifestyles.

2. Write a brief (500-word) essay explaining how and why rapid social change can lead to intergenerational conflict.

3. You are Minister of the Environment in a provincial government. Your job is to find the best way of getting people to leave their cars at home and take public transit to work. Some advisors say that banning single-passenger cars from city streets is the best idea. Others say that more public education is the best approach, and so on. Decide what you are going to do and defend your decision in a 500-word memo to your Premier.

4. Most technological inventions bring both costs and benefits to society. Do a social cost-benefit analysis of one specific technological invention.

SUGGESTED READINGS

1. Chirot, Daniel (1977). *Social Change in the Twentieth Century.* New York: Harcourt Brace Jovanovich. This book attempts to show how the prospects of an individual country depend on how it fits into the world system of "core" and "peripheral" countries. It calls attention to the fact that, for all countries, social change takes place within a "small world."

2. Rifkin, Jeremy with Ted Howard (1980). *Entropy: A New World View.* New York: Bantam. This book outlines the possibility of changing society by changing basic assumptions about the natural world. The authors believe that by changing those basic assumptions we will begin to see the need for a major reorganization of society.

3. Toffler, Alvin (1970). *Future Shock.* New York: Bantam. This book has sold millions of copies. Its theme is the difficulty of trying to cope with the accelerated pace of social change in modern societies. You, for example, may experience such shock when you read a book such as this one—or the daily newspaper for that matter.